TRIAL
ADVOCACY BEFORE JUDGES, JURORS, AND ARBITRATORS
THIRD EDITION

By

Roger Haydock

Professor of Law, William Mitchell College of Law
Member, Minnesota and Federal Bars
Director, National Arbitration Forum
Director, Institute for Advanced Dispute Resolution

John Sonsteng

Professor of Law, William Mitchell College of Law
Member, Minnesota and Federal Bars
Regional Director, National Institute for Trial Advocacy
Executive Director, L.L.M. in United States Law and Practice

Mat #40234780

© 2004 West, a Thomson business
    610 Opperman Drive
    P.O. Box 64526
    St. Paul, MN 55164–0526
    1–800–328–9352

Printed in the United States of America

ISBN 0–314–15225–3

 TEXT IS PRINTED ON 10% POST CONSUMER RECYCLED PAPER

Dedication

To Elaine

To Diane, Michael, David and Molly

*

Preface

Welcome to the real world of advocacy.

This book explains the fundamental advocacy skills and explores the theories, tactics, and techniques involved in preparing and presenting a case to a judge, jury, arbitrator, and administrative judge. The goal of this book is to help you learn how to prepare and present a case in a judicial, arbitral, and administrative forum. Much of this text also applies to other lawyering experiences involving presentations before public and private organizations including boards, legislative bodies, and other decision makers.

Your clients will want you to be an effective, skilled, and trained advocate. They will and should expect you to be able to successfully present their case to a decision maker. This book provides you with what you need to know to meet your clients' expectations.

Chapters 1, 2, and 3 describe considerations involving the advocate, the planning and preparation of a case, and trial and hearing procedures and motions. Chapter 4 covers evidentiary objections and summarizes the law of evidence. Chapter 5 explains the jury selection process. Chapter 6 describes opening statements. Chapters 7, 8, 9, and 10 cover witness examinations including direct examinations, exhibits, cross-examinations, and experts. Chapter 11 describes summation. Chapter 12 concludes this book with an explanation of verdicts and post-trial and post-hearing proceedings.

This third edition reflects the evolutionary change in advocacy. There are now many more cases tried before arbitrators and administrative judges than in previous times. New sections have been included in this edition which explain how advocates can best prepare and present cases before these decision makers. Former sections have been updated to explain how advocates can effectively try a case before a judge or jury.

This edition includes new sections and materials explaining the use of modern technology and computers in advocacy presentations. There have been recent advances in both software and hardware that allow advocates to present evidence and arguments in very persuasive and memorable ways. Chapter 8 includes many new and effective exhibits. Chapter 9 adds new approaches to experts. You will learn new communication and persuasion methods.

The analyses contained in these chapters explain the whys and why nots, and the shoulds and should nots of advocacy and trial practice. Learning about advocacy also requires reading about how lawyers actually try cases. This book presents numerous examples and illustrations of lawyers making statements, examining witnesses, and presenting arguments. These examples reflect the broad range of civil and criminal cases and bring some reality to the explanation of the trial, arbitration, and administrative processes. These illustrations are presented as suggestions and not as examples of what should be said or done. You, as the advocate, need to determine the appropriate approach in the context of each case you try.

The examples presented are based on real and fictional events from the world of history, literature, art, and comedy. We selected events, parties, and witnesses that relate to the topic or skills being explained. Hopefully these illustrations will make interesting, memorable, and entertaining reading.

A brand new and innovative learning method has been added to this edition in the related and separate Supplement. A highly effective way to learn how to be an advocate is to read, review, and analyze the work of successful advocates. Three transcripts—a jury trial, an arbitration, and an administrative hearing—provide you with a firsthand opportunity to study the presentation of complete cases in those three distinct forums. No other law school text provides you with this extraordinarily helpful experience.

You can learn much by studying the individual chapters in this book. You can learn a lot more from reading entire case transcripts with commentary. And, the Supplement also includes the federal rules of evidence and selected civil procedure rules for your handy and ready reference

We hope you will find or have discovered the adventure and excitement that accompanies the practice of advocacy. We encourage you to send us comments, suggestions, stories, anecdotes, and examples that we can include in our next edition. We wish you the best at becoming and being an advocate now and throughout your practice in the future.

ROGER HAYDOCK
JOHN SONSTENG
WILLIAM MITCHELL COLLEGE OF LAW
875 SUMMIT AVENUE
ST. PAUL, MN 55105
(651)227-9171
rhaydock@wmitchell.edu
jsonsteng@wmitchell.edu

June 2004

Acknowledgments

Many persons contributed to the making of this book. We received substantial support and assistance from our families, friends, and colleagues. We thank them all and greatly appreciate their being a part of our lives.

The special individuals whose contributions we acknowledged in the first and second editions deserve continuing recognition for their part in the development of the original book. Without them, this edition would not be. We also want to thank other individuals who have made this third edition a reality.

All the members of our immediate families allowed us the opportunity to work on this book: Roger thanks Elaine, Chuck, Marni, Marci, Jeffrey, Gabe, Kelsey, Cole, Olivia, Emma, Brooks, and Will. John thanks Diane, Michael, David, and Molly.

The students at William Mitchell College of Law, whom we have had the privilege of teaching, and clients, whom we have had the opportunity of representing, deserve our special appreciation.

The staff at William Mitchell with whom we work helped make our ideas appear in print. Jennifer Miller, Kathleen Weston, Jessica Davis, and Linda Thorstad assist us in teaching advocacy.

Our colleagues at William Mitchell, especially Professors Peter Knapp and Ann Juergens provided us with inspiration and encouragement. Deans Harry Haynsworth, Allen Easley, and Eric Janus supported our writing efforts.

Other lawyers and judges, including Hon. Michael Davis, David Herr, Lucinda Jesson, and Edward Anderson also provided us with ideas. The staff at the National Arbitration Forum and the Institute for Advanced Dispute Resolution further supported our work.

The law firm of Robins, Kaplan, Miller & Ciresi provided many of the exhibits appearing in this text. Dianna Case especially provided invaluable assistance to us.

Our research assistants, Lisa Ashley, Lori Bower, Katie Gilbert, Nancy Hylden, Ryan Madison, Andy Roth, and Patty Sturino helped complete the manuscript.

Our publisher and editors at West Group deserve our deep appreciation.

We further acknowledge you who will be reading and using this book. We have written this book for you, for the clients you will represent, and for the system you will serve.

*

Summary of Contents

Table of Contents

CHAPTER 2

PLANNING AND PREPARATION

CHAPTER 3

TRIAL PROCEDURES AND MOTIONS

CHAPTER 4

EVIDENCE AND OBJECTIONS

CHAPTER 5

JURY SELECTION

CHAPTER 7

DIRECT EXAMINATION

CHAPTER 8

EXHIBITS

CHAPTER 9

CROSS-EXAMINATION

CHAPTER 12

VERDICT AND APPEAL

Table of Forms

*

Table of Federal Rules

CHAPTER 1
THE ADVOCATE

REFLECTING ON ADVOCACY

Justice cannot be for one side alone, but must be for both . . . .

—Eleanor Roosevelt

Oh, do not ask, "What is it?"

Let us go and make our visit.

—T.S. Eliot

The Love Song of
J. Alfred Prufrock

§ 1.1 INTRODUCTION

Welcome to advocacy. You will learn how to efficiently prepare and effectively try a case. You will discover what to do, when to do it, where to do it, and why to do it. And, you will know how to plan case strategies and implement trial tactics.

This book is about becoming and being a highly professional, responsible, and competent trial lawyer. Advocates face times of success (!), failure (#%?), excitement (yea!), weariness (sigh), fun (yes!), anxiety (oh, no), satisfaction (ahhh), frustration (ah, me) and peace (it's over). This book is designed to provide you with the theories, knowledge, procedures, skills, and techniques to guide you through these advocacy experiences.

This text explains civil and criminal trial practice in the federal and state court systems, arbitration procedures and hearings, and administrative law processes. Our dispute resolution system includes three primary forums: judicial, arbitral, and administrative, and this book thoroughly covers strategies and tactics applicable to these forums.

The sources of trial "law" include rules of procedure, statutes, case law, constitutional provisions, local court rules, judges' orders and rulings, as well as custom and traditions. The sources of arbitration procedures also include the applicable code of procedure, the agreement of the parties, and the law. The sources of administrative procedural law include statutes, regulations, rules, administrative and judicial opinions.

What occurs during trials and hearings follows common rules and procedures. A case tried in one jurisdiction is tried similarly in another jurisdiction. This book explains these common practices, as well as dissimilar practices.

Further, these materials analyze systems and strategies used by successful lawyers in planning cases. Attorneys learn from each other and adopt successful tactics and techniques. This is not to say that lawyers prepare cases the same way, but often they follow common patterns.

Every chapter describes alternative trial and hearing tactics and approaches. There is no single way to try a case. Much of what occurs during a trial and hearing is determined by the attorney's approach. The illustrations and examples of tactics and techniques presented in this book will assist you in making well-reasoned decisions.

Decisions advocates must make — from the planning of what to do to the presentation of a case — are based on analytical legal reasoning and incisive judgments. This process is a primary focus of this book. Both the theory and practice of why and how advocates effectively think and reason are analyzed.

The psychological and emotional dimensions involved in advocacy are also explored throughout this text. Trying a case can be a trying experience. The information presented in this book is designed to assist you in developing the level of confidence necessary to try a case well.

Advocates make mistakes in every case, and problems commonly occur during cases. The key is not letting the mistakes and problems overwhelm or negate the presentation. Many problems can be anticipated and many mistakes can be eliminated through preparation and an understanding of available solutions described in these materials.

Ethical issues arise during the preparation and presentation of a case. An underlying premise of this book is that advocates must hold themselves to high ethical standards. An understanding of professional rules and guidelines assists in identifying ethical concerns, resolving problems, and becoming a responsible advocate.

The legal profession is a helping profession. The mission of advocates, like all lawyers, is to help their clients. This humanistic dimension of advocacy shapes and influences the work of the advocate. The situations and problems presented in this book — although printed on a page — involve and affect the lives of clients, lawyers, and other people. We encourage you to bring to life what you read so you also can experience to some degree this human dimension of advocacy.

As you read and analyze the textual materials and examples, you will become knowledgeable, curious, wiser, surprised, pleased, and perhaps shocked. Not everything in the real world of advocacy will conform to your expectations and experiences and your notions of the adversary process, the legal profession, and our system of justice. We present the way things are, the way we believe them to be, and the way they should be. Your task as an advocate will be to bring this all together, for yourself, your clients and for those with whom you practice.

§ 1.2 THE ADVOCATE

A. *The Goal of the Advocate*

The goal is to win. A case is tried because other alternative efforts at resolving the dispute — negotiation and mediation — have been unsuccessful. The client obviously expects to win, and counsel must make every reasonable effort to win. However, this goal of winning must be kept in perspective, for this end does not justify all means; and ethical rules and norms must be maintained.

B. Roles of the Advocate

The advocate uses all reasonable approaches to present a case to secure a favorable outcome. An all-out effort is governed by rules, ethics, and common sense. A process that involves acrimony or questionable approaches does not serve the client's interests or the system of justice. The effective advocate must be firm, persistent, and compassionate.

The advocate also has a number of additional lawyer roles during litigation:

- A court officer who follows the ethical norms of the system,
- A counselor who provides well-reasoned advice to clients,
- An investigator who gathers and preserves information,
- A facilitator who considers alternative dispute resolution approaches,
- A negotiator who makes good faith efforts to settle cases,
- A litigator who drafts pleadings and conducts discovery and motion practice, and
- An appellate lawyer who brings or defends an appeal.

The advocate may also perform other professional roles:

- An artist who is creative, imaginative, and intuitive,
- A scientist who is rational, logical, and disciplined,
- A psychologist who understands and predicts human behavior,
- An historian who recreates time past, and
- A director who directs a dispute resolution play where the court or hearing room is the theater, the witnesses are actors, the exhibits are props, and the decision maker is the audience.

C. Character Traits

Our personality and character traits influence our professional approach and behavior. All effective advocates possess integrity, honesty, fairness, sensitivity, and respect for others.

Decision makers must be able to trust attorneys. They rely upon the attorney's word and explanations. An untrustworthy advocate is an ineffective advocate. The attorney must also display a sincere belief in the merits of the client's case. The lack of sincerity may cause the decision makers to conclude that the attorney does not believe in or care about the case. And, lawyers who take advantage of situations or who appear sneaky or underhanded will not be perceived as fair.

Additionally, advocates encounter a full range of personality temperaments in dealing with opposing attorneys, witnesses, arbitrators, judges, and jurors. These individuals may be courteous or rude, cooperative or hostile, friendly or arrogant, pleasant or intimidating, trustworthy or untrustworthy. The advocate must adopt various approaches to deal with this broad spectrum of personalities.

D. Balanced Approach

Advocates suffer stress due to: the pressure to win, unrealistic expectations, fear of failure, money, ego, physical discomfort, fatigue, anxieties, tension, peer pressure, neglect of personal and family matters, emotional withdrawal, and preoccupation with a case. Attorneys may take cases for financial rewards but may also take them to accept a difficult challenge, work with a specific client, obtain publicity, achieve fame, satisfy a legal fantasy, change the law, protect a client's rights, or promote justice.

A number of ways that lawyers can deal with stress and maintain a balanced life include:

- Before accepting a case, reflect on the reasons why you are taking the case and your expectations.

- Maintain a proper relationship with the client. Involve the client in making decisions and avoid overly controlling the case.

- Do not worry about events or matters that cannot be altered. Learn to let go and accept what cannot be changed.

- Expect that relationships with family, friends, and colleagues will be disrupted. Advise them that problems may arise and offer solutions.

- Discuss your feelings and attitudes with family members and other caring listeners.

- Monitor your workload to avoid becoming overworked. Delegate appropriate responsibilities and tasks to support staff. Learn not to interfere unnecessarily and second-guess decisions.

- Exercise your body as well as your mind.

- Avoid tobacco, alcohol, drugs, and other harmful sources of escape.

- Discuss the case with the client and colleagues after its conclusion.

- Celebrate the experience, whether you win or lose.

- Take a break, however brief.

E. Client Relationships

Clients place their legal fate in the hands of advocates. This reliance places enormous responsibility on the advocate to justify the client's trust. The exact relationship between the client and the attorney varies depending upon the needs of the client, the client's familiarity with the legal system, and the client's and attorney's views of the appropriate relationship. The key to effective client/attorney relationships is communication and the continuing involvement of the client in the preparation and presentation of the case.

The client and the attorney in consultation with each other identify the interests and needs of the client, consider potential ways to compromise or win the dispute, and select a course of action to succeed. These decisions involve both the client and the attorney. Clients must decide what their needs are. The more a decision has a substantial legal or nonlegal impact on a client, the more critical it is to have the client involved in making that decision. The more a decision involves professional expertise and skills, the more likely it is that the attorney can make the decision.

§ 1.3 DISPUTE RESOLUTION SYSTEMS

A. *Litigation*

Lawsuits may be brought in federal or state court, whichever has proper jurisdiction. Federal courts resolve disputes involving federal statutes and the federal constitution, disputes between citizens in different states in excess of $75,000, and special cases such as patent disputes and bankruptcy. State courts are courts with general jurisdiction and hear the vast majority of judicial disputes.

A plaintiff begins a lawsuit by serving a summons and complaint on the defendant who can reply with an answer. Litigation proceeds with the parties conducting discovery and bringing motions eventually resulting in a jury or bench trial. Federal and state constitutional and statutory provisions provide parties with the right to a jury trial in most civil cases, particularly those involving money damages. Other cases, including injunctive relief cases, are tried to a judge. Any party with grounds may appeal to an appellate court.

Litigation is often the remedy available to the parties if they are unable to agree to another dispute resolution method. Litigation is typically the last resort parties rely on to have their dispute resolved because the trial process can be very expensive, time consuming, and painful.

B. *Arbitration*

There are two primary types of arbitration. One is a contractual process where a neutral arbitrator (usually an experienced lawyer or a retired judge) conducts a hearing and issues a final, binding award. Procedural rules govern the case, such as The National Arbitration Forum Code of Procedure, which provide for discovery and motions. This system is widely used in numerous types of disputes and is becoming the preferred way businesses, individuals, companies, and consumers are resolving their differences. Arbitration clauses appear in all types of agreements and relationships, including commercial contracts, financial documents, employment relationships, adhesion contracts, health care transactions, insurance contracts, and business agreements. Arbitration is typically much more affordable, a lot faster, and as fair as a trial.

The other is a non-binding process (often called court-annexed arbitration) which is mandatory in some jurisdictions. In this non-binding pretrial proceeding, the arbitrator, who is usually an attorney randomly selected from a panel of arbitrators, hears evidence and arguments and renders a decision. If the decision is acceptable to both parties, the lawsuit is dismissed. If the decision is unacceptable, the case goes to trial.

C. Administrative Hearings

Administrative hearings typically resolve disputes involving government benefits or statutory remedies. A party may file a petition with an administrative tribunal, and an administrative judge holds a hearing and decides the case. Administrative proceedings are similar to bench trials. The availability of discovery and the use of motions may be limited.

Controversies resolved through federal and state administrative hearings include workers compensation claims, unemployment compensation claims, tax claims, social security claims, welfare claims, and other rule based claims. Administrative claims may also involve regulatory procedures. Parties involved in a dispute regarding the enactment or enforcement of government regulations may also appear before administrative bodies to present their case. Examples include utility rate setting cases and environmental cases.

§ 1.4 ALTERNATIVES TO A TRIAL OR HEARING

Before placing their fate in the hands of a judge, arbitrator, or jury, clients and advocates need to consider how else the dispute may be resolved. Parties may be more likely satisfied if they control their fate through a settlement or other alternative dispute resolution (ADR) process. Major dispute resolution methods are discussed below.

A. Negotiated Settlements and Plea Bargains

Negotiated settlements are an essential part of the dispute resolution process. The large majority of civil and criminal cases are settled or plea bargained. Various factors influence the results of negotiation practice, including the willingness of the parties to go to trial and the experience and ability of the attorneys to try cases.

Judges often take an active role in negotiations by encouraging and becoming directly involved in settlement conferences. Judicial approval or consent is not normally required for settlement of civil litigation unless the case involves a class action or an injury to a minor. Many judges require the parties to use a mediator. Arbitrators and administrative judges tend not to become involved in settlement talks as their role is to conduct a hearing and decide the case.

The type of settlement agreement depends upon the nature and circumstances of the civil case. One universal settlement document is a dismissal with prejudice which disposes of the case. The dismissal may be a stipulation signed by the attorneys which dismisses the case, or it may be an order signed by the decision maker based on a stipulation by the parties. The dismissal should specify whether the costs are to be borne by each of the parties or are to be paid by one of the parties. Federal Rule of Civil Procedure 41, similar state court provisions, arbitration rules, and administrative procedures commonly regulate these dismissals.

In criminal cases, the judge usually needs to approve the plea bargain entered into by the prosecutor and defendant. The plea bargain may consist of a guilty plea, a plea to a less serious offense, nolo contendere, or another plea authorized in the jurisdiction, and may also include conditions of probation and sentencing. Pleas of guilty are taken in open court. The defense counsel, prosecutor, and judge all have an obligation to make sure that the defendant understands what is happening and that the plea is complete and legally sufficient to support a conviction.

B. Mediation

Mediation is an informal process where a neutral professional assists the parties in reaching a mutually acceptable agreement. The mediator's primary role is to facilitate a negotiated settlement between the parties. The mediator does not decide any issues or make any decisions but may offer opinions and predict likely outcomes. In some jurisdictions, mediation is compulsory, and the parties must attempt to mediate a settlement in good faith before proceeding to trial. A related process is known as a med-arb proceeding. The parties first attempt to mediate, and if that fails, they arbitrate the dispute.

C. Fact/Issue Finding

Fact/issue finding is an informal process in which a neutral third party selected by the parties or the court reviews the case and submits a written or oral report that identifies and evaluates disputed facts and issues. This process is useful in resolving complex scientific, technical, business, or economic issues where the presentation of proof is extremely difficult, expensive, and time-consuming. The use of a highly experienced neutral assists the parties in reaching agreement on the undisputed and disputed matters. The neutral professional may be appointed by the court under Federal Rule of Evidence 706 or similar state rules.

D. Mini–Trial

A mini-trial is a private, consensual proceeding where counsel for each party makes a short presentation before a panel consisting of a representative of each of the parties and a neutral third person. This process, with the assistance and perspective of the neutral panel member, assists the parties in understanding both sides of the case in an effort to reach a mutually acceptable agreement.

E. Summary Jury Trial

A summary jury trial takes place in a courtroom with a judge, magistrate, or special master and a mock jury selected from the regular jury list, sometimes with the assistance of a private consultant. Counsel for each party makes a presentation consisting of a brief opening statement, the summary introduction of key evidence, and a closing argument. The jury deliberates and renders an advisory verdict or verdicts, which provide the parties with a reliable basis to predict what jurors would do after a complete trial. One party may unilaterally conduct this summary trial privately seeking the help of the mock jurors to evaluate the case. These methods are primarily used in major cases where other ADR methods have been unsuccessful.

F. Moderated Settlement Conference

A moderated settlement conference is a forum for case evaluation and structured settlement negotiations between the parties and their attorneys. The advocates present their cases before a panel of impartial third parties, usually lawyers, who evaluate the case and render an advisory non-binding opinion for use by the parties in settlement negotiations. This method is not widely used.

G. Collaborative Law

A relatively new approach to resolving disputes is known as the collaborative law approach. The parties with the help of a professional versed in dispute resolution agree on their own process to settle their dispute and then proceed to follow the process to a resolution. This approach can be effective in family law cases.

H. Private Judging

Parties to a dispute may agree or be ordered by the court to submit their dispute to a private (usually former or retired) judge for resolution. Parties may prefer a private judge (or arbitrator) because the private judge may have experience resolving the type of dispute and the trial may be able to be scheduled much more quickly than a public trial and conducted more privately. In some states, the decision by the private judge (special magistrate or referee) can be enforced as if it were a judgment or reviewed by a public judge who converts it into a judgment.

I. Court Mandated or Consensual Procedures

A growing number of jurisdictions are mandating the use of one or more of these alternatives to resolve disputes prior to trial. Some states require the parties to attempt an ADR method (usually mediation) before a case may proceed to trial. Other decision makers by statute or rule have discretion to require parties to submit to a dispute resolution procedure.

Parties may also agree to use one or more ADR methods instead of relying on the court system to solve their problems. Some parties believe the judicial system is too costly, too slow, and too unpredictable. They may well prefer and choose private mediation and binding arbitration to resolve their problems.

§ 1.5   FUNDAMENTAL APPROACHES OF PERSUASION

This section explains established methods of persuasion that significantly influence the presentation of a case and that apply to all phases of a case.

A.   *Rely on Values and Principles*

Decision makers often interpret facts, apply the law, and make decisions based on their values, norms, principles, and beliefs. A primary task of an advocate is to attempt to identify these values and predict how a decision maker will make a decision consistent with these principles. Subsequent sections of this text will explore how advocates can best accomplish this task.

B.   *Use Primacy and Recency*

People remember best that which they hear first and last. The doctrines of primacy — what a person hears first — and recency — what a person hears last — may dictate when evidence and statements ought to be made during a case. These doctrines apply to the case as a whole as well as to each stage of the trial or hearing, including the opening statement, witness examinations, and the closing argument.

C.   *Reasonably Repeat Information*

The more times individuals perceive something the more likely they will believe it and remember it. Evidence can be referred to a reasonable number of times to increase the chances that the fact finders will recall and believe it. What is reasonable depends on the facts and the circumstances of the case, how long the case lasts, and how the matter is repeated.

D.   *Use the Rule of Three*

Advocates: explain what happened (opening statement), detail what happened through witnesses and documents (evidence), and summarize what happened (summation). This format follows a rule of persuasion: "Tell them what you are going to tell them, tell them, and tell them what you have told them."

E.   *Employ Visual Senses*

Studies and experience indicate that individuals remember a much larger percent of what they both see and hear compared to what they just hear. And, modern educational and entertainment approaches are designed to involve and influence multiple senses. The use of visual aids and documentary and computer exhibits in advocacy cases increases the likelihood that the fact finder will recall and understand specific evidence and presentations.

F. Use Impact Words

Individuals react to words that are used to describe an event. Descriptive words emphasizing specific facts of a case create more vivid images of an event than nondescriptive words. Descriptive language includes impact words that graphically describe a situation, such as "smashed" instead of "hit," "huge" instead of "large," and "shrieked" instead of "yelled." These impact words affect the fact finder's perception of what happened and are usually more easily remembered by the fact finder.

For example, in an automobile accident case, when the accident is described merely as an "incident" this neutral term will not create a specific image of the accident. When the accident is described as a "collision" or "violent crash," a more graphic image of the accident is portrayed.

Impact words should be factually specific to accurately convey what happened and not exaggerated conclusions unsupported by the evidence. Thesauruses, dictionaries, and works of literature may serve as sources of such words and phrases.

G. Create Images

Individuals learn and understand by forming images in their minds. When fact finders hear a word or listen to a description of an event, they visualize images based on what they have heard from a lawyer or witness.

For example, when an attorney says the word "chair" to a fact finder, each decision maker draws a mental image of a chair. That image might be of a wooden chair, a padded chair, a rocking chair, a desk chair, or a plastic chair. The advocate must make certain that the actual chair involved in the case is the image the fact finders picture in their minds. The more vital the details of this chair are to the case, the more precise the attorney must be in presenting details that give an accurate picture.

As another example, when an attorney asks jurors to assess damages for pain and suffering, the attorney must use words that make the jurors feel the pain and suffering. Injured parties need to describe what the injury really felt like. Witnesses should not merely say they had a headache, but that it felt as if someone was inside their head pounding with a hammer. Witnesses should not merely say that their leg was cut by a saw, but that they felt an intense, burning pain of hot metal slicing through their flesh.

H. Develop Imagination

The images created in the fact finders' minds may be clear or hazy, complete or incomplete. An ideally communicated image should involve the senses and should focus on all details of an event. This, however, is impossible because everything cannot be recreated. The advocate must make the critical images as realistic as possible to enable the fact finder to imagine the event vividly and accurately.

I. Actively Involve the Fact Finder

A fact finder who becomes mentally and emotionally involved in a case is more likely to be interested in the case and more likely to believe and remember evidence. The goal is to present the events in such a way that the fact finders think they are a part of the case, perceive they are observing what actually happened in the past, and feel the emotions of the situation.

J. Use Storytelling Techniques

Effective storytelling techniques are useful to successful advocates. Techniques employed in literature may be adapted to the trial or hearing. Good story tellers immediately draw the reader into the story and maintain the reader's attention throughout. Another technique frequently used in cases is adapted from the theater: the playwright first establishes the circumstances of time and place, introduces the protagonists, develops the problem, and then presents solutions to the problem.

K. Employ Understandable Language

Clarity of expression is critical. Simple and clear language is preferable to complex legalese. Large words used only to show off vocabulary skills turn off the decision maker; while overly simplistic words and explanations sound condescending. The attorney needs to select language appropriate to the decision maker.

L. Make Simple Explanations

The more straightforward and less convoluted an explanation, the more likely it will be accepted as true. The advocate should provide the fact finder with as simple and credible an explanation of what happened as possible. This type of presentation fulfills the need of many decision makers looking for a reasonable, straightforward answer to explain a case, even when the case is difficult and complex.

Unfortunately, lawyers are not always trained to develop simple explanations, but are often taught in law school to present complicated explanations of both sides of a case. For example, in analyzing a criminal case, a criminal defense lawyer could argue that the defendant was not present at the armed robbery, or if the defendant was present, the defendant was not holding a gun, or if the defendant was holding a gun, it was used in self-defense. These possible explanations may generate a high grade in a law school exam, but will only convince a fact finder of the defendant's guilt.

M. *Present Alternatives*

The advocate must obviously avoid presenting mutually contradictory positions. Some situations require a presentation of alternative explanations. These presentations are most effective if they are described as alternative and not contradictory positions by avoiding the use of the terms "but" or "however." It is better to affirmatively state a position and then add another explanation, using such terms as "moreover" or "further."

For example, in an automobile accident case, the plaintiff may contend that she was hit in the crosswalk while the defendant contends that she was hit outside the crosswalk. Plaintiff's counsel could argue that plaintiff was in the crosswalk when she was hit, or even if she wasn't in the crosswalk, she was hit negligently by the defendant outside the crosswalk. A more effective explanation to avoid this contradictory statement would be: "The defendant negligently struck plaintiff where she was walking; moreover, we will prove that she was walking in the crosswalk."

N. *Develop Interest*

Advocates need to make all cases as interesting as possible to hold the attention of decision makers and influence the final decision. Some cases are interesting by their very nature. For example, a wrongful death or murder case is usually dramatic. Other cases, such as those involving commercial litigation and real estate, are not nearly as exciting, but need to be made interesting.

For example, every commercial case is about people making business decisions. The advocate must present these people and these decisions in as stimulating a way as possible. As another example, every real estate case involves a unique piece of property. The advocate might be able to establish the special value of this property to increase the interest level of the case. Even with seemingly boring facts, the advocate must create and develop as much interest as possible so the fact finder will be more likely to understand and remember the events.

O. *Be Reasonably Brief*

Audiences, including judges, arbitrators, and jurors, have limited attention spans, which can be maximized if the presentation is interesting, dramatic, reasonably paced, and otherwise well presented. The length of a presentation must be based not only on what must be said, but on the fact finder's likely attention span. The advocate needs to observe the decision makers and make certain that they are paying sufficient attention to what is going on.

P. *Develop Emotions and Reactions*

An advocate may be able to use the emotions inherent in a case as an actor relies on the emotions inherent in a play. An actor does not become the source of an emotional catharsis; it is the reenactment of an event that creates cathartic reactions in the audience. A good actor leads the audience to the threshold of emotion, and the culmination of that emotion is felt by the audience. An advocate tries to create an atmosphere in which the decision maker is affected by emotions at the right time. In a wrongful death case, the plaintiff's lawyer wants the jurors to feel grief in such a way that their compassion favorably affects their judgment during deliberations.

Q. Establish Realism

A successful play or movie captures the audience so they forget they are at a play or watching a movie. A poorly presented dramatic act makes the audience aware of what they are watching and anxious for the end of the make-believe story. The advocate, paralleling the goal of the playwright, wants the fact finders to forget they are decision makers at a trial or hearing, but instead believe they are observers at an event unfolding before them.

R. Identify With the Fact Finder

Decision makers are more likely to believe a witness or favor a party if they can identify with that individual. Perceiving similarities between themselves and the witness or party helps form this identification. Fact finders may not consciously disbelieve a witness because they do not identify with that witness, but usually the more a witness or party has in common with a fact finder, the more likely the fact finder will identify with and believe that person.

Background information that establishes similarities between the witness and the fact finders should be emphasized. Specific examples of similarities should be described during the direct examination of the witness. The questions should not be so numerous or obvious, however, that the fact finders perceive that the witness is artificially being portrayed to be like them.

§ 1.6 ELEMENTS OF ADVOCACY

There are a variety of approaches to trying a case. These variations reflect the difference in opinions among advocates. This section describes alternative approaches to case presentation.

A. The Persuasive Advocate

Many lawyers believe that advocacy requires them to convince the decision maker of the correctness and righteousness of their client's position by attempting to "sell" the position to the decision maker. Typically, these advocates ask the decision maker to find "in favor of" or "for" or "on behalf of" their client. The underlying premise is that the advocate's client deserves a certain result because the advocate has convinced the decision maker the client is entitled to win.

Another view is that the advocate provides the decision maker with information which would lead reasonable people to come to but one conclusion. This approach does not require that the attorney usurp the decision maker's function. The responsibility remains on the decision maker to reach a decision based on the facts, the law, and justice. Rather than attempt to cajole, sell, or otherwise convince the fact finders, the attorney simply says "here are the facts, here is the law, and the result you should reach is clear."

An approach that combines the benefits of both approaches may be most effective. The benefit of the first adversarial approach is that it can result in a very persuasive and compelling presentation, while a disadvantage is that the advocate may appear to be inappropriately partisan and manipulative. The benefit of the second approach is that the fact finders reach their own conclusion based on the information the attorney presents to them, while the disadvantage is that the attorney may appear to be uncertain and unsure.

B. Involvement of Advocate

The degree to which advocates should involve themselves in cases is a matter of disagreement among advocates. Some argue that attorneys should not emphasize their professional beliefs during the case, while others argue that it is critical to establish this professional belief. Advocates who suggest that the display of involvement is necessary say things like "I will prove to you" and "I will introduce evidence to convince you of these facts." Advocates who suggest that their involvement should be diminished use phrases during the case such as "You will hear evidence and you will conclude. . . . "

These two positions do share common principles and may differ only in the emphasis placed upon them. The decision maker must be given the impression that the advocate believes in the client and the case presented. The decision maker is unlikely to find in favor of a client whose lawyer expresses doubts about whether that client should win.

C. The Objective Partisan

The advocate has a dual role that needs to be balanced: being both a partisan and an objective participant. The attorney as partisan needs to present selective evidence to the fact finder and zealously argue for the client's position. The attorney as objective participant must appear to present evidence in an objective way and provide reasonable explanations. If the decision makers perceive that lawyers are too partisan, they will be less likely to believe lawyers. Likewise, if the decision makers perceive that a lawyer is too objective, then they may be less influenced because the lawyer does not advocate a position.

D. Open–Mindedness of Decision Maker

It is difficult, if not impossible, for the decision maker to have a completely open mind before or during a trial or hearing. Many advocates believe that no decision maker ever has a completely open mind and present their case based on this premise. Some believe that all fact finders have some biases and prejudices, and some of the decision makers may be partial to one side or the other. Decision-making processes in cases parallel similar life experiences.

At the early stages of a case, the decision maker may begin to form impressions about the case, about the attorneys, and about the parties. The notion that decision makers impartially absorb information during a trial or hearing and wait to decide a case is largely inaccurate. Many fact finders, especially jurors, selectively listen for evidence that supports their initial inclination or position. Evidence that does not support their position is rejected, disbelieved, rationalized, forgotten, or not even heard. Many decision makers make up their minds well before the closing argument.

The lack of open-mindedness on the part of the fact finders affects the way an advocate presents a case. The goal of the advocate is to provide the information and reasons sufficient for the decision maker to want to find for the advocate's client early in a case, and then to continue to provide information and reasons to support that decision during the trial or hearing. It is much more difficult to change someone's mind once it is made up or to alter an opinion once it is formed.

E. Memories of Witnesses

In preparing a case, an advocate must determine the degree to which each witness has an accurate recollection of an event. There exists a range of opinions among lawyers regarding people's ability to remember. Some advocates suggest that witnesses remember very little, if anything at all. These advocates believe that witnesses draw on the few recollections they have, collect evidence from other sources (such as other individuals or documents) and use the law of probability to form a recollection. Other lawyers believe that witnesses are able to draw upon the resources of their memory and accurately recall things that happened in the past. The right belief depends upon the ability of that individual to perceive and remember the event, the impact the event had upon the witness, and whether the witness had any reason or expectation to perceive or recall the event.

Cases which arise from situations that the parties did not expect may result in less complete and accurate recollections. For example, in a typical automobile accident case, the parties do not anticipate being immediately involved in an accident and have little reason to focus on the events that occur before an accident. There is little reason for them to concentrate on remembering their speed, distances, or the traffic situation. After the accident, however, witnesses to the event may pay close attention to what is said or how people act because they may expect to be called on to give a statement. It is more likely that the later part of their stories will be more complete and accurate. For another example, in a criminal case the victim may or may not have good reasons to be able to identify the defendant. Some victims are so scared or frightened during the crime that they are unable to look at the criminal, while other victims may want to get a good look so they can later help catch the criminal.

Psychology surveys show that most witnesses add details that they did not perceive and that they do not actually recall. This "filling in the details" phenomenon is often done unconsciously and without the witness intending to exaggerate or lie. Some witnesses, however, intentionally exaggerate or lie. Advocates must present in good faith direct examination stories and must challenge adverse witnesses on cross-examination.

F. Displaying a Relationship With a Client

The nature of the case and the kind of client dictate what relationship should be displayed between an attorney and client. If the fact finder is likely to perceive the client as a credible or a good person, the advocate should display a close relationship with the client by talking with the client and appearing to like the client. In cases in which the fact finder may not identify with or like a client, lawyers disagree as to the relationship they should establish in front of the decision maker. Some lawyers believe that they should distance themselves from this kind of client as much as possible, fearing that the appearance of a close relationship with such a client will hurt the attorney's standing in the eyes of the fact finder. Other lawyers believe that such a client needs visible support from the attorney. They fear the opposite reaction from the decision maker who may not support the client because it appears that the client's own attorney wants little to do with the client.

G. Personal Embarrassments

Inevitably, advocates make mistakes and errors of judgment. The attorney's reaction to these situations increases or decreases the chances of winning. When we make mistakes, we may be naturally inclined to think about ourselves first and what the decision maker will think about us and then find a scapegoat for our errors. When we learn about some surprise information at the beginning of a trial, we may want to blame our client for not telling us about this information rather than ourselves for not properly discovering it. When we ask an awkward question during jury selection, we may want to blame the judge for refusing to ask such a question instead of blaming ourselves for not properly asking it. When the witness makes a misstatement on the stand, we may be inclined to shift the blame to the witness rather than have the decision maker think we did not properly prepare the witness. These reactions are natural and normal, but they must be avoided by the professional advocate.

There is no place for an advocate to be concerned about personal embarrassments during a case. The advocate should not embarrass the client or undercut the client's position. The advocate should usually assume responsibility for the mistake or error and take the blame.

§ 1.7 METHODS OF EFFECTIVE PRESENTATION

All advocates have some talent and capabilities that they can develop and enhance to make them effective advocates. Methodical planning, thorough preparation, and intense practice can make most any lawyer a competent and skilled advocate. This section describes some general principles of effective communication skills. Subsequent chapters contain additional techniques applicable to specific advocacy skills.

A. A Good Person

Be good. A principle of rhetoric is that an effective orator is a "good person who speaks well." Be an advocate who displays good will and character and who presents the case well.

B. Confidence

Appear confident and in control of the case. Thorough preparation develops the necessary confidence, and an effective presentation allows the attorney to remain in control. Successful advocates view the forum as "their" courtroom or hearing room, where they present their client's case.

C. Focusing

Focus on the ideas. In preparing a speech, effective speakers do not focus on the specific words they are to deliver but on the concepts and images they wish to express and evoke. A speech which is simply read from a prepared text is rarely interesting. Similarly, a memorized speech where the speaker merely recites words is also unpersuasive. Focus on the ideas that need to be expressed and explained, practice out loud, and then present the ideas using specific words when needed for impact.

D. Eye Contact

Maintain appropriate eye contact. It is critical to establishing credibility and persuasion. The lack of eye contact causes decision makers to doubt the attorney's sincerity or lose interest in what is being said.

Advocates must speak with their heads up and avoid the extensive use of notes which prevent them from maintaining sufficient eye contact. Some advocates get nervous and lose their concentration while looking a decision maker directly in the eyes. An effective way to look at someone is to focus on the bridge of the person's nose rather than the pupils of the person's eyes. The speaker avoids the intensity of eye contact, while the listener perceives that the speaker is looking at the listener.

E. Body Language

Be natural. Body language is a significant part of the advocate's communication process. The key is congruence, that is, the body language of the attorney should be consistent with the abilities of the lawyer and the message the advocate seeks to communicate. A lawyer whose body language lacks confidence or certainty is unable to be persuasive. An attorney who appears indifferent or uncaring may display an inattentive and insensitive attitude. Advocates are regularly on view in front of the decision maker, and inappropriate body language interferes with communication.

F. Gestures

Act natural. Good speakers employ natural gestures to make a presentation more effective, and an advocate should incorporate appropriate gestures into a presentation.

G. Appearance

Appear natural. A speaker's appearance often affects the listener's perceptions of that person. An attorney who is well-groomed usually appears more professional and credible. The attorney's appearance should be consistent with the personality and approach of the attorney.

Counsel should dress comfortably, in a manner that suits their taste and that conforms to the customs or rules of decorum established or promulgated in a jurisdiction. Many attorneys dress according to a standard they believe is expected of them by the decision maker. Some attorneys prefer to wear a distinctive piece of clothing during a trial to help the jurors remember and identify the attorney.

The dress of an attorney should not become an issue that detracts attention from the client's case. Attorneys may have to put aside personal tastes and conform their dress to the standards of a community or decision maker so as to safeguard and promote the best interests of a client.

H. Vocal Tone and Pace

Use variety. The tone, volume, modulation, and pace of an attorney's delivery affect the listening capabilities of the decision maker. A dull, monotone presentation is as ineffective as a loud, boisterous approach. A balanced and well-modulated approach is usually most effective. Sometimes silence is the best thing that can be used. Silence can be an effective way to highlight a point, to gain attention, or to create a transition.

§ 1.8 ETHICS

The process of becoming an advocate includes an understanding of and adherence to ethical norms and standards. Advocates must reflect on, wrestle with, and come to an understanding of the values, norms, and ethics that should be preserved and that shape the judgment and conduct of the advocate. Attorneys are members of a community consisting of clients, colleagues, opponents, judicial officers, and the public. Each advocate is not only a lawyer but also a person, guided not only by professional or legal ethics but also by individual and community concerns and values. This section specifically describes the shaping of ethical guidelines formed by decision makers within the adversary system, constraints within the system, and professional rules of conduct and behavior.

A. Sources of Decision–Making Power

Attorneys do not have power to control the fates of parties, but attorneys can influence the source of this power. It is the ability of the attorney to convince the decision maker to right a wrong that activates the power within the adversary system. Attorneys influence the results of a case by selecting the theories to be advanced, the evidence to be introduced, and the law to be explained.

B. Constraints

Clients have limited resources. The lack of sufficient funds makes it impossible to do everything that could be done in a case. Many cases do not justify significant monetary expenditures. The advocate must work within these restrictions to do the best possible job.

Lawyers have only limited available time. The time that an attorney can devote to a case is limited by the fee charged, professional hours available, and the lawyer's life outside the practice of law.

C. Professional Rules of Conduct

The rules of professional responsibility and state ethical rules provide both a set of disciplinary rules and guidelines for advocates. Some of the rules deal with the external, objective conduct of an attorney. Many rules deal with internal, subjective thinking of the lawyer. It is often difficult to apply these rules and guidelines to cases where there are two or more versions of what happened, two opponents who may dislike each other, and two advocates who are skilled at creating plausible explanations and portraying questionable behavior as legitimate. Attorneys must develop an internal code of ethics and constantly monitor their own conduct to determine whether it complies with the norms of the profession and their own ethical norms.

Every state has rules that establish standards and impose restraints on a lawyer's behavior. The Rules of Professional Conduct have been adopted with various modifications by the states. These rules codify norms which reflect the collective views and values of lawyers. State rules of procedure, case law, and local customs and traditions also regulate the conduct of advocates. The remainder of this section summarizes ethical rules based on the Model Rules of Professional Conduct that specifically apply to advocates.

1. Abide by Client's Decisions

Model Rule 1.2(a) states:

A lawyer shall abide by a client's decisions concerning the objectives of representation ... and shall consult with the client as to the means by which they are to be pursued. In a criminal case, the lawyer shall abide by the client's decision, after consultation with the lawyer, as to the plea to be entered, whether to waive jury trial and whether the client will testify.

The United States Supreme Court has approved this rule and the following standard:

The decisions on what, when, whether, and how to conduct cross examination, what jurors to accept or strike, what trial motion should be made, and all the strategic and tactical decisions are the exclusive providence of the lawyer after consultation with the client. Jones v. Barnes, 463 U.S. 745, 753 N. 6 (1983).

The advocate has an obligation to discuss the objectives of the case and the strategies that are to be pursued with the client. The attorney must consult with the client in making decisions regarding the objectives of the representation and alternative ways these objectives can be achieved. It is up to the attorney to implement these decisions.

2. Competent Representation

The advocate must provide competent representation and act with reasonable promptness and diligence. Competent representation minimally consists of legal knowledge, thorough preparation, and effective presentation of the case. The lawyer must render candid advice to the client and exercise independent, professional judgment.

3. Confidentiality

What a client tells a lawyer and the advice a lawyer renders to a client is confidential and may not be revealed unless the client consents, or certain situations permit or require disclosure. The factual story a client tells an attorney is disclosed when the client testifies at a deposition, a hearing, or at trial. The legal theories discussed between the client and the attorney often form the basis for the theory of the case which is presented at the trial or hearing.

4. Conflict of Interest

A lawyer may not represent a client if that representation will compromise or be compromised by the lawyer's responsibilities to another client or to a third person. Similarly, if the lawyer's own interests conflict, the case should be referred elsewhere. A client, after being fully informed by the attorney, may willingly waive the conflict and agree to be represented.

5. Good Faith

Model Rule 3.1 states:

A lawyer shall not bring or defend a proceeding, or assert or controvert an issue therein, unless there is a basis in law and fact for doing so that is not frivolous, which includes a good faith argument for an extension, modification, or reversal of existing law. A lawyer for a defendant in a criminal proceeding or the respondent in a proceeding that could result in incarceration may nevertheless so defend the proceeding as to require that every element of the case be established.

Federal Rule of Civil Procedure 11, similar state rules, and related arbitration and administrative provisions contain a similar standard. These rules prohibit an attorney from presenting any claim or defense unless to the best of that attorney's knowledge, information, and belief formed after reasonable investigation and research, it is well-grounded in fact and is warranted by existing law or a good faith argument for the development of new law.

These rules establish an objective standard of conduct as distinguished from a subjective belief. An attorney who has a personal belief that a claim or defense is valid does not meet the standard. The attorney must have an objective basis in law and fact to support the claim or defense. It is insufficient for an attorney to merely have a "pure heart" in asserting a claim or defense. These rules require that an attorney have a "good legal head" and factual and legal support for a claim or defense.

6. Expediting the Case

A lawyer must make reasonable efforts, consistent with the legitimate interests of a client, to expedite a trial or hearing and not delay proceedings for improper reasons. It is inappropriate for an attorney to engage in time-consuming discovery and motion practice if these strategies are not legitimately employed to promote a client's case. It is unethical for an attorney to employ delaying tactics which are used for the primary purpose of causing the opposing party to expend unnecessary resources or for unreasonably extending the time before the case is brought to a final resolution.

7. Evidence

Model Rule 3.3(a)(4) states:

A lawyer shall not knowingly ... offer evidence that the lawyer knows to be false. If a lawyer has offered material evidence and comes to know of its falsity, the lawyer shall take reasonable remedial measures.

Model Rule 3.4(a) further states that:

Lawyers shall not ... allude to any matter that the lawyer does not reasonably believe is relevant or that will not be supported by admissible evidence.

A lawyer may not unlawfully obstruct another party's access to evidence or alter, destroy or conceal a document or other material having potential evidentiary value. The obviously despicable nature of this conduct should not require a rule to prevent it.

8. *Disclosing Controlling Authority*

Model Rule 3.3(a)(2) states:

A lawyer shall not knowingly fail to disclose to the tribunal legal authority in the controlling jurisdiction known to the lawyer to be directly adverse to the position of the client and not disclosed by opposing counsel.

A lawyer must disclose all controlling authority — supportive or adverse — but is not obligated to disclose legal authority if it is not controlling. Precedent from another jurisdiction that does not bind the decision maker need not be disclosed. The attorney may rely upon the law from other jurisdictions and argue that this law ought to apply, requiring the opposing attorney to argue against the application of this law even though it is not controlling.

9. *Influence*

A lawyer may not seek to influence a judge, arbitrator, or juror by means prohibited by law and may not communicate ex parte with such persons unless permitted by law. An advocate should communicate with the decision maker (if permitted) about a matter in a case only if the opposing lawyer is present or involved.

10. *Complying With Rulings*

Model Rule 3.4(c) states:

A lawyer shall not ... knowingly disobey an obligation under the rules of the tribunal except for an open refusal based on an assertion that no valid obligation exists.

A lawyer must comply with the rulings and orders of the decision maker except in extraordinarily unusual situations in which an attorney would decide to face a contempt citation and be penalized for disobeying.

D. *Attorney Misconduct*

A review of attorney disciplinary cases reveals that common reasons for lawyer malfeasance result from greed, alcohol or drug abuse, laziness, and legal incompetence. Many lawyers who operate dysfunctionally will do so until they are caught, and do not stop because of a code of external or internal ethics. A client, colleague, partner, friend, or family member may be the person or persons who get them help.

A review of complaints filed with licensing boards by clients against lawyers reveals that common complaints involve the lack of sufficient or ongoing communications and inappropriate fees. Lawyers can substantially reduce potential client problems by maintaining sufficient, regular communications and explaining the fees charged.

E. *Client Demands and Satisfaction*

Advocates may feel pressure from their clients to win, sometimes at all costs, and sometimes by using inappropriate approaches. They obviously need to avoid submitting to this pressure and explain why they cannot act accordingly, or withdraw from the representation. The demands of clients and the lawyer's need to satisfy their interests must be properly balanced with doing what is ethical and proper.

F.   The Consequences of Misconduct

The most egregious misconduct by an advocate will be handled by the court or arbitrator through a contempt citation or a motion and order for a new trial or hearing, and by the appellate court through a reversal. Lesser misconduct will usually prompt a reprimand by the court or a professional responsibility board or office. Other sanctions may be imposed by state or local ethics committees for misconduct, but this is rare.

Still, the rarity of external sanctions should not be taken as an unlimited license to engage in questionable conduct that may win the case. The primary protection against abuses by advocates lies within each lawyer. The true sanctions are personal and professional, such as the loss of self-esteem, reputation, respect, credibility, and ultimately, cases and clients. It is critical for the advocate to develop and maintain a reputation as an honest, trustworthy, ethical, and professional advocate.

CHAPTER 2

PLANNING AND PREPARATION

REFLECTING ON ADVOCACY

Few things are brought to a successful issue by impetuous desire, but most by calm and prudent forethought.

—Thucydides

Life can only be understood backwards; but it must be lived forwards.

—Soren Kierkegaard

§ 2.1 INTRODUCTION

Before trying a case, the advocate must plan and prepare the case. There is no single, correct way to try or prepare a case; however, experienced advocates share similar approaches to case planning. This chapter explains the preparation process and describes effective planning methods. The following sections cover the stages of a case, the planning process, the selection of case theories, the analysis of evidence, and the submission of jury instructions and verdict forms in a jury trial. Chapter 3 describes additional case procedures including pretrial and prehearing conferences and motions.

§ 2.2 STAGES OF A CASE

A. *Civil Jury Trial*

The trial lawyer must review each stage of a trial and prepare an integrated plan for the presentation of a case. The sequence and stages of a civil trial, after the pretrial litigation process of pleading, discovery, and motion practice has been completed, are as follows:

- Pretrial conference.

- Chambers discussion immediately preceding the beginning of the trial.

- Jury selection, with the plaintiff proceeding first, followed by the defendant (in some jurisdictions defendant proceeds first).

- Opening statement by the plaintiff, followed by the defendant's opening unless reserved until commencement of the defendant's case.

- Plaintiff's case, including the introduction of evidence and direct examinations by plaintiff, cross-examinations by defendant, and redirect and recross examinations.

- Defendant's motion for directed verdict.

- Defendant's case, including the introduction of evidence and direct examinations by defendant, cross-examinations by plaintiff, and redirect and recross.

- Rebuttal (if necessary), with the plaintiff introducing rebuttal evidence followed by any rebuttal by defendant.

- Motion for directed verdict often brought by both the plaintiff and defendant.

- Final selection of jury instructions by judge.

- Closing argument by plaintiff, followed by defendant's summation, followed by plaintiff's rebuttal; or, in some jurisdictions, closing argument by defendant, followed by plaintiff's summation.

- Charge to the jury (in some jurisdictions the judge instructs the jurors before closing arguments).

- Jury deliberations.

- Verdict.

- Post-trial motions, including a motion for judgment notwithstanding the verdict and motion for new trial.

- Notice of appeal.

B. Criminal Jury Trial

The sequence and stages of a criminal trial after a defendant has been arrested and arraigned and after preliminary hearings have been completed are:

- Pretrial conference.

- Chambers discussion immediately before the start of the trial.

- Jury selection, usually with the defendant proceeding first, followed by the prosecutor (in some jurisdictions the prosecution proceeds first).

- Opening statement by the prosecutor, followed by the defendant's opening unless reserved until the commencement of the defendant's case.

- Prosecution's case, including the introduction of evidence and direct examinations by the prosecutor, cross-examinations by defendant, and redirect and recross examinations.

- Defendant's motion to dismiss or for acquittal.

- Defendant's case (unless defendant declines to introduce evidence), including direct examinations by defendant, cross-examinations by prosecutor, and redirect and recross.

- Rebuttal (if necessary), with prosecutor introducing rebuttal evidence followed by rebuttal evidence introduced by defendant.

- Renewal of defendant's motion for acquittal.

- Final selection of jury instructions by judge.

- Closing argument by the prosecution, followed by the defendant's summation, with many jurisdictions permitting rebuttal by the prosecutor, and a few jurisdictions allowing defendant to close last (or in even fewer jurisdictions the defense goes first followed by the prosecution with no rebuttals).

- Charge to the jury (in some jurisdictions instructions are given before closing arguments).

- Jury deliberations.

- Verdict.

- Post-trial motions, including defense motion for judgment of acquittal and motion for new trial.

- Notice of appeal.

C. Bench Trial

The stages of civil and criminal bench trials are the same as jury trials, except that there obviously is no jury selection, jury instructions, jury deliberation or verdict. Instead, there are findings of fact, conclusions of law, and an order for judgment entered by the judge. See Section 2.11.

D. Administrative Hearing

The type of an administrative hearing determines its procedures and stages. Many administrative hearings are identical or similar to a bench trial. The process includes all stages of a bench trial and concludes with a written opinion by the administrative judge which explains the decision. An example of this type of hearing is a worker's compensation trial.

Another administrative hearing format involves the administrative judge as an active participant in the presentation of the case. The judge may initially question the witnesses before the parties have an opportunity to conduct a direct or cross-examination. The administrative judge may ask questions that consist of direct and cross-examination questions. Closing statements may be made by the parties with the judge asking questions or phrasing issues. This type of hearing is common in situations where the parties do not have attorneys representing them, for example, in unemployment compensation hearings.

Other administrative hearings involve regulatory law. The administrative body may receive evidence in different ways. The role of the administrative officers may be to present and submit evidence as well as to consider it. Parties who are directly affected by a potential regulatory ruling may cross-examine witnesses and may present their own evidence. Parties who are permitted to intervene in a case may present evidence or arguments in a more limited role. The staff of the administrative body may act as advocates for specific regulatory rules. Examples of these types of hearings include utility and environmental cases.

E. Arbitration

The stages of an arbitration process include:

- Filing and serving of the arbitration claim and response.

- Selection of an arbitrator.

- Exchange of discoverable information before the hearing.

- Prehearing procedures and issue resolution

- The hearing.

- The award.

Arbitration procedures appear in a set of rules established by the arbitration organization, (e.g., The National Arbitration Forum Code of Procedure).

Parties agree to use arbitration by including a pre-dispute arbitration clause in their agreement or transaction or by agreeing to arbitration after a dispute arises. A claimant may file a claim with the arbitration administrator (e.g., The National Arbitration Forum or the American Arbitration Association or JAMS) to initiate the arbitration process. The claim consists of a detailed explanation of the facts and law supporting the claim, documents which contain relevant information, and the filing fee. The respondent has to respond in writing with a detailed explanation of defenses and available counter-claims, accompanied by supporting documents. After the parties have completed their submissions, a neutral and experienced arbitrator is selected, usually from a panel of arbitrators. The arbitration forum may appoint an arbitrator whom the parties may challenge, or may submit a list of potential arbitrators and the parties may remove one or more of the arbitrators.

Parties may exchange discoverable information, and may obtain from each other relevant and reliable documents. Discovery may range from a limited number of depositions to all the discovery methods available under the federal rules. The arbitrator resolves any discovery disputes between the parties.

The arbitration organization administers the arbitration proceeding. The parties exchange a list of witnesses and exhibits a reasonable time before the hearing. Arbitrators have subpoena power and can require individuals to appear at arbitration hearings if the parties request.

There are two basic types of arbitration proceedings: document hearings and participatory hearings. In a document hearing, the parties submit their case in writing to the arbitrator. Parties may submit documents, exhibits, affidavits, memorandums, and any writing for consideration by the arbitrator. The arbitrator issues an award after a review of these written submissions. Parties do not appear at a document hearing. This type of hearing is especially useful for document cases that can be decided without the need for oral testimony.

A participatory hearing resembles a bench trial. Parties attend that hearing and present their evidence through witnesses and exhibits. Parties may represent themselves or choose to have an attorney represent them. The stages of a participatory hearing include an opening statement, direct and cross-examinations, and summation. Parties may have witnesses appear in person or by a deposition transcript, testify over the telephone or through video transmission. The arbitrator conducts the hearing and admits all relevant and reliable evidence. The case is concluded when the arbitrator issues the award. Parties may also submit additional information or legal memorandums after the hearing. The decision of an arbitrator in a binding arbitration is final and enforceable.

§ 2.3   CASE NOTEBOOK

In order to prepare efficiently, the advocate must develop a systematic approach to each case. The approach must be consistent yet flexible enough to deal with the particular circumstances of each case. Forms and charts are included throughout this book to provide examples of a systematic approach to case preparation.

Preparation for a trial, arbitration, or administrative proceeding includes the creation of a case notebook. This notebook organizes the material needed for trial or hearing, permits new material to be added during case preparation, establishes an orderly approach to each stage of the case, and permits ready access to case material. The notebook should contain separate sections for each stage of the case and can be placed in a three-ring binder with tabs or in individual files in an accordion file. Section topics include:

- Summary of case theory, including legal theories and factual summaries.

- Applicable substantive law, including cases and statutes.

- Applicable procedural rules, including court rules, the arbitration code of procedure, and administrative regulations.

- Pleadings, including a list of allegations that have been admitted.

- Discovery, including discovery responses, witness statements, and deposition testimony that will be introduced as evidence or available for impeachment.

- Motions or requests, including pretrial motions, in limine motions, trial motions, and post-trial motions.

- Pretrial or prehearing discussions, including a list of things to be discussed with the judge or arbitrator.

- Case brief, see Section 3.4(E).

- Objections and applicable rules of evidence and case law decisions to support anticipated evidentiary positions.

- Jury selection, including questions for prospective jurors, the law relating to jury selection, and charts or forms to be used during jury selection.

- Opening statement, including an outline and a list of visual aids.

- Witnesses, including a list of witnesses and the order they will be called.

- Exhibits, including a list of exhibits to be introduced and a chart describing the exhibits, the marking number or letter, the witnesses through whom the exhibits will be introduced, and whether the exhibits have been offered and received in evidence.

- Direct examination, including a list of topics or questions for each witness and exhibits that will be used with each witness.

- Cross-examination, including a list of topics or questions for each witness, prior statements from depositions or hearings, and any exhibits to be used.

- Jury instructions and verdict forms, including proposed general and specific instructions and interrogatory questions to be used.

- Closing argument, including an outline or text of summation and a list of exhibits and visual aids to be used.

- Expenses, including costs, bills, fees, and timesheets.

- Proposed findings of fact, conclusions of law, and order.

- Errors, including a list of prejudicial errors occurring during the trial to support a motion for a new trial and a ground for appeal.

§ 2.4 PLANNING OBJECTIVES

The initial planning for a trial or hearing actually begins with the first client interview. Before a trial or hearing gets underway the lawyers have: gathered facts, researched the law, drafted pleadings, completed discovery, and resolved motions.

The planning process is critical for several reasons:

- Effective preparation develops successful strategies, tactics, and techniques.

- Planning allows for the creation and completion of a written case notebook.

- Preparation helps identify and anticipate problems that may occur and creates responses to those problems.

- Planning builds confidence and reduces anxiety, uncertainties, and surprises.

- Thorough preparation substantially offsets the disadvantage of inexperience.

A. *Beginning at the End*

Begin at the end. The summation is the final destination of the case, and its composition is the first step of case preparation. The outline and content of the closing argument provides a form and structure for the presentation of the case.

Summation contains an explanation of the facts, law, inferences, reasons, and arguments that support a winning decision. This in turn forms the basis for the final selection of case theories, what forum or decision maker should be selected, how the opening should be presented, the evidence that should be introduced, and how the case can best be won. If a fact must be established to support a statement made during the closing argument, the attorney can plan to introduce that evidence through direct or cross-examination. A summation developed early in case preparation will undoubtedly undergo some change as the case progresses.

B. Objective Analysis by Attorney

Assess the facts and analyze the law objectively. As an advocate, it can be difficult to be objective when reviewing the strengths and weaknesses of a client's case. Lawyers must put themselves in the place of the decision maker in assessing the facts, determining the credibility of witnesses, drawing inferences, and accepting arguments.

C. Analyzing the Opponent

Assess the opponent. The assets and liabilities of an opponent affect the presentation of an attorney's case. These factors include: the degree of experience, skill level, demeanor, reputation, habits, relationship with the tribunal, and how the decision maker will perceive and evaluate the lawyer. Information about an opposing lawyer can be obtained from colleagues, attorneys from other firms, and individuals who know the lawyer.

D. Analyzing the Judge/Arbitrator

Assess the decision maker. As explained previously and as expanded on in subsequent sections, an essential approach to succeeding at advocacy is for the advocate to ascertain and predict the values, norms, principles, and beliefs that will influence a decision maker. This analysis will help in selecting evidence and arguments that reflect these values and resonate with these principles. It will be far easier and much more likely for a decision maker to find for a party if the case presented supports the underlying norms and beliefs of the decision maker.

Familiarity with the strengths and weaknesses of decision makers also require assessment. These factors include:

- How are proceedings handled?
- How are rulings made?
- What are the demands or expectations of advocates?
- How are the rules of evidence applied?
- What is the educational and professional background of this decision maker?

Information about a decision maker may be obtained by talking with colleagues, lawyer friends, and others who know the judge or arbitrator.

It is improper for an attorney to contact a decision maker ex parte about a case. Information can also be obtained from computer searches for cases, articles, and statistics and from published listings.

§ 2.5   SELECTING A THEORY OF THE CASE

The "theory of the case" provides the decision maker with the reasons why a client is entitled to win. An effective theory of the case is understandable, persuasive, comprehensive, and compelling. When it is heard, the decision maker will *want* the client to win. It is the most important part of case planning.

A theory of the case can be short and summarized in a few sentences. Or a theory may need more of an explanation. While it is called a theory, the concept blends compelling facts and instructive law into a persuasive statement.

An effective case theory has to work for the client, advocate, and decision maker. The client has to like the explanation. The lawyer has to be able to compose a recognizable legal claim or defense and be able to prove the supporting facts. And, the values and principles advanced in the theory need to reflect the norms and beliefs of the decision maker.

A theory of the case is presented and repeated throughout the trial or hearing. The use of words, phrases, and images contained in the case theory are described in the opening statement, introduced through witnesses and exhibits, and explained in the closing argument.

The issues in a case determine available approaches to crafting a theory. Many civil cases involve responsible or irresponsible conduct. For instance, tort law calls this negligence, and contract law calls this breach of contract. A common civil case theory revolves around who is more responsible for the accident or breach. A case theory can also blend legal doctrines with critical facts to create a compelling explanation. And, eventually the theory of the case is to be fully explained during summation. Three examples follow:

Common Case Example (Tort Case):

For the Plaintiff

This case involves the irresponsible conduct of the defendant country club that invited a lot of members to a party and then made a lot of money by selling them a lot of drinks. But the club did not give them a lot of room. While dancing to a hired band near a very slippery and very crowded pool area the club knew was slippery and crowded, the plaintiff was uncontrollably pushed by the crowd into the pool severely injuring his head and back. The club must be held accountable for its blatant irresponsibility.

For the Defendant

This case is about choices and irresponsibility. The plaintiff choose to come to a fun party for club members and decided to drink so many drinks that he got drunk. That was his choice. He paid for his drinks. No one once forced him to drink. And instead of going home, he choose to stay and find a slippery spot to dance on, right next to the pool and a big sign that says "Caution: Slippery Surface." His falling into the pool was his fault, and not the drinks, not the other members, and not the club. The club workers or members are not to blame. He is.

Blending Law/Fact Example (Products Case):

For the Plaintiff

The Garbomatic Company negligently designed, manufactured and sold the Spinchop garbage disposal to the plaintiff. That disposal was defective when it was designed, defective when it was manufactured, and defective when it was sold. These defects caused the disposal to explode. The metal pieces that exploded out of that defective machine destroyed Alex Wojcik's eye. The Garbomatic Company was negligent and is responsible for what happened to Mr. Wojcik. The Garbomatic Company must be held accountable to him because its defective machine caused his injury.

For the Defendant

What happened to Mr. Wojcik is a tragedy. The Spinchop garbage disposal is a safe, well designed, and expertly manufactured consumer product – when it is installed properly and used as intended. The tragedy is that Mr. Wojcik negligently installed the disposal himself and then negligently used it. He knew he was supposed to install the switch within easy reach of the disposal. He did not, knowing better. He also knew he should not start the disposal if there was silverware in it. But he did, knowing better. Unfortunately, he is responsible for his own injuries, not the Garbomatic Company.

Expanded Summation Example: (Employment Discrimination Case):

For the Defense

Judith Kincade chose to work at the Owen Law Firm. She interviewed with a group of successful, experienced lawyers and decided to join their practice. They allowed her to represent their clients.

What did she have a right to expect? She had a right to expect to be paid fairly, be given the same opportunities as other associates at the firm, and be judged fairly. She was. The firm paid her very generously, provided her with the same opportunities to succeed or fail as other associates, and judged her the way they judged everyone.

What obligations did she have to fulfill? She had responsibilities to work hard, to be productive, and to work well with colleagues. She failed her responsibilities. Her work was reasonable but not up to the billable hour standards of the firm; her legal production was good but she did not generate sufficient new business for the firm; and her demeanor and willingness to work with others was questionable. Ms. Kincade lost her job because she could not do it well. The firm chose others who they felt were much better qualified. So long as there were legitimate reasons for their decision they were wholly within their rights.

Hard work and talent will result in women taking their rightful place in all strata of our society. In order for that to happen, they must be permitted to fail. All of us who work for a living stand on our own two feet. We are subject to the judgment of others. We get knocked down, we get back up, brush ourselves off, get back to work. We learn from our failures. We learn from our mistakes. Let Judith Kincade learn the very same thing.

For the Plaintiff

Judith Kincade had a right to be treated as any other law firm attorney. She was judged by the Owen Law Firm not as an attorney, but as a woman attorney. She is being punished for the very same behavior for which male associates have been rewarded. They were assertive, she was abrasive. They showed leadership, she was bossy. They were businesslike, she was cold.

Nobody told her when she first interviewed with the firm that she would be judged not only by how hard she worked, but by how much fun she was to be around. Nobody told her that her failure to smile or her lack of interest in sports would represent an insurmountable obstacle to advancement. And the reason nobody told her was that the men who interviewed her wanted her to work for them. They knew that this was a bright, driven attorney who could be depended upon to work as hard as possible. They knew it would be six or seven years before they would have to tell her she was not going to make partner. They knew what a good deal they had here.

She now rightfully asks for the good deal they promised her. She lost her job because they discriminated against her, because she was a woman. There is no doubt that the men of the Owen Law Firm are somewhat uncomfortable with Judith Kincade. They may be more comfortable having as partners other men that look and act like themselves. They hired Judith Kincade, worked her hard for seven years, and got rid of her without recognition or reward. They now have to pay for their decision and their comfort. We ask you to make them pay.

§ 2.6 CASE ANALYSIS

When planning, the advocate must analyze the:

- Applicable legal claims and defenses,
- Available facts,
- Story that best blends the law and facts,
- Favorable factual issues,
- Persuasive evidence, and
- Effective strategies.

The following sections describe these six critical assessments.

A. *Selecting Legal Claims and Defenses*

A legal claim or defense is based on an existing law or a good faith argument extending, modifying, or attempting to change existing law. In many cases, the advocate identifies claims and defenses by applying established law. An example is a breach of contract theory for failure to perform an obligation under a written contract. All jurisdictions recognize this claim. In other cases, an attorney advances a claim or defense that expands or modifies existing law. An example is a breach of an implied covenant of good faith and fair dealing in an oral employment contract arrangement. Only a few jurisdictions presently recognize this legal doctrine.

The law supporting the legal theory is found wherever laws are found: in statutes, case law, constitutional provisions, and rules and regulations. Elements of a legal theory appear in jury instructions which can be found in a text of standard jury instruction guides ("JIGs") or by researching the substantive law of a jurisdiction.

Legal claims for civil plaintiffs and prosecutors correspond to the legal elements of the claim or crime. For example, the legal theory of an arbitration claimant who brings a breach of contract action may be based on the following elements: the existence of a contract, performance by plaintiff of the contract, breach by defendant of the contract, and damages resulting from the breach. The legal theory of a prosecutor who charges the defendant with aggravated assault may be based on these elements: intent to do bodily harm, possession of a dangerous weapon, and infliction of injuries.

Legal defenses for civil and criminal defendants arise from a number of sources, including the denial of the allegations of the claim or crime, affirmative defenses, counterclaims, third party complaints, and the joinder of related issues and parties.

In composing an effective legal claim or defense an advocate should:

- *Research all sources of the law,*

- *Assess the strengths and weaknesses of available doctrines,*

- *Consider multiple legal doctrines,*

- *Employ claims or defenses supported by favorable jury instructions or conclusions of law,*

- *Avoid selecting a legal technicality as a claim or defense, and*

- *Select a doctrine readily supported by the facts.*

B. Composing a Factual Summary

A factual summary consists of a description of what happened, and is based upon the evidence that is available and admissible. The story outline consisting of the important facts to be proven and inferences to be drawn is the framework for the factual summary.

A factual summary for a civil plaintiff in an automobile accident case may consist of the following outline:

- The plaintiff was driving home after work.

- The plaintiff stopped the car behind a crosswalk at a stop sign.

- The defendant's car rear-ended the plaintiff's car.

- The defendant was not paying attention.

- The defendant was speeding.

- The plaintiff and the defendant exchanged information.

- The plaintiff suffered injuries, including whiplash.

- The plaintiff paid medical expenses and lost income from work.

- The plaintiff endured pain and suffering.

A factual outline for a prosecutor in a theft case may be:

- The victim was walking down the street to go to the store.

- The crime was committed on the corner.

- The lighting conditions were bright.

- The victim was carrying her purse over her right shoulder.

- The defendant grabbed the purse from behind.

- The victim saw the defendant's face.

- The defendant stole the purse and ran away.

- The value of the contents of the purse amounted to over $1,550.

- The victim gave a description of the defendant to the police.

- The victim identified defendant at a lineup.

- The victim identified defendant in court.

In crafting an effective factual summary an advocate should:

- *Construct a factual summary that will survive a motion for summary judgment or motion to dismiss,*

- *Compose a summary that is supported by credible and persuasive evidence,*
- *Avoid creating inconsistent alternative factual stories, and*
- *Create a story that the fact finder wants to believe in.*

C. Blending Law and Facts Into a Story

An advocate in effectively crafting a story that weaves together the applicable clams and defenses and relevant facts needs to:

1. Assert Affirmative Positions

A story should reflect affirmative, positive positions. Approaches that are purely defensive or negative are usually insufficient. Even a criminal defendant must usually present a story of what happened and not just argue that what the plaintiff/prosecutor says did not happen.

2. Employ an Approach Based on Common Sense

Decision-makers may ultimately resolve the disputed law and facts in the case based upon their common sense, and it makes sense to focus on that approach.

3. Have the Fact Finder Identify With the Story

If the fact finders can identify with a position because they or others have experienced something similar in their lives or the story could reasonably have happened to others, it can be more persuasive.

4. Use an Approach That Results in a Fair and Just Decision

If a position results in a determination that is unfair or unreasonable, the decision maker is less likely to accept the position.

5. Avoid Employing a Position That Requires the Fact Finder to Make a Difficult Choice

The less difficult a decision that has to be made, the more likely a favorable decision will be made.

6. Test the Approach

The advocate can explain positions to colleagues, relatives, or friends to discover strengths and weaknesses of the position and to obtain their favorable or unfavorable response to the approach. In cases with significant resources, the positions can be presented to a mock jury or a focus group which will give their reactions and evaluations of the position.

D. Determining the Factual Issues

Another stage of the planning process is determining what issues the fact finder must decide in a case to render a favorable decision. Effective advocates put themselves in the place of the fact finder to identify the difficult issues that must be resolved in a case:

Issue: *What story to believe?*

Solution:

- Review the evidence and determine which facts are in dispute.
- Determine why the fact finder would believe the supporting facts.
- Determine why the fact finder would not believe the supporting facts and would believe contrary facts.
- List the reasons why the fact finder should not believe these unfavorable facts.

For example, a corporation may defend a fraud case by arguing that there was no intent to deceive the claimant nor reliance on the part of the claimant. The attorney for the corporation should review the facts which establish no intent and no reliance to determine why the administrative judge would more likely accept the story presented by the corporation.

Issue: *What witness to believe?*

Solution:

- List reasons why your witnesses are credible.
- List reasons why opposing witnesses are not credible.

For example, a respondent may claim she never made a specific representation or statement as alleged by the claimant. The defense attorney should list all the reasons why the respondent should be believed and all the reasons why opposing witnesses should not be believed to assist the arbitrator in deciding credibility.

Issue: *What favorable inferences can be made from the evidence?*

Solution:

- Identify all favorable inferences and list reasons why these inferences are reasonable.
- Identify all unfavorable inferences and list reasons why these inferences are unreasonable.

For example, a plaintiff in an automobile accident case may rely upon circumstantial evidence to prove a defendant was negligent. The attorney for the plaintiff should identify all reasonable circumstantial inferences that can be drawn from the direct evidence to support the plaintiff's case.

Issue: *How should facts be interpreted and applied to the law?*

Solution:

- Create favorable interpretations that support a helpful conclusion.
- Determine what unfavorable interpretations negate the opponent's case.

For example, a defendant in a criminal case may rely upon the prosecutor's failure to prove guilt beyond a reasonable doubt as a defense. Counsel for the defendant must present an interpretation and application of the burden "beyond a reasonable doubt" to the fact finder and present the reasons why the facts in the case support "reasonable doubt."

E.   Selecting Evidence

An essential part of the planning process is the identification of evidence that is admissible. The methods available to introduce evidence are:

- *Testimony* of witnesses, including both lay and expert witnesses. See Chapter 7 on direct examination.

- The introduction of *exhibits,* including real and demonstrative exhibits. See Chapter 8.

- *Stipulations.* The parties can stipulate to the introduction of evidence. See Section 3.6(G).

- *Admissions.* Statements made by an adverse party contained in discovery responses, including interrogatory answers, deposition transcripts, and responses to requests for admissions, may be offered by the opposing party as evidence. See Section 3.6(H).

- *Former testimony.* Witnesses who are unavailable for a trial or hearing and who have previously testified at a deposition or hearing may have their testimony admitted as evidence. See Section 3.6(I).

- *Judicial/Arbitral/Administrative Notice.* A party may ask that a judge or arbitrator take notice of certain facts. See Section 3.6(J).

In addition, a lot of information fact finders need to help them decide a case comes from their own life experiences. In every case, the attorneys presume fact finders understand certain information without having to introduce evidence to explain the obvious. For example, in an automobile accident case, witnesses may testify that a car ran a red light, but there will not be general testimony regarding what a car is, or that it has an engine, or what a steering wheel does, unless there is a controversy regarding one of these issues. The attorneys assume that the fact finder is familiar with cars and knows that an automobile has four wheels and that the driver sits behind the steering wheel and uses an accelerator and brake to move and stop the car.

In every case, many elemental facts are presumed to be understood by the fact finder, and the attorneys will not present information regarding these common life experiences. To do so would be a waste of time and insult the fact finder. The advocate must make a judgment regarding what facts should be explained by a witness or document and what should be presumed to be known by the fact finder.

F.   Developing a Strategy

A case strategy is the overall, grand plan designed to win the case. The strategy consists of the numerous tactics to be used in presenting the case. Tactics are the individual approaches, techniques, and applications of the strategy. The effective case strategist:

- *Views the case as a whole* and is able to integrate the various parts and stages of the case,

- *Identifies the arguments* that will most likely influence the decision maker favorably,

- *Thinks creatively* by brainstorming, generating optional strategies, and evaluating these options,

- *Predicts how the decision maker will decide* and fashions a strategy to reflect that process,

- *Identifies weaknesses* and considers ways to reduce or eliminate their impact,

- *Considers risks* attendant with a strategy and attempts to minimize or eliminate those risks,

- *Develops alternative strategies* and tactics as a contingency plan in case the primary strategy fails or falters, and

- *Lists the toughest questions* the decision maker has to make and composes favorable answers to those questions.

Form 2.1 provides an outline for the development of a strategy. The following section demonstrates how a strategy is implemented using supportive tactics and techniques.

FORM 2.1
CASE STRATEGIES

Selecting Theory of Case

Available Legal Theories/Elements of Claims or Defenses:

Factual Summary/Story Outline:

Significant Issues:

Selecting Evidence

    Witnesses:

    Exhibits:

    Stipulations:

    Admissions:

    Former Testimony:

    Judicial/Arbitral Notice:

    Other:

§ 2.7 IMPLEMENTING A CASE THEORY AND STRATEGY

This section demonstrates the implementation of a theory of the case and strategy and the use of supporting tactics and techniques. The example involves an automobile accident. The defendant's theory of the case is that a key witness for the plaintiff misperceived what happened. The strategy is to focus the jury's attention on this issue throughout the trial and to convince them the witness is wrong. This approach is initially introduced during jury selection and repeated and reinforced throughout the trial.

Jury Instruction

The preliminary or final jury instruction given by the judge reads:

> You have to determine the credibility of the testimony of the witnesses. You must assess their interest or lack of interest in the outcome of the case; their ability to see what they say they saw; their distance from the accident and how clear their line of vision was; their memory; their frankness and sincerity; and the reasonableness or unreasonableness of the witnesses' testimony in light of all the other evidence in the case.

Jury Selection

The defense attorney asks the jurors:

> The judge will instruct you regarding credibility of witnesses, that is, their ability to see what they tell you they saw. If the judge tells you that the ability of eyewitnesses to see something depends upon their distance from the event, the direction which they were looking, and their line of sight, would all of you be able to follow that instruction that the judge gives you?

Opening Statement

Defense counsel says:

> Members of the Jury, the plaintiff's case rests on the testimony of an eyewitness who was mistaken about what she saw. The plaintiff will rely extensively on the testimony of Alice Cramden, who the facts will show could not have seen what she said she saw. At the time the accident happened, she was more than half a block away from the intersection, looking in the opposite direction, and her line of vision was blocked by cars.

Cross-examination

During cross-examination of Alice Cramden the attorney asks:

> Q: Immediately before the accident, you were at the bus stop?
>
> A: Yes.
>
> Q: The bus stop is located in the middle of the block?
>
> A: Approximately.
>
> Q: You were waiting for a bus?

A: Yes.

Q: You were sitting on the bench at the bus stop?

A: Yes.

Q: You were looking for the bus coming down the street?

A: Yes.

Q: The bus was coming from the opposite direction of the intersection where the accident happened?

A: Yes.

Q: There were cars parked between where you were sitting and the intersection?

A: There were some cars.

Q: There was traffic on the street between the bus stop and the intersection?

A: Yes.

Direct Examination:

During direct examination of the defendant, the attorney establishes:

Q: Where was the bus stop?

A: In the middle of the block.

Q: In which direction did buses come from to stop there?

A: In the opposite direction of the intersection.

Q: Immediately before the accident, did you see any cars down Main Street?

A: Yes, there were cars parked on both sides of Main Street and there was traffic moving in both directions.

Summation

The defense attorney concludes:

Members of the Jury, the evidence introduced during this case proves to you that Alice Cramden could not have seen what she says she saw. The facts establish that she is mistaken about what happened. She was too far away to get an accurate look. She was not looking in the direction of the intersection before the accident. She was looking for a bus coming from the opposite direction. When did she first look in the direction of the intersection? After the accident happened. After she heard the noise of the collision. Further, the cars parked along Main Street and the traffic going in both directions along Main Street as shown on this diagram show that she is wrong. This mark, that we have labeled Cramden, is where she told us she was sitting. This mark, labeled Accident, is the accident scene. As I now draw a line between the bus stop bench where Ms. Cramden was sitting and the location in the intersection where the accident occurred, you will conclude that it is not possible for her to see what she says she saw.

Verdict

Judgment for the defendant.

§ 2.8   SELECTING THE FORUM

A.   *Selecting the Finder of Fact*

An advocate may have an opportunity to choose a forum in which a matter will be decided. If there is a choice the advocate must consider the facts and law of the case, who the fact finder will be, and the advantages and limitations of the different forums. In litigation, one of the initial and critical decisions the advocate must make is whether the case should be tried to a judge or to a jury. Most cases tried are non-jury trials, also called bench trials, and in many respects are similar to arbitrations and administrative hearings. In some cases the parties do not have a right to a jury trial. In other cases trial attorneys decide to waive the jury trial and try the case before a judge. There are several factors to consider in determining the appropriate forum.

1.   *The Nature of the Factual Issue*

A case primarily involving emotional or sympathy issues may be better tried before a jury than a professional decision maker because judges or arbitrators may be less likely to be swayed by these factors. Conversely, a party opposing these kinds of issues may prefer a non-jury forum.

2.   *The Type of Client*

The personality and nature of a client may be very appealing to a jury of peers while a judge or arbitrator may not be affected by such personal appeal. Also, an experienced decision maker may be less affected than a jury by the traits of a client. For example, while jurors may be unfairly predisposed to favor an individual opposed by a large corporation, a judge may not be unduly influenced by this factor.

3.   *The Nature of the Legal Theory*

If the case involves a legal issue that presents a legal problem, a professional decision maker rather than a jury may be more inclined to provide a recovery. Jurors may be inclined to ignore a point of law if it results in what appears to be an unfair or unjust result.

4.   *The Complexity of the Case*

A jury may or may not be able to understand and decide complex cases as well as a judge. A judge may or may not be able to understand complicated cases as well as an experienced arbitrator or a specialized administrative law judge. Other cases may involve extremely difficult factual or legal issues that may take a very long time to try if presented to a jury and may be much more readily presented to and better decided by an arbitrator who has the requisite expertise.

5. The Efficient Presentation of the Case

Trial procedures are lengthier in a jury trial and the rules of evidence excluding or restricting testimony or exhibits are more strictly enforced. See Section 3.11. These factors may suggest that a bench trial, arbitration, or administrative hearing is preferable because it is more efficient and effective.

6. The Effectiveness of the Advocate

Whether the opposing lawyer will be more effective before a professional or a jury may influence the decision.

7. Preferences of the Client

The client's wishes should also be considered by the lawyer. The client may prefer a decision reached by a jury, or may prefer an experienced arbitrator who can decide the case much more quickly and affordably.

8. The Type of Decision Maker

If the judge assigned to a case may be favorably disposed, a jury trial need not be demanded or may be waived. Some judges may be more empathetic and compassionate than a jury. Parties can select an arbitrator mutually acceptable to them. Administrative law judges may not be able to be effectively challenged and removed.

9. Nature of Potential Appeal

Appellate courts are much less likely to overturn the factual findings of a jury than those of a trial judge because the standards of review are higher in a jury case. See section 12.9. Decisions by administrative law judges who may be given deference are reviewable. Awards issued by arbitrators are reviewable by a judge or appellate panel.

10. Familiarity With Counsel

There may be situations where, either in a social or professional context, an attorney and professional decision maker are favorably acquainted with each other. While this in no way should affect the decision maker's objectivity in hearing the case, it does give this attorney a psychological edge over an opposing counsel not known by the decision maker.

11. Timing of Decision

In litigation, an attorney may initially demand a jury trial regardless of what the previous factors suggest. That demand can later be waived, if, as the case develops, it appears that a bench trial would be better. The demand for a jury trial may increase the chances of an early favorable settlement with an opposing side who may have more to fear from a jury verdict. The timing of the waiver of the jury trial may affect what judge is assigned to hear the case. If an attorney would like to have a certain judge or would like to avoid a certain judge, the timing of the decision to waive may be crucial.

B. Jury Trial

In criminal cases and a variety of civil cases, the parties have a right to a trial by jury. In arbitration, the parties agree to have an arbitrator decide their case and waive a jury trial. In administrative proceedings, the parties may be required by law to proceed before an administrative judge and not a jury. Many more trials and hearings are conducted by judges, arbitrators, and administrative judges than before juries.

In federal court cases, the Seventh Amendment guarantees a jury trial in all actions triable to a jury at common law, and Federal Rule of Civil Procedure 38 preserves this right. Similar state constitutional provisions or rules guarantee the same right in state cases. Criminal cases that may not require a jury are those in which the possible penalty is not incarceration but only a fine. Civil cases that do not require a jury are actions that are primarily equitable in nature, such as cases that do not involve money damages, but rather seek injunctive relief or actions involving statutory claims to be decided by a judge.

Jurisdictions vary on how a party may demand a jury trial. In some courts, a party need not do anything affirmatively to obtain a jury. The filing of the action is sufficient to preserve the right to a jury trial. In other jurisdictions, a party must formally request a trial by jury. In these jurisdictions, a rule or statute specifies how a party must notify the court and the opposing party of a demand for a jury trial. These provisions typically require a party to submit a jury "note of issue" or a separate written demand, or to include a demand statement in the complaint.

Federal Rule of Civil Procedure 38(b) states that a party may make a jury demand at any time after commencement of an action and within 10 days after the close of the pleadings. In federal courts and in state courts that impose a time limit for the jury demand, a party waives the right to a jury trial unless the party complies with the applicable rule. In these jurisdictions, it is common for the party who wants a jury trial to include such a request in the pleading submitted by that party. If the time period has lapsed, a party may move the court for leave to have the case tried before a jury, which the judge has discretion to grant. Once a jury demand is made by either party, the case will be tried to a jury unless the parties agree to a bench trial, or unless a judge orders a bench trial based on a motion to strike the jury demand brought by an opposing party or the court. See, e.g., Fed.R.Civ.P. 39(a).

C. Advisory Jury

A judge may empanel an advisory jury to render a verdict in cases that are not triable to a jury by right. See, e.g., Fed.R.Civ.P. 39(c). An advisory jury may be used whenever the court believes that jurors will assist the court in finding the facts. The jury verdict is purely advisory, and the judge may ignore it or use it as a guide in making findings. Although not often used, advisory juries may be empanelled in cases where the principal dispute centers on the credibility of witnesses, or where some issues are to be decided by a jury and other issues by the judge. For example, if the plaintiff's case has two causes of action, one of which is a common law claim triable by right to a jury and the other is a statutory claim triable only before a judge, the judge may have the jurors deliberate and render an advisory verdict on the statutory claim along with their verdict on the common law claim.

D.   *Role of Judge and Jury*

In a jury trial, the judge administers the trial, manages the attorneys and the participants, rules on motions and the admissibility of evidence, instructs the jury regarding the law, issues orders and enters judgments. In a non-jury trial, the judge is the finder of fact as well. Judges usually maintain notes or minutes of the trial proceedings. These notes may become part of the official record and may also be used by the judge in making rulings.

In a jury trial, the jury is the fact finder. The jurors apply the law given by the judge to the facts. The jurors must deliberate fairly and impartially to reach a verdict and determine liability and damages, guilt or innocence.

In some jurisdictions, jurors are permitted to ask questions by submitting questions to the judge who reviews, approves, and asks the questions. This role changes the function of the jurors from being passive to becoming active participants in discovering evidence. Questions that may be appropriately asked are clarification questions raising new issues or seeking admissible evidence.

E.   *Role of Administrative Judge*

The power and authority of an administrative judge depends upon the type of administrative hearing. Some administrative judges act similarly to judges during bench trials. Other administrative judges have a broader or more restrictive role depending upon the statute and rule that governs the administrative hearing. An advocate may object to an administrative judge exceeding the power and authority applicable in a case.

F.   *Role of Arbitrator*

Arbitrators have the power provided them by the agreement of the parties, the rules of the arbitration organization, and the law. An arbitrator commonly has the same power and authority that a judge has in a bench trial. The arbitrator has broad discretion to conduct and control the hearing and usually has the power to issue any legal relief to which a party is entitled.

G. Roles of Court Personnel

Court personnel assist with and affect the presentation of a case. Court personnel include court clerks, court reporters, law clerks, administrators, and bailiffs. The court clerk administers the oath to the jurors and witnesses, performs general clerical duties during the trial, and enters orders on the judge's instruction. A court reporter marks exhibits and records the trial proceedings with a stenograph machine or computer or an audio recording system.

A law clerk (an attorney or a law student) researches the law and assists the judge in drafting memoranda and orders. An administrative assistant to the judge performs clerical duties. The bailiff or court attendant (often a law enforcement officer) is usually responsible for enforcing order in the courtroom and is responsible for tending to the jury. Some of these functions may be combined so that one person serves as both court clerk and law clerk, or as court clerk and assistant. These court personnel work closely with the judge and usually are willing to answer attorneys' questions regarding the judge's procedures and preferences. Trial attorneys should familiarize themselves with the procedures preferred by the court personnel, flexibly adapt to these procedures, and suggest alternative procedures if the best interests of the client are not advanced by the routine procedures.

H. Role of Arbitration Administrators and Administrative Law Personnel

Arbitration organizations commonly administer the arbitration procedures by filing documents, assigning arbitrators, scheduling the hearing, and issuing the final award. Arbitrations can be filed electronically through computer transmissions. Arbitration organizations may have a website with filing and communication capabilities. (e.g. www.arb-forum.org).

Administrative law personnel process the filing, scheduling, and completion of a case. Clerks and administrators work with the administrative law judges in handling a case. Some administrative proceedings are handled through telephone and computer transmissions.

§ 2.9 JURY INSTRUCTIONS

An essential part of the planning process involves the identification and preparation of jury instructions and verdict forms. Jury instructions are explanations of the law of the case which the judge reads or explains to the jury during or at the end of the trial. Judges may also provide the jurors with a written copy of the instructions during the trial or for use during deliberations.

The instructions describe trial procedures and the legal elements of claims or defenses that need to be proven. Verdict forms contain questions (often called interrogatories) which the jurors must answer or statements they must complete. These forms contain the conclusions the jurors reach during their deliberations.

It is critical that instructions be selected early during trial preparation, even though they need not be submitted to the court until the trial. The instructions contain the legal elements which support the legal theories of the case. A legal theory can only be advanced in the case if it is contained in the jury instruction the court gives to the jury. The jurors only consider the legal theories submitted to them through instructions. The primary goal in composing and submitting jury instructions is to have the judge instruct the jury regarding a legal theory which, if accepted by the jury, supports a verdict in a client's favor.

A. *Right to Jury Instructions*

A party usually has a right to an instruction if evidence has been introduced to support the instruction and if the instruction correctly states the applicable law. The trial lawyer wants the jury instructions to explain the elements of the law involved in the case, the theories underlying the claims or defenses, and any material issues in a case. Instructions are usually given by a judge if evidence has been introduced during the trial which supports the legal issues and if the proposed instruction clearly and properly explains the elements of the law.

B. *Sources of Instructions*

Instructions, also called charges, must be based upon the law of the jurisdiction. Case law, statutes, rules, and other legal authorities provide the basis for the content of the instructions. Nearly all jurisdictions have jury instruction guides, "JIGs" or "pattern instructions," which are generally recognized and accepted charges. Many instructions and verdict forms have been approved by appellate courts.

In determining the applicable instructions and forms, the first source to consider is the set of standard JIGs or pattern instructions used in a jurisdiction. The index of the JIG book reveals which instructions are available. Pattern instructions are readily available for common types of cases, such as negligence and criminal cases. Other sources will have to be researched if there are unsatisfactory JIGs or no pattern instructions available. A second source is the applicable law of the jurisdiction contained in cases, statutes, rules, regulations, or constitutional provisions. A third source is jury instructions used in previous cases in that jurisdiction. A fourth source is the analogous law or jury instructions of another jurisdiction.

Instructions and verdict forms that appear as standard instructions ordinarily reflect current and correct law, but not always. The accuracy and currency of each charge should be verified. Most JIG books and pattern instruction texts are updated periodically. If not, further research may be necessary to confirm that the pattern instruction or JIG is a proper instruction or verdict form.

The instructions submitted to the judge must be complete and correct to avoid creating an appealable issue. The failure to give necessary instructions, or the giving of incomplete or erroneous instructions, presents grounds for a new trial or a reversal of a verdict on appeal.

C. Instructions

There are several types of instructions a judge gives to the jury during a trial to explain trial procedures, to describe the duties of the jurors, and to explain the law applicable to the case. These include preliminary instructions, periodic instructions, cautionary instructions, curative instructions, and final instructions.

1. Preliminary Procedural Instructions

These are instructions the judge gives the jury at the beginning of the case. Preliminary instructions explain to the jury their responsibilities during the trial and may also include an explanation of the law applicable to the case; these instructions may be similar or identical to the final instructions. Some judges have standard preliminary instructions that they give. The trial lawyer may also ask the judge to give some different or additional instructions.

Example:

Members of the Jury, now that you have been sworn, I will give you some preliminary instructions to guide you in your participation in the trial.

First, you should not discuss the case among yourselves or with anyone else. At the end of the trial, you will have as much time as you need to discuss the case. But that is at the end of the trial and not during the trial.

Second, do not read or listen to anything regarding this case in any way. If anyone should try to talk to you about it, bring it to the court's attention promptly.

Third, do not try to do any research or make any investigation about the case on your own.

Finally, do not form any opinion until all the evidence is in. Keep an open mind until you start your deliberations at the end of the case.

It will be your duty to find from the evidence what the facts are. You, and you alone, are the judges of the facts. You will then have to apply those facts to the law as the court will explain the law to you.

---

2. Preliminary Substantive Instructions

At the beginning of the trial, judges may also inform the jury regarding the elements of the claims or defenses that will be presented and the applicable substantive law. These instructions are identical to what will be explained at the end of case.

3. Periodic Instructions

In some trials, particularly those where the issues are complex or unusual, jurors may be assisted by instructions concerning the case or the law given to them periodically during the trial. An attorney who believes these periodic instructions to be helpful should explain this need to the judge, because the judge may not initially consider the use of periodic instructions necessary or helpful. The content of a periodic instruction is identical to the content of a final instruction. Periodic instructions may be repeated during the final charge in the case.

4. Cautionary Instructions

Cautionary instructions are given before recesses and adjournments during the trial to remind the jurors to conduct themselves properly.

Example:

Remember that over the lunch hour you are not to talk to anyone including each other about this case.

---

5. Curative Instructions

During the trial, the judge gives curative instructions after an inappropriate event has occurred, after some inadmissible evidence has been improperly referred to, or after trial misconduct.

Example:

I instruct the jury to disregard the last comment about the defendant attending church. That is irrelevant to this case and should not be considered by you in any way.

---

6. Final Instructions

There are two categories of final instructions: general instructions and specific instructions. General instructions are those charges that apply to all cases and involve the conduct of the trial, such as instructions regarding the role of the jurors, burden of proof, circumstantial evidence, and the credibility of witnesses. Specific instructions include those instructions that contain the legal theories and legal elements of the claims and defenses applicable to a specific case. General instructions are typically found in pattern JIGs. Specific instructions may also be found in pattern JIGs if the case is common. See Section 12.2.

---

§ 2.10 PLANNING AND SUBMITTING JURY INSTRUCTIONS

A. *Planning*

Jury instructions must be selected and drafted to meet several goals. Jury instructions must:

- Reflect the legal theories and factual summaries of the case.
- Be clear and understandable.
- Withstand legal attacks.
- Comply with ethical rules.
- Be drafted as a complete set.

1. *Reflect Legal Theories and Factual Summaries*

The initial draft of jury instructions must contain the legal elements reflected in the legal theories. See Section 2.9(B). These instructions may be modified as the trial preparation develops and as the trial progresses. Final preparations for trial may require revisions in the selection and wording of the instructions. The opponent's submitted instructions may also necessitate revisions and so might discussions with the judge regarding what the judge thinks to be proper or improper.

Jury instructions must also reflect the factual summary. Instructions must be consistent with the evidence presented during trial so that jurors will conclude that the facts support the legal theories. Factual summaries should be reviewed to make certain that instructions covering all important facts are submitted.

2. *Drafting Clear and Understandable Instructions*

Instructions should be drafted to accurately reflect the law and explain concepts, and should use words that are understandable to the jurors and support the client's case theory. The extent to which an attorney may submit a modified standard instruction or compose an original instruction depends upon the use of standard instructions in a jurisdiction and how effectively the attorney has edited or created an instruction.

The use of standard instructions may be so firmly entrenched in a jurisdiction that no proposed change will be acceptable to a judge. Other judges may accept changes that make the instruction more accurate and more understandable. There may be little latitude available to revise the instruction if the source of instruction is a specific and understandable statutory provision or case law opinion. If the source is unclear or incomplete, the judge may be flexible and modify the instruction based upon a reasonable interpretation of the source.

Several guidelines should be followed to draft instructions that will be accepted and used by the judge:

A. The instructions must be legally correct and complete. Only instructions that accurately reflect the law should be submitted.

B. Instructions should be clear and concise. Instructions must be drafted so that jurors, who have no legal training, can readily understand them. Some standard jury instructions drafted by lawyers and judges erroneously presume that jurors are able to understand certain legal terms. A standard instruction must be reviewed to determine whether it is easily understood, and original instructions should be drafted using clear and concise words.

C. Jury instructions should be drafted following principles of effective writing. Some of the more important principles include: the use of simple sentences instead of complex sentences, the use of commonly used words instead of confusing legal terms, the use of active voice instead of passive voice, and the use of affirmative statements rather than negative constructions. An instruction likely to be accepted by a judge is one which includes legal terms that appear in standard instructions and adds an explanation of the terms using common language understandable to the jurors. This reduces the chances that the judge will reject the proposed instruction due to the exclusion of required concepts and phrases.

D. Instructions should be balanced and not biased in favor of one party. While an instruction should support a party's case theory, it should not do so in an overtly biased way. Judges must give objective and impartial jury instructions, not favoring one side or prejudicing the other. However, if there is a choice available between reasonably supportive and impartial words, then the words that most favor a client's position ought to be selected for proposed instructions.

3. Instructions Must Be Able to Withstand Challenges

Opposing counsel will likely challenge proposed instructions by objecting to the use of certain words or phrases. Opposing counsel will argue that their proposed instructions ought to be used by claiming that no evidence supports the use of another instruction or by arguing that any other instruction could be inaccurate or incomplete. The trial judge carefully reviews the submitted instructions to assure they are correct. A high percentage of errors raised on appeal involve jury instructions. Appellate judges review the instructions and decide whether the instructions correctly and completely explained the law to the jurors. By following the suggestions in this section, instructions should be submitted which will survive these challenges.

4. Instructions Must Comply With Ethical Rules

Ethical rules as well as rules of civil procedure prohibit an attorney from knowingly making a false statement of law to the court and from failing to disclose controlling legal authority adverse to the attorney's position. These rules also require that statements of law be based on existing law or a good faith argument for the extension, modification, or reversal of the existing law. Instructions must be drafted to comply with these ethical rules. An attorney who fails to comply with these rules has not only committed an unethical act but may also be sanctioned by the court. Or (dread the thought) may be required to repeat law school, the ultimate sanction.

> 5. *Jury Instructions Must Be Viewed as a Complete Set of Instructions*

Jury instructions cover all legal and factual issues of the case and must be complete and concise. Each individual instruction is part of a set of instructions, and the length and interrelationship of these jury instructions affects their comprehensibility. A set of instructions that is overly lengthy or presented in an unstructured, disorganized manner may confuse and overwhelm the jury. A set of instructions that is too concise and too short may omit necessary explanations. The goal is to submit a balanced set of instructions, with a structure and organization that enhances their meaning.

For example, an automobile accident case may include the following instructions:

- Explanation of duties of jurors,
- Description of claims and defenses,
- Burden of proof,
- Meaning of preponderance of evidence,
- Direct and circumstantial evidence,
- Credibility of witnesses,
- Rulings and objections to evidence,
- Definition of negligence,
- Definition of proximate cause,
- Definition of ordinary care,
- Explanation of comparative fault,
- Violation of applicable statute, ordinance, or regulation,
- Explanation of measure of damages,
- Recoverable injuries,
- Medical expenses,
- Loss of income,
- Pain and suffering,
- Explanation of special interrogatories,
- Selecting foreperson, and
- Concluding instructions.

B. *Submitting Instructions*

Instructions must be submitted in accordance with the applicable rules of procedure. Such rules usually require that requests for instructions be submitted to the court no later than at or before the close of evidence. Instructions must ordinarily be in writing. See, e.g., Fed. R.Civ.P. 51 and Fed.R.Crim.P. 30. Oral requests not made part of the record are ineffective, but some jurisdictions do allow recorded oral requests in place of written submissions. Some courts require or expect a memorandum of law to be submitted in support of significant instructions. It may be advisable, regardless of the rules or practice of the court, to submit a supporting memo to increase the chances the judge will accept and use the instruction.

Many judges want the attorneys to submit instructions at the beginning of the trial; other judges expect instructions to be submitted during the trial; and still others wait until just before closing arguments. Early preparation by the trial lawyer will ensure that instructions are ready at whatever point the judge requests them.

Instructions may be submitted in a variety of ways, depending upon the preference of the judge and the type of instruction. The preferred way to submit important or specific instructions is to submit two sets of instructions. One set includes the text of each instruction on a separately numbered document with a reference to the source or citation for the instruction. The reference to the authority can include an indication whether the instruction is a direct quote from the source or has been edited or revised to reflect the facts of the case. The second set of instructions includes just the text of the instruction with no number or authority. This is a copy the judge can use and give to the jury.

General or less important instructions that appear in the JIG book or pattern instructions may be submitted by providing the judge with a written list of the respective numbers from the pattern JIGs. Depending upon the judge and the jurisdiction, this method of submission is often used in simple cases or short trials. The attorney should ask the judge if this method is acceptable or if the judge prefers a set of proposed instructions in writing, on a computer disk, or as an email attachment. Regardless of how instructions are submitted, the trial attorney must make certain that the judge clearly understands what instructions have been proposed and that there is a record of the requested instructions.

§ 2.11   VERDICT FORMS AND BENCH TRIAL ORDERS

A.   *Types of Verdict Forms*

In jury trials, the jurors are given a verdict form, which they must complete and sign. The form contains the jury's decision. There are three common types of verdict forms.

1.   *General Verdict*

A jury may return a general verdict form, which is signed by the foreperson or by the jurors. In this form, the jury simply finds for or against a party.

Example:

We, the Jury, find for the plaintiff in the sum of $_____.

or

We, the Jury, find the defendant _____

(guilty or not guilty).

2. *Special Verdict*

The judge may submit a special verdict form to a jury that requires the jurors to answer specific questions and make findings of fact on critical factual issues. This form ensures that the jury does not ignore the controlling law, and also makes clear the jury's decision on specific issues.

Example (Product liability case):

(1) Was the product in a defective condition and unreasonably dangerous because of the manufacturing process used to manufacture the product?

Answer: Yes_____ No _____

(2) If your answer to Question No. 1 was "Yes", then answer this question: Was the defective condition caused by the manufacture of the product a direct cause of the plaintiff's injury?

Answer: Yes_____ No_____

(3) If your answer to Question No. 2 was "Yes", then answer this question: Was the defendant manufacturer negligent in the manufacture of the product?

Answer: Yes_____ No_____

(4) If your answer to Question No. 3 was "Yes", then answer this question: Was such negligence a direct cause of the plaintiff's injury?

Answer: Yes_____ No_____

(5) Did the plaintiff fail to exercise reasonable care for her own safety?

Answer: Yes_____ No_____

(6) If your answer to Question No. 5 was "Yes", then answer this question: Was the plaintiff's failure to exercise reasonable care a direct cause of her injury?

Answer: Yes_____ No_____

(7) If you answered "Yes" to Question No. 6, and you also answered "Yes" to Questions Nos. 2 or 4, then answer this question:

Taking all of the fault that directly caused the plaintiff's injury as 100%, what percentage of fault do you attribute to:

Defendant Manufacturer　　　＿＿＿＿％

Plaintiff　　　　　　　　　　＿＿＿＿％

Total　　　　　　　　　　　　100%

3.　*General Verdict Form With Written Interrogatories*

The court may submit a general verdict form with written interrogatories. This form combines both a general verdict and special interrogatories. When this type of form is used, the answers to the interrogatories must be consistent with the general verdict. If they are not consistent, the specific answers usually control. Similar to the special verdict form, this form helps to ensure that the jury will follow the applicable law.

B.　*Proposing a Verdict Form*

The type of case and nature of the issues determine which verdict form should be used. In criminal cases, the general verdict form is usually used. In personal injury cases, special interrogatories are typically used.

The general verdict form is simple and only requires the jury to reach a general conclusion. A special verdict requires the jury to decide the facts and requires the judge to apply the law to the facts and enter a judgment. The special verdict form forces jurors to consider and discuss all the important issues in a case. The use of a general verdict form with written interrogatories combines both the advantages and disadvantages of the two verdict forms. A general verdict form allows jurors to decide a case for whatever reason they wish and, unlike special interrogatories, does not focus the jury's attention on specific factual issues. Special interrogatories, on the other hand, may be improperly or inconsistently answered, and the judge may not be able to understand the basis for the jury's determination.

Procedural rules and case law establish guidelines for the use of verdict forms. Federal Rule of Civil Procedure 49 and similar state rules regulate the use of special verdicts and interrogatories. Usually, during closing argument, counsel can suggest to the jury how they should complete the verdict form. Ordinarily, counsel may also advise the jury of the effect of the answers to special interrogatories. In some jurisdictions, however, counsel may be prohibited from so commenting. These considerations help counsel determine what type of verdict form counsel should propose be used.

C.　*Findings of Fact and Conclusions of Law*

In a bench trial and some administrative hearings, the judge must issue findings and conclusions. In some arbitrations, the arbitrator must support an award with findings and conclusions. Advocates may submit proposed findings of fact and conclusions of law to the judge or arbitrator. See Section 3.11(E). The proposed findings should cover all the important facts contained in the factual summary. Similarly, the proposed conclusions should cover all the elements of the legal theories. The guidelines used in drafting the proposed findings and conclusions are similar to those followed in drafting jury instructions, as explained in the previous sections.

Example:

FINDINGS OF FACT

1. The following events occurred on February 7, 2004, on Grand Avenue, St. Paul, Minnesota.

2. At about noon, plaintiff was walking along Grand Avenue. She approached defendant from behind. Defendant was, at that time, carrying a round bakery product with a sweet topping, commonly known as a bagel with cream cheese and jelly.

3. The bagel was made of tough, chewy dough.

4. As plaintiff passed defendant on the sidewalk, defendant swung around abruptly and unintentionally hit plaintiff in the face with the bakery product.

5. Plaintiff suffered damage as a result of the incident.

CONCLUSIONS OF LAW

1. The statute that applies in this case is Minnesota Statute Section 112.02, which provides:

   Laws, Section 112.02 Assault with a Sweet Roll

   Whoever hits another person with a sweet roll shall be liable to the other person for actual damages and punitive damages not exceeding $1,000.

2. Defendant did not "hit" plaintiff, within the meaning of Section 112.02, because the contact between the two was not intentional.

3. The bakery product involved in this incident was not a sweet roll within the meaning of Section 112.02 because it was not made of soft, flaky dough.

4. Defendant is not liable to plaintiff for damages and is entitled to an order dismissing plaintiff's complaint.

<u>ORDER</u>

1.   This court orders that judgment be entered for defendant.

2.   The parties are to bear their own costs.

———

Judge

---

§ 2.12   BURDEN OF PROOF AND PRESUMPTIONS

For each issue within a case, one of the parties has the burden of proof regarding that issue. The concept, "burden of proof," actually includes two different burdens: the burden of production and the burden of persuasion.

A.   *Burden of Production*

The term "burden of production" (also known as the burden of going forward) requires that a party produce sufficient evidence so that a reasonable person could find on behalf of that party. The judge determines whether sufficient evidence has been produced to meet this burden of production. In legal terms, the burden of production requires a party to introduce evidence of sufficient quality and weight that reasonable and fair-minded persons in the exercise of impartial judgment might find in favor of that party.

An opposing party challenges the burden of production by bringing a motion for a directed verdict in a jury trial or a motion to dismiss in a bench trial, arbitration, or administrative hearing. These motions require the judge or arbitrator to evaluate the evidence and determine whether the evidence is sufficient to meet the burden of production. If the evidence is sufficient, the motion is denied and the case proceeds. If the evidence is insufficient, the motion is granted. A motion for a directed verdict or a motion to dismiss may be brought to resolve an issue, a claim or defense, or the entire case of the opposing party. See Section 3.8(C)(7).

B.   *Burden of Persuasion*

The burden of persuasion (also known as the risk of non-persuasion) requires a party to introduce evidence sufficient to win. The fact finder weighs this evidence and determines whether the party is entitled to a decision. In legal terms, a party must introduce evidence which convinces the fact finder that the elements of the claim or defense have been proven.

C.   *Types of Burdens of Proof*

There are three common degrees of burdens of proof:

1.   *Preponderance of the Evidence*

This burden applies in civil cases. The burden requires a party, usually the plaintiff or claimant, to prove that it is more probable than not that the party's facts are true. In percentage terms, a party carries this burden and wins the case if its facts exceed 50% probability.

2.   Clear and Convincing

This is a standard of proof that applies to some issues in some civil cases that involve a higher burden of proof than that imposed by the preponderance standard. For example, issues of fraud in many jurisdictions are required to be proven by clear and convincing evidence. To satisfy this burden, a party must establish proof greater than the preponderance of evidence. The exact percentage of proof required is unknown, but something more than 50% and less than proof beyond a reasonable doubt is required.

3.   Proof Beyond a Reasonable Doubt

This burden applies to criminal cases. It is the highest of the three burdens of proof. In percentage terms, it is a high percentage, but is not expressed in a number. What is a "reasonable doubt" is left to the determination of the fact finder. It is not the absence of all doubt, and not the existence of some doubt. The fact finder decides what is "reasonable" after hearing the facts of the case.

D.   Allocation of Burdens

The burden of production and the burden of proof for each issue in a case must be allocated between the plaintiff or claimant and defendant or respondent. These two burdens can be allocated in four ways:

- The plaintiff/claimant has both the burden of production and the burden of persuasion.
- The plaintiff/claimant has the burden of production and the defendant/respondent has the burden of persuasion.
- The defense has the burden of production and the plaintiff/claimant has the burden of persuasion.
- The defendant/respondent has both.

The law of a jurisdiction regarding an issue determines how the burdens are allocated. In many civil cases, the plaintiff/claimant has both the burden of production and the burden of persuasion. In civil cases involving a counterclaim or an affirmative defense, the defendant/respondent has both burdens on the counterclaim and affirmative defense. In criminal cases, the prosecution has both burdens. In criminal cases involving an affirmative defense, the defendant may have the burden of production. The allocation of the burden of persuasion and the burden of proof is critical in determining which party prevails.

E.   Practical Implications of Burdens

The legal concepts of burden of proof may be more important to lawyers and judges than to jurors. Regardless of which party has the burden, the jurors want to find on behalf of a party based on truth and justice and not based upon probabilities. Civil attorneys who argue to the jury that they will prove what "probably" happened reduce the persuasive impact of their position. See Section 1.6. This is particularly true in civil cases where the notion is that a party wins even if jurors are only 50.1% sure of what happened. While this may make sense to lawyers and judges, it often leaves some jurors befuddled. Many jurors take the approach that they ought to be able to figure out what happened and which party is entitled to a verdict.

Judges and arbitrators may be more influenced, and rightly so, in cases by the effect of the burden. In close cases, where both parties have presented equally compelling cases, the professional decision maker may decide the case based on which party has the burden of proof. If everything else is equal, the party with the burden will lose. It is the law that the party with the burden has to produce more compelling evidence to win. This concept is more easily understood and accepted by professional decision makers, which is why they can more likely produce a fair result in various cases than jurors could.

The burden of proof has an effective application in criminal cases where the system of justice requires a prosecutor to prove guilt beyond a reasonable doubt and allows the defendant to rely on a presumption of innocence. A criminal defense attorney can explain to the jurors that their role is to render a not guilty verdict if they have a reasonable doubt. Many jurors will nonetheless be skeptical if a defendant does not testify or presents no defense. In these cases the common sense perception of the jurors that an innocent person ought to raise some defense may offset the advantage that the burden of proof provides the defendant.

Another practical problem in relying on the burden of proof is that the jurors may misunderstand or misapply the proper burden. Many jurors have heard the phrase "proof beyond a reasonable doubt" prior to the trial and may improperly rely upon this prior understanding of the burden of proof. They may even apply this criminal standard of proof to a civil case because of their familiarity with the term and their unfamiliarity with the preponderance burden.

The authors have had the opportunity to review hundreds of video-taped jury deliberations of mock trials. During deliberations of criminal trials, many jurors wondered aloud why the defendant did not present a defense unless, of course, the defendant was guilty. On the other hand, other jurors mentioned that they wanted to be "positive" or "sure" before they found the defendant guilty. More often than not during deliberations in civil trials, jurors talked in terms of determining what "actually" happened and not what some lawyer said "probably" occurred. Still other jurors used the phrase "beyond a reasonable doubt" in describing the burden a civil party had. These inaccurate statements by jurors may have occurred because neither the trial attorneys nor the judge accurately explained the applicable burden of proof during the trial. These results, nonetheless, do reflect a preference by jurors to reach a just decision based upon actual facts and not necessarily upon which party has which burden.

F. Presumptions

A presumption is the conclusion a fact finder must reach unless contrary evidence of that conclusion has been presented. A presumption requires that a fact finder conclude fact "B" occurred based on the proof of fact "A" unless contrary evidence of "A" or "B" has been introduced. There are hundreds of legal presumptions established by statute or case law in each jurisdiction. An example of a common presumption is due receipt by mail. If there is evidence that a letter was properly addressed and mailed, it is presumed that the addressee received that letter, unless evidence is introduced to the contrary. The effect of the due receipt presumption is that the fact finder must find that the letter was received unless sufficient evidence has been introduced showing the letter was not written, was not addressed properly, was not mailed, or was not received. In other words, proof that the letter was properly addressed and mailed (fact "A") requires the fact finder to conclude that the letter was received by the addressee (fact "B") unless evidence has been introduced to rebut either fact "A" or fact "B".

The word "presumption" has different meanings which need to be distinguished for trial purposes. A "trial" presumption is a rebuttable presumption. A "substantive" presumption, on the other hand, is irrebuttable. Evidence may be introduced to rebut a "trial" presumption, as in the example of due receipt by mail. Evidence may not, however, be introduced to challenge a "substantive" presumption because it is irrebuttable.

For example, most jurisdictions have a substantive rule of law which states that a person under the age of seven (or other specific age) is incapable of committing a crime. Often, these rules of law use the word "presume": a child under the age of seven is "presumed" to be incapable of committing a crime. This presumption is not a trial presumption because neither party can introduce facts to rebut the capacity of the child to commit a crime. Once it is established that a child is seven years or younger, no rebutting evidence is admissible. Substantive presumptions may, however, be subject to constitutional attack—there must be a rational connection between fact "A" (age of seven) and conclusion "B" (incapable of committing a crime).

G. Inferences

A presumption is not the same as an inference. A presumption has characteristics similar to an inference but its effect is different. Presumptions and inferences employ the same process: from the proof of fact "A" the existence of fact "B" may be presumed or inferred. The difference in their effect is that an inference is permissive and a presumption is mandatory. With an inference, a fact finder *may* infer fact "B" from fact "A". With a presumption, a fact finder *must* conclude fact "B" from fact "A" (unless contrary evidence is introduced).

Common inferences are based on circumstantial evidence. For example, proof of footprints in the sand (fact "A") permits a fact finder to infer that someone walked in the sand (fact "B"), but does not require the fact finder to reach that conclusion. There are many inferences that a fact finder can find in a trial. The law of a jurisdiction determines whether a particular fact leads to an inference or a presumption.

H. Relationship Between Burden of Proof and Presumptions

Presumptions may have an effect on the burden of production and the burden of persuasion. The precise effect depends upon the law of the respective jurisdiction. The following two examples demonstrate the effect presumptions have on the burdens of production and persuasion:

- The presumption may shift the burden of production to the other party. For example, if the plaintiff must prove that the defendant addressee received a letter, the presumption of due receipt may satisfy the plaintiff's burden of production and shift this burden to the defendant to introduce evidence that defendant did not receive the letter. If the defendant fails to introduce contrary evidence to meet this burden, the plaintiff wins because the presumption that the properly addressed and mailed letter was received is sufficient for the fact finder to conclude the letter was received.

- The presumption may have no effect on the burden of proof. The effect of the presumption may vanish if contrary evidence is produced that is sufficiently probative to make it reasonable for the fact finder to find the nonexistence of the presumed fact (also known as the "bursting bubble" presumption). For example, the presumption of due receipt disappears after the defendant introduces reasonable evidence for the fact finder to conclude that the letter was not received. The plaintiff no longer has the advantage of the effect of the presumption and must now introduce evidence to rebut the evidence introduced by the defendant. Some jurisdictions have modified this effect and require the defendant to introduce "substantial" evidence and not just a reasonable amount of evidence to make the presumption vanish.

The significance of the effects of a presumption relate to the strength of the evidence the defendant must introduce to win. If a defendant introduces no evidence regarding a presumed fact, the defendant loses. If a defendant introduces some evidence, the plaintiff still receives the benefit of the presumption, but may lose. If the defendant introduces contrary credible evidence, the plaintiff loses the benefit of the presumption and the defendant should win, unless the plaintiff introduces further relevant evidence.

I. Presumptions, Burdens, Instructions, Findings, and Conclusions

The proper jury instructions to be given in a case depend upon the law of the jurisdiction regarding presumptions and burdens. The impact presumptions and burdens have on jury instructions, findings of fact, and conclusions of law can be substantial. The following alternative instructions, applicable in different jurisdictions, illustrate the differences in the findings the jury may or must make depending upon the facts introduced and how the presumptions and burdens apply in a jurisdiction:

- You shall find that the letter in question was received by the defendant.

- If from the evidence you believe that the letter in question was regularly addressed and mailed to the defendant, you shall find that it was received.

- You shall find that the letter in question was received, unless from the evidence you believe its non-receipt is more probable than its receipt.

- If from the evidence you believe the letter in question was addressed properly and mailed, then you also shall find it was received, unless you believe its non-receipt is more probable than its receipt.

The overlapping concepts of burdens and presumptions can be confusing unless analyzed in a logical, one-step-at-a-time approach. The primary effect presumptions and burdens of proof have in a trial relate to jury instructions and findings and conclusions. Statutes, court decisions, and standard jury instructions in each jurisdiction usually explain the effects that presumptions and burdens have in a particular case. The key to understanding presumptions and burdens involves two steps. First, the concepts must be understood. Secondly, the applicable statute, court decision, evidence rule, procedural rule, or jury instruction that describes the effect of presumptions and burdens applicable in a specific jurisdiction must be found. In many jurisdictions, pattern JIGs provide this information.

CHAPTER 3

TRIAL PROCEDURES AND MOTIONS

REFLECTING ON ADVOCACY

If you're going to play the game properly you'd better know every rule.

—Barbara Jordan

Four things belong to a judge: to hear courteously, to answer wisely, to consider soberly, and to decide impartially.

—Socrates

§ 3.1 INTRODUCTION

This chapter summarizes the various general rules and practices that advocates need to know and follow to prepare and present a case effectively.

§ 3.2 CASE PREPARATION

A. *Scheduling a Trial*

The rules of civil procedure that apply in a jurisdiction govern how an attorney places a civil case on the trial calendar. Typically, a written demand for a jury or court trial, sometimes referred to as a note of issue, is required. After the demand or note of issue has been served upon the parties and filed with the court, the case is placed on the trial calendar. The administrator or clerk of court can provide information on when the case will be called to trial. The timing in each jurisdiction varies depending on the calendar system in use and the number of cases docketed.

Criminal cases are scheduled by the office of the clerk or administrator. Lawyers do not need to file a written request. Statutes, rules, and the defendant's right to a speedy trial govern the scheduling of these cases.

The assignment of a judge for trial depends upon the type of court calendar used by the court. There are three types of calendar systems: a master calendar system, an individual calendar system, and a combination of these two systems.

The master calendar system, or special term system, assigns pretrial motion hearings and trials to judges on a rotating basis. When a pretrial motion is filed with the court, a judge is assigned to hear that motion. When the case is ready for trial, a judge, usually not the same judge who ruled on the previous motions, is assigned. The trial judge first learns about the case shortly before the trial, unless that judge heard a prior motion.

The individual calendar system, sometimes referred to as the block system, assigns entire cases to individual judges. The assigned judge handles all proceedings as well as the trial. In the individual calendar system, the judge is familiar with the facts, law, and attorneys by the time the case is ready for trial. This system is used in federal courts. A magistrate judge assists the judge by hearing discovery and other non-dispositive motions while the judge hears summary judgment and other dispositive motions and tries the case.

Some courts use a hybrid calendar system, combining both the master and individual assignment systems, depending upon the case backlog and court docket. In all systems, a court administrator or clerk assigns the cases on a random basis depending upon the availability and caseload of judges.

B. Scheduling an Administrative Hearing

Administrative hearings are typically scheduled by an administrator from the administrative agency. Administrative hearings are commonly set for a specific, limited period of time.

C. Scheduling an Arbitration

The arbitration organization typically schedules the arbitration proceedings and hearings, depending upon the availability of the arbitrator. The case coordinator with the arbitration organization contacts and advises the parties when and where the arbitration will occur, depending upon their reasonable availability. Some arbitration organizations have the arbitrators schedule their own hearings. It is typical for the parties to estimate the amount of time required for an arbitration hearing, and for the administrator to set specific beginning and concluding times.

D. Readiness of Counsel

Attorneys should commence case preparation as soon as possible after the cause of action arises. The facts are fresh in the minds of witnesses, and documents are available for preservation. Early discovery is usually more productive than later efforts to gather information. Motions typically must be brought to dismiss claims, add parties, complete discovery, and dispose of issues by summary judgment. The schedule for discovery and motions is influenced by many factors, including how soon the case is to be called for trial.

Federal judges and many state judges control the progress of cases by issuing scheduling orders with "cutoff" dates for discovery and motions and a proposed trial date. The parties may submit to the court informational statements, joint or separate, providing stipulated or suggested time periods for stages of the case. The attorneys must complete discovery and have all motions resolved before the termination "cutoff" dates ordered by the judges. Some jurisdictions require attorneys to file a certificate of readiness notifying each other and the court when they are prepared for trial. This notification may terminate discovery unless opposed by one of the parties. It also may be a prerequisite to placing the case on the trial calendar.

Arbitration procedures commonly keep counsel on a reasonably fast track to a hearing, reflective of the issues to be resolved. The time deadlines included in arbitration rules tend to be strictly enforced. One of the benefits of arbitration is the prompt way a case proceeds to a hearing, and counsel need comply with the deadlines and be ready to proceed.

Administrative hearings also often proceed at a faster pace than litigation cases. Rules and regulations of the administrative agency prescribe the timing of procedures. It is the nature of some administrative cases to be scheduled according to firm deadlines, also requiring counsel to be prepared and ready.

E.   The Beginning Date of a Case

Jurisdictions schedule specific starting dates for trials in several ways. Some jurisdictions notify counsel of a "date certain" when the trial will begin. Other jurisdictions advise counsel that they should be prepared to go to trial on a specific day or during a specific week, but that the trial date may be delayed depending upon the court calendar. In other jurisdictions, attorneys select a trial date from alternative dates available at the pretrial conference. Attorneys can ask clerks or administrators how cases are scheduled in a particular jurisdiction and when a particular case is likely to go to trial.

Arbitration organizations or arbitrators schedule the events of an arbitration. The rules of procedure provide for the timing of the hearing. Administrative cases have specific rules and regulations determining the timing of proceedings. Arbitral and administrative forums typically schedule only one hearing before the arbitrator or administrative judge to begin on a date certain, and these hearings can and do begin as scheduled.

The beginning date for trials is often uncertain. This uncertainty of not knowing when a trial will begin can cause problems with preparations for the trial. Witnesses are difficult to subpoena when the attorney is unsure when the trial will begin. This uncertainty can also affect the scheduling of discovery and motions in other cases handled by the attorney. This, however, is part of the life of an advocate. Some jurisdictions attempt to make this life more predictable by using a system that provides some certainty. Other jurisdictions expect advocates to conform to the court's schedule.

§ 3.3   ASSIGNMENT OF THE JUDGE/ARBITRATOR

A.   Assignment of Judge

State and federal courts assign judges to cases on a random basis. In every jurisdiction, judges may be disqualified for several reasons. In some state courts, advocates can remove the first judge assigned to a case without stating a reason. These procedures do not allow an advocate to select a judge, but they do permit an attorney to remove the first judge assigned to the case.

B. *Disqualification of a Judge*

Federal and state codes of judicial conduct determine when a judge must be disqualified. Disqualifying situations include:

- Personal bias or prejudice by the judge toward a party.
- Personal knowledge of disputed evidentiary facts.
- Service as a lawyer representing a party to the case.
- Personal, family, financial, or other interests in the case.
- Relationship within the third degree between the judge and a party or lawyer.

These grounds and others disqualify judges who are not, or may not be, impartial. A judge may also be disqualified because of illness or physical disability. These situations do not arise often. Federal Rule of Civil Procedure 63 and similar state rules provide a procedure to replace judges. Judges often remove themselves from cases where a conflict of interest, appearance of impropriety, or illness exists.

C. *Removing a Judge for Cause*

In cases where judges do not remove themselves, all jurisdictions allow attorneys to request that a judge be removed from a case for cause. An attorney who believes that a judge should be disqualified for cause must bring a motion and establish good cause for removal. Most jurisdictions require that the motion be heard by the judge who is allegedly prejudiced or biased. In some jurisdictions the chief judge appoints another judge to hear such a motion. Situations requiring disqualification occur infrequently, and, consequently, disqualification motions are seldom available and are even less often granted.

D. *Removing a Judge Without Cause*

In states where parties can remove the first judge assigned to a case without cause, attorneys do so in hopes that the second judge will be less biased or more favorable. In this procedure, the advocate files a notice of removal or similar document that requests another judge for the case. The notice need not state any reason for removal. The court clerk or administrator automatically assigns another judge to hear the case.

In some jurisdictions the removal document is referred to as a certificate or affidavit of prejudice and the attorney may have to include a conclusory statement or some perfunctory facts that suggest why the judge may be prejudiced. The clerk must honor the removal request and appoint another judge, usually on a random basis. These procedures permit an attorney to remove the judge initially assigned to a case, but not subsequently assigned judges. A second judge can be removed only through disqualification or by a showing of cause.

Removal documents must be filed promptly. In cases where an attorney receives written notice of the judge assigned, typically several days are allowed to file the document. But in cases where the judge is orally assigned during a trial calendar call, the attorney may have only several minutes to ask for another judge.

The decision by an attorney to file a motion for removal of a judge may be tactically difficult. In some jurisdictions, such requests are routinely made and judges do not know whether a request has been made or which party made the request. In these situations, the strategic decision to file a motion for removal may be easy. In other jurisdictions, such requests are viewed with disdain by the judges. The trial advocate must consider whether it is better to offend potential replacement judges or stay with the initial judge and avoid being talked about by the judges.

E.   *Assignment of Arbitrator*

Parties are able to select their own arbitrator if they can mutually agree. Otherwise, the selected arbitration organization will provide a list of available arbitrators or assign an arbitrator from a list of experienced, impartial neutrals who have no conflict of interest and who are available. The Director of Arbitration typically maintains a list of arbitrators in all communities and appoints a neutral from that list to conduct the hearing. Some arbitrations involve three arbitrators, and the administrator would appoint all three neutrals. Some arbitration clauses provide that each party select an arbitrator and these two arbitrators select a third neutral arbitrator.

F.   *Removing an Arbitrator*

Parties ordinarily have an opportunity to remove or challenge an arbitrator. In arbitrations where the organization appoints a specific arbitrator, the parties may request another arbitrator by challenging the originally appointed arbitrator for a conflict of interest, unfair prejudice, or insufficient expertise. In arbitrations where a list of arbitrators is provided, each party may remove one or more of the proposed arbitrators which results in the surviving arbitrator being the presiding arbitrator. The arbitration organization commonly provides the parties with a professional resume of the arbitrator.

G.   *Assignment of Administrative Judge*

Administrative agencies commonly assign a judge randomly from a pool of judges. Some agencies have their own panel of specialized judges who are assigned to cases (tax judges, for example). Other agencies draw judges from a statewide administrative law judge pool who hear a variety of cases.

H.   *Removing an Administrative Judge*

The procedures for challenging an administrative judge will be established by statute or administrative rules. Some administrative judges may not be removed at the request of a party unless a clear conflict of interest or substantial prejudice or bias exists. Other administrative judges may be removed through a process similar to removing trial judges.

§ 3.4 PRELIMINARY PROCEDURES

A. *Pretrial Statements*

Some courts require advocates, as part of pretrial preparation, to exchange written pretrial statements that summarize aspects of the case. These statements identify and narrow disputed issues, facilitate settlement discussions, help the court understand the case, and assist the lawyers in preparing the case. Such statements typically include the following information:

- Name and address of the client.
- Name and address of the attorney who will try the case.
- The identity of any insurance carriers.
- A summary of the pleadings, issues, claims or defenses.
- A description of discovery that has been completed and that remains to be completed.
- A list of any pretrial motions to be brought.
- The names and addresses of all witnesses who will testify at trial, including expert witnesses and the areas of their expertise.
- A concise statement of the party's version of the facts of the case.
- A list of all exhibits to be offered as evidence.
- Stipulations the parties have agreed to regarding facts, procedures, or evidence.
- The elements of law that must be proved in the case.
- Citations to relevant statutes, ordinances or cases that act as authority.
- An itemized list of special damages, if sought.
- The estimated length of the trial.
- Jury instructions.

The attorney may also submit any additional information that might assist the court.

B. *Pretrial Conference*

Sometime prior to trial, the court will order, or a party may request, a pretrial conference. See Fed.R.Civ.P. 16. These conferences, usually held in chambers, serve many purposes and permit the trial judge to:

- Discuss settlement possibilities or other dispute-resolution procedures with the attorneys.
- Determine whether settlement possibilities have been exhausted.
- Determine all the issues in the case and whether any pleadings should be amended.
- Attempt to simplify issues by inquiring whether:

— any issues in the case may be eliminated, narrowed, or modified by stipulation, motion or dismissal;

— admissions of facts exist;

— undisputed facts can be presented by stipulation or in a summary fashion;

— stipulations regarding the waiver of foundation required for evidence and other agreements regarding certain evidence or exhibits may be reached;

— any preliminary motions concerning the admissibility or exclusion of evidence will be made or any major evidentiary problems may arise during the trial; or

— any critical or unusual legal or factual issues will be presented or arise.

- Determine the advisability of referring issues to a master, referee or magistrate.

- Inquire whether the number of witnesses, including experts, may be reduced.

- Determine the order and sequence of jury selection, opening and closing arguments, and examination of witnesses, especially in multiple party cases.

- Estimate the time required for each part of the trial.

- Prepare for the marking of exhibits before trial and make special arrangements for the use of maps, diagrams, x-rays, videotapes, demonstrations, or viewings by the jury, and other various uses of the exhibits.

- Inquire whether counsel plans to use any visual aids or exhibits during opening statements or final arguments.

- Determine whether any scheduling problems may occur during trial because of other commitments or conflicts that the attorneys, witnesses or the court may have.

- Advise counsel of the hours and days scheduled for the trial.

- Make arrangements for daily transcripts, if needed, and the reporter's fee.

- Certify that a jury has been demanded or waived.

- Review procedures for jury selection and which attorney proceeds first.

- Determine the number of alternate jurors and peremptory challenges.

- Summarize the introductory statement the trial judge plans to make to the prospective jurors explaining the case, issues, and law.

- Review or consider applicable preliminary and final jury instructions.

- Rule on any other motions or requests made by counsel.

Form 3.1 provides a pretrial summary worksheet.

On some matters, the court makes final rulings during or after the pretrial conference that are written or recorded. See Fed.R.Civ.P. 16. On other matters, a judge may make a tentative ruling and reserve a final decision until trial, in order to consider how the issues are presented or how the evidence is offered. Motions, objections, stipulations, and rulings must be preserved on the record. If the judge does not make a record, the attorney must request that a record is made. If a court reporter is present during pretrial discussions, a record is or can be made. If a court reporter is not present, a record can be made at the end of the conference by summarizing, in the presence of the court reporter, all matters that should be preserved.

C. Pre–Hearing Administrative Conference

The existence and scope of a pre-hearing conference for an administrative proceeding depends upon the type of administrative process. In many simple cases, there are no pre-hearing conferences and there is no opportunity for the parties to discuss anything with the administrative judge before the hearing. In other cases, a complete pre-hearing conference may be conducted.

D. Pre–Hearing Arbitration Procedures

Arbitration parties may have an opportunity to participate in a pre-hearing conference with the arbitrator. Issues to be discussed may depend upon the specific arbitration and may resemble similar issues that are resolved at a pretrial hearing. The hearing may occur by a telephone conference call with the parties and arbitrator participating.

E. Case Briefs

Many decision makers expect or require attorneys to submit case briefs or memoranda in support of their case. The content of these briefs varies depending upon the requirements of the jurisdiction. Typically, these memoranda contain a summary of the facts to be proved, a summary of the testimony of key witnesses, an explanation of the law applicable to the facts, the law supporting or opposing evidence motions, and any other useful information, such as the anticipated length of the trial or hearing.

FORM 3.1
PRETRIAL SUMMARY WORKSHEET

Case _____   **File** _____

1. Summary description of case:

2. Description of discovery that remains to be completed:

3. Reasons why case has not been settled:

4. List of pretrial motions:

5. Description of motions in limine or prospective evidentiary problems:

6. Identity of all trial witnesses, including experts:

7. List of all trial exhibits:

8. Concise statement of party's version of facts:

9. Stipulations of facts or undisputed facts:

10. Concise summary of party's claims or defenses:

11. Elements of law that need to be proved:

12. Citations to specific statutes, case law, jury instructions:

13. Case to be tried by: Judge ( )   Jury ( )
    Number of jurors _____ Number of alternate jurors ____
    Number of peremptory challenges:
    Plaintiff/Prosecutor _____ Defendant_____

14. Estimated time for trial_____

15. Other matters to be considered by trial court:

A case brief may consist, in part, of short memoranda regarding various issues in the case. These memoranda may be separated from the main brief and submitted as individual memoranda when needed during the case. The primary purpose of these briefs is to inform and persuade the decision maker regarding claims or defenses and theories of the case. The preparation of a case brief also assists the attorney in planning for the trial or hearing. Case briefs may be submitted to explain the facts and law that support the case, even when they are not requested or required.

§ 3.5 CONDUCT BY THE ADVOCATE

The attorney's conduct is important during every phase of the case because it directly affects the way people react both to that attorney and to that attorney's client. Below are some guidelines for attorney conduct during a case.

A. *Avoiding Familiarity*

The advocate should not display or take advantage of any familiarity with the judge, arbitrator, jurors, parties, witnesses or other counsel. An expression of familiarity in the advocacy setting may be viewed as improper. The judge and attorneys may engage in social banter in chambers, but in the courtroom the relationship displayed should always be professional. The judge instructs the jurors that the attorneys are not allowed to talk with them during the trial or during breaks so the jurors will not consider the attorneys rude.

B. *Use of Names*

A trial or administrative judge should be addressed as "Your Honor" or "The Court" and never by first name. An arbitrator may be addressed as "Arbitrator Surname" or "Your Honor." Some administrative hearing officers who are not judges may be referred to by surname. It is preferred, and required in some jurisdictions, to address all other participants in a case only by their last names to avoid any suggestion of improper familiarity. Some witnesses, such as children, may be appropriately referred to by their first names and some attorneys may prefer to call witnesses by their first names for strategic reasons. The attorney should seek permission from the court to use first names in formal trial and hearing settings.

C. *Interruptions*

An attorney should not interrupt an argument, question or response unless it is patently objectionable or prejudicial. Professional courtesy dictates that opposing counsel may speak without interruption. An examining attorney should wait until a witness has completed an answer before asking another question, unless the witness is making prejudicial responses.

D. *Approaching the Witness/Bench*

An attorney should not wander around the courtroom or hearing room, approach a witness, or approach the bench without first determining whether the judge requires the attorney to request permission to do so. Some judges expect attorneys to make such a request the first time they move about; other judges expect lawyers continually to ask for permission to approach the bench or move around the courtroom during trial. Many decision makers do not require such requests.

E. *Matters to Be Heard Outside the Hearing of the Jury*

Several events that occur during a trial should or must occur outside the hearing of the jury to prevent jurors from being influenced or prejudiced. See Fed.R.Evid. 103(c) and 104(c). Significant evidentiary arguments, offers of proof and supporting arguments, offers to stipulate, motions and oral arguments should all be made at a bench conference, in chambers, or in the courtroom only when the jurors are absent. Additional sensitive areas of evidence such as questions, answers, exhibits, statements, or arguments that may be prejudicial, inflammatory, or inadmissible must be addressed outside the hearing of the jurors. All matters that the jurors should not be exposed to should be resolved by the judge outside the hearing of the jury.

F. *Bench/Sidebar Conferences*

During a jury trial, the attorney must approach the bench and talk quietly with the judge when a topic must not be heard by the jury. The judge may ask the attorney to approach the bench, or the judge will usually grant a request made by the attorney to approach the bench.

The design of the courtroom and the location of the jury box determine where the bench conference occurs. In some courtrooms, the attorneys stand in front of the judge at the bench. In other courtrooms, the conference occurs at the end of the judge's bench, opposite the jury box, which is called the sidebar. Wherever the conference occurs, it should be far enough away or conducted in a quiet enough manner so that the jurors will not hear what is said. The court reporter must record the conference and usually sits adjacent to where the conference is held. In some courtrooms, the court reporter will have to move to hear what is being said during the conference. This awkward and time-consuming procedure is nevertheless necessary.

Attorneys should avoid using conferences for reasons other than to discuss matters that the jurors should not hear. Trips to the bench significantly slow the pace of the trial and cause jurors to speculate about what is being kept from them. Some jurors react negatively to attorneys who repeatedly request bench conferences for no apparent reason.

G. *Counsel Table*

In courtrooms, the tables typically face the bench and witness stand. In arbitrations, the tables may face each other, or the lawyers will sit on opposite sides of a large table. In administrative hearings, the layout may resemble a courtroom or an arbitration room.

In many courts, custom dictates which table is for plaintiff/prosecutor (often the table nearest the jury box) and which is the defense table. In other forums, the attorney who arrives first selects a table. In arbitration and administrative hearings, the arbitrator or judge may assign placements. Whatever table is used, it is critical that the lawyer appear organized and that the table is kept neat. A disorganized, cluttered, or sloppy counsel table may cause the decision maker to think the attorney's case is similarly confused.

In a jury trial, the advantage in having the table nearest the jury is that the attorney can more easily observe the jurors. The advantage in having the table farthest from the jury is that the attorney can watch the entire courtroom, including opposing counsel. Some trial advocates have strong preferences about which table they want; others are flexible.

H. Setting the Stage

Requirements vary regarding whether counsel should stand or sit during the various stages of a trial or hearing. In trials and formal hearings, counsel typically stand during the opening statement and the closing argument. Where counsel stands in relation to the decision maker, and whether counsel must stand behind a lectern, depends upon local rules and the decision maker's preference. Some judges require counsel to stand at counsel table or behind a lectern during witness examination and at counsel table during the making of objections. Other courts allow or require attorneys to be seated for witness examination and objections. In arbitrations and administrative hearings, it is common to sit during all stages of the case, and may be preferable to stand during formal presentations.

Many courts restrict attorneys' movements in the courtroom. Some judges do not allow attorneys to move away from the lectern or counsel table during witness examinations unless they introduce or use an exhibit. Some courts do not permit counsel to move around the courtroom during opening or closing. Arbitrators have similar rules and preferences.

The effective advocate may seek permission from the court to stand, sit or move in order to enhance the persuasiveness of the argument or witness examination. An attorney must become comfortable and familiar with the acoustics, distances, furniture, and physical setting of the courtroom. The layout affects where the attorney stands during opening statement and closing argument and how the attorney presents evidence.

The decision makers need to have an unobstructed view of the advocates, the witnesses, and exhibits. Some courtrooms have inadequate space, poor acoustics, uncomfortable jury chairs, and other problems that the attorney should know about. The decision concerning where to stand or sit or move should be based on an analysis of where in the courtroom or hearing room the attorney will be most effective in presenting information or making an argument.

I. Room Equipment

Courtrooms typically include an easel, a black or white board, and a shadow box to display x-rays. Some courts also have available video equipment, overhead projectors, and presentation equipment. Modern courtrooms will also have electronic white boards, document cameras, monitors for viewing, and easy computer access. Arbitration rooms and administrative hearing rooms may contain equipment appropriate for the type of case to be heard. In complex cases, or cases involving many exhibits, arrangements must be made to store evidentiary exhibits and visual aids. File cabinets, storage lockers, or other equipment may need to be brought in to the courtroom to accommodate these items.

Tribunals are adapting to the growing use of computer equipment used in the preparation and presentation of a case. Recently built or remodeled courtrooms can accommodate this equipment. Arbitral and administrative hearing rooms may also be able to do so. The advocate must determine what is provided and what is needed so that the proper equipment is present and in working order. See Section 8.3.

J. Case Materials

Advocates commonly bring a variety of materials and books to the trial, including the case notebook, exhibits, deposition or preliminary hearing transcripts, parts of the case file, the rules of evidence and procedure, and a laptop. Additional supplies that many trial lawyers bring are: markers, highlighters, folders, calculators, paper, tape, scissors, white-out, disks, and other presentation materials. Experienced trial lawyers maintain a "kit" in a large briefcase that contains these commonly used books and supplies for ready accessibility during the case. Many documents may be stored in a computer laptop drive or be available online via access by a computer and internet connection.

K. Requests by Counsel

Any request by counsel, including requests to mark an exhibit, go "off the record," read something into the record, or take a recess should be addressed to the judge or arbitrator and not to the reporter or clerk. Usually the reporter stops recording only if the judge so indicates, and the clerk will honor an attorney's request only with the judge's approval, unless the court permits attorneys to direct such requests to court personnel, such as "Please mark this exhibit."

L. Demeanor of Counsel

Counsel should act with respect for all participants in the case at all times. This professional demeanor should not prevent counsel from being assertive, insistent, or aggressive in appropriate situations. However, displays of anger, rudeness or any other inappropriate conduct should not occur during the case.

Counsel should avoid exaggerated facial expressions, body language, head shaking, gesturing, shouting or other conduct that indicates disagreement or approval of rulings, statements by the judge or arbitrator or events that happen during the case. While an opposing lawyer makes a presentation or conducts questioning, the attorney should refrain from reacting improperly, either verbally or nonverbally, because the decision makers watch the attorneys and expect professional courtesy from them.

§ 3.6 THE TAKING OF EVIDENCE

A. *Scheduling Witnesses*

Counsel should attempt to schedule witnesses in an efficient manner to avoid unnecessary delays. Attorneys should exchange good faith estimates regarding the sequence, timing, and length of witness examinations. The examining attorney has the responsibility to make certain that the witness is present when needed. Usually a witness' testimony should be pursued until it is concluded and should not be interrupted by the taking of other evidence. This helps the fact finder minimize confusion about the testimony and is also more convenient for the witness.

B. *Subpoenaing Witnesses*

Counsel should always subpoena their witnesses, including supportive witnesses, to make certain they appear to testify. The subpoena reminds witnesses of the date of the trial and location of the court. A subpoenaed witness who fails to appear can be ordered by the judge or arbitrator to appear at a rescheduled time. An unsubpoenaed witness who fails to appear may be precluded from later testifying because the witness was not properly subpoenaed by the examining attorney.

Subpoenas are commonly issued by judges and arbitrators and obtained from a court clerk's office, the arbitration forum or arbitrator, and the administrative law clerk or judge. Most jurisdictions and forums require that a witness fee be tendered to the witness along with the subpoena. A statute or rule usually establishes the amount of this fee, which includes reimbursement for mileage and a small payment such as $25. Lay witnesses are not paid for their testimony or reimbursed for lost income. Expert witnesses may be and typically are reimbursed for their time in court by a flat fee or an amount equal to their hourly rate.

A witness who fails to abide by a subpoena may be subject to a contempt citation and arrest. See Fed.R.Civ.P. 45(e). A warrant may be issued if the service of the subpoena and attendant fees are proper and if no reasonable excuse exists for the failure of the witness to attend. The attorney who subpoenaed the witness should make diligent efforts to obtain the witness' appearance or to determine whether the witness' failure to appear was reasonable.

C. *Sequestering Witnesses*

The judge or arbitrator has the power and discretion to sequester — that is, to exclude or separate — witnesses during a case. Before the trial or hearing begins, an attorney may request that witnesses be excluded from the room to prevent them from hearing and being influenced by others' testimony. Parties to a case, including individuals and designated corporate representatives, have a right to be present during trial and ordinarily cannot be excluded. Criminal defendants cannot be excluded, although restraints can reasonably be placed on them if they unreasonably interrupt the trial. The rules of evidence may also affect whether witnesses can be excluded from the trial or hearing. Federal Rule of Evidence 615 and similar state rules prohibit the exclusion of a party or of a person whose presence is essential to the presentation of a case, such as an expert witness.

The granting of a motion to sequester most commonly bars witnesses from the courtroom or hearing room except when they testify. A witness remains excluded until testifying, until the party calling the witness has rested, or until rebuttal evidence has been completed. Whether the judge or arbitrator will grant a motion to sequester depends upon the applicable rules and local practice. If a rule confers this right on a party, the motion is usually granted. If a rule makes the granting of the motion discretionary, the judge or arbitrator usually considers what difference, if any, it makes to restrict the attendance of witnesses.

Sequestration orders may or may not serve an effective purpose. On the one hand, witnesses usually know from their preparation by counsel what other witnesses will say and what evidence will be introduced. On the other hand, if they listen to each other's actual direct and cross-examinations, witnesses may gain valuable information and better present their stories in a consistent way. The effectiveness of a sequestration order depends on the type of witnesses, how thoroughly the attorney has prepared them, how familiar they are with the stories of other witnesses, and whether the sequestration order prohibits contact among witnesses outside the courtroom or hearing room.

D. Use of Interpreters

A witness or party may need an interpreter in order to testify or understand the case presentation, and courts will have available interpreters. The party calling that witness needs to advise the court in advance of this need. An interpreter provided by the examining attorney may be sufficient if that person is reliable; otherwise, the judge or arbitrator will select an interpreter to ensure that the testimony is interpreted fairly and completely.

E. Order of Examinations

The mechanics of the trial, administrative, and arbitral processes and the method and order of interrogating witnesses is left to the discretion of the judge and arbitrator. Federal Rule of Evidence 611(a), similar state rules, and related arbitration provisions provide that a judge or arbitrator shall exercise reasonable control to make the witness examination effective for the ascertainment of truth, to avoid needless consumption of time, and to protect witnesses from harassment or undue embarrassment. These rules make it clear that the judge or arbitrator bears the ultimate responsibility for the proper conduct of the case and the manner of receiving evidence.

F. Scope of Examinations

1. Direct Examination

A competent witness may testify to any relevant matter unless excluded by a specific rule, statute or case. See Fed.R.Evid. 401 and Section 7.2.

2. Cross–Examination

A witness may be cross-examined regarding any matter covered on direct examination, or related to credibility, or any relevant matter permitted within the discretion of the judge or arbitrator, even if not covered on direct examination. See Section 9.2(D). Cross-examiners are typically provided with wide latitude and substantial leeway to ask questions. Cross-examination topics ordinarily relate directly or indirectly to a subject matter of the direct examination or to a matter affecting the credibility of the witness. See Fed.R.Evid. 611.

3. Redirect, Recross, and Subsequent Examinations

Redirect examination is confined to new matters brought out on cross-examination and cannot merely repeat matters brought out on direct examination. Recross examination is limited to matters brought out on redirect examination. Subsequent examinations are confined to the scope of matters covered during the previous examination. The judge or arbitrator has discretion to permit questions on matters not covered in the previous examination. An opposing party has the right to inquire into new matters brought out on redirect, recross or subsequent examinations. See Fed.R.Evid. 611(b).

4. Rebuttal

After the defense has rested, the plaintiff/claimant/prosecutor may present additional evidence in rebuttal. The scope of this evidence is limited to those material areas covered during the defense case that were not covered during the initial case. Rebuttal is limited to new and significant areas of evidence and cannot be used to repeat evidence.

Rebuttal typically consists of a witness who can deny or contradict what a defense witness has stated or a document that contains contrary information. Judges and arbitrators have broad discretion in permitting or limiting rebuttal. An attorney offering rebuttal evidence should establish its importance to the case and how it expressly rebuts contrary evidence. Some may deny rebuttal evidence if they believe it should have been introduced during the proponent's case in chief. Others may deny rebuttal to both sides, convinced that neither side is entitled to the last word. Witnesses may be precluded from further rebuttal testimony if they had been sequestered but sat in on the trial or hearing after their testimony.

After the plaintiff/claimant/prosecutor has introduced rebuttal evidence, the defense may offer rebuttal evidence. Following the defense rebuttal evidence, the plaintiff/claimant/prosecutor may offer new rebutting evidence. This, however, is not often allowed, because judges and arbitrators place reasonable limits on additional evidence and because enough is enough.

G. Stipulations

Stipulations present evidence in a case without calling witnesses. The parties may stipulate to specific facts, authentic exhibits, or witness testimony. A stipulation is reduced to writing and signed by the attorneys or made orally on the record. The stipulated facts are presented to the fact finder at an appropriate time in the case, usually during the case in chief of the offering attorney. A stipulation may be read by one of the attorneys, a witness, the clerk, or by the judge or arbitrator.

Example:

Counsel:

Your Honor, at this time I wish to offer Exhibit No. 23, which we have already marked for identification. It has been provided to the court upon agreement of counsel this morning before we started. This stipulation involves the testimony of A.D. Pythagoras.

Judge:

Is that correct, counsel?

Opposing Counsel:

Yes, your Honor.

Judge:

It is received. You may proceed.

Counsel:

Your Honor, at this time I would like to read to the jury the stipulated testimony.

Judge:

You may, counsel. Members of the Jury, you are to accept these facts you are about to hear as true and undisputed.

Counsel:

Members of the Jury, opposing counsel and I have agreed that were A.D. Pythagoras called to testify, he would tell us that he is the owner of the Pythagoras Accounting Service, and that as the owner of the accounting service, he has checked the books and records of Harvester Corporation. He has learned that the gross sales of farm equipment by the Harvester Corporation in 2002 were $7,355,000,000 and that the gross sales of farm equipment by the Harvester Corporation in 2003 were $825,000,000.

H. Admissions

Statements made by an opposing party may be admitted as evidence against that party. Federal Rule of Evidence 801 and similar state rules render admissible out-of-court statements made by an opposing party and out-of-court conduct of that party. In civil cases, admissions occur in written documents and discovery responses such as interrogatory answers, deposition answers, and responses to requests for admissions.

The party seeking to introduce admissions must affirmatively offer them into evidence. Typically, the offering attorney introduces the statements by introducing into evidence the document containing the admission. For example, the offering attorney asks the judge or arbitrator to accept in evidence the relevant points of the discovery document, marked as an exhibit. The attorney also can call the opposing party as an adverse witness and ask the party to admit such statements. If the opposing party denies making the statements, the statements can then be introduced as an exhibit. The offering attorney should decide whether it is better tactically to have the admission read by the attorney, clerk, or judge, or to have the opposing party admit the statements.

In criminal cases, admissions made by the defendant may be contained in a confession, which can be introduced through a witness, usually a law enforcement officer who heard the oral confession or who can authenticate the written confession.

I. Former Testimony

Situations arise where witnesses are unavailable to testify during a case. In civil cases, the previous testimony of a witness who is not available may be presented as substantive evidence. The previous testimony must usually be made under oath, at a deposition or hearing, and the opposing party must have had an opportunity to cross-examine the witness at that time. The witness must be unavailable to testify because of illness or death, or more commonly, because the witness is beyond the subpoena power of the tribunal. Section 7.10(A) explains these situations and procedures in detail. In arbitrations and administrative hearings, witnesses may be able to appear by telephone if they cannot be present in person. In criminal cases, former testimony is usually inadmissible because of the constitutional right of the defendant to confront witnesses during the trial.

J. Judicial/Arbitral/Administrative Notice

Facts that are indisputable or highly authoritative and widely accepted may be introduced through judicial, arbitral, or administrative notice. Notice may be taken of facts known as adjudicative facts, which are facts generally known within the territorial jurisdiction of the forum, or those that can be accurately and readily determined by highly reliable sources. See Fed.R.Evid. 201.

Examples:

Geographic and Historical Facts:

Notice may be taken of the location and existence of places, events, and things, such as streets, intersections, and landmarks. For example, The White House can be established as being located in Washington D.C.

Accurate and Verifiable Facts:

Notice may be taken of calendars, census findings, weather reports, and almanac information. For example, a specific day can be established as a legal holiday (September 2, 2003, a Monday, was Labor Day).

Scientific Facts:

Notice may be taken of scientifically verifiable or undisputed facts such as the laws of nature and the operations of machines and scientific equipment such as radar, intoxilizers, and breathalyzers. For example, the boiling point of water at sea level is 212 degrees Fahrenheit.

The party offering evidence by way of notice must supply the information and request that it be admitted into evidence. A judge or arbitrator may also take notice on their own initiative. A judge may accept judicially-noticed facts at any time during the proceeding and may inform the jury of the facts. In civil cases, judicially-noticed evidence is conclusive of the facts and jurors cannot find otherwise. The judge instructs the civil jury that they must find the fact as judicially-noticed. The party offering such facts need not introduce any other evidence of the fact. In criminal cases, judicially-noticed evidence is not usually conclusive and jurors can find otherwise. The judge instructs the criminal jurors that they need not accept or believe the judicially-noticed facts.

K. *Evidence Summaries*

In lengthy, legally complex, or factually complicated cases, time-saving evidence summaries may be needed. The judge or arbitrator may order, or the parties may stipulate to, several types of summaries, including a summary of the testimony of a witness based upon a deposition, a summary list of exhibits and their contents, summary outlines of information, or any other summary that makes the evidence more understandable to the fact finder. See Section 8.6(H).

L. *Planning the Introduction of Evidence*

Form 3.2 provides a format to identify and select evidence that needs to be introduced in a case. This approach or a similar plan is helpful to properly prepare for trial or hearing.

§ 3.7 COURT INTERVENTION

A. *Court–Appointed Experts*

A court may, on its own motion or on the motion of any party, appoint its own expert witness to testify in a case. The rules of civil procedure or evidence in a jurisdiction usually cover the procedures involved in such an appointment. Federal Rule of Evidence 706 and similar state rules govern the appointment of court experts. A judge may perceive the need for an expert to clarify confusing points or assist the fact finder in determining certain issues. This rule is seldom invoked. Arbitrators are unlikely to have this power. Administrative judges may have this power, especially in regulatory proceedings.

FORM 3.2

SELECTING EVIDENCE

Elements of Claim/ Defense	Facts to be Proven	Witness	Exhibit	Stipulation	Admission	Former Testimony	Hearing Testimony	Judicial/ Arbitral/ Administrative Notice	Other

B. Court Witnesses

The court may, on its own motion or on the motion of any party, call a witness who has not been called by a party. All parties are entitled to cross-examine the witness. Federal Rule of Evidence 614(a) and similar state rules authorize the court to call any person as a witness, with the exception of a criminal defendant. This rule is rarely invoked. An arbitrator is unlikely to have this power. Administrative judges may have this power if the hearing is one which is not solely adversarial.

C. Questioning by the Court

A judge may question any witness. See Federal Rule of Evidence 614(b) and similar state rules. Questioning by a judge occurs more often in bench trials than in jury trials because the judge is the fact finder in a bench trial. The judge may examine a witness during, or more commonly, after the parties have completed their questioning. Most judges limit their questions to areas that need clarification. After the judge has finished, the attorneys may further examine the witnesses on matters covered by the judge. Attorneys have a right to object to questions asked by the judge, and to the court's appointment of an expert and the calling of a witness. See Section 4.5(F) and Fed.R.Evid. 614(c).

D. Questioning by Jurors

In some jurisdictions, jurors are permitted to ask questions of witnesses. Usually the jurors submit written questions to the judge, who reviews the questions and determines if they may be asked. In a few courts, the jurors may be able to ask questions orally after the attorneys have completed their questioning. The attorneys may object to any questions asked.

Traditionally, jurors do not participate in a trial by asking questions of witnesses. That responsibility is to be performed by the lawyers and occasionally by the judge. A growing number of judges and lawyers recognize that permitting jurors to ask questions may assist them in their determination of the facts. Some advocates and judges oppose permitting jurors to ask questions because what they ask may be prohibited by the rules of evidence and non-answers may prejudice a party. Questions that are appropriate and screened by the judge and lawyers may be quite helpful to all participants.

E. Master/Referee

In certain cases, a judge may appoint a master or referee to assist with the factual or legal matters in a case. Some jurisdictions have magistrates or referees who assist the judge with preliminary discovery and pretrial matters. Federal Rule of Civil Procedure 53 permits federal district courts to appoint masters or referees for cases involving complicated issues, complex damages or accounting matters. The judge may allocate the costs of appointing a master or referee to the parties.

In complex or multi-party cases, the judge may appoint a special master to assist with the case. The special master may serve a variety of roles including reviewing disputed discoverable information, recommending to the judge what documents are privileged or discoverable, assisting parties with pretrial procedures, and acting as a mediator. The fees of the special master are commonly paid by the parties.

F. Administrative Proceedings

Administrative judges may be very active or very passive in a case. In some administrative hearings, it is the role of the judges to present evidence, call witnesses, and raise issues. In other administrative hearings, the judge acts similarly to a trial judge or an arbitrator.

G. Arbitration Proceedings

Arbitrators may ask questions of witnesses to clarify evidence and may ask questions of parties regarding legal issues. Arbitrators typically cannot raise new issues or call their own witnesses, unless the parties agree or are permitted to by the applicable rules and law.

H. Complex or Multidistrict Cases

Cases that are complex, prolonged or geographically located in more than one jurisdiction present special problems that require special handling. In federal court, the Manual for Complex Litigation provides procedures applicable to the management and conduct of cases that are complicated or venued in more than one district. The administration of large or multi-jurisdictional cases takes place during the early stages of the case, and matters that affect the trial are usually resolved well before trial.

Complicated or very lengthy cases may involve changes in the stages of the trial and the introduction of evidence. Summation may occur periodically during the trial with the attorney summarizing parts of the evidence as the trial progresses. The background of witnesses and the qualifications of experts may be introduced through written resumes. Numerous documents may be submitted through evidence summaries. See Section 8.6(H). These and other efficient procedures may be used in an effort to reduce the duration of the trial and to prevent an overwhelming amount of evidence.

Federal cases that are filed in different federal districts that have common issues of law and fact may be transferred to one federal judge who administers all discovery and pretrial proceedings. The Federal Multi–District Litigation Panel transfers these cases in accord with the applicable federal MDL statute. Nationwide or multi-state products liability cases and disaster cases are examples of the same or similar case that is filed by individual or class action plaintiffs in numerous districts against the same defendants. Thousands of cases may be filed across the country, and this method helps coordinate proceedings. The transferee judge assigns lead counsel, liaison attorneys, and a plaintiffs steering committee to represent the interests of all plaintiffs. Defense counsel may also join together and more easily defend in this singular proceeding. A special master can be appointed to further coordinate the litigation proceedings.

There is no similar procedure to coordinate cases filed in different state courts around the country. State court judges in one state have no power over cases filed in other states, and federal judges likewise cannot control state court cases. The state court plaintiff and defense lawyers can and do cooperate with each other in an effort to avoid unnecessary and duplicative litigation efforts.

§ 3.8 MOTIONS

Any request, oral or written, made by an attorney seeking an order or some relief from a judge or arbitrator is a motion. Many requests are often not formally referred to as motions by counsel. More typically, lawyers orally ask the judge or arbitrator that something be done or prohibited. Federal Rule of Civil Procedure 7(b) and similar state rules allow oral motions "during a hearing or trial." These oral motions may be made in the courtroom or in chambers.

Motions are much more frequent in litigation. Motions may also be brought in arbitrations (often called "requests") and administrative hearings (sometimes called "petitions"); but some motions are unnecessary or unavailable in arbitration and administrative cases. For example, summary judgment motions are often inappropriate in these cases because the hearing is promptly scheduled and the parties can more efficiently and effectively present their entire case to the arbitrator or administrative law judge, obviating the need for an early preliminary decision. The frequent use of motions in litigation is one of the reasons why judicial cases are more expensive and take much longer to resolve.

Motions should be brought if the relief sought has a significant impact on the status, progress or outcome of the case. If granting relief through a motion may substantially increase the chance of obtaining a favorable decision, then the motion should be vigorously pursued. If the relief sought has only marginal influence on a favorable decision, then the motion should be reconsidered.

The specific relief sought in any one motion must be considered in the context of the entire case. If motions are brought on overly technical or minor points, or if too many motions clutter the proceedings, they may have an adverse impact on the moving attorney. An advocate's ability is evaluated in part on how effectively the attorney handles procedural matters such as motion requests.

A. Motion Documents

Some motions should be — or must be — presented in writing. Written motion documents include:

1. Notice of Motion

The notice of motion advises all parties of the time and place of the motion hearing, and typically identifies the judge who will hear the motion. Anywhere from five to thirty or more days may be required to give timely notice of the hearing. Written trial motions are commonly heard by the trial judge at the final pretrial conference. Whether a written notice is required depends on the motion, the relief sought, and the impact on opposing counsel. Sufficient written notice should be given to prevent the opposing party from claiming unfair surprise or prejudice in arguing against the motion. Arbitration rules and administrative law regulations may delineate the timing and deadlines of available motions.

2. Affidavits

An affidavit is a sworn statement containing facts or opinions. Affidavits are used in motion practice to support or oppose a motion. An affidavit is necessary when no facts in the file or record support the motion, or if the facts are based on the personal knowledge of the moving attorney.

3. Memorandum of Law

Most forums require (and most decision makers expect) written legal authority supporting or opposing a motion. The submission of a persuasive memorandum of law increases the chances that the motion will be granted.

4. Proposed Order

Most jurisdictions and judges require submission of a proposed order by the moving party. The proposed order makes clear to the judge what is requested and enables the judge to grant the motion more expeditiously. Some judges sign the proposed order if it reflects their decision. Other judges draft their own order, often based on the proposed order. Proposed orders may be submitted to an arbitrator and administrative judge.

B. Opposing Motions

Generally, there is no need for the opposing attorney to bring a motion seeking to deny the relief requested in the moving party's motion. Orally opposing the motion at the hearing may be sufficient to obtain an order denying the motion. Whether the opposing party should submit any written documents depends on the rules of the forum, the timing of the motion, and case strategy. Court rules ordinarily state whether the court requires submission of any written opposition documents. A written motion submitted on the eve of trial or hearing may not provide sufficient time for the opposing lawyer to reply in writing, making an oral response both appropriate and sufficient.

In many situations, it is usually not necessary — although it may be advisable — to submit opposing affidavits. Affidavits may need to be submitted if the facts do not appear in the file or record or if the facts claimed to be accurate by the moving party are not true or complete. In most situations, an opposing memorandum, however brief, is necessary and advisable. The submission of a memorandum opposing the motion may provide the decision maker with legal authority to deny the motion. See Section 3.9(D). Similarly, the submission of a proposed order denying the motion may sway the decision maker to decide against the relief sought in the motion.

C. Types of Motions

Many types of motions may be made before or during a trial or hearing, depending upon events. The more common judicial motions include the following:

1. Motion to Amend Pleadings

Procedural rules usually permit amendments of civil pleadings during the preliminary stage of a case and during a trial. The procedure to amend pleadings at the trial stage is commonly known as a motion to amend to conform the pleadings to the evidence. See, e.g., Fed.R.Civ.P. 15(b). This amendment is ordinarily allowed if the parties expressly or impliedly consent to the evidence offered during the trial. Express consent means that the parties agree to the introduction of evidence that supports or contradicts a claim or defense not appearing in the original pleadings but presented during the trial. Implied consent occurs if a party submits evidence on an issue not contained in the original pleadings and the opposing party does not object to its introduction. The introducing party may then move the court to amend the pleadings because there is evidence to support the claim or defense. The opposing party must make a timely objection to the introduction of the evidence to exclude such evidence and to oppose the motion successfully.

The requirements of the motion to amend the pleadings ensure that one party does not surprise the other party at the trial or hearing. If a party attempts to introduce some new or undisclosed evidence in support of a new theory, the opposing lawyer is usually able to claim prejudice and the judge usually excludes the evidence. The purpose of the motion is to permit the introduction of evidence that might be barred by an overly technical and formal application of the pleading rules, and to allow the fact finder to consider all evidence that bears on a related issue in a case. A motion to conform the pleadings to the evidence is used infrequently because the situations that require its use seldom arise.

2. Motion in Limine

A motion "in limine" seeks to exclude from the trial, usually a jury trial, the introduction of inadmissible evidence. This motion may be made before the trial begins in anticipation of certain evidence being offered, or during the trial immediately prior to the introduction of such evidence. An in limine motion often requests an advance ruling from the judge to prevent the opposing party from offering objectionable evidence during the trial in the presence of the jury. The motion is meant to prevent the prejudicial effect the mere disclosure of such evidence would have on the jurors. An in limine motion may also ask the court to permit the moving party to introduce evidence during trial without being interrupted by an objection from opposing counsel. Seeking an advance ruling of an in limine motion promotes trial efficiency and permits the judge more time for reflection. Section 4.5(A) explains motions in limine in detail.

3. *Motion for Summary Judgment*

A summary judgment motion resolves all or part of the issues in a case and is dispositive because the case, some of the claims, or some of the defenses are resolved by the judge without a full trial or hearing. Rules of procedure and case law establish two grounds for the motion: no disputed issues of material fact exist, and as a matter of law a party is entitled to judgment. See Fed.R.Civ.P. 56. If there is no controversy regarding the material facts, then there is no need for a jury to determine the facts. The judge may apply the law to the facts and render judgment. The judge does not decide any facts, but only determines whether or not there are disputed material facts. If there are disputed facts, the case must go to trial.

Typically, a summary judgment motion (called a demurrer in some jurisdictions) is a pretrial motion and is brought before the case has been set for trial, most often after discovery has been completed. This eliminates the need for a trial, or at least reduces the number of triable issues. In some situations, a summary judgment motion may be appropriately made at the final pretrial conference or immediately before the trial begins. If the undisputed facts support the motion, then the motion is timely and proper. Summary judgment motions are ordinarily supported and opposed by affidavits and discovery responses that supply the facts. A case that is ready for trial has all the facts developed and available, making affidavits unnecessary.

In some cases a summary judgment motion is available when there are undisputed facts regarding one or more issues in a case. Summary judgment sought on fewer than all the issues in a case is known as partial summary judgment. For example, in a contract case, the facts regarding liability may be undisputed, and summary judgment may be entered on the issue of liability; then only the claim for damages would be submitted to a jury at trial.

Ordinarily, summary judgment motions are written and noticed for hearing. In many jurisdictions, an oral summary judgment motion may properly be brought before the trial begins. At that stage, the undisputed facts have been established and need not be proven, and all of the disputed facts have been developed. In such cases, there is no need for formal written notice, because neither party can claim prejudice nor legitimately request more time to develop contrary facts.

Example:

Defendant moves this court pursuant to Federal Rule of Civil Procedure 56 for a summary judgment on the grounds that no disputed issue of material fact exists and that Defendant is entitled to a judgment as a matter of law. Defendant bases this motion on the attached affidavits, Plaintiff's answers to Defendant's interrogatories, pages 61 to 69 of Plaintiff's deposition, Plaintiffs responses to Defendant's requests for admissions, and on the submitted memorandum of law and proposed order.

Arbitration rules may not permit summary judgment because there is no procedural need for this motion. The arbitration agreement of the parties may include a summary judgment provision, permitting its use. Administrative law regulations may permit a summary judgment, especially in lengthy or complex cases.

4. Motion to Strike

A motion to strike is made during trial in reaction to some objectionable matter such as an improper question by the attorney, an inadmissible answer from the witness, or some inappropriate behavior. The purpose of the motion is to make clear that the improper statement or conduct is to be ignored by the fact finder.

Nothing is actually ever stricken from the record. The court reporter does not delete anything when the court grants the motion. The record contains the objectionable remark, the objection, the motion to strike, and the ruling. The reason that nothing is stricken is to provide a complete record for the appellate court.

This type of motion may be anachronistic. The objecting attorney really does not want what was objectionable stricken from the record. If the objecting party loses the case, then that party will want the appellate court to review the objectionable matter on the record.

In a jury trial, a curative instruction from the judge is necessary and should be requested instead of, or in addition to, the motion to strike. In a bench trial, the motion serves no real purpose because the judge knows that the inadmissible matter cannot be used in the findings of fact. But, even in bench trials, many judges expect to hear such motions and require them to be made. Additionally, for many lawyers the motion to strike is automatic and instinctive, and so they use it in all situations, even if it doesn't make sense.

5. Motion for a Curative Instruction

A motion for a curative instruction is a request for the judge to advise the jury to disregard some objectionable matter. The curative instruction is an attempt to repair the harm done by an improper question, inadmissible answer, or inappropriate behavior. The curative instruction is meant to reduce or avoid the influence the statement might have had on the jury. For example, if an attorney refers to inadmissible evidence during opening statement, the opposing lawyer should object and request an instruction from the judge that the jury ignore that statement.

The use of the curative instruction has advantages and disadvantages. The request by the attorney for the instruction calls the jury's attention to the harmful matter, and the instruction by the judge may reinforce the jury's memory of it. If an objectionable remark or event is not significant, seeking an instruction may do nothing more than highlight the remark. If the harmful matter is significant, the instruction should be requested because the jury will have doubtlessly taken notice of the matter. They may be influenced by the improper comments but, with a curative instruction, will ordinarily not rely on such information in forming a verdict. If the matter is severely objectionable, a motion for a mistrial should be made. Section 4.5(D) explains the use of curative instructions in detail.

6. *Motion for Involuntary Dismissal*

In a bench trial, arbitration, and administrative hearing, after the presentation of evidence by the plaintiff/claimant/prosecutor, the defendant may move for dismissal of the case on the ground that the no right to relief has been demonstrated or the asserted claims have not been proven. Usually the motion is made orally, after the plaintiff/claimant/prosecutor rests. In judicial jurisdictions, this motion is used in bench trials and not jury trials. See Fed.R.Civ.P. 41(b).

In deciding whether to grant the motion, the judge or arbitrator usually asks the moving attorney to identify what elements or facts supporting the cause of action have not been proven. The judge or arbitrator may rule on the motion at this stage of the trial, or reserve judgment until the close of all the evidence. This motion requires a determination regarding whether the evidence is sufficient to present a question of fact for the fact finder. In making this decision, the judge or arbitrator must view all the evidence and draw every reasonable inference in favor of the plaintiff/claimant/prosecutor. This determination is the same standard applicable to a directed verdict motion in a jury trial.

The motion for involuntary dismissal is seldom granted. In a bench trial, the judge, who is also the fact finder, usually decides the case on the merits by weighing the evidence and determining the credibility of the witnesses. A motion to dismiss does not permit the judge to weigh the evidence or assess the credibility of the witnesses. Rarely in civil cases are judges prompted to grant motions to dismiss. Arbitrators and administrative law judges are similarly disinclined to grant the motion unless it is clear there is no need to hear additional evidence. Criminal cases, with their higher burden of proof, may involve insufficient facts to support a judgment and prompt a judge to grant the motion. Some judges prefer to resolve those cases with a judgment on the merits after a full trial and not a motion to dismiss. An order granting an involuntary dismissal operates as an adjudication on the merits.

7. *Motion for Directed Verdict or Motion to Dismiss*

In jury trials, a motion to challenge the legal sufficiency of the evidence may be brought at the close of a party's case or after the close of all the evidence. This motion may be called a motion for a directed verdict, a judgment as a matter of law, a dismissal for failure to prove a prima facie case, a nonsuit, or, in a criminal case, a judgment of acquittal. The motion asks the court to direct a verdict on the ground that the opposing party has not proven the facts or elements of law supporting the claim or defense. Such a motion is brought only in jury trials and is identical to the motion for involuntary dismissal available in bench trials.

Any party may bring a motion for a directed verdict. Ordinarily, after the plaintiff rests, the defendant automatically brings this motion. Likewise, after the defendant rests, the plaintiff usually brings a directed verdict motion. After rebuttal, or at the close of the evidence, the defendant again brings this motion. In some jurisdictions, a directed verdict motion may be brought after the opponent's opening statement if the opening makes no reference to facts supporting the party's assertions. In making this motion, the attorney usually specifies what elements or facts have not been proven. The other party may then rebut this argument or seek leave of the court to produce additional existing information.

A motion for directed verdict should not be made unless a party has sufficient grounds to support such a motion or unless the rules of a jurisdiction require a motion to be made in order to preserve the opportunity to bring a motion for a judgment notwithstanding the verdict. See Section 12.5(B). A party who brings a motion for a judgment as a matter of law must state the specific grounds supporting the motion.

The motion creates a question of law regarding whether sufficient evidence exists to support a verdict for the nonmoving party. The precise grounds for granting or denying the motion vary among jurisdictions. Typically, in deciding a motion, the judge cannot weigh the evidence or determine the credibility of the witnesses, but must instead draw all reasonable inferences and view all the facts in the light most favorable to the party opposing the motion. If any evidence exists to support the opposing party's version of the case and if a reasonable person could possibly find in favor of this party, then the judge will deny the motion, even if the judge would find for the moving party.

Judges seldom grant these motions because the losing party is deprived of a jury determination on the merits. A trial court holding will be more likely affirmed by the appellate court if the judge submits the case to the jury and then rules on the sufficiency of the evidence in a motion for judgment notwithstanding the verdict after a jury has returned a verdict. Denying the directed verdict motion allows the judge, in effect, to defer ruling until the jury decides. If the jury decides in favor of a party which has produced insufficient evidence as a matter of law, then the judge may correct the jury's error and grant the motion for judgment notwithstanding the verdict. See Section 12.5(B).

8. *Motion for Leave to Reopen a Case*

If a motion to dismiss or a directed verdict motion is granted, the losing attorney may move for leave to reopen the case and present additional evidence, if such evidence exists. Judges and arbitrators usually grant this motion if the evidence is readily available and substantial enough to raise a question of fact sufficient to deny the directed verdict motion. Tribunals prefer that cases be decided on the merits based on all available evidence and not upon an oversight by counsel.

9. *Motion for Mistrial*

Incidents may occur during a jury trial that give rise to a motion for a mistrial. Grounds that support a mistrial motion include statements or conduct by counsel, witnesses, jurors, court officials, or the judge that:

- Are substantially and unfairly prejudicial,
- Constitute gross misconduct,
- Intentionally violate a court order,
- Deliberately and unfairly attempt to influence the judge or jury,
- Provide false evidence,
- Improperly and adversely affect the substantial rights of a party,
- Result in substantial irregularities in the trial proceedings, and
- Otherwise make a fair trial impossible.

These and other errors are the same as the grounds for a new trial after a verdict. Examples of errors supporting a motion for mistrial include: opposing counsel intentionally making inflammatory remarks, an adverse witness testifying to inadmissible and unfairly prejudicial evidence, a judge making improper comments manifesting a bias in favor of an opposing party, and juror misconduct.

The grounds for a mistrial must be so severe and uncorrectable that a party is denied a fair trial. The mere occurrence of misconduct is not sufficient to support the granting of the motion. The misconduct must significantly influence the judgment of the jury or judge to a degree that adversely affects the substantial rights of a party. The adverse effect can ordinarily be reduced by providing the jurors with a curative instruction to disregard the misconduct or by admonishing the offending person.

The status of the case influences both an attorney's decision to move for a mistrial and the judge's ruling. If an attorney perceives that the case is going well, moving for a new trial may not be advisable. If the attorney believes the case is not going well, the attorney may want to pursue a mistrial motion. A trial judge is not likely to terminate a lengthy trial because of the time and efforts invested. A trial that is just beginning stands a better chance of having a judge grant a mistrial motion.

Few cases result in a mistrial. In a criminal case, the constitutional rights of a defendant coupled with prosecutorial misconduct may justify the granting of a new trial. In civil cases, curative instructions and admonitions usually remedy the damage done. The granting of a mistrial motion results in a new trial.

10. *Motion to Reconsider*

Once a motion is decided, that ruling is the law of the case for that that case, and it cannot be changed by asking the judge to rethink and change the decision. The motion decision is final and controlling. Even if another judge becomes the trial judge, a previous ruling by a different judge is still the law of the case, and a party does not get a second chance to win just because there is a different trial judge. Judges have lots to do and ought not to asked to do things twice, and they may ignore motions to reconsider or may even consider them frivolous and harassing.

But even at the trial stage, lawyers may be inclined to bring a motion to reconsider after losing a motion. This tactic–as in pretrial and post trial practice–should be resisted unless the very, very narrow grounds for reconsideration are available, which are even less likely for trial motions. The primary ground — and sometimes only legitimate ground — for reconsideration is that the law changed between the time of submission and decision that controls the motion. It is usually not sufficient that the law changed after the decision, unless it is clear that the new law is retroactive.

If allowable, most courts require a party to bring a motion requesting the opportunity to bring a motion to reconsider, before actually submitting the reconsideration motion. A party must have existing, legitimate grounds in that jurisdiction to support such a motion.

If it not clear by now: judges do not like, do not want to see, and will not review motions to reconsider unless there is clear and evident reason to do so. They view this motion as a party seeking a second chance, which is not available. The losing party naturally believes the judge is wrong, but being wrong in the view of a party–however strongly believed or seemingly supported by existing law–is not a ground for a motion to reconsider.

11. *Additional Motions*

Many other motions may be made during a case. The following list includes commonly available motions:

- Motion for jury or court trial,
- Motion to recuse or disqualify judge,
- Motion to disqualify counsel,
- Motion for jury selection examination,

- Motion to strike juror for cause,
- Motion for court reporter to record proceedings,
- Motion to sequester witnesses,
- Motion for recess or adjournment,
- Motion to limit testimony of witness,
- Motion to interrupt order of witnesses because of unavailability,
- Motion to exclude testimony or exhibits,
- Motion to make offer of proof,
- Motion to receive testimony or exhibits,
- Motion for judicial notice,
- Motion to instruct jury,
- Motion to sequester jury,
- Motion to discharge jury, and
- Motion to poll jury.

Post-trial motions are explained in Section 12.5 and include:

- Motion for judgment notwithstanding the verdict (j.n.o.v.),
- Motion for new trial,
- Motion for amended findings of fact, conclusions of law, and order of judgment,
- Motion for additur,
- Motion for remittitur,
- Motion for a stay of entry of judgment,
- Motion for a stay of judgment,
- Motion to enforce judgment,
- Motion for interests and costs, and
- Motion for attorney's fees.

§ 3.9   MOTION ARGUMENT

Some motions include oral argument scheduled at a hearing, while other motions are decided by judges on the briefs presented without oral argument. Some courts have rules which determine what motions include oral argument. An advocate who prefers to orally argue a motion may request a hearing. The preparation of an argument in support of or in opposition to a motion requires the same degree of preparation as any other facet of advocacy.

A. *Available Time*

Whether a specific time limit is set for a motion argument depends upon the forum, judge, or arbitrator. Some forums schedule motions for a specific and limited amount of time; other forums schedule motions in sequence and allow attorneys a reasonable time for argument. The amount of time allocated depends on the importance of the motion, the length of the case, and how much time can be devoted to the entire case. The attorney must decide how much time is necessary and how the available time should be used. If more time for argument is needed than is allocated by a court, the attorney may request additional time.

B. Preparation by the Judge

An attorney must ascertain whether the judge has read or is familiar with the motion, the case, and the applicable law. Some judges review the file before the hearing; others do not have time to do so. The extent of the judge's familiarity with the motion determines the content of the motion argument. If a judge is not familiar with the motion, then the moving attorney must inform the judge about the motion. Otherwise, the judge may spend the first few minutes looking through the file rather than listening to the beginning of the attorney's argument.

A judge who is familiar with the case may not need much background information about the case. The extent of a judge's preparation may be learned from experience, by contacting the law clerk and inquiring about the judge's knowledge of the case, or by simply (and diplomatically) asking the judge if the judge had the opportunity to review the file and motion. Arbitrators and administrative judges are usually familiar with the motion because they schedule a specific time to hear and decide the motion.

C. Supporting Memorandum

Some jurisdictions require that a memorandum or citation of authorities be submitted in support of a motion. Motion memoranda are usually submitted prior to the oral motion argument, but may also be submitted after the argument if some issues were raised during argument which need briefing. An attorney may also suggest that a memorandum and reply be submitted, or a judge or arbitrator may request submissions from the attorneys.

A memorandum should be concise and contain a summary of the vital facts and the legal authorities supporting the position asserted by the attorney. A short memorandum that identifies the issues and supporting legal authorities and citations or highlighted copies of judicial opinions, statutes or rules is often sufficient. A lengthy, detailed memo should be reserved for complex, complicated issues.

D. Opposition Memorandum

Submitting a written memorandum in opposition to a motion is required in many jurisdictions and forums and expected in many others. An opposing memorandum should obviously explain why the motion should be denied. An effective reply memorandum should address and refute arguments made in the opponent's motion memorandum. This review of the other side's statements should focus on revealing weaknesses and mistakes such as factual misstatements or omissions, legal errors, inadequately supported legal or factual conclusions, inappropriate issues, illogical arguments, inconsistent positions, and concessions. An opposing memorandum need not be submitted in all situations. Some positions advanced by the other side deserve no rebuttal while others may be rebutted adequately during oral argument.

E.   Location of Argument

Trial motions are argued in the judge's chambers or in the courtroom. Some judges may prefer to discuss the merits of the motion on an informal basis in chambers, where the attorneys and the judge are seated around the judge's desk or a conference table. Most judges prefer the formality of a courtroom. For presentation of a motion in a courtroom, the attorney usually stands and argues before the judge, who sits at the bench. If the attorney believes that the presentation of the argument or the determination of the judge would be enhanced by arguing the motion in either chambers or the courtroom, then the attorney should make that request of the judge. Lawyers may appear in person or by telephone if they are distant from the court. It is wise to seek the approval of the court ahead of time if the lawyer will appear by phone, so the judge can make the technical arrangements for a speaker phone. Arbitration and administrative proceeding motions are argued by telephone, or in writing, or in person, and some day soon, by e-mail.

F.   Sequence of Argument

The moving party usually argues first. Then the opposing attorney is given an opportunity to speak in opposition to the motion. Rebuttal arguments are permitted by both lawyers as long as the statements are responsive and not repetitious.

G.   Recording of Argument

The practice of recording the oral arguments of attorneys varies among jurisdictions and judges. There may be no reason for the argument to be recorded. In such instances, the attorney need not be concerned with the making of a record. But if the attorney wants a record made, the presence of a court reporter should be requested. Arbitration motion arguments are commonly not recorded. Some administrative motion arguments may be recorded in cases involving significant issues.

The making of a record usually influences the tenor and content of statements made by the attorneys and the judge, and reduces the likelihood that injudicious or extraneous statements will be made. A record preserves everything that is requested and argued by the lawyers and everything that is decided by the judge. Further, a transcript can be used to present grounds for a new trial motion or an appeal and can be made available for a client who is not present. An alternative to having the court reporter present to record the entire motion argument is to argue the motion off the record and then have the moving attorney summarize the motion and the relief sought and have the judge explain the ruling on the record.

§ 3.10 MOTION ARGUMENT TECHNIQUES

Oral motion argument techniques do not differ significantly from other oral argument situations. An effective, efficient, and economical presentation in support of or in opposition to a motion must address the following question: What information does the decision maker need to decide the motion in favor of the client? After determining this information, the advocate must then present the information persuasively.

A. Brevity

Be brief!

B. Conversational, Interesting Approach

Many lawyers present motion arguments in a formal manner, as if they were in a debate or making an appellate argument. This approach may not be as effective as a conversational approach in which the attorney converses with the judge or arbitrator and invites questions. To be an effective "conversationalist" in this setting, an attorney must adopt a persuasive style, display familiarity with the facts and the law, demonstrate confidence, and persist when necessary. Rapport, eye contact, voice tone, diction, pace, and gestures are among the many factors which influence the effectiveness of a presentation.

C. Preface

An attorney should preface the substance of an argument with a brief outline of what will be covered. An argument is more easily followed when the decision maker is advised what topics will be discussed. The judge or arbitrator may suggest to the attorney certain matters that need not be covered because they are already familiar with them and may even have already resolved them. A judge or arbitrator may also be inclined to postpone asking questions about a matter until that point is reached during the argument.

The moving attorney who speaks first may also want to include as a preface a short description of the motion, its grounds, and the relief sought, to remind the decision maker about why the attorneys are there. The moving attorney may also wish to provide some background regarding the nature and history of the case in order to put the motion in perspective. An opposing lawyer may supplement this information.

D. Structure

The argument following the prefatory remarks made by an attorney must be structured in an effective, persuasive manner. The optimum order for an argument depends significantly on the type of motion presented. Any lengthy argument must be carefully structured so that it can be easily followed. The motion, memorandum, proposed order, affidavits, or other motion papers may provide an attorney with an outline for structuring the argument.

E. Substance of Argument

What an attorney says and what relief is requested depends upon the type of motion presented. The presentation should contain an explanation of the facts and the law mixed with reason, logic, emotion, and equity. Considerations that increase the persuasive value of an argument should be reviewed, including:

- Is the motion a common, routine request or an unusual request?

- Should the strongest position be asserted first, with the second strongest position last and other, weaker positions explained in between?

- Should key words, phrases, or positions be emphasized and repeated throughout the argument?

- Should the circumstances causing the motion to be brought be mentioned?

- Should the failure or refusal of the opposing attorney to cooperate with the moving attorney in resolving or compromising the issues of the motion be mentioned?

F. The Law

Legal explanations should be accurate and understandable. Many arguments lose their effectiveness because the applicable law is exaggerated or explained in a confusing way. An attorney should carefully select the references to the law to be explained during argument. Leading cases, supporting statutes, and persuasive quotations should be used when necessary. Cases from other jurisdictions, peripheral legal authorities, and overly technical explanations should be avoided. Legal matters should be argued if they can be explained more effectively in oral argument than in a brief. Legal matters which may be effectively presented in a memorandum need not be repeated orally, unless the attorney anticipates the judge will not read the memorandum, or unless the arguments need clarification.

References to the law should also be concise. Quotations from cases or statutes should be woven into an argument and should not be read at length. Long quotes and specific citations should be provided in a memorandum, brief or outline of authorities.

G. The Facts

Many motions revolve around questions of law and the facts of the case may not make a significant difference in the outcome of the motion. Other motions depend upon the development of the facts. Facts in a motion hearing are often presented by submitting affidavits which contain the relevant and necessary information. Some motion hearings involve the presentation of live testimony through witnesses and the introduction of exhibits. Such evidence offered during a motion hearing usually mirrors the direct and cross-examinations of the witnesses.

H. Factual Descriptions

A description of the facts should include a complete and accurate recitation of the relevant evidence. Some attorneys tend to ramble during motion arguments, providing the court with factual information not appearing in an affidavit, in the file, or in the record. An opposing attorney should point out the inadequacy of this information and the inappropriateness of an attorney attempting to testify or provide evidence in an improper manner. Other attorneys may exaggerate or stretch the facts to match a point of law. These tactics usually backfire because the inherent weakness of such positions are readily apparent to an opposing attorney and to the decision maker.

I. Notes

Arguments should not be read. Notes outlining the essential points of an argument may be used as a guide during a presentation. A lack of notes may indicate a lack of preparation by an attorney and may make a complete and logical presentation difficult. The use of notes, however, should not detract from the presentation of the argument. Attorneys should be flexible and not "glued" to their notes because they may be interrupted with questions about other issues not anticipated in the prepared notes. The attorney must be so well prepared that interruptions and digressions by the judge or arbitrator do not fluster or confuse the attorney.

J. Exhibits

Exhibits, including real and demonstrative evidence, or visual aids such as diagrams, charts, graphs, and computer generated exhibits may assist an attorney's presentation, and may help a judge or arbitrator in understanding an argument. Exhibits should be used if they enhance the persuasiveness of an argument, but not, obviously, if they prolong or confuse the argument.

K. Interruptions

An attorney should avoid interrupting an opposing attorney or the judge or arbitrator. Interrupting the opposing counsel is unprofessional and discourteous, unless the opponent's statements are unfairly prejudicial, bear no relation to the motion, or mischaracterize something that requires immediate correction. Attorneys who make unnecessary interruptions are likely to be admonished. A more effective approach is to note any misstatements of fact or law and comment on them after the opposing lawyer has completed an argument.

A lawyer should direct all statements to the judge or arbitrator and should avoid arguing directly with the opposing attorney. Some situations may require that a lawyer request that opposing counsel be directed to apologize for a remark or be admonished for making disparaging statements.

L.   Opposition Weaknesses

An argument should contain references to the weaknesses of the opponent's case or to the inappropriateness of a position taken by the other side. This requires an attorney to anticipate positions taken by an opposing lawyer and counter those points during the argument. If this is not possible or appropriate, rebuttal will afford an opportunity to expose the weakness in the opponent's case. An argument sounds more persuasive if made in a positive, constructive manner. A defensive argument that merely attacks the opposition appears weak.

M.   Candor and Compromise

An attorney must be candid during an argument. If the facts and supporting law provide a judge with the discretion to grant or deny a motion, a moving party should not argue that the judge has no discretion. If the facts and supporting law provide a moving party with a reasonable position, an opposing lawyer should not unnecessarily criticize the position or pretend that precedent mandates the arbitrator to deny the motion.

An attorney may also have to compromise during a motion hearing. Many judges view the hearing as an opportunity to force attorneys to negotiate a resolution to the problem. Attorneys who maintain set positions during a motion hearing must be prepared to propose or accept alternative positions to resolve a matter. A motion hearing may provide a forum for the arbitrator to mediate a solution to a problem the attorneys were unable to resolve on their own.

N.   Questions by the Judge or Arbitrator

Questions asked by the judge or arbitrator should be answered at the time asked. Rarely should answers be postponed. Questions are expected to be answered when asked. An attorney should answer questions directly and completely and should avoid being evasive. An attorney should admit to not knowing an answer, if the answer is unknown.

Efforts should be made to provide answers in a light most favorable to the client's position. An attorney must be prepared, if necessary, to concede a point in a response to avoid arguing an issue unnecessarily. Any concession should be put in perspective, and the attorney should continue on with another point.

Questions from judges and arbitrators should be encouraged. An attorney may want to ask if the judge or arbitrator has any questions. It is critical for the attorney to address and resolve the issues the decision maker is considering, and an effective way to ascertain these issues is to invite questions.

O. Involving the Decision Maker

The attorney should prepare and present an argument in such a way as to involve the decision maker in the motion. Some judges and arbitrators are inclined to be active while others are more inclined to be passive during oral argument. An effective presentation by an attorney often develops an interchange between that attorney and decision maker. The more the decision maker participates in a motion discussion, the more likely the motion will be understood and the right decision made.

P. Rulings

After hearing arguments on a trial or hearing motion, the decision maker will usually make the ruling orally, on the record, if there is one. If a proposed order has been submitted, the judge or arbitrator may sign that order. The rulings and orders a judge makes during a trial are interlocutory orders and are appealable along with the final judgment entered in the case after the trial. A few rulings or orders, which involve significant issues dispositive of a case, may be immediately appealable. See Section 12.9(F).

The determination whether to grant or deny the motion is not always based on the law and the facts of the case. Other considerations may influence a judge's decisions. Some judges believe that a case ought to be settled, and realize that if a motion is decided in a certain way, settlement will be more likely to occur. Other judges believe that one party has a much stronger case than the other party and rule on a motion to increase the chances that the party with the stronger case will prevail. Motions provide an opportunity for a judge to influence the result of a case, and some judges take advantage of this opportunity.

Q. Written Arguments

For those motions not allowed by the court to be argued orally, the written brief may need to be composed to reflect the lack of oral argument. The questions that need to be addressed are:

- What would have been stated in oral argument that is not contained in the initial draft of the brief?

- Is there an argument that seems inappropriate for briefing but appropriate for oral argument?

- What, if anything, is being left out of the brief that would have been argued at a motion hearing?

- Might the judge have questions the answers to which are not addressed in the draft brief?

The answers to these questions may require the brief to be redrafted, if it the sole means an advocate has to present an argument. It may well be that the primary purposes of a motion argument are to allow the judge an opportunity to ask questions and to increase the chances that the judge will fully understand why the motion should be granted or not granted. In those cases, the lack of oral argument may not be a significant loss.

§ 3.11 PREPARATION AND PRESENTATION TO A JUDGE OR ARBITRATOR

This section discusses additional considerations applicable to making a case presentation to a trial or administrative judge or an arbitrator. These decision makers are professional decision makers, having made decisions before in cases. Jurors are usually first time legal decision makers and some advocacy approaches that are effective with them will not be effective before judges and arbitrators, especially if they have heard the same argument before in previous cases. But there are many similarities among all types of decision makers, and experienced judges and arbitrators can be successfully influenced and affected by many of the same approaches that work with jurors and inexperienced professional decision makers.

A. *Opening Statement*

Opening statements should be made unless the decision maker is very familiar with the case. A discussion with the decision maker before the start of the trial or hearing — in which the theory of the case and the significant facts and issues have been discussed — may be a sufficient substitute for an opening statement. If an advocate believes the judge or arbitrator knows enough about the case to proceed to the presentation of evidence, then an opening may be unnecessary. Many advocates prefer to make an opening statement, even a brief one, because of the informative and persuasive impact it has. In some administrative hearings, an opening may not be permitted. And if trial judges or arbitrators insist they do not need to hear openings, it may be waste of time for advocates to do so.

B. *Evidentiary Rulings*

The judge or arbitrator who must decide both the facts and the admissibility of evidence may have a difficult time avoiding the influence of inadmissible evidence. When deciding whether to admit or deny the introduction of certain evidence, a decision maker must understand what the evidence is. Judges and arbitrators may not rely on inadmissible evidence in reaching their decision, but it may be difficult for them to disregard the impact of this evidence, and they may have to hear an offer of proof. See Section 4.5(B).

Fact finders are more inclined to admit evidence than to exclude it. They may believe they need to know or they may be curious. Trial and administrative judges realize that appellate courts are more likely to overturn a court decision if key evidence is omitted than if the evidence is admitted. Many of the exclusionary rules of evidence, discussed in Chapter 4, are primarily designed to restrict the introduction of evidence in jury trials and not bench trials, arbitrations, or administrative hearings.

C. Introduction of Evidence

The presentation of evidence through witnesses and documents must obviously be addressed to the fact finder in as persuasive and effective a way as possible. Some attorneys are less formal and less careful in presenting evidence to an arbitrator or administrative judge, but this approach can result in an inadequate presentation. Professional decision makers need to hear all relevant, persuasive evidence about the case and need to hear testimony that establishes the credibility of witnesses.

On direct examination, advocates may more likely ask leading questions to speed the case up or may eliminate foundation questions because the judge or arbitrator has heard these facts before in previous cases. But it is critical to the determination of witness credibility for the professional decision maker to hear the witness testify and not counsel through too many leading questions. And it is critical for the judge or arbitrator to hear all compelling evidence, and not just a summary version, to make sure they understand the complete and accurate factual stories that support the theory of the case.

On cross-examination, some areas of cross may not need to be as thoroughly examined with a judge or arbitrator as they would need to be with a jury. For example, impeachment with a prior inconsistent deposition statement need not include questions to the witness which explain deposition procedures. If a judge or arbitrator understands what happened in a specific case, cross-examination to establish those facts may be unnecessary.

D. Summation

The attorney needs to craft a closing argument that has a compelling impact on the decision maker. The decision maker will most likely be leaning in favor of one party and may have already decided the case before closing arguments. A summation must be presented in a way that assists and persuades the decision maker to interpret and apply the facts to the legal elements in favor of the advocate's client. Judges and arbitrators may ask questions of the attorneys during summation, usually regarding matters they have not resolved. It is wise to be prepared for and to invite questions during summation.

Some closing argument approaches may be inappropriate or ineffective if delivered before a professional. For example, arbitrators usually know the applicable law and there may be no need for an attorney to engage in an explanation of its basic elements. Further, an explanation about our legal system, or an emotional plea may have an impact on a jury, but probably will not have a favorable impact on a judge who has heard the explanation or plea before.

An attorney should not underestimate the persuasive impact of a closing argument before a professional, however. Many judges and arbitrators have decided cases based on arguments made during summation. The closing argument ought to be prepared, planned, and presented in the most eloquent, interesting, and compelling manner possible.

E. Findings of Fact, Conclusions of Law, and Proposed Orders

In a bench trial, the judge must complete written findings of fact, conclusions of law, and an order for judgment. See, e.g., Fed.R.Civ.P. 52. Procedural rules may require attorneys to submit proposed findings, conclusions and an order, or the judge may request that the attorneys do so. Arbitrators who have to render a detailed award and administrative judges who have to issue an explanatory decision may also have to compose findings and conclusions. An example of findings, conclusions, and an order appear in Section 2.11(C). Tactically, it is advisable to submit findings and conclusions because they provide the judge with a summary of the party's case and the specific relief sought, and they may favorably influence or assist the judge in making a decision. Section 12.5(I) describes the use of a post-trial motion to amend findings and conclusions.

§ 3.12 MAKING A RECORD

A. Purpose

The primary purpose of making a record is to establish and preserve grounds for appeal. A trial record usually consists of a transcript of the proceedings, exhibits, jury instructions, the jury's completed verdict form, pleadings, discovery requests, motions, memoranda, orders, the judgment, the notice of appeal, and any other filed documents. See Fed.R.App.P. 10. Final and binding arbitration proceedings may not be recorded because there is no factual appeal. Administrative proceedings which are appealable commonly retain a record.

The attorney must continually be aware of the need to make the record complete for possible appellate review. Appellate courts may not consider anything other than the trial record when making a review. Appeals can be lost due to faulty or incomplete records.

Most appellate courts require compliance with certain procedures to properly raise an issue for appeal. Typically, the trial record must reflect the following:

- A record of the ruling, order, conduct, or event creating the grounds for appeal;

- An objection by the attorney to an error in the trial;

- An offer of proof showing what the evidence would have proved if an evidentiary objection has been sustained;

- A request for a curative instruction by the judge to the jury if the error occurred within the hearing of the jury; and

- The submission of a post-trial motion to the judge, identifying the error and requesting a new trial.

These requirements are intended to prevent appeals unless the attorney has properly objected at the trial level, thereby providing the trial judge an opportunity to correct or reduce the impact of the error. Some issues, such as the sufficiency of the evidence to support the findings, will be appealable even if an objection was not made at trial. If manifest injustice could result from the denial of an appeal, some courts allow an appeal where issues have not been preserved for appeal.

There are several conditions that must be met for an appellate court to reverse a trial judge's ruling:

- The trial judge must commit an error;

- The error must have been objected to by the advocate;

- The mistake must be preserved in the trial record;

- The error must not have been cured or waived or abandoned; and

- The error must have been prejudicial.

B.　Complete and Accurate Record

The advocate must ensure that all rulings, orders, findings, verdicts, and judgments are entered on the record. Also, advocates should attempt, to the greatest extent possible, to have the reasoning of the judge reflected in the record. If the judge has adopted the opponent's reasons or if the reasoning is apparent from the situation, there may be no need to have the reason appear on the record. If, however, the reasoning differs from that advanced by either party, or is not apparent from the circumstances, the advocate should ask the judge to state the reasoning on the record for appellate purposes. In some situations the losing party may not want the judge's reasoning to appear on the record, either because a well-reasoned ruling or order may make it more difficult to win on appeal or because the losing party intends to argue that the judge abused discretion or exceeded authority due to the absence of any supportive reasoning.

The advocate must make a complete and accurate record during all stages of the trial or hearing, including pretrial and post-trial proceedings. The advocate should review the record periodically throughout the case to make certain that all written or oral rulings have been made and are recorded.

C.　Court Reporter

The general rule is that if an appealable case is worth trying, a court reporter should be present to transcribe all proceedings. If something is not recorded, there is no transcript available for an appeal. The presence of a court reporter also holds judges and lawyers accountable and causes them to be more careful and thoughtful regarding what they say.

The trial court supplies the court reporter. In federal courts and most state courts, court reporters are available during all stages of the trial. In some jurisdictions, the trial advocate may be responsible for making certain a court reporter is available. In some of these jurisdictions, the court reporter may not routinely be available for pretrial proceedings, and the advocate should contact the court ahead of time to make certain a court reporter is present.

A court reporter should be present for all trial proceedings, including everything that occurs in the courtroom and in chambers. Not all judges and jurisdictions follow this general rule. In many jurisdictions, court reporters are present only at the conclusion of discussions or proceedings held in chambers and only transcribe a summary of the motions and rulings. The judge typically makes such a summary, supplemented by comments from the attorneys. The advocate should make certain that any matter that may be an issue for appeal is fully reflected in the summary transcription. In many jurisdictions, a court reporter may not be present during jury selection. Anticipating that something may happen that may need to be preserved for appeal, the advocate should request that a court reporter be present to record all questions and responses made during jury selection.

If a judge refuses to honor the request that a court reporter be made available, the advocate can ask that an independent court reporter, to be paid by the party, be obtained. If this request is denied, the attorney should make every effort to preserve the judge's ruling regarding the denial of the court reporter. The advocate can ask the trial judge to sign a written order denying the attorney's motion for a court reporter, or at the next stage of the trial, when the court reporter is present, ask the court for permission to summarize on the record the previous motion and adverse ruling.

If the judge refuses to grant the attorney permission to comment on the record (even by threatening contempt if the attorney attempts to place such information on the record), the only available avenue the attorney may have is to compose an affidavit summarizing these events and offer the affidavit into evidence as a trial exhibit. Determining whether to have a court reporter present or to summarize events is a matter of judgment and discretion for the trial attorney.

D. Log of Trial

A losing attorney may not need or want to pay for the costs of an entire transcript. It is helpful for the advocate to maintain a log of the transcribed proceedings to assist in determining what portions of the transcript should be ordered. This log can identify the stage of the case, the date of the event, the reporter or method of reporting, and a concise explanation of what happened or why a transcript might be needed.

E. Assisting the Reporter

The reporter is responsible for making sure that a complete and accurate transcript is made. Attorneys can assist the reporter in fulfilling this responsibility by:

- Speaking clearly and making certain the witnesses speak clearly,
- Proceeding at a pace appropriate for the reporter,
- Spelling difficult names and words or providing a written list of them,
- Providing the reporter with any necessary information to assist them in understanding the nature of the case and the identity of witnesses,
- Avoiding blocking the reporter's view of the witness or anyone else talking in the courtroom,
- Avoiding speaking simultaneously with others,
- Describing all conduct, gestures, inaudible responses, nonverbal behavior, and any other event that may not appear on the record. Many judges expect the attorney to ask permission from the judge to have the record reflect what occurred. For example, the attorney may preface the description with the phrase: "Your Honor, may the record reflect that. . . . " Other judges allow the attorneys to describe on the record whatever occurred without requesting such permission,
- Avoiding superfluous comments (O.K., now, let me ask you this, I see), repeating answers, and making unnecessary comments, and
- Properly referring to exhibits by number or letter. Section 8.5 describes in detail the marking and handling of exhibits.

The judge controls going on and off the record. If an attorney wishes that something not be on the record, the attorney should ask permission of the court to go off the record. After discussion off the record, either one of the attorneys or the judge may want something that was said off the record summarized on the record. The judge can do this independently, or the attorney may do this by requesting permission of the judge.

F. Administrative Hearings and Arbitrations

Administrative hearings which are reviewable are commonly recorded by electronic recording devices operated by the administrative judge. Some proceedings are recorded by a reporter. The purposes and tactics involved in these recorded cases are similar to the approaches discussed with regard to trial proceedings.

Arbitration awards are reviewable by judicial judges, but the factual determinations of arbitrators are not usually reviewable. And so, there is typically no need for a contemporaneous record in arbitrations. Arbitrators by agreement of the parties or as required by the forum code of procedure may need to rely on applicable substantive law in support of their decisions. This aspect of the award is reviewable de novo by a judge, and a transcript is usually unnecessary for the scope of this legal review.

§ 3.13   TRIAL PROBLEMS

A.   *Problem Decision Makers*

Judges may do or say things during a trial that may constitute misconduct. A judge may make adverse comments about an attorney, improper remarks regarding evidence, or unfair comments regarding the testimony or credibility of a witness. A judge may incorrectly prohibit an attorney from presenting the case or may engage in facial grimaces, body language, or non-verbal conduct that disrupts an attorney's presentation. All these occurrences should be placed on the record by counsel. The record should indicate what has happened and the objections to the behavior that were made. This can be a delicate and difficult task, but may be necessary to correct the judge's behavior and protect the client's best interests. The attorney who is objecting to this behavior may prefer to approach the bench initially and, out of the hearing of the jury, request that the judge refrain from such conduct.

B.   *Attorney Problems*

If the opposing counsel creates problems for the attorney by making improper statements, behaving in a distracting manner, or engaging in any other inappropriate behavior detrimental to the case, the attorney should object on the record, and the court should be asked to intervene and admonish opposing counsel. An attorney should avoid arguing with opposing counsel. Some lawyers attempt to engage opposing counsel in improper and inappropriate arguments, but such behavior should be avoided.

C.   *Problem Witnesses*

An attorney who examines a witness on direct examination must be prepared to direct and control the testimony given. Likewise, a cross-examiner must control the responses of an unfavorable witness. An attorney may need to admonish an unresponsive witness by politely but firmly insisting upon a response or by seeking assistance from the judge, who may or may not agree to admonish the witness. An attorney should initially make one or more attempts to control the responses of a witness before seeking the intervention of a judge, and should know ahead of time whether the judge is likely to intervene or force the attorney to control the interrogation alone. See Section 9.3(D).

D.   *The Response*

When facing these and other problems that arise, it is critical for the advocate to consider how the best interests of the client are affected. If adversely, the advocate will need to do something during the presentation of the case to rectify or resolve the problem, so the client has the best chances of succeeding. And later, after the case is over, the aggravating and stressful situations may make wonderful stories for the next bar convention.

CHAPTER 4
EVIDENCE AND OBJECTIONS

REFLECTING ON ADVOCACY

We arg'ed the thing at breakfast, we arg'ed the thing at tea,
And the more we arg'ed the question the more we didn't agree.

—Will Carleton

Betsey and I Are Out

He that wrestles with us strengthens our nerves and sharpens our skill.
Our antagonist is our helper.

—Edmund Burke

§ 4.1   INTRODUCTION

A. *Purposes*

An objection is the procedure used to oppose the introduction of inadmissible evidence, to oppose the use of improper questions, and to contest inappropriate conduct or improper procedures during a case. Evidentiary objections are used to exclude evidence that should not be considered by the fact finder, or to change the form of questions improperly phrased by opposing counsel. Objections also may be used to control the behavior and statements of an opposing attorney, a witness, the judge, or other participants or to prevent a witness from being harassed.

Objections create a record of the error and preserve that error as a ground for a new trial or an appeal. The failure to make an objection usually waives any error as a ground for a new trial or appeal, unless the error is so prejudicial and obvious that the substantial rights of a party are adversely affected.

Objections may also accomplish tactical objectives. Tactical reasons for objecting are only proper if there is a good faith legal basis that supports the objection. Objections with no legal basis made solely to interrupt or bother the opposing lawyer are unethical and violate the rules of practice.

An attorney may tactically object to emphasize an opponent's evidentiary problems, to force the opponent to alter the introduction of evidence, or to alter the presentation of the case. An attorney may also object to help a witness testify. For example, if a witness becomes confused or has difficulty answering questions, an objection may allow the witness a short break to regain composure and plan a responsive answer.

An objection may also be used to interrupt the flow of testimony. When an examination is proceeding very smoothly, an objection may break up the rhythm and flow of the examination. An experienced lawyer may object in an effort to confuse or distract an inexperienced lawyer who may become nervous and ineffectual. These tactical objectives, however, must always be supported by a good faith legal basis and are not to be used improperly.

B. Case Type: Judicial, Arbitration, Administrative

Rules of evidence govern the admissibility of evidence in trials. This chapter explains objections to the introduction of evidence in both bench trials before a judicial judge and jury trials.

Arbitrations and administrative hearings are governed by rules of evidence which usually are less numerous, more broad, and applied with greater flexibility and discretion. The general rule for arbitrations and administrative hearings is that evidence is admissible if it is relevant and reliable.

Relevant is a similar concept to relevancy for trial purposes. Reliability includes admissible substantive evidence, such as hearsay and authentic documents, whose reliability outweighs its unreliability. The concepts and strategies explained in this chapter apply to arbitrations and administrative hearings as well as court trials. All the references to judges include arbitrators and administrative hearing officers.

Proper foundation, reliable testimony, and appropriate question format make evidence more persuasive in all types of proceedings. When used properly, the rules of evidence are excellent guides to aid in preparing and presenting a case. For example, while the hearsay exceptions are not strictly enforced in arbitrations and administrative hearings, the reasons supporting the exceptions aid in determining the reliability of a hearsay assertion.

The initial sections of this chapter explain objection procedures, and remaining sections explain substantive evidentiary objections. Objections made during jury selection, opening statement, and summation appear in those respective chapters. Some readers may prefer to first read the substantive rules of evidence explained in Sections 4.6 through 4.9 and then read about objection procedures described in Sections 4.2 through 4.5.

C. Considerations

Objections should be planned around the following considerations:

The approach of the judge. The judge's knowledge of the rules of evidence and inclination to make rulings is a major factor. Some judges sustain minor, technically correct objections while other judges apply a broader approach and overrule such objections. The attorney who interposes too many questionable objections may lose favor with the judge. There may be little advantage in making an objection the judge will overrule. While the mere fact that the judge disagrees is not a reason to avoid objecting, it is a consideration.

The effect of an objection. An objection may call a mistake or an omission to the attention of the opponent who may then correct the error. Objections should not necessarily be made where they may help the opponent.

The reaction of the jury. Incessant objections, whether sustained or overruled, may annoy or alienate the jury. The jurors may perceive that the objecting attorney is attempting to hide evidence or is acting unfairly by making technical or numerous objections.

The nature of the evidence. A lawyer should consider objecting to anything that lacks probative value, is unclear or confusing, is collateral to the issues in dispute, or breaches a rule of evidence.

Highlighting specific evidence. An objection tends to highlight the evidence to which it is directed. A lawyer might refrain from objecting, knowing that an objection will unduly emphasize the evidence and increase its weight.

Creation of a clear and complete record. If something objectionable and prejudicial occurs during trial, an objection should be made to hold the offending participant accountable for such conduct.

Preservation of an error for post-trial motions and appeal. Even if a lawyer anticipates that an objection will be overruled, the objection should be made to preserve the error properly.

The ability of an opponent. An opponent may have little knowledge of evidence law and may not be able to properly ask questions or lay foundations. Sustained objections may disrupt the presentation of a poorly prepared attorney.

Strategic impact. A lawyer might consider making appropriate objections that are sure to be sustained early in the trial. Successful objections early in the trial give the lawyer the appearance of being in control and knowledgeable. As a result, the judge will be likely to pay attention to subsequent objections; the opponent will be less inclined to offer inadmissible evidence; witnesses will be easier to control on cross-examination; and a jury might pay more attention to the argument of a lawyer who has demonstrated competence and skill.

§ 4.2　PREPARATION

Objections are based on violations of the rules of evidence, statutes, trial practice, civil and criminal procedure, case law, common sense, and fairness. The judge makes the final determination whether grounds for objections exist and are proper. Not all judges recognize all objections. The understanding and interpretation of evidence law varies among judges. An attorney must adapt to the rules as applied by the judge and assert those objections which the judge recognizes. Forms appear at the end of this chapter that provide a method to anticipate and plan for evidentiary problems.

A. Anticipating Evidentiary Problems

Anticipating evidentiary problems and planning how to handle them are elements of proper preparation. The goal of an examining attorney is to present evidence that is not objectionable. When preparing and presenting evidence, the attorney must recognize and understand potential objections that may be asserted and structure questions to avoid evidentiary infirmities. The opposing attorney must anticipate potentially inadmissible evidence and prepare objections to that evidence. A motion in limine may be brought before the trial begins or before a witness testifies to obtain a court ruling on the admissibility of evidence before it is introduced. See Section 3.8(C)(2).

B. Admissibility and Weight

Two questions must be resolved regarding the introduction of evidence:

1. Is the evidence *admissible* under the law?

2. What is the *weight* or probative value of the evidence?

The judge decides the first question, and, in a jury trial, the jury decides the second. Federal Rule of Evidence 104 and similar state rules require the court to make preliminary decisions regarding the admissibility of evidence. The judge reviews the sufficiency of the initial evidence and then decides whether to allow the introduction of further evidence. The judge determines whether the facts introduced are sufficient to support a finding a reasonable fact finder may make based on those facts.

For example, judges decide whether sufficient evidence has been introduced to establish that a person is qualified to be a witness, that a privilege exists, that a duplicate document is admissible, and that a hearsay statement falls within an exception rendering it admissible. After sufficient evidence has been introduced, the jurors then determine whether they find the admissible evidence probative, credible, and persuasive. In situations when a close question exists regarding the sufficiency of the evidence, most judges are inclined to admit the evidence and let the jurors determine what it is worth.

C. Learning How to Make Evidentiary Objections

The process of making evidentiary objections includes two separate questions:

1. Is there a legitimate, *good faith* available *objection* supported by the law of evidence?

2. Is there a favorable *strategic or tactical reason* for making the objection?

It is difficult enough to make these decisions in a calm, cool, detached atmosphere, such as while reading this chapter. It is much more difficult to make a quick decision amidst the tension and commotion of a trial. During the trial, an objecting attorney must make split-second judgments while concentrating on all other aspects of what is happening in the courtroom. This skill is enhanced with practice and experience.

There are a number of things that can be done by inexperienced trial lawyers to increase their ability to think quickly, make instant judgments, and assert objections during trial:

- *Become familiar with the types of common objections.* Review a list of available objections and organize the objections in a format that permits you to easily remember and apply these objections. Form 4.1 and the lists of common objections at the end of this chapter provide a usable framework that can be modified for such use.

- *Learn to recognize types or patterns of evidence that create objectionable situations.* These include:

  — Lengthy direct examination questions are often objectionable because they are leading.

  — Questions that involve conversations may trigger hearsay objections.

  — Questions calling for the witness' observations require proper foundation and may be objectionable based on a lack of foundation.

  — Questions calling for a lay witness to give an opinion may give rise to an objection based on an improper conclusion.

  — Documents must be authenticated, otherwise an objection based on lack of authentication may be appropriate.

  — Answers that include prefaces such as "I'm not certain, but," may support an objection based on speculation.

  Sections 4.6 through 4.8 explain these and other commonly available objections.

- *Prior to trial, prepare a list of specific objections to the anticipated evidence.* This planning process will assist in quickly and accurately identifying objections during trial.

- *During trial, concentrate on the evidence being introduced.* Although many things are going on while the evidence is being introduced, focus on the evidence.

- *Listen attentively and watch the examination.* The sound of a question or answer, or the demeanor of the attorney or witness, may be objectionable.

- *Rely on common sense.* Many events occurring during a trial are objectionable and obviously improper and unfair.

- *Over prepare.* Extra preparation helps in applying the rules of evidence to the evidence introduced at trial.

- *Be prepared to lose an objection.* Valid objections are overruled and inadmissible evidence is sometimes admitted.

- *Be willing to make mistakes.* Expect that the judge will disagree with your objections and think you are wrong. Sometimes you will be.

- *Prepare to be surprised.* Sometimes evidence comes in differently than anticipated, and judges exercise their discretion in unexpected ways.

- *See if the judge wants you to object.* The judge may invite an objection by sighing, making faces or by appearing impatient with the testimony. However, an attorney should not necessarily object at the judge's apparent invitation. The attorney may misinterpret the judge's behavior, or the attorney may not want to object for tactical reasons.

- *Rehearse making objections to anticipated evidentiary problems.* Imagine how opposing counsel may make evidentiary mistakes and imagine asserting objections in these scenarios.

D. Deciding Whether to Make Objections

Whether an objection should be made even when there is legal support for the objection and the judge will most likely sustain the objection depends on the strategic impact the objection has on the admissibility of the evidence. The more critical the evidence is to the theories of the case, the more likely the objection should be made. There are four basic guidelines determining whether to object to inadmissible evidence:

- If the evidence is clearly admissible, the trial lawyer should not object. Rather, the attorney should try to minimize the effect of the evidence through cross-examination or rebuttal and then argue its lack of weight in final argument.

- If the offered evidence is clearly inadmissible and harmful, the lawyer should object. The law of evidence should be used to exclude improper evidence that hurts an objecting party's case. The objecting attorney should try as hard as possible to exclude this evidence and use all available means to do so.

- If the evidence is probably inadmissible but not harmful, the attorney should consider not objecting, or may object but not pursue the issue if the judge overrules the objection. The potential problem of weak evidence may be overcome on cross-examination or final argument. The trial lawyer may establish on cross-examination that the testimony or witness is unreliable, and can argue the slight probative value or the implausibility of the evidence during final argument.

- If the answer to a question will reveal favorable or neutral information, then no objection should be made.

Objections are best reserved for those situations that meet the considerations listed in Section 4.1. In some trials, there may be no need to interpose objections. Trials between skilled and well prepared lawyers are often tried with few or no objections.

E. Alternative Objections

There may be more than one objection that can be made to a question or an answer. Part of the planning process is formulating a series of potential objections to anticipated evidence. Objections that may be available to the same piece of evidence include:

- *Improper form of the question.* The question may be leading or otherwise improper.

- *Irrelevant.* The topic may not have any logical relevance to the case.

- *Cumulative.* The evidence has previously been introduced and this item of evidence is unnecessarily repetitive.

- *Unfairly prejudicial.* Even if the item is relevant, it may be unfairly prejudicial.

- *Lack of foundation.* The witness may not be competent to lay a foundation for the introduction of this item of evidence.

- *Improper opinion.* The witness may testify to an inadmissible opinion.

- *Hearsay.* The source of the information the witness knows may be from an inadmissible hearsay source.

- *Original writing (best evidence) required.* The evidence is being offered to prove the contents of a writing, and the writing must be introduced.

F. Explaining Why No Objection is Made

In some situations during trial an objection may seem appropriate, but the attorney does not want to object. In such situations, the attorney may want to explain to the jury why no objection is being made. Instead of sitting silently in the courtroom or saying "Your Honor, we have no objection," the attorney may state: "We want the jurors to hear this testimony," or "We agree that the jurors should see this exhibit," or "We want the jurors to have the benefit of this evidence."

G. Invitation by Judge

Judges occasionally look at opposing counsel when evidence is being introduced and ask "Any objection?" Some judges ask these questions neutrally without suggesting that an objection exists in order to provide opposing lawyers with an opportunity to interpose an objection. Other judges do this to signal that they will sustain an appropriate objection. Even if the opposing lawyer did not plan to make an objection, the attorney should consider whether to object in this situation because the judge apparently suggests that there is something objectionable. An attorney should not object merely because the judge believes an objection ought to be made, but rather the attorney should reconsider and assert an objection if a strategic reason exists for doing so.

§ 4.3 PRESENTATION

A. *Stand to Object*

Whether an attorney should stand or remain seated while objecting depends on the jurisdiction and judge. Most judges require or expect the attorney to stand when addressing the court. The seated attorney may say "Objection, your Honor," and then stand to state the grounds. The extra half second gained by standing may help in framing an objection. An attorney may remain seated or request to remain seated, especially if the objection is made quickly and the judge immediately rules, or if there is a series of objections. Most objections and rulings are made in front of the jurors unless an argument must be made on the objection. See Section 4.3(D). Arbitration and administrative forums allow the objecting attorney to stay seated.

B. *Timing*

An objection must be timely made. If a question is improper, the objection must be made before the answer is given. For example, objections to the form of a question must be made immediately after the question and before the answer. If a question is proper but the response is inadmissible, an objection should be made as soon as the inadmissible evidence becomes apparent. For example, if a witness begins to testify to inadmissible hearsay, the opposing attorney should interrupt and make an objection. An objection interjected too late, however meritorious, is ordinarily overruled by the judge. Late objections are also ineffective because the jury has already heard part or all of the inadmissible evidence. Furthermore, the error may not be preserved for appeal.

Attorneys should avoid making premature objections. If an objection to the content of a statement is available, the attorney must object to the question that introduces the objectionable content. For example, an objection to the preliminary question, "Do you have an opinion about the defendant's condition?" is premature, but the attorney should object to the follow-up question seeking an improper opinion, "What is that opinion?" Similarly, a hearsay objection to the question, "Did you have a conversation with the witness?" is premature, the proper objection should be made to the next question, "What did the witness say?"

This task is made more difficult by the fact that witnesses often are not prepared to respond to the precise wording of the questions. The question "Do you have an opinion?" often produces the opinion rather than the anticipated "Yes" answer. If the examiner has not adequately prepared the witness, an objection may have to be made to the preliminary question in order to prevent these nonresponsive answers. The judge may, however, overrule the premature objection, and the attorney will need to restate the objection following the next question.

Example (Direct Examination):

Examining Attorney:

Q: Did you and Ms. Wells–Barney speak to each other?

Objecting Lawyer:

I object your Honor, that question calls for hearsay.

Judge:

The objection is premature, the witness may answer.

A: Yes, we did.

Examining Attorney:

Q: What did Ms. Wells–Barney say?

Objecting Lawyer:

Objection, hearsay.

Judge:

Sustained.

When the witness responds to a question calling for a yes or no response with a further response, the attorney should object to the answer because it goes beyond the scope of the question.

Example (Direct Examination):

Examining Attorney:

Q: Dr. Oppenheimer, do you have an opinion as to the effectiveness of the Fermi Accelerator?

A: Yes, I do. It is probably the only ...

Objecting Lawyer:

Your Honor, I object. The question has been answered.

Judge:

Sustained.

The witness should stop answering the question once the objection is made. If the witness continues to answer, the opposing attorney should interrupt and ask the judge to instruct the witness to stop answering. If the examining attorney is asking questions too rapidly, or if the witness is answering questions too quickly, the judge may be asked to instruct the attorney or witness to proceed at a reasonable pace, which provides an opportunity to object before the witness responds.

C. *Phrasing an Objection*

The proper way to object in most jurisdictions is to say "objection" and state the specific ground or grounds with a few identifying words. This method is simple, quick, and advises the judge of the ground(s) of the objection. The applicable rules of evidence ordinarily require the objecting attorney to state the specific reason supporting the objection. See, e.g., Fed.R.Evid. 103(a)(1). More than one ground may support an objection, and an attorney should state all applicable grounds. If the attorney does not advance a specific reason and the ground for the objection is apparent from the context of the evidence, an objection may be sustained by the judge.

Using the name or title of the rule involved is usually sufficient: "Your Honor, objection, hearsay" or "We object, your Honor, on the grounds of hearsay." Proper courtroom etiquette may require the attorney to preface an objection with the phrase "Your Honor." Also, the addition of a descriptive term to an objection in a jury trial is advisable so the jury better understands the grounds for the objection: "Objection, unreliable hearsay." Some judges expect attorneys to use specific words in making an objection, requiring the attorneys to be very precise. Other judges require objecting attorneys to refer to specific evidence rule numbers.

D. *Outside the Hearing of the Jury*

Trial proceedings should be conducted so that inadmissible evidence, arguments, and statements are not heard by the jury. Comments by counsel, arguments, lengthy objections, and offers of proof must be made outside the hearing of the jury. Jurors should not be influenced by inadmissible evidence or the explanations of counsel.

"Speaking objections" — arguments in front of the jury — are rarely appropriate. If an attorney needs to explain an objection further, permission to approach the bench should be requested and the arguments made at the bench. If an objecting attorney persists in arguing an objection in front of the jury, the other lawyer should interrupt and request permission to approach the bench. When an attorney argues at a bench conference, in a voice loud enough for jurors to hear, the judge should be asked to admonish the attorney and instruct the jury to disregard the argument.

A fine line exists between appropriate, descriptive statements and improper speaking objections. For example, an objection may be stated: "Counsel is attempting to present unreliable and untrustworthy hearsay through this witness." This statement explains the grounds of the objection and helps the jury understand the evidentiary problem. While some judges may allow this, others prohibit this lengthy a statement.

An attorney needs to adapt objection procedures to the judge's preferences. Some judges prefer a lengthier explanation of an objection instead of a few descriptive words, and the attorney should provide the judge with that information. Some judges inappropriately allow "speaking objections'' instead of requiring bench conferences. This practice results in attorneys making evidentiary arguments in the hearing of the jury.

E. Legal Support

When an anticipated objection is made to a vital piece of evidence, it is sometimes useful to have a short, one or two page memorandum supporting or opposing the objection. This issue brief provides the judge with precedent, eliminates the need to make an extemporaneous argument, and shows the judge that the attorney is serious about a position. These factors may sway the judge regarding a close evidentiary ruling.

F. Attorneys' Demeanor

Objections should be made in a firm, clear voice and in a professional and reasonable manner. Objections and responses should always be directed to the judge and not to opposing counsel. Arguing with opposing counsel may draw an admonition from the judge and should be avoided. A calm, low-key approach is usually most effective, unless the situation dictates that an attorney be vigorously assertive or talk in a louder voice to interrupt an improper question or response.

Responses to adverse rulings by the judge should also be professional and respectful. Statements of disapproval or nonverbal behavior demonstrating disappointment are usually inappropriate and rarely necessary even to highlight outrageous improper evidence or conduct.

G. Responding to the Judge

An attorney may need to respond to a judge who attempts to unduly restrict the attorney's ability to make or explain objections on the record. Judges want the case to proceed as quickly as possible, and some judges pressure attorneys not to make objections. Occasionally a judge may make comments in front of the jurors about what the judge perceives to be wasteful and time consuming objections. The attorney cannot always please the judge or do whatever the judge demands. It is the responsibility of the attorney, not the judge, to prevent the opposing attorney from introducing inadmissible evidence and to preserve a record for appeal. If the judge improperly interferes with the assertion of objections, the objecting attorney may make a record that the judge's interference is adversely affecting the case.

H. Continuing Objections

If an objection has been overruled and subsequent questions are asked on the same subject, the objecting attorney may consider making a ''continuing'' objection to every subsequent question and answer on the subject. A continuing objection may eliminate the need for the attorney to repeatedly object after each question or answer. Not all jurisdictions recognize continuing objections. A problem with their use is that there is no specific objection on the record to individual questions or answers, and it may be unclear regarding what questions and answers are included in the objection.

The lawyer should define the scope of the continuing objection as precisely as possible. Instead of saying, "I object to this entire line of questioning," the attorney should say, "I object to all the testimony about the witness' identification of Exhibit No. 8 on the ground that...." The lawyer should also be alert to additional grounds that arise during subsequent testimony. If another ground becomes apparent during the line of questioning, that ground should be added to the continuing objection. If the scope or grounds cannot be made clear with a continuing objection, a more effective tactic may be to repeat objections to specific questions and answers. While repetitive objections may be annoying and disruptive, they remove any doubt regarding the ground and scope of the objection and avoid the inadvertent waiver of objections.

I. *Responding to Objections*

Usually the examining attorney need not say anything in response to an objection. Sometimes the judge asks the examining attorney to argue against the objection. If the examining attorney wants to make a brief statement in opposition to an objection, it may be stated in front of the jury. If the attorney wants to argue further, the attorney should approach the bench and make the argument there.

J. *Presenting Contrary Evidence*

An objecting attorney may have an opportunity to introduce contrary evidence — to show that an objection should be sustained — before a judge rules on an objection which seeks to exclude evidence. These situations arise when a judge must determine whether sufficient evidence exists to support the admissibility of additional evidence, or if there is a factual or legal impediment to further testimony. Section 4.2(B) explained that the judge reviews preliminary evidence to determine whether subsequent evidence is admissible.

There are two ways an opposing attorney may introduce contrary evidence. The first and typical way is by questioning the witness to lay the grounds for an objection. The second way, which is used only in unusual circumstances, is through extrinsic evidence.

1. *Questioning the Witness*

The most common way for an attorney to introduce contrary evidence is to request permission to interrupt the examination to ask questions of the witness for the purpose of establishing the grounds for an objection. The procedure — also known as "voir dire" of a witness — consists of the attorney examining the witness, usually through leading questions, to establish facts in support of a ruling by the judge that subsequent evidence is inadmissible. For example, the witness may identify a document which the proponent offers. The opposing attorney may question the witness in an attempt to show the witness cannot sufficiently authenticate the document.

Judges permit "voir dire" questioning of a witness if the attorney appears able to establish the inadmissibility of the evidence. Usually the opposing attorney can ask a reasonable number of questions to establish the lack of admissibility. These questions, which interrupt the direct examination, may not develop into questions that should be asked on cross-examination. Questioning that extends beyond proper "voir dire" and into cross-examination should be objected to as improper. Some lawyers attempt to use "voir dire" to disrupt the direct examination. This tactic is improper unless there is a good faith basis to establish contrary evidence supporting the objection.

Example (Direct Examination):

Examining Attorney:

Q: Ms. Naples, please describe all the contents of the frozen pizza that you purchased.

Objecting Lawyer:

Your Honor, may I voir dire the witness by asking a few questions to lay the foundation for an objection?

Judge:

Yes, you may.

Objecting Lawyer:

Q: You are not a food scientist are you?

A: No.

Q: You did not test any of the ingredients in the pizza did you?

A: No.

Q: You did not read the label did you?

A: No.

Q: You never ate the pizza?

A: No.

Q: And by looking at it you could not tell precisely what it was made of.

A: That's for sure.

To the Court:

Your Honor, I object to any further testimony by this witness about the contents of the pizza on the grounds of lack of foundation.

Judge:

Sustained.

2. Extrinsic Evidence

Extrinsic evidence is evidence from a source other than the witness on the stand, such as another witness or document. Extrinsic evidence may be admissible if an opposing attorney challenges the competency of a witness or claims the existence of a privilege. For example, a witness testifies on direct examination that she is not married to the defendant and that she had a conversation with the defendant. The opposing attorney may object on the grounds of marital privilege and offer into evidence a marriage certificate as extrinsic evidence. The primary reason the situations involving the use of extrinsic evidence are rare is that these problems are usually taken care of through a motion in limine before trial or before the witness testifies.

§ 4.4 RULING BY JUDGE/ARBITRATOR

A. Discretion

Judges and arbitrators have broad discretion in ruling on the admissibility of evidence. The standard used to determine the admissibility of evidence is whether there exists "evidence sufficient to support a finding" of the proposition sought to be proven. See Fed.R.Evid. 104(a) and (b). If there is insufficient evidence to support a finding by the fact finder regarding that proposition, the evidence is inadmissible.

B. Ruling

Ordinarily, the judge or arbitrator rules immediately after an objection and says "sustained" (the objection is valid) or "overruled" (the objection is denied). Usually the judge does not state a reason for the ruling because the reason is the same ground the objecting attorney stated. Most judges do not sustain an objection unless the opposing lawyer correctly states the ground for the objection. Usually then, the examining lawyer knows the defect in the question or answer. Even if a question or answer is objectionable, many judges do not sustain an objection if the attorney states an incorrect ground. While judges and arbitrators have the discretion to exclude inadmissible evidence on their own (in the absence of any objection or in the absence of any specific supporting grounds), many do not exercise this discretion.

C. Provisional Ruling

In some situations, a judge or arbitrator may make a provisional, or conditional, ruling which can be readily reconsidered at a later stage of the case. The opportunity is reserved to change the ruling depending on subsequent events in the case that may affect the admissibility of the evidence. Objections based on irrelevancy, lack of foundation, or improper lay or expert opinion may result in conditional rulings that allow evidence to be admitted subject to reconsideration. For example, a judge may overrule a relevancy objection because the examining lawyer advises the judge that the relevancy of this evidence (Evidence A) depends upon the later admission of related evidence (Evidence B). The judge may overrule the objection and allow Evidence A on the condition that Evidence B is later presented. If Evidence B is not subsequently admitted, the objecting attorney may renew the objection to Evidence A and the court will sustain the objection and instruct the jury to disregard Evidence A.

Example (Direct Examination):

Examining Attorney to the Judge at the Bench:

Your Honor, at this time we offer Exhibit No. 35. We realize that we need to provide another witness in order to establish the technical foundation for chain of custody. We will do that through Ms. Phaedra, who is not available as a witness until tomorrow. We are asking the court to provisionally admit Exhibit No. 35 with our assurances that we will connect up the foundation with Ms. Phaedra.

Judge:

With that assurance I will conditionally accept Exhibit No. 35 into evidence.

D. *Inquiring About a Ruling*

If an objection is sustained or overruled and the reasoning of the judge or arbitrator is unclear, the attorney may ask the judge to explain the ruling. In some jurisdictions, the attorney even has a right to such an explanation. The judge may ask the objecting lawyer to explain the ground for the objection.

If the lawyer believes the judge made an incorrect ruling, the attorney may approach the bench and request that the judge reconsider the ruling. Judges do not often change their rulings, and this tactic may waste time. The judge may simply have an understanding of evidence — whether right or wrong — that is different from the lawyer's, and no purpose is served by arguing with the judge. If, for example, the judge sustained a leading objection, the examining lawyer should merely rephrase the question rather than trying to persuade the judge that the situation created an exception to the leading question rule. However, in some situations an explanation to the judge of the reasons that support the question or answer may be effective. For example, the judge may sustain a relevancy objection because the judge does not see any issue that the evidence supports. An explanation of the issue and its connection with the facts may cause the judge to change the ruling and allow the evidence.

E. Renewing an Objection

In jury trials, if the judge overrules an objection, the opposing lawyer can ask to approach the bench for argument. Judges often refuse this request because they are confident of their decision. A more effective practice for the opposing lawyer is to object to the next related question or answer. Perhaps the judge will better understand the grounds for the objection as it applies to the subsequent question or answer and sustain it. The objecting attorney should be persistent and respectful in pursuing objections.

F. Pursuing Objections

A judge or arbitrator may overrule an objection that is premature, as explained in Section 4.3(B). The attorney should make objections to subsequent questions to make certain the judge rules consistently. For example, an attorney may object to the question "Did you form an opinion after your examination?" anticipating that the witness may give a narrative response. The judge may overrule the objection because this question calls for a permissible yes or no answer. The attorney then should interpose objections to subsequent questions regarding the content of the opinion.

G. Obtaining a Ruling

A judge or arbitrator may fail to make a ruling on an objection, either by mistake or as an attempt to avoid deciding. Some judges have figured out that if they don't make any ruling they can't be reversed on appeal for making a wrong ruling. Attorneys have a right to a ruling and should insist on one if necessary.

Example (Direct Examination):

Examining Attorney:

What did Mr. Morse say about this new invention?

Objecting Lawyer:

Objection, hearsay.

Judge:

All right, go on, continue.

Objecting Lawyer:

Your Honor, before we continue, I objected to the last question on the grounds of hearsay.

Judge:

Overruled.

Witness:

He said, "What hath God wrought?"

Examining Lawyer:

Whom was he quoting?

Objecting Lawyer:

Objection, irrelevant and hearsay.

Judge:

Next question.

Examining Lawyer:

Your Honor, may the witness answer the last question?

Judge:

No, sustained.

Examining Lawyer:

Your Honor, may we approach the bench to make an offer of proof?

Judge:

You may

---

§ 4.5　OBJECTION PROCEDURES

A.　*Evidentiary Motions Before Trial: Motions in Limine*

A motion in limine (meaning at the threshold) seeks an advance ruling from the judge regarding the admissibility or inadmissibility of evidence. In criminal cases, these rulings are commonly sought through suppression motions to attack the admissibility of evidence on the grounds that the evidence violates constitutional rights, statutory provisions, or the rules of evidence. See, e.g., Fed.R.Crim.P. 41. Motions in limine are also common in civil cases to obtain an advance evidentiary ruling.

1.　*Purposes*

Motions in limine may be brought for several purposes:

- *To prohibit opposing counsel from introducing or mentioning objectionable evidence in the presence of the jurors.* A ruling can be sought prohibiting the use of evidence that is barred by any exclusionary rule of evidence, such as unfairly prejudicial and irrelevant evidence and inadmissible hearsay. A favorable ruling prevents the jurors from becoming aware of, and being influenced by, inadmissible evidence and from suspecting that the objecting attorney is trying to hide evidence from them. Examples of this type of evidence include the questionable admissibility of a prior criminal conviction of a party, or of subsequent remedial measures taken by a defendant in a tort case.

- *To require opposing counsel to obtain a ruling on admissibility before evidence is offered.* This motion in limine seeks a ruling from the judge requiring opposing counsel to lay a proper and complete foundation before the evidence will be admitted. Examples of such evidence include the foundation required to authenticate a document and the foundation required to comply with the original writing (best evidence) rule.

● *To obtain a preliminary ruling by the court that evidence offered by the proponent is admissible.* This motion is made by the proponent of the evidence who seeks an advance ruling by the court that certain evidence will be admitted during trial. A proponent may have some evidence which the opposing party will oppose. The proponent of this evidence may want to know prior to trial whether the evidence will be admitted in order to properly prepare and plan the trial presentation. Examples of this type of evidence include photographs that contain relevant but grisly depictions, or expensive demonstrative evidence. Before parties spend money creating an elaborate chart, a complicated model, or a videotape, they may prefer to obtain a preliminary ruling by the judge that such demonstrative evidence can be used during the trial.

A motion in limine brought for this purpose presupposes that the opposing party plans to object to its introduction. The advantage of this type of motion is the certainty obtained by a ruling assuring an attorney that certain evidence can be referred to during opening statement. Plans can also then be made to introduce the evidence during the trial. The disadvantages are that the importance of certain evidence is highlighted and opposing lawyers may be prompted to object where otherwise they may not have done so.

Motions in limine are commonly brought prior to jury trials to avoid the prejudicial impact of inadmissible evidence on the jurors, but they also serve a purpose in non-jury trials. Obtaining an advance ruling makes clear what questionable evidence is or is not admissible in a bench trial. This ruling will assist in determining what the most effective theory of the case will be and what facts will be considered by the judge.

2. *Motion Procedure*

Motions in limine may be made either in writing or orally on the record, depending on the nature of the issue and local court rules. There is usually no specific limit regarding the number of motions that may be brought, but strategy and common sense ordinarily restrict such motions to important items of evidence. A judge who faces a barrage of motions regarding routine evidentiary problems may be inclined not to consider such motions seriously.

Motions in limine usually require that reasonable, advance notice be given to the opposing attorney. The timing of the notice depends on the nature of the motion, the rules of the jurisdiction, and the evidence in question. Many jurisdictions require that motions in limine be brought in writing a reasonable time prior to trial to provide the opponent with an opportunity to respond. Other courts permit motions in limine to be made orally on the eve of trial and during trial. If a party plans to offer or seeks to exclude questionable or critical evidence, it is best to submit a written motion with notice to the opposing attorney so that memoranda can be submitted and a full hearing held on the issues. When an attorney seeks to introduce or oppose the introduction of routine real evidence or standard demonstrative evidence, an oral request made on the eve of trial or just before a witness testifies may be sufficient.

A motion in limine should state the specific relief sought and the grounds supporting the motion. Supporting authorities should be provided to the judge in a written memo form or by providing the court with copies of supportive rules, decisions or statutes. The moving attorney should also make clear during argument why an evidentiary motion is brought prior to trial rather than as an ordinary objection during trial. Many judges prefer deferring or denying motions in limine until they see and hear the evidence introduced during the trial. A moving attorney has to overcome this predisposition by explaining to the court why a preliminary ruling is necessary.

3. Order

The order granting the in limine motion must specify the evidence that is excluded or ruled inadmissible. An order that is overly broad may exclude otherwise admissible evidence and become the ground for a new trial or reversible error. An order that is ambiguous may permit opposing counsel to refer to related evidence while still complying with the order. The order, whether written or recorded orally, must be specific and clear as to what evidence is to be excluded or admitted. If there is any doubt about the scope or meaning of an order, counsel should ask to have the order clarified.

A trial judge has broad discretion and several options when ruling on a motion in limine:

- The judge may refuse to hear the motion because it is untimely. Advance written notice of a motion provided to the opposing attorney and to the judge prevents the opposing attorney from claiming surprise and prejudice and reduces the likelihood the judge will refuse to hear the motion.

- The judge may defer ruling on the motion until later. The judge may reconsider the motion immediately prior to the time during the trial when the evidence is sought to be introduced. The judge may decide it is impossible or difficult to make an advance ruling because it is not clear from the arguments whether the evidence is admissible or inadmissible. The judge may prefer to wait until the evidence is developed during the trial and observe how the evidence is being introduced before making a ruling.

- The judge may deny the motion but permit the moving attorney to bring the motion again during the trial for the judge's reconsideration. A judge may do this for the same reasons that were explained in the previous paragraph.

• The judge may grant only part of the relief sought in the motion in limine. If the motion seeks to totally exclude a piece of evidence, the judge may permit a part of the evidence to be introduced. Or, if the motion seeks to exclude evidence which is offered to prove several things, the judge may limit the effect of the evidence to prove only some of those things. See section 4.5(E) on limited admissibility.

• The judge may enter a conditional order requiring that specific facts be introduced during the trial as a condition for the introduction of the disputed evidence. If the specific facts are not introduced during the trial, then the conditional ruling takes effect and the evidence is precluded. A conditional order is sometimes entered when the court needs to hear certain facts in order to make a proper evidentiary ruling. The intent of the conditional order is to advise attorneys that certain facts must be introduced before a final ruling can be made. See section 4.4(C).

• The judge may grant the motion in limine and preclude any introduction and reference either directly or indirectly to the inadmissible evidence.

4. Preserving Error

A court's ruling on a motion in limine usually preserves that evidentiary issue as a ground for a new trial and an appeal. In most jurisdictions, there need not be any further evidentiary offer or objection made during the trial because the previous ruling is on the record. In some jurisdictions, a party who loses a motion in limine may need to take further steps during the trial to preserve the evidentiary issue. In these jurisdictions, if a motion in limine is denied, the losing attorney may need to object to the introduction of the evidence during the trial to preserve the issue properly.

5. Violation of Order

The violation of an order granting a motion in limine may result in reversible error, especially if the trial court does not properly instruct the jury to disregard the excluded evidence. The intentional violation of an order should also subject the offending attorney to sanctions from the court. Sanctions may include a reprimand and the imposition of attorney's fees. An inadvertent violation of an order may be excusable if it is not the result of negligence. Attorneys have an obligation to inform their witnesses of the effect of a ruling on a motion in limine. If the court grants a motion and excludes evidence, the attorney must advise witnesses not to volunteer such evidence during the trial.

Example (Motion In Limine and Order):

Motion in Limine

Defendant Dr. Craig moves this court for an order in limine ordering that the Plaintiff St. Elsewhere Hospital makes no reference to the contract between St. Elsewhere and Dr. Craig dated August 16, 2004, on the grounds that it is irrelevant and unfairly prejudicial. Defendant supports this motion with a memorandum of law and a proposed order in limine.

Attorney for Defendant

Order in Limine

This court orders that Defendant Dr. Craig's motion in limine is granted and orders Plaintiff St. Elsewhere Hospital to make no reference during this trial to the August 16, 2004 contract between Dr. Craig and St. Elsewhere Hospital.

Judge

B. *Offers of Proof*

When an objection is sustained and evidence excluded, the examining attorney must make an offer of proof to preserve the error for appellate review. The offer of proof provides a description of the excluded evidence so the appellate court can review the offered evidence and determine the significance of its exclusion. Offers of proof must conform to the rules of evidence, and opposing counsel may make other objections after the offer has been made.

There are three ways to make an offer of proof, each of which occurs on the record outside the hearing of the jury. All these involve an explanation to the judge of the anticipated testimony and the grounds for its admissibility.

  1. *The Examining Attorney May Summarize the Proposed Evidence at the Bench*

This is the most common way of making an offer of proof.

Example (Direct Examination):

Examining Attorney:

Q: During that afternoon conversation, what was the first thing Ms. Lopez said to you?

Objecting Lawyer:

Objection, hearsay.

Judge:

Sustained.

Examining Attorney:

Your Honor, may I make an offer of proof at the bench?

Judge:

Yes, approach the bench.

Examining Attorney:

Judge, the witness will testify that Ms. Lopez told him that she had known that the repairs on the golf cart were not completed on July 1.

---

2. *Counsel May Ask the Witness to State What the Testimony Would Be in a Question/Answer Format*

This method is the most time consuming but is also the most complete and accurate. Such a format reflects the exact questions and answers excluded and not just a summary.

3. *The Offering Attorney May Submit a Written Statement of the Proffered Testimony*

The first and third methods are usually adequate to create a sufficient record. The second method is used primarily in situations where the record should contain an exact transcript of the precise evidence to be offered.

The offer of proof provides an opportunity for the judge to reconsider the original ruling. Sometimes, after hearing the proposed evidence, the judge understands why it is not objectionable and overrules the objection. The offer of proof also provides an opportunity for the examining lawyer to explain why the evidence is admissible. This argument, coupled with proposed evidence, may convince the judge to admit the evidence.

Example (Continued):

Examining Attorney:

Judge, at the time Ms. Lopez made the statement about the golf cart repairs she was still an employee of the defendant, and the statement is an admissible party admission.

Objecting Lawyer:

Your Honor, Ms. Lopez did not have personal knowledge of the repairs.

Judge:

An employee need not have personal knowledge if the statement refers to matters within the scope of employment. I will change my ruling and overrule the objection.

C. *Motion to Strike*

A motion to strike usually occurs after an attorney has made an objection and the court has granted the relief. The purpose of the motion is to make clear that the improper statement or inadmissible evidence is not to be considered by the fact finder. Section 3.8(C)(4) explained the procedure for making motions to strike. Although a motion to strike may clarify the scope and extent of the excluded evidence, a motion to strike should not be made unless it serves a valid purpose, or unless making such a motion is a common practice in the jurisdiction.

D. *Request for Curative Instruction*

A motion for a curative instruction attempts to repair the harm done by an improper question or inadmissible answer. After an objection has been sustained, the attorney may immediately ask the judge to instruct the jurors that they must disregard what they heard. While completely ignoring some facts may be difficult, jurors usually follow the judge's admonition. If told that they cannot consider some inadmissible evidence, they usually will comply, particularly if the party causing the error appears to be acting unfairly.

Example:

Objecting Lawyer:

Objection, your Honor. The response from the witness is inadmissible hearsay and I ask that the jury be instructed to disregard that answer.

Judge:

Members of the Jury, you are to disregard the testimony concerning the conversation between this witness and Saint Augustine.

E. *Limited Admissibility*

Evidence which is admissible for one purpose but not for another may be admitted by the court. An attorney may request that evidence be admitted for a limited purpose. See Fed.R.Evid. 105. For example, a repair bill may be admissible to prove that the bill was paid, but inadmissible hearsay to prove that actual repairs were completed. The bill can be received in evidence only for the limited purpose of proving it was paid.

A judge has several options in determining what to do with evidence that is admissible to prove some facts but not others:

- The court could admit the evidence and instruct the jury regarding its import.

- The court could admit the evidence without comment.

- The court could exclude the evidence if it is unfairly prejudicial and the impact outweighs the probative value of the evidence.

- Separate trials could be held regarding severed issues or claims.

The first option is probably the most common solution. The court admits the evidence but limits its scope and instructs the jury accordingly.

Example:

Judge:

Members of the Jury, some evidence in this case is now being introduced for a limited purpose. When you receive this evidence now, and when you consider it during your deliberations, you are to use it only for (state proper purpose). You are not to use it for any other purpose. You are not to use it for (state prohibited purpose). You are only to use it (repeat proper purpose).

The judge may repeat the limiting instruction after the evidence has been received or a line of questioning completed, depending upon the nature and impact of the evidence. Further, a judge usually repeats the limiting instruction during final jury instructions at the end of the case.

Limiting instructions have limits. The jurors who hear the evidence may disregard the limiting instructions and broadly use the evidence to prove other matters. For example, if the repair bill is received with a limiting instruction, the jurors may nonetheless infer that the repairs were properly completed because the party would not pay the bill unless the repairs were done.

F. Objections to Questioning

All jurisdictions permit a judge to ask questions of witnesses in a bench trial. Most jurisdictions, including federal courts, provide the judge with discretion to ask questions of a witness in a jury trial. Many judges do not ask any questions of witnesses because they do not believe it is their role to do so. Some judges will occasionally ask questions to clarify an important matter, and others may periodically ask questions to supplement the questions asked by the attorneys. Whatever approach the judge takes, a judge may not take over the questioning of a witness, unnecessarily interfere in witness examinations, or unduly influence a jury by questioning witnesses.

In some administrative hearings, the judge will initiate the questioning and ask a lot of questions allowing the attorneys to ask follow-up questions. In arbitrations, the arbitrator usually only asks clarifying questions. Objections may be made to improper questions asked by an administrative judge or arbitrator.

An attorney may object to any question asked by a judge that violates a rule of evidence and may ask the court to rule on the propriety of the question asked by the court. This objection is difficult to make because the attorney is challenging the judge and may be concerned about the possibility of alienating the judge who has asked the question. Further, the judge is not apt to sustain an objection to the question asked. Nonetheless, the attorney should object to exclude inadmissible evidence and to make a record for appeal. It is, of course, easier said than done, but it may need to be done.

Example:

The family of a mentally impaired patient sues the state for causing his injuries. The plaintiff is called as a witness. The judge has trouble understanding him, interrupts and asks the following questions.

Judge:

Q: You said your nurse hit you, Mr. McMurphy. When did that happen?

A: When it snowed.

Q: And she hit you every time it snowed?

Objecting Lawyer:

I object to the court's questions. Your Honor, your question was leading and may cause the jurors to place undue weight on the response.

Most state court systems prohibit a trial judge from commenting on or expressing opinions about the evidence in a jury trial. State judges usually adhere to this policy and do not comment on the evidence.

The federal court system permits judges to comment on the evidence and express opinions on the weight or sufficiency of the evidence and the credibility of witnesses. Federal judges often make such comments at the time they instruct the jurors. If a federal judge comments on the evidence to the jury, the judge must also advise the jury that they are the sole finders of fact and they may reach a conclusion contrary to the judge's comments. If a judge improperly refers to the evidence, the attorney should make an appropriate objection to such a misstatement.

Example:

Objecting Lawyer:

Objection. We respectfully submit that your Honor has (improperly commented on the evidence, has improperly expressed an opinion regarding the weight of the evidence, has improperly made remarks concerning the credibility of witnesses, or has otherwise made an improper statement).

G. Preserving the Evidentiary Error

An evidentiary error is properly preserved if steps are taken to make a record of the error and to provide the trial court with notice and an opportunity to correct the error or reduce its prejudicial impact. Section 3.12(A) explained this process. In most jurisdictions to preserve an evidentiary error for appeal, the trial attorney must:

- Timely object on the record.

- Specifically state all available grounds. The failure to state a ground usually waives the omitted ground, unless it is readily apparent from the context.

- Include the evidentiary error in a motion for a new trial.

- Raise the specific evidentiary issue on appeal.

If the error occurs as a result of a party or witness introducing inadmissible evidence, the opposing attorney must also request a curative or limiting instruction, and may make a motion to strike, if appropriate. If the objection is sustained, the examining attorney must make an offer of proof.

H. Motion for Mistrial

Inadmissible evidence that has been improperly admitted may be a ground for a mistrial. See Section 3.8(C)(9). The inadmissible evidence must be so unfairly prejudicial that a party is denied a fair trial because of the impact of the evidence on the minds of the jurors. Usually, a curative instruction is sufficient to reduce the impact of inadmissible evidence. If the impact of some evidence cannot be cured by an instruction, a mistrial may be granted.

Example:

Objecting Lawyer:

Objection, your Honor. Counsel has referred to evidence that your Honor previously ruled inadmissible. I now move for a mistrial on the grounds that this misconduct is so unfairly prejudicial that my client is denied a fair trial. A curative instruction will not remove from the minds of the jurors what they have heard. This inadmissible and highly prejudicial information counsel has presented prevents them from considering the evidence in a fair and impartial manner. Furthermore, I ask that the court admonish counsel for such improper misconduct.

I. *Prejudicial Error*

In order for an evidentiary error to be a prejudicial (reversible) error, the error a trial judge makes must adversely affect a substantial right of a party. Section 12.5(F) generally describes the requirement of a prejudicial error to support a trial judge's or appellate court's ruling to order a new trial. Many evidentiary rulings are incorrect, but only amount to "harmless error." Harmless error in an evidentiary situation is an error that does not substantially prejudice a party. Most evidentiary errors during a trial are harmless and not sufficiently prejudicial to warrant a new trial or reversal. An appellate court does not often order a new trial solely on the grounds of evidentiary error.

An error of great magnitude may occur during the conduct of the trial, and the appellant's attorney may fail to timely and properly object. The "plain error" doctrine permits the appellate court to reverse a decision based on an error that is obvious and that adversely affects substantial rights of a party, even though the error was not properly preserved on the record. See Section 12.9(D)(1)(c). This reversal seldom occurs.

J. *Appellate Review*

Appellate courts allow judges wide latitude in deciding when to admit or exclude evidence. This latitude affects the judgment of trial judges in making evidentiary rulings. Many trial judges are inclined to admit questionable evidence and overrule objections which seek to exclude borderline evidence. These judges reason that the jurors can assess the weight afforded such evidence and base their verdict on reliable, credible evidence. An appellate court is more likely to reverse an evidentiary ruling if a judge excludes evidence, than when the judge admits the evidence. The appellate courts reason that the exclusion of this evidence from consideration by the fact finder may deny a party a substantial right to a trial based on relevant, reliable evidence. Consequently, trial judges, in ruling on close evidentiary issues, are more inclined to admit rather than exclude evidence.

The standard of review an appellate court employs depends on the evidentiary error the trial judge has made. Section 12.9(G) explains the various standards of review, which are also applicable to evidentiary rulings.

§ 4.6 OBJECTIONS TO DIRECT EXAMINATION QUESTIONS

This section explains common objections to the improper form of questions asked on direct examination. The cross-examiner can use these objections to force the direct examiner to ask proper questions. Some of these objections may apply to questions asked on cross-examination. See Section 4.7.

A. *Leading*

Generally, asking leading questions during direct examination is improper. Fed.R.Evid. 611. Leading questions are questions that contain and suggest the answer. The problem with leading questions is that the attorney is testifying instead of the witness. Leading questions are permitted in limited situations during direct examination. See Section 7.7(B). Leading questions are permitted on cross-examination, unless, in some jurisdictions, the witness is clearly sympathetic and supportive of the party represented by the cross-examiner.

Example (On Direct Examination):

Examining Attorney:

Q: Mr. Frost, when the two roads diverged in a yellow wood, you took the one less traveled by, right?

Objecting Lawyer:

Objection, your Honor. Leading question.

Or

Objection, counsel is testifying and leading.

Judge:

Sustained.

Usually a leading question is one that can be answered by a "yes" or "no" or a specific one or two word answer contained in that question. However, not all questions that call for "yes" or "no" or a short specific answer are leading. In order for a question to be leading, it must also *suggest* and *contain* the answer to the witness. Even if leading questions are asked, there may not be any tactical advantage in objecting to them. Leading questions are often ineffective on direct examination because the fact finder does not hear the witness testify about the facts, since the lawyer is telling the story and the witness is merely affirming the lawyer's testimony.

Responses to a leading objection:

● Rephrase the question and ask a non-leading question.

● Explain to the judge that the leading question falls within one of the permissible uses of leading questions on direct examination. See Section 7.7(B).

● Explain to the judge that you are trying to speed the trial up by asking a reasonable number of leading questions. Judges sometimes prefer efficiency over the rules of evidence.

B. Narrative

An objection may be made to a question that calls for a narrative answer or to an answer that turns into a narrative. Fed.R.Evid. 611. An improper narrative question allows the witness to tell a long, uncontrolled story. For example, "In your own words, Mr. Jefferson, tell the jury everything that happened to you on July 4."

Narrative questions allow the witness to interject inadmissible testimony without giving the opposing attorney a reasonable opportunity to object in a timely manner. Sometimes a witness will give a narrative response to an otherwise permissible question. A narrative answer may be objected to as being a narrative answer or as being non-responsive. As a tactical consideration, however, the attorney may not want to object to a witness' narrative if the "rambling" testimony tends to make the opponent's direct examination ineffective.

Example:

Examining Attorney:

Q: Ms. Kellogg, what happened as you pushed your shopping cart down the cereal aisle at Ortiz's market?

A: I went to the center left aisle to pick up my six-year-old's favorite cereal. When I reached for a box of Frosted Flakes, my right foot suddenly slid sideways. I kept sliding. I didn't notice the slippery floor. My ankle turned, and I fell down on my right hip. I couldn't move. I felt nauseated. I then saw the wet spots on the floor. Everything went black and white. I closed my eyes. I heard people talking, but I couldn't look up to answer. When I looked up, there was a cast on my right leg and an IV in my arm, and I felt ...

Objecting Lawyer:

Objection. Improper narration.

Judge:

Sustained.

A narrative answer is improper because our adversary system requires specific answers to specific questions and not narrative answers to broad questions. A judge has discretion to sustain or overrule a narrative objection and will consider the scope of the question, the timing of the question, the apparent preparation of the witness, the ability of the witness to be responsive, and the ability of the attorney to control the examination.

During a trial, seemingly objectionable narrative questions will be allowed because the judge realizes the witness will only give a brief response and the attorney can control the examination. For example, the attorney may ask the witness "Then what happened?" This question, if literally answered, would permit the witness to provide a narrative response explaining everything that happened. A well-prepared witness will ordinarily give a short response, and the examining attorney will follow up with a responsive question, such as "Then what happened after you arrived at the Temple?"

Responses to a narrative objection:

- Politely interrupt the witness and stop the rambling.

- Ask a specific question to maintain control of the direction of the examination.

- Explain to the judge that these open-ended questions save time.

- Explain that the narrative answers cover uncontroverted, preliminary, or insignificant matters and do not cover significant issues in the case.

- Say to the witness: "I will now ask you some specific questions to which you can give specific answers."

C. Non-responsive

A non-responsive or volunteered answer occurs when a witness provides information not required by the attorney's question. Any response that extends beyond the specific information required is objectionable. Fed.R.Evid. 611. Some authorities believe that only the examining attorney can make this objection. In practice, however, the vast majority of judges will sustain an opposing lawyer's objection if the witness on direct examination testifies in a non-responsive manner.

Example:

Examining Attorney:

Q: Ms. Leary, when did you become a maintenance manager?

A: Well, I had three brothers, and I was the only girl in the family after Mom died. The whole time we were growing up, I was competing with the guys. They were always fixing cars and working on engines and motors, mowing, painting, and doing things like that. It all looked like fun; so I tried to keep up, and I learned how to do those things right along with them .

Objecting Lawyer:

Objection. Witness is non-responsive.

Judge:

Sustained. Just answer the question asked of you.

Responses to a non-responsive objection:

- Interrupt the witness politely and stop the non-responsive answer.

- Ask more specific questions which require the witness to give shorter answers.

D. Vague and Ambiguous

A question should be clear and understandable so that the witness can understand what is being asked. Vague and ambiguous questions are subject to objections. Fed.R.Evid. 611. Questions may be vague as to the time and circumstances of an event, or may be ambiguous in the choice of words used.

Example:

Examining Attorney:

Q: Socrates, who attended your class?

Objecting Lawyer:

Objection. Vague and ambiguous. The witness has taught different classes in Athens and Thermopolis.

Judge:

Sustained.

There may not be a tactical advantage to objecting to vague and ambiguous questions asked on direct examination if the jurors become confused with the line of questioning. An objection to a vague and ambiguous question may only assist the direct examiner in making clear to the jurors something that is being presented in a confusing manner. The better tactic may be not to object but to allow the jurors to remain confused.

Responses to a vague and ambiguous objection:

- Rephrase the question to make it clearer.

- Ask the witness if the question was understood.

- If the objection is overruled, request that the court reporter read back the question to show how clear the question was and how opposing counsel is attempting to interrupt a proper examination.

E.   *Cumulative*

Cumulative evidence is repetitious evidence. The trial court has the discretion to control cumulative and repetitive evidence. Fed.R.Evid. 403 and 611. Evidence is cumulative when a series of witnesses testify to the same thing or when a series of exhibits provide identical information. If the evidence is important, however, more witnesses or exhibits may relate to the same facts without being cumulative. But when many witnesses testify to the same event or when many nearly identical exhibits are offered, they serve no useful purpose and are therefore cumulative. Cumulative evidence is objectionable because it is repetitive and unnecessary.

Example:

Examining Attorney:

Q: The defense calls Citizen Kane.

Objecting Lawyer:

May I have a sidebar hearing, your Honor?

Judge:

Approach the bench.

Objecting Lawyer:

Your Honor, I believe that counsel, through Citizen Kane, is trying to introduce more evidence of the plaintiff's alleged bad faith. This evidence is unnecessarily cumulative as this is the fourth witness testifying to the same thing.

Examining Attorney:

Your Honor, we have a right to prove up our counterclaim based on the plaintiff's bad faith in bringing this action.

Judge:

I overrule the objection. The defense may introduce this evidence of the plaintiff's intent to intimidate and harass in bringing the lawsuit. However, this is the last witness you may call on this point.

Responses to a cumulative objection:

- Explain to the judge that this evidence is not repetitive, but adds important details to evidence already admitted.

- Explain to the judge that the evidence is not improperly cumulative. Rather, the corroborative evidence from additional sources is needed to buttress the facts being proved.

- If the objection is sustained, continue on with the questioning and return to the evidence during a later stage of the witness' examination.

F. Misstatement of Evidence

Misstatement or mischaracterization of evidence is objectionable because it inaccurately describes evidence. Fed.R.Evid. 611. This objection may be used to object to responses by witnesses as well as questions. A misstatement or mischaracterization of evidence may be done inadvertently or intentionally. An opposing attorney or witness may not remember exactly what was said in previous testimony or the characterization may be a description of a piece of evidence that can be described with more than one term. For example, a letter opener may arguably be referred to as a knife-like object. Whether the problem is caused inadvertently or intentionally, an objection should be asserted and the court should be requested to instruct the opposing attorney or witness to make proper reference to the evidence or testimony.

Example:

Examining Attorney:

Q: What kind of meals did you receive while you worked on the ranch, Ms. Cartwright?

A: They were like poison. My father doled out stale sandwiches and watery soup as though we were prisoners of war.

Objecting Lawyer:

Objection. The witness is mischaracterizing the evidence. I request the jury be instructed to disregard that answer and the witness be instructed to properly answer the question.

Judge:

Objection sustained. The jury is instructed to disregard that answer. The witness is directed to answer the question and not to add unnecessary and improper descriptions.

Responses to a mischaracterization objection:

- Point out to the court that evidence has already been introduced that refers to the question or answer.

- Explain to the court that there is a source of evidence that will be introduced which will support this question or answer. Request that the court conditionally accept the answer subject to the introduction of supportive evidence.

- Explain that the characterization in the question or answer is a proper admissible opinion.

- Explain that the characterization by the witness is the way this witness ordinarily talks and expresses facts.

G. Assuming Facts Not in Evidence

This objection is used to object to questions that assume facts that have not been introduced in evidence. See Fed.R.Evid. 611. A direct examiner who faces this objection may revise the question to eliminate the assumption of fact or may tell the court that the assumed fact will be proven later. If the latter course is taken, the assumed fact must be proven. If that fact is not proven later, the opposing attorney may request that the judge advise the jury to disregard such evidence.

Example:

Examining Attorney:

Q: Ms. Penelope, when did your husband, Mr. Ulysses, begin his search for you?

Objecting Lawyer:

Objection. There has been no evidence introduced about any search.

Judge:

Sustained.

Responses to an assuming facts objection:

- Revise the question to bring out the questionable facts.
- If the witness can describe the facts, allow the witness to testify to the facts.

§ 4.7   OBJECTIONS TO CROSS–EXAMINATION QUESTIONS

This section explains common objections to improper questions asked on cross-examination. The direct examiner can use these objections to protect the witness from being asked improper questions. While some of these same objections may also be available during direct examination, the examples in this section illustrate cross-examination situations.

A. *Repetitious*

If a question has been asked and answered, an attorney may object to similar questions as repetitious. See Fed.R.Evid. 403 and 611. This objection prevents the opposing attorney from gaining undue advantage by repeating testimony. The form of the questions does not have to be absolutely identical in order to raise this objection. If a new question calls for an answer previously given on cross-examination, the question is objectionable as repetitious. This objection is also referred to as "asked and answered."

Example:

Examining Attorney:

Q: Mr. Hur, at the time you purchased this chariot, Ms. Spartacus handed you a written warranty, didn't she?

A: Yes.

Q: And you had an opportunity to read that warranty over, didn't you?

A: Yes.

Q: And Ms. Spartacus explained to you the length of that warranty so that you understood how long the warranty would run, didn't you?

A: Yes.

Q: So, there was no question in your mind that you understood the length of time of that warranty, isn't that correct, Mr. Hur?

Objecting Lawyer:

Objection, your Honor. Repetitious.

Judge:

The objection is sustained.

Responses to a repetitious objection:

- Explain that the point needs to be emphasized on cross-examination.

- Explain that the witness is attempting to be evasive, thus requiring similar and related questions to pin the witness down.

- Move on to the next line of questioning and emphasize this point during summation.

B. Misleading or Confusing

A question must be reasonable, clear, and specific so that the witness knows what is being asked. See Fed.R.Evid. 403.

Example:

Examining Attorney:

Q: Mr. Quixote, since you ran away, you don't know whether Sancho did a good job or not, do you?

Objecting Lawyer:

Objection, your Honor, the words "good job" are vague and ambiguous.

Judge:

The objection is sustained.

Responses to a misleading objection:

- Ask if the witness understands the question.

- Rephrase the question so it is not misleading or confusing.

C. Multiple or Compound Questions

A multiple or compound question presents two or more questions within a single question. These types of questions are objectionable because the answer will usually be ambiguous. Fed.R.Evid. 403 and 611. An example of a compound question is, "The defendant was wearing tap shoes and she was dancing?" Answers to multiple or compound questions, which sometimes seem straightforward and understandable in the courtroom, can become extremely confusing when reviewing the record.

Example:

Examining Attorney:

Q: On the day of the alleged threat to Caesar's life, you talked to Brutus about Caesar's gladiator training, not the threat, and then you visited the defendant at his villa the same night to talk about minting new coins, didn't you?

Objecting Lawyer:

Objection, your Honor. Counsel is asking Mr. Augustus two questions at the same time.

Judge:

Sustained.

Response to a multiple question objection:

- Repeat one of the questions and ask the witness to answer that question and then ask the other question.

D. Mischaracterization of Evidence

This objection is often used to object to questions on cross-examination that include facts that are not in evidence or statements that improperly misstate or mischaracterize the evidence. Fed.R.Evid. 611. The improper or mischaracterized statement may be an attempt to trick the witness and may also be an argumentative question. The issues for a cross-examiner are similar to those for a direct examiner who misstates or mischaracterizes the facts (see Section 4.6(F)), but a cross-examiner has more latitude to ask questions which fairly test the credibility or memory of a witness.

Example:

Examining Attorney:

Q: Mr. Newton, when you stood under the tree a kumquat hit you on your foot, correct?

Objecting Lawyer:

Objection. There are no facts to support these inaccurate assumptions.

Judge:

Sustained.

Responses to a mischaracterization of evidence objection:

- Introduce the evidence before asking this question. Laying a foundation makes this objection inappropriate.
- Explain that evidence has been introduced which supports the question and refer the judge to such evidence.

- Explain to the court that such evidence will be introduced at a later stage of the trial, and request that the judge conditionally accept this evidence subject to subsequent proof.

- Argue that one of the purposes of cross is to test the memory and credibility of a witness and that the witness can deny the asserted facts if the witness disagrees with the assertion.

E. Argumentative

Any question that is essentially an argument is improper. See Fed.R.Evid. 611. The role of the attorney is to question and not to argue. An argumentative question either elicits no new information or harasses the witness. Argumentative questions often assume a sarcastic tenor: "Do you mean to tell me ... " or "Doesn't it seem strange that.... " Such statements should be saved for closing arguments.

Example:

Examining Attorney:

Q: Ms. Starl, had you been keeping a proper look out, you must realize you would never have recklessly run over Lassie.

Objecting Lawyer:

I object to counsel arguing his case through this witness.

Judge:

Objection sustained. The jury will disregard counsel's statement.

Responses to an argumentative objection:

- Re-ask the question and eliminate the objectionable comment.

- Re-ask the question and change the tone so the question does not sound argumentative.

F. Improper Impeachment

Improper impeachment is an attempt to incorrectly discredit a witness. Fed.R.Evid. 613. Section 9.4 explains impeachment in detail. Improper impeachment may occur in a variety of ways. A cross-examiner may attempt to impeach the witness on a collateral, unimportant, or irrelevant matter, or may attempt to impeach the witness with a prior statement that is not materially inconsistent. In considering whether to object in these situations, the attorney should weigh the consequences of the impeachment testimony against any damage caused by objecting.

Example:

Examining Attorney:

Q: Ms. Daedalus, in a prior statement you said that Icarus was wearing wings made of yellow wax, not golden wax, true?

Objecting Lawyer:

Objection, your Honor. The color of the wax is not inconsistent, and this impeachment effort is improper.

Judge:

Sustained.

Response to an improper impeachment objection:

• Explain how the impeachment is not collateral or is materially inconsistent.

• Ask additional cross-examination questions to establish the relevancy and importance of the impeachment.

G. Beyond the Scope

Any questions that go beyond the permissible scope of an examination are objectionable. Fed.R.Evid. 611. Cross-examination is limited to the subject matter of the direct examination and matters relating to the witness' credibility. Credibility usually permits a broad range of questions. If the cross-examiner wishes to go beyond the permitted scope of the direct, the cross-examiner must usually call the witness and ask questions on direct examination. The cross-examiner may raise new matters, however, if the court permits. Many judges view the scope of cross-examination liberally and permit wide-ranging examinations as long as the questions are relevant to the case.

Example:

Examining Attorney:

Q: Ms. Ingalls–Wilder, you later lived in a little house on the prairie, didn't you?

Objecting Lawyer:

Objection, your Honor. The question goes beyond the scope of the direct examination which was limited to the townhouse in Bearpath.

Judge:

Sustained.

Responses to a beyond the scope objection:

• Point out the testimony from direct examination which relates to this question on cross-examination. The attorney may need to remind the judge about the question or answer on direct examination that touched on the subject. If an objection to the scope of cross-examination is anticipated, listen carefully during the direct examination for a related topic so that the judge can be shown that this topic or a related topic was asked during direct examination.

- Explain that the questions relate to the credibility of the witness or another witness.

- Explain to the court that the judge has substantial discretion to allow questions to be asked beyond the scope of direct examination.

- Explain to the judge that if these questions are not permitted at this stage of the trial, the witness will be recalled at a later stage which will only take more time and cause inconvenience to the witness.

§ 4.8   OBJECTIONS BASED ON THE EXCLUSIONARY RULES OF EVIDENCE

This section explains common objections used to exclude evidence. The judge initially decides whether an evidence rule requires the exclusion of evidence. The exclusionary rules of evidence can be grouped into several categories:

- *Irrelevant and unfairly prejudicial evidence.* The judge determines whether the probative value outweighs its unfairly prejudicial impact.

- *Privileged information.* The judge decides whether there is sufficient evidence to support a finding that a privilege exists.

- *Lack of personal knowledge and improper opinion.* The judge determines whether a witness has personal knowledge of a fact or a permissible opinion.

- *Lack of foundation for documents and other exhibits.* The judge decides whether there is sufficient evidence to support a finding that the exhibit is what it purports to be.

- *Constitutional limitations on evidence in criminal cases.* The judge determines whether evidence is inadmissible because the defendant's constitutional rights were violated during a seizure or arrest, or whether compelled testimony is admissible.

- *Hearsay.* The judge decides whether sufficient preliminary facts exist to establish that a statement is not hearsay or falls within a hearsay exception.

Exclusionary rules may not be as strictly enforced in a bench trial and even less so in administrative hearings and arbitrations. The exclusionary rules are still useful in these forums to evaluate the impact of evidence. The advocate can explain in summation how unreliable evidence is based on the rationale underlying the applicable exclusionary rule.

A. *Irrelevant and Unfairly Prejudicial Evidence*

1. *Irrelevant (Fed.R.Evid. 401 and 402)*

Evidence must be relevant in order to be admissible. Relevant evidence has probative value, which is the tendency to make more or less probable any facts of consequence to the outcome of the case. Relevant evidence may be excluded when the probative value of that evidence is outweighed by its unfairly prejudicial effects. Fed.R.Evid. 403.

Relevant evidence may be either direct or circumstantial. Direct evidence is that which is proved by witnesses who testify to what they saw, heard, or experienced, or by physical evidence of the fact itself. Circumstantial evidence is that which can be reasonably inferred from other facts proven in the case. Most relevancy objections involve circumstantial evidence that requires the drawing of inferences, possibly weak or remote, to establish the probative value of the evidence.

Example:

Evidence:

The defendant, Jennifer Moriarty, is identified as the robber of a convenience store. The owners have testified that the store was robbed at 9:45 a.m. The robber wore a neon green jogging suit. A resident of an apartment building one block from the store identified the defendant as the person who ran past her building at 9:45 a.m. wearing a neon green running suit.

Objection:

Irrelevant.

Ruling:

Overruled.

The identification of defendant is admissible. The close proximity in time between the robbery and the neighbor's observation has a tendency to prove through circumstantial evidence that the defendant was the robber running from the store.

What is or is not relevant depends upon the particular evidence and the issues of each case. In offering evidence, an attorney must have an explanation for the evidence's relevance supporting its admissibility. In planning to introduce evidence, the attorney must consider what issue the evidence supports.

After an objection of irrelevancy is made, the judge may or may not ask the examining attorney about the relevancy of the evidence, depending upon whether or not the relevancy is apparent in the context of the case. Many judges prefer to ask before ruling. If the attorney can explain a connection between an issue in the case and the evidence offered, the judge will be inclined to overrule the objection. If the offering attorney anticipates that the judge may sustain the objection, the attorney may ask to be heard before the judge rules and explain the relevancy to the judge. If the objection is sustained, the offering attorney should make an offer of proof and explain the relevancy to the judge, which may change the judge's mind.

Judges often defer to the judgment of the attorney if the judge believes the attorney has properly planned the introduction of evidence. If the attorney can immediately explain to the judge the reasons supporting the relevancy of the evidence, the judge will more likely overrule an objection. If an attorney hesitates in explaining why a piece of evidence is relevant, the judge may believe that the attorney does not know why the evidence is being offered or has not properly prepared for trial. In these situations, a judge is more likely to sustain an objection.

2. Immaterial (Fed.R.Evid. 401 and 402)

Evidence is material if it has some logical relationship to the case. Materiality has been subsumed by Federal Rules of Evidence 401 and 402 and similar state rules. The concept of materiality relates to the concept of what is of "consequence" to a case. What is of consequence depends on the scope of the pleadings, the theories of the case, and the substantive law. Materiality is included in an objection based on relevancy, and is no longer recognized as a distinct objection in most jurisdictions because immaterial evidence is almost always irrelevant.

Example:

Evidence:

Plaintiff Cinderella seeks to prove that the defendant's improper maintenance of a stairway also contributed to the falls of two other residents of the defendant's apartment building. The other accident victims were hurt when they caught their heels in loose carpeting and tripped.

Objection:

Irrelevant.

Ruling:

Overruled.

Admissible if plaintiff shows that all the relevant circumstances were substantially identical to her own accident: the accidents all occurred on the same stairway, the same carpeting was in the same loose condition, the same means of securing the carpeting to the stairs was used, and the lighting conditions and other circumstances were the same.

---

3. Conditional Relevancy

The relevance of a specific item of evidence may be conditioned upon the proof of other facts. In these situations, the court may conditionally admit the proffered evidence, subject to the proof of the additional facts. If those additional facts are not proved, the opposing attorney can object to the admissibility of the previous evidence, request that the evidence no longer be admitted, and ask for a curative instruction. The process is sometimes referred to as "connecting up." If the evidence is never connected up, it is inadmissible.

Example:

Objecting Lawyer:

Your Honor, this court allowed into evidence testimony from Madam X regarding a telephone conversation that supposedly took place on January 2. We objected, and counsel for plaintiff said that she would later offer evidence establishing the date of the conversation. Such evidence has never been established, and the jury should be instructed to disregard the previous evidence because there are no facts to support a finding that a telephone conversation took place on January 2.

Judge:

The previous objection is sustained and the jury is instructed to disregard the testimony.

---

4.   *Unfairly Prejudicial (Fed.R.Evid. 403)*

Relevant evidence is inadmissible when its prejudicial effect substantially outweighs its probative value. The key to a successful assertion of an objection based on prejudicial evidence is that the evidence is unfairly prejudicial. All evidence is prejudicial in the sense that it hurts one party and helps the other party. Only evidence that is *unfairly* prejudicial may be excluded. This objection may be made against evidence that appeals to the passion or prejudice of the jurors, to exhibits that unnecessarily display injuries, or to an event or a scene described in overly graphic or gruesome detail.

Inadmissible prejudicial evidence includes the following categories specifically barred by the Federal Rules of Evidence and similar state rules of evidence.

a.   *Improper Character Evidence (Fed.R.Evid. 404 and 405)*

The general rule is that evidence of a person's character traits are not admissible to prove that the person acted in conformity with those traits on a particular occasion. For example, evidence that the accused has stolen things in the past should not be allowed to prove that the accused stole money on a later occasion.

Section 7.10(D) explains the situations and methods under which character evidence may be admissible in criminal and civil cases. If character evidence is introduced in situations other than those permitted by the rules, then an objection should be made. If character evidence is introduced by an improper method, an objection to the way the evidence is being introduced should be made.

Example:

Evidence:

Doctor Afuhruhurr is accused of medical malpractice for transplanting plaintiff's brain. Plaintiff's attorney presents evidence that Doctor Afuhruhurr is an arrogant, uncaring, overly demanding, and rude physician.

Objection:

Unfairly prejudicial. Improper character evidence.

Ruling:

Sustained.

This evidence of the doctor's character is not admissible to prove the doctor's negligence in the civil case. The doctor may be an arrogant and rude physician, but that information is unfairly prejudicial because the jurors may be influenced improperly and find the doctor negligent in this case because of the doctor's bad general character.

b.   *Improper Habit Evidence (Fed.R.Evid. 406)*

Improper habit evidence is inadmissible. Section 7.10(E) explains the introduction of proper habit evidence on direct examination. An objection should be made as evidence of improper habits is being introduced. An example of an improper "habit" that is usually excluded involves evidence of intemperance. Evidence of excessive drinking is ordinarily inadmissible to prove drunkenness in accident cases. Similarly, evidence of other assaults is usually inadmissible in a civil assault case. These types of evidence are usually deemed inadmissible because they are unfairly prejudicial. The jurors may be unfairly inclined to find the party guilty or liable because of past conduct and not decide the case based on the facts of the present case.

Example:

Evidence:

Plaintiff testified that the defendant, Cameron, backed his car out of Ferris Bueller's driveway without looking, and ran into Plaintiff's car. Cameron claimed that he didn't see Plaintiff's car before he backed out because Plaintiff was speeding. Cameron's witnesses would testify the defendant periodically drove them to school, and he usually looked both ways before backing up.

Objection:

Improper habit evidence.

Ruling:

Sustained.

This testimony is inadmissible evidence of habit. There is insufficient evidence to establish Defendant's looking both ways as a matter of habit.

---

c. Subsequent Remedial Measures (Fed.R.Evid. 407)

The term "subsequent remedial measures" refers to actions taken after an event which, if taken before the event, would have made the event less likely to occur. An example is fixing a car's brakes after an accident caused by faulty brakes. Evidence of subsequent remedial measures is not admissible to prove negligence or fault in a previous event. Such evidence is considered to be unfairly prejudicial and misleading because the repairs inaccurately imply a recognition of liability or may divert the jury's attention from the real cause of the accident.

For example, evidence that a railroad installed a crossing gate and warning lights after an accident should not be admissible to prove the railroad's fault because, in hearing the evidence, the jury might incorrectly infer that the railroad admitted it was negligent. If this type of evidence were admissible to prove fault, many types of repairs would not be made for fear that liability would be imposed on the person making repairs.

The exclusion of subsequent remedial measures does not apply where the issue to be proved involves controverted matters of ownership, control, feasibility of precautionary measures, or impeachment of a witness. These reasons make subsequent remedial measures admissible in many cases.

Example:

Evidence:

Plaintiff Rose DeWitt Bukater slipped on the ice on the deck of the ship. Defendant knew that this slippery condition was likely to occur but claimed that it would be too expensive to make the ship safe. After Plaintiff's accident, Defendant radioed for bags of de-icer to spread around the deck.

Objection:

Unfairly prejudicial evidence.

Ruling:

Sustained.

If offered to show Defendant's fault, but overruled if introduced to show feasibility of precautionary measures, even if the ship sank.

---

d. Offers of Compromise (Fed.R.Evid. 408)

Evidence of offers to resolve a dispute or attempts to settle a lawsuit out of court is not admissible, because the evidence might be misinterpreted as an admission of liability. Parties are encouraged to negotiate and settle cases before trial, and all statements, discussions, and admissions made during settlement talks are excluded from evidence. However, evidence of a compromise offer to prove bias of a witness or to rebut a contention of undue delay may be admitted as an exception to the general rule.

Example:

Evidence:

Mr. Ferrari and Ms. Porsche were involved in an automobile accident where Mr. Ferrari's fender was dented. Each party believed the other was at fault, and an argument ensued. Ms. Porsche didn't want the hassle of going to court and gave Mr. Ferrari some money to fix his car. A few months later Mr. Ferrari developed some health problems that he claims were caused by the accident. Mr. Ferrari sued Ms. Porsche for personal injury, and attempted to present evidence at trial that the defendant paid for the plaintiff's damaged car after the accident.

Objection:

Unfairly prejudicial evidence

Ruling:

Sustained.

The jury might interpret the defendant's payment to fix plaintiff's car as an admission of liability for the accident, and for plaintiff's later health problems.

---

e. Payment of Medical Expenses (Fed.R.Evid. 409)

Evidence of payment, promises to make payment, or offers to make payment for medical expenses by the opposing party may not be offered to prove liability for an injury. This evidence may be admissible to prove other issues in a case, however.

f. Plea Bargains (Fed.R.Evid. 410)

A person accused of a criminal offense may offer to plead guilty to a lesser offense rather than plead not guilty and go to trial. The person may also decide to plead nolo contendere, which means that the person neither admits nor denies guilt, but agrees that if the case went to trial there would be sufficient evidence for a jury to make a finding of guilt. Offers to plead guilty to a lesser offense and pleas of nolo contendere are not admissions of guilt, and may not be used as evidence against the person in a later action. Once a guilty plea is accepted and entered by the court, the guilty finding may be admissible under very limited circumstances. If a guilty plea is entered and later withdrawn, however, it becomes inadmissible.

g. Liability Insurance (Fed.R.Evid. 411)

The existence or nonexistence of insurance coverage is not admissible regarding an issue of negligence or wrongful actions. This is because the jury may believe that an insured person does not use as much care as an uninsured person or may improperly decide to give the insurance company's money to a needy plaintiff. Evidence regarding insurance is admissible if offered to prove issues of agency, ownership, control, bias, or impeachment.

h. Religious Beliefs or Opinions (Fed.R.Evid. 610)

Evidence of a person's religious beliefs or opinions is not admissible to show that the person is more or less credible.

Example:

Evidence by prosecuting attorney on cross-examination of a witness for the defense:

Q: Are you sure you heard the victim cry out on the night of the accident?

A: Oh, yea. Real clear.

Q: But you also hear voices when you speak in tongues at church, right?

Objection:

Unfairly prejudicial.

Ruling:

Sustained.

The jury might adversely use the religious beliefs of the witness.

B. Privileged Communication (Fed.R.Evid. 501)

A privileged communication consists of a communication between persons having a confidential relationship. The policy behind the privilege is to encourage open, honest communication between certain persons. A valid objection based on privilege will bar the underlying communication from being disclosed.

Common privileges include: attorney/client, doctor/patient, spousal communications, parent/child, clergy/penitent, trade/business secrets, and news sources. Executive privilege is not as common. Local statutes and case law must be consulted to determine available privileges in a jurisdiction.

Every privilege has a number of elements that must be proved. The privilege may not be successfully asserted unless evidence is introduced to show the existence of these elements. Attorney/client, doctor/patient, and spousal communication are the three most common privileges that are asserted.

1. Attorney/Client Privilege

The establishment of an attorney/client privilege requires:

(a) A professional relationship between an attorney and a client who seeks legal advice, involving

(b) A communication made in confidence

(c) Between an attorney (or agent of the attorney) and client, who is the holder of the privilege.

2. Doctor/Patient Privilege

The establishment of a doctor/patient privilege requires:

(a) A doctor/patient relationship in which the patient seeks medical assistance, involving

(b) A communication regarding medical information, including examinations, reports, tests, and notes made

(c) Between a doctor (or medical assistant) and a patient, who is the holder of the privilege.

3. Marital Communications Privilege

A limited privilege recognized in most jurisdictions protects confidential communications made between spouses during marriage. Neither spouse can testify, during or after marriage, concerning certain communications made between the spouses while married. Both spouses are holders of the privilege.

The establishment of a marital communication privilege requires:

(a) A marriage relationship, involving

(b) Confidential, private communications

(c) Made during the marriage.

4. Waiver of Privilege

Any privilege may be waived if:

• The holder or attorney, with the consent of the holder, knowingly and expressly waives the privilege;

- Voluntary disclosure of the privileged information occurs during discovery or trial testimony;

- No objection is made to a question eliciting privileged communications;

- A privileged matter is discussed in the presence of a third person;

- An eavesdropper without using surreptitious means, overhears a privileged communication; or

- The holder raises a claim or defense that places the privileged matter in issue.

If a privilege has been waived, an objection asserting the existence of a privilege will be overruled.

Example:

Evidence:

In the hallway outside the courtroom, Defendant Christine Vole discusses strategy with her attorney. A witness who plaintiff intends to call to corroborate evidence is sitting about two feet from defendant and defendant's attorney. In direct examination, opposing counsel questions the witness about the substance of what the witness overheard in defendant's communication with her attorney.

Objection:

This information is protected by the attorney/client privilege.

Ruling:

Overruled.

Ordinarily, an attorney may assert the privilege for the holder and seek to exclude the confidential communication. However, in this example, the defendant voluntarily communicated within the earshot of the witness. This constitutes waiver in most jurisdictions.

C. Lack of Personal Knowledge/Improper Opinion (Fed. R.Evid. 601 and 602)

A witness must be competent to testify. Competency embodies four factors: an understanding of the oath or affirmation, the perception of events, the recollection of those events, and the ability to communicate. Section 7.2(A) describes each of these factors.

Generally, a witness is presumed competent to testify unless challenged by the opponent or the court on its own motion (which judges rarely do). Objections to the competency of a witness are usually made before a witness takes the stand. If a witness does not appear competent while testifying, the opposing attorney may object and "voir dire" the witness to establish that the witness is not competent because the witness does not understand the oath, did not perceive a relevant event, does not remember the event, or cannot communicate. Because witnesses are usually competent, opposing lawyers rely on cross-examination to reduce the weight of the witnesses' testimony.

Example:

Evidence:

Witness saw collision between a meteor and an asteroid.

Examining Attorney:

Q: How fast was the meteor traveling?

Objecting Lawyer:

Objection. Your Honor, this witness is not competent to testify to the speed of the meteor. She did not see it for a sufficient amount of time before the collision because it was out of her view as she running to her bunker.

Ruling:

Sustained.

Some judges would overrule the objection and allow the evidence in for what it is worth. These judges tend to allow the jurors to determine the credibility and persuasive value of the evidence.

---

1. Lack of Personal Knowledge (Fed.R.Evid. 602)

A witness may not testify to any matter unless evidence is introduced which is sufficient to support a finding that the witness has personal knowledge of the matter. If the proponent does not establish that the witness has personal knowledge of the matters about which the witness will testify, an objection should be interposed. Whenever a witness is about to testify, the opposing attorney should silently ask: "How does the witness know this information?" or "What is the source of the information the witness is about to give?" If the opposing attorney knows the witness has firsthand knowledge and the information is reliable, no objection ought to be made. If the opposing attorney believes the witness does not have firsthand knowledge or that the source of information is unreliable, an objection should be made. The proper objection is either lack of personal knowledge or lack of foundation.

Example:

Examining Attorney:

Q: What happened in the fencing room?

A: I told D'Artagnan and Aramis that I no longer was going to be a Musketeer and then I left the room, and they continued to talk about. . . .

Objecting Lawyer:

Objection. Your Honor, the witness has no personal knowledge of what D'Artagnan and Aramis said after he left the room.

Judge:

Sustained.

---

2. *Lack of Foundation (Fed.R.Evid. 901 and 903)*

Foundation is preliminary information which must be established before some evidence is admissible. Section 7.2(C) describes and provides examples of foundations. A lack of foundation objection is used to prevent the introduction of evidence or simply to force the opposing attorney to provide the missing element of foundation.

Example:

Examining Attorney:

Q: Ms. Toad, what happened to your car on the way home?

A: It broke down.

Q: What caused the car to break down?

Objecting Lawyer:

Objection. There's been no foundation laid for this witness to respond to that question.

Judge:

The objection is sustained.

If the objection does not keep the evidence out but forces the opposing attorney to establish the missing element of foundation, it may be strategically inappropriate to object because the additional foundation may make the evidence appear more credible. This is usually true if the opposing attorney can supply the missing foundation.

Example:

Examining Attorney:

Q: Before your car broke down, Ms. Toad, what did you first notice?

A: I saw black smoke coming out of the engine compartment.

Q: What did you see next?

A: I heard this explosion and the hood of the engine blew off, and I saw it land about a hundred feet to the side of the car.

Q: Then what happened?

A: I saw a huge ball of fire erupt from the engine compartment.

Q: What happened after you heard this explosion and saw this huge ball of fire erupt from the engine compartment?

A: The car broke down.

A better tactical approach in this instance may be to not object, but later argue that the proponent failed to prove the missing element, causation.

3. Opinion

There are two types of opinion testimony: that given by an expert, and that given by a lay person.

a. Expert Opinion (Fed.R.Evid. 702 and 705)

Expert opinion is admissible to provide conclusions or inferences beyond the abilities of the fact finder. Experts can give opinion testimony after the trial judge determines that:

- The subject matter of the opinion is not one of common knowledge but one of scientific, technical, or other specialized knowledge.

- The opinion will assist the trier of fact to understand evidence or determine a fact in issue.

- The expert, by way of knowledge, skill, experience, training, or education, possesses sufficient expertise to render an opinion.

- The basis of the opinion is reliable and will assist the trier of fact.

Objections should be made if these four factors have not been met. Chapter 10 explains the intricacies of expert witness examination.

Example:

Evidence:

Annie Oakley testifies that she is qualified as a ballistics expert and that on the basis of the tests conducted on the handgun found in William Cody's possession, it is her opinion, based upon her education, training, and experience in ballistics analysis, that the bullet that killed the buffalo was fired from Mr. Cody's gun.

Objection:

Improper expert opinion.

Ruling:

Overruled.

Ballistics is a widely accepted area of expertise in the courts; the witness is qualified as an expert; and the expert opinion will help the fact finder.

---

b. Lay Witness Opinion (Fed.R.Evid. 701)

Lay witnesses may render opinions and conclusions if such statements are rationally based on the perception of the witness and helpful to a clear understanding or determination of a fact in issue. Lay witnesses can render opinions if they have personal knowledge to support their perceptions and if there is a rational basis for the conclusion. For example, a witness may not testify to what a person was thinking but may render an opinion regarding the appearance of the person from which the fact finder may infer what the person was thinking. For another example, a lay witness may not testify that someone had a specific type of fracture, but may conclude that the person had a broken arm.

There are many opinions and conclusions a lay witness may render. Permissible lay opinions may be given regarding speed, distance, time, appearances, conditions, emotions, age, health, sobriety, value of personal property, and other rational perceptions. Lay witnesses may testify that a person appeared nervous, happy, sad, scared, excited, or drunk. Inadmissible lay opinions are those that exceed the perception of the witness, are not rationally based, or do not assist the fact finder. An objection based on improper opinion should be made unless the witness can establish the foundation to support the opinion.

Lay witnesses may testify to a conclusion in some situations even though they are unable to explain specific observations that support the conclusion. The most common example involves the formation of an instantaneous opinion regarding matters that are observed, referred to as the collective facts doctrine. For example, an eye witness to an accident in which a pedestrian was hit by a car can testify to the conclusion that the car could not have swerved in time to avoid hitting the pedestrian. It would be difficult, if not impossible, for the witness to testify to specific, detailed facts that support the opinion. This type of conclusion assists the jury in determining the facts and is admissible in most jurisdictions.

Example:

Examining Attorney:

Q: What did you see, Mr. Kegger?

A: I saw the defendant holding a can of beer in one hand and staggering as he walked over to me. His eyes were bloodshot, he smelled like a brewery, and he slurred his words.

Q: Describe his condition.

A: He was drunk.

Q: What else did you conclude?

A: He was negligent when he drove the car while drunk and he caused the accident.

Objecting Lawyer:

Objection. Improper opinion.

Judge:

Sustained.

While the witness may testify that the defendant was drunk when he talked to him, the witness cannot draw the conclusion that the defendant was negligent because he did not perceive the event and the opinion infringes on an ultimate issue of the case.

---

4. *Speculation (Fed.R.Evid. 602 and 701)*

Any question that asks the witness to guess or engage in conjecture is objectionable. Speculation on the part of a witness as to what could have happened is usually of little probative value. Words like if, should, could, and similar phrases in a question may render a question susceptible to this objection.

Example:

Examining Attorney:

Q: How close were you to Lancelot when he was knocked off his horse?

A: About fifteen feet away.

Q: Could Gwenivere have avoided Lancelot if she had been cantering instead of galloping her horse?

Objecting Lawyer:

Objection, the question calls for speculation.

Judge:

Sustained.

The witness' opinion is speculative and has little probative value.

D. Documents

Four evidence rules determine the admissibility of a document:

- *Relevancy*, explained in Section 4.8(A);

- *Hearsay*, explained in Section 4.8(F)(1);

- *Original writing*, explained in this section; and

- *Authentication*, explained in this section and Section 8.6.

Whenever a document is introduced, an opposing attorney should review the document for potential objections and determine whether these objections have been overcome by the attorney offering the document. Parts of a document may also be objectionable, and the attorney should scrutinize the entire document to make sure all the paragraphs, sentences, phrases, and words are admissible. If any one of these objections may preclude the introduction of part of a document, an objection should be made to exclude that portion of the document which is objectionable. Section 8.4(F) explains the process of redacting parts of documentary exhibits.

Example:

Examining Attorney:

Your Honor, Ms. Emily Dickinson offers Plaintiff's Exhibit No. 640, the poem, as evidence.

Objecting Lawyer:

I object, your Honor, to the admission of a part of this Exhibit. I object to the introduction of the handwritten notes in the margin of this document. There has been no foundation made to authenticate the handwriting, and this handwritten statement constitutes inadmissible hearsay.

Judge:

Sustained. The handwritten notes in the left margin are excluded from evidence and are to be removed. The remainder of Plaintiff's Exhibit No. 640 is received into evidence.

---

1.   Original Writings (Fed.R.Evid. 1001 and 1007)

The modern "original writings" rule permits originals and duplicate originals to be introduced to prove the contents of a writing, unless a question exists regarding the authenticity of the original or if it would be unfair to introduce a duplicate. This rule is also known as the "best evidence" rule, which is a misleading term. There never has been, and is not now, any requirement that the "best" or most persuasive evidence be introduced. The traditional "best evidence" rule required that the original of the document be introduced to prove its contents, and did not permit copies of the original. Modern evidence law recognizes that there may be a number of "originals" of a document and that mechanical reproduction machines or computer printers produce accurate and reliable duplicate originals. Documents covered by the original writings rule include all written documents, recordings, and photographs. Neither the modern rule nor the traditional rule applies to oral testimony.

The modern rule specifically provides that duplicates are admissible to the same extent as an original unless there is a question about the authenticity of the original, or some other unfairness. The modern rule also provides that if neither the original nor a duplicate exist, if the original and copies have been inadvertently lost or destroyed, or if the documents cannot be obtained by any available judicial process or subpoena, other evidence of the contents of the writing is admissible.

Example:

Examining Attorney:

Q: Ms. Jurassic, what did your lease set out as the rules about giant frilled lizards?

Objecting Lawyer:

Objection. The best evidence of the terms of that lease requires that the written lease be introduced instead of oral testimony.

Judge:

Sustained.

Some evidence that is written in a document may be admissible through oral testimony without the need to introduce the document. There are three specific situations where oral testimony provides accurate and reliable evidence without the need for the available document to be admitted.

a.   Signs, Labels, Tags

A witness may testify to the contents of a writing inscribed on a sign, label, or tag. Because there are only a few words on these items, the testimony is reliable. If an item contained a lengthy statement, then the original writing rule would apply. For example, a witness can testify that a sign read "no trespassing," but cannot testify regarding a sign containing several detailed sentences of information.

b.   Independent Facts

Facts that exist independently of a document and that are known to a witness may be established without requiring that the document be produced. For example, a witness may testify that a payment was made and not have to produce a canceled check or a copy of a paid bill. For another example, a tenant may testify to the amount and due date of the rent paid without having to produce the original lease. In these examples, the facts are independently known without reliance on the document because the witness paid or received the money. On the other hand, a written document is required to be introduced to establish facts that are not independent of the document, such as detailed terms or provisions.

c. Collateral Matter

If the writing, recording, or photograph is collaterally (indirectly) related to the issue to be proved, and the need for producing the original is minimal, secondary evidence by way of oral testimony will be permitted. For example, if a witness testifies to a date that appears in a diary calendar, the original of the diary calendar need not be introduced if the actual date is not significant to the case.

2. Lack of Authentication (Fed.R.Evid. 901 and 902)

Writings must be authenticated to be admissible, that is, they must be shown to be what they purport to be. Authentication is a foundational requirement for the introduction of writings. Section 8.6 explains specific authentication requirements for various documents. A lack of authentication objection is identical to a lack of foundation objection.

Example:

Evidence:

In a copyright case, Shakespeare introduces a signed letter that he claims was written by Roger Bacon.

Objection:

The letter is not authentic because there is no testimony that the signature of Roger Bacon is genuine and Mr. Bacon denies writing the letter.

Ruling:

Sustained

If evidence of the authenticity is admitted, the exhibit is admissible.

---

3. Parol Evidence Rule

The parol evidence rule provides that a written agreement cannot be contradicted or modified by oral or written evidence of a prior or contemporaneous agreement. Exceptions to this rule are when the contract is ambiguous, when the writing is not intended to be a complete and final expression of the agreement, or when fraud or mistake was committed in the formation of the contract.

Example:

Evidence:

Phineas Fogg agreed to buy a hot air balloon from Jules Verne for $25,000. Verne said he would supply propane gas for one *month without charge. Fogg and Verne signed a contract which stated that Fogg purchased the balloon for $25,000, but did not mention anything about the gas. When Fogg later attempted to obtain the propane gas, Verne told him he would have to pay for it. Fogg sued Verne, and Fogg now attempts to testify about the agreement for free fuel.*

Objection:

The parol evidence rule prohibits testimony contradicting or modifying a writing.

Ruling:

Sustained.

If the agreement regarding the gas was indeed part of this contract, it should have been in writing.

E. Constitutional Limitations in Criminal Cases

Evidence that may be reliable under the rules of evidence may be excluded in a criminal case because it was not obtained by the government in a fair way. The Bill of Rights and the Fourteenth Amendment establish limitations on the government. Criminal constitutional exclusionary rules were developed by the federal and state courts to exclude evidence obtained in a way that violated the defendant's constitutional rights. For example, if evidence or statements were obtained from a defendant through an unconstitutional search or improper interrogation of the defendant by the police, they will not be admissible even though they would be admissible under the general rules of evidence.

F. Hearsay (Fed.R.Evid. 801 and 804)

Hearsay is an out-of-court statement offered to prove the truth of the matter asserted. See Fed.R.Evid. 801. Hearsay occurs when a witness repeats an out-of-court statement in court. The out-of-court statement is made by a declarant, who can be either the testifying witness or another person. Hearsay is excluded because it involves one or more defects making it unreliable and untrustworthy:

- The fact finder has no opportunity to observe the credibility of the declarant when the statement was made, to gauge the sincerity, perception, or memory of the declarant, or to resolve ambiguities in the declarant's statement.

- The out-of-court statement may not be restated accurately because the witness may have misheard or misunderstood the statement.

- At the time the statement was made the declarant was not under oath.

- It may not be possible to cross-examine the declarant.

Most hearsay statements are admissible in a trial, either because the statements do not meet the legal definition of hearsay or because an exception provides for their admissibility. While the rules of evidence state that hearsay is inadmissible, the reality of trial practice is that most hearsay statements are admissible.

This section provides a method of analyzing out-of-court statements to assess whether they are or are not hearsay and then to determine whether exceptions exist to admit the hearsay statements. This section defines hearsay, explains why many out-of-court statements are not hearsay, and describes the more common exceptions to the rule against hearsay.

1. Definition (Fed.R.Evid. 801)

There are three essential factors to a hearsay statement. If any one factor is absent, the statement is not hearsay.

The first factor is that the "statement" must be an oral or written assertion or nonverbal conduct intended to be an assertion. Hearsay statements may be oral, written, or asserted conduct. Oral testimony and written documents are hearsay statements, but not all conduct is a statement within the meaning of hearsay. Only assertive conduct constitutes hearsay. Assertive conduct is conduct that is intended by the actor to be an assertion. For example, during a line-up, the victim points her finger at the defendant. This is assertive nonverbal conduct. The statement implied in that conduct is "the defendant did it."

The second factor is that the statement must be an "out-of-court" statement. A hearsay statement is a prior statement made by a declarant outside the courtroom which is repeated by the witness in court. Three examples illustrate this factor:

- If the witness, Ichabod Crane, on the stand states, "Brom Bones said the horseman is headless," that statement is an out-of-court statement.

- If witness Ichabod Crane on the stand states, "I said the horseman is headless," that statement is also an out-of-court statement.

- If witness Ichabod Crane on the stand states, "I saw the Headless Horseman," that testimony is not hearsay.

The first two examples are out-of-court statements because they were made outside of the courtroom and were repeated in the courtroom. The third example is not a restatement of a prior statement, but a description of an event.

The third factor is that the out-of-court statement is offered to prove the truth of what the statement says. If the statement is offered for any other purpose, it is not hearsay. One way of determining whether the third factor has been met is to compare "what the statement proves" with "what the proponent is trying to prove." If there is a match, the statement is hearsay. If there is not a match, the statement is not hearsay. For example, a witness testifies that Mr. Black Elk said it was snowing on Mt. Rushmore on May 1. If the statement is offered to prove that it was actually snowing on Mt. Rushmore on May 1, the statement is hearsay. If the statement is offered to prove that the witness could identify the voice of Mr. Black Elk, the statement is not hearsay.

2. *Out-of-Court Statements That Are Not Hearsay (Fed.R.Evid. 802)*

Out-of-court statements that are admissible include:

- Statements not offered for the truth of the matter asserted.

- Nonassertive conduct.

- Non-propositions.

- Verbal acts.

- "Statements" by a declarant who is not a person.

a. *Statements Not Offered for the Truth of the Matter Asserted*

As a general rule stated above, an out-of-court statement offered to prove the truth of the matter asserted is inadmissible hearsay. A statement offered to prove a fact other than the truth of the matter asserted may be admissible. For example, a witness overheard the groom say "I do. I do." If offered for the truth of the matter asserted — that the groom said "I do. I do." — it is inadmissible hearsay. If offered for some other purpose, "I do. I do." it is not hearsay.

For example, if the statement is offered to prove that the groom was alive at the time the statement was made, it is not hearsay. If offered to prove the groom could talk, it is not hearsay. When offered for another purpose, the contents of the statement need not be believed for the evidence to be relevant. The mere fact that the statement was made independent of its truth is what is relevant and reliable.

A statement may appear to be offered for its truth but is primarily offered for another purpose. Common examples of such statements include statements offered to prove that an individual had notice or knowledge of something. For example, if a service station attendant tells a driver that his engine needs oil, that statement may be introduced at trial to determine a breach of warranty claim brought by the driver. The statement is introduced primarily to show that the driver had notice that his engine needed oil and not for the truth of the matter asserted.

b. *Nonassertive Conduct*

Nonassertive conduct — conduct not intended by the actor to stand for the matter to be proved — is not hearsay. For example, an issue at trial is whether it was cold and windy at an intersection, and Sherlock Holmes testifies that, "I observed from my window people standing at the intersection all faced in one direction, wearing heavy coats, with their collars upturned, and their hands in their pockets." The nonverbal conduct by the pedestrians is nonassertive conduct because they did not intend their acts to stand for the proposition sought to be proved at trial — that it was cold and windy. Nonassertive conduct is admissible because it is reliable.

c. Non-propositions

Statements are hearsay only if they contain a "proposition," that is, a statement that is offered for the truth of its contents. A common non-proposition statement is a question. Questions are usually not hearsay because they often do not contain any proposition. For example, a statement "I said, 'What did you say?'" is usually not hearsay, but the statement "I said, 'Elaine, who is with you at the toy store on Michigan Avenue?'" is hearsay because it contains a proposition that Elaine is at the Michigan Avenue toy store.

d. Verbal Acts

Statements known as "verbal acts" or "operative words" are not considered hearsay because they are not offered for the truth of the matter asserted, but, rather, for their legal or logical significance. The making of the statements creates legal duties or obligations irrespective of the truth asserted.

The most common examples are statements which constitute the words of an offer or acceptance creating a contract, or defamatory words spoken to establish slander. For example, in a contract case, the witness can testify that "I heard the President say 'I will sell you these jellybeans if you sell me those hog rinds.'" Further, in a defamation case, a witness can testify "Chambers said Hiss was a communist."

A verbal act may also logically permit a statement to prove the declarant spoke. For example, in a personal injury case, if the defendant claims the accident rendered the plaintiff unconscious, the plaintiff could introduce a statement from a witness bystander who heard the plaintiff crying out after the accident. Whether the plaintiff was crying out "Wow that hurts" or "Call for help," the statement proves the plaintiff was conscious.

e. Declarant Not a Person

A statement is hearsay only if made by a person. A "statement" not made or produced by a person is not hearsay. A result produced by an inanimate object such as a machine or the conduct of an animal is not hearsay. For example, the number produced by a radar device which displays the speed of an automobile is not a hearsay statement; a dog that was trained to smell narcotics and who points to a package does not make a hearsay statement; a witness who testifies that her watch said "two-thirty" is not making a hearsay statement because the watch is not a person. These situations raise foundation issues to determine admissibility.

3. Statements Not Defined as Hearsay

Some out-of-court statements that are offered for the truth of the matter asserted are defined by both federal and state rules of evidence as non-hearsay. These include:

- Party admissions,
- Prior statements by witnesses, and
- Prior identifications.

a. Party Admissions (Fed.R.Evid. 801(d)(2))

Any statement made by an opposing party or the party's agent, employee, or representative is not hearsay and is admissible when offered against that party. An admission is defined as a statement made or an act done by a party to a lawsuit. A working definition of party admissions is: Anything an opposing party ever said or did that has anything to do with the case will be admissible. A plaintiff can testify to what a defendant said, and a defendant can testify to what the plaintiff said. A witness can testify to what any party said if offered by the opposing party against the declarant party.

Statements by an opposing party are admissible because the party should assume responsibility for statements made and because the party has a full opportunity to explain why the statement was made to place it in proper context. Admissions extend to statements made by agents, authorized persons, co-conspirators, and to adopted or approved statements made by other representatives of the party. For example, Casey, an engineer of defendant's train, tells an investigator, "The brakes did not work, and I was not looking where I was going." The investigator can be called by the plaintiff to repeat Casey's statements.

Some state jurisdictions treat party admissions as an exception to the hearsay rule, rather than as non-hearsay statements. This treatment yields the same results as the federal rule.

b. Prior Statements by Witnesses (Fed.R.Evid. 801(d)(1))

Prior inconsistent statements made by witnesses under oath at a trial, hearing, deposition, or other proceeding are admissible as substantive evidence of the statements made. Prior consistent statements are admissible to rebut an indirect or express charge against the witness of recent fabrication, improper influence or motive. The declarant must testify at trial and be subject to cross-examination. The federal rules and similar state rules admit prior inconsistent statements in evidence as substantive proof. Some states only permit prior statements to be introduced for impeachment purposes and do not permit them to be considered by the fact finder as substantive proof.

For example, during a deposition, Paul Revere states "There was one lamp in the belfry arch." After the deposition, Paul Revere makes changes in his deposition testimony and now states "There were two lanterns in the belfry." During direct examination at trial, Paul Revere says "There were two lanterns in the belfry." On cross-examination, Paul Revere can be asked: "Prior to this trial, you stated that there was one lamp in the belfry arch." This statement is offered to prove the truth of the matter asserted — that there was only one lamp — and also offered to impeach the witness.

During redirect examination, Paul Revere can testify that he said after the deposition that there were two lanterns. This statement is offered to corroborate the direct testimony and to rebut the impeachment by the prior inconsistent statement. In states that do not follow the federal rules, the prior statements are only admissible to impeach and to rebut impeachment and not to prove there was one lamp.

c. Prior Identification (Fed.R.Evid. 801(d)(1))

Prior identification of a person made by a witness after observing the person is admissible if the declarant testifies at trial and is subject to cross-examination. This rule allows a witness to testify to a prior identification statement made during or shortly after viewing the person or after identifying a photograph of the person.

For example, a witness, Cole Porter, who saw an assailant, tells the police that the assailant was "Five foot two with eyes of blue." At trial, Mr. Porter can say: "I told the police that the person who attacked me was five foot two with eyes of blue." Also at that trial, the police officer can state: "Mr. Porter told me that the suspect was five foot two with eyes of blue."

G. Hearsay Myths

A number of myths exist regarding hearsay. These myths arise from a misunderstanding of the application of the hearsay rules. An explanation of some of these myths may clear up some of the misperceptions regarding hearsay.

- Myth: *All out-of-court statements are inadmissible hearsay.* Most out-of-court statements are admissible at trial.

- Myth: *A witness on the stand can testify to whatever the witness has said in the past.* A witness on the stand who repeats what he or she has said in the past is testifying to an out-of-court statement that may or may not be admissible under the hearsay rules. The declarant's mere presence on the stand does not automatically make any prior statements admissible.

- Myth: *If a witness can be cross-examined, all prior statements of that witness are admissible.* Merely because a witness has testified or is available to be cross-examined does not automatically make all prior statements by that witness admissible. The hearsay rules determine whether out-of-court statements by that declarant are admissible.

- Myth: *If the proper foundation is laid to authenticate a relevant document, the document is admissible.* Authentic and relevant documents are admissible only if they contain admissible out-of-court statements. The contents of the document must comply with the hearsay rules to be admissible.

- Myth: *Affidavits (statements made under oath) are admissible.* An affidavit, though made under oath, is a hearsay statement, and must satisfy a hearsay exception, such as past recollection record-ed, to be admissible.

- Myth: *Affidavits are admissible if the witness is unavailable.* An affidavit made by a person who is unavailable to testify is not a substitute for the testimony of that person and constitutes inad-missible hearsay.

- Myth: *Res gestae makes much of hearsay admissible.* The phrase "res gestae" (which means "the things done") has been replaced by modern rules of evidence. The phrase means different things to different advocates, and is only recognized in a few jurisdictions.

- Myth: *Judges flip a coin when ruling on hearsay objections.* Most judges base their ruling on the applicable hearsay rules. Some judges are inclined to overrule hearsay objections because of the unlikelihood that an appellate court would reverse their evidentia-ry ruling and grant a new trial. Some judges misunderstand or misapply the rules of hearsay and improperly overrule hearsay objections. Hearsay objections should, however, be made in an attempt to exclude unreliable evidence and to make a record for appeal.

- Myth: *After a hearsay statement has been admitted, little can be done about its impact.* Even if questionable hearsay is allowed in, much can be done to reduce its effect. Cross-examination ques-tions can demonstrate its unreliability, and the defects of the evidence can be pointed out during summation.

- Myth: *No one understands hearsay, so who cares?* Ninety percent of the hearsay situations and rules are relatively easy to under-stand and apply. It is the remaining ten percent that require further analysis.

- Myth: *Hearsay is fun to learn and not at all frustrating.* The most frustrating aspect of hearsay is that different judges and lawyers have different understandings of the hearsay rules. Hearsay can become less frustrating if the advocate flexibly adapts to the judge's view on hearsay, and offers evidence consistent with those views.

- Myth: *There is always a hearsay exception that makes the hearsay statement admissible.* A hearsay statement must meet the require-ments of a hearsay exception to be admissible

There are a reasonable — but nonetheless limited — number of hearsay exceptions.

H. *Hearsay Exceptions (Fed.R.Evid. 803 and 804)*

Many hearsay statements are admissible because one or more excep-tions to the hearsay rule make them admissible. Federal and state jurisdictions have developed numerous exceptions. The federal rules of evidence have codified twenty-nine separate exceptions, and many states recognize more.

There are a number of rationales as to why these exceptions have been developed. A common rationale is that the hearsay exceptions recognize that some hearsay statements are reliable and trustworthy. If the traditional defects of unreliability and untrustworthiness do not exist, the statement ought to be admissible.

A second rationale supports those hearsay statements where the declarant can be cross-examined. If there is an opportunity to cross-examine the person who made the hearsay statement, it may be appropriate to allow that statement to be admitted.

A third rationale is there is no efficient or economical way of proving the fact except through the hearsay statement. Some exceptions to the rule against hearsay have been created in part to respond to the pragmatic needs of introducing evidence. If there are no other practical means of proving something critical to the case, hearsay may be admissible.

The following sections explain the most commonly recognized hearsay exceptions. Most jurisdictions, including the federal system, divide hearsay exceptions into two general groups which depend upon the availability of the declarant to testify at trial.

Hearsay statements which are excepted from the hearsay rule *regardless of whether the declarant is available to testify* at the trial include:

- Sense impressions,
- "State of mind" assertions,
- Records, and
- Reputation evidence.

Additional hearsay statements which are excepted from the hearsay rule *only when the declarant is unavailable to testify* include:

- Former testimony,
- Statements against interest,
- Statements of personal or family history, and
- Dying declarations.

In addition to these exceptions, some hearsay statements will be excepted from the rule if certain specific requirements of reliability are met. The federal rules and many state jurisdictions designate this exception as the "residual" exception.

1.   General Hearsay Exceptions

a.   Sense Impressions

This exception includes two types of statements: present sense impressions and excited utterances.

i. Present Sense Impressions (Fed.R.Evid. 803(1))

Statements describing or explaining an event or condition made while the declarant was perceiving the event or condition, or immediately thereafter, are admissible as present sense impressions. This is a broad exception and covers many statements made by persons involved in or who observe an event. This exception has two specific requirements:

- The statement describes or explains an event or condition, and

- The statement is made immediately or shortly after the declarant perceives the event or condition.

These spontaneous statements are deemed reliable because of the lack of time for reflective thought which can result in a changed perception of the event, and because the witness is likely to have a fresh memory of the event at the time the statement was made.

Example:

Bo Jangles falls on a dance floor and is injured. Mr. Jangles' attorney calls Ms. Cherise, a witness, to testify about Bo's accident.

Examining Attorney:

Q: Where were you standing?

A: I was standing next to Ms. Caruthers, and both of us were standing near Bo when he fell.

Q: What did Ms. Caruthers say when Mr. Jangles fell?

Objecting Lawyer:

Objection. Hearsay.

Judge:

Overruled.

A: Ms. Caruthers said to me "This dance floor is very slippery, I almost fell myself a moment ago."

Q: What did you do next?

A: I walked over, slowly, to help Bo.

Q: What did Mr. Jangles say?

Objecting Lawyer:

Objection. Hearsay.

Judge:

Overruled.

A: He said "This floor has some slippery goo on it."

Both objections are overruled because both declarants, Mr. Caruthers and Mr. Jangles, made statements about a condition immediately after perceiving the event. The statement by Mr. Jangles is not a party admission because it is not being offered against him, but rather is being offered on his behalf.

ii. Excited Utterances (Fed.R.Evid. 803(2))

Statements made by the declarant while under stress or excitement caused by a startling situation, and which relate to that situation, are admissible as excited utterances. This exception only applies if:

- The statement is made by the declarant while under stress,
- The declarant has personal knowledge of the event by participating in or observing the event,
- The statement is prompted by the startling event, and
- The statement relates to the event.

The rationale for this exception is that spontaneous statements made under stress or during a startling event are reliable because a person does not have time to fabricate such statements.

Example:

In a personal injury case, Jill witnesses a startling event and testifies at trial that she said, "Oh no, the handle of the pail cracked and Jack fell down and broke his crown!" The opposing lawyer, representing the landowner, anticipating Jill's response, would object to the statement as hearsay. The judge would overrule the objection because the statement is an excited utterance, and is also a present sense impression.

Many statements are both excited utterances and present sense impressions. An excited utterance statement differs from a present sense impression in two aspects:

- While an excited utterance usually occurs during or immediately after an event, it need not occur at those times. As long as the declarant is still upset by the event when the statement is made, it is an excited utterance. The present sense impression must be made at the time of the event or immediately thereafter.

- The excited utterance need only "relate" to the startling event, while a present sense impression must "describe or explain" an event or condition.

b. State of Mind or Body Exceptions

There are two related exceptions that involve statements regarding the declarant's state of mind or body: Existing mental, emotional, or physical conditions, and medical treatment statements.

i. Existing Mental, Emotional, Physical Condition (Fed.R.Evid. 803(3))

Statements by a declarant involving the declarant's existing state of mind, emotion, sensation, or physical condition (such as intent, plan, motive, design, mental feeling, pain, and bodily harm) are admissible. These statements are reliable because of their spontaneous nature. They are made at the time the declarant experiences the mental, emotional, or physical condition.

Example:

In a products liability case, a witness called by the plaintiff testifies that he heard the plaintiff, Knievel, state right after the jumping accident: "My head is throbbing. I got the chills. I feel depressed. I hate the guy who sold me this motorcycle. I am going to go back to the cycle store and complain." All these statements are admissible as statements of existing physical, emotional, and mental conditions.

This exception does not include statements of past conditions. For example, if Knievel also said: "Last week, my back hurt," the statement is inadmissible hearsay because it refers to a past condition. If Knievel also said: "My back hurts," the statement is admissible because it refers to a present, existing condition.

ii. Medical Treatment Statements (Fed.R.Evid. 803(4))

Statements made by one person who describes medical history, past or present pains, or symptoms to a medical professional for purposes of medical diagnosis or treatment are admissible. These statements are deemed reliable because the declarant who seeks medical treatment has little or no incentive to lie.

Example:

In a personal injury accident, the plaintiff's treating physician is called to testify at trial on behalf of the plaintiff.

Examining Attorney:

Q: When did you examine Whiplash Willy?

A: About two weeks after the accident.

Q: What did Mr. Willy tell you about his injuries at that time?

Objecting Lawyer:

Objection. Hearsay.

Judge:

Overruled.

A: He said that right after the accident his neck hurt a lot and that up until the day before he saw me he could not turn his head to the right or left.

Q: What else did he say about his injury?

Objecting Lawyer:

Objection. Hearsay.

Judge:

Overruled.

A: He said he had hurt his neck when his head hit the headrest.

Q: What else did he say about the cause of the injury?

Objecting Lawyer:

Objection. Hearsay.

Judge:

Sustained.

The first objection is properly overruled because the testimony consists of a medical diagnosis. The second objection is also properly overruled because the cause of the injury is a relevant part of the information the doctor needs to properly diagnose and treat the injury. The third objection is properly sustained because any further statement, such as "It was defendant's reckless driving that caused my neck injury," is not a part of the patient's medical history.

c. *Records*

Several hearsay exceptions permit the admissibility of specific categories of records. These records are deemed reliable because the information they contain is usually entered and maintained in an accurate, trustworthy manner including:

- Business records,
- Public records,
- Specific records,
- Absent records, and
- Past recollection recorded.

i. *Business Records (Fed.R.Evid. 803(6))*

Records kept in the ordinary, regular course of a business or other organization are admissible. Records include memoranda, reports, data compilation, documents, or any other type of written information. Recorded information includes facts, opinions, and other information. The term "business" includes any business, institution, association, profession, occupation, and organization, whether profit or nonprofit. The records are admissible hearsay written statements if:

(1) The entries are made at or near the time of the event or act,

(2) A person with knowledge records the information or transmits the information to someone who records it,

(3) The records are kept in the course of a regularly conducted business activity or duty,

(4) The recording of the specific information is a regular practice of that business,

(5) The custodian or the qualified witness testifies to these facts, and

(6) The records are reliable and trustworthy.

Example:

In a commercial arbitration case, Ms. Euro testifies that she is the manager of the business loan department, that it is the business of the bank to make and maintain records of loans, that Defendant's Exhibit No. 3 contains loan documents made contemporaneously with the information recorded on the documents, and that the documents were made in the regular course of the business of the bank. Exhibit No. 3 is admissible.

The records witness must testify to the requirements of the business exception rule, which usually requires the examining attorney to ask leading questions to establish these requirements. In most civil cases and many criminal cases business records are introduced through a stipulation or in response to a request for an admission. There is usually no need to waste time during trial to subpoena a witness to lay the foundation for the hearsay exception. Many of these records will also be self-authenticating under the rules of evidence and may be introduced through a witness who can testify to their relevance.

ii. Public Records (Fed.R.Evid. 803(8))

Public records are reliable because government officials record the information pursuant to a public duty or the law and have no interest in recording information that favors one side or the other. Several types of public records maintained by government agencies are admissible:

- Records that describe or explain the activities of an office or agency, such as published reports by the government summarizing what the office or agency does. An example is a document published by a department of transportation which explains how it conducts drivers' licensing exams.

- Records of matters observed and recorded pursuant to a duty imposed by law. Documents maintained by government officers concerning their official activities are examples of such records. Another example is public housing records listing the names of tenants and their addresses. Public reports containing observations of police officers or other law enforcement personnel are not generally permitted in criminal cases under this exception.

- Factual findings resulting from investigations made pursuant to authority granted by law, such as reports prepared by government investigators. Only those parts of an investigation report that are factual findings, factual conclusions, and historical facts will be admissible. Conclusions or opinions are not admissible. For example, a fire investigative report which includes a description of the accident is admissible, but a portion of the report that concludes the Chicago fire was caused by arson and not a cow because the defendant was in a desperate financial situation is inadmissible. In some cases, determining what is an admissible "factual finding" and what is an inadmissible "conclusion" is difficult. Courts have held that "factual conclusions" are admissible under the public records exception. The resolution in each case will depend upon the exact words contained in the report.

- Land records and property documents maintained in a public office, including deeds, certificates, entries in ledgers, and computer data relating to property interests. These documents are reliable and admissible.

iii. Other Specific Records

The rules of evidence in most jurisdictions render admissible the following specific types of documents:

- Market reports and commercial data. Hearsay statements are contained in market reports, financial summaries, commercial documents, and business transaction data. These statements include facts, opinions, and evaluative or interpretive information. Examples are market quotations, stock prices, lists of financial information, business directories, and other compilations. The rationale for their admissibility is that since the financial and business world relies upon them, so should the law. (Fed.R.Evid. 803(17)).

- Records of vital statistics, including birth, death, and marriage information. (Fed.R.Evid. 803(9)).

- Records of religious organizations, including birth, marriage, divorce, death, and other personal or family records kept in the ordinary course of a religious organization's activities. (Fed. R.Evid. 803(11)).

- Marriage, baptismal, and other certificates. (Fed.R.Evid. 803(12)).

- Family records, including personal or family history or facts contained in Bibles, engravings, inscriptions, and other sources. (Fed.R.Evid. 803(13)).

- Ancient documents and statements contained in authentic documents in existence for 20 years or more. (Fed.R.Evid. 803(16)).

- Judgments of previous convictions and judgments involving personal, family, history, or boundary data. (Fed.R.Evid. 803(22) and (23)).

Many records are admissible under more than one hearsay exception. A record may qualify as a business record, public record, and a specific record. Some records may appear to be admissible under a rule but have been held to be inadmissible by the courts. For example, police reports are not admissible in criminal cases, even though such reports may technically qualify as business records or public records, because the defendant has a constitutional right to cross-examine witnesses, and a record cannot be cross-examined. Case decisions or statutes may expand or narrow the rules of evidence governing the introduction of various types of records.

iv. Absence of Business or Public Records (Fed.R.Evid. 803(7) and (10))

The lack of an entry in a business or public record is admissible to prove an event did not occur. Before the lack of a record or entry is admissible, the attorney must establish that the information was the type of information that would have been recorded and that a search has been made of the records. Most jurisdictions allow two ways to prove the absent record search. A witness with personal knowledge may testify to the search that was undertaken, or the proponent may offer a self-authenticating certificate which describes the diligent but unsuccessful search.

v. Past Recollection Recorded (Fed.R.Evid. 803(5))

Records concerning a matter that a witness no longer remembers, but that the witness once knew and accurately recorded when the matter was fresh, will be admissible evidence. Written records of prior events are admissible if:

(1) The testifying witness does not presently fully or accurately recall the event,

(2) The witness has personal knowledge of the record,

(3) The witness made the record or adopted it as correct at a time when the memory of the witness was fresh, usually close in time to the occurrence of the event, and

(4) The witness testifies that the report is accurate, or testifies that the record would not have been signed or adopted if it were inaccurate.

Section 8.6(J) describes the introduction of a past recollection recorded document.

Example:

In a computer antitrust case, the witness maintained a database of email conversations made three years before the trial describing an event. At trial, the witness is not likely to be able to remember the details of a three-year-old email conversation, however rich. The relevant database may be admitted as past recollection recorded by having the witness establish the existence of the four foundation factors for past recollection recorded.

vi. Learned Treatises (Fed.R.Evid. 803(10))

A learned treatise is a book, periodical, article, pamphlet, or magazine established as reliable authority on a matter, ordinarily the subject of expert opinion, which is relied upon by an expert in direct examination or called to the attention of an expert witness during cross-examination. Sections 10.5(G) and 10.7(B)(14) describe the introduction and use of learned treatises.

d. Reputation Evidence (Fed.R.Evid. 802(19), (20), and (21))

Reputation evidence is a collection of hearsay statements in which specific hearsay exceptions render certain types of reputation evidence admissible. Reputation evidence concerning personal or family history, such as marriages, births, deaths or other events of family significance are admissible. Fed.R.Evid. 803(19). Reputation evidence regarding general history or land boundaries or customs is also admissible. Fed.R.Evid. 803(20). Reputation evidence of a person's character among associates or in the community is likewise admissible as a hearsay exception. Fed. R.Evid. 803(21). Section 7.10(D) explains when reputation evidence is relevant. If relevant, then this specific hearsay exception renders the hearsay admissible.

2. Declarant Unavailable Exceptions (Fed.R.Evid. 806)

Some hearsay statements are only admissible if the declarant is unavailable to testify at trial. Fed.R.Evid. 804(a).

The "unavailability" of a witness includes situations in which the declarant:

- Is absent from the hearing and the proponent of the statement is unable to procure attendance through a subpoena or other process.
- Is unable to be present because of an existing physical or mental illness or death.
- Testifies to a lack of memory of the subject matter of the statement.
- Is exempted from testifying by a court ruling on the ground of privilege.

- Persists in refusing to testify despite a court order.

Hearsay statements that are admissible if the declarant is unavailable include:

- Former testimony,

- Statements against interest,

- Statements of personal or family history, and

- Dying declarations.

a. Former Testimony (Fed.R.Evid. 804(b)(1))

In a civil trial, the testimony given by a witness at a deposition or another hearing may be admitted if the party against whom the testimony is offered had an opportunity to previously examine the witness. The most common use of former testimony in a civil trial involves the introduction of deposition testimony because the lay or expert witness is unavailable. In criminal cases, this hearsay exception is less often applicable because of the defendant's constitutional right to cross-examine witnesses during the trial. Section 7.10(A) explains the introduction of prior testimony.

b. Statements Against Interest (Fed.R.Evid. 802(b)(2))

A statement made by a person contrary to that person's interests is admissible. The contrary interests include statements adversely affecting a person's pecuniary or proprietary interests or which tend to subject the person to civil or criminal liability. The rationale for this rule is that reasonable individuals do not make statements against their own interests unless those statements are accurate. This exception need only be used where the declarant is not a party. If a party makes such a statement, the statement is admissible as a party admission. See Section 4.8(F)(3).

Example:

In a civil case, the user of an addictive product has sued the manufacturer of the product. An employee of the manufacturer made a statement to an agent of the Food and Drug Administration. The plaintiff calls the FDA agent to testify.

Examining Attorney:

Q: What did Mr. Marlboro tell you when you investigated the claim?

Objecting Lawyer:

Objection. Hearsay.

Judge:

Overruled.

A: Mr. Marlboro told me that he and others routinely added candy to the tobacco in violation of company policy.

---

c. *Statements of Personal or Family History (Fed.R.Evid. 803(b)(4))*

Statements regarding the personal or family history of the declarant are admissible. These statements are generally allowed as long as the declarant was related to a person or intimately involved in a family and likely to have accurate information even though the declarant had no means of personally knowing the matter.

Example:

In a probate case, a daughter is called to testify to what her father had told her.

Examining Attorney:

Q: What did your father tell you about his family?

Objecting Lawyer:

Objection. Hearsay.

Judge:

Overruled.

A: My father told me he had one brother who had nine heads and that his name was Hydra.

---

d. *Dying Declaration (Fed.R.Evid. 803(b)(2))*

A statement concerning the cause or circumstance of the declarant's impending death which is made by the declarant who believes death is imminent is admissible. The rationale is that the declarant, who faces death, is telling the truth.

Example:

In a murder case, the victim's husband is called to testify by the prosecution.

Examining Attorney:

Q: After your wife was shot, what did you do?

A: I ran over and knelt next to her.

Q: What did she say?

Objecting Lawyer:

Objection. Hearsay.

Judge:

Overruled.

A: She said, "I'm not going to make it." And then she told me, "The butler did it."

---

3. *Residual Hearsay Exception (Fed.R.Evid. 803(24) and 804(5))*

Hearsay statements that are not covered by a specific hearsay exception may be admissible if:

- The statement is offered as evidence of a material fact,
- No other evidence exists which is more probative,
- Its admission will serve the interests of justice, and
- The offering party provides opposing counsel with prior notice of the introduction of such a statement.

This "residual" or "catch-all" exception to the hearsay rule may render other reliable, trustworthy hearsay admissible. This exception is useful in limited situations where no other rule or exception permits reliable and trustworthy hearsay to be admissible. This exception is not intended to and has not been interpreted by courts to make inadmissible hearsay admissible. The exception is reserved for unusual circumstances in which a reliable and trustworthy hearsay statement should be admissible in the interests of justice because no other exception covers the situation. For example, hearsay statements made by consumers who report their experiences with a product in a consumer survey may be deemed to be admissible under this residual exception.

4. *Multiple Hearsay (Fed.R.Evid. 805)*

A statement may contain more than one hearsay statement. This multiple form of hearsay is called "hearsay within hearsay." Each statement must be analyzed to determine whether there is multiple hearsay and whether each part of the statement fall within an exception or are defined as non-hearsay.

Example:

Curley sues Moe for civil assault. At trial, Curley testifies that "Moe said to me, 'I meant to poke you in the eyes because Larry said he was in a lot of pain because you had just slapped him.'" The attorney for Moe objects to this multiple hearsay. There are two statements within this testimony: the statement by Moe to Curley and the statement by Larry to Moe. The first statement — that of Moe to Curley — is a party admission and is admissible. See section 4.8(F)(3)(a). The second statement — that of Larry to Moe — is admissible as a hearsay exception, either as a present sense impression or as a statement of an existing physical condition. See Section 4.8(H)(1)(b). The entire statement is admissible.

A common situation of multiple hearsay occurs with documents. Documents introduced during trial commonly contain hearsay information. The document may contain admissible statements and inadmissible hearsay. Each document must be analyzed to determine which sentences, phrases, and words are admissible and which are not. See Section 8.6(B).

Example:

A plaintiff lays a foundation through a medical record custodian that a hospital record falls within a business record exception to the hearsay rule. See Section 4.8(H)(1)(c).

The witness is a medical record custodian, Patch Adams. The exhibit is the medical record of plaintiff Worf offered by the plaintiff. The witness testifies that he is the Director of the Emergency Room, that it is the business of the hospital to make such medical records, that this exhibit was made contemporaneously with the events recorded, and that the record was made in the regular course of the business of the emergency room. The record falls within the business record exception to the hearsay rule. Parts of the record may be admissible or inadmissible depending upon the application of hearsay exceptions. The record contains the following statements:

- A statement by Dr. Schutt: *"Administered alien steroids to the patient."* Admissible. Business record exception.

- A statement by Dr. MacNeil: *"Set patient's broken antenna in a cast."* Admissible. Business record exception.

- A statement by the plaintiff Worf: *"My third eye hurts."* Admissible. Statement by person made for purposes of diagnosis.

- A statement by the defendant Picard: *"I was warping around 2000 light years when I hit the rear end of his tractor beam."* Admissible. Party admission offered against that party.

- A statement by a bystander in the Twilight Zone: *"Wow, its (referring to the plaintiff) head was all covered with green blood right after the accident."* Admissible, by most judges. Present sense impression.

- A statement by a Wookie who observed the accident: *"Picard sure looked euphoric to me when I saw him later after the accident."* Inadmissible, by most courts. No exception applies.

---

§ 4.9   QUESTIONABLE OBJECTIONS

Certain objections — some of which are commonly made — are improper, inapplicable, inappropriate, or not recognized in a jurisdiction.

These improper objections vary among jurisdictions, and include the following:

Irrelevant, Immaterial, Incompetent. This broad objection may be inappropriate because it is too general. Irrelevancy is a proper ground for an objection. "Immaterial" is no longer a term recognized by the Federal Rules of Evidence. "Incompetent" refers to the ability of a witness to testify and not to specific questions or answers.

Improper and Unfair. This objection is too general and does not specify the ground of an objection. A reference to a more specific reason must be made, or this objection will usually be overruled.

Self-Serving. This objection is usually groundless. In a general sense, every item of evidence the opposing side attempts to introduce is self-serving, that is, it will serve that side's best interests and harm the other side's case.

Prejudicial. This objection is also improper, for reasons similar to the inappropriateness of the self-serving objection. It is not sufficient that evidence is prejudicial for it to be excluded, the evidence has to be "Unfairly prejudicial." See Fed.R.Evid. 403.

Invades the Province of the Jury. This objection may be too ambiguous to be useful. An expert witness can testify to an ultimate opinion; lay witnesses are able to testify to many common opinions. These admissible responses can be said to invade the province of the jury.

§ 4.10 OBJECTION ANALYSIS

The following lists provide a summary of trial objections and a worksheet to prepare for evidentiary objections.

Common Objections
IMPROPER FORM OF QUESTION

Leading
    FRE 611
        Lawyer Testifying

Multiple Questions
    FRE 611
        Compound Questions

Narrative
    FRE 611
        No Question Before
        Witness

Assuming Facts Not in Evidence
    FRE 611 & 701-704
        Inaccurate
        Hypothetical

Non-Responsive
    FRE 611
        Volunteered

Misstatement of Testimony
    FRE 611
        Mischaracterization of
        Evidence

Cumulative/Repetitious
    FRE 403 & 611
        Asked and Answered

Argumentative
    FRE 611
        Badgering

Vague
    FRE 401-403
        Ambiguous
        Confusing
        Misleading
        Unintelligible

Improper Impeachment
    FRE 613
        Collateral Issue

Beyond Scope
    FRE 613

Common Objections
EXCLUSIONARY RULES OF EVIDENCE

Relevancy
    FRE 401-411
        Irrelevant
        No Probative Value
        Unfairly Prejudicial
            Improper Character
            Improper Habit
            Subsequent Reme-
              dial Measures
            Offers of Compro-
              mise
            Payment of Medi-
              cal Expenses
            Plea Bargains
            Liability Insurance
            Religious Beliefs/
              Opinions

Privileges
    FRE 501
        Attorney/Client
        Doctor/Patient
        Spousal Testimony
        Marital Communica-
            tions
        Clergy/Penitent
        Trade/Business
         Secrets
        Informer Identity
        Governmental Informa-
        tion
        News Sources
        Other

Competence
    FRE 601-602
        Incompetent
        Lack of Personal
            Knowledge
        Lack of Memory

Foundation
    FRE 601-602
        Lack of Foundation

Lay Opinion
    FRE 701
        Impermissible Opinion
        Impermissible Conclu-
         sion
        Speculation

Expert Opinion
    FRE 702-705
        Unqualified Witness
        Impermissible Opinion

Authentication
    FRE 901-902
        Lack of Authenticity

Original Writings
    FRE 1001-1007
        Signs
        Independent Facts
        Collateral Matter
        Unauthentic Copy
        Non-genuine Original

Parole Evidence
        Statutory or Case Law

Criminal Constitutional Issues

Common Objections
SUMMARY HEARSAY ANALYSIS

Hearsay
    Declarant
        Not Under Oath
        Not Subject to Cross
        Credibility Not Observ-
            able

Definition FRE 801
    Offered to Prove Truth of
        Statement?
    Out-of-Court Statement?
    Assertive or Nonassertive?
    Non-propositions
    Verbal Acts
    Declarant Not Person

Non-hearsay 801(d)
    Party Admissions
    Prior Statements

Hearsay Exceptions
    Sense Impressions
        Present Sense Impres-
           sion 803(1)
        Excited Utterance
           803(2)
    State of Mind
        Existing Mental/Emo-
           tional/Physical
           Condition 803(3)
        Treatment Medical
           Statements 803(4)

Records/Documents/
    Writings
    Business Records 803(6)
    Public Records 803(8)
    Past Recollection
        Recorded 803(5)
    Vital Statistics 803(9)
    Absent Entries 803(7)
        &(10)
    Commercial Data
        803(17)
    Property Records
        803(14) & (15)
    Official Certificates
        803(11) & (12)
    Family Records
        803(13)
    Ancient Documents
        803(16)
    Learned Treatises
        803(18)
    Previous Convictions
        803(22)
    Other Judgments
        803(23)

Reputation
    Character 803(21)
    Family 803(19)
    General History 803(26)

Declarant Not Available
    Former Testimony 804(b)(1)
    Statement Against Interest
        804(b)(3)
    Personal History 804(b)(4)
    Dying Declaration 804(b)(2)
    Reliable Hearsay 803(25)
        & 804(b)(5)

FORM 4.1
OBJECTION PLANNING WORKSHEET

Case _____ File _____

Anticipated Objections to be Made by Adversary

Witness/ Exhibit	Evidence	Objection	Grounds for Objection (Rule/Statute Case Law)	Response to Objection	Other Sources of Evidence	Offer of Proof	Limited Admission

Anticipated Objections to Adversary's Evidence

Witness/ Exhibit	Evidence	Objection	Grounds for Objection (Rule/Statute Case Law)	Limited Admission	Curative Instruction

Pretrial Evidentiary Motions

Motions in Limine	Anticipated Ruling	Alternative Way to Introduce Evidence

CHAPTER 5

JURY SELECTION

REFLECTING ON ADVOCACY

A jury consists of twelve persons chosen to decide who has the better lawyer.

—Robert Frost

The audience is the most revered member of the theater ... Without an audience there is no theater ... They are our guests, our evaluators ... They make the performance meaningful.

—Viola Spolin

§ 5.1　INTRODUCTION

Jury selection is the first stage of the jury trial. During jury selection, the court selects prospective jurors from whom the lawyers will de-select those they do not want, leaving the panel that decides the case.

The primary purpose of jury selection is to identify and select jurors who can fairly determine a party's case. Voir dire, another name for jury selection, means to "speak the truth." The jurors answer questions asked by the judge, and in many jurisdictions, by the attorneys, to reveal their impartiality and fairness, biases, and prejudices.

Jury selection may be the first opportunity the attorney has to establish personal contact with prospective jurors and the only opportunity attorneys may have to enter into a dialogue with the jurors. During the remainder of the trial, the attorneys either speak to the jurors or present evidence through witnesses to the jurors.

The process of selecting jurors is actually a process of deselecting jurors. Attorneys on both sides attempt to remove jurors apparently unfavorable to their side or favorable to their opponent. The process has some limits. Some factors, such as race and gender, cannot be a reason for removal. Attorneys use peremptory challenges and, occasionally, motions to strike for cause to properly remove prospective jurors from the panel of jurors.

This process of deselection is a difficult task because of the limited amount of time available for jury selection. Attorneys are only able to obtain a relatively limited amount of information from jurors in attempting to make a determination about the jurors. It would take an extensive amount of questioning and a long period of time for attorneys to obtain enough information to make thoroughly informed judgments. With the limited amount of time available, the best an attorney can hope to accomplish is to obtain enough information to make a reasonable judgment.

This chapter explains jury selection procedures, how to prepare for and conduct jury selection, effective selection approaches, various types of jury questions, procedures for the removal of jurors, and strategies and tactics involved in this selection process.

A. Role of the Attorneys

The role of the attorney in jury selection varies among jurisdictions. In all jurisdictions, attorneys may bring motions to strike jurors for cause and may exercise peremptory challenges to remove jurors. In those jurisdictions where the judge asks all questions of the prospective jurors, the role of the attorney is limited to submitting proposed questions to be asked by the judge and to making the final decision to remove jurors from the panel. In jurisdictions where the attorneys may question the prospective jurors, the role of the attorney becomes much more extensive.

The process of asking questions of the jury panel involves a number of intricate skills. Attorneys direct questions to the prospective jurors and engage them in a dialogue about matters that often relate to their personal lives. The attorneys must make immediate, intuitive judgments regarding the nature and scope of questions, whether issues should be probed, and when some jurors should not be submitted to further questioning.

Jury selection is not as predictable or structured a process as other parts of the trial. The attorneys usually do not know the answers they will receive and must quickly assess biases and prejudices jurors may have, based on the answers to their questions. And the attorneys must continually assess the effect questions and answers have upon all prospective jurors and the group dynamics of the panel.

B. Client Participation in Jury Selection

The extent to which clients are involved in jury selection is a matter of personal preference. Many trial attorneys feel that the client's input is extremely valuable, while others seldom consult with the client. In deciding to what degree the client should be used as a resource the attorney should consider:

- The ability of the client to make informed decisions about jury selection,
- The underlying approaches that have been chosen for jury selection,
- The relationship with the client,
- The impression made on the jurors when an attorney and client "team" effort is demonstrated,
- The ramifications of a disagreement with the decision that the client has made about a certain juror, and
- The lawyer's belief in the proper role of a client in a case, and the corresponding ethical obligations involved.

C. Role of the Judge

The role of the judge varies among jurisdictions and the preferences of individual judges. In jurisdictions where the judges ask all the questions, some judges may ask only a limited number of questions, while other judges may ask many of the proposed questions submitted by the attorneys. In jurisdictions where the attorneys also ask questions, some judges may be actively involved in asking questions of the jurors while others may be more passive.

Active judges may limit their questioning to standard questions, allowing the attorneys to ask specific questions about the case. Passive judges may ask few, if any, questions, and permit the attorneys to conduct whatever questioning the attorneys believe appropriate.

D. *Familiarity With Procedures*

The advocate must become completely familiar with the jury selection procedures used by the judge. Prior to trial, the attorney may learn how a judge conducts jury selection by watching the judge conduct jury selection in other cases. Colleagues, clerks, and bailiffs are also sources of information about a judge's preferences for the jury selection process.

During the pretrial conference or immediately before jury selection begins, specific procedures for jury selection should be discussed thoroughly with the judge and opposing counsel. If the judge or opposing counsel suggests that jury selection be conducted in the "usual" way, the attorney should not presume to know what the "usual" way is, but should ask the judge to describe the procedures. There is a tendency by inexperienced attorneys to pretend they know how judges conduct jury selection in order to avoid revealing their inexperience. There is no standard way to conduct jury selection. Even the most experienced trial lawyers ask the judge to explain what procedures the judge prefers to follow, suggest alternative procedures, and request permission of the judge to conduct the jury selection process in a way that helps the party's case.

§ 5.2 OBJECTIVES OF JURY SELECTION

There are six objectives trial attorneys may try to achieve during the jury selection process:

- Obtain information to make challenges for cause;
- Obtain information to exercise peremptory challenges;
- Educate the jury about the case, facts, clients, parties, witnesses, and the law;
- Develop rapport with the jurors;
- Neutralize negative and build on positive juror attitudes, opinions, and beliefs; and
- Seek commitments from the jurors.

The extent to which the objectives can be achieved depends upon the rules of a jurisdiction, the practice of the judge, and the attorney's ability to question jurors.

A. *Support a Challenge for Cause Motion*

Questions concerning objective factors that establish obvious or apparent bias or prejudice on the part of a juror determine whether grounds exist to support a motion to challenge for cause. Areas of such questioning include: prior knowledge of the case, familiarity with the parties or attorneys, employment status, existing attitudes regarding issues in the case, and similar areas. Questions asked by the judges usually include these types of questions. Examples of such questions appear in Section 5.7(A).

B. *Exercise Peremptory Challenges*

These questions seek information about the jurors to discover obvious or apparent opinions, feelings or attitudes that may prejudice a juror against a party or bias a juror in favor of the opposing party. Areas of such questionings include all aspects about jurors including: their hobbies, what they do in their leisure time, literature they read, television or movies they watch, their family background, where they grew up, and other relevant bits of information about the person. Examples of such questions also appear in Section 5.7(A).

C. *Educate the Jury*

Attorneys may use jury selection to educate the jury about the facts, the client and parties, the witnesses, and the strengths and weaknesses of the case. Jury selection is the first opportunity the attorneys have to describe the case to the jurors. As explained in previous chapters, the first impression the jurors have about a case may significantly influence their verdict. Trial attorneys attempt to inform the jurors about aspects of the case through questions asked of the jurors. See Section 5.7(B).

Information questions may be asked that explain the theories of the case. Questions may also be asked that reveal persuasive facts supporting the story of the case. Weaknesses or problems in the case may include concerns that are applicable to all cases as well as those that are individual and specific to the case. Some case weaknesses include: the type of client (for example, a large corporation against a sole proprietor), the type of remedy (a substantial amount of money), the nature of the case (sexual harassment or criminal sexual abuse), the type of defense (consent or self-defense), the type of witness (a felon), and the facts involved (drugs). Problems that are specific to the case depend upon the particular circumstances of the case.

The attitudes and feelings of the jurors regarding these problems and weaknesses must be explored for several reasons. These topics are important areas to probe for prejudices that may significantly affect a juror's ability to be fair and impartial. An open discussion of these topics may reduce the chances that the jurors will use these weaknesses to adversely decide the case. Further, affirmatively revealing problems reduces the impact of the weaknesses and prevents the jurors from first hearing it from the opposing party. Finally, the questioning attorney may be able to obtain a commitment from the jurors to base their decision on all the evidence presented and not just on isolated bits of information.

Jury selection questions can be designed to anticipate and counter efforts by opposing counsel to educate the jury regarding case theories and weaknesses. Questions can be asked that explore the jurors' reactions to the other side's theory of the case and weaknesses. These questions may reveal biases jurors have in favor of the opposing side which may not be able to be remedied, requiring the removal of these jurors. Further, in situations where the opposing attorney conducts jury selection second, initially revealing the other side's case theories and weaknesses may change the perception the jurors have about the other side's case from a favorable perception to a neutral or negative perception.

D. Develop Rapport With the Jurors

Trial attorneys want the jurors to like, respect, and trust them, and to have a favorable impression of their client. These goals can be achieved through a dialogue of questions and answers, which establishes a rapport between the jurors and the attorneys. An attorney who engages in an effective conversation with jurors substantially increases the likelihood that the jurors will perceive the attorney to be caring, sincere, and honest. See Section 5.7(C).

E. Neutralize Negative and Build on Positive Juror Attitudes, Opinions, and Beliefs

The questioning process provides an opportunity to discover biases and prejudices and also may be used to overcome negative opinions, attitudes, and reactions. Questions can also build on positive feelings that the jurors may already have toward the case and client. See Section 5.7(D).

F. Obtain Commitments

An effective method of gaining support from jurors is to obtain their commitment to an issue in the case. Trial attorneys may seek to have jurors promise that they will not hold weaknesses in the case against the client, or that they will be fair and impartial, or that they will follow the law as explained to them by the judge. These commitments will, the lawyer hopes, guide the jurors during deliberations. Not all courts permit these commitments. See Section 5.7(E).

§ 5.3 PROCEDURE

Jury selection procedures are controlled by statutes, rules of procedure, local court practice, and the preferences of individual judges. This section briefly summarizes procedures followed in federal and state jurisdictions which will be described in more detail in subsequent sections of this chapter.

A. Jury Pool

Jurors are obtained from the community where the case is heard. The area of this community is usually the same as the venue boundaries of the court, such as the district or county boundaries where the court is located. The names of prospective jurors are obtained from public records including voter registration cards, driver's licenses, utility records, property documents, telephone directories, city directories, and tax records. The process used to identify potential jurors must meet constitutional standards, which require that the jury pool include individuals from all segments of the community and not exclude any class of people.

B. Juror Summons

The clerk of court (known as the court administrator in many jurisdictions) sends a summons to individuals living in the community selected to serve as jurors. The summons tells the prospective jurors to appear at the courthouse on a certain day and time and usually includes an explanation of how an individual may be excused from jury duty. A statute or court rule will typically list the legitimate reasons for which a juror may be excused, for example, severe physical illness, personal or family emergencies, or employment status (such as judges). Most jurisdictions reject common excuses (e.g., inconvenience, work) and require representative members of the community, including lawyers, to serve jury duty.

Jurors are ordinarily scheduled for jury duty for a set period of time, such as a few weeks. Jurors complete their jury service after this time period has elapsed or after they reach a verdict in a case for which they sat as a juror. Some individuals called for jury duty never serve as a juror because they are removed or because they are not needed.

C. Jury Orientation

Prospective jurors arrive at the courthouse on the scheduled day and time and typically complete a written information form. The clerk may review this information to determine whether any of the jurors should be excused because of personal or special employment situations. Many jurisdictions make the information forms available to the attorneys who will be selecting from among these prospective jurors. The clerk usually conducts an orientation program for the jury pool, including a lecture regarding jury duty, the distribution of a pamphlet explaining jury service, or the showing of a videotape or DVD describing the roles of jurors.

After orientation, the jurors may stay at the courthouse and wait to be called for a case or may leave for home or work. If they stay at the courthouse, they usually wait in a room where they may read, talk, play games or watch television. If they leave, they may be told to return on a specific day or may be contacted by the clerk in the future if they are needed for a case.

D.   *Jury Panel*

The clerk selects from the pool of individuals summoned for jury duty a panel of prospective jurors for a specific case. A bailiff or other court official escorts this panel to the courtroom in which the trial will occur and typically seats the prospective jurors in the back of the courtroom.

E.   *Number of Prospective Jurors*

The total number of prospective jurors in a panel usually includes the following: the number of jurors who will deliberate, plus one or more alternate jurors, plus the number of individuals equal to the peremptory challenges the attorneys may exercise, plus additional individuals to replace any juror who may be removed for cause. For example, a panel of prospective jurors in a civil case may include: the 6 jurors who will make up the six-member jury; 1 alternate juror or 2 alternates if the trial is expected to last several days; 4 additional persons who will be struck when the plaintiff and defendant each exercise their two peremptory challenges; and a few extra individuals who may replace the jurors who may be removed for cause, for a total of 14 jurors plus extras.

In other cases, the panel will consist of more jurors. If a case requires twelve jurors to deliberate, additional alternative jurors will sit and more peremptory challenges are provided each party. For example, in a criminal case, there may be a need for 12 jurors, a minimum of two alternates, eight more for possible peremptory challenges, and additional individuals for replacements for those removed by challenges for cause, totaling a minimum of 26 jurors plus extras.

F.   *Seating Prospective Jurors in the Courtroom*

The court clerk randomly selects prospective jurors from the pool by drawing their names from a box or drum and having them take a seat in the jury box. In some jurisdictions only those members of the pool selected to be prospective jurors are seated in the jury box to be questioned; the remainder return to the waiting room. In other jurisdictions, the remaining members of the jury panel remain seated in the back of the courtroom until they are needed, if at all, and then return to the jury waiting room. If more jurors are needed, they are obtained from the pool of jurors in the jury waiting room.

G.   *Preliminary Information About Panel*

A list of the prospective jurors may be available and provided to counsel, along with information about each of the individuals. This data may include their name, address, employment status, family status, and information obtained from the form completed during orientation. If the names of the prospective jurors are not provided to counsel, the attorneys must write down the names as the clerk calls their names. Most lawyers write down the phonetic pronunciation so they will be able to pronounce the names properly. If no preliminary information about the jurors is provided to counsel, questions should be asked by the judge or attorneys to obtain this preliminary information.

H. Jurors' Oath

The prospective jurors take an oath or affirmation, usually given by the clerk, to answer all questions asked of them truthfully and completely.

I. Preliminary Remarks

The judge ordinarily makes introductory remarks to the prospective jurors. These remarks typically include an explanation of the purpose and procedures of the jury selection process; an introduction of the parties, attorneys, and the court officials; a brief description of the case; and instructions regarding the role of jurors in the case. The nature and extent of these introductory remarks vary among jurisdictions and judges. The comments usually cover information needed by the prospective jurors to understand what is happening. The judge then typically asks questions to gain information from the prospective jurors about their familiarity with the parties and the attorneys, their knowledge of the case, and their previous jury trial experience.

Example (Judge):

Members of the Jury, this is a medical malpractice case. The plaintiff, Laura Fischer, is seated at the counsel table to your left, next to her attorney, Frank Galvin. The defendant, Wesley Brophy, is seated at the other table, next to his attorney, Ed Concannon, from the law firm of Concannon and Kaplan.

The plaintiff claims that the defendant negligently diagnosed and failed to properly treat her condition when she sought medical treatment from him for her severe headaches. The defendant denies he was negligent and asserts that the plaintiff did not tell him about the severity of her headaches. The plaintiff seeks to recover damages for the injuries and pain she has suffered as result of defendant's alleged negligence. Defendant denies he is responsible for those damages.

Q: Are any of you familiar with, or have any of you heard about, the incident that I described to you? Please raise your hand if you have.

A: (No affirmative responses).

Q: Are any of you familiar with, or do any of you know, any of the parties or attorneys that I have introduced to you?

A: (No affirmative responses).

As you know, I am Judge Anderson. Two other court officials who will be assisting me with this trial are Alvin Bednarz, who is the clerk of court, and Samantha Cabrara, who is the court reporter.

This part of the trial is the jury selection process. We need an impartial jury that can decide this case fairly. To determine which of you can be fair and impartial, I and the attorneys will be asking you some questions. We ask these questions to obtain information about your ability to sit as a juror in this case. You must answer the questions honestly and completely. We do not ask the questions to pry into your private lives but only to seek helpful information so that the parties in this case can obtain what you would want in this case if you were a party: a jury made up of fair and impartial individuals.

In some jurisdictions, the judge may decide not to make some or all of these comments, instead, allowing the first attorney to address the jury to make some of the preparatory remarks. An attorney who is first to make such remarks may gain an advantage by being able initially to establish some rapport with the jurors. The attorney who is second may then add whatever preparatory remarks the first lawyer did not cover or add other remarks about the case that were omitted.

§ 5.4   QUESTIONING THE PANEL

The panel of prospective jurors is questioned either by the judge and the attorneys or by the judge alone. This process, as explained earlier, varies among jurisdictions. The Federal Rules of Civil and Criminal Procedure and similar state rules provide judges with discretion in conducting jury selection. These rules give the court the authority to conduct the entire examination or to permit the parties or their attorneys to conduct the examination of prospective jurors. See, e.g., Fed.Rule Civ.Proc. 47(a) and Fed.R.Crim.Proc. 24(a).

A. *Questioning Exclusively by the Judge*

Judges ask all jury selection questions in about one-fifth of the state courts and approximately two-thirds of the federal courts. The attorneys may — and usually do — submit questions to the judge which the judge may ask. The rules in most jurisdictions require that the court allow the attorneys to submit proposed questions in writing or orally.

An advantage of the judge asking all the questions is efficiency. The jury selection process is shortened, often taking less than thirty minutes, because the attorneys are not given an opportunity to ask questions to extend the jury selection process. The disadvantages are that the judge does not know the case as well as the attorneys and therefore may not ask necessary questions; the jurors may be hesitant to answer some questions in a forthright manner because the judge is an authority figure; and the lawyers have little opportunity to work with the jurors to educate them, neutralize their attitudes, develop rapport with them, or obtain commitments from them.

After a judge asks the questions, the attorneys may request that the judge ask some clarifying or additional questions, making certain that the record contains a list of the questions proposed by the attorneys the judge did not ask. After the questioning has been completed, the attorneys may bring motions to strike for cause, which the judge may grant or deny, and then the attorneys are able to exercise their peremptory challenges. See Section 5.8.

B. *Questioning by Judge and Attorneys*

In most state courts and in some federal judicial districts, the judge and attorneys share the questioning. In these jurisdictions, the judge typically asks initial questions to determine grounds for challenges for cause, followed by questions from the attorneys to complete the jury selection process. The extent to which a judge is involved in the questioning of potential jurors depends primarily on the philosophy and preferences of the judge.

State court rules and procedures vary widely with regard to the specific ways jury selection is conducted. In major civil and criminal cases, the lawyers commonly conduct intensive and extensive examinations. In most civil cases, the judges often limit the scope and number of questions asked by the attorneys and set a time within which the jury selection process must be completed.

The advantage of this system of shared questioning is that the attorneys are able to obtain relevant information from the jurors in order to properly exercise their challenges and to establish rapport. The disadvantage is that the process is time consuming and attorneys may misuse the system by attempting to argue their case instead of obtaining information from the jurors. The attorneys make their challenges for cause during or after all the questioning has been completed and exercise their peremptory challenges after all the questions have been asked.

1. *Questions Directed to the Panel*

Ordinarily, jurors are questioned as a panel. The lawyers first ask general questions of the entire panel and then question individual jurors. It is important to determine just how those questions are phrased, which questions are directed to the entire panel, and which are asked of individual jurors. When jurors are questioned as a panel, the attorneys make their challenges for cause and exercise their peremptory challenges after all the questioning has been completed.

2. *Questions Directed to Individual Jurors*

In some courts, the attorneys individually question each prospective juror on the panel. The attorneys ask all questions of one prospective juror before questioning another member of the panel. After questioning an individual prospective juror, the attorneys make a motion to challenge for cause, exercise a peremptory challenge, or accept the juror. The attorney then questions the next prospective juror on the panel, and the process continues until the required number of jurors has been selected.

3. *Questions Directed to Individual Jurors Outside the Presence of the Panel*

Prospective jury members may be individually questioned by attorneys outside the presence of the other prospective jurors. In these cases one juror at a time is brought in the courtroom and questioned individually to prevent a response from prejudicing or influencing other members of the panel. The attorneys then make a challenge for cause, exercise a peremptory challenge, or accept the juror. Jury selection is completed when the required number of jurors have been selected. This time consuming process is not often used but is available in most jurisdictions for significant criminal cases and some major civil cases. Additional prospective jurors are added and questioned if the original panel of prospective jurors is insufficient in number because of successful challenges made for cause.

C. *Introductory Remarks by Attorneys*

In jurisdictions which permit the attorneys to ask questions, the lawyers are usually able to make some short introductory remarks about the case before beginning questioning. The scope of these remarks depends upon what the judge and opposing attorney have said to the jurors. The remarks can include identifying the client, the purpose of jury selection, and a concise explanation of the factual story and legal theories of the case.

Example (Plaintiff's Attorney):

Members of the Jury, I represent Maria Martinez, the plaintiff in this case, who sits here next to me. My name is Alex Rajharsha. Ms. Martinez, an accountant, is in court to obtain money from the defendant for breach of an employment contract that Ms. Martinez had with the defendant, entitling her to be paid a salary.

As the Judge has explained, I will be asking you some questions to obtain information regarding the issues in this case. Both sides need to know your attitudes and feelings regarding these issues in order to determine that you will be fair and impartial. My questions are not intended to make you uncomfortable or nervous, although it is normal and natural for you to feel that way because we all are nervous when we are in court. If you do not understand a question I ask, please tell me and I will rephrase the question and make it understandable. I will be asking some questions directed to all of you and I will be asking some questions directed to individuals. If you have any information, regarding any question that I ask, please raise your hand or answer the question.

It is improper for an attorney to make argumentative comments during the introductory remarks to jury selection.

Example (Improper Comments):

This case is about an extremely hardworking and trustworthy employee, Bob Cratchit, who is the poor plaintiff who had to sue Scrooge to obtain his meager salary. Bob signed a valid and enforceable employment contract with the very rich defendant, who wrongfully and unfairly has refused to pay Mr. Cratchit the salary he rightfully deserves. At the end of this case, we are certain you will right this terrible wrong.

D. *Mechanics*

1. *Presence of Judge and Reporter*

While most judges are usually present during the jury selection process, some may leave the bench while the jury is being questioned. In some jurisdictions a court reporter may not record the jury selection, and the judge may not be present to monitor the process. When there is no record of the questions being asked or when the judge is not in the courtroom, it is more difficult to control the questioning by opposing counsel. An attorney should usually request that a court reporter make a record of the questioning and that the judge remain in the courtroom.

2. *Attorney Movement*

The lawyers may be permitted to walk around while questioning jurors or may be required to remain at a lectern or at counsel table. The physical arrangement or the acoustics of the courtroom may prevent movement or require the lawyers to move to a particular location so they can be heard.

3. *Order of Questioning*

In many jurisdictions, defense counsel is the first attorney to ask questions, followed by the plaintiff/prosecutor. Other jurisdictions have the plaintiff/prosecutor go first, followed by the defense. Knowing who goes first is obviously important. An attorney who plans to ask many preliminary questions and then realizes that the other side gets to ask those questions first may be left without much to ask. As a result, the attorney may look unprepared or be unable to accomplish specific objectives.

4. Discussion of Law

Generally, a discussion of the law by the attorneys is not permitted, although what is permitted varies among judges. An inappropriate discussion of the law may result in a reprimand from the judge.

5. Amount of Time Available

Some judges strictly limit the amount of time the lawyers are permitted to question the jury. Even if the court does not have strict time limitations, there is a common sense tolerance level that restricts the amount of time spent on questioning. This tolerance level varies, depending on the seriousness of the case, the interest factors provided by the case, any pretrial publicity, the lawyer's ability, and the patience and schedule of the judge.

6. Open Courtroom

The press and the public are always permitted in the courtroom during the jury selection process, as well as during all other stages of the trial. The judge rarely considers setting limits on who may be in the courtroom, and then only in those cases where there is an overriding interest that requires protection through privacy. The constitutional right of a defendant in a criminal case and the substantial interest of the public and press makes the presumption of openness extremely difficult to overcome.

7. Jury Selection Materials

Effective advocates organize and have readily available the materials they need for jury selection. This information includes the questions to be asked, a summary of the case theories, a list of witnesses and exhibits about which the jurors may be questioned regarding their knowledge, information about the jurors gathered from questionnaires completed by the jurors, the law regarding challenges for cause and peremptory challenges, and objections that might be made during jury selection.

8. Recording Information During Jury Selection

The lawyer or co-counsel must usually take notes and record information obtained from juror interviews. This information may include observations of the juror's behavior and dress, juror responses to questions, and other factors which may help to rate prospective jurors as favorable or unfavorable. The extent of the note taking depends upon the lawyer's approach and the desired objectives.

Note taking can also create some problems during jury selection. It may unnecessarily interfere with and delay asking questions. Some jurors may be suspicious, bothered or offended by note taking. Overly extensive note taking can distract the lawyer from observing and listening to the jurors.

Notes should be taken in an organized manner. A large number of written notes containing excessive information may be difficult to organize and impossible to apply. A recording system should be designed so that there is sufficient room for all relevant information, and so all notes can be easily reviewed. Some lawyers develop a shorthand method that is neither distracting nor offensive, while others do not take notes at all, preferring instead to pay closer attention to what the jurors say and how they say it. Co-counsel, an assistant, or the client may also take notes during the process, allowing the trial attorney to ask questions without having to be concerned about note taking.

A jury chart is indispensable as a means to record information about the jurors. See Form 5.1. A chart used to record information may be constructed as the court clerk reads the names of the prospective jurors, or the information to create the chart may be provided by the court clerk in advance. Information obtained during jury selection can be recorded by using abbreviations, symbols, or initials. For example, the letter "M" can signify married, and the letter "S" can signify single. Symbols can be used to rate prospective jurors.

§ 5.5   JURY SELECTION QUESTIONS

A. *Types of Questions*

The scope and type of jury selection questions depend on what the lawyer wishes to accomplish with the questions. The wording of the questions also depends on what questions the judge has already asked the jurors, what information is already available to the lawyer, and whatever the attorney believes is necessary to achieve the objectives of jury selection.

There are several types of questions the lawyer may ask:

- Open-ended questions,
- Close-ended questions,
- General questions to the entire panel,
- Specific questions directed to the entire panel,
- General questions to an individual juror, and
- Specific questions directed to an individual juror.

1. *Open–Ended Questions*

Open-ended questions give jurors a chance to talk in their own words and to express their own opinions.

Examples:

Q: Mary Tyler Moore, what do you do on a typical evening in the newsroom?

Q: What do you like to do in your spare time away from television?

FORM 5.1
JUROR INFORMATION

Name _____

Address _____

Approximate age/
    demeanor/dress _____

Knowledge about case _____

Knowledge about attorneys/ parties/witness _____

Occupation _____

Employer _____

Education _____

Marital status _____

Spouse's occupation/employer _____

Children _____

Past claims/lawsuits _____

Similar case experience _____

Past/present jury duty _____

    Civil _____

    Criminal _____

Opinion about case _____

Attitude toward client/case _____

Hardships _____

Other _____

2. *Closed Ended Questions*

Closed ended questions gather a relatively small amount of information from a juror and they are phrased to obtain a "yes" or "no" response. They are generally used to obtain factual information, to obtain commitments, and to educate the juror.

Example:

Q: Ms. Segal, have you had any business dealings with Mr. Capone?

A: Yes.

Q: Have you been at his store here in Mercer?

A: Yes.

---

3. *General Questions to the Entire Panel That Require an Explanatory Response*

Examples:

I am going to ask some general questions about the Hockey Hall of Fame and follow up with some more specific questions.

Q: How many of you have visited the Hockey Hall of Fame?

Q: Tell us about your experience at the Hall of Fame.

---

4. *Specific Questions Directed to the Entire Panel Requiring "Yes" or "No" Answers and That May Require Follow-up Questions*

Examples:

Q: Have any of you attended a presidential auction?

Q: Have any of you bought anything at a presidential auction?

---

5. *General Questions to Individual Jurors Requiring Narrative, Explanatory Responses*

Examples:

Q: Ms. Benz, you said that you were involved in an automobile accident. Please tell us about that experience.

Q: Mr. Du Bois, you raised your hand when I asked if any of you knew any members of the union. How do you know someone with the union?

6. *Specific Questions Directed to Individual Jurors Requiring "Yes" or "No," or Short Explanatory Responses*

Examples:

Q: Both parties want this case decided not on sympathy but on the evidence presented to you. You will be able to do that, won't you?

A: Yes.

Q: Ms. Kachina, you said you attended ceremonial dances on the reservation, did you participate in the dances?

A: Yes.

Q: About how many ceremonial dances did you attend?

B. *Selecting Types of Questions*

The type of questions that should be asked depends upon the preference of the lawyers, the responses of the jurors, the nature of the case, the time available for juror interviews, and the purpose for asking the questions. General questions directed to the panel as a whole are usually appropriate if "yes" or "no" answers or short explanations are expected. Specific questions directed to an individual juror may be asked as follow-up questions or to probe new areas.

The jurors also need to know how they are expected to respond to questions. The lawyer, particularly in asking questions of the entire panel, should make clear whether the jurors should respond verbally or by raising their hand.

Some types of questions should be directed to the panel as a whole, while other types should be asked of jurors individually. The nature of the questions and the anticipated answers often determine when and what types of questions should be asked of jurors. Attorneys often ask questions of the entire panel during the beginning of the jury selection process, postponing individual questions until they establish some rapport with the jurors. Questions seeking grounds for challenges for cause are commonly asked of all members of the panel because the questions are less threatening when every juror is asked the question. Questions involving sensitive or personal matters may also be more effectively directed to the entire panel because the impact of the questions will be less intrusive on individual jurors.

Questions should be asked in a manner that involves all jurors. A mix of general and specific questions usually maintains the attention of the entire panel. All jurors should be treated equally. However, if a lawyer knows for certain that a juror will be struck, then it may not be necessary to question that juror in the same way the other jurors are questioned.

C. Concluding Questions

The concluding questions of jury selection should elicit a positive and affirmative response that supports a verdict for the client.

Example (Civil Plaintiff):

Members of the Jury, after we present evidence proving Ms. Vegas' case, will each of you be able to return a verdict in favor of the plaintiff?

Example (Civil Defendant):

Will each of you agree that you will not decide this case until you have heard all the evidence, and that you will keep an open mind and wait until we have presented our case on behalf of Mr. Kingpin, the defendant, before reaching any decision?

---

§ 5.6   THEORIES OF JURY SELECTION QUESTIONING

Successful trial lawyers have developed their own jury selection theories to determine whether a juror will be favorable or unfavorable. Theories used to determine which jurors will be biased or prejudiced are almost as diverse as the number of lawyers who appear in court. Whatever theory is used, it is important to remember that jury selection theories are merely guides and are by no means conclusive.

Listing all potential jury selection theories is impossible. Attorneys develop and employ their approaches based largely on their experience, judgment, intuition, and feelings. These variables produce approaches not necessarily based on objective, discernible factors. Many theories do not have consistent validity applicable to each individual sitting as a juror, and particular approaches should not be used without a great deal of consideration given to their predictive accuracy.

The following paragraphs present several theories used by trial lawyers in removing prospective jurors.

A. Impressionistic Evaluations

This approach relies largely on the intuition of the attorney and frequently on the intuition of the client as well. The attorney, or the attorney and the client, determine which jurors the attorney and client like, and which jurors seem to like the client, the case, and the attorney. These intuitive judgments are based upon the attorney's subjective assessment of each juror. It may be based on the simple analysis of "I like this juror" and "This juror appears to like me."

B. Generalizations and Stereotypes

Many attorneys select jurors based upon generalizations regarding people. The attorney relies upon selective characterizations to predict how a juror will react and vote. Some of these generalized stereotypes may have merit (bank officers are often fiscally conservative); other stereotypes may be speculation (rural inhabitants dislike corporations); still other stereotypes are nonsensical (obese individuals whose grandparents came from Crete favor defendants). The stereotyping of an individual based on generalizations applicable to a class of people can be detrimental or helpful, depending on the validity of the stereotype.

C. Character and Personality Traits

Some attorneys identify favorable jurors based upon the apparent character and personality traits of the juror. The attorney obtains information and observes the jurors to determine their character and personality traits. The attorney then determines which of these jurors may be most favorable to a client. Examples of character and personality traits include: how authoritative or assertive the juror is, how good a communicator or listener the juror is, and how honest and open the juror appears.

D. Nonverbal Behavior

Attorneys may rely on the nonverbal behavior revealed by jurors in addition to their verbal responses to assess their real attitudes and feelings. They closely observe the jurors for positive and negative body language and attempt to interpret this behavior in assessing the jurors' biases and prejudices.

E. Improper Theories

It is improper to rely on some factors to select or remove jurors. It is unconstitutional to use race or gender as the sole or primary reason in choosing jurors. Other immutable characteristics of a person may also be illegal factors in some jurisdictions. If a prohibited factor appears to be the reason why a juror is being struck, the advocate has the burden to establish the primary, legitimate reasons why a juror is being removed.

F. Jury Profile

This approach is based upon a jury profile developed in advance of trial to indicate in general terms how a particular juror will make a decision in a case based on generalizations from a larger group in society. A jury profile describes the characteristics of the ideal, mythical juror. This juror is someone who will like a client or case and return a winning verdict. Some lawyers do not find this procedure worthwhile because it is too speculative, and they feel that the chances of finding an ideal juror on the panel is remote. However, many lawyers believe it is worthwhile to create a profile which can be used as a reference point to evaluate the prospective panel of jurors.

A psychologist, sociologist, or an expert with experience in jury selection may help design a juror profile. If sufficient economic resources are available, this approach might be useful in supplementing the attorney's assessment of prospective jurors. This information may also be obtained less expensively from books, articles, and treatises. A jury profile may be created by reviewing the factual and legal theories, considering how jurors might identify with the client, witnesses, and the attorney, and predicting how jurors might react to the issues in a case. Jurors are then selected from the panel who most closely match the characteristics of people who identify with the case theory, the participants, and the issues.

A jury profile of unfavorable jurors may also be designed. This anti-juror profile corresponds to the opponent's favorable, mythical juror. Characteristics and traits of individuals who are least likely to identify with the case theory, the participants, and the issues are identified. During jury selection then, prospective jurors who have these characteristics and traits are challenged or struck from the panel. A jury profile should not be used to replace the responsibility of the attorney to select jurors.

G. Social Science Data

Some attorneys, in cases where clients have the resources to pay for the development of this information, rely on social science data to select jurors. This approach identifies demographic characteristics that favorably correlate with a case theory. Social scientists research appropriate demographic factors and sample the community to determine which jurors may have these characteristics. Information about the juror's financial status, job, marital status, neighborhood, and hobbies reveal information which may match these favorable demographic factors. This approach relies upon the expertise of social scientists, however, and many lawyers are reluctant to rely extensively upon the judgment of non-lawyers in selecting jurors.

§ 5.7 QUESTIONS AND APPROACHES TO ACHIEVE OBJECTIVES

The judge has discretion to allow or disallow questions depending upon the purpose and nature of the question. In all jurisdictions where the attorneys may ask questions, the attorneys generally have a right to ask questions about possible grounds for a challenge for cause. In these jurisdictions, the attorneys also have a right to ask reasonable questions to obtain information needed to exercise their peremptory challenges.

Judges have broad discretion to permit questions that serve the other jury selection objectives. Many judges allow the attorneys to ask a wide range of questions that educate, develop rapport with, and obtain commitments from jurors. Other judges restrict the scope of these questions. Still other judges prohibit these types of questions. The attorney should obtain information about what limitations the judge places on the questions. See Section 5.4. The Almanac of the Federal Judiciary provides information about federal judges.

Many jurisdictions limit jury selection questions to areas that establish bias or prejudice and prohibit or limit questions designed to educate or indoctrinate prospective jurors. However, many jurisdictions do permit attorneys to question jurors to achieve broader objectives. Categorizing jury selection questions into those that are designed to show bias or prejudice and those that are designed to educate or indoctrinate the jury is often difficult. Many questions serve multiple purposes, and legitimate questions in all jurisdictions designed to elicit bias and prejudice may also properly serve to achieve broader objectives.

Effective jury selection questioning should follow some common sense communication guidelines. Attorneys should:

- Engage the jurors in conversation.

- Be receptive and responsive.

- Encourage the jurors to give complete and honest answers.

- Listen carefully to answers.

- Observe nonverbal demeanor.

- Reward helpful answers through verbal and nonverbal responses.

A.　*Obtaining Information*

1.　Information About Jurors

In order to identify favorable jurors, the lawyer should collect and review as much information as possible about the prospective jurors. In most cases, the attorneys do not know who the jurors will be until the jurors arrive in the courtroom, limiting the opportunity to obtain preliminary information. In some jurisdictions, information about the prospective panel of jurors may be obtained before trial. Addresses of the panel provide generalized information concerning the neighborhood, home, and socioeconomic status of the prospective jurors. Information about size of family, occupation, prior jury duty, and other background information may also be useful.

In jurisdictions that provide advance information and with a client that has substantial resources available, an investigation may be conducted of the prospective jury members. Investigators may contact neighbors and friends to gather information about panel members, but no personal contact may be made directly with prospective jurors. In some jurisdictions, books are maintained about jurors' prior jury service. Prosecutors, criminal defense counsel, plaintiff's personal injury trial lawyers, or defendant's insurance attorneys may also maintain information about jurors, particularly in smaller communities.

2. *Information About Jury Duty*

Trial attorneys need to review the jury orientation program to discover what information prospective jurors receive before they appear in the courtroom. This may be done by obtaining a copy of the written information, by watching the film or videotape, or by talking with court personnel. Where jurors wait during jury duty and what they do during this wait may also influence their perception about the legal system. The trial attorney should become familiar with the waiting room, what kind of magazines or books the jurors have access to, what kind of card games or other activities the jurors participate in, and where jurors are likely to have lunch. The more the attorney learns about what happens to the jurors prior to jury selection, the better able the attorney is to ask appropriate questions.

3. *Information from Observations of Jury Activity in the Courtroom*

a. *Prospective Jurors in the Courtroom*

The trial attorney should begin observing the jurors as they enter the courtroom. The lawyer should observe the appearance of the jurors, including their conduct, any apparent physical discomforts, with whom they talk, and whether individuals appear talkative, quiet, nervous, or alone. This first impression may be helpful in making a final selection, as well as in asking questions.

b. *Prospective Juror Associations*

Some of the prospective jurors may have spent a substantial amount of time together and may have formed friendly or unfriendly relationships. Particular attention should be paid to these relationships, as they will affect the cohesiveness of the jury. Attention should also be paid to those jurors who appear to emerge as leaders, as they may influence the other jurors.

c. *Juror Body Language and Appearances*

Nonverbal cues prior to jury selection and during the selection process may help determine if a juror is more or less favorable. Did the juror make more eye contact with you or your opponent? Did the juror appear to be more interested or alert during your questioning or the other side's questions? Did the juror seem more at ease in answering your questions or the other side's questions? Jurors who appear to be impressed with the courtroom, the judge, and the court setting may be indicating a willingness to follow instructions more readily than someone who is familiar with the system.

d. *Observations by Team Member*

Another trial team member may sit in the courtroom to observe the jurors during jury selection and advise trial counsel with regard to those observations. This individual, not occupied with asking questions, has a greater opportunity to observe the conduct and nonverbal behavior of the jurors.

4. Factual Information

If a question seeks specific information, the question should be phrased to generate a specific response. There are several areas of questions that should be considered with every juror. The following examples provide sample questions that may be asked during jury selection.

Examples:

Employment Status

Q: Where do you work, Maynard G. Krebs?

Q: What kind of work do you do?

Q: Do you supervise other people?

Q: How many people do you supervise?

Q: What are your responsibilities as a supervisor?

Q: How do you feel about being a supervisor?

Family Status

Q: You said you have five children. What is the age of the oldest? Youngest?

Q: Are the other children in school?

Q: Do you ever get the chance to help out at school?

Q: What does your oldest child do?

Educational Level

Q: After high school, did you take any courses at any other school?

Q: Have any of you taken courses where the law has been taught or discussed?

Q: What kinds of courses were they?

Life Experiences

Q: What do you do on a typical Saturday? Sunday?

Q: What are your hobbies?

Q: What do you do with your vacation time?

Previous Jury Experience

Q: Have you ever sat as a juror before?

Q: What kind of a case was it?

Q: Was the jury able to reach a verdict in the case?

Q: Do you have any positive or negative feelings about our system of justice based on your experience?

Experience With the Court System

Q: Have any of you ever been involved as a plaintiff or defendant in a case?

Q: Have any of you been involved as a witness in any case?

Q: Have you ever appeared in court for any reason?

Q: Would you please tell us about that experience?

Q: Does that experience affect how you may consider this case?

Experience in Fields Relating to the Case

Q: Do you have any relatives or friends who are familiar with the field of medicine?

Q: Do you know anyone or have any of you ever been the victim of a crime?

Knowledge of case

Q: Because you have heard of the defendant company, do you have any feelings, one way or the other, that may affect your judgment about my client which is a corporation?

---

5. *Relationships With Parties, Lawyers, and Witnesses*

These questions are often asked by the court in the initial process of jury selection. Counsel may inquire further if the jurors have some additional information.

6. *Opinions and Attitudes*

These questions seek opinions and attitudes of the jurors, may be phrased either as open-ended or leading questions.

Examples:

Q: Have you heard about the concept of a living will?

Q: Have you heard about the concept that people, before they die, can choose to have life support ended if they have a terminal illness and there is no hope for continued life?

Q: The fact that this case involves Eden Prairie Hope Hospital which employs people in this community will not influence you one way or the other in reaching a verdict based on the facts, will it?

---

7. *To Demonstrate a Bias*

Example:

Q: Ms. Anton, you have told us that it would be very difficult for you if your child were to marry someone of a different race and that your feelings about race are very strong feelings. You know that this is a race discrimination case. Because your feelings are so strong, would you agree that it would be impossible for you to be neutral as you evaluate the evidence in this case?

8. *Pretrial Publicity*

Newspapers, pictures, and television and radio may have an influence on the ability of the jurors to listen to the case.

Examples:

Q: What do you remember seeing on television or reading in the newspapers about this case, Ms. Hearst?

Q: How do you feel about the defendant in this case based on what you have heard?

The words people use to describe the publicity may reveal their attitudes and provide a basis for asking further questions about their views.

B. Educating the Jury

Questions may be asked that provide information to the jurors. Questions can be designed to tell the jurors a great deal about the evidence, the law, and other facets of the case.

1. *About the Case and Facts*

Examples:

Q: Are you all aware, from what the judge told you, that this is not a criminal case involving Ms. Simpson, but is a civil case?

Q: Do you understand that civil cases differ from criminal cases?

Q: In this case the plaintiff is saying that the defendant unlawfully caused the death of a person, her husband, Homer. Do you understand that this is unlike a criminal case, and in this case no one will go to jail if you find that the defendant is responsible?

2. About the Clients or Parties

Example:

Q: The judge asked you if you knew Mr. Baden Powell, who is the plaintiff in this case. He is a widower. His wife, Lady Baden Powell, died last fall. She was very active in community affairs in our city. Did any of you know her?

Example:

Q: The plaintiff in this case emigrated from Vietnam thirty-five years ago. Because of that move, he lost everything and had to start anew in this country. The plaintiff was a doctor in Vietnam but because of our medical regulations he cannot practice medicine. He has taken laboring jobs to provide for his family. Do any of you know anyone or had any experience with someone who has moved from another country and has had those types of problems?

Example:

Q: Coco Chanel is a fashion designer and consultant and she will testify in this case as an expert witness. Have any of you read any of her books or attended any of her seminars?

---

3. About the Witnesses

a. Lay Witness

Example:

Q: Cass Gilbert is the only eyewitness who will be testifying in this case. He is an architect, and he will tell you that after work he had two bottles of beer and left the bar to go home. Then he saw the accident. Do any of you doubt that someone like Mr. Gilbert who has had two beers can observe an accident clearly and remember it?

---

b. Expert Witness

Example:

Q: Dr. Rose Mayo will be testifying and will be telling you that she is a graduate from the University of Minnesota Medical School and is an orthopedic surgeon. Will all of you be able to weigh her expert testimony based on her qualifications, training, and experience, and not be influenced because Dr. Mayo is from a different part of the country?

4. About the Law

a. Burdens of Proof

The different degrees of proof — "beyond a reasonable doubt" and "preponderance of evidence" — are unfamiliar terms to many people. Since it is easy for jurors to be confused as to the different standards of proof, it is very important that they understand the differences from the beginning so they do not apply the wrong standards.

Examples:

Q: In a criminal case the defendant does not have to take the stand and testify. Do you understand that?

Q: Do you understand that as Agatha Christie sits here in this courtroom, she is presumed innocent?

Q: It may be that some people might consider the defendant guilty if she does not testify. Will you be able to set aside any such thought and follow the law which allows the defendant not to testify?

Example:

Q: Do you understand that the burden of proof in a civil case is by a preponderance of the evidence which is less than the burden of proof beyond a reasonable doubt that you might have heard about in a criminal case?

b. Liability

Examples:

Q: One of the issues in this case is whether the defendant Hand Gun Holster Company is strictly liable for what happened. Has anyone heard of strict liability?

Q: What that term means is that in this case, if the holster was defective, whether or not the company that made the holster knew about the defect or not, that company would still be responsible for the injuries caused by the defect. Does that general concept bother any of you?

Q: Do you think it is unreasonable to say that the company that made the product is responsible for the deaths of others caused by the defect, even if it didn't intend to cause any injuries or was unaware of a problem?

c. Defenses

Examples:

Q: In this case the defendant Mandrake the Magician is going to tell you that he was somewhere else with his friends and couldn't have committed the crime. That is called an alibi. Are all of you familiar with that term?

Q: Do you think it's likely that a person can be accused of something and actually be the wrong person?

---

d. Elements

Jury selection also provides the opportunity for the lawyer to teach the jurors about elements of a case.

Examples:

Q: Do you understand that in any case where the truth is out there and someone has been killed, there are a number of different possible offenses that describe what might have happened?

Q: Do you understand that the term "manslaughter" is a lesser offense than first-degree murder?

---

5. *About Weaknesses and Strengths in the Case*

The attorney may acknowledge weaknesses during jury selection. If dealt with in a straightforward manner, there will be no surprise and the later effect of the weaknesses will be diminished.

Example:

Q: Mehmet Robie has a criminal record. Three years ago he was convicted of burglary. He will take the stand and tell you when he testifies on his own behalf that his days of being a "cat burglar" have long been over. Will you be able to decide the case on the evidence presented in court about what happened in this case and not what happened five years ago?

C. *Developing Rapport With the Jury*

Jury selection questions must be asked in a way that develop a positive rapport with the jury. The trial lawyer who makes a favorable impression during jury selection benefits from the lasting effect of this impression. Jurors' initial perceptions of the lawyer and the client influence the ability of the attorney to persuade the jury as the trial progresses.

Rapport can be created and developed in several ways. The attorney must project a sincere and honest attitude in the case. The attorney must also direct questions to the jurors to make them feel important, while also paying attention to the jurors in an attempt to reduce their anxiety. A respectful attitude, a caring approach, appropriate eye contact, attentive listening, and a genuine interest help reduce anxiety and build rapport.

The lawyer must also be well prepared. Poorly phrased questions, inappropriate inquiries, and aimless questioning portray the attorney as ill-prepared and unprofessional. The more comfortable and at ease the jurors become with the attorney and client, the more attention and concentration they can devote to the case.

1. Developing Rapport Begins When the Jurors Enter the Courtroom

The jurors will be watching the attorney and the client as soon as they come into the courtroom. The preparation, setting up the tables, and orienting the clients and witnesses to the courtroom should occur before the jurors enter to avoid appearing disorganized or unprepared. The jurors will be watching the lawyer, the client, and witnesses as they deal with other persons in the courtroom. They may even watch the attorneys as they discuss matters in the hallway and as they talk to clerks, bailiffs, and other court personnel. The attorney must appear comfortable and confident in the courtroom in front of the jurors.

2. Properly Addressing the Panel

Jurors should be addressed by their last names. Using the appropriate form of address or title for each juror is important. While some jurors may be more sensitive to this issue than others, every effort should be made to make sure of the juror's preference. A military person may expect to be addressed by a title such as "Captain" or "Sergeant." A scientist or medical doctor may prefer to be addressed by the title "Doctor." Attorneys should ask the jurors their preference, or the attorney could request that the judge or clerk obtain that information before the lawyer questions the jurors.

3. Using Body Language and Appearances to Develop Rapport

Attorneys and clients must consider how they initially wish to appear and whether they appear that way in the eyes of the jurors. Section 1.7 discussed considerations of physical appearance, clothing style, gestures, body language, and related considerations. These factors should be used to effectively enhance rapport with the jurors.

4.   *Using Questions to Develop Rapport*

a.   *Manner of Asking Questions*

Questions should be delivered with a calm voice using appropriate pauses and interesting modulation. This helps the attorney appear interested in the question as well as the juror's answer. Questions that are read or delivered in a monotone voice appear to be routine questions and, while they may get some information, they do little for developing positive rapport.

b.   *Recognizing Jurors' Discomfort / Anxiety*

If the attorney recognizes that a juror is uncomfortable or anxious about being questioned, the attorney should sincerely acknowledge that juror's discomfort and should attempt to help the juror relax. However, overly solicitous behavior should be avoided because it will probably appear insincere.

Example:

Q: It appears to me that you are troubled with the question I've asked you. I'll rephrase it so it makes better sense.

---

c.   *Questions That Permit the Juror to Clarify or Expand on Previous Statements*

The attorney will appear to be receptive and sensitive to a juror's problem when the juror is given a chance to clarify an answer or save face.

Example:

Q: Earlier I asked you some questions about damages and you indicated that you would award damages to someone who has proved pain and suffering. However, later you said you felt that it would be hard to judge pain because people feel pain so differently. Will you be able to make a fair judgment about the pain the plaintiff suffered in this case, Ms. Prozac?

---

d.   *The Style and Tone of the Questions*

A juror may be bothered by an awkward question or by the tone in which a question is asked. The lawyer must accept the blame for asking that kind of question and rephrase it, rather than implying that the juror is at fault.

Example:

Q: What I am really trying to ask is prior to the last question that I asked you, before I was speaking to you about the following information ... I'm sorry, that just didn't make sense. Let me try it again, Ms. Malaprop.

5. Dealing With Hostile Jurors

Questioning a juror who is obviously hostile or angry with either the client, the case, or the attorney is difficult. One approach is simply not to ask a hostile person any questions, with the idea that the person will be removed later on a peremptory challenge. In so doing, the attorney may avoid the risk of a hostile juror influencing other jurors through negative answers to questions. However, an open, direct approach to anger or hostility may go a long way toward developing rapport with the other jurors, or may work towards diffusing the anger so that the juror becomes an asset rather than one who has to be removed with a peremptory challenge. If this approach fails, a basis for a challenge for cause may be established by showing the hostile juror to be prejudiced against the case, the client, or the attorney.

Example:

Q: Ms. Nightingale, you appeared to be angry when I asked you about lawsuits against surgeons. You told us that you thought these doctors were a bunch of overpaid prima donnas.

A: Yes, I did.

Q: Do you ever go to a doctor yourself for any kind of treatment?

A: I've been to some doctors, but never a surgeon.

Q: Have you ever been treated in a hospital?

A: Fortunately not.

Q: Now, you have told us that you have children. Have they ever gone to a doctor?

A: I've never taken them. My husband does.

Q: You haven't taken them to have shots or any kind of preventive treatment or health care?

A: I don't like dealing with doctors.

Q: Would you agree that it would be very difficult for you to be fair to a doctor and listen to all the evidence before making up your mind?

A: I can't trust what they say. I don't believe them.

6. Avoid Embarrassing Jurors

In some cases, attorneys must ask questions that are personal and potentially embarrassing to the jurors because the answers to those questions may be vital to the selection process. Attorneys must be sensitive to the juror's situation and the possible reaction to personal inquiries. Questions should be worded carefully in order to minimize adverse reactions on the part of the jurors.

Example:

Q: Mr. Marx, if you were out on the street one day and a news reporter stopped you and asked you whether you saw yourself as a liberal or conservative, how would you describe yourself and why?

Q: Ms. Brooks, if you had the chance to go back and see your favorite high school teacher and that teacher asked you how things were going for you, what would you say?

7. Humor

Artificial humor and jokes are dangerous because it is possible that the attorney will appear flip and uncaring. Natural humor, appropriate to a situation as a response to a juror's humor, may work to relate to a juror or reduce some tension.

8. Giving the Jurors a Chance to Talk

When an attorney asks an open-ended question, the attorney should listen to the full answer and not interrupt the juror's response. Encouraging broad juror responses generates more information about them. If the juror appears to be hesitating, the attorney can be supportive by using a silent pause, an affirmative head nod, or phrases like, "Go on," "I see," or "Please continue."

9. Thanking Jurors

The attorneys may recognize the willingness of the prospective jurors to be jurors in a case. It is appropriate to thank the jurors for answering questions and for being candid and open.

Example:

Thank you very much for being so direct with me and for answering all my questions honestly. We all appreciate the fact that you have been thoughtful in answering these questions, even the difficult ones concerning personal matters in your life.

D. *Neutralizing Negative and Building on Positive Attitudes, Opinions, and Beliefs*

Jurors bring their beliefs and life experiences with them to the courtroom. All jurors have some biases and prejudices and hold misperceptions about trials, jury duty, what trial lawyers do, and what clients deserve. People have difficulty publicly admitting their biases and prejudices, especially in a courtroom in front of strangers. Sometimes jurors may believe they are being truthful when their answers are, in fact, false, misleading, or half-truths.

Example:

Q:　Except for what the judge has told you about this case, you don't know anything about the case, do you?

A:　That's right.

Q:　As you sit here now, you have no strong feelings one way or the other about this case, do you Mr. Data?

A:　I don't.

Q:　You don't have any biases or prejudices that would unduly influence you one way or another toward either the plaintiff or the defendant in this case?

A:　That's right.

Q:　And the only evidence you are going to rely on to decide this case is the evidence presented during this trial?

A:　Yes, I will.

Of course, those answers are not quite accurate. Nobody is completely neutral. Jurors' biases, prejudices, and life experiences influence their decision making, and one of the objectives of the jury selection process is to learn about these attitudes. Questions that are designed to discover bias and prejudice should also be used to neutralize negative attitudes and build upon positive feelings that the jurors may have toward the case, client, or attorney.

Example:

Q:　Real trials are not like television programs such as "The Practice" and "Law and Order." And, you know, of course, lawyers don't behave in real courtrooms like they are so often portrayed in the movies, don't you?

More importantly, attorneys must break down any inappropriate stereotypes regarding the client or witnesses.

Example:

Q: You are going to learn that Tom Joad, the plaintiff in this case, is unemployed. He has not worked for a number of years and has received assistance, which he is entitled to receive from the government to live. The fact that Mr. Joad has not worked does not affect in any way his feelings of pain and hurt in this case. Will all of you be able to set aside any feelings that you might have about unemployed people in making the decisions in this case?

The jurors may have preconceived notions about things such as injuries that cannot be seen, soft tissue injuries, psychiatric problems and psychiatric testimony, high monetary verdicts that have been paid to individuals, or feelings about lawsuits similar to the kind of suit that is at issue. These feelings may need to be explored.

Example:

Q: This case involves corporate acquisitions and stock transactions. Do you have any feelings one way or another that would be negative or positive about people who are involved in company takeovers?

E. *Obtaining Commitments*

The lawyer may attempt to obtain a promise from the jurors to not hold some fact or weakness against a client or a witness. Such a request should be phrased as a question seeking a "yes" or "no" response.

Example:

Q: In this case Mata Hari is going to tell you on the stand that she was sexually assaulted by the defendant. She will also tell you that although she is a prostitute, she told the defendant that she did not want to have sexual relations with him. He then forced her to have sex with him by threats and beat her and hit her. Do you believe that everyone, no matter who they are, has the right to make a voluntary decision about their own sexual partners?

While there is some debate about whether it is proper to attempt to obtain commitments, most jurors will hold themselves and other jurors to such promises. Studies of videotaped jury deliberations confirm that some jurors speak up and remind the others about a commitment if that subject arises as a factor in making a decision. Commitments made during jury selection can be used during final argument to remind the jurors that they must approach the deliberations with the understanding that they made commitments and should honor them.

§ 5.8 CHALLENGES

Attorneys may remove a juror based on two primary types of challenges: challenges for cause and peremptory challenges. A third type of challenge, rarely available, is a challenge to the array. This third challenge claims that the process used to select the pool of jurors was unlawful or unconstitutional because the selection system excluded or restricted certain classes of people from being part of the jury pool.

In the past, prospective jurors in some jurisdictions were selected only from voter registration records which excluded those classes of people who were not registered voters. Jurisdictions have developed lawful and constitutional procedures to identify and obtain jurors from all parts of the community. Prior to trial, attorneys should be knowledgeable of the process used to select jurors in the jurisdiction in which the case is to be tried in order to determine if a successful challenge to the entire panel exists.

A. *Challenges for Cause*

A motion to challenge for cause seeks to remove a prospective juror from the panel for a particular reason. A trial attorney requests that the judge rule a prospective juror be excluded for one or more of three reasons:

- A lack of juror qualifications (e.g., a person has a disability which makes it impossible to be a juror),
- Actual bias or prejudice (e.g., a juror has expressed some bias or prejudice), or
- Implied bias (e.g., a juror has a relationship with a party or witness).

Statutes, rules, or case law ordinarily establish the grounds supporting a challenge for cause. Certain types of persons who may otherwise be impartial may be automatically disqualified for jury duty. These persons may include judges and relatives of attorneys and parties. The judge or a clerk often screens the jurors and disqualifies those individuals who are excluded by law.

A challenge for cause may be based on either actual or implied bias. Actual bias is present when the juror has a state of mind regarding a particular case, the parties, or witnesses that prevents the juror from acting with impartiality and without prejudice to the substantial rights of either party. For example, a juror may admit that she strongly dislikes the defendant car dealer because of previous bad experiences in having her car serviced by the dealer. Implied bias may be based on existing relationships between a prospective juror and any of the other parties or witnesses even without a showing of actual bias. For example, a juror who is a good friend of a party will be excluded.

1. Establishing Bias or Prejudice

In order to be granted a challenge for cause it must be shown that the juror is so obviously sympathetic or prejudiced that it would be impossible for the juror to be fair. In establishing a challenge for cause, having jurors simply admit that they are biased or prejudiced is usually insufficient. Their answers must indicate the reasons why they are unable to be fair and impartial followed by conclusory questions that establish their bias or prejudice.

Example:

Q: Would those reasons make it very difficult, if not impossible, for you to be fair and impartial in this case, Ms. Van Buren?

Q: You would agree that it would be better for you if you served as a juror in some other case that does not involve the issues involved in this case, is that correct?

Example:

Q: Ms. Paige, you understand that the plaintiff is claiming that the defendant struck her on the head with a baseball bat. Is there anything about this case, before having heard any evidence, that may cause you to feel that you could not be fair and impartial to both sides?

A: Yes.

Q: Could you tell us, please, why you feel that way.

A: I have been at Little League games and have seen how parents get out of control. I'm terribly bothered by anyone assaulting another person. I believe it could happen, and probably did in this case. The whole thing makes me very angry.

Q: As you sit here, I understand that it would be difficult or impossible for you to sit as a fair juror in this case.

A: That's true. My mind is pretty well made up.

---

2. Procedure

An attorney challenges a juror by moving the court to strike the juror for cause. An attorney may indicate acceptance of a juror by advising the court that the attorney finds the juror acceptable or by using a phrase such as "I pass this juror" or "I waive the right to challenge this juror." Some judges ask the attorneys whether they wish to challenge any juror, while other judges expect the attorney to affirmatively make such a motion to challenge a juror. If no challenges are desired, the attorney can state to the court "Both my client and I are satisfied with these jurors and find them to be fair and impartial."

An attorney who challenges a juror for cause must state the motion and grounds on the record.

Example:

Your Honor, it is clear from Mrs. Olsheski's answers that her past experiences with the staff at Good Samaritan Hospital make it impossible for her to be fair and impartial toward my client. She agreed that she would not be able to put aside her negative attitudes and feelings about the hospital in reaching a verdict in this case. For these reasons, we request that Mrs. Olsheski be excused as a juror.

In some jurisdictions, this challenge is made at a bench conference or in chambers. In other jurisdictions, this challenge is made in front of the jurors.

Preferably, challenges should be made outside the hearing of the jury. If an attorney announces in front of the jury: "We challenge Mr. Wallace for cause because it is clear that he could not be fair and impartial in this case," problems may arise. The making of the challenge may diminish rapport with jurors who have befriended Mr. Wallace, or may create a bad impression on other jurors. If the court denies the challenge, the attorney will have to exercise a peremptory challenge to remove Mr. Wallace because of the natural, adverse reaction Mr. Wallace will have toward the challenging attorney. It is a better practice for the challenging attorney to explain the reasons for a challenge outside the hearing of the rest of the panel.

It may be effective to move to strike a juror in front of the entire panel if a particularly prejudiced juror can be challenged in a way that provides positive and helpful information to the rest of the jurors. Challenges for cause stated in front of the panel must always be stated in such a way as to not embarrass a juror or diminish rapport between the challenging attorney and other jurors. The challenging attorney may say: "We ask the Court to excuse Mr. Wallace so that he may be a juror in another case, and thank him for his time in court today."

3. Numbers of Challenges

There are no limits to the number of challenges for cause that may be made. However, courts are conservative in granting these challenges because removing a juror extends the jury selection process and delays the trial. Judges realize that most jurors have some biases and prejudices and consequently require a showing of substantial prejudice, adversely affecting the juror's ability to be fair and impartial, before granting a challenge for cause.

Judges also realize that some jurors may not want to sit as a juror and may admit to a bias or prejudice to avoid jury duty. Judges do not want to encourage jurors to exclude themselves and combat this by not allowing other prospective jurors to be removed too easily. Judges who grant challenges reluctantly also decrease the chances that attorneys will make unnecessary challenges and superfluous motions.

4.   Strategies for Exercising Challenges

In most jurisdictions, attorneys must bring challenges for cause before exercising peremptory challenges. The timing for challenges for cause depends upon the procedures of the jurisdiction. In some courts, the cause challenge must be made as soon as the possible ground surfaces during the questioning. In other jurisdictions, the cause challenge cannot be made until the questioning of a juror is completed. In some other jurisdictions, the cause challenge cannot be made until all the prospective jurors have been questioned.

An attorney must consider several factors in determining whether to exercise a challenge for cause:

- Sufficiently objective reasons must be established before a cause motion can be made. If objective reasons have not been established, the attorney should either ask further probing questions or pass the juror.

- An attorney must assess whether the judge freely or grudgingly grants motions to remove for cause. The judge's practice influences whether an attorney brings or declines to bring a cause challenge.

- The type of case may also determine whether a challenge for cause is more likely to be granted. Challenges for cause are more likely to be granted in criminal cases, especially if requested by defense counsel. A challenge for cause is more likely to be granted in a civil case when the case involves a substantial sum of money or significant issues.

- If peremptory challenges may not be available to remove all unfavorable jurors, a motion for cause is more likely to be made. If there are a sufficient number of peremptory challenges, there may be no need to make a challenge for cause.

- Attorneys should compare the replacement jurors from the panel with the prospective jurors in the jury box to determine whether the replacement jurors might be better or worse.

5.   Options for the Challenging Attorney

An attorney has four options regarding the removal of a juror for cause. First, the attorney can convince the prospective juror to state explicitly that the juror is unfair and biased and under no circumstances can sit as a juror in the case. This option might not be available with judges who do not want jurors to remove themselves because they feel such procedures unnecessarily lengthen the jury selection process.

Second, the attorney can hope the judge will decide to excuse the juror without a request from the attorneys. This may occur in situations where a juror has obvious prejudices, or objective factors have been revealed that make it unlikely that the juror will be fair. This option is available before those judges who take an active role in the jury selection process, but may not be available before judges who take a passive role.

Third, the attorney can hope that opposing counsel will challenge a juror for cause. This situation occurs when a juror is unfavorable to all parties.

Fourth, the attorney can challenge the juror for cause.

6. *Options for the Opposing Attorney*

An attorney who faces a challenge for cause brought by the opposing counsel has a number of options. The attorney can oppose the challenge for cause and argue that the juror is qualified. The attorney can request that the judge ask rehabilitative questions. The attorney can ask permission of the judge to ask rehabilitative questions. Or, the attorney can join in the challenge for cause and ask that the juror be excused.

This latter option may be appropriate and effective in situations where it is clear to everyone in the courtroom that the juror would not be able to be fair and impartial. In these situations, the attorney may be perceived by the judge and jurors as being fair and trustworthy by agreeing that an obviously biased juror be excused and replaced with an impartial juror. There may be a tendency to oppose the cause challenge or to ask for rehabilitative questions, acting on the adversarial theory that an attorney should oppose whatever the other lawyer requests. However, this situation presents the attorney with an opportunity to gain an advantage by not opposing the other lawyer.

7. *Rehabilitation Procedures*

After an attorney has asked questions to establish grounds for a challenge for cause or after the challenge for cause has been made, an opposing attorney or the judge may ask questions of the prospective juror for "rehabilitation" purposes. These questions are an effort to establish that the witness can be fair and impartial.

Example:

Q: You have just told us that you have a particular bias against car dealers, Ms. Greyhound. In this case there will be car dealers who will be called as witnesses. If the judge tells you that you must set aside your biases and decide the case solely on the facts presented to you, will you be able to follow the instruction that the judge gives you?

A: Yes.

Q: If the judge tells you that it is your duty not to let your feelings or attitudes about the case influence you, could you follow the judge's instructions and be fair to both sides?

A: Yes, I will be able to do that.

Rehabilitation questions permit new information to be developed to rebut any facts or inferences supporting a challenge for cause and to help establish the degree of bias or prejudice the juror may have. The judge may also wish to rehabilitate in order to avoid having to call a replacement juror, which would extend the length of the jury selection process. In permitting or asking rehabilitative questions, the judge must determine if the juror can be fair and if it is appropriate to require opposing counsel to exercise a peremptory challenge instead of granting a challenge for cause.

Example (By the Judge):

Q: You have just told us that you had a particular bias against car dealers, Ms. Greyhound. If I were to tell you that you must set aside your bias and decide the case solely on the facts presented to you, and if I tell you that it is the law, I take it that you will be able to set aside that bias and decide the case solely on the evidence given to you in this case. Isn't that true?

A: Yes.

Rehabilitation may force the opponent to use a peremptory challenge if the challenge for cause is unsuccessful. If rehabilitation establishes that the juror can be fair and impartial, the challenging attorney will need to exercise a peremptory challenge to remove the challenged juror, thus reducing the number of peremptory challenges available for other jurors.

8. *Reversing Apparent Bias or Prejudice*

An attorney may not be able to bring a motion for cause or have a sufficient number of peremptory challenges available to remove all questionable jurors. Many jurors have an appearance of a prejudice against a party that further questioning may be able to neutralize. In these situations, the attorney may need to ask questions of a juror to either reduce the apparent prejudice so the juror may be kept, or to reveal a prejudice by that juror against the other side, causing opposing counsel to consider exercising a challenge. The goal of the examining attorney is to establish reasons why the juror can be impartial and to obtain a commitment from the juror to be fair.

Example:

Q: Would it be difficult for you, Ms. Ogala, to be fair and impartial in this case because the defendant is an executive who has a job similar to yours?

A: I don't think so.

Q: Would you be able to set aside your attitudes and feelings about your job and decide this case upon the evidence presented to you?

A: Yes.

Q: You would be able to determine whether the conduct of the defendant in this case was legal or illegal based upon what you hear in this case and not based upon what has happened in your company?

A: Yes.

Q: You would hold the defendant in this case to the standards of a reasonable employer and not to some higher standard you may have experienced in your professional life?

A: Of course.

Q: If the facts establish to your satisfaction that the defendant illegally fired the plaintiff in this case, you would be able to find in favor of the plaintiff, correct?

A: Sure.

Q: As an executive, have you had to fire an employee if there was good cause to fire that employee?

A: Unfortunately, yes.

Q: But you yourself have never been fired?

A: Not yet (laughter). Seriously, no.

Q: You believe you can be fair and impartial in determining the credibility of the plaintiff in this case?

A: Yes.

Q: And you promise us to be fair and impartial as a juror in this case?

A: I do.

This line of questioning, if successful, can establish the importance of setting aside biases and prejudices all the jurors have in deciding the case. It may also result in one or more jurors bending over backward during deliberations to appear to be fair and impartial.

If this line of questioning works, opposing counsel may even become concerned with the juror developing a bias in favor of the opposing party and with the possibility of the examining attorney establishing overly effective rapport with the juror. If this approach does not work, however, the examining attorney may still be able to exercise a peremptory challenge and remove the juror.

9. Replacement Jurors

When a juror has been removed for cause, a replacement juror takes that juror's place. The replacement juror may be called from the panel that is seated in the courtroom or may be called from the jury waiting room. If the replacement juror has been in the courtroom during the selection process, many of the preliminary questions may have already been asked. However, if the replacement juror has not been in the courtroom, preliminary matters must be repeated. If the replacement jurors are in the courtroom during the interviews of the prospective jurors, as much attention as possible should be paid to the replacements because it is possible that an unknown replacement juror is less favorable than the juror who was removed from the panel for cause.

B. Peremptory Challenges

Peremptory challenges permit the attorney to remove a limited number of prospective jurors from the panel without any reason or explanation to the court, with some limitations. An improper basis, such as race or gender, cannot support a peremptory challenge. A statute or court rule determines the number of peremptory challenges available to each party, which number varies among jurisdictions and depends upon the type of case.

In civil cases, each party may have two or more peremptory challenges. In criminal cases, each party usually has more than two peremptory challenges. In federal criminal trials, if the offense is punishable by imprisonment for more than a year, the government is entitled to six peremptory challenges and the defendant is entitled to ten peremptory challenges. If the offense is punishable by imprisonment for no more than a year, each side is entitled to only three peremptory challenges. See Fed.R.Crim.P. 24(b).

An attorney has two options when exercising a peremptory challenge: the attorney can use a challenge and remove a juror, or the attorney can hope opposing counsel removes the juror by using a peremptory challenge. The actual process of making peremptory challenges varies widely and it is important that the attorney know which process will be used. Three common ways include:

- At the conclusion of the questioning, both sides approach the bench where plaintiff strikes the permitted number of jurors. The defense then strikes a similar number leaving a final panel.

- When questioning is completed, a chart containing the names of jurors not removed for cause is passed between the attorneys. The defense first strikes one juror, followed by the plaintiff, with remaining strikes made alternately until the appropriate number of jurors are removed.

- Following completion of questioning and motions for cause, each side independently lists the names of the jurors to be removed. The judge compares the lists and seats the first six or required number of jurors not removed.

The limited number of peremptory challenges makes it difficult for attorneys to remove as many undesirable jurors as possible. For example, the plaintiff may want to get rid of five jurors but has only four strikes. If the plaintiff thinks that one of those jurors is bad but is as undesirable for the defense as for the plaintiff, the plaintiff's attorney can make an educated guess that the defense will strike the juror. This gives the plaintiff the chance to strike the other four jurors.

If the jurors are struck alternately, each side can watch the progress and an extremely bad juror can be struck last if the other side has not removed the juror already. However, if each side strikes four jurors independently and the judge seats the first six unchallenged jurors, neither side can rely on the other to remove the undesirable juror. If both sides strike the juror, the strikes overlap and fewer unacceptable jurors will be removed.

C. *Alternate Jurors*

Alternate jurors are included in most trials, particularly in lengthy or complex trials. An alternate juror is selected to sit as an extra juror throughout the trial and will be called to replace a juror who becomes ill during the trial, is unable to attend the trial, or is unable to deliberate. The selection of alternate jurors occurs at the same time and is identical to the procedure used for selecting regular jurors.

The court usually permits an additional peremptory challenge when alternate jurors are selected. Typically, one alternate juror will be selected for a six-person jury and two to three alternates for a twelve-person jury, depending on the potential length of the trial. Alternate jurors may be excused from duty when the jury begins deliberations.

D. *Removing Jurors From the Panel*

The last decision the attorneys make in the jury selection process is to exercise peremptory challenges and to strike individuals from the panel. What the striking process presumes is that the attorneys have obtained enough information about the prospective jurors to make an accurate determination about the people they want to have sit on the jury, and those they want to remove. As Section 5.8(B) explained, the number of peremptory challenges and choices are limited. A successful determination about whom to strike depends on the lawyer's ability to obtain useful information about each juror, to analyze this information, and to make accurate judgments about people.

Making an accurate final decision is difficult.

Example:

Judge:

Counsel, are you prepared to exercise your first peremptory challenge?

Counsel O:

Your Honor, may co-counsel and I have a few minutes to confer?

Judge:

Yes, you may.

(Counsel O and Z conferring)

Counsel O:

I think that we should strike juror No. 5 first. He does not fit my profile.

Counsel Z:

What do you mean?

Counsel O:

We have an emotional, sympathetic case and I don't believe that he will react favorably to our client or our case. He is middle aged, owns his own business, lives in a wealthy suburb, reads conservative magazines, and drives a very expensive European car. My profile shows that he would be a very bad juror for our side.

Counsel Z:

Wait a second. That juror grew up in poverty. His parents died when he was young and he was raised by his grandparents. He made his own way and worked his way through college washing dishes in the college cafeteria. He told us that he volunteers for Boy Scouts and is very involved in developing educational programs for underprivileged children. I think he's terrific.

Counsel O:

But he is of Polish descent and likes the color pink and that is a sure sign that he will not vote our way.

Counsel Z:

You've got to be kidding. Where in the world did you get that stuff?

Counsel O:

I read about it somewhere.

Counsel Z:

Let's strike juror No. 2. She doesn't look at us at all. When I questioned her, she sat with her arms folded and a scowl on her face. I don't think I related to her. She made me feel uncomfortable.

Counsel O:

I think that we should keep her. Her experience fits my profile.

Counsel Z:

I also think that we should strike juror No. 8. He just doesn't seem to think the way anybody else thinks. I can't understand what he is talking about, and he regularly watches professional wrestling, and local cable channels.

Counsel O:

But he's perfect for our case. He is a head nodder, appears, upbeat, and looks like a lot of fun. He will react with empathy, and that's what we want.

Counsel Z:

Right! He fits your profile. Let's ask our clients who they prefer to decide their case.

---

§ 5.9   MISCONDUCT AND OBJECTIONS

State and local rules of procedure, the Model Rules of Professional Responsibility, rules of decorum, and common sense establish standards for proper conduct by attorneys and jurors during jury selection.

A.   *Inadmissible Evidence*

Any questions or behavior by counsel designed for the sole purpose of prejudicing the jury are improper. For example, questions that inform the jury that a defendant is wealthy or an atheist, if not relevant, are not permitted, are objectionable, and probably constitute grounds for a mistrial. The general rule is that evidence may be referred to in jury selection as long as it bears upon an issue at trial and will be brought out at trial. In addition, questions must be designed to provide a basis for determining whether to exercise a challenge for cause or a peremptory challenge.

B.   *Improper Questions*

Questions asked to meet improper objectives may not be asked during jury selection. Whether a question is legitimate or inappropriate depends upon the law of the jurisdiction and the discretion of the judge. For example, questions seeking solely to educate or indoctrinate jurors may be proper in one court but improper in another.

C.   *Improper or Questionable Topics*

Questions that touch on improper areas of inquiry must be phrased carefully. For example, in a personal injury case it is improper to mention insurance coverage. When a particular insurance company is a party to a lawsuit, however, jurors may be asked if they have an interest in, or a relationship with, that insurance company.

Questions must be asked in good faith. For example, if a question is asked for the sole purpose of informing the jury that either the defendant or the plaintiff is insured, the question is improper and may be grounds for a new trial. However, an attorney may inquire whether any of the jurors work for an insurance company to legitimately determine their bias or prejudice.

In situations involving questionable or potentially prejudicial topics, the attorney may ask the judge to ask such questions. This technique avoids mistakes being made by the attorneys.

D. Currying Favor

Communication with jurors before and during trial is forbidden except in the course of official proceedings. "Currying favor," or trying to seek or gain favors through flattery of the jurors, is improper. This kind of flattery may include an overstated expression of concern for jurors' comfort.

Juror concerns or discomfort should not be resolved directly by an attorney. Instead, the problem should be brought to the attention of the judge who will then assist the juror. Similarly, social and business arrangements with jurors should be avoided. The judge will, or should, advise the jurors that the lawyers are prohibited from talking to the jury during the trial, and that if the attorneys appear to act rudely to the jurors during the recess, it is because they are not allowed to communicate with jurors in any way.

E. Juror Misconduct

Jurors commit misconduct if they answer jury selection questions falsely, violate any rules of court or fail to follow the directions of the judge. Trial lawyers have a duty to inform the court of any jury misconduct immediately upon learning about it. Acts of jury misconduct cannot be kept secret and used later as grounds for a new trial.

F. Improper Conduct by Attorneys

Attorneys must maintain a fair and impartial relationship with prospective and actual jurors before, during, and after the trial. It is improper and unethical for attorneys to:

- Talk with jurors individually or in a group,
- Contact any friends or relatives of jurors, or
- Indirectly have a colleague contact a juror.

G. Objections

Counsel may object to the jury selection questions and conduct of opposing counsel. In determining whether to object or not, an attorney should consider strategic factors including:

- The prejudicial impact of the questioning;

- The extent that opposing counsel is actually using jury selection for purposes other than to determine challenges for cause and peremptory challenges; and

- Whether the judge has a reputation for taking control of jury selection after becoming frustrated with prolonged questioning that strays from challenges.

1. Arguing the Case, the Law, or the Facts

Questions may be asked concerning the case, the law, and the facts; however, in most jurisdictions, it is improper to present arguments in these areas during jury selection.

Example:

Objection. Counsel is conducting improper jury selection by arguing the case, the law, and the facts.

Response to Objection:

- Rephrase the question to seek information from the jurors rather than making a statement to the jurors.

- Alter your voice tone to make the question sound appropriate.

- Advise the judge prior to the beginning of questioning that questions may appear to be objectionable. Explain to the judge why these types of questions must be asked.

- Explain to the judge that you need to question the jury about the case, the law or the facts to properly exercise your challenges.

2. Improperly Indoctrinating the Jury

In many jurisdictions, questions that attempt to indoctrinate the jurors are improper. What are appropriate education questions varies among judges and attorneys. Section 5.7 explained the use of jury selection questions to provide proper information to the jurors through the use of questions.

Example:

Objection. Counsel is indoctrinating the jury through improper questions.

Response to Objection:

- Rephrase the question to avoid arguably objectionable phrasing.

- Explain to the judge the need to obtain answers from the jurors regarding their positions and reactions to the questions.

- Explain that a promise from the jurors to vote in favor of the client is not being sought, but that the jurors are being asked whether they can keep an open mind after hearing certain evidence.

3. Referring to Inadmissible Evidence or Topics

Inadmissible evidence and prejudicial topics may not be referred to during jury selection. Section 5.9(C) explained inappropriate areas of inquiry during jury selection.

Example:

Objection. Counsel has mentioned inadmissible evidence and improper topics during jury selection. We request that the court instruct the jurors to disregard what counsel mentioned.

Response to Objection:

- Explain why the evidence is admissible or why the topic is not improper.
- Explain that while the area is a sensitive topic, the subject must be explored in this case because of some specific reasons.

4. Repeating Questions

Areas of jury selection already explored by the judge or opposing counsel may not be repeated. Counsel may, however, clarify or ask more detailed questions in areas already explored by the judge or opposing counsel. Whether or not the questions are repetitive or appropriate is a matter of discretion for the judge.

Example:

Objection. Counsel is improperly repeating questions or asking questions in areas already covered during prior jury selection.

Response to Objection:

- Prior to jury selection, advise the court and opposing attorney that certain areas may be explored that the court and opposing counsel may also wish to explore.
- Explain that additional information must be gathered from areas previously covered in order to obtain more complete information from the jurors.

5. Asking the Jurors to Prejudge the Case

Questions that ask the jurors to prejudge the case are improper. Questions that seek commitments from the jurors regarding an issue or evidence in the case may be improper because the scope of the commitment may exceed that which the jurors may properly promise.

For example, a party who has a previous felony conviction may be impeached with the introduction of that felony conviction. The attorney for this felon may properly inform the jurors of the conviction during jury selection to obtain a commitment from them that they will base their verdict on the evidence in the case and not automatically discredit the story of the party merely because the party has a felony conviction. In most jurisdictions the attorney may not ask the jurors to promise that the felony conviction will not influence them because the conviction is a credibility factor the jurors may consider.

Example:

Objection. Counsel is asking the jurors to prejudge the evidence.

Response to Objection:

- Rephrase the question to avoid seeking a commitment or promise from the jurors.

- Rephrase the scope of the commitment or promise sought from the jurors.

6.   Irrelevant Questions

An attorney may not ask irrelevant questions regardless of how educational or entertaining those questions might be.

Example:

Objection. Counsel is asking questions that are irrelevant regarding the qualifications of the jurors and is improperly attempting to educate the jurors.

Response to Objection:

- Explain to the judge how the information sought in the question relates to a challenge for cause or peremptory challenge.

- Rephrase the question to avoid the appearance of it being to educate the jurors.

7.   Questions that Improperly or Incorrectly Explain the Law

Questions that ask the jurors if they understand or will apply the laws as explained by the judge are appropriate. Questions that improperly or incorrectly state the law are objectionable.

Example:

Objection. Counsel is improperly explaining the law to the jurors.

Response to Objection:

- Explain why the attorney needs the response of the jurors to the legal issues stated in the question.
- Rephrase the question by advising the jurors that the judge will explain the law.
- Restate the law correctly.

8. *Questions that are Unfair, Embarrassing, or Pry Too Deeply Into the Personal and Private Life of a Juror*

Questions that seek legitimate information about jurors are appropriate. Overly sensitive, embarrassing, or unfair questions that seek inappropriate personal information about jurors are improper.

Example:

Objection. Counsel is asking unfair and embarrassing questions of the jurors.

Response to Objection:

- Apologize to the jurors and to the court.
- Stop being insensitive.

H. *Improper Reasons to Remove a Juror*

Discriminatory reasons that are used to support a peremptory challenge or a motion to remove for cause may be illegal. A prospective juror cannot be removed for racial or gender reasons. Some jurisdictions prohibit removal for other protected, immutable traits. An attorney may object to an improper removal. It if appears to the judge illegitimate factors are being used, the advocate will need to explain why legitimate reasons support removal.

CHAPTER 6
OPENING STATEMENT

REFLECTING ON ADVOCACY

The best way to win an argument is to begin by being right....

—Jill Ruckelshaus

Speeches cannot be made long enough for the speakers, nor short enough for the hearers.

—James Perry

§ 6.1 INTRODUCTION

A. *Purposes*

The opening statement provides the advocate with the opportunity to explain the evidence to the fact finder and to describe the issues to be presented during the trial or hearing. An opening statement has a significant impact on the decision maker's initial understanding and impression of the case. Judges have reported that they often form an early impression of a case during a trial and hearing based on the opening statement. Jury surveys have established that during final deliberations jurors often vote consistently with the early positions formed during the opening statement. This result may be caused by other trial events such as the effective introduction of evidence, credible witnesses, or a persuasive closing statement. Nonetheless, the more effective an opening statement is, the more likely a favorable decision will be obtained.

The purposes of an opening statement are to:

- Explain the evidence to the fact finder,
- Tell an interesting and compelling story,
- Describe what the case is about including theories, issues, claims, defenses, and positions,
- Persuade the fact finder of the merits of the case,
- Motivate the fact finder to want to render a favorable verdict,
- Establish an appropriate atmosphere in the court or hearing room.

Opening statements should always be made in jury trials, and they should be also be made in bench trials, arbitrations, and administrative hearings unless there is a good reason not to. In bench trials and arbitrations, if the advocates have been able to explain the case and the significant factual events to a judge or arbitrator, then it may be unnecessary to present a whole opening statement. It may be sufficient to conduct a short opening providing the judge or arbitrator with the essential information that has not been communicated. In administrative hearings, this approach also works unless opening statements are not permitted by any party in the case.

Some judges and arbitrators may suggest or tell the lawyers not to conduct openings because they believe they already know enough or to save time. It may not make sense to deliver an opening to a decision maker who does not want to hear it, but the advocate should press to make an opening if the advocate believes it will increase the knowledge of the judge or arbitrator and help win the case. A well presented, concise opening may actually shorten the case presentation as the decision maker better understands the theory of the case and a summary of the evidence.

B. What Can Be Presented

This chapter describes the presentation of opening statements in jury trials. Most of the strategies and techniques described in this chapter also apply to bench trials, arbitrations, and administrative cases, but there are important differences as explained in Section 3.11.

1. Facts and Opinions

An opening statement presents facts and opinions which will be introduced as evidence. The facts that can be described include direct and circumstantial evidence and reasonable inferences drawn from this evidence. The opinions that can be described include admissible lay and expert opinions. In a jury trial, an opening statement consists primarily of statements based on evidence.

The goal of the attorney is to tell a story about the evidence. Any admissible evidence, even if in dispute, can be presented. An attorney can refer to evidence from any source, including evidence introduced by opposing counsel. Not all evidence will be referred to during the opening. A skilled advocate selects significant facts and opinions that meet the purposes of an effective opening without including all the details of the case or insignificant information.

2. Theories and Issues

Section 2.5 described the importance of selecting a case theory to support a favorable verdict. During the opening statement the advocate should use theme words and phrases to introduce and establish the case theories and issues.

3. Argument

The general rule in jury trials is that it is improper to present arguments during an opening. An attorney cannot provide explanations, propose conclusions, comment on the evidence, or otherwise advance arguments. The attorney should, however, present the most persuasive opening possible, and a skilled advocate attempts to present an opening statement that touches the line of argument but does not cross over that line.

There is often a fine line between what argument is and what may be stated during an opening statement. There is often a fine line between what is a fact supported by the evidence and what is a conclusion drawn by the attorney. Different decision makers disagree as to where these lines are to be drawn.

Advocates presenting openings before judges and arbitrators have great latitude in the scope and content of their opening. Opening statements presented before professional decision makers may include some argument as well as factual and legal statements. These openings can effectively raise the issues and identify the questions that have to be decided by the judge or arbitrator. Summation is the more appropriate and more effective opportunity to argue the case. Trial lawyers opening to a jury will be held close to the proper boundaries of openings.

4. Issues

Before jurors, the best opening is a story, and it also may be helpful to tell the jurors the issues they will need to resolve. These statements need not identify all specifics of the issues but can generally state the decisions the jurors need make. For example, in a criminal case, references may be made by defense to the jury finding the defendant not guilty.

Before professional decision makers, advocates may specifically advise the judge or arbitrator about the issues they need to decide. If there are several issues, they could be numbered and provided on a chart or exhibit. Issue statements make clear what needs to be decided and provides guidance to the judge or arbitrator, presuming the issues as stated are accurate and complete.

5. The Law

In a bench trial, arbitration, and administrative hearing, the advocate can ordinarily discuss the law and explain legal issues. In a jury trial, the judge explains the law to the jury. The trial attorney may make short, accurate references about the law during the opening in almost all jurisdictions. The lawyer can concisely refer to the legal issues in the case, the elements that comprise a claim or defense, and the burden of proof. The attorney can also show how the facts establish the issues, prove the elements, and meet the burden of proof. A lawyer may briefly show how the law applies to the facts or how the facts support the law.

6. A Test

One effective "test" to determine whether an attorney can include information during opening to a jury is to determine whether a witness, a document, or some other form of evidence will provide such information. If the answer is yes, the statement may be made during the opening; if no, then that statement is probably inappropriate and objectionable.

Adherence to this conservative test minimizes objections to an opening statement. Strict adherence, however, may deprive an opening statement of the persuasive explanation needed to be most effective, including an appropriate explanation of the case theory. Most judges and opposing lawyers allow more latitude in an opening statement than described in this test.

Ideally, an effectively presented opening statement would result in the decision maker jumping up, hugging the advocate, and telling the client that the remainder of the case is a mere formality and the client will win. This fantasy does not happen very often. Actually, there is no recorded instance of this ever occurring in the annals of trial practice, but it is an aspiration.

§ 6.2　PREPARATION

The preparation of an opening statement includes the selection of the evidence to be explained, the theories to be described, the law to be explained, the most effective way to present the information, and additional planning considerations discussed in this section.

A.　Pretrial Evidentiary Rulings

When determining which evidence to present during the opening statement in jury trials, the attorney must ascertain whether an in limine ruling is necessary before presenting that evidence. An opening statement may not refer to evidence that is inadmissible during trial. Pretrial evidentiary rulings permit the attorney to plan an opening statement knowing exactly what evidence will be admissible during trial.

Section 3.8(C) described the procedure of bringing a motion in limine to obtain a pretrial evidentiary ruling. An attorney may want to obtain an advance ruling to avoid an objection by the opposing lawyer to questionable evidence. An opposing attorney may want to obtain a pretrial ruling to prevent the jurors from hearing information that will not be admissible evidence during the trial.

Not all evidentiary problems will be resolved in a pretrial motion. The judge may defer ruling on admissibility until that point in the trial when the evidence is actually introduced. An attorney may decide not to seek a pretrial ruling for tactical reasons. An attorney may prefer to assume the evidence will be admissible, or may not want to suggest to the opposing counsel or to the judge that some evidence might be objectionable. In these and other situations the attorney may need to plan the opening statement without the benefit of a pretrial ruling, and without knowing exactly what evidence will be admitted during the trial.

B.　Opening Based on Trial Events

An opening statement should be based in part on what has happened during the judge's initial explanations and jury selection. Remarks made during jury selection and during preliminary instructions by the judge to the jury may affect what should be said and how it should be said during opening. In jurisdictions where jury selection questioning has been extensive, it may not be as necessary for the attorney to spend time establishing a rapport with the jurors. But, where jury selection is limited, the attorney may need to provide the jurors with more information and may need to make certain the jurors have a favorable impression of the attorney during the opening. In a similar fashion, where the judge provides an objective explanation of the issues in a case, it may not be necessary for the attorneys to detail the claims and defenses. But, where the judge gives few preliminary instructions, a detailed explanation of the issues, claims, and defenses may be necessary during the opening.

C. Opening Based on Final Argument

The final argument constitutes the foundation for the opening statement. The final argument must be planned before the trial starts. See Section 11.3(A). If a fact, opinion, theory, issue, or position is not going to be a part of the closing statement, it should not be part of the opening statement or the rest of the case. The opening statement must be consistent with what will be presented in summation and should be based on what will be included in the final argument.

D. Anticipating Opponent's Positions

When preparing an opening statement, an attorney needs to review the case from the perspective of the opposition. The advocate must anticipate and attempt to diffuse the other side's opening statement, theories, evidence, and case. The more accurately an attorney anticipates the other side's positions, the more effective the attorney can be in presenting an opening statement that rebuts what the other side has said or will say.

E. Selecting Visual Aids and Exhibits

An attorney must decide whether to use visual aids or exhibits during the opening statement. Consideration should be given to the persuasive impact these devices may have on the decision maker and how they will make the opening statement more understandable and interesting. The use of visual aids and exhibits is described in Section 6.4(G) and Chapter 8.

F. Order of Opening Statements

In bench trials, arbitrations, and administrative hearings, opening statements occur at the beginning of the case. In jury trials, opening statements usually occur immediately after jury selection. In some administrative proceedings, opening statements may not be common or permitted.

The general rule is that the party with the burden of proof gives the first opening statement. A plaintiff/claimant/prosecutor has the burden of proof in a case and makes the first opening. The defendant/respondent then has an opportunity to present an opening immediately or may delay the opening until after the plaintiff/claimant/ prosecutor has presented evidence and rested, as explained in Section 6.2(H). In cases with multiple parties, the order of the opening statements is determined by the decision maker, usually based on one or more of the following factors: which party has the more substantial burden of proof, the chronology of the factual events, and which party has the more substantial defense, affirmative defense, or counterclaim.

G. Length of Opening Statement

The opening statement should be long enough to explain what needs to be explained, yet short enough to maintain the attention of the fact finders. Some opening statements may only last five minutes, others will extend for an hour or more. Many opening statements last between ten to twenty minutes. There is no optimum length for an opening statement because each opening depends upon the evidence and circumstances of the case and the speaking ability of the attorney. Some decision makers may set limits on the length of an opening if it is anticipated that the attorney may take an unreasonable amount of time. An attorney who anticipates that the opposing lawyer may exceed reasonable time limits may ask for a time limit for the opponent.

H. Waiving or Reserving the Opening Statement

An opening statement may be waived. In a jury trial, however, an opening statement should never be waived because of the advantage an effective opening statement provides. In a case before a judge or arbitrator, an opening statement may be waived for tactical reasons if an attorney has had an opportunity to fully explain the case to the judge or arbitrator prior to the trial or hearing.

Federal and state court jurisdictions permit the defendant to present an opening statement immediately after the plaintiff/prosecutor or to reserve the opening statement until the plaintiff/prosecutor rests and the defense case begins. Local rules or practice may prohibit or restrict the defense option of delaying the giving of an opening. In the vast majority of civil cases and in most criminal cases, the defendant should give the opening statement immediately following the opening by the plaintiff/prosecutor. This approach provides the jury with an explanation of both sides of the case, places the plaintiff/prosecutor's case in perspective, and counters an effective opening statement. When the defense opening is delayed, the jury may attach undue weight to the initial opening statement and not fully consider available defenses.

In civil cases, because of liberal discovery rules, pretrial conferences, and settlement negotiation efforts, the defense knows what issues the plaintiff will attempt to prove and what evidence will be introduced. In these cases, the advantages in immediately giving the opening usually far outweigh any advantage gained from delaying the opening. The defendant's own story is explained in full at the outset, and the jurors are provided with additional information and perspectives to be considered while the plaintiff presents evidence.

In criminal cases, there may be an advantage to the defendant in reserving an opening statement, especially where the prosecutor has had limited discovery and does not know what the defense will be. Reserving the opening statement in such situations prevents the prosecution from modifying the presentation of its case to reduce the impact of the anticipated defense. Also, in a case where alternative defenses exist and a defense attorney is unsure what defense to use, it may be more effective to make that decision after the prosecution has presented its evidence. In some cases where the defense attorney is not certain whether the defendant will testify, delaying the opening may also be a useful tactic. Not giving an opening, however, may create an impression that the prosecution's case is stronger than it is.

I. *Written Outline or Detailed Script*

The material for an opening statement should be organized into an outline format. The outline should include the introduction, the body, and the conclusion. The use of an outline helps organize the facts and theories of the case into a readily accessible format. As the attorney prepares other aspects of the case, this outline may be modified or altered and should remain flexible. Form 6.1 is an example of an outline of elements to be considered.

Some attorneys find it advantageous to prepare a complete opening statement. This draft may then be reviewed and improved. With this format, the attorney knows that the final script of the opening statement will contain everything that needs to be presented. The drawback of using a script during an opening statement is the temptation to read it. A better approach is to prepare a key word outline of the script. After becoming completely familiar with the script, the advocate should be able to present the opening statement using only the key word outline. When notes or outlines are used, they should be used in a candid, forthright fashion.

J. *Rehearsal*

After the attorney has prepared the outline or script, practice is necessary to be adequately prepared for the presentation. Opening statements should not be read aloud from a written script, nor should they be memorized. The attorney should not necessarily try to remember exact words used during the practice sessions, but rather express the ideas that have been rehearsed in these sessions.

The attorney may want to think through the opening statement silently and then practice verbally, concentrating on content. As the content of the opening statement is mastered, the attorney can work on stylistic improvements. After this preparation the attorney should continue rehearsing the opening statement. The attorney may use an audience of colleagues, family, a mirror, or videotape for review and critique.

The attorney should rehearse until the story can be told in a persuasive, compelling manner. The key to an effective presentation of an opening statement is that the attorney knows the ideas and important phrases that need to be conveyed, is comfortable with this story, and can make a sincere, believable, and understandable presentation.

FORM 6.1
OPENING STATEMENT PLANNING WORKSHEET

Case _____ **File** _____

Case theory

Theme words of case

Significant issues

Structure

Introduction

Significant story facts

Event/circumstances

What/how/why it happened

Parties/witnesses

References to the law

Visual aids/exhibits

Case weaknesses

Request for verdict

Conclusion

Other tactics/approaches/techniques

Possible objections adversary may make

K. Specific Requirements

The attorney should determine before the trial or hearing whether the judge or arbitrator has any special requirements or limitations or whether applicable rules set limits on the opening statement. This determination avoids having the opening statement interrupted and reduces the chances of opposing counsel making objections.

§ 6.3 ORGANIZATION

A. *Structure*

Opening statements must be presented in a structured fashion. The structure should allow the entire case to be framed in the opening and should help the fact finder understand the facts and theories easily. The following are examples of various structures:

1. *Chronological*

A chronological description of events is relatively easy to remember, makes sense, and is easy to understand. The attorney describes the events in the order in which they occurred. For example, in an employment law arbitration, the opening can begin when the plaintiff was hired and conclude with the events occurring on the date the plaintiff was fired.

2. *Flashback*

The beginning of the opening can explain the end of the story, and the remaining story can be told by flashing back to earlier events. For example, in a murder trial, the murder can be described first, followed by the events leading up to the murder, including the preparation and planning.

3. *Parallel Actions*

The actions of the plaintiff and the defendant or victim and criminal defendant can be told separately with the conclusion being the final event at which they came together. For example, in an automobile accident case, the routes of the plaintiff and defendant can be described with the conclusion being the collision.

4. *Claims, Defenses, Topics*

The opening can be structured around the claims, defenses or related topics that will be proved during the trial. For example, in a breach of contract arbitration, the opening can describe the elements: creation of a contract, its breach, and the resulting damages.

5. *Order of Evidence*

The opening can be structured to reflect the order in which the evidence is presented, the witnesses testify, and the documents are introduced. For example, in a real estate administrative hearing involving lay and expert witnesses and numerous documents, the opening statement can follow the order in which the witnesses will testify and documents will be introduced.

6. *Liability and Damages*

In civil cases, the opening can first discuss liability and then damages. For example, in a personal injury case, the story can describe how the accident happened and then what injuries the plaintiff suffered.

7. *Mixture of Substructures*

A number of these approaches can be used for parts of the opening, as substructures. For example, a civil case could begin with the flashback technique, use chronology to present the liability facts, and explain the damages in the order in which the witnesses will describe the damages.

B. *Parts of the Opening Statement*

An opening statement has at least three major parts: the introduction, the body, and the closing.

1. *Introduction*

An opening should begin with an introduction that draws the fact finder into the case. At the beginning of the case, and especially at the beginning of the opening statement, the fact finder is usually alert. The principles of advocacy and persuasion explained in Sections 1.5 and 1.6 apply with special force to the introduction of the opening statement.

Starting the statement in an interesting and dramatic way may be the most effective way to begin an opening. Beginning remarks in an opening statement need to take into account what has occurred previously in a case. In a case before a judge or arbitrator, if the decision maker is very familiar with the case, the opening may be limited to outlining the major issues to be decided. In a jury trial, the beginning depends in part upon what introductory remarks and instructions the judge may have given and what information the jury has learned about the case during the jury selection process. An illustration of a judge's explanation follows.

Example (Judge):

Members of the Jury, at this beginning stage of the trial the attorneys will now make what is called an opening statement. Each of them will tell you the evidence that will be introduced in this case. After these opening remarks, each of the parties will present their case. The plaintiff will proceed first, and present her witnesses and introduce documents which support her case. Defense counsel will then have an opportunity to cross-examine the plaintiff's witnesses. After the plaintiff introduces all her evidence, the defendant will then present witnesses and exhibits, and the plaintiff will have a chance to question the defense witnesses. After both parties have completed presenting their evidence, the attorneys will have an opportunity to summarize and explain the case to you in final argument. I will then instruct you on the law by explaining the law that applies to this case. You will then go to the jury room, deliberate and reach a verdict which will conclude this trial.

Counsel for plaintiff will now make the initial opening statement.

Ordinarily a judge provides a similar or even more concise explanation to the jury describing how the trial will be conducted. If the attorney is uncertain whether the judge will give any instructions, the attorney can request that the judge provide particular instructions and preliminary remarks concerning the purpose of the opening statement and the identity of the parties and attorneys. If a judge does not explain to the jury the trial procedures, the attorney may provide that information at some point during the opening statement.

a. *Explanation of Purposes*

An opening statement may begin with an explanation of who the attorneys are, who they represent, and the purposes of an opening statement. The following examples of introductory comments demonstrate how some lawyers begin their opening. The remarks provide a comfortable way to begin an opening statement, helping to get rid of initial nervousness.

Example (Purpose):

Members of the Jury, this opening statement allows me to explain to you the evidence that you will hear and see in this case. The evidence will be presented in bits and pieces and not in the order in which the events happened. This opening will provide you with an overview of the case and help you understand what happened.

Example (Explanation):

My name is Atticus Finch. I represent Tom Robinson, who is sitting here. I now have the privilege of speaking to you about the evidence that will be introduced during this trial. This case will be presented to you like a jigsaw puzzle. Each witness who testifies and each document that is admitted will be a piece of that puzzle. At the end you will be able to put that picture together by yourselves. In the beginning, this opening statement allows me an opportunity to describe to you each of the pieces so that you will be better able to understand the complete picture.

Example (Personal Injury):

Ms. Duncan, the plaintiff, has suffered severe and permanent injuries caused by the negligent driving of the defendant, Mr. Bugatti. As you know, I am Max Steuer, the attorney representing Ms. Duncan. As the judge explained, this opening statement permits me to talk with you about what happened to cause that accident and to cause those disabling injuries. I will tell you the story of what happened and a summary of what the witnesses will describe.

Example (Employment Contract Case):

You have already met the plaintiff, Ms. Hussein. She is in court today to be paid the salary the defendant promised to pay her. I am here today to present the facts through witnesses and documents which show that she is entitled to that money. You are here today to listen to that evidence and award her the money owed her.

The advantage of these or similar preliminary remarks is that the jurors may better understand the purpose of the opening statement and the identity of the attorneys and parties. The disadvantage of such remarks is that they may not be the most persuasive way to begin the presentation of the case to the jury. The jurors should initially be told about the facts and case theory, and not about opening statement procedures or the name of the attorney.

b. *Explanation of Theme*

An opening statement may begin with an explanation of the case theory described in a compelling and dramatic way to develop interest and persuade the fact finder. The advantage of this approach is that the fact finder gains a favorable impression of the case and is more likely to recall the theme words used to describe the important facts and issues. The disadvantage of such an approach is that issues may be overstated, or the opening made too melodramatic. This approach can be especially effective in all types of cases before all types of fact finders.

Example (Personal Injury):

This case is about the life and death of a man, a husband, a father, and a productive member of this community. His name was Ward Nelson. He was killed when the Jeep he was driving rolled over, throwing him out of the Jeep and over the cliff where he fell to his death. He was thirty-one years old with a family, a wife, two boys, and a full life ahead of him.

Example (Product Liability Plaintiff):

You are going to hear a case of corporate deception and the greed by one of the largest pharmaceutical manufacturers in the world. The case is about the marketing of a product, the Precon

Shield, an untested and unsafe product. The case is about the selling of this product to thousands of women without caring about the serious injuries these women suffered because of this dangerous and defective product.

Example (Criminal Prosecution):

Members of the Jury, on a clear summer evening on July 15, Della Southern got off the commuter train in Elmhurst. She was coming from work in downtown Mitchell where she works as a legal assistant. The train pulled away from the station. She crossed the tracks and began walking towards her car parked a block from the train station in a parking ramp. As she walked into the entrance of the parking ramp, she heard a noise. She turned to her right and confronted that man (looking at the defendant). On behalf of the people of this state, I am here today to tell you the facts of what happened when she confronted that man (pointing to the defendant). After hearing those facts, it will be clear beyond a reasonable doubt that that man (turning to the defendant) brutally assaulted Ms. Southern and stole her purse, her money, and her sense of security and peace of mind.

Example (Criminal Defense):

This is a case of mistaken identity. Mr. Ramirez did not commit any crime on the evening of July 15. He is innocent of what the prosecutor has claimed he did. Under our system of justice, the prosecution has the burden to prove to you beyond a reasonable doubt that my client is guilty. Under our system of justice, Mr. Ramirez is presumed to be innocent. Indeed he is innocent as he sits here in this courtroom. The facts that you will hear in this case will convince you that there is more than a reasonable doubt that my client was anywhere near the scene of the crime. The case for the prosecution consists of one eyewitness who attempts to identify my client. That identification, Members of the Jury, was made under circumstances which make it totally unreliable.

---

2. The Body

The content of the opening depends upon what the fact finder knows. A judge or arbitrator may know some aspects of the case, and the content should cover matters not known. Jurors may only know a bit about the case depending upon the extent of jury selection and preliminary statements made by the judge. The advocate should design a presentation to explain the unknown facts and elements of the case in understandable terms.

An opening statement may answer six questions: who, what, how, where, when and why? Who is involved, what happened, how did it happen, where, when and why did it happen? The most effective way this information can be presented is usually by the attorney telling a compelling and complete story. This factual story constitutes much of the content of the opening statement. The story should parallel the substance of the evidence, and the summary that will be given in the closing argument. The attorney, particularly a defense counsel, may need to explain what the evidence will not show as well as what the evidence will show. Section 6.4 provides many examples of the components of the body of an opening.

3. Conclusion

An opening statement should have a strong conclusion. This may be achieved with a concise summary of the vital facts, with a compelling statement justifying a decision, or with a dramatic summary of the major theme of the case. A strong conclusion will have an impact because the fact finders often remember what they hear last. A strong presentation can be hindered by an apologetic or weak conclusion. The final words should be well thought out, so that no matter how lost the attorney gets, the conclusion will be effective both in words and delivery.

Example (Civil Plaintiff):

Members of the Jury, at the end of this trial, after you have heard all the evidence, we'll ask that you find the defendant responsible for the damages suffered by Ms. Didrickson and that you find that the defendant must compensate her for her medical expenses, for the wages and income that she lost, and for the pain and suffering she has suffered as a result of the defendant's negligence. We're confident that you will return this verdict which will right the wrong the defendant inflicted on her.

Example (Civil Defendant):

Those facts clearly establish the defendant was not negligent and has no responsibility to the plaintiff in this case. At the end of this case, based on this evidence, you'll conclude the defendant did no wrong and bears no responsibility. We'll ask you, at that time, to return a verdict on his behalf, a verdict in support of Edmund Fitzgerald against the plaintiff.

Example (Criminal Prosecution):

At the conclusion of this trial, I'll have an opportunity to talk with you again. I'll discuss some of the things I've said today and the evidence you will hear in the trial. I'll ask you at that time to return a just and fair verdict and find the defendant Bonnie Clyde guilty of robbery.

Example (Criminal Defendant):

At the end of this case, I'll discuss what you have heard and seen during the trial. By that time, you will have more than reasonable doubt that Mr. Baggins was involved in the incident. By that time, you will be convinced that Mr. Baggins did not steal the ring and is not guilty. By that time you will know he is innocent, and that you must return a verdict on his behalf.

C. *Opening Statement Critique*

Questions that may assist in determining whether an opening statement has been properly constructed include the following:

- Does the opening statement tell what happened?
- Does the opening statement tell why to find for the client?
- Does the opening statement make the decision maker want to find for the client?
- Does the opening statement tell how to find for the client?
- Does the opening statement have a structure that is clear and simple?
- Is the opening statement consistent with what will be proved and with what will be argued in summation?

§ 6.4 CONTENT

The exact content of an opening depends upon the facts and circumstances of the case and the strategic and tactical decisions of the attorney. The following factors should be considered when preparing the opening statement.

A. *Prefatory Phrases*

Advocates may use a variety of prefatory phrases during opening statements. Some common prefaces include "I will prove" and "the evidence will show." Whether prefatory phrases should be used is a matter of debate among advocates. Some lawyers suggest that none of these phrases should be used but that the attorney should simply tell a story without any qualifying prefaces. Some advocates believe the attorney must use phrases like "I will prove to you" or "I will present evidence" to establish the attorney's position in a case and to have as powerful an influence as possible on the fact finders. Other advocates believe that more objective phrases such as "the evidence will show" or "you will learn" are the more appropriate phrases. Some decision makers expect or require lawyers to preface their remarks with these phrases. In cases before these decision makers, counsel will need to comply with the decision maker's preference.

The use of some phrases during an opening may prevent a presentation from sounding like an argument. A neutral qualifying introduction such as "you will learn" or "the evidence will show" may be an effective way of preventing an objection. If this tactic is overused, however, and it becomes apparent it is being used to argue or to introduce otherwise inappropriate information, the decision maker will sustain appropriate objections.

Example (Criminal Case):

I will prove the defendant did not intend to shoot the gun. I'll present evidence to you that will establish this incident was all a tragic accident.

Example (Civil Case):

You'll learn from the evidence the defendant was negligent. Because he was negligent he is responsible for what happened. The facts will prove that, because the defendant is responsible, he must be held accountable and must compensate the plaintiff for what he did to her.

B. An Effective Story

The opening statement story should be told with simple language, in as dramatic a fashion as is appropriate, and in an interesting way. Things that make a story very interesting and very believable appear in great works of literature, art, and theatre, and they are the same things that make an opening statement very effective. See Section 1.5(J).

Example (Commercial Case):

This is a case of a lost business opportunity, a lost invention, a lost dream — lost by an inexperienced individual to a large corporation. On February 14, Dr. Kostrzewa, while working hard and long hours, by herself for herself, in her home work-shop, invented a new and innovative electronic computer device. Sometime later she visited the offices of the defendant — a very large corporation. She offered the defendant an opportunity to buy this invention. The lawyers for that corporation drafted an 18 page, single-spaced contract. The executives of that corporation told the plaintiff that if she wanted to market her invention she would need to sign this contract. She signed it. They signed it. She lived up to her end of the bargain. They have not lived up to their end of the contract. They breached the terms of that contract. They did not do what they told her they would do. They have not paid her what they told her they would pay her. We are here today to hold them to their promise, to their word, to the written contract.

Example (Negligence):

On the evening of July 20, Jamie Dancingwolf was just finishing the last half mile of her three mile run down Highway 100 here in Culver City. Mr. Bung had just finished drinking his fourth or fifth martini at the Mermaid bar. As Jamie was running about four miles an hour on the marked jogging path along Highway 100, Bung was weaving his car from side to side about 60 miles per hour along southbound Highway 100. Jamie never saw the car that ran her over. Jamie never saw the driver that killed her. She is gone. Her life is over. But we can see him, he is with us. He sits in that chair over there. This trial is to hold Mr. Bung responsible for the reckless killing and negligent homicide of Jamie Dancingwolf — a tragedy that should never have happened.

C. Details

The facts presented during an opening statement should be as detailed as necessary to provide a clear and complete story. The advantage of providing a very detailed story is that the story is usually perceived by the decision maker as more credible and more persuasive. Detail that provides necessary information for a full understanding and explains sources of corroboration or credibility usually bolsters the essential aspects of a case. The disadvantage of detailing specific facts is that the subsequent presentation of that evidence may not be as specific as the opening statement suggested. Further, too much detail is boring and unpersuasive.

Example (Personal Injury):

In this case defendants violated school district safety rules regarding gym activities. These rules require gym mats to contain two and a half inches of thick foam. The defendants were using two inch thick pads. The school district rules require one supervisor for every ten kids using the gym mats. The defendants had only one supervisor for twenty kids.

Example (Technical Data):

We will hear a lot of technical data about this machine. We will see instruction manuals, diagrams, blueprints, and other documents. And although these engineering details may appear very complicated and technical, the basic issue in this case is simple and understandable. We will be focusing on one part of the machine which was properly designed, was safely used, and did not cause the accident.

D. Parties/Witnesses

Information about the parties and witnesses can be explained during opening. The advocate can explain who will testify and what each person will say. Witnesses should be described in a way that will make their story understandable and their testimony credible.

The fact finder needs to understand or be reminded that a case involves people and not merely abstract legal problems. The more a party and key witnesses are personalized and described as individuals who will testify to what happened, the more likely they will be perceived as believable. Statements should be made which help the fact finder identify, relate to, and empathize with the witnesses.

Whether every witness needs to be identified during opening statement depends on the facts of the case and the importance of the witness to the case. The more critical the individual is to the case, the more essential it is to identify that individual. If the testimony of the witness should be highlighted, identifying the witness in the opening statement will help to do so. If a distinguished expert will testify, identifying that expert will help.

Fact finders may have a difficult time identifying with witnesses who are not described during an opening. They have no way of forming a picture in their mind of the witness. A party or witness who is present can be identified. Key witnesses may be present during the opening so the attorney can introduce them. The names and identities of the witnesses can be written on a visual aid.

Many fact finders will not remember the names of witnesses, and identifying witnesses may only distract them from remembering more important details of the opening. Highlighting the source of the evidence by generically describing the witness (an eyewitness to the accident, a bank vice president, a police officer) may be sufficient. This identification helps the fact finders understand the facts without burdening them with unnecessary names.

Statements about the background of a witness may also be included. This information can be effective if the fact finders have things in common with the background of the witness or if the description portrays the witness as a responsible individual who can be believed. The backgrounds of minor or problem witnesses need not be detailed in the opening statement.

Describing a witness during the opening commits the attorney to calling that witness to testify. Only witnesses who are sure to be called ought to be described. If there is uncertainty about whether a witness will testify, no specific reference ought to be made to that witness. A defense attorney may decide not to call a witness to testify based on the way the plaintiff/claimant/prosecutor proved a case and should not specifically refer to these optional witnesses in the opening.

Whatever is said about a witness and testimony should be proved during the trial or hearing. An advocate should not offer incomplete information or exaggerate the background or testimony of the witness. Exaggeration may create unfulfilled expectations with the fact finder. Misstatements provide an opportunity for opposing counsel to correct the inaccurate or incomplete description during opening or comment during final argument on the failure to prove such statements.

Example (Corporation):

The Polaris Company is a group of people, of individuals, who work at all levels of the business to provide services to consumers. The people of this company include workers, managers, and shareholders. Excelsior Henderson, who sits here, represents all those individuals involved in the company. He'll stay throughout the entire trial, and he will also take the stand and testify.

Example (Witnesses):

Please consider the testimony of the witnesses carefully. Consider what they say and assess their believability. See which one has a position to protect or a reason to be less than honest. See which one was in the best position to observe what happened. We know what Ms. Polaris will say in this case because we had an opportunity to ask her questions under oath before trial. We are sure she'll tell you the same things she told us. This is what she will tell you.

Example (Experts):

Rachel Carson will testify that in her opinion this product is harmful to the environment. We'll hear all about her environmental expertise, her extensive professional experiences, the many articles she has written, the teaching positions that she holds, and her reputation in her profession. We will also hear her expert opinion, the facts that support that opinion, and the reasons why that opinion is correct.

E. The Event

The description of the incident, occurrence, or event is a typical part of an opening statement, particularly when that occurrence is important. The description should be accurate and complete and should enable the fact finders to create a clear picture in their minds. Verbal descriptions of scenes can become complicated if too much detail is given, or if complex descriptions are made. Only those details that portray the scene accurately should be given. It can be difficult for fact finders to follow directions or visualize matters in the abstract. References to compass directions (north, south), degrees (a 90 degree turn), angles (a sharp right turn), and similar references are difficult to visualize. Visual aids and exhibits may be used to describe scenes in order to ensure a better understanding.

Example (Use of Computer Generated Diagram in Civil Case):

The streetcar was headed east, in this direction on the diagram, along Main Street. The bus stopped at this intersection here at the southwest corner of University Avenue. Main Street runs east and west, and University Avenue runs north and south along this line. The plaintiff, Stella Kowalski, got off the streetcar at this intersection. She waited for the lights to change and waited for the walk sign to be lit up and then began walking in the crosswalk across Main Street to the northwest side of the intersection of Main and University to this spot.

F. Circumstances

Information about the circumstances surrounding the incident or event may be important and may need to be explained during the opening. Explanations of the time, date, weather, vehicles, equipment, and other information should be provided to the extent necessary. The more important the circumstance is to the story, the more detail should be provided. If the time of the day is critical to the case, the precise time should be mentioned. If the exact weather conditions are important, atmospheric details should be provided. The extent to which details need to be described depends upon how precise the witnesses will be and how necessary it is that the fact finder visualize an accurate picture. It may be enough to describe a car as a "car" if a further description is not necessary. If it is important that the fact finder accurately visualize the bumper of a car, then a photograph of the bumper or an actual bumper should be introduced.

Example (Criminal Case):

As Georgia O'Keefe walked down the first block towards her studio, she saw a number of apartment buildings on her left and to her right she saw a gas station, a grocery store, and a few homes. As she walked down the second block, she could see more apartments and more homes on both sides of the street. It was twilight. The street lamps were on. There were three street lamps on the second block: one in the middle and one at each end. The apartment buildings all had exterior lights that were turned on. The evening sky was clear.

G. Visual Aids and Exhibits

The use of visual aids and exhibits significantly increase the effectiveness of an opening statement. These devices help the fact finders understand the facts and details of the case and help the advocate accurately and persuasively present the opening.

Visual aids may be created exclusively for use during opening statement. Exhibits that will be real or demonstrative evidence during the trial or hearing can also be used. Exhibits vary from simple diagrams to video presentations to computer generated reconstructions of events. Some jurisdictions have restrictions on the use of visual aids and exhibits. Permission for their use should be sought from the decision maker before the opening to avoid an interruption or objection from opposing counsel. Most decision makers routinely permit their use. Some decision makers may be reluctant to permit the use of visual aids or exhibits because many lawyers do not use them in opening, and these decision makers may not be familiar with the use of exhibits.

Example (Injuries):

You will see some photographs of the plaintiff's injuries and computer generated graphics of the operation during this trial. Some of them may be difficult to look at. But you need to see them so that you can understand the full extent of the plaintiff's injuries. They are not shown to you for their shock effect. If they do shock you somewhat, remember that they are really only a pale imitation of what the real injuries were and much less shocking than if you saw the real injuries in the flesh. I am going to show you a few now. This first one is how the plaintiff looked one day after the accident.

Example (Product Liability):

Please look at the monitors in front of you. Here is a chart listing the design and manufacturing defects. We want to review each of these items with you. This first column lists the defects. This second column lists the dates when the defendant first knew about the defects, and this third column lists what injuries the defects caused. This chart will help you understand what went wrong and why it went wrong.

H. What Happened

The fact finder obviously needs to know what happened. The facts and circumstances of a case dictate the parameters of this part of the story. A description of what happened includes references to the parties, the scene, and circumstances. An effective description includes statements that are objectively accurate, complete, and believable. A description that is too abstract, too subjectively biased or incomplete is not persuasive.

Example (Criminal Case):

Mr. Jordan was holding the straps of the duffel bag in his right hand as he walked toward the gym. The defendant came up to him and grabbed one strap of the duffel bag and attempted to steal the bag from Mr. Jordan. Mr. Jordan immediately looked right at the defendant, and instinctively gripped the handle of the duffel bag tightly. As the defendant tried to pull the bag from Mr. Jordan, he again looked at the defendant and pulled the duffel bag towards himself. The defendant held onto that bag, and was pulled closer towards Mr. Jordan until the defendant's face was only about a foot away from Mr. Jordan's face.

I. How it Happened

Usually an issue in a case will revolve around the question of how something happened, and an explanation will be part of the opening. An explanation of the facts that describe the "how" of what happened is essential.

Example (Civil Case):

Ms. Moffetal suffered a ruptured disc in the accident. We will learn from the doctors who will testify that the spinal column is made up of a number of bones or vertebrae, one on top of the other. Between each of these bones is something called an intervertebral disc. It is shaped like a donut and acts like a shock absorber. The center of the donut is filled with something called nucleosis pulpesis, a gelatin or jelly-like substance. If the vertebrae are jammed together pressure can be put on these "donuts" and the "jelly" squirts out the side (descriptive gesture). This is a rupture and the injury is called a ruptured disc. This model shows the vertebrae and discs.

Example (Civil Case/Third Party Defendant):

The evidence will show that it was Cornelius Krum who was at fault. Mr. Krum didn't oil the machine, and did not check to see if parts were worn. The machine was not faulty. Cornelius Krum ran the machine way too fast. The defendant did not cause the machine to explode, it was Mr. Krum. The defendant did not cause the plaintiff's injuries, it was Mr. Krum. The evidence will show that the defendant is not responsible for what happened, but rather Cornelius Krum was and is responsible.

J. Why it Happened

Explaining the what and the how of a story may not be sufficient if the why has not been explained. The why may not be of critical importance in a legal sense, but the fact finders will be curious about why something happened. If a good reason exists to explain the "why," then a concise explanation should be included in an opening. If no good reason exists to explain an event, then an explanation should be avoided.

Explanations of why something happened usually are limited in an opening because a detailed or lengthy explanation may go beyond the evidence of a case and become improper argument. If an explanation cannot be based on direct or circumstantial evidence, then an explanation should be reserved for final argument.

Example (General):

Why were the defendants in a hurry? Because they were late for a skittleball game.

Example (Medical Negligence):

This is a case about medical negligence. Doctor Romano was careless when she performed surgery on the plaintiff. She is not a bad doctor. She is not unfit to practice medicine. She made a serious mistake and must be held responsible the same way any professional must be held responsible for a serious mistake that causes pain and suffering and damages. She made the mistake, in part, because she was tired. She had been up all night working at the hospital and had not slept.

K. Disputed Issues

The decision maker needs to focus on the disputed issues between the parties. A reference to the conflict in the evidence or testimony helps define what needs to be decided.

Example (General):

There will be a dispute in the evidence presented to you—a disagreement about who said what. Ms. Scarlett will say the light was red, while Mr. Teal will say the light was green. The lawyers and the witnesses know about this dispute because we have had the opportunity to learn about the facts of this case before coming to trial and we know who will say what. After hearing both sides, we believe you will agree that Ms. Scarlett is mistaken and Mr. Teal is correct and find that the light was green.

L. Claims and Defenses

In most cases references to the claims or defenses should be made. These explanations focus the jury's attention on what they must decide.

Example (Civil Claimant):

The evidence will show that Mary Kay signed this contract and failed to deliver the goods that she promised to deliver to

Amway according to the terms of this contract. The issue you will need to resolve is whether the goods that defendant did ship were the goods the plaintiff ordered under the agreement.

Example (Civil Respondent):

The primary question you will need to answer in this arbitration is whether this piece of paper is a legally enforceable and binding contract. The evidence will show that this paper is not a contract and that Amway is not responsible to Mary Kay. Counsel for plaintiff has told you the type of goods the plaintiff expected to receive from the defendant. That is not the main issue. The main issue is whether this piece of paper is a legal contract.

M. The Law

The advocate may refer to the law and may blend an appropriate discussion of the law with the facts. Trial counsel may not explain the law in detail to a jury. See Section 6.4(M).

Example (Negligence by Defendant):

You will learn that there was a stop sign at the intersection of Boardwalk and Park Place and that a person driving through that intersection must come to a complete stop and look in both directions before proceeding. The evidence will show that the defendant failed to come to a full, complete stop at the stop sign at the intersection of Boardwalk and Park Place as she was required by law to do.

Example (Lack of Negligence):

Judge Davis will instruct you that negligence is the failure to exercise ordinary care or the failure to do something that a reasonable prudent person would have done under the same or similar circumstances. You will apply this legal standard to the facts of this case. When you do, it will be clear that the defendant did exercise ordinary care when she drove the buggy and is not responsible for the accident.

N. Burden of Proof

If the decision maker in preliminary instructions does not explain to the jury the burden of proof in the case, it may be appropriate to briefly mention the burden in the opening statement. A reference regarding the burden should be brief because references to matters of law must be limited. A reference to the burden should be made if doing so is tactically advantageous. Section 2.12 discussed burden of proof strategies in detail.

Example (Civil Case):

This is a civil case. The burden of proof in a civil case is called "preponderance of the evidence." That means that the plaintiff wins if it is more probable than not that her story is true. We will prove that it is more likely than not that what the plaintiff said happened, actually happened. The burden of proof is not beyond a reasonable doubt, which is a much heavier burden. That applies in criminal cases, not in civil cases like this one. Judge Hand will explain this lesser burden of proof later during the trial, and we will apply it to this case to show you why the plaintiff is entitled to your verdict.

O. Damages in a Civil Case

In a civil case the plaintiff needs to explain the types of injuries, expenses, and other damages. Damages that are recoverable under the claim brought by the plaintiff should be mentioned. In a contract case, the damages may be computed by referring to the terms of the contract or by establishing the lost income or profits. In a tort case, personal injury damages should include an explanation of the injury, diagnosis, treatment, and prognosis.

Example (Personal Injury):

This case is about what happened to Clark Kent as a person. He was one person before the accident and a different person after. Your task is to put a value on the differences between what Clark was and what he has become and will remain for the rest of his life.

Example (Pain and Suffering):

Margaret will tell you the horrors she went through during four months of intensive burn treatments. She will tell you that her twice daily bath was so excruciatingly painful she screamed. She will tell you that she has never experienced any pain like the pain caused from her burns. She will explain that she could not use enough drugs to eliminate the pain because the drugs made her even sicker. She will describe to you the pain with which she has to live.

P. Amount of Damages

Lawyers who prefer a detailed description of damages want the fact finder to know from the outset the extent of the damages sought. Mentioning a dollar amount creates a frame of reference, provides some guidance during the case, establishes the extent of the damages, suggests that the attorney knows what the case is worth, and preconditions the fact finder to a request in summation for a large damage award. Lawyers who prefer a minimal description of damages want the fact finder to first hear the details during the presentation of the evidence. Not mentioning the dollar amount during the opening delays the disclosure of damages to the introduction of damage evidence, creates suspense, avoids locking the attorney and witnesses into set positions, and gives the fact finder an opportunity to hear the witnesses describe the injuries before a request for specific damages is made.

If the injuries that caused the damages are slight, less emphasis should be placed on them. If the injuries that caused the damages are great, more emphasis should be placed on them during the opening. In jury trials, references to damage amounts may also be made during jury selection which may influence what should be said during the opening.

Example (Damages Described):

This case involves the amount of responsibility that the International Olympic Committee bears as a result of this tragedy. The law measures the amount of responsibility in dollars. You will hear evidence about the substantial injuries Mr. Decathlon has suffered as a result of the accident. These damages amount to $12,256,000, which is a substantial amount of money — but an amount which is fair and reasonable because the responsibility the defendant has in this case is equally substantial.

Example (Damages Reserved):

At the conclusion of the case, we will discuss the evidence that you have heard. We will ask at the conclusion of the case that you return a verdict that will fairly and adequately compensate Ms. Universe for what she has been put through. We will also ask you to return a verdict which will include punitive damages-damages which punish World Wide for gross misconduct. Punitive damages are available under the law in cases of this nature when a manufacturer recklessly makes a product. Punitive damages tell the defendant it did something wrong and shouldn't ever do it again. The defendant corporation has a net worth in excess of $500 million, that is over one half a billion dollars. At the end of the case, I will come back and request you to award the plaintiff an amount of money that will compensate her for what happened and award her additional money that will tell the defendant what it did was reckless.

Q. Request for Relief

An opening statement should contain an explanation of the decision or verdict that the facts will support. This explanation should be clear and distinct so the fact finders understand what conclusion they must reach to find for a party. Some attorneys will say that the facts require that the fact finder return an award or verdict because the client is entitled to or has a right to such a verdict. Other attorneys explain that the fact finders have an opportunity, and even a duty, to decide based upon the facts of the case.

Example (Civil Arbitration):

That concludes my opening. You will hear from the witnesses just what happened, and you will have documents that will support that testimony. At the close of this arbitration, I am going to ask you to issue an award in favor of ADRI.

Example (Criminal Case):

The facts will prove that the Defendant is guilty of murder in the first degree beyond a reasonable doubt. The testimony and exhibits will prove that the Defendant shot and killed J.R. Ewing. The evidence will prove that the Defendant intended to shoot J.R. Ewing, intended to kill J.R. Ewing, and that the Defendant thought about it for three days beforehand. These facts will prove that the verdict you are to return at the end of this case is first degree murder.

---

§ 6.5   TECHNIQUES

The following sections involve techniques that apply to the presentation of an opening statement. These approaches need to be reviewed to determine their applicability to an opening statement in a particular case.

A.   *Offensive/Defensive Approaches*

An opening statement should lead the fact finder to a conclusion that the client is entitled to win. The plaintiff/claimant/prosecutor will naturally take the "offensive" and explain the story in a positive way. Some defense counsel may think it appropriate for the opening statement to be explained in a "defensive" way because the other side has the burden of proof. A more effective tactic may be for the defense to take the offensive and explain what the defendant's evidence will prove and then defend the case by stating what the other evidence will not prove.

Counsel for the defendant who presents an opening after the opening by the plaintiff/claimant/prosecutor must decide whether and how to respond to the opening by the opposing attorney. Defense counsel should be careful not to appear weak by responding in a completely defensive way. The opening should describe the case of the defendant/respondent and, after that has been explained, respond to the extent necessary to statements by the other side in the initial opening statement. Even in a criminal case where the defendant will not testify, the opening statement for the defense should be as positive as possible. The defense will present evidence through cross-examination of the prosecution's witnesses, and this information can be used to support reasonable doubt.

At the end of the opening statement for the plaintiff/claimant/prosecutor, counsel may raise some questions or make some remarks which counsel suggests the defense lawyer should respond to or address during the opening for the defendant. The lawyer for the defendant should present the prepared opening statement and should avoid directly responding to this ploy, unless a response is necessary or would be more effective than not responding.

Example (Civil Case):

At the end of her opening statement, counsel for the plaintiff suggested to you that I should tell you what facts we had which differed from the facts she explained to you. You may have wondered why I did not respond to the questions she raised until now. The facts that I just explained to you, that you will hear from the witnesses who take that stand and which you will read in these documents, will answer those questions. There is no need for me to do what plaintiffs counsel asked. You will do that later during your deliberations.

B. *Anticipating Defenses*

After making an opening statement, the plaintiff/claimant/prosecutor has no opportunity for rebuttal after the defense opening. Defenses need to be anticipated and dealt with in the opening. In civil cases, the plaintiff will usually know the defenses the defendant will raise and can explain away such defenses.

Example (Accident Case):

The defendant will try to avoid responsibility in this case by telling you the accident was Alice's own fault — that she wasn't watching where she was walking. But after hearing all the evidence, you will learn this was an area that people walked all the time and no one — including Alice — would expect there to be a hole in the ground.

Example (Automobile Case):

Now I must tell you that the defendant will try to put some of the blame for this accident on James Dean. The defendant will claim that Mr. Dean should have stopped his car or swerved to avoid the accident. But you will learn the defendant came into that blind intersection so fast there was no way Mr. Dean could have avoided the collision — he just could not see or avoid the defendant's car.

In criminal cases, the constitutional rights of the defendant limit comments that can be made by the prosecution. The prosecutor may not directly comment on evidence the defense may produce. A prosecutor can explain evidence that will be introduced during the prosecutor's case and state indirectly that such evidence overcomes potential defenses, but the prosecution cannot comment on possible testimony by the defendant because the defendant need not and may not testify or present any witnesses.

C. Asserting Promises

A "promise" to the jury that certain evidence will prove a certain fact can be effective as long as the attorney can fulfill that promise. A promise that is not kept causes the jury to lose confidence in the attorney and other facts as well. A promise is a tactical approach that must be employed carefully. If a lawyer does make promises during an opening or otherwise asserts that certain evidence will be proved, the opposing lawyer should note all these statements and mention during summation all promises not kept.

Example (General):

I promise you that I will present evidence showing the defendant lied to the plaintiff about the value of her land. After hearing this evidence, you will conclude that the defendant misrepresented the facts and defrauded the plaintiff. At the end of this case, I will ask you to put us to the decisive test: Did we prove to you what we said we would prove? If we have, we will ask you then for a verdict in favor of the plaintiff against the defendant.

D. Making a Compact With the Jury

The attorney may make a compact with the jury during the opening. The attorney may promise the jurors that the attorney will never mislead or misdirect them or intentionally misstate any evidence or exaggerate the facts. The attorney may ask the jurors to hold the attorney to this statement and to hold the opposing lawyer to the same strict standard. This approach impresses the jury with the sincerity of the lawyer and reduces the chances the opposing lawyer will engage in misdirection or exaggerations. This tactic ought to be reserved for those situations where there is a reasonable concern the opposing lawyer will present an unfair and improper opening statement.

Example (General):

Everything that I have told you in this opening about the evidence is what you will hear from this witness stand and see and read in this contract. I will prove that the events in this case happened the way I described the facts. I ask you to hold the other parties to this same standard.

E. Employing Understatement

Understatement can be a useful credibility-building device for an opening statement presentation. Understating a case sets the expectation of the fact finder at a level that will be exceeded during the trial or hearing. The presentation of the evidence will then surpass the fact finder's expectations, enhancing the credibility of the case and the attorney. Understatement may also arouse curiosity. If the attorney does not describe all the details of an event or a conversation during the opening, the fact finders may pay special attention because they have been eagerly waiting to hear or see the evidence. The use of understatement does have disadvantages. It may reduce the attorney's ability to explain the facts in a persuasive way, and a fact finder may initially perceive an understated case to be weaker than the attorney intended.

Example (Civil Case):

Judy and Doralee talked that day about Violet and her future with the group. They will take the witness stand and tell you what they said. When you hear what they said, you will understand the plans they had for Violet.

F. Avoiding Overstatement

The attorney should avoid the use of overstatement during an opening statement. The fact finder may be initially impressed, but this initial impression will not last long once it is realized that the evidence does not match what the attorney stated during the opening statement. Further, opposing counsel may comment during closing argument about the absence of the exaggerated evidence from the case.

Example (Criminal Case):

Many normal people drink in moderation. Many normal people have car accidents. Many do both. They aren't hauled before the court as public menaces. My client is no more a public menace than they are.

G. Asserting Difficult Positions

The facts and issues in some cases will be more difficult for fact finders to accept than in other cases. Usually, it is easier to prove that a person was negligent, failed to do something, or made a mistake rather than having to prove that a person intentionally did something, acted very unreasonably, or lied. For example, in a negligence case where contradictory statements were made by the plaintiff and defendant regarding the color of a traffic light, the plaintiff can win by proving that the defendant could not accurately see the color of the light or was confused about the color of the light without proving the defendant is a liar. In some cases the difficult and uncomfortable position is necessary as part of the proof and these difficult facts must be addressed in the opening statement. For example, a discrimination case requires the plaintiff to prove the defendant committed a discriminatory act. In the opening statement, the attorney needs to state exactly what will be proved.

Example (Civil Plaintiff):

We will prove to you that the defendant stated that he didn't want "them" working for him, and if it is not now appropriate for me to call the defendant a racist, by the end of the case it will be clear to you that he is a racist.

Example (Criminal Defendant):

I will prove to you that the witness for the prosecution is a liar. Jim Carrey, whom the prosecutor has described as the key witness in this case, has lied a number of times in the past regarding what he did on the night of February 14th. He lied to the police when they questioned him. And he took an oath to tell the truth and lied to a judge at a court hearing.

H. Describing Case Weaknesses

An attorney must consider whether to describe weaknesses in a case. Weaknesses that will be brought out in testimony must be presented in a candid and forthright manner. Weaknesses in a case that have not been explained and that most likely will be mentioned during the opposition's opening statement or later in the case should be addressed during opening statement. An open and candid disclosure of this information usually increases the appearance of sincerity and credibility of the attorney while reducing the impact of the opposition's strong points.

Example (Negligence):

A moment ago, I told you that I would describe everything that happened. You will learn that Mickey Morissey had stopped at a local bar on his way home from work. Mr. Morissey will tell you himself that he had dinner and two or three glasses of wine with dinner a couple of hours before the accident. The evidence will show, however, that that had nothing to do with the accident, which happened only because the defendant's car crossed over the center line.

Example (Contract):

We told you that we would put everything before you, the good and the bad. You will learn in this case that Leona Stuart has a criminal record — she was convicted of income tax evasion over five years ago. But that has nothing to do with the fact that she had an employment contract with the defendant and that she has a contract right to her salary.

Example (Personal Injury):

In the interest of fairness, and holding nothing back, you will hear evidence from J.J. Gittes that he was a trespasser — he did not have permission to be on the property when he got hurt. But you will learn that the owner, the defendant, must take care not to injure people who are on her property whether they have permission to be there or not.

I. Explaining the Absence of Evidence

During the opening the attorney can describe what facts will not be proved, what documents will not be introduced, and what evidence will not be presented, and briefly explain why such information will not be offered during the case. Usually this explanation is appropriate where evidence does not exist or was not preserved. Fact finders may wonder why some evidence is not introduced, and this tells them what they will not hear or see.

Example (Missing Witness):

The van was behind schedule when Ms. Rayette boarded it. She will tell you it was about five minutes late. The driver of the van will not be able to tell you how late the van was because he moved away from our city over a year ago and cannot be located despite our very best efforts to find him.

Example (Absent Evidence):

The evidence will be that Overland Motors did no testing on the Model C–11. Our expert, Dr. Necessiter, will testify that in his opinion proper testing would have shown the C–11 to be unreasonably dangerous and defective. Evidence will be before you that there was no warning.

J. Qualifying Remarks

Some attorneys emphasize to the jurors that what an attorney says during opening does not constitute evidence. Other attorneys may explain that the jurors' function is to determine the facts after hearing the evidence during the trial. Comments like this reduce the impact of an opening statement presentation and are often unnecessary because the same statement may be contained in the judge's preliminary instructions to the jury. Defense counsel may want to make such comments in an attempt to reduce the effectiveness of a particularly persuasive plaintiff's opening statement and to remind the jurors that they must wait to determine the evidence as it is introduced during the trial.

Example (General):

You will hear a lot of lawyer talk in this case. You have just listened to the opening statement for the plaintiff. What we lawyers say is not evidence. The judge will tell you that you are not to decide this case based upon what we as lawyers have said but rather on what the evidence will prove. You are not to rely on lawyer talk in reaching the verdict in this case. You are to rely on the testimony of the witnesses who will come before you and testify and the documents that will be read to you. Now let me describe to you what the evidence will show.

---

§ 6.6   PRESENTATION AND DELIVERY

The manner in which the attorney delivers the opening statement affects the fact finders' understanding of the facts of the case, significantly influences their initial impression of the attorney and the strengths and weaknesses of the client's case, and shapes their perspective of the entire trial. The following factors are matters that will affect the quality of the opening presentation. These factors supplement the considerations relating to presentation and delivery explained in Section 1.7.

A.   *Location of the Presentation*

The attorney is usually more effective standing in front of the fact finder and not behind a lectern or table. This is not to say that an effective opening cannot be presented using a lectern, but a lectern may unnecessarily interfere with an attorney establishing an effective presence. In arbitrations and administrative hearings, the opening may be delivered sitting down. This can be effective as long as the advocate has a direct view of the decision maker.

In some courts, local court rules require that the attorney stand behind a lectern when presenting the opening statement. In these situations, the attorney should ask permission of the court to stand away from the lectern in order to make a more effective presentation. If the attorney must remain at a lectern, visual aids or exhibits may be used to emphasize points and to provide some opportunity for movement away from the lectern.

B.   *Movement*

Some movement is useful, particularly if the opening is long. Movement and stance should be orchestrated so as not to be distracting. An attorney may use movement as a transition or to provide emphasis. Movement that appears purposeless is usually distracting and should be avoided.

C. Appropriate Distance

The attorney must maintain an appropriate distance from the fact finder. This distance should neither be so far away that personal contact is lost nor so close that the fact finders feel uncomfortable. A distance of between five and ten feet can be used as an appropriate guide, but the optimum distance varies in different circumstances. An attorney should observe the fact finders' reaction and move close when appropriate and stand further away when necessary. For example, when the attorney approaches the jury box, the attorney may stand in front of jurors in the front row, speak with a lower voice, and make primary eye contact with jurors in the second row.

D. Gestures

The attorney should use gestures that are appropriate to the content of the opening statement and that appear natural to the attorney. Gestures should be made even if the attorney stands behind the lectern. Fact finders will become bored with a talking head, which is all that they might see if the attorney sits stock still or stands behind a lectern without using any gestures, movement, or visual aids.

E. Eye Contact

One of the most effective ways to establish credibility and sincerity is to look directly at the fact finder during the opening statement. Good eye contact also helps hold attention and allows the attorney to observe reactions. Eye contact does not mean staring. The eye contact must be varied, sufficiently long to establish a contact but not so long that it makes people uncomfortable.

F. Transitions

The opening statement is more effective if the attorney employs transitions in the presentation. Prefatory remarks, silence, a louder voice, a softer voice, visual aids, movement, and gestures are all devices which can signal a transition.

G. Observing the Fact Finder

The attorney must observe the fact finders' reactions during the opening statement and adjust the presentation to their reactions when necessary. Some will express reactions regarding the facts of the case during the opening statement. The initial impressions displayed during the opening statement will also be useful in determining how the evidence is later presented and what might be an effective closing argument position. However, it is difficult to determine accurately what people are thinking just by watching them during a presentation. Care

must be taken not to overreact and not to change an approach completely because of a perceived reaction.

H. Notes and Outlines

When notes are used, the attorney should not pretend not to use
them or try to sneak a peek. An obvious use of notes done openly can be
effective. Fact finders understand the need to use notes.

Prepared outlines can be effectively employed in an opening conducted with the use of visual aids. A prepared diagram, whiteboard, easel
paper, or computer screen may contain an outline of the opening which
highlights important matters for the jurors and assists the attorney in
explaining the facts.

§ 6.7 OBJECTIONS AND MOTIONS

A. Improper Comments

Certain statements and comments made during an opening are
objectionable. References to the following evidence and the following
comments are improper:

1. Referring to Inadmissible or Unprovable Evidence

Counsel must not refer to inadmissible evidence or unprovable facts
during opening statement. This prohibition extends to evidence excluded
by pretrial rulings, or likely to be excluded by the rules of evidence, as
well as facts, opinions, or inferences that are not supported by evidence.
The standard for determining whether an attorney may refer to specific
evidence is whether the attorney has reasonable, good faith grounds to
believe the evidence will be admissible. The standard to determine
whether a matter can be proved is whether there is a source of available
evidence to prove the matter. The opening statement is not to be used as
a subterfuge to present inadmissible or nonexistent evidence to the jury
or to circumvent the rules of evidence and professional responsibility.

Objection:

Counsel has referred to evidence that is neither admissible nor
provable in this case. We request that the jury be instructed to
disregard such evidence and that counsel be admonished for
making such references.

Response to Objection:

- Explain the evidence law that supports the admissibility of the
  questioned evidence.

- Describe the source of evidence that will support the statement
  made.

- Advise the judge and opposing counsel before the opening that there will be a reference to potentially objectionable evidence, and seek a preliminary ruling by the judge as to its admissibility.

2. Explaining Details of the Law or Jury Instructions

The attorney should not explain details of the law or give instructions to the jury. While making brief references regarding the law in the case is proper, lengthy descriptions or detailing of the law is not proper. These descriptions are only appropriate in summation.

The precise extent to which an attorney may refer to the law during an opening varies among jurisdictions and among decision makers. Some courts strictly limit an attorney's explanation of the law during opening statement, and some courts permit reasonable latitude to the attorneys to explain the law applicable to the facts. See Section 6.1(B).

Objection:

Counsel is improperly explaining the law or jury instructions during opening statement.

Response to Objection:

- Avoid lengthy or detailed references to the law or jury instructions.

- Briefly mention the law or jury instructions several times during the opening, rather than describing it in one lengthy explanation.

- Combine a description of the facts with an explanation of the law to make these statements sound more factual in nature.

- Use prefatory remarks such as "The evidence will show" before explaining the law.

- Remind the jurors that it is the judge and not the attorneys who will explain the law to them.

3. Making Argumentative Statements

Counsel should not make argumentative statements during the opening. The opening statement is primarily an opportunity for counsel to present the evidence that will be introduced and not to argue the facts, the law, or the case. See Section 6.1(B).

Objection:

Counsel is arguing to the jury.

Response to Objection:

- Immediately request a bench conference to avoid being admonished by the court in front of the jury.

- Explain that the reference to the facts, law, or case is proper and necessary for the jury to hear during opening statement and is not an argument.

- Avoid speaking with an argumentative tone of voice, or with over-emphatic gestures, or in a loud, aggressive manner.

4.   Stating Personal Beliefs and Opinions

The attorney should not give the jurors a personal opinion or belief concerning the evidence or the case. The jury is to determine the case based upon the facts and the law and not upon the personal statements of counsel. Phrases such as "I personally believe" or "It is my opinion" are objectionable. The lawyer may state, "I will prove" or "I submit" because the lawyer is not stating a personal position.

Objection:

Counsel is stating a personal belief or opinion.

Response to Objection:

- Rephrase the remarks and avoid interjecting personal opinions.

- Use phrases such as "We will present evidence to you that will show" and "You will learn that" rather than phrases that suggest your personal beliefs.

5.   Putting the Jurors in the Place of the Party

Counsel may not ask jurors to put themselves in the place of a party or witness in determining an issue. The jurors are to base their verdict on the evidence and not substitute their personal experiences or reactions for that of the evidence presented in the case.

Objection:

Counsel is asking the jurors to improperly put themselves in the place of a party.

Response to Objection:

- Avoid suggesting the jurors put themselves in the place of a party or witness.

- Save references to the common life experiences of the jurors until final argument.

- Use general references to real life or common sense. The jurors will put themselves in the place of the witness or party without being asked to do so. For example, "Mr. Burns did what most people would do" and "Ms. Allen used common sense when she turned to the right."

6. *Speculating About the Other Side's Case*

A prosecutor in a criminal case cannot suggest what the defense will prove because the defense has no obligation to prove anything. Speculation as to the other side's case in a civil matter is argumentative, does not represent what the evidence will show, and is usually improper.

Objection:

Counsel is improperly speculating regarding what we will prove.

Response to Objection:

* Explain the statements relate to evidence the other side will introduce and are proper.

* Explain it is necessary to describe facts the other side will prove in order that the jurors understand all the facts of the case.

7. *Making Disparaging Remarks*

Counsel may not make remarks during opening statement which disparage opposing counsel, the opposing case, the opposing party, or witnesses. Such conduct is improper, unfairly prejudicial, and unethical. The decision maker should reprimand the offending attorney. Severely disparaging remarks may be a ground for a mistrial.

Objection:

Counsel is making improper remarks. Counsel has said I was mendacious and I ask your Honor to admonish counsel and insist she apologize to me.

Response to Objection:

* Try to explain that the remarks are not improper.

* Admit a mistake and apologize.

* Accept an admonition from the court without argument.

8. *Additional Prohibitions*

The issues involved in specific cases may further restrict certain references made during opening statements. In a personal injury case, references to insurance are inappropriate. In a criminal case, a prosecutor cannot comment on the failure of the defendant to testify. In all cases, counsel may not refer to matters that may affect the passion or prejudice of the jury, such as appeals to the family circumstances of a party or references to the wealth or poverty of a party.

B. Objections

If an objection is made during opening, the decision maker will rule on the propriety of the objection. If the objection is sustained, the attorney should correct the mistake and continue with the opening. If the objection is to the content of the opening statement, then the subject ought to be avoided. If the objection is to the form of the statement, the statement can be rephrased. If the objection is overruled, the attorney should continue with the opening and may repeat or emphasize the statement, and may preface it with "As I was saying" or "Before the interruption."

Tactically, an attorney may decide not to object but rather write down what was said and use this against the opposing attorney in closing argument. Many attorneys extend a professional courtesy to one another and do not object during opening statement unless the opponent is saying or doing something that is clearly improper and damaging to the case. Most attorneys want the openings to be presented zealously and without interruptions. However, an objection and a request for a curative instruction may be necessary to preserve an issue for appeal.

C. Curative Instructions

After an objection has been sustained, the attorney making the objection should consider asking the decision maker to instruct the jurors to disregard the improper comment. This curative instruction may reduce the negative impact of the improper comment. Some jurisdictions require the curative instruction be requested to preserve an issue for appeal. A request for a curative instruction may call more attention to the improper statement, however, and ought not to be made if the disadvantage caused by highlighting the improper comment outweighs the effectiveness of the curative instruction. See Section 4.5(D).

D. Opening Statement Motions

An opposing party may bring a motion to dismiss or for a directed verdict on an issue in the case based on admissions made by counsel during opening statement. Admissions made during the opening statement can have a binding legal effect on the party. Because the opening statement is part of the record of the case, facts conceded by counsel during the opening statement may be admissions. This motion is seldom available because rarely will the opposing counsel make such adverse admissions.

A motion to dismiss or for a directed verdict may also be brought on the ground that the opposing party has failed to establish a prima facie case during the opening. Generally, the failure to mention specific evidence in the opening does not preclude subsequent introduction of the evidence at trial. As long as the pleadings and pretrial proceedings have placed matters in issue, the rules of evidence and not the scope of the opening statement determine what evidence will be admissible and inadmissible.

In a civil case, a trial court has the discretion to grant a summary disposition based upon the opening statement of counsel. If an opening statement contains admissions or fails to refer to sufficient supporting evidence, there may be grounds for a motion to dismiss, a summary judgment, or directed verdict. In criminal cases, a decision maker may direct a verdict for the defendant on the basis of the prosecutor's opening statement if no reasonable juror could convict the defendant based upon the facts stated in the opening statement.

The purpose for a summary disposition based upon the opening statement is judicial economy. A trial is unnecessary if, based on the opening statement, it is obvious that no claim, defense, or case exists. Summary dispositions are rarely granted. Opening statements usually contain more than enough information to support a claim or defense. If a case is so weak that no facts exist to support a claim or defense, the weakness will be apparent at the pretrial stage and the case should be dismissed or settled at that time. If counsel fails to refer to facts sufficient to support a claim or defense, the trial judge may allow the case to go to trial. If such a summary disposition motion is granted, and evidence exists which was not described in the opening, the losing side should move to reopen the case and supplement the opening statement.

Other possible motions include:

- A motion to have the court set restraints on the opponent's opening regarding time, scope, detail, and demeanor. If an attorney exceeds the reasonable standards for an opening, this motion may be granted.

- A motion by plaintiff to present additional facts in rebuttal to defendant's opening. This unusual motion may be appropriate in a situation in which the defendant raises unanticipated issues.

CHAPTER 7

DIRECT EXAMINATION

Reflections on Advocacy

Any fact is better established by two or three good testimonies than by a thousand arguments.

—Nathaniel Eramens

If you can't be direct, why be?

—Lily Tomlin

§ 7.1 INTRODUCTION

A. Purpose

Testimony from witnesses is a primary source of evidence in our dispute resolution system. An advocate asks questions, and the witness becomes the storyteller. The focus of attention — the spotlight — is on the witness and the story that is being told.

Direct examination requires an advocate to present evidence that will:

- Be legally sufficient to survive a motion for a directed verdict or a motion to dismiss.

- Meet or exceed evidentiary admissibility requirements.

- Be easily understood and readily remembered by the fact finder.

- Convince the fact finder of the truth of the story being told.

- Stand up to the test of cross-examination.

- Anticipate, counter, or contradict evidence submitted by the opposition.

The direct examiner must ask questions that permit the witness to recreate an event so that the fact finder will see, feel, hear, sense, and perceive the event exactly as perceived by the witness. The story told by the witness must be clear, interesting, credible, and convincing. It is the responsibility of the direct examiner to ask questions to develop this story and enable the witness to communicate effectively.

A good direct examination sounds and looks easy. The witness describes the events in a clear and persuasive way while being credible. The fact finder is engrossed in the story. There are no interruptions and the examination flows. The opposing attorney can make no objections that would be sustained. And, all the evidence needed to prove the case is introduced.

It may appear that a good direct examination depends on an effective witness, an easy case, or just plain luck. But, the success or failure of a direct examination depends primarily upon the abilities of the direct examiner. The advocate orchestrates the telling of an interesting and persuasive story through a credible and convincing witness.

B. *Taking of Testimony*

The taking of the testimony of witnesses in court trials is done orally and in open court. The process begins with the judge asking counsel to call a witness, or counsel saying: "The plaintiff calls Ms. Heather as our first (or next) witness." The judge or clerk may ask the witness, who is seated at the counsel table or in the back of the courtroom, to come forward and stand in front of or enter the witness box. Witnesses are asked to raise their right hand, and in some jurisdictions, are asked to place their left hand on a Bible. The clerk or judge then administers an oath or affirmation. A witness may choose to affirm to tell the truth rather than swear to an oath that includes the word "God." Then, the witness sits in the witness box.

The clerk or judge may then ask the witness: "Please state your full name and spell your last name for the record." In some jurisdictions, witnesses may also be asked to give their address. The judge may then state to counsel, "Counsel, you may proceed," or the attorney may automatically begin asking questions. The direct examiner need not have witnesses repeat their name and address and can begin the direct examination with a new, relevant question.

In arbitrations and administrative hearings, the process is similar to court trials with the decision maker often administering the oath or affirmation. In lieu of testifying in person, witnesses may alternatively testify over the telephone, video transmission or by other satellite, electronic, or cable means.

§ 7.2 EVIDENCE CONSIDERATIONS

Four primary evidentiary considerations apply to direct examination:

1. The witness must be *competent* to testify.

2. The testimony must be *relevant.*

3. *Foundation* questions must establish the *reliability* of the testimony.

4. The *form* of the question must be proper.

A. *Competency*

There are four competency requirements: A witness must:

- Give an *oath* or an affirmation,
- *Perceive* something,
- *Remember* what was perceived, and
- *Communicate* this information.

The judge or arbitrator determines when a witness meets these requirements. The rules regarding competency reflect practical decisions made by direct examiners. A witness who fails in one of these four requirements is obviously not going to be helpful and will not be called to testify.

1. Oath or Affirmation

A witness must agree to tell the truth either in response to an oath ("I do") or an affirmation ("I affirm that what I will say will be the truth"). The witness must be able to understand the meaning of an oath or affirmation. The competency of most witnesses will be obvious and go unchallenged.

Witnesses may be challenged if they are unable to understand what it means to tell the truth. Such witnesses include young children or people with mental, learning, memory, or communication disabilities. It may be necessary for the direct examiner to ask a series of questions that demonstrate the witness' ability to understand and tell the truth.

Example:

Lawyer examining young child:

Q: Jeff, how old are you?

A: Seven.

Q: What does it mean to you when someone asks you to tell the truth?

A: It means I shouldn't lie.

Q: What is a lie?

A: It's when I don't tell the truth about something.

Q: What happens to you when you don't tell the truth?

A: Ah, I have to go to my room, or I can't do something that I want to do.

Q: Has that happened to you?

A: Yea.

Q: What will you tell us today?

A: What happened to me.

Q: Will it be the truth?

A: Yes.

In jury trials, it may be necessary to conduct a hearing outside the presence of the jury for the judge to determine whether a witness is competent. An attorney who plans to conduct a direct examination of a questionable witness may ask the court to rule on the competency of the witness before that witness takes the stand to avoid the opposing party from objecting to a witness in front of the jurors. The direct examiner may ask questions of the witness to lay a foundation to establish competency. A judge may prefer to meet the witness in chambers and talk with the witness to determine competency.

2. Perception

The degree to which a witness must perceive something depends upon the nature of the testimony. A witness is competent to testify if the witness has personal knowledge of the matters about which the witness is to testify. The rules of evidence exclude testimony concerning matters the witness did not observe or had no opportunity to observe. See Fed. R.Evid. 602. Witnesses acquire personal knowledge through any of their senses. Witnesses who hear or see something can testify to what they heard or saw. See Section 4.8(C).

A lay witness can testify to an opinion if the opinion is rationally based on the perception of the witness and the opinion is helpful to either a clear understanding of the testimony or determination of the fact in issue. Witnesses can testify to opinions within the realm of common experience and which help the fact finder understand an issue. Common lay witness opinions include speed, time, distance, emotions, feelings, age, health, and sobriety. See Section 4.8(C)(3)(b).

A witness may be qualified to testify as an expert witness if the testimony is not generally within the knowledge of the fact finder and the testimony will assist the fact finder in understanding the case or will help establish a fact in issue. Expert testimony includes scientific, technical, or other specialized knowledge outside the scope of the common experiences of the fact finder. A witness is qualified as an expert when the witness has sufficient knowledge, skill, experience, training, or education to render an opinion. Unlike a lay witness, an expert need not witness an incident. For a detailed explanation of expert witnesses, see Chapter 10.

3. Recollection

A witness must be able to recall what was perceived. A witness whose memory may somehow have been affected between the time of observing an event and trial may be challenged as incompetent. For example, witnesses may be incompetent if they suffered an injury adversely affecting their ability to remember.

4. Communication

A witness must be able to communicate. Witnesses must be able to narrate what they perceived either through their own words or those of an interpreter. A witness with communication difficulties may be assisted by the direct examiner who can ask leading questions to help the witness testify. See Section 7.7(B). This tactic must be carefully employed to avoid highlighting the inability of the client to testify independently of the attorney.

B. Relevance

Testimony must be relevant before it may be considered by the fact finder. Relevant testimony has a tendency to make more or less probable any facts of consequence to the case. Fed.R.Evid. 401 and 402. See Section 4.8(A). If the testimony has probative value, it is admissible. If the testimony has no logical relationship to the case, it is not relevant and therefore not admissible.

While almost all relevant testimony is admissible, there are some exceptions. If the prejudicial value of the evidence unfairly outweighs its probative value, or if the testimony confuses the issues, misleads the fact finder, causes undue delay, or is a needless presentation of cumulative evidence, the evidence will not be permitted even though relevant. Fed.R.Evid. 403. In addition, there are other types of unfairly prejudicial evidence described in Section 4.8(A)(4) that will not be permitted even if relevant: improper character evidence (Fed.R.Evid. 404 and 405), improper habit evidence (Fed.R.Evid. 406), subsequent remedial measures (Fed.R.Evid. 407), offers of compromise (Fed.R.Evid. 408), payment of medical expenses (Fed.R.Evid. 409), plea bargains (Fed.R.Evid. 410), and liability insurance (Fed.R.Evid. 411).

C. Foundation

Evidence based upon unknown or unreliable sources is not admissible. Foundation consists of the facts that establish the reliable source of the evidence. Before evidence of "Y" can be introduced, evidence of "X" must be established. The "X" is the foundation testimony. See Section 4.8(C)(4).

Example:

Examining Attorney:

Q: What happened when you arrived home?

A: Someone was in the kitchen with Dinah.

Q: Who was it?

Objecting lawyer:

Objection: Lack of foundation.

Judge:

Sustained.

Examining Attorney:

Q: What did you do when you got to the house?

A: I walked into the kitchen.

Q: What did you see?

A: I saw someone in the kitchen with Dinah.

Q: What did you see this person doing?

A: Strummin' on the ol' banjo.

Q: What else was this person doing?

A: He was singing "Fee Fi Fiddley I Oh."

Q: Did you recognize this person?

A: Yes.

Q: How?

A: I had seen and heard him strum his banjo and sing this song at the Grand Ol Opry.

Q: Who was he?

A: Corky Wharton.

Q: Who?

D. Reliable Evidence

The evidence introduced through direct examination must be assessed to determine its reliability. The following questions assess the admissibility of evidence:

- Does the witness have personal knowledge of the matter? Fed. R.Evid. 602.
- Has a sufficient foundation been laid to establish the source of the information? Fed.R.Evid. 901 and 903.
- Is the opinion testimony rationally based on the perception of the witness? Fed.R.Evid. 701.
- Is the out-of-court statement not defined as hearsay? Fed.R.Evid. 801.
- Is the testimony admissible based on an exception to the hearsay rule? Fed.R.Evid. 803 and 804.

If these questions are answered in the affirmative, the evidence is admissible. The following examples illustrate questions establishing reliable testimony:

Example: (Description of an event):

Q: What happened with the harpoon?

A: The harpoon was launched, striking the whale.

Q: What did the whale do?

A: The stricken whale flew forward and dove beneath the sea.

Q: What happened with the harpoon line?

A: With igniting velocity the line ran through the groove until it ran afoul.

Q: What happened after the line ran afoul?

A: Captain Ahab stopped to clear it, but the flying line caught him around the neck.

Q: Then what happened to Captain Ahab?

A: He was shot out of the boat, voicelessly as Turkish mutes bowstring their victim.

Q: What did you see?

A: He was gone. He disappeared into the depths of the sea.

Q: What did you see next?

A: After a while, the whale breached. It shot out of the water.

Q: Did you see Captain Ahab?

A: Yes.

Q: Where was he?

A: He was strapped to the whale, bound by the harpoon lines.

Q: How did he look?

A: Peaceful. His arm was waving at us, beckoning us to follow him.

Q: Did you hear Captain Ahab say anything?

A: Yes.

Q: What did he say?

A: He said, "I spend my last breath on thee."

Example (Description of sensations):

Q: Shortly before you saw the fire, did you smell anything, Ms. Nero?

A: Yes.

Q: What did you smell?

A: I smelled smoke.

Q: Did you hear anything shortly before you saw the fire?

A: Yes.

Q: What did you hear?

A: A fiddle.

Example (Identification of a speaker):

Q: Do you know Jan Dean?

A: Yes, I do.

Q: How?

A: I was his friend for years.

Q: Did he talk to you about the accident?

A: Yes, he did.

Q: What did he say?

A: He said, "Gosh, I sure wish that I hadn't gone so fast around Dead Man's Curve."

Example (Description of opinions):

Q: What did Norma Rae do?

A: I saw her run over to the foreman and shake her fist at him.

Q: How far away from them were you?

A: About three feet.

Q: Did you see how Ms. Rae looked?

A: Yes.

Q: How did she look?

A: She was quite flushed and very excited.

Q: What did she do next?

A: She grabbed a sheet of paper and began writing on it.

Q: How long did you see Ms. Rae?

A: For about a minute.

Q: How would you describe her actions?

A: She was very angry.

Example (Explanation of an incident):

Q: What did you see, Mr. Frost?

A: Two roads diverged in a yellow wood.

Q: What were you thinking?

A: Sorry I could not travel both and be one traveler.

Q: What happened next?

A: Long I stood.

Q: What did you see as you were standing there?

A: I looked down one as far as I could see.

Q: What did you do?

A: I took the one less traveled by.

Q: Why?

A: Because it made all the difference.

---

§ 7.3 PREPARATION

A. *Overall Preparation*

The preparation of direct examination begins with a review of the legal theories, actual story, and significant issues of the case. Evidence that is necessary to support a theory, fact, or issue needs to be established through direct examination.

1. Legal Theories

The elements of each claim or defense must be reviewed to ascertain what direct examination testimony is needed to prove these legal elements. A review of the jury instructions in a jury trial and the proposed findings of facts in a bench trial provide this information.

2. Factual Story

A direct examination must introduce those facts and opinions the witness knows or holds that are part of the factual story of the case. The direct examination of a witness must also establish the foundation for the admissibility of exhibits the witness can identify. Further, the direct examiner must anticipate the cross-examination of the witness and plan to reveal information that reduces the effectiveness of the anticipated cross-examination questions. The direct examiner must also review the theories, facts, and issues of the opposing party's case and determine whether additional information should be introduced that contradicts or rebuts the opposing side's evidence.

3. Significant Issues

The direct examiner must review the significant issues in a case to determine whether a witness should be asked questions regarding those issues. A witness who has information that corroborates important facts, buttresses the credibility of another witness, provides additional information from which the fact finder may draw favorable inferences, or has any other helpful information, should testify to this evidence on direct examination.

B. Evidence/Witness Chart

Form 7.1 provides an analytical framework to prepare a direct examination.

C. Written Preparation

The presentation of an effective direct examination requires the preparation of written materials. These materials may be an outline of topics, a list of questions, or a combination of topics and questions. A written outline provides an organized and structured approach to the examination and includes the major topics about which the witness will testify. The detailed list of questions acts as a script for the direct examination and contains the sequence of questions to be asked. The materials should be written in large, easy-to-read print, with important words, phrases, and questions highlighted.

A combination outline/script provides the advantages of both while reducing the disadvantages of each. An outline may be effective for easy questions and simple topics, but may be inadequate for complex or difficult foundations or subjects. A detailed script provides a complete list of questions to be asked, but may not permit sufficient flexibility and may encourage the attorney to read questions instead of asking questions in a conversational manner. A well-prepared outline/script contains a comprehensive list of topics to be covered and specific questions to be asked in certain areas. These topics and questions ensure the direct is complete and comprehensive and provides the attorney with an easy to follow format.

In preparing written direct examination materials:

- Write out all the topics that need to be covered.

- Organize and sequence the topics by grouping together ones that are related.

- Write out questions for those topics that need prepared written questions.

- Edit and supplement the materials during witness and trial preparation.

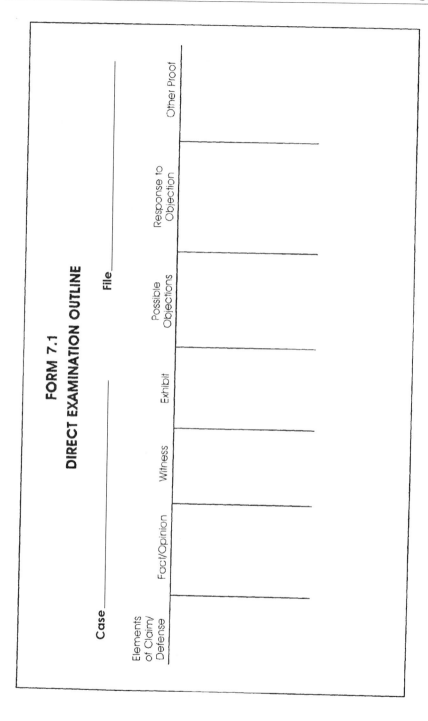

FORM 7.1
DIRECT EXAMINATION OUTLINE

Witness Preparation Example for Personal Injury Auto Accident:

Background

Name

Address

Family

    Spouse

    Children

Education

    High school

    College

    Degrees

Hobbies

Job

    Present

        Duties

        Duration

        Responsibilities

    Prior

        Duties

        Duration

        Responsibilities

Day of Accident

    Date–March 3, 2004

    Location-999 Westview Drive, Green Acres

Before accident

    Where

    When

    From-to

At accident

    Where standing

    Lighting

    Weather conditions

    Other cars

    Busy intersection

    Other witnesses

    Arrival of police

Scene

    Intro diagram: fair and accurate representation

    NE corner-corner where standing-gas station

    SE corner-opposite corner-straight ahead-corn field

    NW corner-corner to left-grocery store

    SW corner-diagnoal opposite-ball diamond

Action

    Blue Chevy going west — right to left on Westview Drive

    Red Ford going east — left to right on Westview Drive

Foundation for speed of Chevy

    How long in view

    From what distance

    From where to where

        Drove car for 20 years

        Estimated speed of own car and other cars

        Opinion: 30 m.p.h.

Collision

    Standing on corner

    Waiting to cross street

    Watching traffic

    Saw collision

    Describe collision

    Front end of Chevy hit driver's door of Ford

After collision

    Ran over to Chevy

    Passenger opened car door and got out

    How did the passenger appear to you?

    Did the passenger say anything to you?

    What did the passenger say?

Leave scene

    Went home

        Contacted by investigator

D. Practice/Rehearsal

An effective way to prepare a direct examination is to practice asking the questions out loud, following the prepared outline/script. There is no need initially to have a witness provide the answers.

Verbalizing the questions familiarizes the attorney with the direct examination, makes the attorney more comfortable with the questions to be asked, and increases the attorney's level of confidence. Changes to the written outline/script can be made after this rehearsal.

Successive rehearsals allow the attorney to experiment with pacing, timing, voice modulation, gestures, and movement. The direct examination should be practiced until the attorney knows the material and is comfortable and confident while conducting the practice direct examination.

§ 7.4 WITNESS PREPARATION

An attorney must develop a system to ensure that all witnesses who will testify on direct examination have been contacted and subpoenaed. All witnesses, even friendly witnesses, should be subpoenaed a reasonable time before testifying to assure attendance as well as generate neutrality. Form 7.2 provides a checklist for witness selection and preparation.

Witnesses should be prepared and familiar with the testimony they will give at the trial or hearing. Factors that may influence the witness' impressions include:

- Who conducts the preparation? Does the witness feel important because the attorney conducts the preparation?
- When does preparation occur? Will the witness be more comfortable if the preparation takes place at a time convenient to the witness?
- Where does the preparation occur? The location, the furniture, and physical layout may affect the impression of the witness.
- Why does the preparation take place? Does the witness understand the role of the witness in the trial and the issues in the case to the extent necessary to be an effective witness?

A. Obtaining Information

The gathering of information from witnesses occurs before the initiation of the lawsuit and continues through pretrial proceedings. The attorney must determine how the information is to be gathered. Every contact with the witness should be viewed as an opportunity to prepare the witness for trial.

The attorney must determine:

- What facts the witness knows,
- What opinions the witness has,
- What exhibits the witness can identify,
- Prior statements the witness has made,
- Weaknesses that may be established by the cross-examiner, and
- Prior experience as a witness.

FORM 7.2
WITNESS INFORMATION WORKSHEET

Case _____   **File** _____

Name of Witness   _____

Address   _____

Phone: Home _____ Work   _____

Employer   _____

Statement taken _____ Deposition completed _____

Subpoena/Duces tecum served   _____

Witness given copy of statement/
   Deposition to review   _____

   Deposition transcript summarized   _____

Former testimony to be used   _____ _____

Purpose(s) of witness   _____

   _____

Exhibits to be introduced through witness   _____

   _____

Witness prepared   _____

Appearance date _____   Time   _____

The trial attorney may attempt to shape the story of the witness before or during the time the witness is being prepared. After the attorney obtains this information, the attorney needs to consider:

- What can this witness contribute to the case?

- How important is this witness to the case?

- What are the strengths and weaknesses of this witness?

- What are the abilities of the witness to observe, perceive, remember, and communicate?

- How vulnerable is this witness to cross-examination?

B. *Extent and Methods of Preparation*

The advocate must meet with the witness in order to fully and properly prepare that witness for direct examination. The type and extent of preparation varies from case to case, from attorney to attorney, and from witness to witness. Areas to be covered include the legal theories, the factual summary, and significant issues. The more critical the witness is, the more thorough this explanation must be.

There are a variety of ways advocates prepare witnesses. Some attorneys prefer to conduct a mock interrogation and dress rehearsal, complete with questions and answers, of a direct examination and the probable cross-examination, conducted by the attorney or a colleague. Some attorneys videotape witnesses so the witnesses can view their answers and their demeanor. Other attorneys prefer to prepare a witness by outlining the structure of the examination without rehearsing specific answers to specific questions.

Attorneys may take the witness to the courtroom or hearing room where the case will be tried. When the court is in session, the witness can see where everybody sits and watch the proceedings for awhile. When the court is out of session, the witness can sit in the witness chair and walk around the courtroom and become more comfortable with the surroundings. Whatever the approach taken, the witness must be properly prepared to testify in a way that is credible and does not appear contrived.

Witnesses may be prepared individually, in groups, during one interview or several interviews. The appropriate method depends upon the type of case, the ability of the witnesses, and the time available. Some witnesses may have problems that require special consideration before trial. Children, people with communication disabilities, and extremely nervous people are among witnesses who may need special care during preparation. Doctors, linguists, therapists, or interpreters may assist attorneys with these witnesses. Some witnesses may be rambling, defensive, arrogant, or sarcastic, and the advocate must discuss these problems with the witness to reduce or eliminate their negative impact.

The goal of witness preparation is to have the witness testify truthfully and be believed by the fact finder. Some attorneys overly prepare a witness by "sandpapering" and "sanitizing" their testimony. All witnesses have some weaknesses and problems that need to be dealt with in an open and forthright way throughout the trial. An attorney should adjust the approach to each lay and expert witness depending upon the experience the witness has in testifying, the importance of the testimony, the witness' ability to testify, and the witness' effectiveness in communicating information.

In addition to personally meeting with a witness, there are other ways an attorney can provide information. The attorney can send the witness a letter or booklet which explains general information about the trial process and specific information about the case. If the witness is a client, this written information will most likely be protected by the attorney/client privilege and not be discoverable by the opposing attorney, except to the extent the information refreshes the recollection of a witness. If the witness is not a client, the written information will most likely be discoverable by the opposing attorney if requested. Another means of witness preparation is the viewing by a witness of a videotape providing general information to the witness about the case process, including direct and cross-examination.

After preparation and before the trial, the attorney should instruct the witnesses to keep the attorney informed of their whereabouts and of any new information concerning the case, and to bring their individual subpoena to court.

C. *Preparation for Direct Examination*

Witnesses must know what is expected and what will happen at the trial or hearing. Areas to be covered with a witness include explanations about:

- The stages of the trial or hearing.
- The role of the judge, jury, arbitrator, witnesses, attorneys, and court personnel.
- Objection procedures, including the meaning of the words "overruled" and "sustained."
- Practical matters such as transportation to the trial or hearing, the meaning of a subpoena, the location of the trial or hearing, when to appear, the place to meet the attorney, the place to wait before testifying, and what to do after testifying.
- Preparation of diagrams or demonstrative evidence to be drawn on or used by the witness.
- Explaining what the attorney may do if the witness forgets something, such as the use of leading questions and other ways to refresh recollection.
- The need to testify only to what the witness saw, did, said, or heard.
- Avoiding speculation, guesses, and assumptions.

- Avoiding memorizing answers.

Directions the advocate must give a witness include:

- When you are called as a witness, walk confidently to the witness stand or witness chair and remain standing upright while taking the oath. Say "I do" clearly so that everyone can hear.
- Tell the truth.
- Speak clearly and loudly and do not cover your mouth with your hand.
- If you will be testifying regarding an event, attempt to recreate in your mind the details of that event. Picture the scene, the persons present, what happened, what was said, and other details.
- Listen carefully to the questions and make sure you understand them before answering. If you do not understand, ask me to repeat the question. If you still do not understand the question, say so. Never answer a question you do not fully understand or before you have thought your answer through.
- Answer with positive, definite answers. Avoid saying "I think," "I believe," "I'm not real sure," or "In my opinion" when you actually know the facts. If you are uncertain or do not know an answer, say so.
- If your answer was incorrect or unclear, correct it. It is appropriate to say "I want to clarify something."
- Use your own words and language, not my language or someone else's words.
- When testifying, imagine you are having a conversation with the fact finders.
- Look at and speak to the fact finder when testifying.
- Answer the question asked; do not second guess why I asked the question.
- Be aware of body posture.
- Dress neatly and appropriately as if the trial or hearing was a serious event.
- Do not bring any written notes or material unless I tell you to do so.
- Immediately stop when an attorney objects or when the judge or arbitrator interrupts. Do not try to sneak in an answer.
- If there is an objection to the question, listen to the objection and what the attorneys and judge say. You may learn something about the question and how it should be answered from these statements.
- Be courteous, and avoid disagreeing with me or making jokes.
- Do not make gestures or facial expressions which are distracting.

- Do not ask the judge or arbitrator for advice. I will assist you.

- Anticipate being nervous; it is normal and expected.

- If you feel ill, excessively nervous, or fatigued, ask for a break or for a glass of water.

An attorney may need or wish to provide witnesses with additional information. If the witness is a client, obviously that person will need to be involved in all aspects of the case and know everything about it.

D. Suggestions for Cross–Examination

Directions the advocate should give before a witness testifies include:

- Answer directly and simply, with a "Yes" or "No," if appropriate. Do not volunteer information or attempt to explain an answer. I may have you explain something on redirect examination if I think it's appropriate.

- If your answer is complete and truthful, remain quiet. Do not say more even if the cross-examiner looks at you expecting you to say more. If the examiner asks you if that is all you recall, say "Yes" if that is the truth.

- Testify to only what you have personally seen, done, said, or heard. Do not speculate, guess, or assume anything. If you do not "know" something because you have not seen, done, said, or heard it, your answer should be, "I don't know."

- Testify only to your best recollection. If you do not recall something, do not hesitate to say so, even if you fear this may make you appear to look foolish.

- Do not exaggerate, and avoid adjectives and superlatives such as "never" or "always."

- Take your time if you need to in answering a question.

- If information is contained in a document and you are uncertain of an answer, ask to see the document, or state you do not recall the answer.

- If you are asked a question which was asked during a deposition or a prior statement, answer the question if you recall the answer. Otherwise, say you do not recall.

- Do not allow the cross-examiner to put words in your mouth. Do not accept the cross-examiner's characterization of time, distances, or events. If a question is inaccurate, state "I cannot answer that question" even if the attorney tries to force you into agreeing or disagreeing with the question or saying yes or no.

- If you say something that is inconsistent with your prior testimony, do not collapse. Mistakes will happen. If you make a misstatement, correct it. If you make a mistake, admit it.

- Expect the cross-examiner to obtain some information that may weaken your story. Every lawsuit has two sides, and the cross-examiner is attempting to tell the other side of the story.

- If the cross-examiner seems confused, do not attempt to help.

- Answer trick questions properly:

"Have you talked to anyone about this case?"

> Explain with whom you have talked about the case, including the lawyer or other witnesses, or anyone else. It is normal and expected to talk with these individuals.

"Are you being paid to testify in this case?"

> You are not being paid to testify. You may be receiving some compensation for the time spent in court away from your work.

E. Client Guidelines

A client who sits throughout the case at the counsel table may need to be advised about certain procedures. The client should be told that:

- The client will be periodically watched by the decision maker and should always be conscious of being observed.

- The client should periodically maintain eye contact with the decision maker. This helps personalize the client.

- The client should not interrupt the attorney unless necessary or when the attorney seeks advice. It may be preferable for the client to write a note to the attorney.

- The client must pay attention throughout the case and concentrate on the evidence and arguments and watch the decision maker. The client may be able to catch something the attorney missed.

F. Sequence of Witnesses

The order in which witnesses testify in a case is a critical aspect of how a case is presented. There are numerous factors that a trial attorney must consider in determining the most effective sequence of witnesses.

- *Chronology.* Witnesses can be called in the order in which the story unfolds.

- *Topical Order.* Witnesses may be called in the order in which the attorney presents topics to the fact finder.

- *First and Last Impression.* The witness that provides the best first or last impression about the case should be called first or last.

- *Overview Witness.* A witness who provides a general overview of important events should be called first or early during the case.

- *Party Witness.* The party can be called early during their case in chief to provide the fact finder with the opportunity to see and hear this key witness near the outset.

- *Adverse Witness.* If a party calls the opposite party as an adverse witness, and if the adverse witness must testify to damaging admissions, this evidence should be presented at a time during the case that presents the best impact.

- *Foundation Witness.* A witness who has information needed to establish the foundation for the introduction of other evidence should be called before that evidence is offered.

- *Critical Exhibits.* In a case involving important exhibits, it may be necessary to introduce the exhibit at the outset of the case and to call the witnesses necessary to lay the foundation for the introduction of the critical exhibits.

- *Corroborating Witnesses.* A witness who has information which corroborates testimony of a main witness should follow the main witness.

- *Repetitive Information.* If several witnesses will testify to the same facts, it may be effective to separate these witnesses in order to reduce the impression that their stories have been prepared in advance or rehearsed.

- *Weak Witness.* An unimportant witness or an important witness who may have credibility problems or who may be boring should be called when their negative impact is at a minimum.

- *"Sandwich" Sequence.* Strong witnesses should be called in the beginning and at the end, with weak witnesses called in between.

- *Lay Witnesses Before Expert Witnesses.* Lay witnesses who establish facts which support the opinion of an expert witness should be called before the expert witness testifies.

- *Availability of Witnesses.* Some witnesses, particularly expert witnesses, may only be available at predetermined days and times, limiting when they can be scheduled. Their scheduling needs must be accommodated in order for them to appear and testify.

- *Deposition Testimony.* In civil cases, when witnesses are unavailable to testify in person, their deposition transcript may be read or their deposition video shown to the fact finder. The advantage is that the video can be edited to provide concise and relevant testimony. The disadvantage is that this means of providing testimony is often not as interesting or persuasive as live testimony.

- *Time of Day/Place in Case.* The time of the day when witnesses testify and the place they testify in a multi-day trial or hearing may affect the impression they make on the fact finder. Important or complex evidence may be better received when the fact finder is more alert in the morning or after an afternoon break. The period before or after a lunch or recess may be less productive because the fact finder is thinking about lunch, taking a break, or going home and may be least alert and awake.

- *Concluding Witness.* The last witness in a case should serve one or more purposes, such as: highlighting the case theory, emphasizing important facts, and providing compelling evidence. The concluding witness should not be vulnerable to cross-examination. In a case involving expert witnesses, strong expert witnesses typically make effective final witnesses.

- *Rebuttal Witnesses.* An important witness should never be saved for rebuttal. If the opposing side chooses not to present the anticipated information needed for the witness to rebut, the witness may not be allowed to testify. See Section 3.6(F).

Whatever order of witnesses an attorney selects, the attorney must be prepared to change that sequence. Flexibility may be needed because witnesses may be late or become unavailable on a scheduled day. The prediction the attorney made regarding the time needed to introduce evidence may be wrong, and witnesses may need to be called out of order. The planned sequence of witnesses may need to be adjusted during the trial. The attorney may request that the judge or arbitrator allow for a recess or a break in the case, but it is unlikely this request will be granted because of other scheduling conflicts.

§ 7.5   ATTORNEY PRESENTATION

A.   *Location and Movement*

Many courts have established rules that restrict the attorney's location and movement in the courtroom during direct examination. Some courts require the attorney to stand at a lectern while questioning, and some of these courts go so far as to require the attorney to stand behind the lectern at all times, permitting the attorney to move only a short distance on either side of the lectern. Other jurisdictions, including arbitration forums and administrative law tribunals, require the attorney remain seated at counsel table during questioning, unless the attorney addresses the judge or arbitrator. Still other jurisdictions provide the attorney complete freedom, and the attorney can decide whether it is best to stand, sit, or move about the courtroom.

An attorney who is in a jurisdiction which restricts location and movement may ask permission to ask questions from a different location. Permission should be sought if there exists a tactical advantage in conducting the examination the way the attorney wants. Such requests may be summarily denied or readily granted. If the judge or arbitrator asks for a reason, the attorney should explain that the witness will be better able to testify and the fact finder better able to hear or see the evidence.

The direct examiner should consider selecting a location that works for the witness, fact finder, and reporter. The place from which the attorney conducts the direct examination should be a place that permits the fact finder to easily hear the witness and see exhibits and allows the reporter, if there is one, to hear and see what is said to ensure a complete and accurate record.

In jury trials, some direct examiners prefer to place the jury between the witness and the direct examiner. This placement encourages both the witness and the attorney to speak loud enough so that the jurors can easily hear, focuses the jurors' attention on the witness because the attorney is out of their line of sight when they look at the witness, and encourages the jurors to move their heads periodically back and forth between the witness and the attorney, keeping the jurors more alert.

B. Approaching the Witness

Judges and arbitrators permit attorneys to approach the witness when the attorney needs to show the witness an exhibit. Some judges, especially those who are conservative in permitting movement, require the attorney to ask for permission before approaching a witness. See Section 3.5(D).

Example:

Examining Attorney:

Q: What did you do with the gold medal, Ms. Quann, when you picked it up?

A: I scratched my initials on it.

To the Court:

Your Honor, may I approach the witness with the exhibit that has been marked for identification as Exhibit No. 14?

Judge:

Yes, you may.

Many judges do not require the attorney to ask for permission to approach the witness. They assume that if the attorney approaches the witness, it is for a good reason. Those judges that do require attorneys to ask for permission may only expect the request to be made the first time an attorney approaches the witness. It is usually unnecessary for the attorney to ask to approach the witness on subsequent visits to the witness stand. See Section 3.5(D).

C. Procedures

Formal and informal rules and idiosyncratic preferences by judges and arbitrators may affect how aspects of direct examination proceed. The advocate attorney needs to be familiar with, or ask the judge or arbitrator about, specific procedures that must or should be followed.

§ 7.6 STRUCTURE OF DIRECT EXAMINATION

Every direct examination must be organized in a manner that most effectively achieves its purposes. A structure should be selected to enable the witness to tell an interesting, persuasive, and credible story.

A. *Beginning of Direct Examination*

A common and effective way to begin a direct examination is to establish the background of the witness. Background questions accomplish a number of direct examination goals. They:

- Relieve some of the initial anxiety and nervousness of the witness and put the witness at ease. Questions regarding employment, family, and hobbies are usually easy to answer.

- Build confidence in the witness to provide longer and more detailed answers as the examination proceeds.

- Help establish a witness' personality and credibility. Easy to answer questions humanize witnesses and reflect the way they naturally talk.

- Identify similarities between the witness and the fact finder, especially jurors. Any similarities strengthen the credibility of a witness because the jurors unconsciously or consciously identify with the witness, which strengthens their perception regarding the sincerity and integrity of the witness.

- Establish a foundation to support a witness' statement or opinion in the case. Statements should be sought about the background of the witness that strengthen the witness' ability to testify. For example, if a witness testifies to detailed facts, there may be some prior experiences the witness had which affect the ability of the witness to observe or remember detailed facts.

The extent to which an attorney can develop the background of a witness depends on the type of forum, the relevance of the testimony to a legal issue in the case, the kind of decision maker, the predisposition of the judge to allow a reasonable number of background questions, and the tactical decision by the opposing attorney to object to unnecessary background questions. Administrative law cases may focus on specific, limited issues to which the background of the witness is irrelevant. Many background questions are not legally relevant to a case. For example, whether an eyewitness to an accident has a family or has lived in the community for a long period of time is legally irrelevant to the issues in the case.

Most judges allow a reasonable number of background questions, even though the questions are technically irrelevant, as long as they establish the background of the witness. The more important a witness is in a case, the more likely judges permit extensive background questions. Opposing attorneys may object to background questions that are too numerous or go beyond the boundaries of reasonable background information. The judges overrule these objections if the direct examiner can establish a link between the background question and an issue in the case.

Background questions typically begin a direct examination, unless the case is an administrative hearing where these questions may have no place. Some background questions with some witnesses may be more effectively asked at a later stage of the direct examination. For example, the hobbies of a car crash victim may have more impact on damages when explained by the witness after the witness has related the injuries suffered which prevent the witness from pursuing the hobbies. Background questions that relate to a specific issue the witness will address should be delayed until the witness testifies regarding such an issue.

Example:

Examining lawyer:

Q: Then what happened?

A: He came right up to me and demanded all my money.

Q: What do you do for a living, Ms. Clinique?

A: I am a beauty consultant.

Q: How long have you been doing this?

A: Fifteen years.

Q: What are some of the things that you do on your job?

A: One of the most important things I do is pay attention to the detail of people's faces.

Q: Why?

A: In order to make the correct decisions about what is best for the beauty of my clients.

Q: What have you done to help you with your job?

A: Actually, I study people's faces. Sometimes I am embarrassed because I get caught staring at people.

Q: When you were robbed, what did you do?

A: I stared at the man so I would be able to remember the details of his face.

Q: Describe his facial features.

A: He had brown eyes, brown hair, large cheekbones, a small triangular shaped chin, thin lips, and a bent nose.

B. Structure

The following are ways to construct a direct examination:

1. Chronology

The witness can describe the events in the order in which they occurred.

2. Elements of Claim or Defense

The witness can testify in the order in which the elements of a claim or defense need to be proved. For example, in civil cases, a witness can first discuss the facts which establish liability and then explain the facts which support damages. For another example, in a criminal case, the witness can establish the facts which show a conspiracy and then describe events that explain the criminal act.

3. Flashback

The witness can summarize an event and then describe the event in detail. The direct examiner can ask the witness short narrative questions that provide an overview of the entire event and then ask the witness detailed questions that explain the event step by step. Subsequent specific questions present the details of the incident and are not repetitious of the broad answers.

Example:

Examining lawyer:

Q: Ms. Daa'e, please briefly tell us what you did at 8: 00 p.m. on November 2.

A: I attended a play.

Q: What play?

A: Phantom of the Opera.

Q: What happened after the play?

A: A man came into the box where I was seated.

Q: What did you notice about the man?

A: He was wearing a mask.

Q: Then what happened?

A: He grabbed me and carried me away through a trap door in the stage.

Q: Where did he take you?

A: To the pit.

At this point the direct examiner can have the witness describe the incident in detail.

Q: I want you to tell us what happened step by step that night. What time did the play end?

A: Around 10: 00 p.m.

Q: What is the very first thing you saw immediately after the
play ended?

A: I saw. . . .

§ 7.7 PROPER QUESTION FORM

A witness will not be permitted to answer direct examination
questions that are phrased improperly. Each question asked on direct
examination must be assessed to determine whether its form complies
with the rules of evidence. The following analysis provides a method of
determining whether questions are proper as to their form.

- Does the question suggest the answer? If so, it is a leading
  question. Fed.R.Evid. 611.

- Does the question call for a narrative response? If so, it may be
  overly broad and improper. Fed.R.Evid. 611.

- Is the question a multiple question? If so, it may result in an
  improper compound answer. Fed.R.Evid. 611.

- Is the question vague or ambiguous? If so, it may be confusing or
  unintelligible. Fed.R.Evid. 401 and 403.

- Is the question repetitious? If so, it may produce cumulative,
  unnecessary evidence. Fed.R.Evid. 403 and 611.

A. *Leading Questions*

A leading question is a question that contains and suggests the
answer. Every question is leading to some extent in that it suggests a
topic or a result. Pure non-leading questions are: What? Where? Who?
Why? When? How? Direct examiners would not get very far if forced to
ask these neutral, broad questions, such as "What?" instead of "What is
your job?" A question is not leading and is a proper direct examination
question if it does not suggest the answer. A direct examination question
may suggest something happened, may refer to a topic, may ask whether
someone spoke, and may suggest a result, as long as it does not suggest
the answer.

Example:	**Explanation:**
Q: Did you go anywhere? A: Yes. Q: Where? A: Downtown.	These two questions do not give information but let the witness tell the story. They are not leading.

Example:	**Explanation:**
Q: Where did you go? A: Downtown.	This question suggests that the witness went somewhere, but does not tell where and is proper.

Example:	**Explanation:**
Q: Did you go downtown? A: Yes.	This question suggests that the witness went somewhere and suggests the place. Although it does not actually suggest the answer, it is more leading than the first two examples and may be improper.

Example:	**Explanation:**
Q: You went downtown, Ms. Petula Clark, didn't you? A: Yes.	This question is leading and suggests the answer, and may be permitted only under an exception.

Leading questions are prohibited on direct examination because the witness is to testify and not the attorney. Leading questions may draw objections which interrupt the flow of testimony, and leading questions do not allow the witness the opportunity to tell the story. The witness, who should be the focus of attention, may fade into the background as the attorney "testifies" through leading questions. A fact finder cannot accurately judge the credibility of a witness who has not spoken much and may react negatively to the attorney who is taking over and testifying.

B. *Permissible Leading Questions*

The general rule that "leading questions are not permitted on direct examination" is a rule of limitation and not an absolute prohibition. Proper leading questions can:

- Help a witness testify by suggesting familiar topics.
- Provide an opportunity to introduce variety into the examination.
- Demonstrate honesty by bringing out negative information.
- Speed up the presentation of information.
- Demonstrate the attorney's knowledge of the facts.
- Make the testimony more interesting and compelling.

Federal Rule of Evidence 611(c) and similar state rules permit leading questions when they are necessary to develop testimony. Rule 611(c) has been interpreted to mean that leading questions are permitted in the following situations:

- To bring out preliminary matters;

- To reduce stress and help the witness become comfortable;

- To elicit non-controversial or undisputed facts;

- To establish inconsequential facts;

- To suggest new topics;

- As transitions;

- To bring out negative facts;

- To examine an adverse witness;

- To question a hostile witness or a witness predisposed against the case;

- To lay the foundation for certain exhibits;

- To establish complex foundations;

- To examine a witness who has difficulty communicating because of age or a disability;

- To refresh a witness' recollection;

- To lay a foundation for past recollection recorded;

- When asking a witness to contradict a statement made by another.

Not all judges recognize these exceptions. Many judges will not permit the use of leading questions in all of these situations. Judges in bench trials and administrative hearings and arbitrators may be more inclined to permit leading questions because they believe it is a faster way to introduce evidence. Some of them will also encourage advocates to lead witnesses, to save even more time. The advocate should resist this push if the witness and not the attorney should be the source of the evidence.

The following examples illustrate permissible leading questions recognized by most judges and arbitrators:

Preliminary Matters

Example:

Examining lawyer:

Q: Mr. Dulles, you were Secretary of State in the Eisenhower administration?

A: Of course.

Q: That was a cabinet level position?

A: Yes. I was part of the kitchen cabinet.

Witness Comfort

Example:

Examining lawyer:

Q: On the fifth day of August, at noon, you were at the Monterey Mall?

A: Yes.

Q: Where had you been?

A: At work.

Q: Now, you work for the city, don't you?

A: Yes.

Q: What do you do, Clint ... excuse me, Mr. Eastwood?

A: I am the mayor of the city.

Q: Why were you at the Mall?

A: I was there to give a talk at the opening of the new city child care center.

Eliciting Non-controversial or Undisputed Facts

Assume the example below involves a motorcycle accident in which the issue is fault, not the identity of the rider.

Example:

Examining lawyer:

Q: Mr. Lawson, you were driving Mr. Robert's motorcycle, right?

A: Yes.

Q: It was a V–Max, wasn't it?

A: Yes, it was.

Establishing Inconsequential Facts

Example:

Examining lawyer:

Q: You were planning to visit the Great Wall of China, weren't you, Ms. Buck?

A: Yes.

Q: So, much of your conversation was about the trip?

A: Yes.

Suggesting a New Topic

Example:

Examining lawyer:

Q: Dr. Ezekiel, what was your occupation?

A: I was the medical examiner for the county of Galilee.

Q: How long were you medical examiner?

A: Fifteen years.

Q: What do you do now?

A: I am retired.

Q: Before you retired you performed an autopsy on the body of Lazarus, didn't you?

A: Yes, I did.

As a Transition

Example:

Examining lawyer:

Q: Captain Nord, what did you do on Monday?

A: I destroyed documents in my office using my portable shredder.

Q: Now, on Tuesday you stayed home with your kids?

A: Yes.

Q: What did you do on Wednesday?

A: I again shredded documents in my office.

Bringing Out Negative Information

Example:

Examining lawyer:

Q: What did you see?

A: I saw a munchkin run right down the middle of the road.

Q: You don't know who the munchkin was?

A: No, I don't.

Q: Did you see where the munchkin went?

A: Yes.

Q: Where?

A: Straight down the yellow brick road.

Q: Out of sight?

A: Yes.

Q: And you have never seen the munchkin since that day, have you?

A: Never. Only some hobbits.

Examining an Adverse Witness

Occasionally, the only person who has information necessary to prove a critical element in a case is the opposing party or a person closely identified with the opposing party, such as an employee or agent. The general theory behind direct examination is that witnesses called by one side cooperate with the direct examiner and give information candidly and truthfully, but this is not necessarily true with an adverse witness. An adverse party will obviously not be willing to cooperate, and an adverse witness may favor the opposing party and attempt to use every opportunity to provide information that could damage the case. The adverse witness may be examined as if on cross-examination.

Example:

Examining lawyer (To the Court):

Your Honor, may I call the defendant, Mr. Earnheart, as an adverse witness?

Judge:

You may.

Examining lawyer:

Q: You are a successful race car driver, aren't you?

A: Yes I am.

Q: On April 17, you were driving your car, correct?

A: Yes.

Q: Your car is a 1936 Pierce–Arrow?

A: Yes. It's a beauty.

Q: You drove your car into the back end of the plaintiff's car?

A: Yes.

Q: Immediately before the collision, your foot slipped on your gas pedal?

A: Yes.

Q: It was embarrassing for you to have your foot slip?

A: Of course.

Q: So, that is why you told the police the plaintiff had backed her car into yours at a speed of 25 miles per hour?

A: I'm afraid so.

Questioning a Hostile Witness

An independent witness who demonstrates a reluctance to testify or hostility toward a party becomes a hostile witness, and at that time it is within the discretion of the judge or arbitrator to permit the direct examiner to cross-examine as if the witness were an adverse witness and ask leading questions. A showing of actual hostility in the courtroom and surprise answers by the witness is often a predicate, but surprise is not always a necessary element. If it is clear in advance of the case that the witness will be hostile, the attorney should make a preliminary showing of anticipated hostility. Some witnesses may become hostile during an examination, and the lawyer can then ask for the witness to be treated as a hostile witness.

Example:

Examining lawyer (To the Court):

Your Honor, this witness is a hostile witness. She is angry with the police and my office for prosecuting her friend. While she initially said she would not talk about how much the defendant had to drink, she is now willing to do so but with much reluctance. I am uncertain what she will say. I request the opportunity to use leading questions during the direct examination under the provisions of Rule 611(c).

Judge:

You may do so.

Examining lawyer:

Q: Are you the defendant's friend?

A: Yes.

Q: You are angry with the police for arresting him for drunk driving?

A: That's very true.

Q: Do you want to help the defendant?

A: Yes.

Q: You don't want to be here to testify for the prosecution, do you?

A: No.

Q: You told the police that you did not want him to go to jail, and that you would not tell anybody about how much you saw him drink?

A: Yes.

Q: It is true that you saw the defendant drink an entire bottle of wine and then drive his car?

A: Yes, that's true, but it was an exquisite 1991 French Bordeaux that had extraordinary clarity.

Foundation for Exhibits

Example:

Examining lawyer:

Q: Mr. Noah, I have just handed you a photograph which has been marked for identification as Exhibit No. 2. Do you recognize it?

A: Yes, I do.

Q: What is it?

A: It is a picture of our Ark.

Q: How do you know?

A: Well, it looks just like we left it when we beached it on Mount Ararat.

Q: Is Exhibit No. 2, marked for identification, a fair and accurate representation of how your Ark looked the day before the flood?

A: Yes.

Establishing Complex Foundation

Example:

Examining lawyer:

Q: As a laboratory analyst, Ms. Curie, based on your education, training, experience, and the testing of this substance, do you have an opinion to a reasonable degree of scientific certainty what this substance is?

A: Yes.

Q: What is your opinion?

A: It is law school vending machine food.

Examining a Witness Who Has a Difficult Time Communicating Because of Age or a Handicap

Example:

Examining lawyer:

Q: How old are you, Gretel?

A: Four.

Q: Do you remember what happened to your brother, Hansel?

A: Yes.

Q: He's not here anymore, is he?

A: No.

Q: Do you know what happened to him?

A: Yes.

Q: What happened?

A: We were playing in the woods.

Q: What did you see in the woods?

A: A house.

Q: Did you go into the house?

A: Yeah.

Q: What happened?

A: I saw the old lady put Hansel in the oven.

Refreshing a Witness' Recollection

A witness may have a memory lapse on the stand. A previous statement or a leading question may help the witness recall the answer. It is not unusual for a witness under the stress of an examination to forget something and need their memory jogged.

The examining lawyer may show a document to the witness to refresh the witness' memory. The examining attorney must first establish that the witness now has no memory of the answer about which the witness is being questioned. The witness may review the statement and then must set it aside before answering, since the answer must not be from the document itself, but must be from actual refreshed memory.

The witness should not read from the statement for two reasons. First, it is improper and objectionable. If the witness reads a prior statement, that statement is actually being introduced as past recollection recorded. Federal Rule of Evidence 803(5) requires a specific foundation for the introduction of a document as a previously recorded recollection. See Section 4.8(H)(1)(c).

In practice, the difference between refreshing recollection and past recollection recorded is often ignored and witnesses are frequently permitted to review their notes or statements while testifying. Second, if the witness reads from a statement or document, the witness becomes vulnerable to cross-examination questions which highlight that the witness has no independent recollection of what occurred and may not be believable.

Documents used to refresh recollection do not need to be marked, because they are not offered as evidence, unless the judge or arbitrator requires them to be marked. The cross-examining lawyer has a right to see the written statement or document or item used to refresh, and can use it during cross-examination. See Fed.R.Evid. 612. The opposing attorney may have the document marked and introduce it into evidence for impeachment or as an admission.

In some situations witnesses may bring notes with them to help refresh recollection. Police officers, administrators, and some experts often bring a file with them to the witness stand and use it to refresh their memory during testimony. The opposing lawyer may insist that the notes be used properly. That is, the lawyer may either ask the judge or arbitrator that the witness put the notes away and testify independently without reference to the notes or have the examining attorney lay the proper foundation.

Example:

Use of leading question:

Q: Mr. Chase, when you loaded up the car for your national vacation, what did you pack?

A: Picnic gear, raincoats, regular clothes, suitcases, Wally World map, Aunt Edna ... oh, let's see, I think that's it.

Q: Do you remember putting anything else in the trunk?

A: That's all I can remember.

Q: Did you pack five sets of scuba gear and five pairs of snow skis?

A: How silly of me, of course.

Example:

Use of document:

Q: Mr. Chase, do you remember putting anything else in the trunk?

A: That's all I can remember. There may have been more.

Q: Is there anything that would help refresh your recollection as to what else you might have put in the trunk?

A: Yes, my letter to the insurance company. I listed everything that was stolen.

Q: I have just given you a letter. Do you recognize it?

A: Yes, it is my letter to the insurance company.

Q: Read it please.

A: All right.

Q: Does reading that letter refresh your recollection as to what else you put in your trunk?

A: Yes.

Q: May I have it back, please?

A: Yes, here is the letter.

Q: Do you now remember what else you put in the trunk?

A: Yes.

Q: What?

A: Five sets of scuba equipment and five pairs of snow skis.

Asking a Witness to Contradict a Statement Made by Another

Example:

Examining lawyer:

Q: Ms. Frazier you heard your son testify that the noisy argument took place out on the patio deck, didn't you?

A: Yes, I heard that.

Q: Is that what you recall about the argument?

A: No, it isn't.

Q: Where did the argument take place?

A: The argument occurred in the hallway.

C. *Narrative Questions*

A narrative question may be proper or improper, depending upon the scope of the question, the timing of the question, the ability of the witness to answer, and the ability of the attorney to control the witness. A narrative question is improper if:

- The witness responds with a long, uncontrolled story, or

- The narrative response denies the opposing attorney the opportunity to anticipate objectionable evidence and the ability to make a timely objection, or

- The narrative question reduces the ability of the examining attorney to control the direction or the scope of the examination.

Judges and arbitrators have broad discretion in permitting or limiting the use of narrative questions. In determining whether to allow their use, the decision maker:

— assesses the capabilities of the witness to properly testify and the capabilities of the direct examiner to control the examination,

— is unlikely to allow a witness to answer a narrative question if the witness may be unable to provide a concise response or has a tendency to introduce objectionable testimony,

— will not permit a narrative response if the witness is unprepared or the attorney is insufficiently experienced to interrupt and control the witness who begins to ramble,

— is likely to permit narrative questions asked by an effective examining attorney or by a witness who has properly answered narrative questions without rambling,

— will allow narrative responses to establish background or foundation, or to complete the description of an event.

Specific forms of narrative questions are commonly asked during direct examinations. Narrative questions that are limited in scope or that act as transition questions are usually appropriate, such as "What happened next?" or "Then what happened?" A proper narrative question avoids allowing the witness to tell the entire story, but acts as a directed question allowing the witness to continue telling part of the story.

Example:

Examining lawyer:

Q: Mr. President, what happened in the voting booth on the second Tuesday in November?

A: I voted for Alfred E. Neuman.

Q: Then what happened?

A: I lost the election.

Q: Pleased explain how that changed your life.

D. Improper Question Forms

1. Vague or Ambiguous Questions

All questions must be reasonably clear and specific so that the witness knows what is being asked, the other side knows whether to object and the fact finder can understand the testimony. It may happen that the attorney's mind is racing ahead and what is asked makes little sense, or that lawyer uses the wrong words. Vague, ambiguous, confusing, unintelligible, and misleading questions must be avoided.

Example:

Examining lawyer:

Q: Did you, subsequent to your oral conversation with the professional investigator, affix or otherwise impress your distinctive signature to a testimonial document satisfying the statute of frauds?

A: Well ... Huh?

Q: Let me rephrase the question. Did you sign the piece of paper that Mike Hammer gave you?

A: Oh! Yes, I signed it.

---

2. Repetitious Questions

A witness is generally permitted to describe what happened only once, and an advocate is not permitted to gain unfair advantage by repeating favorable testimony. The form of the question need not be identical to be repetitious. Questions may be asked during direct examination to clarify prior responses, add descriptive details to a story, and emphasize testimony. The key is to avoid asking questions that sound repetitive or produce answers which are repetitive.

Example:

Examining lawyer:

Q: What happened next Ms. Samsonite?

A: I held on to the strap of the briefcase, and he had hold of the other end and was pulling it away from me. I tried to pull it away from him, and then he yanked real hard and pulled it out of my grasp.

Q: How did you try to pull it away from him?

A: I had the newspaper in my left hand, and I gripped the strap with my right hand, and pulled my arm towards my body.

Q: How did he yank the briefcase away from you?

A: He grabbed on to the bottom of the briefcase with both hands and pulled it right out of my hands.

Q: How did he grab on to the briefcase?

A: With both hands.

When more than one witness provides the same information, it becomes cumulative. While it is certainly permissible for witnesses to corroborate each other, it is within the discretion of the judge or arbitrator to place limits on the extent of the cumulative testimony.

2. Multiple Questions

Multiple or compound questions are impossible to understand and create a jumbled court record. It is often unclear what part of the multiple question the witness answered. Compound questions should be withdrawn and rephrased.

Example:

Examining lawyer:

Q: When did you wake up, and what did you see when you awoke? Excuse me. I'll withdraw the question and rephrase it. What day did you wake up, Mr. Van Winkle?

---

§ 7.8 QUESTIONS AND ANSWER TECHNIQUES

This section presents a variety of questioning techniques that can be employed to produce effective testimony.

A. *Background*

1. Putting a Witness at Ease

Questions can be asked to help put the witness at ease as well as establish that the witness is competent.

Example:

Examining lawyer:

Q: Cole, is your last name Bond?

A: Yes.

Q: How old are you, Cole?

A: I am going to be eight.

Q: When are you going to be eight?

A: When my birthday comes.

Q: Who are your Mom and Dad?

A: They're over there.

Q: What is your Dad's name?

A: Chuck.

Q: And Mom's name?

A: Marni.

Q: Do you have any brothers or sisters?

A: Olivia and Brooks and Kelsey.

Q: What do you like to do most of all?

A: Play with my computer.

Q: What is your favorite computer program?

A: I like Lawyer Hunt.

2. Establish a Witness' Background and Personality

The background of the witness is necessary to establish a personality and the credibility of the witness.

Example:

Examining lawyer:

Q:　Tell us your name please.

A:　Vanna Gray.

Q:　Ms. Gray, what is your occupation?

A:　I am a hostess for a television game show.

Q:　What does that involve?

A:　All that I am really required to do is to dress fashionably and to turn letters on a big board as contestants guess them.

Q:　Is that it?

A:　Yes, it is.

Q:　Do you have to do much talking on the show?

A:　No.

Q:　How did you get into that business?

A:　When I finished college, I moved to California and for the fun of it, I auditioned for the job and got it.

Q:　When did you move to California?

A:　About ten years ago.

Q:　Where did you go to college?

A:　The University of Linguistics.

Q:　What did you get your degree in?

A:　I received a degree in etymology.

---

3. Demonstrate Credibility

The experiences of a witness help establish the credibility of that witness. Information which establishes a connection between the experiences of a witness and the evidence should be established.

Example:

Examining lawyer:

Q: Mr. Chan, were you requested to investigate an automobile accident in which Ms. Miyamoto was involved?

A: Yes, I was.

Q: What did you do to investigate this accident?

A: I went out to the accident site and saw Ms. Miyamoto's black Stingray Rickshaw and the other car. I photographed the scene from many different vantage points and photographed the vehicles as they were parked in a parking lot near the intersection. I noticed the skid marks on the street, measured their length and photographed them. I also took close-up photographs of all the damaged parts of both vehicles. I wrote up fact sheets on all of my observations and attached the developed pictures to each of the appropriate fact sheets.

Q: Describe the training that you have had in photography and particularly in taking pictures of accident scenes?

A: I worked as a member of a highway patrol crime and accident scene team for twenty-five years until my retirement three years ago. In the last three years, I have had my own business, Cannon Ball Investigative Services. I have taken forty hours of training in photography through Kodak company and I have studied photography at the University.

Q: Can you estimate how many accident scenes you have investigated and photographed over the last twenty-eight years?

A: Yes.

Q: How are you able to do that?

A: When I started my business, I knew it would be important to be able to provide that information in order to show my experience in the field if I was called upon to testify in court. I went back to the department and went over all of my reports through the use of the computer and was able to determine how many accidents I had investigated. Since I started my own business, I have kept careful records.

Q: How many accident scenes have you investigated and photographed over the last twenty-eight years?

A: Very close to 4,000.

4. *Display the Sincerity of the Witness*

When witnesses are given the opportunity to talk about their lives, jobs, friends, and acquaintances, in their own words, they can demonstrate they are honest and sincere persons.

Example:

Examining lawyer:

Q: Mr. Cassidy, as a bank robber, what kinds of things do you have to do?

A: I have to plan every robbery, buy the bullets, feed the horses, keep track of the money, and be able to shoot accurately.

Q: What details do you plan?

A: We must plan each robbery with great detail. We must know how many persons are working in each bank and how many guards are on duty. We must determine how long we can be in each bank before the sheriff shows up; and, of course, we have to know when the payroll arrives at the bank.

Q: How often do you rob banks?

A: Quite regularly. In the winter we head south. In the summer we head north.

Q: Do you take any breaks between bank robberies?

A: Yes.

Q: How do you take these breaks?

A: Well, every robbery is a little bit different, and so are the breaks. We usually take a week break between banks, sometimes longer, if we get chased.

Q: Where do you usually go?

A: To Hole-in-the-Wall.

Q: Are these breaks important?

A: Yes.

Q: Why?

A: Well, there is some strain in robbing banks and to relieve tension and make sure that we don't make mistakes, me and Sundance and the boys take regular breaks to relax and to help us keep our skills sharp.

---

5. Identify Similarities Between the Witness and the Fact Finder.

It can be helpful to identify similarities between the witness and fact finder.

Example:

Examining lawyer:

Q: Tell us your name?

A: Mr. Spock.

Q: Where do you live?

A: Live?

Q: Yes, where are you from?

A: I see. I am from the Planet Vulcan and that is where I make my home when I am not working.

Q: Where do you work?

A: I am assigned to the Star Ship Enterprise.

Q: And where is the Enterprise now?

A: In the Milky Way — coordinates star point 4896.12.

Q: What is your assignment on the Enterprise?

A: I am the first officer.

Q: Do you have any time for hobbies?

A: Yes, I do.

Q: Tell us please what your hobbies are.

A: Well, I do like to travel. I enjoy camping. One of my favorite places is Yosemite. I like sports, particularly bowling. I enjoy reading, especially twenty-first century history.

B. Establish Foundation to Support Facts

1. Establish Perception

Facts must be established to show that the witnesses saw or heard what they say they saw or heard.

Example:

Examining lawyer:

Q: What happened next?

A: I saw this man walk up to my ticket window and stand right in front of me.

Q: What were the lighting conditions like at that time?

A: There were bright lights on both sides of the ticket window, and there was a light on in the ticket window.

Q: Describe the ticket window you were looking through when you saw the man standing in front of you.

A: It's a clear plate glass window, about 2 feet wide and 3 feet high with a 6 inch opening to pass money and tickets.

Q: What condition was it in on that day?

A: It was clean, and there was nothing blocking my view.

Q: Describe the man you saw, Ms. Ortega.

2. *Enhance Foundation*

Foundation questions should be asked that enhance the reliability and accuracy of the story told by the witness.

Example:

Examining lawyer:

Q: Mr. Fife, where were you at 3:00 in the afternoon last April 2?

A: I was at the northeast corner of the intersection of Lexington and Grand Avenues in our city.

Q: What were you doing?

A: I was working as a crossing guard, watching traffic.

Q: What did you see?

A: I saw a collision between a red Honda and a blue Toyota.

Additional foundation questions further enhance the reliability and accuracy of the witness' story.

Example:

Examining lawyer:

Q: What is your educational background, Mr. Fife?

A: I have a degree from Mayberry High School.

Q: How long ago?

A: Thirty-three years.

Q: Since you graduated from high school, what further education have you had?

A: Courses that helped me in my career like driving school, traffic training, weapons training, not with real bullets, of course, and other police courses needed to sharpen my keen law enforcement skills.

Q: Since graduation what has been your work experience in the field?

A: Well, I haven't worked a lot in the field but I have worked here in town for twenty-five years as a deputy for Sheriff Andy Taylor.

Q: Have you had any special titles?

A: Yes, I am the Guard in Charge of the Mayberry Elementary School crossing.

Q: What are your responsibilities?

A: It is my duty to make sure that all the children get across the street safely, and that means that I have to watch the cars and the children very carefully.

Q: Have you had any special training for this assignment?

A: Yes.

Q: What?

A: Well, Sheriff Taylor sent me to traffic training where I learned the most modern methods of school crossing techniques. And then during the day when the kids are in school, I go out and practice at the crossing, making cars stop and go.

Q: Please describe to us what you saw at the intersection of Lexington and Grand Avenues at 3:00 p.m. on April 2, last year.

---

3. *Establish Foundation to Support an Opinion*

Before a witness can render an opinion, questions need to be asked which show that the witness perceived events which support the opinion or conclusion.

Example:

Examining lawyer:

Q: Were you in the room when John Greystoke signed the will?

A: I most certainly was.

Q: Did you see what he was doing before he signed the will?

A: Yes, I did.

Q: What was he doing?

A: He was swinging from the chandelier, chattering like a baboon.

Q: How long had you know Mr. Greystoke?

A: Twenty years.

Q: How often had you seen him?

A: Weekly over that time.

Q: Had you ever seen him swing from the chandelier before?

A: Only a few times.

Q: How did he sign the will?

A: He first tried to squash his banana on it.

Q: Then what?

A: His butler gave him a pen and he made a "T" on the will.

Q: Do you have an opinion if Mr. Greystoke knew what he was doing when he signed the will?

A: Yes.

Q: What is that opinion?

A: He had no idea what he was doing.

C. Setting the Scene

Most stories, plays, motion pictures or re-creations of actual events must be placed in a setting that the audience can visualize. The same is true with a direct examination. The scene must be established before the action can make any sense. Once that scene has been established by primary witnesses, later witnesses may be placed at the scene to confirm the accuracy of what has been established and then to describe the action from their perspective. As the action shifts to a new location, the scene must be set again by witnesses. The extent to which a witness must set the scene depends on the order of witnesses, the importance of the witness to the case, and the witness' relationship to other witnesses. The direct examiner must determine what can be left to the imagination of the fact finder and what must be carefully described verbally or by exhibits.

1. View of the Witness

The direct examiner should focus the witness and the fact finder on the perspective from which the examiner wants them to see the scene. The scene may be described from two perspectives: through the eyes of the witness or from an overview. The first has the witness act as a storyteller and use phrases "I saw" and "I could see," and is generally more effective. The second has the witness act like a historian and describe a scene and can be more difficult to picture. The ideal goal may be to create a vision for the fact finder to be at the actual scene with the witness.

Example:

Examining lawyer:

Q: As you were walking up the cobblestone driveway, what did you see directly in front of you?

A: I saw large, old oak trees and magnolia trees lining both sides of the path.

Q: As you were looking around, tell us what you saw to your right?

A: I could see a large home with white columns and ivy growing on the brick walls.

Q: And what did you see as you looked to your left, Ms. O'Hara?

A: I saw the burned-out shell of the house that was destroyed by the explosion and fire.

Q: As you continued walking toward your house, please describe what you saw next.

2. Detail

The determination of what to describe and what to leave to the imagination of the fact finders should not be left to chance. The fact finders should be told every detail necessary to accurately understand the scene as the attorney wants them to understand it to satisfy their reasonable curiosity.

Example:

Examining lawyer:

Q: What kind of neighborhood was there, Mr. Matzeliger?

A: It was a residential neighborhood, with large old homes on two corners, an empty lot on one, and a newer building that contained apartments for adults only on the other corner. There was a small food store in that building.

Fact finders may interpret this response differently. What does "residential neighborhood" mean to a twenty-year-old college student juror, a sixty-five-year-old judge, or an arbitrator who was an architect? What do "large old houses" mean to an arbitrator who lives in a rural area, an inner city juror who grew up in a two-room flat, or a judge who grew up in a suburban house? Is the "food store" one of a chain of stores or an independently owned store located in the basement of the apartment building?

The details necessary for the fact finder to get an accurate picture should be included in the examination, and unnecessary details omitted.

D. Describing the Action

A witness can describe events as they happened. The direct examiner should ask questions in a structured way so that it is easy for the witness to explain events to enable the fact finders to clearly visualize what happened. A chronological order is usually easy to follow. Most people describe an event the way it happened and expect a story to be told in the same way.

1. Detailed Description of a Person

Example:

Examining lawyer:

Q: After you came downstairs and went into the living room, what did you see?

A: I saw a man standing by the fireplace.

Q: How were you able to see him?

A: The table light and the Christmas tree lights were on.

Q: What was he wearing?

A: A red outfit.

Q: Please be more specific.

A: He was dressed in fur, from his head to his foot.

Q: Were his clothes clean or dirty?

A: They were all tarnished with ashes and soot.

Q: Describe his general build for us?

A: He was chubby and plump.

Q: What did his face look like?

A: His eyes twinkled. He had dimples and appeared merry.

Q: Go on?

A: His cheeks were like roses, his nose like a cherry.

Q: What was his mouth like?

A: He had a droll little mouth which was drawn up like a bow, and he had a beard on his chin that was as white as the snow.

Q: Did he have anything in his mouth?

A: Yes.

Q: What?

A: Well, he had a stump of a pipe which he held tight in his teeth.

Q: Was he carrying anything?

A: Yes.

Q: What?

A: He had a bundle of toys which he had flung on his back.

Q: What did he look like?

A: He looked like a peddler just opening his pack.

Q: What else can you remember about this man?

A: He had a broad face and a round little belly that shook when he laughed, like a bowl full of jelly.

Q: Is there anything else that he did besides laugh?

A: Yes, he winked at me and twisted his head.

Q: What did you feel when he did that?

A: I felt that I had nothing to dread.

---

2. *Detailed Description of an Event (Criminal case)*

Example:

Examining lawyer:

Q: What is your name please?

A: Officer Lenny Briscoe.

Q: Where do you work?

A: For the City of New York.

Q: What do you do for the City?

A: I am a police officer.

Q: How long have you been a police officer?

A: Ten years.

Q: Were you working on May 1st this year?

A: Yes.

Q: At 11:00 p.m. on May 1st this year were you on duty?

A: Yes, I was.

Q: Where were you at 11:00 p.m.?

A: I was at the intersection of 71st Street and Newton Avenue.

Q: Were you on foot or in a car?

A: In a police car.

Q: What did you see?

A: I saw a bright red Chrysler Roadster.

Q: Which way was it traveling?

A: North to south on Newton Avenue.

Q: What did you see about the car?

A: It was traveling on the wrong side of the road and appeared to be traveling very fast.

Q: What did you do?

A: I began to follow the car.

Q: What was the car doing?

A: It was weaving wildly from side to side of the entire road. Twice it drove up on the curb and bounced back down on the road.

Q: Was your car equipped with radar?

A: No, it was not.

Q: Were you able to determine how fast the car was traveling?

A: Approximately.

Q: How?

A: I sped up and got behind the car. At that time, I was able to match my speed with the car for about one block. I stayed about 150 feet behind the car because of its weaving from side to side. My speedometer indicated that my car was traveling 40 miles per hour.

Q: Do you know what the posted speed limit is on Newton Avenue where you were?

A: Yes, I do.

Q: What is it?

A: Thirty miles per hour.

Q: What did you do?

A: I followed the red Chrysler for about 2 blocks and then I turned on my overhead red lights and siren.

Q: What happened?

A: The car kept on going on the wrong side of the street for another block and then it finally stopped on the wrong side of the street.

Q: What did you do?

A: I shined my spotlight on the car and walked up to the driver's side.

Q: What did you see when you approached the car?

A: I saw a man in his early sixties sitting behind the wheel. He was wearing a white suit, no tie.

Q: What else did you notice?

A: When the man rolled down the window of his car, I could smell a strong odor of what I believed to be alcohol coming from inside the car.

Q: What did you do next?

A: I asked him to get out of the car and he did. I asked if he had a driver's license.

Q: Did he give you a license?

A: No.

Q: Did he say anything to you?

A: Yes, he did.

Q: What?

A: He said that he did not have a license, had never had one, and didn't need one.

Q: How did he speak?

A: His speech was very slurred. I could hardly understand what he said.

Q: Could you see his face clearly?

A: Yes.

Q: How?

A: I had my flashlight shining near his face, the police car spotlight shined on us, and we were standing directly under a street light.

Q: Describe his face for us.

A: His face was flushed and reddish. He appeared to be sweating, and his eyes were bloodshot, glassy, and watery.

Q: Could you smell his breath at that time?

A: Yes.

Q: How close were you when you could smell his breath?

A: About two feet.

Q: What could you smell?

A: I could smell the strong odor of an alcoholic beverage.

Q: What did you do next?

A: I asked him to take what are called "field sobriety tests."

Q: Why do you ask a person to take field sobriety tests?

A: To determine the ability of a person to coordinate movements, retain balance, follow simple directions and perform simple tasks.

Q: What is the first test that you asked him to perform?

A: I asked him to stand erect with his feet together and his arms outstretched. I told him to close his eyes and touch the tip of his nose with first his right index finger and then with his left.

Q: How did he do when he tried to touch his nose with his right hand?

A: First he started to fall over and I caught him and stood him up. However, he did not open his eyes. He then touched the middle of his forehead with his index finger and slid it down along his nose to the tip.

Q: How did he perform with his left hand?

A: He touched the side of his upper lip and slid his finger up to his nose.

Q: Did you ask him to perform another test?

A: Yes, I did.

Q: What?

A: I asked him to say the alphabet.

Q: How did he do?

A: He did fine until he got to the letter "K" and he then said "K" eight or nine times and finally said, "I can't remember any more."

Q: Did you ask him to take any more tests?

A: Yes.

Q: What test?

A: I asked him to walk a straight line, one foot in front of the other.

Q: Did he take that test?

A: No.

Q: Did he tell you why?

A: Yes.

Q: What did he say?

A: He said, "I ain't takin' any more tests. I'm as drunk as an old skunk. You've got me now and you know it."

Q: What did you do then?

A: I placed him under arrest for driving while under the influence of an alcoholic beverage. I then drove him to the county jail and offered him a breath test.

Q: What happened when you offered him a breath test?

A: He refused to take a breath test. I then offered him a chance to provide a urine or blood sample.

Q: Did he give you any samples?

A: No.

Q: What did you do then?

A: I left him at the jail with the county sheriff and went back on patrol.

Q: Did he ever tell you his name?

A: Yes, he said his name was Bacchus.

Q: Just Bacchus?

A: That's right. He said that was the only name he had.

Q: In the years on the police force have you arrested people for driving under the influence of alcohol?

A: Yes, hundreds of times.

Q: Do you ever drink alcoholic beverages?

A: Yes, I do, on occasion.

Q: Have you seen other people drink?

A: Yes.

Q: Have you seen some of these people come under the influence of alcohol?

A: Yes, I have.

Q: Based upon your own experience, your observations of others, and your observations of Mr. Bacchus, do you have an opinion whether he was under the influence of alcohol the night that you arrested him?

A: Yes, I do.

Q: And what is that opinion?

A: He was very much under the influence of alcohol.

---

3. *Detailed Description of an Event (Civil case)*

Example:

Examining lawyer:

Q: What did you do on that Thanksgiving holiday?

A: My daughter, Molly, and I were going to be alone that day, and we were invited to go into the country for dinner at the home of some people with whom I work.

Q: What is their name?

A: Mr. and Mrs. Baskerville.

Q: How old was Molly at the time?

A: She was six.

Q: What time did you arrive?

A: We were invited for dinner at two p.m., and we arrived a few minutes after that as we got lost on the way.

Q: Had you ever been to the Baskervilles' home before that day?

A: No, I had not.

Q: What did you do when you got there?

A: Their farm is quite a long ways off the county road. We drove up the driveway by the barn and parked in front of the house by the gate.

Q: Where is the barn located in relation to the house?

A: It is across the driveway.

Q: How far is the barn from the house?

A: About 100 feet.

Q: How far from the house did you park?

A: About 30 feet. There is a fence around the front yard, and we parked right by the fence.

Q: What did you do?

A: I got out of the car and waited for Molly to walk around the front of the car.

Q: What happened?

A: As Molly was walking in front of the car, something caught my attention out of the corner of my eye from the direction of the barn.

Q: What did you do?

A: I turned my head to see what it was.

Q: What did you see?

A: I saw an enormous shaggy brown dog running right towards Molly.

Q: Did it make any noise?

A: No, it was running real fast and was making no noise at all.

Q: How big was this animal?

A: It was huge. Its head was higher than my waist. It had a huge mouth, and I could see its teeth.

Q: What did you do?

A: I screamed and ran to Molly.

Q: What happened?

A: I grabbed her and started to pick her up and as I started to do that the beast leaped at us and bit Molly in the back of her neck.

Q: Go on.

A: We fell to the ground. I could not get my hand loose, and the dog was biting and snarling and tearing at us. There was blood all over, and we were both screaming and crying for help.

Q: What was the next thing that happened?

A: I heard a woman yelling.

Q: What did she say?

A: I heard something like, "Down Hound! Stop that! You naughty dog! You should be ashamed of yourself!"

Q: What did the dog do?

A: It let go and sat there snarling and growling at us.

Q: Did you see who the woman was?

A: Yes, Mrs. Baskerville.

Q: What did the dog look like?

A: It was a huge filthy hound. It had long, shaggy, matted brown hair covered with dirt. It smelled just awful. It had an enormous head with yellow eyes. It had huge teeth and was growling, drooling, and quivering as it sat there.

Q: What happened next?

A: Mrs. Baskerville took us inside the house and tried to stop the bleeding while her husband called an ambulance.

Q: Did she say anything to you?

A: She said that the darn dog was always jumping on people and that they should have locked the dog in the barn.

Q: Had she ever said anything to you about a dog before you came to the house that day.

A: Never! I never even knew that they had a hound.

E. Conversations

The foundation needed to admit a relevant conversation is fairly easy when the conversation occurs face-to-face and the witness can identify the person making the statement. However, foundation is more difficult with telephone conversations, as the witness has to be able to identify the voice in order to show that the conversation relates to the case.

Example (Prior familiarity with voice):

Examining lawyer:

Q: Did you conduct an investigation of the collapse of the ski lift gondola?

A: Yes, I did.

Q: What did you do?

A: I called up Stein Eriksson, the owner of the resort, on the telephone.

Q: Had you ever spoken to Stein Eriksson before?

A: Yes, many times.

Q: Did you recognize his voice when you called him?

A: Yes.

Q: How?

A: I recognized the sound of his voice and his accent.

Q: Did he identify himself to you in any other way?

A: Yes.

Q: How?

A: When he answered the phone he said, "Allo, dis is Stein Eriksson speking."

Q: Then what did he say?

A: He said, "I sure vish we had fixed da dern cable car."

Example (Subsequent identification of a voice):

Examining lawyer:

Q: What did you do on the fifth of January?

A: I called up a man to talk about the show.

Q: Did you talk to the man?

A: Yes.

Q: Did you know the man?

A: No.

Q: Did you recognize his voice?

A: No.

Q: Have you heard his voice since that conversation?

A: Yes.

Q: Where?

A: In the courtroom today when he testified for the plaintiff.

Q: How can you recognize his voice?

A: It is very distinctive high pitched—and he has a silly laugh.

Q: What is the name of the man whose voice you heard today?

A: Peewee Herman.

Q: What did he tell you about the show when you phoned him?

A: He said that he wanted a prime time show.

Example (Extrinsic sources of identification):

Examining lawyer:

Q: Had you ever spoken to Groucho Marx before March 3 of last year?

A: No.

Q: Have you ever spoken to him since?

A: No.

Q: On March 3, what did you do?

A: First, I went to the city telephone book and looked up the phone number of Groucho Marx Productions.

Q: Then what?

A: I called the number and a woman answered "Groucho Marx Productions."

Q: What did you do?

A: I asked to speak to Groucho Marx.

Q: What happened?

A: First, there was silence, then the phone rang and a man answered and said, "Mr. Marx's office."

Q: What did you do then?

A: I asked to speak to Groucho Marx.

Q: And then?

A: A man answered and said, "Marx here, whadda ya want?"

Q: What did you say?

A: I identified myself and then asked him why he had shot the duck.

Q: What did he say?

A: He said, "You wodda too if you had the dumb thing flying down at you all the time."

F. Persuasive Questions

The direct examiner should ask understandable questions that develop an interesting story. The following factors should be followed in phrasing effective questions.

1. Simple Words

Simple, everyday conversational words are generally more effective as they are easy to understand and reflect the language fact finders, especially jurors, use. Complex, multi-syllable words or legalese sound snobbish and can be confusing. The ordinary language used in the community is most effective, excluding vulgar or crude language, unless such language is a relevant part of the case. The advocate should not underestimate the intelligence of the fact finder. More sophisticated language can be effective with professional decision makers.

Example:

Examining lawyer:

Simple:

Q: Before the accident, where were you?

Complex:

Q: Prior to the accident, where were you situated in relation to this event?

Simple:

Q: Did you see something?

Complex:

Q: Did you have occasion to observe anything material at all?

Simple:

Q: What happened on December 14?

Complex:

Q: Calling your attention to the date of December 14, what, if anything, occurred on that date, if you recall?

---

2. Short Questions

Short questions make it easier for the lawyer to control testimony and to direct a witness to provide detail. Long, drawn out questions delay the testimony, waste time, and interrupt the flow of the testimony.

Example:

Examining lawyer:

Q: What were you doing?

A: I was the scorekeeper at the basketball game.

Q: Where were you?

A: I was sitting at mid-court at the scorer's table, about four feet back from the sideline.

Q: Who was playing?

A: Cannon Falls and Pine Island.

Q: What did you see shortly before the end of the first half?

A: I saw a man wearing a Pine Island jacket jump out of the bleachers and run right up and punch the coach of the Cannon Falls team right on the nose.

---

3. Narrative and Specific Questions

The following examples demonstrate three comparative approaches to the development of a story: a story elicited with a narrative question, with specific questions, and with a combination of the two.

a. Narrative

Example:

Examining lawyer:

Q: Tell us what you remember about that afternoon.

A: When the kids got home from school and had their snack, I sent them out to play. They had on light jackets and boots. The golf course across the street has a pond. The kids had skated there all winter. After they left, I thought they might head for it, so I went out looking for them. When I got to the pond, the ice had given way. I ran out to pull them from the water. I first got Amy on the shore and then I waded back into the water to find Mike. He was below the ice and I couldn't see him. I went under the ice as fast as I could and felt with my hands until I felt his arm. I grabbed him and pulled him out, and he was blue.

---

b. Specific

Example:

Examining lawyer:

Q: What is the first thing that happened when Amy and Mike came home from school on March 15?

A: They had a snack—crackers and milk.

Q: After the snack, what did they do?

A: They put on their play clothes and jackets to go outside.

Q: What kind of jackets?

A: Light, spring jackets.

Q: Why didn't they wear winter jackets?

A: Because it was a very mild day. The snow was melting.

Q: Where do the children like to play?

A: They like to play on the golf course in the winter because there are hills for sliding and a pond that they skate on.

Q: Where is the golf course?

A: Right across the road.

Q: On that day, did you tell them anything about the ice on the pond?

A: Yes.

Q: What?

A: I told them to stay off the ice because it was unsafe.

Q: After the children got dressed, what did they do?

A: They went outside.

Q: What did you do?

A: I thought they might head for the pond, so I went out looking for them.

Q: Did you see them?

A: No.

Q: What did you do?

A: I ran over to the pond and saw that the ice had broken through.

Q: What did you do?

A: I jumped into the water to find my kids.

---

c. *Combination Narrative and Specific*

An effective direct examination employs a mix of questions that call for short, narrative responses combined with short, controlled questions that elicit appropriate details. This mix of questions guides the witness in telling the story, permits the attorney to control the direction of the story, provides clarifying details, and holds the interest of the fact finder.

Example:

Examining lawyer:

Q: After the children got dressed, what did they do?

A: They went outside, and I saw them run towards the golf course.

Q: What did you do after you saw the children run towards the golf course?

A: I thought they might go to the pond, so I got dressed and ran after them. I was scared they would fall through the ice.

Q: Then what happened?

A: The ice had already given way, and both children were out of sight. I ran out to pull them from the water. I took my cardigan off and held one arm of the sweater and swung it out to Amy so that she could grab the other arm. I got her on the shore, and then I waded back into the water to Mike.

Q: Where was Mike?

A: He was below the ice, and I couldn't see him.

Q: What did you do?

A: I went under the ice as fast as I could and felt with my hands and after a little bit I felt his arm. I was so frightened.

Q: After you felt his arm, what did you do?

A: I grabbed him and pulled him out. I saw he was blue, and I cried out for help.

---

4. Completing a Sequence

Sometime during an examination, the direct examiner realizes that something has been left out of an earlier part of the examination. Important information may need to be added in the right sequence.

Example:

Examining lawyer:

Q: What happened to you Ms. Dewey?

A: Well, the man attacked me. He was hitting and kicking me. I was yelling for help and trying to get away.

Q: And were you able to get away?

A: Yea, I ran back to the library as fast as I could.

Q: By the way, I didn't ask you earlier what time you got off work at the library after you finished cataloging the decimal system. When did you get off work?

A: About 4:30 p.m.

Q: And about what time did you get away and run back to the library?

---

5. Impact Words

A careful choice of impact words can have an effect on how testimony is perceived. Impact words are graphic words that vividly describe something in support of a perception the witness is trying to portray. See Section 1.5(F).

Neutral words:

Q: What was the *speed* of the two cars?

Impact words:

Q: How *slowly* were you driving?

Q: How *fast* was the other car going?

Neutral words:

Q: What was the *distance* between you and the other woman?

Impact words:

Q: How *close* were you to the other woman?

Q: How *far* away were you?

Neutral words:

Q: How *much* water was in the glass?

Impact words:

Q: How *full* was the glass?

Q: How *empty* was the glass?

---

6.   Double Direct

"Double direct" is a technique in which part of a previous answer is used as a preface to the next question. This tactic emphasizes critical information so the fact finder hears the information more than once and should be reserved for important evidence.

Example:

Examining lawyer:

Q: When you finished studying, what did you do?

A: I went out to jog around the stadium.

Q: Which way did you go to get to the stadium?

A: I came off Arapahoe and headed toward the track.

Q: What time was that?

A: 6:00 p.m.

Q: What happened next?

A: I jogged towards the track. When I got about 150 feet off Arapahoe, I passed a large hedge on my right. I heard branches scraping and twigs snapping.

Q: When you heard branches scraping and twigs snapping in the hedge, what did you do?

A: I ran faster, and I felt someone running up behind me.

Q: How do you know?

A: I heard the running steps and then my arm was grabbed from behind and was twisted hard behind my back.

Q: What happened when your arm was twisted?

A: I lost my balance and fell into the hedge.

Q: What happened when you fell into the hedge?

A: The person put a knife to my throat.

Q: As the person put a knife to your throat, were you able to see the face of this person?

A: Oh, yes. I looked right into that face.

---

7.   *Clarifying Answers*

The lawyer needs to ask questions that clarify answers that the fact finder needs to know. This can be difficult because the advocate knows the case better than the fact finder. It is helpful to hear the answers from the perspective of the fact finders to make sure the witness tells what they need to know.

Example:

Examining lawyer:

Q: Detective Sipowicz, where were you going?

A: To the NYPD police station.

Q: What happened on the way there?

A: I saw a man run out of a store carrying a shotgun. I reached for my gun in my holster under my arm.

Q: Under your right arm or left arm?

A: I carry my gun in a shoulder holster under my left arm and that's where it was, and I grabbed it with my right hand.

---

8.   *Listening Carefully*

The attorney must listen carefully to every response. Witnesses frequently misunderstand a question, make mistakes, or assume that the attorney wants an answer not called for by the question. And the attorney may be preoccupied with other thoughts, such as the next question or problems with opposing counsel or the judge. Or the attorney may expect certain answers and not pay attention when the witness says something different.

When a witness makes a mistake or does not answer the question precisely, the attorney must correct the witness. There will be occasions when the witness has made a factual mistake, or is rambling out of control, or has added information that is improper and the attorney must interrupt. Occasionally, the answer in itself is not a problem, but the lack of demonstrated control may cause a problem if the witness continues to testify. Controlling the witness demonstrates that the attorney seeks only proper, responsive answers, bolstering the credibility of the attorney and the witness.

Example:

Examining lawyer:

Q: What did you see, Ms. Sturgis?

A: *(At a very rapid pace.)* There was this strange looking creature with a head of rainbow colored hair and who was wearing a boa. He was jumping up and down and dribbling a basketball towards me and he must have really been excited and I really thought that he was going to dunk the ball in the basket I was carrying and then he started yelling at me and he said . . .

Q: I am going to have to stop you right here for a moment. We are going to have to take it one step at a time. I'm going to ask you some simple questions and ask you to give a responsive answer. Okay?

A: Oh, yes.

Q: You can't tell us what this gentleman said to you because that's hearsay and not allowed in this trial. Now when he did speak to you, were you looking at his face?

A: Yes.

Q: Did you see if he was wearing a pierced nose ring?

A: Oh yes, I did.

Q: Was he?

A: Yes, several.

9. *Explaining Terms*

The attorney should make sure the witness explains terms that have specialized or multiple meanings. A direct examiner should not assume the jury understands what the witness understands.

Example:

Examining lawyer:

Q: What was the man like?

A: He was a huge man.

Q: Describe what you mean by huge.

A: He was at least 7 feet tall and weighed about well over 300 pounds.

Q: Who was he?

A: Paul Bunyan.

---

10.   *Volunteering Weaknesses*

Weaknesses in the witness' background or testimony may need to be presented during the direct examination to minimize its impact and to enhance the credibility of the witness and the attorney. Negative information about the witness or testimony that is not revealed on the direct examination and is first exposed on the cross-examination can be harmful. Weaknesses revealed on direct examination demonstrate that neither the attorney nor the witness has anything to hide, reducing the adverse affect of the weakness. In addition, the witness has the opportunity to explain the weakness in the witness' terms, not in the opposing counsel's words. Weaknesses should be addressed in a matter-of-fact way, and explained with as little embarrassment or concern as possible.

The decision to admit weaknesses can be difficult. If a weakness cannot be excluded by the rules of evidence, and the cross-examiner is expected to expose that weakness, the weakness should be brought out on the direct examination. It is possible to deal with a weakness on redirect examination in the hope that the cross-examiner will not bring up the matter or that the explanation will be so good that the cross-examination will appear foolish. This, however, is a defensive and difficult position to assume and often backfires.

Example:

Examining lawyer:

Q: What color was the light?

A: Green.

Q: Did you talk with Lieutenant Columbo the day of the accident?

A: Yes.

Q: Did he write up a statement?

A: Yes, on a scrap of paper.

Q: Did that statement say the light was fuchsia?

A: Yes.

Q: Did you sign the statement?

A: Yes.

Q: Can you explain why you did that?

A: Yes, I can.

Q: Tell us please.

A: When Lt. Columbo was taking the statement, I was in the hospital and was in a lot of pain. I did not read the statement. I just signed it to get rid of him. He was always hanging around asking me questions. I did not realize that the statement said that the light was fuchsia.

---

10. *Exhibits*

Exhibits should be used in a way that enhances the testimony of a witness and introduced at an appropriate time during an examination. Exhibits can be important to a case and helpful to a witness and the fact finder. A separate chapter focuses on the proper and effective use of exhibits. See Chapter 8.

§ 7.9   REDIRECT EXAMINATION

The direct examiner has an opportunity to conduct a redirect examination after the completion of the cross-examination. Redirect examination provides the direct examiner with the opportunity to have the witness clarify or explain points raised on cross-examination and to cover new material raised by the cross-examination that was not dealt with on the direct examination.

With proper preparation, the direct examiner can predict the areas of cross-examination and may cover those areas on direct examination and limit the effectiveness of a cross-examination. In addition, a redirect examination can be planned in advance so that the anticipated areas of weakness or vulnerability can be clarified or explained. Important testimony and significant issues need to be addressed on direct, and a direct examiner should not reserve vital evidence to be introduced during redirect.

A. *Limited Scope*

The general rule is that redirect examination may only cover new material raised by the cross-examination. Redirect should not be used to go over the same information covered by the direct examination or raise new areas not covered by either the direct or cross-examinations. If this occurs, most judges and arbitrators will sustain an objection that the redirect examination is repetitious or beyond the scope of the cross-examination. The application of these restrictions is uneven with a broad scope allowed by some judges and arbitrators, while others are more restrictive.

Example:

Cross-Examination of an Eyewitness:

Q: Have you ever seen someone you thought you recognized and waved at that person only to realize the person was a complete stranger, Ms. Sybil?

A: Yes, that has happened to me.

Q: It was embarrassing to have that happen, wasn't it?

A: Well, yes it was.

Q: I have no further questions.

Redirect Examination of the Same Witness:

Q: Ms. Sybil, when you thought you recognized a stranger, did that stranger stand two feet in front of you, face-to-face and demand all your money as the defendant did in this case?

A: Never. The only time I have been robbed is by that defendant.

B. *Foregoing Redirect Examination*

A well-prepared case and a good direct examination often make a redirect examination unnecessary. In making the decision whether to conduct a redirect examination, the following factors should be considered:

- The witness may not have been prepared for certain redirect questions and should not be asked surprise questions.

- The witness may not understand the point the attorney wants to make and misspeak.

- Having the last word is not the most important thing. The same information need not be repeated over and over again just to get in the last word.

- Continuing with redirect examination may bore or bother the fact finder and add nothing to the information already provided.

- Closing argument may be a much better time to explain the important parts of the case, rather than redirect examination.

- Cases may be damaged by asking too many questions. A witness who repeats answers may look rehearsed, and mistakes can be made in regard to the same testimony.

- Redirect examination gives the opponent the opportunity for a recross-examination.

C. *Question Form*

The same rules of evidence apply to redirect and direct examination, with the same restrictions applying to the use of leading questions. There may be a greater latitude allowed by some judges and arbitrators who permit the use of leading questions during redirect in order to permit the attorney to focus on matters within the scope of the cross-examination and to speed the redirect to completion. Since the witness has testified on both direct and cross-examination, the redirect examiner may refer to previous answers and lead the witness to a specific topic through the use of this prior testimony. The opposing attorney might not object because the cross-examination consisted of leading questions, and the attorney may be so used to such questions that leading questions on the redirect may not sound improper.

D. *Correcting Mistakes/Refreshing Recollection*

Redirect examination may be used to refresh the witness' recollection if the witness has misstated or forgotten information during the cross-examination. See Fed.R.Evid. 612.

Example (Redirect examination):

Examining lawyer:

Q: During the cross-examination you told us that the man held you by the throat with his left hand while he had a knife in his right. Are you sure that he had the knife in his right hand, Mr. Bowie?

A: Oh my, did I say right hand? I didn't mean to say that. He had the knife in his left hand and was choking me with his right.

Q: How do you know that?

A: Because I had grabbed his left hand so I wouldn't be knifed.

E. *Reserving the Introduction of Evidence*

A witness should be permitted to describe all necessary facts on the direct examination. Information should not be withheld for later presentation during a redirect examination. An attorney who reserves important evidence runs the risk of not being able to present this important element of the case because the opposing attorney may not cross-examine at all or may not cover that particular area, rendering some areas beyond the scope of the cross. It can be dangerous to run the risk of not being able to present reserved evidence for the tactical purpose of getting the last word or outwitting the opponent.

There are some occasions where the delaying of the introduction of information is worth the risk of not being able to present the evidence. If the direct examination is structured in such a way so that the cross-examiner is quite likely to cross-examine on the topic and damage will not be done to the case if the evidence is not dealt with, evidence may be reserved for redirect.

Example:

During the direct examination, the main eyewitness to a robbery has identified the defendant as the robber and has said that he looked carefully at the defendant for about a minute during the course of the robbery. The robbery took place in a well-lit store. The witness has testified that when he was seen staring at the defendant, he was told to knock it off, but kept looking at him. He was then struck, knocked to the floor, and kicked until he became unconscious.

On both the direct and cross-examination he testified that he was scared, that the robbery happened quite fast, and that he was concerned for his young child and for the other people in the store. He testified that he had a great deal of money in his possession and was angry that it was being stolen. He also testified that he had never seen the robber before the day of the robbery and the only other time that he had seen him was in court at the trial where the defendant was seated next to his attorney. He has testified further that he has not seen any photographs of the defendant prior to trial and never participated in any line-up identification.

Redirect Examination:

Q: Mr. Phocus, we have asked you a number of things about the robbery, but one of the things that neither I nor the other attorney has asked you is this: Why did you keep staring at the robber even after you were told to stop?

A: I never wanted to forget the face of the man that would terrorize and steal from us. I hoped that I could help catch him someday.

Q: I have no further questions.

If a topic was not covered either on the direct or the cross-examination, some courts will permit the direct examiner to reopen the direct examination to permit the witness to be recalled to cover the new topic. The decision to permit the reopening of a direct examination of a witness is not automatic and is within the discretion of the judge or arbitrator.

§ 7.10 DIRECT EXAMINATION SITUATIONS

This section presents several direct examinations of specific types of witnesses involving special considerations.

A. Former Testimony

In civil trials, testimony of a witness may be introduced through former testimony given at a deposition or another hearing. This testimony is either read to the jurors, or if videotaped, shown to them. Former testimony is admissible in lieu of live testimony if the previous testimony was given under oath, the witness is unavailable to testify at the trial, and the party against whom the testimony is offered had the opportunity to previously examine the witness, or another party with substantially the same interest or similar motive had that opportunity.

The most common use of former testimony in a civil case involves the introduction of deposition testimony because the lay or expert witness is unavailable. Many civil cases include this type of evidence. Depositions are often taken to preserve testimony when the offering attorney anticipates that lay or expert witnesses will be unavailable at the trial, arbitration, or hearing. The deposition of these witnesses is taken and their testimony is recorded stenographically, or the deposition is videotaped. It is very common that the testimony of expert witnesses, who are unavailable because of their professional schedules, is presented in these ways.

The procedure to introduce the former testimony is similar to the introduction of live testimony. The videotaped testimony can be shown to the fact finder. If there is only a transcript available, a judge or arbitrator can read the testimony. In jury trials, the transcript can be read to the jury, usually with the attorney reading the questions and another person sitting in the witness stand supplying the answers. The offering attorney should select a person to read the answers who looks credible and sounds persuasive to gain as much impact as possible from the reading of the deposition. The offering attorney should also attempt to make the reading of the transcript as interesting as possible.

Prior to the reading of the transcript or showing of the videotape, the opposing attorney may object to questions or answers contained in the former testimony. The judge or arbitrator rules on each of the objections, and if sustained, the inadmissible question or answer is deleted. If a deposition transcript is read, the portions of the transcript ruled inadmissible are not read. If the videotape is used, the portions ruled to be inadmissible are not shown to or relied on by the fact finder.

There are a number of mechanical ways this can be done. If evidentiary rulings are made a reasonable time before the videotape is shown, an edited copy of the original tape can be made and that edition shown. Otherwise, the tape can be fast-forwarded to eliminate the inadmissible portions, or the monitor turned off, or the sound muted while the tape continues to play. In jury cases, neither the written deposition transcript nor a videotape of the deposition go with the jury to the jury room during deliberations. This is to avoid the jurors giving such evidence more weight than other oral evidence heard by them from live witnesses during the trial.

Example (Deposition transcript):

Examining Attorney:

Your Honor, William Mayhew, an eyewitness, is unavailable to testify. Mr. Mayhew testified in a previous deposition. Both I and opposing counsel were present and examined him at that deposition. We now request permission of the court to read the deposition transcript of Mr. Mayhew to the jury.

Opposing Counsel:

We have reviewed those parts of Mr. Mayhew's former testimony that the plaintiff plans to introduce, and we have no objection to the introduction of that evidence. After counsel for plaintiff completes the direct examination of Mr. Mayhew, we will introduce our cross-examination questions and answers.

Judge:

Members of the Jury, at this time counsel for plaintiff will present to you the testimony of a witness who is unavailable to be here today to testify. You are to consider the testimony of this witness with the same degree of attention and consideration that you give the testimony of any other witness. Counsel, you may proceed.

Counsel:

I will read the questions, your Honor, and a colleague from my firm, Elmer Gantry, will read the answers.

Court:

Mr. Gantry, you may come forward and sit in the witness stand. Counsel, begin the questions and answers.

Example (Video Deposition):

Examining Attorney:

Your Honor, Dr. Livingston, one of our expert witnesses, is unavailable to testify. We previously videotaped a deposition of his testimony, and counsel was present at that deposition. Your Honor has reviewed this videotape and has ruled on defendant's objections. Those questions and answers you ruled inadmissible have been edited from this videotape. We now request permission of the court to show to the jury the videotaped testimony of Dr. Livingston.

Judge:

You may proceed.

In criminal cases, former testimony is usually inadmissible because the defendant has a constitutional right to be confronted by live witnesses and to cross-examine them. Former testimony in a criminal case may be admissible when there is a retrial of the same defendant, or if the defendant stipulates to its admissibility.

B. Past Recollection Recorded

When a witness has no present recollection and efforts to refresh recollection have failed or would fail, the introduction of past recollection recorded may be used to present evidence on direct examination. Federal Rule of Evidence 803(5) provides an exception to the requirement that a witness testify verbally in court.

The examining attorney will have prepared a witness for the use of past recollection recorded. It should not come as a surprise when a witness has no current recollection of an event. Statements introduced as past recollection recorded need to be marked and offered into evidence because they constitute the substantive evidence substituted for the verbal testimony of the witness. The foundation for the introduction of the recorded item includes:

- The witness has no present, independent recollection,

- The witness at one time personally knew information relevant to the case,

- The information was written down or recorded by the witness at the witness' direction,

- The writing or recording was created or adopted when the information was fresh in the witness' memory,

- The writing or recording accurately contains the information, and

- The witness authenticates the exhibit.

Some witnesses (police, investigators, doctors, experts) may have to rely upon prior statements and reports to assist them during testimony. In many routine cases involving such testimony, the decision makers do not expect and do not require the laying of a full foundation for these documents as past recollection recorded because they have heard the foundation laid many times before in similar cases, and they want to save time and move the case along. The opposing attorney may not be satisfied with this informal custom and may want to object to the lack of proper foundation.

Example:

Examining Attorney:

Q: What do you do for a living?

A: I'm a state highway trooper.

Q: How long have you been a state highway trooper?

A: Fifteen years.

Q: What are your primary duties?

A: To enforce highway traffic laws and to assist on highway accident scenes.

Q: Do you know how many tickets you generally give each year?

A: Approximately.

Q: How many?

A: Between twelve hundred and fifteen hundred a year.

Q: Do you remember the details of all the accident scenes you have investigated?

A: No.

Q: Do you remember the details of all the traffic tickets that you have written?

A: No.

Q: What is your procedure when you give a ticket?

A: After I give a ticket, I immediately write a report while sitting in my police car on the front and back of the ticket describing all the important details of the incident.

Q: Do you recall giving a ticket to the defendant in this case on June 1, last year?

A: Yes, I remember giving him a ticket.

Q: Do you remember the details of the incident?

A: Not completely.

Q: What do you remember?

A: I remember it was a careless driving violation.

Q: Do you remember any other details?

A: No.

Q: How come?

A: Because I see so many reckless driving and speeding cases I can't accurately and completely remember all the details.

To the Court:

Your Honor, may I approach the witness?

Judge:

Yes you may.

Examining Attorney:

Q: Trooper Estrada, I have just handed you what has been marked for identification as Exhibit No. 1. Do you recognize it?

A: Yes.

Q: What is it?

A: It is my copy of the ticket I was speaking about.

Q: Do you recognize it?

A: Yes I do,

Q: How?

A: I recognize my handwriting, my trooper number; I recognize the name of the defendant on it; and I recognize the date and time.

Q: Does reading this document, Exhibit No. 1 for identification, help refresh your recollection as to the details of the incident?

A: No it does not.

Q: Do you have any recollection of the details of that incident as you sit here today?

A: No I do not.

Q: At the time that you wrote down this report, did you remember the details of the incident?

A: Yes.

Q: When you wrote it down, did you write down the true and correct version of what you had observed?

A: Yes.

Q: Would you have signed it if it had not been a true and correct version of what you observed?

A: No, I would not have.

To the Court:

At this time your Honor, I offer Exhibit No. 1 as past recollection recorded.

Judge:

Any objections Counsel?

Opposing Counsel:

No objections.

Judge:

It is received.

Examining Attorney:

At this time, Trooper Estrada, would you please read what you wrote down in the report.

A: Yes, I will: "I was proceeding on routine patrol on my CHP motorcycle when I observed the subject vehicle, a stunning new silver Porsche with exquisite Boxster red leather interior plus the twin turbo spoiler and sporting 18″ performance wheels, go past me on the right-hand shoulder at a very high rate of speed."

Q: Go on.

A: "At that time...."

C. *Witnesses With Communication Problems*

A child or mentally challenged witness requires special consideration as a direct examination witness. The decision maker must determine if the witness is competent to testify. Often a questionably competent witness is the only person who can testify in a case, such as a child abuse, sexual assault, incest, neglect and dependency case. Federal Rule of Evidence 611(c) permits leading questions to assist this witness in communicating. However, the more the attorney asks leading questions, the less competent the witness will appear to be and the less persuasive the testimony becomes.

A witness who has communication problems must be made to feel at ease in the courtroom or hearing room. The preparation may require that the witness be brought to the room, rehearse testifying, and even be allowed to spend additional time in the room to become comfortable with an unfamiliar and potentially scary place. A mix of leading and nonleading questions assists the witness in testifying, and helps the attorney lead up to critical testimony which should be given without the use of leading questions.

D. *Character Evidence*

Character evidence is evidence of a trait or characteristic of a person offered to prove that the person acted in conformity with such character. The evidence rules of almost all jurisdictions are consistent with the common law doctrine that character evidence is not admissible to prove that an individual acted in conformity with the individual's character on a specific occasion. Evidence of wrongs, bad acts, or crimes is generally inadmissible to prove that a party is a bad person or possesses a bad character. For example, evidence that a party has a trait for speeding while driving a car to prove that party was speeding is inadmissible. Conversely, evidence of good character, good deeds, or an exemplary life is inadmissible to prove that a party is a good person or possesses a good character. For example, proof that a defendant is a careful driver is inadmissible to prove that the defendant was not negligent. Character evidence may be relevant, but the unfair prejudice and confusion of the issues resulting from the character evidence outweighs the probative value of such evidence.

1. *Civil Cases*

In a civil case, character evidence is usually inadmissible to prove that the person acted in conformity on a particular occasion, but may be admissible in the following instances:

- Evidence of the character of a person or a pertinent trait may be admissible to prove motive, opportunity, intent, preparation, plan, knowledge, identity, or absence of mistake or accident.

- Evidence relating to the character for untruthfulness may be offered against the person testifying.

- Evidence of the truthful character of a witness is admissible after the character of the witness for untruthfulness has been attacked.

- If character is an issue or an element of liability or damages, evidence is admissible on that issue. Civil cases in which character is an issue include defamation cases (reputation of plaintiff).

2. *Criminal Cases*

In criminal cases, character evidence is admissible in the following situations:

- An accused may offer evidence of a pertinent personal trait. The defendant who claims self-defense in an assault case may offer evidence regarding the defendant's reputation for peacefulness.

- The prosecution may offer character evidence to rebut the pertinent trait offered by the accused. In a self-defense case, the prosecutor can offer evidence of the defendant's reputation for violence.

- The accused may offer evidence of a pertinent trait of the character of a victim and the prosecution may offer evidence in rebuttal.

- The prosecution may offer evidence of a character trait of peacefulness of the victim in a homicide case to rebut evidence that the victim was the first aggressor.

- Evidence relating to the character for untruthfulness may be offered against the person testifying.

- Evidence of the truthful character of a witness is admissible after the character of the witness for untruthfulness has been attacked.

- Character evidence may be admissible to prove motive, opportunity, intent, preparation, plan, knowledge, identity or absence of mistake or accident.

- Character evidence which may be otherwise proper may be deemed inadmissible as unfairly prejudicial. See Section 4.8(A)(4).

3. *Introduction of Character Evidence*

There are three ways in which character evidence may be introduced during direct examination of a witness:

A. Opinion testimony: A witness may testify to a personal opinion about the character of a person if a foundation is first established concerning what the witness knows or has observed about the person over a period of time.

> "I have personally known the defendant for 30 years, and I consider him to have an excellent reputation."

B. Reputation testimony: A witness can testify to the reputation of a person in the community if a foundation is first established concerning what the witness has heard expressed about that person in a defined community. Reputation is the expressed community consensus about an individual.

> "I have lived in the community for 30 years, and I have heard that the defendant's reputation is excellent."

C. Specific instances of conduct: A witness may testify to firsthand knowledge about a person.

"The defendant has been a youth counselor and Red Cross volunteer for 10 years."

In all cases, character evidence is admissible by reputation testimony and opinion testimony. Federal Rule of Evidence 803(21) and similar state rules make such testimony admissible hearsay. Testimony of specific instances of conduct is not admissible to prove character on direct examination. Specific instances of conduct may be more convincing, but such specific evidence also has the potential to arouse the greatest prejudice, to confuse the issues, and to consume unnecessary time. Reputation and opinion testimony are less convincing, less prejudicial, and take less time.

Where character evidence has been admitted on direct examination, specific instances of misconduct may be explored during cross-examination. A witness who testifies on direct examination that a party has good character may be cross-examined regarding knowledge about specific instances of bad character about that person. This line of inquiry may show that the witness may not have known about these specific instances, or ought not to be believed.

In cases in which a character trait of a person is an essential element of the case, proof of the trait may be made by specific instances of conduct. If a character trait is a direct issue in a case, then specific instances of good conduct may be introduced on direct examination to prove such issue. Specific instances of bad conduct may be raised on cross-examination to disprove such issue, and specific instances of bad conduct may be introduced on direct examination through a witness testifying on behalf of the adverse party to further disprove the character established. All questions regarding specific instances of good conduct or bad conduct must be asked in good faith and must be based on facts. Attorneys cannot make up such situations, or suggest such instances by innuendo, or ask unsubstantiated questions.

Example (Direct examination):

Examining Attorney:

Q: How long have you lived in Washington?

A: 10 years.

Q: What do you do now?

A: I'm a consultant.

Q: Before you were a consultant, what did you do?

A: I was a senator.

Q: How long were you a senator?

A: Six years.

Q: Why did you quit being a senator?

A: I was defeated in an election.

Q: Do you know Congressman Doodle?

A: Yes.

Q: How long have you known him?

A: Ten years.

Q: Have you ever socialized with him?

A: Yes.

Q: How often?

A: At least once a month over the last 10 years.

Q: Do you know other people in the Washington area who have socialized with Congressman Doodle?

A: Yes.

Q: How many?

A: Hundreds.

Q: Can you tell me some of the people that you know who have socialized with the Congressman?

A: Yes.

Q: Please tell us.

A: Other senators, representatives, employees of the House and Senate, and other consultants like myself.

Q: Have you ever talked to these people about Congressman Doodle's drinking habits?

A: Yes.

Q: How often?

A: Hundreds of times.

Q: Have you ever seen the Congressman drinking?

A: Yes.

Q: How many times?

A: On every occasion that I was with him.

Q: What is the most recent experience that you have had with the Congressman?

A: Last week.

Q: Based on your own observations and your discussions with others, do you know Congressman Doodle's reputation for sobriety in the community of Washington?

A: Yes, I do.

Q: What is that opinion?

A: Congressman Doodle's reputation is that he is a very sober person when he is not drinking.

E. Habit Evidence

Evidence of a particular habit of a person or the routine practice of an organization is admissible to prove that a person or organization acted in conformity with that habit on a particular occasion. If the evidence of an otherwise relevant habit is unfairly prejudicial, an objection is proper and will be sustained. See Section 4.8(A)(4).

Federal Rule of Evidence 406 does not define habit. Definitions may be found in treatises, statutes, case law and local rules. Habit is generally defined as a regular response to a repeated specific situation. It is within the discretion of the judge or arbitrator to determine if the specific situation has been repeated enough to assure that a true habit exists.

§ 7.11 IMPROPER DIRECT EXAMINATION

This section describes improper uses of direct examination which are unethical and grounds for an objection, mistrial, new trial, or new hearing.

A. Facilitating the Presentation of Perjured Testimony

The knowing use of fraudulent, false or perjured testimony is prohibited. Attorneys have a duty to prevent the misrepresentation of testimony. If the client in a civil case insists on testifying falsely, the attorney must inform the tribunal of the fraud in some manner. Disclosure may occur by making a record of the fact that the client is taking the stand against the advice of counsel or by actually telling the decision maker about the perjury. If a client in a criminal case insists on presenting false testimony, the attorney has the same duty but may be limited by constitutional considerations in determining how or if the perjury may be revealed. A criminal defense lawyer may have to allow the defendant to testify but may not ask the witness any questions or use the false testimony as a part of the final argument. If an attorney knows that a witness, who is not a client, will offer perjured testimony, the lawyer may not call that witness to testify.

In both civil and criminal cases, an attorney may request to withdraw from the case, but the request may be denied. Denial of the request to withdraw usually occurs when the trial is well underway and the withdrawal will cause unfair delay which may cause prejudice to the opponent or the administration of justice.

B. Soliciting Inadmissible Responses

It is improper for an attorney to solicit inadmissible responses. For example, it is highly improper for a plaintiff's counsel to ask, "Did you ever take photographs of that automobile before the repairs were made?" anticipating the witness will respond with, "No, but the insurance company did." A direct examiner must comply with the exclusionary rules of evidence and cannot attempt to prompt an inadmissible response from a witness, even with a question that is not objectionable. A direct examiner who attempts to contravene the rules of evidence commits misconduct which may result in a mistrial or a reversal. Further, the integrity of the attorney will be severely damaged, and the decision maker may conclude the attorney is untrustworthy. Ultimately, the attorney may be reported to the governing professional responsibility or lawyer licensing body.

C. Inadvertent Witness Misconduct

The inadvertent blurting out of inadmissible evidence by a witness can result in an admonition or even a mistrial or reversal. The examining lawyer needs to control the witness. This can be achieved by a preparation session before trial in which the witness is advised of the dangers of volunteering information and in not responding to the questions. Some witnesses disregard such advice and want the decision maker to know certain information, which is excluded by the rules of evidence. For example, a witness may want to tell about some rumors and gossip the witness heard about a party, which is inadmissible hearsay. The direct examiner must explain to the witness what information is inadmissible and the impropriety of attempting to disclose inadmissible evidence.

D. Allowing the Client or Witness to Disrupt the Trial or Hearing.

Allowing a client or witness to disrupt a case may bring disciplinary action against the lawyer. Lawyers should not stand mute as their clients misbehave. Not only may the lawyer be sanctioned, but a client or witness can be cited for contempt as well.

E. Using Tricks to Confuse Identification

The deliberate substitution of someone other than a party at the trial or hearing is improper. An attorney must disclose to the tribunal the name of the client that the attorney represents. In a case in which identification is an issue, it may be unethical for a lawyer to seat someone other than the client at counsel table for the purpose of eliciting an erroneous identification or to test an eyewitness' identification. However, full disclosure of the tactic to the judge or arbitrator and opposing counsel beforehand may permit the use of this technique.

CHAPTER 8
EXHIBITS

8.9 Objections to the Introduction of Exhibits
    A. Preparing for Objections

B. Responding to Objections
C. Questioning the Witness

D. Common Objections

REFLECTING ON ADVOCACY

Few things are harder to put up with than the annoyance of a good example.

—Mark Twain

A pleasant illusion is better than a harsh reality.

—Christian Nestell Bovee

§ 8.1 INTRODUCTION

Judges, jurors, and arbitrators often expect to see evidence as well as to hear about it. Exhibits meet this expectation. Well-prepared and well-presented exhibits help parties and attorneys communicate and present an interesting and persuasive case.

Outside the court and hearing rooms, learning is often accomplished through images and graphics. Adults absorb flashy news magazines, amazing television programs, dazzling movies, and the visual world of the internet. They expect to learn and to be entertained.

It takes more than the spoken word to keep people interested. It takes illustrative aids to help people learn and remember. This is just as true in the courtroom and in the hearing room as it is anywhere else.

An exhibit is anything other than testimony that can be perceived by the senses and presented as evidence. A presentation that combines verbal and visual evidence is much more likely to be understood and remembered than a presentation that only uses one of these sources. The successful outcome of a case may depend on how well the evidence is perceived and received by the fact finder.

There are three major types of exhibits: real evidence, demonstrative evidence, and visual aids. This chapter explores their use and effect, and explains the application of modern technology to twenty-first century dispute resolution.

A. *Real Evidence*

Real evidence consists of exhibits which are objects or writings that are facts in a case. Real evidence includes physical objects and documentary writings, such as the knife used in a homicide, DNA material found on a victim, the blender involved in a product liability case, and a written contract in a contract case. These tangible items of real evidence are probative in and by themselves. Real evidence is admitted into evidence as part of the record, and is usually made available for a jury to view during deliberations in the jury room.

Example:

Examining lawyer:

Q: I have just handed you an exhibit which has been marked for identification Exhibit No. 1. Do you recognize Exhibit No. 1?

A: Yes.

Q: How do you recognize Exhibit No. 1?

A: I recognize it by its title and by my initials which I wrote on it right after I took it from the defendant's hands.

Q: What is Exhibit No. 1?

A: It's the book entitled *Ghandi* that I saw the defendant use to hit the plaintiff over the head.

Q: Is Exhibit No. 1 in the same condition as it was when you saw the defendant hit the plaintiff over the head with it?

A: Yes.

To the Court:

Your Honor, at this time I offer Exhibit No. 1 in evidence.

Real evidence adds another dimension of proof in a case. A physical object or document provides the fact finder with a lasting impression of certain trustworthy facts. For example, the claw hammer murder weapon can be seen; the defective medical implant can be touched; the signature on the lengthy, small-print contract can be viewed; the emailed libelous statement can be seen.

B. Demonstrative Evidence

Demonstrative evidence refers to those exhibits that are not a part of the "real" event or transaction. These exhibits are usually created after the fact. Demonstrative or illustrative evidence includes diagrams, charts, graphs, models, videotapes, computer graphics and anything else that augments verbal testimony. These exhibits are admissible if they:

1. Assist a witness in testifying, or

2. Help the fact finder understand the evidence.

The attorney should request permission of the judge or arbitrator to use demonstrative evidence. While demonstrative exhibits are usually admitted into evidence and become a part of the record, many judges do not permit them to be used by jurors during deliberations in a jury room because they are not real evidence.

Example:

Examining lawyer:

Q: You have in your hands what is marked for identification as Exhibit F. Do you recognize it?

A: Yes.

Q: What is Exhibit F, Mr. Michelangelo?

A: It is a three dimensional model of the sculpture.

Q: Is the diagram a fair and accurate depiction of the sculpture that you created five hundred and fifty years ago?

A: Yes.

Q: Would this model assist you in explaining the birth of the Renaissance?

A: Yes, it would.

To the Court:

Your Honor, at this time I offer Exhibit F as illustrative evidence, and ask that the witness be allowed to use it during his testimony.

Demonstrative evidence adds a powerful visual dimension to the trial. A prepared diagram can provide an overview of an event; a photograph can bring to life the details of a scene; a videotape can show the lengthy, deliberate path the defendant took going to the murder scene to establish premeditation; a working model with movable figures can demonstrate a product; a metal diagram of an intersection with magnetic cars can assist a witness in telling the story of an accident; a computer generated recreation of an airline accident can bring to life the final fatal moments. See Sections 8.7. and 8.8

C. Visual Aids

Visual aids are created and used by attorneys to effectively communicate information to the fact finder and to help the fact finder understand the attorney's presentation. Visual aids are neither real nor demonstrative exhibits and are not considered evidence. Visual aids may be used during final argument, opening statement, and direct and cross-examination. Examples of visual aids include: a prepared chart summarizing evidence; overhead transparencies summarizing expert testimony; a part of opening statement prepared on a poster board; a blown-up verdict form to be used during final argument; a whiteboard, flip chart, or easel paper written on by the attorney listing words, dates, amounts, or other testimony of a witness during direct or cross-examination, and a computer generated flowchart of events, dates, and amounts.

Example:

To the Arbitrator:

We have prepared a list of each transaction between Wookie and Hans Solo involved in this case. We can display this summary evidence on the monitor screen. It will help us present our summation and assist you in understanding the multi-galactic transactions. We ask permission to use it.

Arbitrator:

You may do so.

Visual aids can persuasively emphasize evidence and arguments. A line or bar graph can be designed that favorably portrays evidence. Summaries of testimony can highlight evidence. Prepared lists of words and phrases placed on taped or Velcro-backed strips can be placed on a chart creating an outline of an argument. A software program can recreate and dramatize a story.

Visual aids are usually not marked as exhibits and are not received in evidence as a part of the file or record. Although there is no specific foundation that ordinarily must be established to use visual aids, it is usually necessary to either advise the judge or arbitrator of their intended use or to obtain permission for their use. Some judges expect visual aids to be handled like demonstrative exhibits and require them to be marked, introduced, and received in evidence. The judge has discretion to permit the use of visual aids or deny their use if they are confusing, unclear or distorted. See Section 8.8. Visual aids are usually not available to a jury during deliberations.

§ 8.2   PREPARATION OF EXHIBITS

The process for planning and using exhibits includes several preliminary considerations:

- Identifying potential exhibits.
- Assessing the use of exhibits.
- Planning a professional presentation.
- Managing exhibits.

A. *Identifying Potential Exhibits*

The identification of exhibits occurs during the investigation, discovery, and preliminary stages of a case and throughout its duration. Real evidence is located, gathered, and preserved. Demonstrative evidence is created during the case and before the trial or hearing. Visual aids are developed and produced a reasonable time before their use.

B. *Assessing the Use of Exhibits*

Advocates select exhibits that effectively communicate the case theory, present substantive information to the fact finder, emphasize important areas of evidence, refute the opponent's evidence, and persuade the fact finder of the truth of what happened. The following questions help assess useful exhibits:

- Will the exhibit enhance the ability of the witness to testify more effectively? Or the ability of the advocate to present evidence?

- Will the fact finder better understand and remember the evidence portrayed by the exhibit? If the exhibit distracts or confuses the fact finder, it should be not be used.

- Can the foundation for the exhibit be established through the testifying witness? Some exhibits involve a "chain of custody" foundation, and may require more than one witness to testify before an exhibit is introduced or used. See Section 8.4(C).

- Will the exhibit take too long to introduce or use? The examining attorney should efficiently introduce and use the exhibit.

- Does the relevant, probative value of the exhibit outweigh any unfair prejudicial impact? If the exhibit shocks the fact finder, is vulgar or in bad taste, or is unnecessarily cumulative or repetitive, it should not be offered.

- What is the cost and amount of time needed to make or obtain the exhibit? The expense, in dollars and time, should not exceed the exhibit's overall usefulness. The decision to use an exhibit must be made far enough in advance so the exhibit can be created.

- Will the exhibit be perceived by the fact finder as unfair? Expensive or numerous exhibits used by one side and not employed by the other side may cause the fact finder to perceive the case as one party with significant resources overwhelming a party of lesser resources.

- What technical problems might there be with the exhibit? Does the court room or hearing room have the facilities to present the exhibit? Have adequate steps been taken to ensure these problems can be overcome?

C. Planning the Presentation

Advance preparation is needed for exhibits. The attorney should prepare and rehearse the use of exhibits ahead of time to effectively present them. A selected and qualified witness or witnesses must identify and lay a foundation for the admission of the real or demonstrative exhibit. A lawyer usually explains the use and purpose of visual aids. Exhibits may also be admitted as evidence by a stipulated agreement of the parties.

D. Managing Exhibits

Organization is of particular importance in introducing and using exhibits. There is so much going on during a case that necessary foundation questions can be easily forgotten, and exhibits too easily misplaced. The attorney should have specific reference lists itemizing the exhibits to be used, the necessary foundation for those exhibits, and the witnesses who will provide that necessary foundation.

This organized format helps assure the exhibit is introduced and received in evidence. Forms 8.1 and 8.2 illustrate an effective system. Many exhibits can be included in an exhibit notebook, and copies can be provided to the fact finder, opposing lawyer, and witness.

FORM 8.1
EXHIBIT FOUNDATION WORKSHEET

Case_____ File_____

Exhibit

Elements of Admissibility	Which witness will provide	What witness will say
(1)		
(2)		
(3)		
(4)		
(5)		
(6)		
(7)		
(8)		
(9)		
(10)		

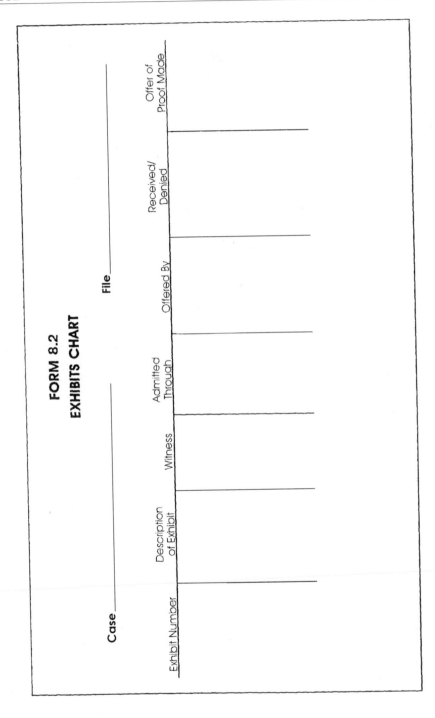

FORM 8.2
EXHIBITS CHART

Case _____

File _____

Exhibit Number	Description of Exhibit	Witness	Admitted Through	Offered By	Received/ Denied	Offer of Proof Made

§ 8.3 MODERN TECHNOLOGY

A. *Introduction*

The use of modern technology may be an option or a necessity in advocating a case. When properly used, technology helps present evidence and allows fact finders to quickly comprehend information. When used poorly, technology inhibits effective communication.

Attorneys must be prepared to use technology in two ways. They must understand the technology available and when its use is most appropriate and effective. And, they must know how to lay the necessary foundation and present the high tech evidence so that the judge or arbitrator will allow the evidence to be presented.

Technology in the courtroom is not new, and today's courtrooms and hearing rooms are being equipped with new multimedia systems. Many judges and arbitrators use or have access to computers during cases. Attorneys, administrators, clerks, and reporters use computer technologies to track evidence and create exhibits.

Communication technology permits the use of a variety of exhibits:

- Photographs,
- Documents,
- Financial summaries,
- Deposition excerpts,
- Animations,
- Diagrams,
- Charts,
- Timelines, and
- Video/audio recordings.

To learn about available technologies before a trial or arbitration, the lawyer should visit the courtroom or hearing room or contact the administrator to learn what systems are available. And, the lawyer should find out how familiar the judge or arbitrator is with exhibit technology.

B. *Technology Systems*

Technology systems generally fall into two categories: permanently installed equipment and portable equipment.

Permanent. Court and hearing rooms across the country are being equipped with technology systems, and there is a chance that your potential hearing room has a technology system already installed.

Portable. If a courtroom does not already have technology equipment, you need to determine whether or not the room has the capability for portable equipment to be used.

Laptops, power supplies, monitors, and speaker systems are just some of the equipment needed. A layout or drawing of the court or hearing room is helpful when deciding what supplies are necessary and how the setup will be completed. Equipment can be rented and set up from vendors located near the hearing or trial.

C. *Use of Technology*

The introduction and use of technology equipment is left to the discretion of the judge or arbitrator and the judgment of the advocates. Exhibit limitations as well as room factors, including layout and size, determine which methods are appropriate.

1. *Monitors/Screens.* Many court and hearing rooms have screens, and some rooms are outfitted with television or computer monitors allowing the participants to view the evidence. Judges usually have ultimate control over jury viewing, through override switches they control from the bench. For a bench trial or arbitration, three or fewer monitors are sufficient. For a jury trial, five or fewer monitors are optimal. Or, one large monitor screen may be used if it can be seen by all. When using monitors, it is also necessary to have an amplifier to broadcast the signal from the laptop or document cameras.

2. *Document Cameras/Projectors.* If using monitors, no projector is necessary for either the laptop or document camera. With a portable screen, the projector is needed for the laptop and document camera. Or, a document camera with a built-in projector may be used.

3. *Smart Boards.* A growing number of court and hearing rooms are equipped with smart boards that are connected with computers and can display large images. They can be written on with special markers that make an image that can be preserved in the computer. Printed copies can be made for display and for the record.

4. *Sound systems.* Audio equipment may be needed depending upon the size of the room and the number of participants. Most courtrooms have some sort of sound projection equipment; however, very few have lapel microphones.

5. *Power lecterns.* Many courtrooms have installed adjustable lecterns for the comfort of advocates. Tall or shorter advocates can adjust the height of the lectern.

6. *Live testimony transcriptions.* Reporters in some court and hearing rooms are entering testimony into viewable, "real time" files, which can be searched, reviewed by lawyers and witnesses, and referenced during the proceeding.

7. *Bar code technology.* In a case with numerous exhibits, this technology permits an advocate to pull up a document, and

quickly scroll to a particular page and paragraph, all on a screen for all to see instantly. Documents are marked or filed with a bar code.

8. *Extension cords, scissors, staples, white out, glue, sticky markers, highlighters, marking pens.* Advocates need to bring their own, even with all the new technology.

Effective use may still be made of traditional methods, such as easels with flip charts, white boards with markers, and chalk boards, augmenting newer equipment.

D. *Communication Technology*

There are basically two approaches to using technology with the right hardware and software: electronic and digital.

1. *Electronic Evidence Presentation*

Document cameras, also referred to as visual presenters, are electronic devices that combine a video camera with projection equipment. As the witness examines a document during testimony, the exhibited document is placed on the document camera and is shown to the fact finder. Typically, the document camera is either hooked up to an LCD projector that reflects the image onto a screen, or is connected to monitors in the court or hearing room.

The document camera is really nothing more than a video camera connected to a monitor or projector. Unlike other technology equipment, there is no need to scan documents and photos ahead of time. Hard copies of documents, as well as tangible exhibits, can be placed on the document camera surface. Documents can be highlighted during testimony on the document camera, promoting interactivity with the witness' testimony.

Video evidence can be presented electronically through VCR or DVD equipment. Deposition or prior trial or hearing testimony can be presented as if the witness were testifying in person.

There are limitations. Document cameras are often formatted with landscape (11″ x 8.5″) orientation, making it difficult to see detailed portrait (8.5″ x 11″) documents without zooming in each time on particular data. And, it is difficult to compare two or more documents.

2. *Digital Evidence Presentations*

Digital evidence presentations most commonly include a laptop with files to display case information through the use of an LCD projector or monitor. Original exhibits, such as documents and photographs, are scanned in and made into digital files, then loaded into a laptop and viewed with various software applications. Effective case presentation systems allow lawyers to retrieve documents in any order, and not just sequentially, as well as compare multiple documents and zoom, highlight, and draw on documents during the presentation.

Once documents and other evidence are digitized, files can be stored in multiple directories, locations, and searchable formats. When presenting evidence using a laptop, there is no paper shuffling or document rummaging. Presentation software allows lawyers to type in a code or use a bar code to retrieve documents, making use very smooth and efficient during evidence presentation. Features allow the advocate to bring up more than one document at a time, zoom in when needed, or focus on several areas at once. Presentations can be prepared which add facts, one at a time.

Video evidence can be copied onto a CD–ROM and synchronized with a typed transcript so the two can be shown at the same time. Attorneys can present computer-generated animations to supplement the testimony of expert and fact witnesses. Such presentations can have a powerful impact in helping fact finders understand complex events, processes, and transactions.

Overuse of technology can clutter the case. Some attorneys can become so fascinated with technology that they forget that simple presentations are often the most persuasive. There may also be a problem of rich versus poor, and the side with all the "stuff" may seem to have an unfair advantage. And, the technology may distract the fact finder from focusing on the evidence.

§ 8.4 EVIDENTIARY CONSIDERATIONS

Real and demonstrative exhibits are subject to the rules of evidence like any other item of evidence. Some exhibits, like physical objects, may be easy to introduce. Other exhibits, such as documentary evidence, have to satisfy evidence rules regarding the admissibility of hearsay and original writings before being received into evidence. Chapter 4 on Evidence and Objections described the applicable procedures and rules for all forums including jury and bench trials. Exhibits used in administrative hearings and arbitrations may be subject to less formal and rigid admissibility requirements.

The following sections discuss additional exhibit issues:

- Relevancy and unfair prejudice.
- Levels of foundation.
- Chain of custody.
- Demonstrative evidence.
- Exhibits used for limited purposes.
- Redaction of an exhibit.
- Exercise of discretion by the judge or arbitrator.

A. *Relevancy and Unfair Prejudice*

An exhibit must be relevant to be admissible. An exhibit is relevant if it has any tendency to make more or less probable the existence of any fact that is of consequence to the determination of the action. See Section 4.8(A).

Example:

Examining Attorney:

Q: I am showing you what has been marked for identification as Exhibit No. 10. Do you recognize it, Mr. Dumbo?

A: Yes.

Q: How?

A: I brought it with me.

Q: What is it?

A: It is a peanut shell. I ate the peanut part before I took the stand.

Q: Why did you eat the peanut?

A: To help my memory so I can testify better.

To the Court:

Your Honor, I offer Exhibit No. 10.

Opposing Counsel:

Your Honor, I object to this exhibit. It has nothing to do with this case and is irrelevant.

Judge:

Objection sustained.

Even when an exhibit is relevant, it may be excluded from evidence if it tends to confuse the issues or mislead the fact finder, causes undue delay, wastes time, is needless and cumulative, or if the probative value of the exhibit is substantially outweighed by its unfair prejudicial impact. The attorney should consider bringing a motion in limine and presenting any potentially prejudicial or gruesome exhibits to the trial judge and opposing counsel prior to trial to seek a ruling regarding their admissibility. See Section 4.5(A).

Some exhibits may be susceptible to a claim of undue prejudice because of their visual impact. This impact may indeed be prejudicial to the opponent, but such harm is not necessarily unfair. For example, a photograph showing injuries that a plaintiff has suffered demonstrates the extent of the injury and communicates to the jurors the pain and suffering the plaintiff endured. The impact of this photograph is undoubtedly more harmful to the defendant's case than if the plaintiff orally described the injuries. This harm does not rise to the level of unfair prejudice as defined by the rules of evidence unless the exhibit is unnecessarily gruesome.

Some exhibits may be excluded because of the unnecessary impact they have in a case or the way they distort the evidence.

Example:

In a criminal trial, presume the prosecution is introducing a series of photographs of the deceased victim through a police officer.

Examining Attorney:

Q: Officer Furillo, I am showing you what has been marked for identification as State's Exhibit No. 84. It is a photograph. Do you recognize this photograph?

A: Yes, I do.

Q: What is it?

A: It is another photograph in the series you have just shown me of the body of the victim.

Q: Is that also, like the other five photographs I have shown you, a fair and accurate representation of the victim's body as you saw it on the day of the murder?

A: Yes, it is.

To the Court:

Your Honor, I offer State's Exhibit No. 84.

Opposing Counsel:

Your Honor, I object to the introduction of Exhibit No. 84 on the grounds that it is unduly prejudicial, a waste of time, needless and cumulative.

Judge:

Your objection is sustained.

Example:

In a civil trial, presume the witness is an eyewitness to an auto accident that occurred at 9:00 p.m. on a summer night.

Examining Attorney:

Q: Ms. Avalon, I show you what is marked for identification as Defendant's Exhibit C. Do you recognize this photograph?

A: Yes.

Q: What does it show?

A: It shows the intersection where the accident happened.

Q: Is Defendant's Exhibit C a fair and accurate representation of the scene of the intersection that you saw?

A: Yes, for the most part.

To the Court:

Your Honor, I offer Defendant's Exhibit C into evidence.

Opposing Counsel:

I object, your Honor, to the introduction of Defendant's Exhibit C. This photograph was taken during the day and does not show the intersection as the witness saw it at dusk, after the sun had set. The photograph distorts the evidence and is likely to confuse and mislead the jury.

Judge:

Sustained.

B. Levels of Foundation

There are two levels of foundation for exhibits that must be met during a case. The first is the legal foundation which must be established before the exhibit can be admitted as evidence, and the second is the persuasive foundation. The judge or arbitrator always determines whether the minimum legal foundation has been met and whether the exhibit is admitted in evidence. The fact finder, including the jury in a jury trial, determines the persuasive weight and whether the exhibit is believable.

The threshold legal foundation is the absolute minimum requirement for the admissibility of an exhibit. While the admissibility foundation for the introduction of an exhibit may be quite easy to meet, the attorney must expand, simplify, or clarify the foundation to increase the weight the fact finder will give to that exhibit. Testimony by a witness must be developed so that sufficient evidence has been introduced that meets both levels of foundation.

1. Legally Sufficient Foundation

The judge or arbitrator determines whether there is sufficient evidence to support a finding that the exhibit is what it purports to be. The foundation for real evidence is established by a witness testifying that the tangible object or document is what it is claimed to be. Federal Rule of Evidence 901(b)(1). There are two primary types of real evidence:

- Evidence that is *readily identifiable* because it is unique or singular, and

- Evidence that is *fungible* and which lacks unique or readily identifiable characteristics.

The minimum evidentiary foundation is established for a piece of real evidence when a witness can identify the object by its distinctive characteristics and can state that the object is in substantially the same condition as it was at a relevant time. Federal Rule of Evidence 901(b)(4) permits identification by "distinctive characteristics" such as "appearance, contents, substance, internal patterns, or other distinctive characteristics."

Example:

Examining Attorney:

Q: I show you what is marked for identification as Exhibit No. 101. What is it?

A: It is my rubber duckie.

Q: How do you recognize it?

A: It looks identical to my rubber duckie. It is the same shape and color. It feels the same. And it has the same exact water marks on it from the last time I used it.

Q: Is Exhibit No. 101 in the same, or substantially the same, condition now as it was when you last saw it in your bathtub?

A: Yes.

To the Court:

Your Honor, we offer Exhibit No. 101, a rubber duckie, into evidence.

Evidence law does not require that a witness be completely sure or state with absolute certainty that an exhibit is the identical object. An exhibit will be admitted as long as there is reasonable evidence to support a finding that the exhibit is what it is claimed to be. A qualified identification of an exhibit may affect the weight the fact finder gives to the exhibit but does not affect admissibility.

2. *Persuasive Foundation*

After a judge or arbitrator has ruled that sufficient evidence has been established to admit an exhibit, additional testimony may be needed to convince a fact finder that the exhibit is real, accurate, complete, or true, depending on the type of exhibit. The more relevant and compelling facts that are admitted regarding the authenticity or accuracy of an exhibit, the more likely that the fact finder will conclude the exhibit is what it is claimed to be.

The following example illustrates the levels of evidentiary foundation and persuasive foundation with respect to the opinion testimony of an expert regarding an exhibit.

Example:

Presume J.E. Hoover has been qualified as an expert crime laboratory analyst and has analyzed two separate bullets: one from the body of the deceased and the other from the test gun.

Examining Attorney:

Q: You have told us that you examined what has been marked for identification as State's Exhibit A—a bullet from the body of the deceased?

A: Yes.

Q: Did you examine State's Exhibit B, which is the bullet you told us was fired from the test gun?

A: Yes.

Q: Did you compare them?

A: Yes.

Q: How did you do that?

A: With a comparison microscope.

Q: What is a comparison microscope?

A: A comparison microscope is an instrument which allows me to put two bullets under separate eyepieces so they can be rotated, and I can look for similarities in both the vertical and horizontal markings on the bullets.

Q: Based on your examination with the comparison microscope, do you have an opinion whether the bullet from the body of the deceased matches the bullet fired from the test gun?

A: Yes, I do.

Q: What is it?

A: They match identically.

Q: Describe to us how you made this comparison.

A: The markings on both bullets, which are known as striations, matched.

Q: What caused the striations?

A: Striations are caused by scratches and imperfections in the barrel of the pistol which causes marks or striations on the bullet.

Q: How do these striations help you make bullet comparisons?

A: These striation markings will be the same on every bullet fired from the same gun.

Q: Do you have an opinion whether the bullets, Exhibits A and B, were fired from the same gun?

A: Yes.

Q: What is the opinion?

A: They were fired from the same gun.

Q: How do you know?

A: I rotated the bullets so I could see that the scratches or
     striations on the two bullets were identical.

C. Chain of Custody

The foundation for most exhibits can be established through a
witness who testifies that an exhibit looks or feels like the real thing.
Some exhibits, particularly physical objects, may not be identifiable
through the senses of a witness. Objects that are not unique, that do not
have distinctive characteristics, or that have not been marked in any
identifiable way, may require a "chain of custody" foundation to make
the exhibit admissible.

A chain of custody accounts for the whereabouts of the exhibit
during all relevant times of the case. Examples include: in a drug case,
the plastic bag containing the drug needs to be accounted for from the
time the bag was seized from the defendant until its transportation to
the courtroom; in a criminal case, a bloody glove found at the scene must
be carefully marked and preserved; in a contaminated beverage case, the
glass bottle needs to be accounted for from the time of consumption until
the time of trial or hearing.

There are two primary ways of establishing an unbroken chain of
custody:

- The exhibit has been *at all times in the continuing,* safe, and sole
  possession of one or more individuals; or

- The exhibit itself was *distinctively identified,* or was sealed and
  placed in a safe, tamper-proof container.

Testimony from one or more witnesses must show there have been
no significant breaks in the links of the chain of custody. Typically,
evidence need not establish an unbroken chain or the whereabouts of an
exhibit over the entire period of relevant time. Judges and arbitrators
recognize that a chain of custody is flexible and that qualified evidence is
sufficient to meet the admissibility foundation. Additional evidence may
be necessary to meet the persuasive foundation and convince the fact
finder that the exhibit is the actual real evidence and there has been no
loss, misplacement, mix-up, unexplained changes, or tampering.

Example:

*This example illustrates how the chain of custody is established
when the exhibit has been in the continual, sole possession of
individuals.*

Examining Attorney (First witness establishing foundation):

Q: On May 2, at 12:00 noon, where were you?

A: I was at the Mudville Ball Park.

Q: What were you doing there?

A: I was there with my wife and my son, and we were having a picnic before the team began batting practice for the big game.

Q: What happened?

A: One of the baseball players was walking out toward home plate before anyone else even arrived.

Q: Did you know who it was?

A: Yes.

Q: Who?

A: Casey.

Q: How do you know it was him?

A: I recognized him. I had seen him many times before at games and in town.

Q: What was he doing?

A: Swinging a big bat.

Q: Then what happened?

A: I heard the sound of a crack of a bat.

Q: Then what?

A: Well, I was quite surprised.

Q: Why?

A: Because it was long before any batting practice or the game.

Q: What happened next?

A: I was suddenly hit on the head by a ball.

Q: What happened to you?

A: I ended up with a big cut on my head.

Q: What did you do?

A: I picked up the ball.

Q: Then what did you do with it?

A: I gave it to my son.

Q: Did you look at it carefully?

A: No, I was bleeding a lot.

Q: Can you identify the baseball that hit you on the head?

A: Not specifically. It looked like any baseball.

Examining Attorney (Second witness establishing chain):

Q: You are the son of the plaintiff who was hit in the head with the baseball, correct?

A: Yes.

Q: Describe for us what happened?

A: My dad cried out, and I turned and he handed me a baseball.

Q: Did you see your dad get hit with the ball?

A: Not really.

Q: What did you do with the ball?

A: I have kept it in my possession since that time.

Q: Why did you do that?

A: Well, I watch Court T.V. and thought maybe Dad might have a good lawsuit.

Q: How did you keep it?

A: Well, I carried it home with me.

Q: Then what did you do with it?

A: I locked it in my desk drawer and put the key on a chain and carried it around my neck.

Q: Does anyone else have a key to your desk drawer?

A: No.

Q: When did you remove the baseball?

A: I took the key from around my neck today, removed the baseball, and brought it with me to court.

Q: Do you have that baseball with you right now?

A: Yes, I do.

Q: Will you hand it to me, please?

A: Yes.

Q: I am showing you what has been marked for identification as Plaintiff's Exhibit No. 1. What is it?

A: It is the baseball that I kept in my possession since my dad gave it to me, that I just took out of my pocket and gave to you.

Q: By the way, how did Casey do that day?

A: He struck out.

Example:

This example deals with an exhibit that cannot be specifically identified but which has not been tampered with because it has been kept in a sealed container.

Examining Attorney:

Q: What were you doing on September 5?

A: I was in my dorm room with a professor.

Q: What was his name?

A: Professor Kingsfield.

Q: What were you doing?

A: We were smoking marijuana.

Q: What did you do after you smoked the marijuana?

A: I picked up this partially smoked marijuana cigarette that had been smoked by the professor.

Q: What did you do with it?

A: I placed it in a standard letter-sized envelope, sealed the flap, wrote my name over the seal, and the date and the time.

Q: Why did you do that?

A: Well, I thought that some day Professor Kingsfield might be up for an appointment to the World Court.

Q: I am showing you what has been marked for identification as Exhibit No. 1. Do you recognize it?

A: I do.

Q: What is it?

A: It is the envelope upon which I wrote my name and the date after putting in the marijuana cigarette.

Q: What did you do with this envelope, Exhibit No. 1.

A: I placed it in a box in my house in the attic.

Q: Where Exhibit No. 1 been for the past year?

A: In that box in my house in the attic.

Q: Has the envelope been opened?

A: No, it has not.

Q: How do you know?

A: It is still sealed and has my name over the flap. The envelope is intact.

D. Demonstrative Evidence

Exhibits that are not real evidence may involve issues relating to authenticity depending on the nature of the particular exhibit. Witnesses must be able to testify that they are familiar with or know that the information portrayed or contained in or on the exhibit is accurate. Illustrative aids that are plainly visible, including prepared diagrams and models, can be described by the witness. Exhibits such as video, DVD, and computer generated demonstrative aids require a witness to establish that the images or information has been reviewed and is accurate. See Sections 8.7 and 8.8 for examples.

E. Limited Purposes

An exhibit, like any other form of evidence, may be admitted for a limited purpose. Federal Rule of Evidence 105 and similar state rules authorize evidence to be offered for a limited purpose. See Section 4.5(E). The contents of some exhibits may be admissible for one purpose but inadmissible for other purposes. In these situations, the offering lawyer should indicate the limited purpose the exhibit serves.

Example:

Presume the plaintiff has testified the injuries she sustained in an accident due to the defendant's negligence have caused her to lose physical control over her arm and she is now unable to write. A defense witness has testified he saw the plaintiff write a note which is being introduced as real evidence.

Defendant's Counsel:

Your Honor, I offer Defense Exhibit No. 1.

The Court to Plaintiff's Counsel:

Do you have any objections?

Plaintiff's Attorney:

Not to the introduction of the written note, your Honor, but we do to its contents, which are unflattering to the plaintiff. May we have an instruction to the jury that Defense Exhibit No. 1 is being offered for a limited purpose?

Judge:

Yes, you may. (To the jury): Members of the Jury, I am instructing you at this time that Defense Exhibit No. 1 is being offered for the limited purpose to show that the plaintiff wrote a note. The content of the note itself is not evidence in this case and should not be considered by you as such.

Example:

Presume the defendant consumer testified that he paid for repairs done to his Silver Heritage Special motorcycle and he has identified a $297 repair bill, Defendant's Exhibit No. 2, as the copy of the bill that he received marked "Paid."

Defendant's Counsel:

I offer Defendant's Exhibit No. 2 into evidence for the limited purpose of proving that the defendant paid this bill.

Plaintiff's Attorney:

Objection, your Honor. This bill contains hearsay information that repairs were done on the defendant's motorcycle and is inadmissible.

Defendant's Counsel:

Your Honor, we do not offer the bill to prove the repairs were performed, but only to prove that the defendant paid money and received a receipt.

Judge:

Objection overruled. Defendant's Exhibit No. 2 is received for the limited purpose explained by counsel.

F.   *Redacting an Exhibit*

Some exhibit documents contain admissible and inadmissible evidence. The examining attorney should offer only those parts of the documents that are clearly admissible. In jury trials, when the judge sustains an objection to part of a document, the ruling will require that the inadmissible portions of the document be redacted (removed) before the jurors see the document. The examining attorney may anticipate such objections and prepare an alternate exhibit which does not contain the inadmissible statements, which can be shown to the jury in lieu of the original document.

Example:

Examining Attorney:

Your Honor, we offer Plaintiff's Exhibit No. 12 into evidence which is a copy of the manuscript, *Paradise Regained,* written by John Milton. My client, the plaintiff, wrote some comments in the margins which contain statements that are irrelevant to this case. Counsel for defendant has seen those comments and agrees with us that they are inadmissible. We eliminated those comments from this exhibit manuscript by whiting them out.

Opposing Counsel:

Your Honor, we have no objection to the admissibility of Plaintiff's Exhibit No. 12 with those comments removed.

Judge:

Plaintiff's Exhibit No. 12 is received.

There are a number of ways that inadmissible portions of a document may be eliminated. If only a few words or phrases need to be redacted, they may be easily obliterated by using white-out or a marking pen. If substantial portions of a document need to be deleted, those parts can be covered up with a piece of paper and a copy made of the document, or the document can be scanned, word processed, and edited. If the form of the document is unimportant, the admissible portion of the contents may be recreated on a blank page and that new document admitted into evidence. Whatever method is employed, the jurors should only be allowed to see the admissible portions of the document. Taping a piece of paper over the inadmissible parts of a document is not wise because the jurors may be tempted in the jury room to peek under the taped portion.

Example:

Examining Attorney:

Your Honor, we offer Plaintiff's Exhibit No. 7, a dental report prepared by the plaintiff's dentist, Dr. Olivier, into evidence.

Opposing Counsel (At the Bench):

Your Honor, we object to the second and third sentence of the first paragraph of the report. Those sentences contain statements that are inadmissible hearsay because they were not made to the doctor for purposes of diagnosis or treatment.

Judge:

Sentences two and three of the first paragraph of Plaintiff's Exhibit No. 7 are ruled inadmissible. The remainder of the exhibit is received into evidence. Counsel, before you may show this exhibit to the jurors, you must remove those two sentences.

Examining Attorney (At the Bench):

Yes, your Honor. We have them removed on this copy.

Opposing Counsel (At the Bench):

Your Honor, we ask the court to instruct the jurors to disregard that portion of the dental record that is removed and that they not guess about what was contained in the document.

Judge:

Members of the Jury, you may review the dental record of the plaintiff, but you are not to consider those statements that were omitted. You are to disregard them and not draw any inference or guess what was included in the document or why it was removed.

G. Judicial Discretion

The judge or arbitrator has discretion in ruling on the admissibility and use of exhibits. This discretion is limited in regard to real evidence. Since the admissibility of real evidence is determined as a matter of law, real exhibits are admissible if the proper foundation is established.

Discretion is much broader in regard to demonstrative evidence and visual aids. The determination is more one of fact than law in the question of admissibility of demonstrative evidence and visual aids. These types of evidence will not be permitted if the judge or arbitrator decides that the illustrative evidence does not assist the witness or does not help the fact finder.

§ 8.5   INTRODUCTION OF EXHIBITS

A. *Legal Terminology*

Many exhibits require the examiner to use precise legal terminology for their introduction and use. Specific questions, which are often artificial and formalistic, must be asked to establish the proper foundation. Most witnesses would never be able to come up with these words by themselves, and so the attorney is allowed — and required in many situations — to state the foundation words in the form of leading questions. This "litany" of questions elicits the precise elements of foundation necessary for the introduction and use of exhibits and reduces the time a witness would need to testify to such matters if leading questions were not used. Other reasons may also justify the use of leading questions in laying the foundation for exhibits. See Section 7.7.

Examples:

Q: Is this photograph a fair and accurate representation of the scene as you saw it on February 14, Ms. Valentine?

Q: Are these records made in the ordinary and regular course of your travel business, Mr. Gulliver?

Q: Is this musket in substantially the same condition as it was the day you first saw it at the scene of the shooting, Mr. Crockett?

B. *Steps for the Admissibility of Exhibits Into Evidence*

The introduction of exhibits requires several steps that the attorney should master and commit to memory. The witness must provide testimony which establishes the necessary foundation for the particular exhibit. Specific illustrations of the foundation required for various types of exhibits appear in Section 8.6. While the precise steps vary among judges and arbitrators and differ among types of exhibits, the following steps provide a general format:

1. Qualify the witness by laying the *foundation* for the witness to identify the exhibit.

2. Make certain the exhibit has been pre-marked before the trial or hearing or before the witness testifies, or have the item *marked* as an exhibit during the examination.

3. Ask permission from the judge or arbitrator to *approach the witness*. Many do not require this.

4. Request that the witness *examine* and *recognize* the exhibit.

5. Have the witness *identify* the exhibit.

6. *Offer* the exhibit into evidence by referring to its exhibit number or letter.

7. Provide *opposing counsel* the opportunity to *review* the exhibit, if not done previously.

8. *Respond to* any *objections* made by opposing counsel if necessary.

9. Obtain a *ruling* from the arbitrator or the judge on the record.

10. If admitted, *show* the exhibit *to* the *fact finder* in an appropriate way.

ILLUSTRATION OF ADMISSIBILITY STEPS

Plaintiff's Examining Attorney:

Q: What is your name, sir?

A: Mr. Little.

Q: Where were you last June 1 at 3 o'clock in the afternoon?

A: Out in the chicken yard.

Q: What happened?

1. FOUNDATION

A: A brick fell into my yard and nearly hit me.

Q: What did you do?

A: I picked it up.

Q: Why?

A: I thought the sky was falling.

Q: What did you do with the brick you had picked up?

A: I scratched my name on it with a nail.

2. MARKED

To the Court Reporter:

May I have this marked for identification as Exhibit No. 1?

Court Reporter:

Your exhibit has been marked for identification as Exhibit No. 1.

3. APPROACH

To the Court:

Your Honor, may I approach the witness?

Judge:

Yes, you may.

4. EXAMINE AND RECOGNIZE

Q: I have just handed you a brick which has been marked for identification as Exhibit No. 1. Do you recognize it?

A: Yes.

Q: How?

A: I recognize the size and the shape and I recognize my name that I scratched on it with a nail.

5. *IDENTIFY*

Q: What is Exhibit No. 1 for identification?

A: The object that fell in my yard last June 1.

Q: Is Exhibit No. 1 for identification in the same condition as it was last June 1?

A: Yes.

6 & 7. *OFFER AND REVIEW*

To the Court:

Your Honor, at this time I offer Exhibit No. 1, and I am handing it to opposing counsel.

8. *RESPONSE*

Opposing Counsel:

No objection, your Honor.

9. *RULING*

Judge:

Exhibit No. 1 is admitted.

10. *SHOW TO FACT FINDER*

Plaintiff's Attorney:

May the brick be shown to the jurors?

Judge:

Yes. You may pass it to them.

Plaintiff's Attorney:

Your Honor, may I wait just a minute before I ask any further questions of this witness so the jurors have a chance to look at the exhibit?

Judge:

You may have just a short time, counsel, and then proceed.

The following paragraphs explain each of these steps in detail.

1. Qualifying the Witness (Foundation)

Questions need to be asked of the witness to lay the foundation for the witness to identify the exhibit. The witness must testify that the witness saw the exhibit and is able to recognize it.

Example:

Q: What happened after the conference?

A: I signed the pact, and I saw Mr. Chamberlain sign the pact.

Example:

Q: What did you see?

A: I saw the defendant, Ma Barker, holding the machine gun.

In these two examples, after the witness testifies to the existence of the evidence, the attorney can begin asking questions to introduce the exhibit.

2. Marking the Exhibit

Most exhibits will be pre-marked before the trial or hearing or before the witness testifies. Many judges and arbitrators require the attorneys to have all the exhibits marked by the court reporter or clerk before the start of the trial, and administrative judges and arbitrators may ask the attorneys what exhibits they plan to introduce before the hearing and mark them at that time. In a situation where an exhibit is not pre-marked, the attorney can have the exhibit marked during the trial or hearing.

Exhibits will be marked either by a number or a letter. The practice among tribunals varies. In many forums, the exhibits are marked with consecutive numbers. In other forums, all of the plaintiff's exhibits are marked with numbers and the defendant's exhibits with letters. The person marking will know the proper system, and the attorney need not suggest whether a number or letter should be used. The judge or arbitrator or reporter will also usually maintain a list and keep track of the sequence of exhibits, and will know the next letter or number that should be used.

3. Approaching the Witness

Some judges and arbitrators require the attorney to request permission before approaching the witness with an exhibit. Some expect the attorney to seek such permission only with the first exhibit, or the first witness. Most do not require or expect the attorney to ask for such permission, because they recognize the attorney must approach the witness in order to show the exhibit to the witness. The attorney can ask the judge or arbitrator about the preferred practice if the attorney is uncertain whether a request should or need be made. See Section 3.5(D).

4. Examination and Recognition of Exhibit by the Witness

The attorney needs to describe on the record (if there is one) the handing of the exhibit to the witness. The attorney should always clearly refer to the number or letter marked on the exhibit to identify the exhibit for the record. There are a number of alternative phrases that may be used:

Examples:

I am handing you what has been marked as Plaintiffs Exhibit No. 1 for identification.

You have in your hands.

I hand you. . . .

I have just handed you. . . .

Here is . . .

I show you.

I am showing you.

The witness must be able to recognize the exhibit and explain how the witness is able to do so.

Example:

Q: Do you recognize Exhibit No. 6 for identification?

A: Yes.

Q: How?

A: I recognize the size and shape of the blue diamond that I wore and its distinctive blue color.

Q: Anything else?

A: Oh, yes.

Some judges require all references to an exhibit not yet received in evidence include the phrase "marked for identification." Most judges consider this an unnecessary technicality and do not require the use of this phrase.

With some exhibits the attorney may appropriately describe the exhibit when it is handed to the witness. If it is obvious to everyone in the courtroom what the exhibit is, or if the identification of the exhibit is not in issue, the attorney may generically describe the exhibit.

Examples:

Q: I hand you what has been marked as Plaintiff's Exhibit No. 2. Do you recognize this telescope, Mr. Galileo?

Q: Here is Plaintiff's Exhibit No. 3. It is a computer printout, Ms. Gates.

5. *Identification of Exhibit by the Witness*

The witness identifies the exhibit with a brief description of the exhibit.

Example:

Q: Please look at Defense Exhibit C for identification, Mr. Daguerre, and tell us what it is.

A: It is a photograph I took of the cathedral of Notre Dame de Paris.

Example:

Q: Mr. Fitzgerald, what is Plaintiff's Exhibit No. 3?

A: It is a letter I received from Zelda.

It is improper for the attorney to describe an exhibit which is not identifiable by sight or is an issue in controversy.

Example:

Examining Attorney:

Q: I show you Defendant's Exhibit No. 1, which is a Lawyer Hunt CD game.

Opposing Counsel:

Objection, Counsel is testifying. There is no foundation as to what that exhibit is.

Arbitrator:

Objection sustained.

6. *Offering the Exhibit Into Evidence*

The attorney must offer the exhibit into evidence. The attorney must refer to the exhibit by the assigned number or letter and direct the offer to the judge or arbitrator.

Examples:

Your Honor, I offer Plaintiff's Exhibit No. 1 into evidence.

Defendant offers the disk marked as Exhibit E.

The attorney should avoid using unnecessary words in making the offer, such as "I would like to offer into evidence" because it does not matter what the attorney "would like" to do. A short, simple declarative statement is sufficient. "I offer . . . " is enough.

7. *Examination of the Exhibit by Opposing Counsel*

After the exhibit is offered by the proponent, the opposing attorney may object to its admission. The opposing attorney must usually wait until the proponent has offered the evidence before an objection regarding admissibility can be made, unless there is a reason for making an earlier objection. Early objections to the admissibility of an exhibit may be made through a motion in limine before trial, before the witness testifies, or before the exhibit is shown to the witness. The opposing attorney may also need to object to an exhibit if displaying it is unfairly prejudicial or otherwise objectionable, or if the examining attorney asks improper questions in an effort to lay a foundation for the introduction of the exhibit.

Some attorneys show the exhibit to opposing counsel at the same time they offer the exhibit into evidence. The attorney may walk over to counsel's table and hand it to counsel if the examining attorney wants the opposing counsel to look at the exhibit, or if the opposing counsel wants to look at the exhibit. The offering attorney may remark that counsel has been provided with an opportunity to see the exhibit before the trial or hearing. The attorneys have usually seen the exhibits and know what they are, and it may be unnecessary to physically show the exhibit to opposing counsel because of counsel's familiarity with the exhibit.

In some jurisdictions the exhibit may be shown to opposing counsel at an earlier time during the case. In some tribunals, the exhibit is shown to opposing counsel before it is shown to the witness. In these jurisdictions, it may be necessary for the examining attorney to first hand the exhibit to the opposing counsel before showing it to the witness. In other forums, the exhibit is shown to opposing counsel after it is shown to the witness but before it is offered in evidence. Whatever the requirements are in a jurisdiction, the examining attorney should follow them.

8. *Responding to Objections*

The examining attorney may need to respond to any objections which the opposing attorney has made to the introduction of the exhibit. The judge or arbitrator often rules immediately and overrules the objection without expecting any response from the offering attorney. If a response is expected or if the examining attorney believes the objection may be sustained, the attorney should explain why the exhibit is admissible. If an objection is sustained, the examining attorney should ask additional questions to remedy the evidentiary deficiency, or should make an offer of proof if the exhibit is excluded. See Section 4.5(B).

9. *Showing the Exhibit to the Fact Finder*

How an exhibit is shown to the fact finder depends upon the type of exhibit, the exhibit's importance to the case, how the attorney prefers to present the exhibit, and how the judge or arbitrator wants the exhibit presented. In bench trials, administrative hearings, and arbitrations, the judge or arbitrator may be able to easily and readily review the exhibit. In jury trials, a number of options may be available.

a. *Tangible Objects*

Objects that are large, easily seen or dangerous need not be handed directly to the jury. The jurors can see these tangible objects while the witness is on the witness stand. For example, it is sufficient for the jurors to see a gun from a distance, and it may be unnecessary or inappropriate for them to individually handle the gun.

Some tangible objects may need to be handled and individually seen by the jurors. Objects that are small or difficult to see from a distance may need to be shown to the jurors up close. If the actual weight of an object is in issue, or if the use or function of an object is in dispute, the jurors may individually need to handle the object.

(i) *Documents*

There are a variety of ways documents may be shown to the jury. A document may be:

- Read to the jury panel by the attorney or clerk (a neutral person),
- Passed among the jurors,
- Copied, with one copy distributed to each juror,
- Blown-up, placed on an easel, and explained by the witness, or
- Displayed on a monitor screen.

The attorney should decide which method will be the most effective and efficient and make appropriate arrangements for that distribution or display in advance of the trial.

(ii) *Photographs and Videotapes*

Photographs may be taken and used in a variety of cases for a variety of purposes. In automobile accident cases, photographs of the scene, the automobiles, and injuries to the injured parties are common. A videotape of the day in the life of a severely injured and handicapped plaintiff may be made and shown to the jury. Photographs of the scene of the crime are typical in criminal cases. Aerial photographs may be used in condemnation proceedings. Computer generated graphics may display recreations of events with three dimensional, rotating views.

Photographs are usually demonstrative evidence. Some photographs constitute real evidence. A film of a bank robbery taken with a surveillance camera or a videotape of a physical injury may be actual evidence of facts in a case.

The foundation for real or demonstrative photographs is usually the same. The witness' testimony that the photograph or videotape accurately depicts what appears is sufficient to establish foundation. In some cases, a witness may have to testify as to how the videotape or CD–ROM presentation was made, if the making affects the authenticity or accuracy of the reproduction.

(iii) Diagrams, Drawings, and Computer Displays

A witness may use a prepared diagram or may create a freehand drawing on a whiteboard, on an easel paper using marking pens or a computer screen using a mouse. While freehand drawings may have to be used because of time or financial constraints, prepared diagrams are much more effective because few witnesses draw well.

(iv) Visual Aids

During opening statement and final argument, an attorney may use a prepared chart of key facts, a list of damages, or a summary of evidence. This information may be presented on a board or a monitor screen.

In a jury trial, during final argument, an attorney may refer to enlarged copies of the jury instructions or the verdict form, which are placed on an easel in front of the jury. During witness examination, the attorney may write key words of the witness' testimony on an easel pad, or may have an expert outline testimony on a computer screen.

b. Duration of Display of the Exhibit

How long an exhibit is displayed depends upon the type of exhibit. Items of real evidence are usually left on counsel table or on the clerk's table during a case, unless their presence is unfairly prejudicial or otherwise objectionable. Demonstrative evidence is displayed during the testimony of a witness who uses the exhibit. If an opposing lawyer does not want the evidence to be displayed after the testimony of the witness, the opposing attorney may either physically move the exhibit, ask the examining attorney to put the exhibit away, or ask permission to have the exhibit removed. The same procedures are available for visual aids.

c. Attention of Fact Finders

The examining attorneys should provide the fact finders with sufficient time to understand, view or touch evidence before continuing with the examination of a witness or the introduction of other evidence. If an exhibit is being read by a judge or arbitrator or if jurors are reviewing exhibits, the attorney should delay continuing a witness examination until the fact finders can devote their full attention to the additional evidence.

C. Exceptions to the Usual Steps

1. Stipulations

Advocates may stipulate to the foundation of an exhibit to avoid the need to ask detailed questions during the case. Stipulations can significantly reduce trial and hearing time and should be voluntarily entered into between counsel if there is no real dispute concerning the authenticity or accuracy of the exhibits. Judges and arbitrators, especially in bench trials and arbitrations, encourage or expect certain types of evidence to be admitted by stipulation. For example, hospital records will often be entered into evidence by stipulation because these records are usually reliable. A written stipulation should be introduced during the trial or hearing, or an oral agreement summarized before the arbitrator or judge or on the record. The offering attorney must request permission to introduce the stipulation by reading it or have someone read the content of the stipulation.

Example:

Claimant's Attorney:

Ms. Arbitrator, at this time I offer Exhibit No. 13. It is a print out of email messages sent between the parties on September 30, the admissibility of which both I and counsel for the Respondent have agreed to through stipulation.

Arbitrator (To Counsel for Respondent):

Is that correct, counsel?

Respondent's Counsel:

Yes it is your Honor.

Arbitrator:

Exhibit No. 13 is received.

Even when adverse counsel are likely to be cooperative and agree to stipulate to the admission of exhibits, there are occasions when laying the foundation is advantageous and may be important for persuasive foundation. In these situations, counsel should ask questions which establish a complete foundation for the exhibits. Counsel may need to reject a proffered stipulation from the other side or resist the urgings of the judge or arbitrator to accept such a stipulation. In rejecting a stipulation, the examiner must decide that laying the foundation is strategically necessary for its persuasive value.

2. Pleadings, Admissions, and Discovery Responses

Pleadings and discovery documents are a part of the case but are not considered as evidence by the fact finder unless or until an attorney affirmatively offers such information as evidence during the case. The evidence may be offered during the direct or cross-examination of the witness who originally provided the information, or may be read directly during the offering party's case in chief or on cross-examination.

Example:

Plaintiff's Attorney:

Your Honor, we offer Plaintiff's Exhibit No. 1, the letter containing the libelous statement made by the defendant about Oscar Wilde. The authenticity of the letter was admitted in Defendant's Answer, paragraph three, making it admissible.

Example:

Defendant's Counsel:

Your Honor, at this time I offer Defendant's Exhibit No. 25. It is a copy of the first page of the Street Legal Road Lawyers Website that is in issue in this case, the admissibility of which has been obtained pursuant to Federal Rule of Civil Procedure 36. The admission can be found in Plaintiff's Response No. 4 to Defendant's Request for Admissions.

---

3. Abbreviating the Foundation

When there is a series of exhibits for which the foundations are similar, the attorney may abbreviate the process of laying foundation after the first few exhibits have been introduced. The attorney can ask the witness whether the response given to the foundation questions for the previous exhibits would be essentially the same for subsequent exhibits which are to be introduced. Once the judge or arbitrator and opposing attorney know that the attorney is prepared to present an extensive foundation, the actual presentation of that foundation may not be necessary.

Example:

Presume the witness has testified that she seized ten items from the defendant's airplane hangar and that she used a marking pen to mark each item with her name and the date.

Examining Attorney:

Q: I am showing you what we have already marked for identification as Plaintiff's Exhibit No. 1. Do you recognize it?

A: Yes.

Q: How do you recognize it?

A: I recognize it by the fact my name and the date are written on the blade.

Q: What is Plaintiff's Exhibit No. 1 for identification?

A: It is the propeller I found in the defendant's hangar.

Q: Where did you first see Plaintiff's Exhibit No. 1 for identification?

A: I saw it when I seized it from the defendant's garage.

Q: When did you put the markings on it?

A: At the time I seized it from the defendant, Mr. Wright.

To the Court:

Your Honor, we offer Plaintiff's Exhibit No. 1.

Judge:

With no objection, it is received.

Examining Attorney:

Q: I am showing you what has been marked for identification as Plaintiff's Exhibit No. 2. It is a map of Kitty Hawk. It has writing on the top in the surface. Is that your writing?

A: Yes.

Q: Is that your name, and the date?

A: Yes.

Q: Is that also an exhibit you found in the defendant's hangar and marked in the same way as Plaintiff's Exhibit No. 1?

A: Yes.

And so on with the following eight exhibits.

4. Self–Authenticating Documents

Some exhibits are self-authenticating. Federal Rule of Evidence 902 and similar state rules make it unnecessary to introduce evidence to authenticate certain exhibits including:

- Domestic public documents under seal.
- Domestic public documents not under seal.
- Foreign public documents.
- Certified copies of public documents.
- Official publications issued by public authorities.
- Newspapers and periodicals.
- Trade inscriptions.
- Acknowledged and notary public documents.
- Commercial paper and related documents.

After the attorney establishes that an exhibit falls into one of these categories, the attorney need not introduce any other evidence to establish its authenticity. The exhibit may be offered, unless some other evidence rule has not been met.

Example:

Examining Attorney:

I offer Exhibit No. 5 for identification into evidence. It is a computer chip. The chip has the trade name "X–Files" and is inscribed with "The Truth is out there." This exhibit is self-authenticating.

Arbitrator:

Received.

---

§ 8.6 THE ELEMENTS OF EVIDENTIARY FOUNDATION FOR VARIOUS EXHIBITS

The necessary evidentiary foundation questions vary from exhibit to exhibit but, typically, responses are sought that establish the exhibit, its existence, identity, authenticity, and accuracy. The following checklists of foundation elements and examples demonstrate the legal grounds for admissibility in introducing various exhibits.

A. *Physical Objects and Properties (Including Products, Clothing, Appliances, and Weapons)*

To admit a tangible object into evidence, the following elements must be proved:

- The exhibit is relevant to the case.
- The witness recognizes and can identify the exhibit.
- The witness can recall what the exhibit looked like at the previous relevant time.
- The exhibit is now in the same or substantially the same condition as when the witness saw it at the previous relevant time.

Example:

Examining Attorney:

Q: When you entered the Borden house, where did you go?

A: The bedroom.

Q: What did you see?

A: I saw an axe.

Q: Where was it?

A: On the floor.

Q: What did you do?

A: I picked it up.

Q: Why?

A: Because it was covered with blood.

Q: Was there anything else you noticed about the axe?

A: Yes, it had a chip on the handle.

Q: What did you do with it?

A: I took it back to the police department and put it in my evidence locker.

Q: How long was it there?

A: Until today.

Q: What did you do with it today?

A: I took it out of the evidence locker and brought it to court.

Q: Officer, I have just placed on the table in front of you what I have had marked for identification as State's Exhibit No. 1. It is an axe. Do you recognize it?

A: Yes.

Q: How do you recognize it?

A: I recognize the chip on the handle, the size, and the red stain.

Q: What is it?

A: It is the same axe I found in the living room of the Borden house.

Q: Does it appear to be in the same condition as it was when you picked it up?

A: Yes, except the red stain is now dry.

To the Court:

Your Honor, I offer State's Exhibit No. 1 into evidence.

B. Documents (Including Letters, Contracts, Leases, E-mail, and Other Signed or Acknowledged Documents)

To admit documents into evidence the following elements must be proved:

- The document is relevant to the case.

- The document contains a signature, was handwritten, was composed on a computer only accessible by a password, or bears some other identifying characteristics.

- The signature, handwriting, or characteristic belongs to or identifies a person.

- The witness saw the person sign, write, or compose the document; or

- The witness knows, is familiar with, or can recognize the signature or handwriting; or

- The witness recognizes and can identify the characteristics of the document; or

- The witness is a party and admits signing, writing, or composing, or identifies the contents of the document; or

- A handwriting expert states that the signature or writing is by a certain person or that the document can be identified by its characteristics.

- The document is authentic.

- The document is an original or an admissible duplicate or other copy.

- The document is now in the same condition as when it was made and has not been altered.

Example (Letter):

Examining Attorney:

Q: Mr. Abelard, do you know a woman by the name Heloise?

A: Yes.

Q: How do you know her?

A: We have been friends.

Q: How long?

A: We met twenty years ago. Then I went into a monastery and she went into a convent.

Q: How was your relationship continued?

A: Through letters over twenty years.

Q: How often did you correspond?

A: Frequently. Often on a weekly basis.

Q: Did you write to her?

A: Yes.

Q: Did she write to you?

A: Yes.

Q: Can you recognize her signature?

A: Of course.

Q: How?

A: Well, I had seen her sign her name before I went in the monastery, and I received hundreds of her letters over the past twenty years.

Q: I have just given you a piece of paper with handwriting on it which I have had marked for identification as Plaintiff's Exhibit No. 1. Do you recognize it?

A: Yes.

Q: How do you recognize it?

A: By the signature, Heloise, on the bottom, and by the date.

Q: What is it?

A: The last letter I received from Heloise.

To the Court:

Your Honor, I offer Plaintiff's Exhibit No. 1.

Example (Signed Document):

Examining Attorney:

Q: Tell us your name please.

A: John Hancock.

Q: Where were you on July 4, 1776?

A: I was in Constitution Hall in Philadelphia.

Q: Why were you there?

A: To attend a meeting of the signing of the Declaration of Independence.

Q: Did you see the document being signed?

A: Yes.

Q: Whom did you see sign the Declaration?

A: Some other chaps and myself.

Q: Would you recognize the Declaration if you saw it again?

A: Yes.

Q: How?

A: By my signature on it, and I remember the words of the document.

Q: I have just given you what has been marked for identification as Defendant's Exhibit No. 6. Do you recognize it?

A: Yes.

Q: How?

A: I recognize the words and I recognize my signature.

Q: Your signature is rather large, isn't it?

A: Yes.

Q: How come?

A: I was feeling particularly revolutionary that day.

Q: Would you tell us please, what is Defendant's Exhibit No. 6?

A: It is the same Declaration of Independence that I and others signed on July 4, 1776.

Q: Has it been changed or altered in any way?

A: No.

To the Court:

Your Honor, I offer Defendant's Exhibit No. 6.

Example (Contract):

Examining Attorney:

Q: You said you entered into what you thought was a contract for employment as a first year associate?

A: Yes, I did.

Q: Did you negotiate that contract?

A: Yes, I did.

Q: With whom?

A: Brachman, the senior partner of the law firm.

Q: What term or terms did you negotiate?

A: The starting salary.

Q: How much was that for?

A: $199,999.99 a year.

Q: Did you sign the contract?

A: Yes.

Q: Who else did?

A: Brachman.

Q: I have just handed you what I have marked for identification as Exhibit No. 5. It is a piece of paper. Do you recognize it?

A: Yes, I do.

Q: How do you recognize it?

A: I recognize the signature of Brachman, the senior partner, my signature, and the contents.

Q: Have there been any additions or subtractions to that piece of paper since you signed it at the office of the senior partner?

A: No.

Q: What is Exhibit No. 5?

A: It is the contract that I signed last year on April 18.

To the Arbitrator:

I offer Exhibit No. 5.

C. Business Correspondence (Including Letters, Memos, Notes, Email, and other Correspondence)

Business correspondence has similar foundation requirements as documents. Some correspondence may require additional foundation evidence to prove it was sent or received. In these instances, the additional elements include:

- The correspondence was addressed or routed to a certain person.
- The witness saw or signed the original, duplicate original, or a copy of the original.
- The witness placed the correspondence in an accurately addressed delivery envelope; or sent the message to a current email address; or the witness supervised a person who in the normal course of business sends such correspondence.
- The envelope was placed in a mailbox or given to another carrier; or the message was sent through the regular computer network; or the witness supervised a person who in the normal course of business sends such envelopes or messages
- The copy of the original is an accurate duplicate.
- The original correspondence was received by the addressee or never returned to the sender.

Example (Business Documents):

Examining Attorney:

Q: Tell us your name.

A: Colonel Tom Parker.

Q: For whom did you work?

A: Elvis Presley.

Q: What did you do?

A: I was his business manager.

Q: You are holding a piece of paper which has been marked for identification as Defendant's Exhibit No. 3. Do you recognize it?

A: Yes, I do.

Q: How do you recognize it?

A: I typed it, and I remember the words. These are my initials on the bottom, and I recognize Mr. Presley's signature.

Q: How?

A: I have seen him sign his name hundreds of times.

Q: What is Defendant's Exhibit No. 3?

A: It is the letter suggesting a personal interview that I prepared for Elvis Presley which he signed and I mailed.

Q: Do you remember what you did with that paper that you prepared after it had been signed by Elvis?

A: Yes. I mailed it.

Q: How did you mail the letter?

A: I placed it in an envelope and sealed the envelope.

Q: Did the envelope have any writing on it?

A: Yes.

Q: What was the writing?

A: It was addressed to: Publisher, National Enquirer, Eden, MN 55347.

Q: Do you know how the address got on there?

A: Yes.

Q: How?

A: I wrote it on myself before I placed the letter in it.

Q: What did you do next?

A: I licked the stamp and put it in the upper right-hand corner.

Q: Then what did you do?

A: I walked outside to a mailbox.

Q: Then what?

A: I dropped it in the mailbox and went back to work.

Q: Did you ever get the envelope and letter returned to you?

A: No. Never.

To the Court:

Your Honor, I offer Defendant's Exhibit No. 3.

Example (Oral Contract Reduced to Writing):

Examining Attorney:

Q: On March 19, Sir, in the year 2010, did you receive a phone call about 16:00 hours?

A: Yes.

Q: Did the caller give any form of identification?

A: Yes. He identified himself.

Q: What did the caller say?

A: The caller said that he worked for the husband of the President. He said that the First Gentleman had a hobby workshop in the basement of the White House and the First Gentleman wanted to start whittling carbon fiber replicas of the President.

Q: Did he say anything else?

A: Yes. He said he wanted to order a digital force power titanium implanter.

Q: What do you do for a living, sir?

A: I manufacture hammers.

Q: What did you do next?

A: I told him I needed an order in writing from the person ordering the goods from my company.

Q: Did you talk about anything else?

A: Yes. The caller told me that he was willing to pay up to $1,000 for the tool.

Q: What happened then?

A: Well, I was kind of excited because our usual hammer only sells for $9.70. At that time, in anticipation of the letter, I set our design staff working on a model hammer.

Q: Did you ever receive any orders?

A: Yes. One week later I received a letter.

Q: Showing what I've marked for identification as Claimant's Exhibit No. 1, do you recognize that?

A: Yes, I do.

Q: How do you recognize it?

A: Well, it has a White House label and it says from the office of the First Gentleman and is signed with the name of the First Gentleman.

Q: Anything else?

A: Yes. It is an order for a digital force power titanium implanter.

To the Arbitrator:

We offer Claimant's Exhibit No. 2.

Examining Attorney:

Q: What did you do after that?

A: Well, we worked for a couple weeks and came up with a modified new hammer model. We packaged this hammer in a designer container and included a letter of acceptance and a bill for $723.45.

Q: How was the package delivered?

A: I addressed the package to the First Gentleman at the White House and completed the Express Delivery form. Then I put it in the "Delivery" box on my desk.

Q: What is the pick up and delivery procedure in your office?

A: Our company procedure is that all packages are picked up periodically by our messenger. She goes through all the offices, picks up everything from the "Delivery" boxes and sends them.

Q: Did you ever notice in your "Delivery" basket that the package was no longer there?

A: Yes, I did. Later that same day, the basket was empty.

Q: I am showing you what has been marked for identification as Claimant's Exhibit No. 2. Do you recognize this?

A: Yes, I do.

Q: How?

A: By its contents.

Q: What is it?

A: Exhibit No. 2 is a copy of the letter that I sent to the First Gentleman along with the hammer.

Q: Who made the copy?

A: I did.

Q: Why did you do that?

A: Well, as a matter of policy in our business, whenever anyone composes a letter a copy is printed on our printer and the original is saved to a file in our computer database. I recognize this exhibit as an exact printed copy of the letter that I wrote, signed, and placed in the package that was sent.

To the Arbitrator:

Claimant offers Exhibit No. 2.

D.   *Business Records (Including Memoranda, Reports, Writings, or Data Compilations)*

Records maintained in the ordinary course of business may be introduced through a witness who does not have personal knowledge of the recorded information but does have personal knowledge concerning the business recording process. The introduction of this information is allowed by the foundation elements detailed in Federal Rule of Evidence 803(6) and similar state rules. The term "business" includes any business, hospital, institution, organization, association, profession, occupation, and calling of any kind including nonprofit agencies. The content of business records may include facts, acts, events, conditions, opinions or diagnoses that are relevant to the case. The elements to be proved under Federal Rule of Evidence 803(6) include:

- The report must have been "made at or near the time" of the occurrence which gave rise to the report.

- The record was made by "a person with knowledge" of the information or was made "from information transmitted by" a person with knowledge.

- The record was made "in the regular practice of that business activity."

- The record was kept "in the course of a regularly conducted business activity."

- The witness is the "custodian" of the documents or is in some other way a "qualified witness."

Example (Hospital Records):

Examining Attorney:

Q: What is your name, sir?

A: Charles Drew.

Q: Where do you work?

A: Metropolitan Medical Center.

Q: What is your job?

A: I am the medical records librarian.

Q: As a medical records librarian, what do you do?

A: I am the custodian in charge of all the hospital records of the Metropolitan Medical Center.

Q: Do you have a staff working for you?

A: Yes. They all work at my direction and control.

Q: Do you have a policy in your hospital concerning the making of records?

A: Yes, we do.

Q: What is that policy?

A: All medical records must have been made at or near the time of the occurrence of the information contained in them. The record must be made by a person with knowledge of the information or from information given to that person by someone with knowledge.

Q: I am showing you what has been already marked for identification as Plaintiff's Exhibit No. 23. Can you tell us what it is?

A: Yes, they are medical records obtained from our medical records library of a patient with the patient number 2345, which corresponds with the name Mabel Stampers.

Q: Are these records kept under your control?

A: Yes.

Q: You reviewed these records?

A: Yes.

Q: Reviewing these records, did you determine whether these records were made at or near the time of the occurrence of the information contained in them?

A: Yes, they were.

Q: How do you know that?

A: The different occurrences are dated and timed and the time of the dictation of the information is also dated. My examination of both the records and the dictation notes shows that they were made at or near the time of the occurrence.

Q: Looking at these records, can you determine whether the records were made by a person who had knowledge of the information contained in the records?

A: Yes, I can.

Q: How?

A: In each of these cases the person making the dictation was a doctor, and the doctor was assigned to the case by patient name and number.

Q: Are these records kept in the course of the regularly conducted business of your hospital?

A: Yes, they are.

Q: Was this record made in the regular practice of that business or hospital activity?

A: Yes, it was.

To the Court:

I offer Plaintiff's Exhibit No. 23.

Computer data may readily qualify as business records. When computer records will not qualify as business records, additional foundational questions relating to the input, storage, and retrieval methods of the computer system and its reliability will be necessary.

Example (Computer Data):

Examining Attorney:

Q: Ms. Lopez, at Fidelity Finance Company has it been the regular practice that a person with knowledge of the data enters that information on computer?

A: Yes.

Q: As custodian of Fidelity's computer records are you familiar with the method of entry, storage, and retrieval of data in the system?

A: Yes, I am.

Q: Is that system reliable?

A: Yes.

Q: Are there safeguards capable of detecting and correcting errors in the system?

A: There are.

Q: Does the computer printout reliably contain the retrieved data?

A: Yes.

Q: Is the information necessary for notices of delinquent accounts programmed into the computer at or near the time invoices are sent out?

A: Yes, on the first working day of each month.

Q: Do you know Fidelity's procedure for keeping records of the delinquent accounts and its notifying customers in default in March, 2004.

A: Yes.

Q: Please explain those default and notification procedures.

A: The data reflecting all activity on the account are verified by hand. Then the verified data is keyed into the terminal and copied on a hard drive. Every working day the processor merges the new data with the information already on the accounts record for the month. The computer, by the 15th of the month, finds all accounts not currently paid. To find these accounts, the computer uses instructions from a program to search and identify delinquent accounts. As instructed, the computer prints up these accounts. This printout is held five days. If the account is paid up within that time, no additional interest is assessed, but additional interest is assessed if the account remains unpaid. As programmed, all the accounts, delinquent or otherwise, are put into monthly statement form. Using the program, the computer prints the statement for each Fidelity Finance account, prints out the next payment's due date, folds, and stuffs the statement into a window envelope, meters the letter for first-class mailing, seals the envelope, and lines the envelope up in trays for delivery to the post office.

Hundreds of thousands of accounts are handled like this every month.

Q: What steps does Fidelity take to ensure the computer finds and identifies delinquent accounts so accurate notices of default notify customers?

A: Special control procedures are built into the system. Transcriptions of data are verified by two different terminal operators. In the computer the two sets of data are verified. Accounts identified as unpaid by the 15th are rechecked. If these accounts remain unpaid during the next five days, notices are printed and included with the statement, folded, and put in a window envelope with Fidelity's return address for return delivery.

Q: I'm showing you what's been marked Respondent's Exhibit No. 8. It purports to be a delinquency notice attached to a Fidelity Finance Company's statement. Is that what this document is?

A: Yes. It's Mr. Genander's delinquency notice.

Q: How do you recognize it?

A: This is a duplicate of the statement on our computer system.

Q: Was this duplicate printed in the regular course of business?

A: Yes.

Q: Was this notice and statement prepared by the computer system and program you have described for us this afternoon?

A: Yes.

Q: Is the information on Exhibit No. 8 correct?

A: It is correct for the date stated.

To the Arbitrator:

I offer Respondent's Exhibit No. 8.

Opposing Counsel:

Your Honor, may I examine the witness for the purpose of laying a foundation for an objection?

Arbitrator:

Yes, you may.

Opposing Counsel:

Q: Ms. Lopez, Exhibit No. 8 was printed up on March 20, 2004 wasn't it?

A: Yes.

Q: You did not make any data entry on this statement and notice of delinquency from which Exhibit No. 8 was made, did you?

A: No. The accounts receivable operators and the computer system read the data, and the computer program carries out the accounting procedure.

Q: Does the computer itself read documents like the statement, Exhibit No. 8?

A: Only if the computer is equipped with an optical scanner.

Q: But your computer does not have such a scanner, does it?

A: It does not.

Q: And your computer cannot read this statement, can it?

A: No, only the data stored on the disk.

Q: How often does the computer store account information?

A: Daily, but only on accounts that have had activity. The transcription of daily activity is run through the system to merge with the last cumulative tape. The computer, by program, performs the necessary accounting on active accounts and the data base is updated.

To the Arbitrator:

We object. Claimant's Exhibit No. 8 is unreliable hearsay. The witness admits no personal knowledge of input or retrieval.

Arbitrator:

Overruled. The exhibit is a business record made by Claimant's computer in the regular course of its business. Claimant's Exhibit No. 8 is received.

E. *Copies/Duplicates*

Modern copying equipment creates accurate copies of original documents and records. These "duplicate" originals are admissible. However, the original may be the most persuasive and, if available, should be offered to prove its content. See Fed.R.Evid. 1002. A duplicate original may be routinely admitted unless it is of questionable authenticity or it would be unfair to admit a copy. See Fed.R.Evid. 1003. A copy may also be admissible if the original has been lost or destroyed, is in the possession of the opponent, or is otherwise not obtainable. See Fed. R.Evid. 1004.

Example:

The witness has testified that he saw and read the original agreement.

Examining Attorney:

Q: Brother Timothy, I am showing you Exhibit No. VII marked for identification. Do you recognize it?

A: Yes.

Q: What is it?

A: It is a copy of the rental agreement for the monastery.

Q: How do you know?

A: I recognize all the words and terms.

Q: Do you have the original?

A: No.

Q: Was this copy made from the original?

A: Yes.

Q: How do you know?

A: I saw the landlord use his office photocopy machine right after I signed the original lease. The landlord handed me the copy, and I saw the landlord put the original in a filing cabinet. I brought this copy home and put it in the monastery vault.

Q: Has it changed in any way?

A: No.

Q: Is this the copy, Exhibit No. VII, that you removed from your vault?

A: Yes.

To the Court:

Your Honor, I offer Exhibit No. VII.

F. *Electronic Recordings (Including Audio, Video, Digital, and Computer Recordings)*

The elements necessary to establish a sufficient foundation for the introduction of recordings are:

- The electronic recording is relevant to the case.
- The operator of the equipment was qualified to run the equipment.
- The recording equipment was checked before its use and operated normally.
- The witness heard or saw the event being electronically recorded.
- After the event had been recorded, the witness reviewed the tape and determined that it had accurately and completely recorded the event.

- The witness can recognize and identify the sounds or images on the recording.
- The recording is in the exact same condition at the time of trial as it was at the time of the taping.

Example (Video Event):

Examining Attorney:

Q: Sheriff, where were you on the 24th day of November, 1963?

A: I was in the Dallas jail.

Q: Where in the Dallas jail?

A: I was in the basement garage by the exit ramp.

Q: What did you see?

A: I saw a man I later learned was Jack Ruby point a gun in the direction of Lee Harvey Oswald and shoot at him.

Q: Sheriff, I have given you a videotape which has been marked for identification as Defense Exhibit No. 155. Do you recognize it?

A: Yes, I do.

Q: How do you recognize it?

A: Well, I wrote my initials on the label of the tape that I saw before coming into this courtroom today. After I saw it, I also wrote my initials on this card which indicates that I have seen the tape.

Q: What is on the tape?

A: It's a tape of what I just described ... of the shooting I saw on the 24th day of November in 1963.

Q: Is this videotape a complete and accurate representation of what you saw that day?

A: Yes, it is.

To the Court:

I offer Defense Exhibit No. 155.

Example (Sound Recording):

Examining Attorney:

Q: Mr. Caul, what do you do for a living?

A: I install electronic sound recording instruments.

Q: Have you ever installed sound recording instruments for the President?

A: Yes, I have.

Q: When was that?

A: A short time before he left office.

Q: Where did you do the installation?

A: In the Oval Office of the White House.

Q: What did that consist of?

A: I set up a secret tape recording device in the desk in the Oval Office. I put the receiving device in another room.

Q: Did you ever test the device?

A: Yes, I did.

Q: How did you do that?

A: I started the machine running, went in the other room, and watched it record. It recorded for one hour.

Q: What did you do after that?

A: I removed the tape and played it on my tape player.

Q: Did you recognize the voice of anybody on the tape?

A: Yes.

Q: Whose?

A: I recognized the voice of the President.

Q: What did you do with the tape?

A: I took the tape and put it in a special envelope and sealed it, and I have kept it in my safe in my office until I brought it here to court.

Q: Did you listen to the tape before you came in here?

A: Yes.

Q: Whose voices are there?

A: There is only one voice.

Q: Whose voice is it?

A: The tape just contains the voice of the President.

Q: Have you made any additions or subtractions or changes to that tape?

A: No, I have not.

Q: You have in your hand Plaintiff's Exhibit No. 23. Do you recognize it?

A: Yes, that's the tape.

Q: How do you recognize it?

A: I removed it from the envelope that I had previously sealed.

Q: Was the envelope sealed at this time?

A: No, it was not. I opened it in the court's chambers before trial started and after that I gave it to you.

To the Court:

I offer Plaintiff's Exhibit No. 23. Counsel, this is the tape that we gave to you in discovery before this trial started.

Judge:

It is received.

Examining Attorney:

Q: May I play the tape at this time, your Honor?

A: Yes, you may.

G. Test Results (Including X–Rays, Laboratory Work, Computer Analysis)

Exhibits containing results from tests, x-rays, and other procedures require special foundation information to be introduced at trial. These are the elements to be proven:

- The exhibit is relevant to the case.
- The witness is qualified to operate the equipment.
- There exists a procedure which regulates the testing, x-ray or analysis process.
- The witness personally conducted or supervised an operator who conducted the testing, developed the x-rays or completed the analysis.
- The equipment was in normal operating condition.
- The witness can recognize and identify the results, x-rays or analysis.
- The results, x-rays or analysis are in the same condition as when they were completed.

Example (X–Ray):

Examining Attorney:

Q: Mr. Igor, you are an x-ray technician employed by Share Health, aren't you?

A: Yes, I am.

Q: Were you on duty on Tuesday, July 3, at the Spring Lake Center Clinic?

A: Yes.

Q: Mr. Igor, I'm handing you what's been marked for identification as Exhibit No. 2. Do you recognize it?

A: Yes, I do.

Q: What is it?

A: It's a flat plate abdominal x-ray I took on July 3 of last year.

Q: How do you know?

A: My initials, I.I., are in the corner next to the date and the patient's identifying number. That number is from the patient's chart, the medical record at Share Health.

Q: Mr. Igor, I'm handing you Exhibit No. 1, already stipulated as Mr. Frankenstein's chart and received into evidence. What is the medical record number?

A: (Reading) 01B146203.

Q: Now I'm handing you what's been marked as Exhibit No. 2, the x-ray. What number is it that indicates the patient's chart?

A: It's next to the date.

Q: What is that number?

A: (Reading) 01B146203.

Q: Are you a certified technician?

A: Yes.

Q: How did you prepare this x-ray?

A: I made the exposure.

Q: Was the machine functioning properly?

A: Yes, there was no problem.

Q: After you made the exposure, what did you do?

A: I developed it, put my ID, the date, and the patient's ID on it, then I printed it and sent it up to the radiologist to interpret.

To the Court:

I offer Exhibit No. 2.

H. Summary Exhibits

Summaries of evidence may be introduced as an efficient and effective means to explain evidence to the fact finder. Summary exhibits may include a chart detailing the testimony of one or more witnesses or a summary description of documents. Federal Rule of Evidence 1006 and similar state rules permit summaries of writings to be introduced as evidence. The elements for introduction of summaries include:

- All the information summarized must be relevant.

- The witness has knowledge concerning the information contained in the summary.

- The witness has reviewed the exhibit and verified that it is an accurate summary of the evidence.

Example:

Examining Attorney:

Q: Now you have told us you recently graduated from law school and are a law clerk for our law firm?

A: Yes.

Q: What have you done in preparing this case for trial?

A: I have prepared a CD-ROM photo exhibit of the 457 exhibits containing a photo of each of the items that have been admitted in this case as having come from King Tut's tomb.

Q: I am showing you what has been marked for identification as Exhibit No. 458 which is a CD-ROM disk. Are you familiar with this disk?

A: Yes.

Q: How are you familiar with it?

A: I personally prepared the entire data base on this disk.

Q: What does it contain?

A: Photos of the 457 exhibits indexed with a bar code system.

Q: Is it a fair and accurate portrayal of each one of the exhibits?

A: Yes.

To the Court:

Your Honor, at this time we offer Exhibit No. 458, the exhibit summary of all the plaintiff's exhibits introduced into evidence.

I. Judicial Arbitral/Administrative Notice

A judge or arbitrator may take notice of facts, at any time during a proceeding, that are accurate, verifiable by reliable sources, and undisputable. See Fed.R.Evid. 201 and Section 3.6(J). These facts may appear in an exhibit.

Example:

Plaintiff's Attorney:

Your Honor, it is critical to this case that we prove what day December 7, 1941 fell on, as well as the days of the week upon which other dates fell in 1941. I have marked a 1941 calendar as Plaintiff's Exhibit A for identification. At this time I request the court take judicial notice of the accuracy of this calendar and admit Plaintiff's Exhibit A into evidence.

Judge:

I will take judicial notice of Plaintiff's Exhibit A and admit Exhibit A into evidence.

J. *Past Recollection Recorded*

A witness who, at the time of trial, does not have an independent recollection of an event may have previously made a record of that event and that record may be introduced at trial as an exhibit of real evidence. The elements to establish the foundation of past recollection recorded exhibits appear in Section 4.8(H)(1)(c) and include:

- The witness has no present recollection of the relevant event.

- The witness once had knowledge of the event.

- The witness made a record of the event when the matter was fresh in the witness' memory.

- The recorded recollection accurately reflects the knowledge of the witness.

- The exhibit is in the same condition now as when it was made.

Example (Lack of Memory):

Examining Attorney:

Q: Mr. Gilligan, on February 18, 1969, do you remember what happened to you after you boarded the S.S. Minnow?

A: I was injured in a boating accident when the tiny ship was tossed, if not for the courage of the fearless crew the Minnow would have been lost.

Q: Do you remember any other details of that accident?

A: No, I do not. I have not been able to remember the details since the day after my accident.

Q: The day of the accident, did you give a statement to anyone?

A: Yes, I did.

Q: To whom did you give a statement?

A: I gave a statement to a Coast Guard officer.

Q: At the time you gave the statement, did you remember what details occurred to you at the accident?

A: Yes, I did.

Q: Do you have a memory of those details now?

A: I do not.

Q: At the time you gave the statement to the Coast Guard officer, what did you do?

A: I read it, and I signed it.

Q: Showing you what has been marked by the court reporter as Exhibit No. 50 — it's a three-page handwritten, water-stained statement with your signature on each page and the date, February 18, 1969 — do you recognize this document?

A: Yes, I do.

Q: What is it?

A: It is a statement I wrote and signed the day of the accident.

Q: Would you please read the statement silently to yourself.

A: Yes.

Q: Having read the statement, does it refresh your recollection as to the details of what happened in the accident?

A: No, I really don't remember.

Q: Would you have signed this statement if it had not been accurate?

A: No, I would not have.

To the Court:

Your Honor, at this time I offer Exhibit No. 50 as past recollection recorded.

Example (Detailed Facts):

Examining Attorney:

Q: Ms. Ames, do you recall going to Van Line's warehouse on April 18 last year?

A: Yes, I do.

Q: And you accompanied Mr. Andrews, the defendant, who was inventorying the library shipped from his mother's Galveston, Texas home?

A: Yes.

Q: How did you assist Mr. Andrews?

A: As he opened each box and told me the contents and condition of each book, I used a digital dictator recorder to record the information.

Q: Each box was inventoried?

A: Yes.

Q: What did you do after you completed the inventory?

A: We returned to the office, and I downloaded the dictation disk to my computer system.

Q: Does the data include all the information from the recorder?

A: Yes, and it includes the value for each title based on its condition and rarity.

Q: When did you obtain the value?

A: Thursday, after I inputted the information. Mr. Andrews told me what value to put by each book, and I did so.

Q: Do you remember the valuation of the volumes written by Virginia Woolf?

A: Not really.

Q: Would it help you to look at the printed list where those editions are valued?

A: Yes, it would.

Q: Ms. Ames, here is Defendant's Exhibit E marked for identification. Do you recognize it?

A: Yes, this is the list I printed from the warehouse database and these are the values I inserted next to each title after Mr. Andrew's appraisal.

Q: Is the list in the same condition as it was when you prepared it?

A: Yes, it looks the same.

To the Arbitrator:

I offer Defendant's Exhibit E into evidence.

Arbitrator:

Received.

Examining Attorney:

Q: Ms. Ames, please read the Virginia Woolf titles and their value as set out on page four of that list.

---

§ 8.7 DEMONSTRATIVE AIDS

A. *Types*

Various types of demonstrative evidence may be useful during the presentation of a case. Witnesses may testify more accurately, comfortably, and effectively with illustrative aids, such as:

- Photographs and prints,
- Diagrams,
- Charts,
- Models,
- Drawings,
- Overhead transparencies,

- Slides,

- Videotapes/DVDs, and

- Computer generated graphics, maps, animations, simulations.

B. Design

Exhibits should be designed in such a way that they are user friendly and visually attractive. There are three pertinent questions to ask when designing demonstrative evidence:

1. *What does the fact finder need to understand from the exhibit?*

2. *What is the minimal amount of information needed to provide this information?*

3. *Which type of exhibit is the most effective, efficient, and affordable to convey the information?*

Demonstrative exhibits that are properly designed will be the most effective. Demonstrative evidence need not be exact, but must not inaccurately portray the facts. Some exhibits do not have to be drawn to scale, while others may need to be. Design considerations for the primary demonstrative exhibits are:

Photographs and Videotapes.

These exhibits should be sufficiently large and clear to be seen by the fact finders. A photograph may be enlarged so that jurors can see it, or an individual copy of smaller photographs may be provided to the judge or arbitrator. Color photographs will be more realistic, unless only a black and white photograph is available or is necessary because of the unfairly prejudicial impact of a color photo. See Section 4.8(A)(f). Photographs may be mounted on a solid backing or affixed to paper hung on an easel. Digital photos may be displayed on a monitor screen. A videotape or computer file may be created to explain a procedure or to recreate an event.

Diagrams, Drawings, and Computer Displays. Enlargements of simple prepared diagrams can be made inexpensively and quickly. Displays of lists or transactions may be easily presented through a computer program and monitor.

Charts/graphs. There are several types of charts and graphs

- Line — This graph is helpful to display timelines, trends, and prices. Avoid placing plots too close together or including too many plots.

- Pie — This chart is best used for a division of one number or percentages. Avoid pie charts with more than seven slices and charting numbers that are so small they disappear when compared to other pie pieces.

- Bar — This graph has a wide variety of uses, including comparisons for single or multiple numbers, events, or groupings of data. Make sure the labels and colors are distinct.

Exhibit Boards. Minimum size for a board is 30″ x 40″, and recommended sizes are 36″ x 48″ for an average-sized room and 45″ x 60″ for a large room. The greatest benefit of using boards is that unlike computer and document camera exhibits, boards can remain displayed during other evidence presentation. The disadvantage of using exhibit boards is the difficulty of placing the boards where everyone can see the information.

Computer slide/video projectors. Portable projectors are available that can be connected directly to the laptop, and also to camera equipment or videotape players. This technology easily displays various sizes of exhibits. Modern projectors display accurate renditions, while old style slide projectors may distort part of an exhibit and require the room to be darkened.

Notebooks for written/printed exhibits. Some exhibits can be copied and placed in individual notebooks with tabs for use by the fact finders, lawyers, and witnesses.

C. Composition

Demonstrative exhibits need to be carefully designed to have their greatest impact. Factors to consider are:

Format. Proper formatting creates the right size, not too small or large.

Font. Big is often better.

Lines. Too many lines clutter the exhibit. Five lines with five words is a reasonable guide.

Spacing. The use of white space and margins is important to keeping the viewer focused on the display contents.

Color. Color tends to hold a viewer's attention longer than black-and-white and has more retention value.

Contrast. Viewers need to be able to distinguish the contents.

Orientation. Either a landscape (11″ x 8.5″) or a portrait orientation (8.5″ x 11″) can be used.

Other features. Additional methods for computer exhibits are: (1) split screens e.g., (side-by-side presentations of conflicting testimony/documents), (2) call-outs (highlighted text segments "brought out" from their location on a displayed document page in larger font), or (3) builds (sequential additions to a graphic exhibit) that show the evidence along with the testimony.

D. Admissibility

The introduction and use of demonstrative evidence is subject to a variety of approaches depending upon the practice in a jurisdiction and the preferences of the judge or arbitrator.

In some forums, the examining attorney need not formally offer a demonstrative exhibit into evidence but need only ask permission for the witness to use the demonstrative exhibit. In these jurisdictions this permission makes the exhibit part of the file or record. In other tribunals, a demonstrative exhibit is not offered into evidence until after the witness has used it during testimony or has marked on it. The record should indicate what the demonstrative evidence is and how it is being used.

In cases where more than one witness uses or marks a demonstrative exhibit, the procedures for its introduction may also vary. If a second witness uses or marks the exhibit, the demonstrative evidence may have to be re-offered because new information now appears on the exhibit. The markings may be distinguished by the use of a different color marker or by the placement of a clear, plastic sheet over the drawing or chart which the witness draws on to distinguish those markings from the markings of the first witness.

The following examples demonstrate the admissibility and use of major demonstrative exhibits.

Photographs

The elements to be proven to admit photographs into evidence are:

- The photograph is relevant to the case.

- The witness is familiar with the scene displayed in the photograph at the relevant time of the event.

- The photograph fairly and accurately depicts the scene at the time of the event.

There is no need to establish the type of camera used, film speed, focal lens, shutter speed, lens opening, other photography details, or even when the picture was taken, unless these facts are an issue in a case.

Example—Photograph

Examining Attorney:

Q: Ms. Jetson, on July 1, 2988, at approximately 2:00 sundial time, were you at the intersection of Lunar Pad and Galaxie Avenue?

A: Yes, I was.

Q: What were you doing there?

A: I was waiting for the space shuttle.

Q: While you were waiting for the shuttle, what did you observe?

A: I saw two cars, a Masarocket and a Lambomissle, enter the intersection and collide.

Q: I show you what has been marked as Plaintiff's Exhibit No. 1 for identification and ask you to examine it. Do you recognize it?

A: Yes, I do.

Q: What is it?

A: It's a photograph of the intersection where the accident occurred.

Q: Is the scene on the photograph in any way different from the scene that you observed on July 1, 2988?

A: No.

Q: Is the photograph a fair and accurate depiction of the scene of the accident that you observed on July 1.

A: Yes, it is.

To the Court:

I offer Plaintiff's Exhibit No. 1.

Diagrams, Charts, Drawings

The elements to be proven in order to establish the foundation for the introduction of a diagram, chart, or drawing are:

- The witness is familiar with the scene or event.

- The witness recognizes the facts depicted in the diagram or chart or is familiar with the exhibit.

- The exhibit will assist the witness in explaining testimony or will aid the fact finder in understanding the testimony.

- The exhibit is reasonably accurate (or is drawn to scale) and is not misleading.

A copy of the diagram may be introduced as part of the record. A Polaroid photograph may be made of a freehand drawing as part of the record.

Example—Prepared Diagram

Examining Attorney:

Q: Ms. Monroe, are you familiar with the intersection of Hollywood and Vine in Hollywood, California?

A: Yes, I am.

Q: Do you remember what the intersection looked like on April 4, four years ago?

A: Yes, I do.

Q: How do you remember?

A: That was the day that, as I was leaving the drugstore, I saw an accident.

To the Court:

Your Honor, may I approach the witness?

Judge:

Yes, you may.

Examining Attorney:

Q: Ms. Monroe, I am showing you a diagram marked as Plaintiff's Exhibit No. 1 that has already been prepared. Have you seen it before?

A: Yes, I have.

Q: Is this diagram a fair and accurate representation of the location of the streets and the buildings at the intersection of Hollywood and Vine on April 4, four years ago?

A: Yes, it is.

Q: Would this diagram assist you in describing to the jury what you saw that day?

A: Yes, it would.

To the Court:

Your Honor, I offer Plaintiff's Exhibit No. I for demonstrative purposes.

Judge:

It is received.

Examining Attorney:

Your Honor, may I place it on the easel and have the witness approach the diagram?

Judge:

Yes, you may.

Examining Attorney:

Q: Ms. Monroe, there is an arrow on the diagram indicating north is to the top of the diagram. Is that correct?

A: Yes.

Q: Which way does Hollywood run?

A: It runs from north to south.

Q: And that is from top to bottom on the diagram?

A: Yes.

Q: Would you take the red marker and mark an "M" to indicate where you were at that intersection when you saw the accident?

A: I was right here.

Q: You have placed an "M" on the northeast corner of the intersection. Is that right?

A: Yes.

Q: Now, what did you see?

A: I saw one car coming from the east and one car coming from the west, and they met head-on in the middle of the intersection.

Q: Did you learn who was driving the car from the east?

A: Yes, he told me his name was Clark.

Q: What about the car from the west?

A: The driver said his name was Paul.

Q: Will you label the car coming from the east and one from the west with the names Clark and Paul placed in the center of the cars?

A: Yes.

Q: Will you draw a line from the cars from the east and west showing where they collided in the intersection?

A: Yes, I will.

Q: Will you mark with an "M" the spot of the crash?

A: All right.

To the Court:

Your Honor, at this time I re-offer the exhibit as marked.

Judge:

It is once again received.

Example—Model

Examining Attorney:

Q: Dr. Pierce, did you have the opportunity to examine the knee of my client, Mr. Radar?

A: Yes, I did.

Q: Did you do any surgery on Mr. Radar's knee?

A: Yes, I did.

Q: Would a model of a knee assist you in explaining to us what you saw during the visual and surgical examination of my client's knee?

A: Yes, it would.

Q: You have in your hand now what has been marked for identification as Plaintiff's Exhibit No. 1. What is it?

A: It is an anatomical model of a person's knee.

Q: Is that an exact model of a person's knee?

A: Yes, it is.

Example—Freehand Drawing

Examining Attorney:

Q: Now you said earlier that you have had an idea for some kind of cartoon character?

A: Yes, I did.

Q: What kind of character?

A: A rodent.

Q: Would it assist you in explaining your idea to us if you would draw your idea on this computer screen using your mouse?

A: Yes, it would.

Q: Now sir, I see you have drawn some sort of animal on the screen.

A: It's a rodent.

Q: Are you sure that's a rodent, it looks like a rat?

A: It is a rodent.

Q: What are you drawing on the rodent?

A: Pants and shoes.

Q: And now what are you drawing?

A: Three-fingered gloves.

Q: Do you have a name for this character?

A: Yes, I do.

Q: And what is that name?

A: I have been thinking about Ralph.

E. Demonstrations

Live demonstrations or experiments in court are difficult and dangerous. They may work well at rehearsal before trial, but can fail too easily. An effective alternative is to prepare a videotape of the experiment or demonstration or a computer generated recreation before the trial or hearing and if it works and is effective show it during the case.

A simple demonstration that can be easily performed may be conducted if appropriate. A witness who displays an injury or shows how an object was held can assist the fact finder in understanding what happened. Anything more complex should be videotaped or recreated before the trial or hearing, or, if resources do not permit, not done at all.

Problem Example (Demonstration):

Examining Attorney:

Q: Ms. Chiquita, where were you on June 1, two years ago?

A: I was in the produce department of the Foods Unlimited supermarket.

Q: Did anything happen to you there?

A: Yes.

Q: What?

A: I was walking down the aisle when I slipped on a banana peel that was lying on the floor.

Q: Did you see the banana peel before you slipped?

A: Yes.

Q: When?

A: Just as I stepped on it, I looked down and saw it under my left foot.

Q: What happened?

A: Both feet went out from under me. My feet went up in the air and I came down hard on my right elbow.

Q: What happened to you?

A: I felt terrible pain in my elbow and saw a bone sticking out of my arm and lots of blood.

Q: Would you be able to demonstrate how you fell in the store?

A: Yes.

Q: Would that assist you in explaining to us what happened?

A: Yes.

To the Court:

May the witness please step down from the stand and demonstrate to us what happened?

Opposing Counsel:

I have absolutely no objections.

Judge:

Are we insured for this kind of thing?

F. *Displaying Demonstrative Exhibits*

Advocates may have options in presenting demonstrative exhibits in a court or hearing room. All participants need to view the exhibits. When using exhibits, advocates may move about the room.

Diagrams 8–1 and 8–2 show some options for the placement of exhibits and movement in the courtroom while examining witnesses with an exhibit and demonstrative evidence.

DIAGRAM 8–1

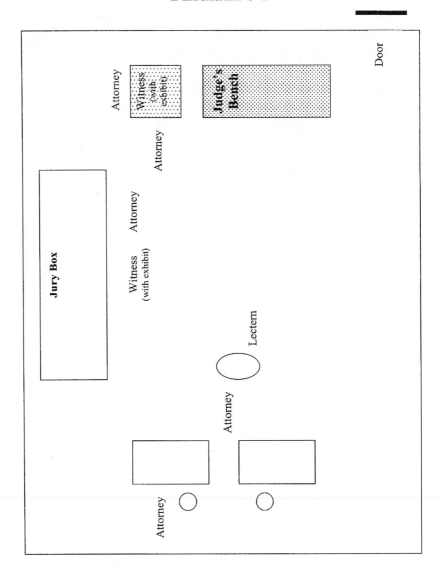

DIAGRAM 8–2

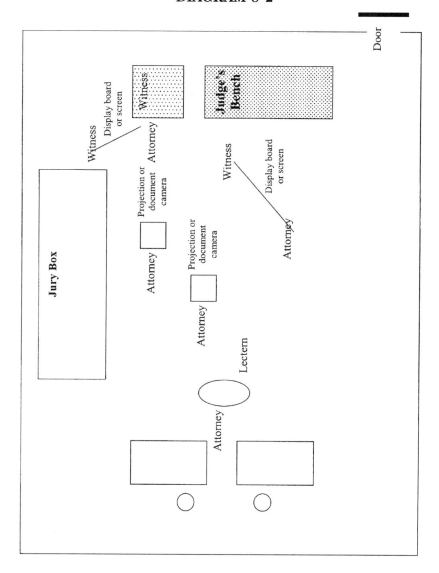

Photographs 8–3 and 8–4 show optional layouts of courtrooms with high tech equipment.

PHOTOGRAPH 8–3

PHOTOGRAPH 8–4

Diagrams 8–5 and 8–6 show optional layouts of court rooms with high-tech equipment.

DIAGRAM 8–5

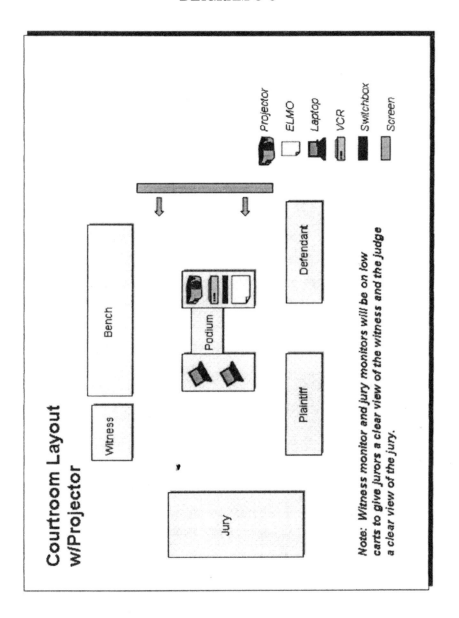

DIAGRAM 8–6

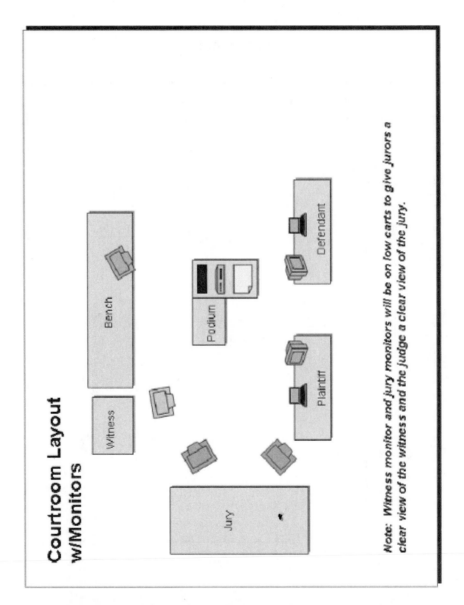

G. *Keys to Effective Visual Presentation*

1. Plan well enough ahead to create demonstrative exhibits.

2. Review the resources available for exhibits development.

3. Select the best medium for your presentation.

4. Prepare exhibits that are simple, clear, and understandable.

5. Be familiar with the court or hearing room and preferences of the judge or arbitrator.

6. Use professional, persuasive exhibits.

7. Practice using the equipment and exhibits before the trial or hearing.

8. Test run the technology to display exhibits.

9. Double check viewing distance, readability, and comprehension of presented information.

10. Present the information confidently and as part of the overall introduction of evidence.

§ 8.8 EXHIBIT DISPLAYS

The following examples demonstrate a variety of display options for exhibits.

A. *Photographs*

PHOTOGRAPH 8–7

PHOTOGRAPH 8–8

B. Models

MODEL 8–9

MODEL 8–10

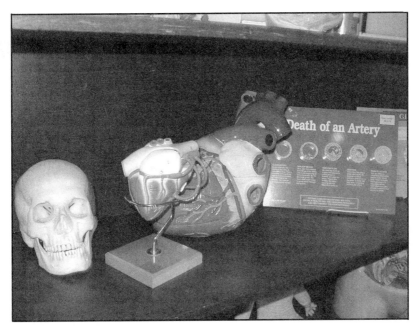

C. *Computer models*

COMPUTER MODEL 8–11

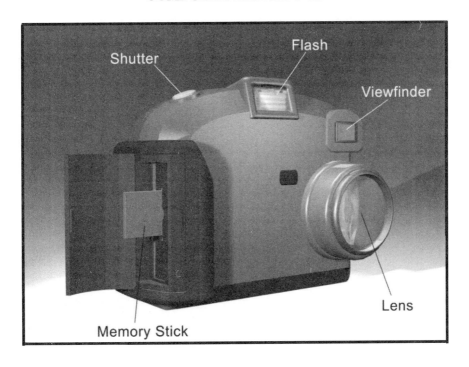

COMPUTER MODEL 8–12

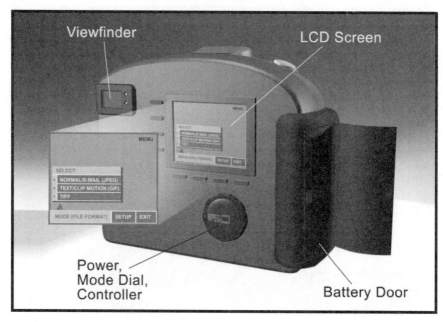

D. Display Board

Display Board 8–13

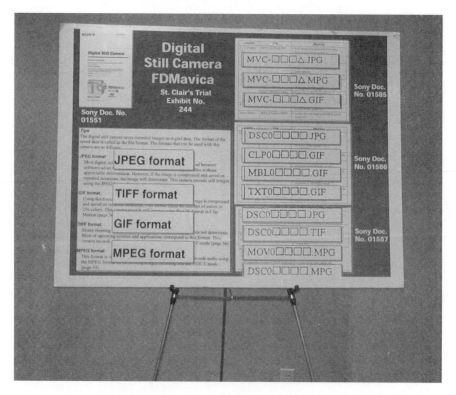

E. *Diagrams: Simple*

DIAGRAM 8–14

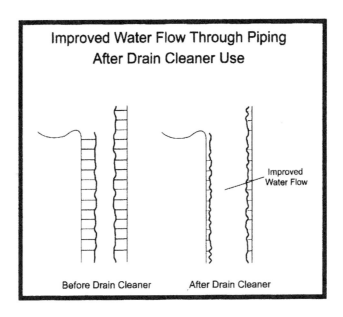

DIAGRAM 8–15

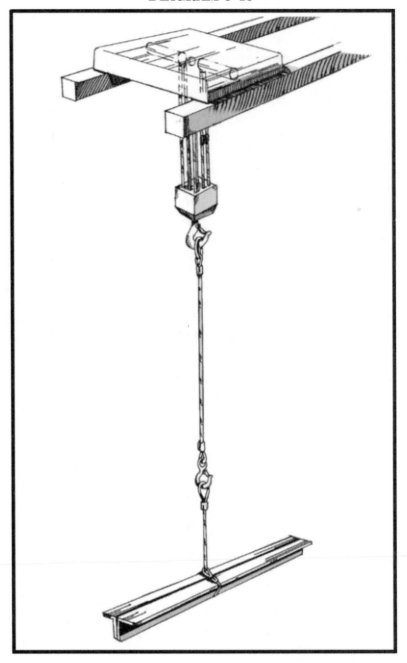

DIAGRAM 8–16

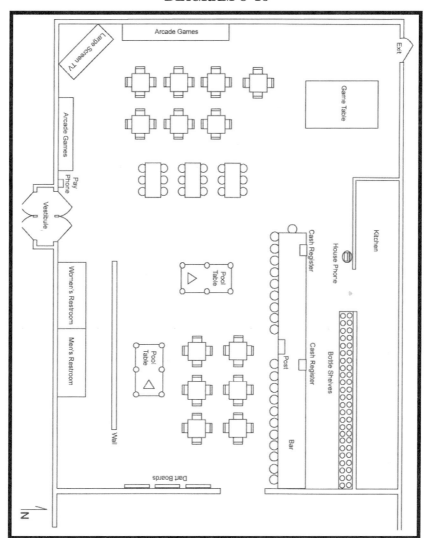

DIAGRAM 8–17

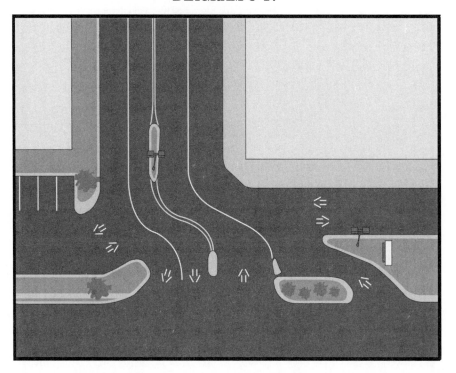

DIAGRAM 8–18

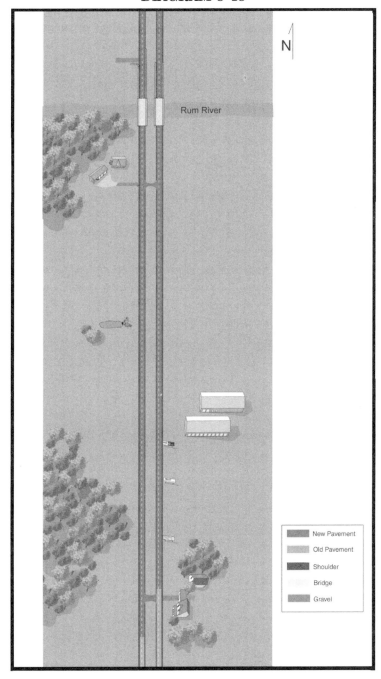

F. *Diagrams: Complex*

DIAGRAM 8–19

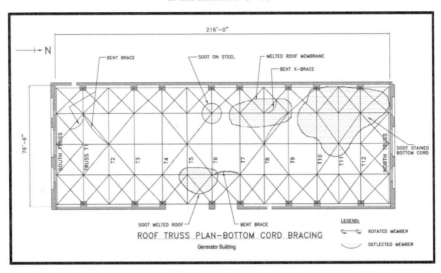

ROOF TRUSS PLAN—BOTTOM CORD BRACING
Generator Building

DIAGRAM 8–20

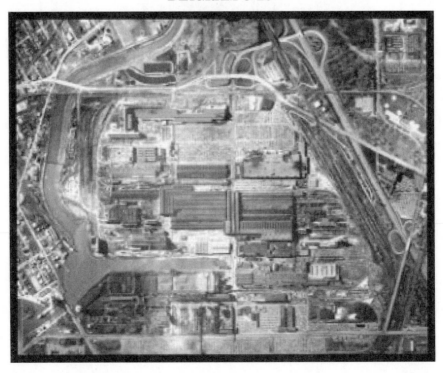

G. Diagrams: Cutaway

DIAGRAM 8–21

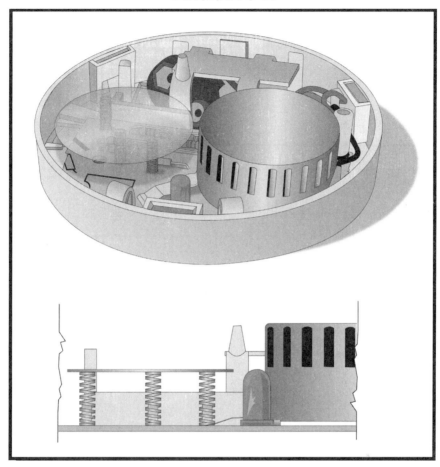

H. Time Lines

DIAGRAM 8–22

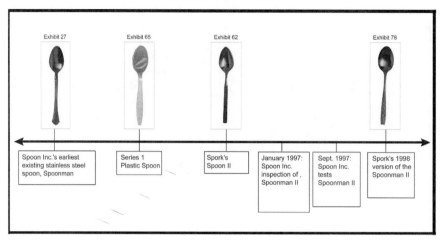

DIAGRAM 8–23

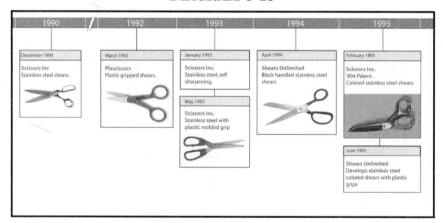

DIAGRAM 8–24

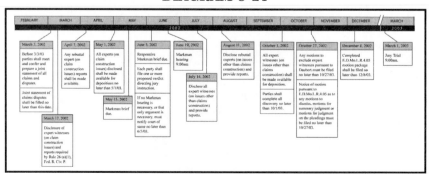

I. *Anatomical Drawings*

DIAGRAM 8–25

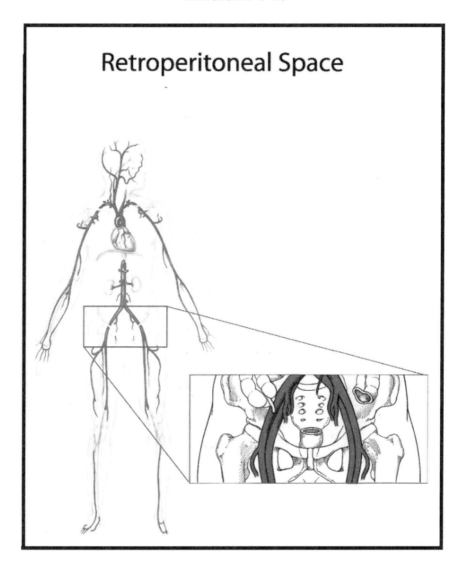

Retroperitoneal Space

J.   ***Charts and Graphs***

DIAGRAM 8–26

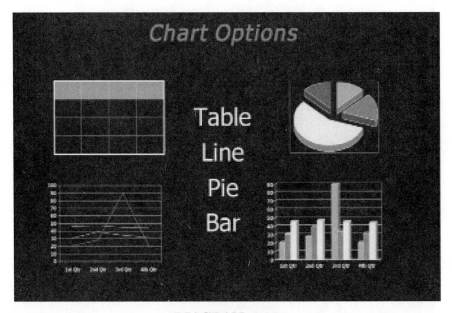

DIAGRAM 8–27

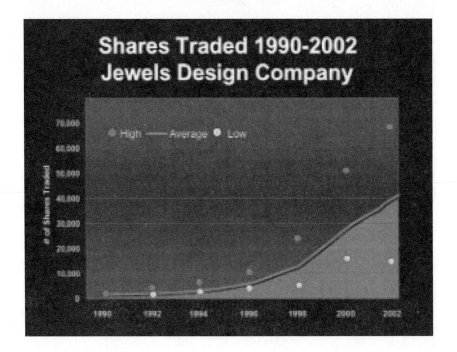

DIAGRAM 8–28

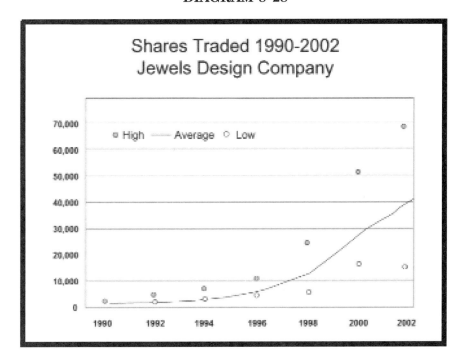

DIAGRAM 8–29

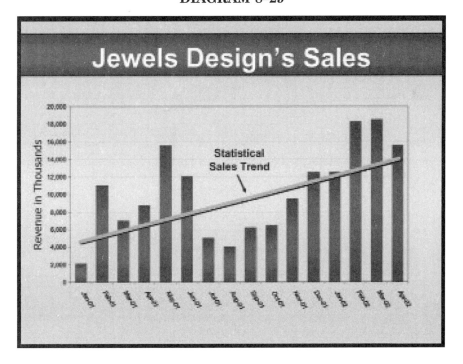

DIAGRAM 8–30

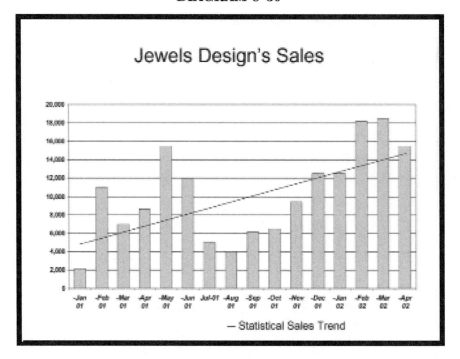

DIAGRAM 8–31

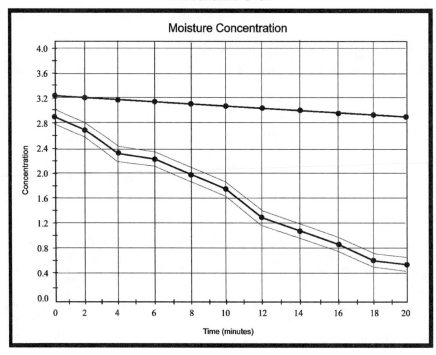

DIAGRAM 8–32

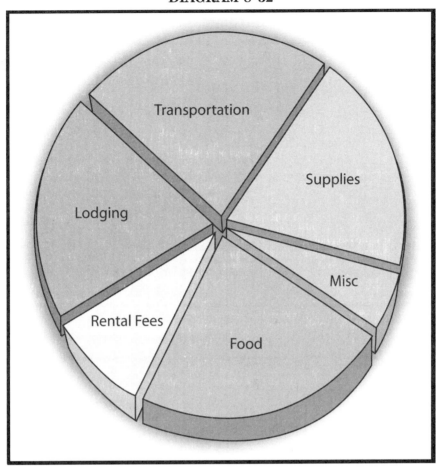

K. Schematics

DIAGRAM 8–33

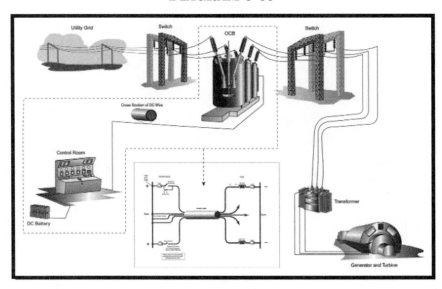

DIAGRAM 8–34

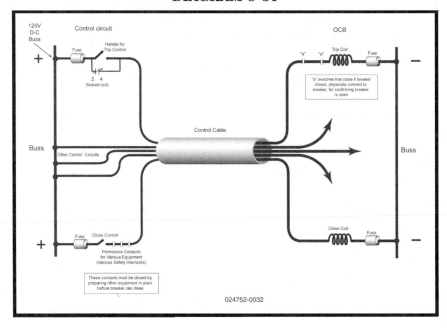

024752-0032

L. Concepts

DIAGRAM 8–35

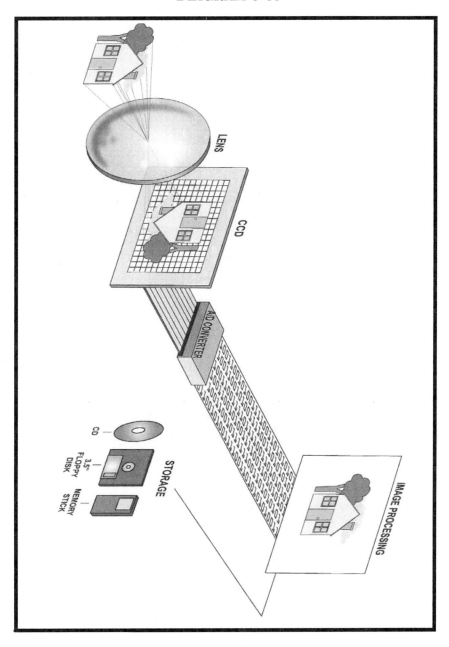

M. *Documents: Highlights*

DIAGRAM 8–36

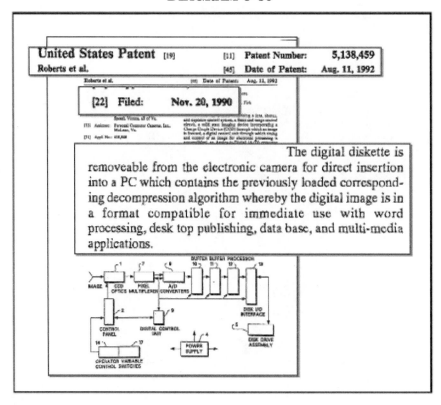

N. Comparisons

DIAGRAM 8–37

Mr. Anderson's	Mr. Smith's
"The spoon is the best utensil. Period. You can cut with it if it has a nice sharp tip and you can scoop. What more do you need?"	"The best utensil? I'd say a knife. There's so many varieties of knives. Sharp knives, butter knives, serrated knifes. I could go on forever. "
"Why use anything other than a spoon? Can you scoop with a fork? I don't think so. The only other utensil I would ever consider would be a spork. But even that is pushing it."	"Granted, it is hard to eat with a knife with out cutting up your mouth, but have you ever tried cutting a steak with anything else? Its worth the pain."

DIAGRAM 8–38

Georgia-Pacific Corp. v. U.S. Plywood Corp.
Factors to Consider

Licensing	Financial / Business	Technical
1) Royalties received by the patentee for the licensing of the patent in suit tending to show an established royalty rate	5) Commercial relationship between the licensor and licensee	9) Utility and advantages of the patent over old modes or devices
2) Rates paid by the licensee for the use of other comparable patents	6) Effect or value as a generator of sales on non-patented items	10) Nature, character and benefits of the patented invention to users
3) Nature and scope of the license	8) Profitability, commercial success and popularity of products made under patent	11) Extent of use by infringer and evidence probative of the value of that use
4) Licensor's established policy and marketing program to maintain patent monopoly	12) Portion of profit customary to allow for use of the patented invention	
7) Duration of the patent and term of license	13) Portion of realizable profit that should be credited to the patented invention	
	14) Opinion testimony of qualified experts	
	15) Hypothetical negotiation between licensor and licensee	

Plaintiffs' Trial
Exhibit 4130

O. *Computer Animation*

DIAGRAM 8–39

DIAGRAM 8–40

§ 8.9   OBJECTIONS TO THE INTRODUCTION OF EXHIBITS

A. *Preparing for Objections*

The advocate must anticipate and prepare for any possible objections to the introduction of an exhibit which opposing counsel might raise. An objection, whether sustained or overruled, slows the presentation of the exhibit and the case. Protracted legal discussions interrupt the flow of the presentation.

B. *Responding to Objections*

If an objection to the introduction of an item of real evidence is sustained, the offering attorney has a number of options.

- Make an offer of proof explaining the exhibit and the grounds for its admissibility. See Section 4.5(B).

- Offer the exhibit for a limited purpose. See Section 4.5(E).

- Offer the exhibit as demonstrative evidence, and not as real evidence.

The foundation for demonstrative evidence is less than that required for the introduction of real evidence and may permit the exhibit to be received for illustrative purposes. For example, in an assault case, if the offering attorney cannot prove the actual baseball bat used during the assault is the bat offered as real evidence, the attorney could offer the bat as demonstrative evidence to assist the witness in testifying and to help the fact finder understand what happened.

C. *Questioning the Witness*

Opposing counsel may question the witness after an exhibit has been offered to determine if there is a basis for an objection or to lay a foundation for an objection. Counsel may ask questions (also called voir dire) to determine whether the required foundation for the exhibit is lacking.

Example:

Q: Your Honor, may I ask some questions of this witness for the purpose of laying a foundation for an objection to the introduction of this exhibit?

Section 4.3(J) explains this questioning procedure. The scope of this voir dire examination is very limited. The questions should not be about the weight to be given the exhibit but only about the foundation. Voir dire examination should not be used unless the exhibit is likely to be excluded. Cross-examination is a more effective tool to reduce the evidentiary effect of an exhibit. The proponent of the exhibit has the right to object if the questioning goes beyond the scope of the intended purpose of that questioning.

D. Common Objections

Exhibits like other evidence are subject to any available and appropriate evidentiary objectives. Some common objections include:

- Irrelevant. Fed.R.Evid. 401 and 402.

- Unfairly prejudicial or gruesome. Fed.R.Evid. 403.

- Misleading or inaccurate. Fed.R.Evid. 403.

- Waste of court's time or undue delay. Fed.R.Evid. 403.

- Exhibit does not assist the witness or aid the jury. Fed.R.Evid. 401.

- Cumulative or repetitious. Fed.R.Evid. 403.

- Lack of foundation, authentication, and identification. Fed. R.Evid. 901 and 903.

- Inadmissible hearsay. Fed.R.Evid. 801 and 803.

- Violation of original writing rule. Fed.R.Evid. 1002.

- Constitutional objections in criminal actions (i.e., denial of right to cross-examine).

This section provides examples of specific objections that may be made to improper or questionable exhibits.

1. Unfairly Prejudicial Exhibits

Example:

The prosecutor wishes to introduce a two foot by three foot color photograph displaying the victim's dead body found at the scene of the crime.

Prosecutor:

Your Honor, the state offers State's Exhibit No. 3, a photograph of the victim's body, which shows there were two separate shotgun blasts; one to the head, and one to the knees.

Defense counsel:

Objection, your Honor. This exhibit is revolting, gruesome, and unfairly prejudicial. It has little probative value because the state's medical expert already testified to the cause of death. There is no reason for the jury to be shocked by the display of this photograph.

Prosecutor:

Your Honor, may I be heard?

Judge:

Yes.

Prosecutor:

This photograph establishes there were two separate shots, supporting the state's claim of premeditation. It is essential for the jurors to see this photograph.

Judge:

The objection will be sustained as to State's Exhibit No. 3. It is unnecessarily large and unfairly prejudicial.

Prosecutor:

Your Honor, we have a smaller 8–inch by 10–inch color photograph of the same scene which we now offer as State's Exhibit No. 4.

Defense Counsel:

We continue to object, your Honor. There is no need for this photograph to be introduced and no need for it to be in color.

Judge:

Objection overruled. State's Exhibit No. 4 is received.

Defense Counsel:

Your Honor, we request that the photograph only be briefly shown to the entire panel of jurors and that it not be used by the state again during this trial.

Judge:

I will allow each individual juror to view the photograph and permit the state to refer to the photograph during summation.

Problems can be anticipated and resolved in advance. The offering attorney can:

- Prepare alternative pieces of demonstrative evidence if the initial exhibit is held not to be admissible. Some attorneys will also have prepared a large black and white photograph as another alternative exhibit, if the judge refused to allow a color photograph into evidence.

- Explain to the judge the exhibit provides the jury with relevant and realistic facts which are essential to an understanding of the case.

- Bring a motion in limine to obtain a preliminary ruling as to its admissibility.

2. *Emotionally Laden Exhibits*

Example:

The plaintiff lost both legs in an accident. The defendant provided plaintiff with prosthetic devices as artificial legs. The plaintiff sues the defendant for a defective prosthesis.

Examining Attorney:

Your Honor, we offer as demonstrative evidence Plaintiff's Exhibit No. 12, a videotape which shows the difficulty the plaintiff has in putting on and wearing the prosthesis and the defects in the product.

Objecting Lawyer:

Objection, your Honor. This videotape is unfairly prejudicial as it plays to the passion and prejudice of the jury, which substantially outweighs its minimal probative value. Further, your Honor, this evidence is repetitive because the plaintiff has already testified to the difficulty he has had with the prosthesis. However, we are willing to stipulate to the introduction of a still photograph of the plaintiff wearing the prosthesis.

Judge:

Overruled. The plaintiff is entitled to show the jury how improperly the artificial limb fits.

In preparing the exhibit, the attorney may:

- Prepare a realistic videotape and not a staged effort that exaggerates what is displayed.

- Introduce the demonstrative evidence before substantial evidence has been introduced which may trigger an objection on the grounds of repetition.

- Have the witness perform a live demonstration instead of the video demonstration. This is not recommended because live demonstrations frequently fail, and the demonstration may not establish what is being attempted to be proved.

3. Misleading or Time Consuming Exhibits

Demonstrative evidence may mislead or confuse the fact finder or distort the facts. Drawings which are not drawn to scale, photographs taken of the scene at a time far removed from the incident, models that are not substantially similar to the real evidence, are examples of misleading situations.

Example:

In a wrongful death action in which the plaintiff died from injuries sustained in an automobile collision, the plaintiff's accident reconstruction expert witness recreated the accident with a computer program.

Examining Attorney:

Your Honor, Plaintiff offers Plaintiff's Exhibit No. 10, a disk containing a recreation of the scene prepared by our expert witness to reconstruct what happened on that day.

Opposing Counsel:

Objection, Your Honor. This recreation is misleading and confusing and distorts the facts. The expert who recreated this event has no personal knowledge of the accident, this recreation is not drawn to precise scale, and the recreation does not include all of the evidence in this case to be introduced concerning the accident.

Examining Attorney:

Your Honor, in response to the objection, this computer recreation will help the jurors understand the testimony by our expert witness and will help the fact finder understand the facts in this case.

Court:

Overruled. Plaintiff's Exhibit No. 10 received.

Sometimes a presentation of demonstrative evidence may be time consuming or require extensive preparation. In these instances, the value of the demonstrative evidence must be weighed against the cost of time and delay. Demonstrative evidence that does not significantly add to the case will frequently be rejected; for example, when the evidence will take a long time to be presented or when alternative ways of introducing the evidence, through oral testimony by witnesses, may be sufficient. Demonstrative evidence that does not aid or assist the fact finder in understanding testimony of a witness or the facts of a case is also objectionable and unlikely to be allowed by the court.

4. *Unconstitutional Exhibits*

In criminal cases, the introduction of demonstrative evidence may be objectionable as a violation of the defendant's constitutional right to cross-examine the witnesses. The defendant may not be able to cross-examine the person who created the exhibits. This objection is best used in conjunction with another ground supporting an objection.

Example:

Prosecutor:

Your Honor, I offer State's Exhibit N—the police report.

Defense Counsel:

Objection, your Honor. This is not within the public record exception to hearsay. The report is conclusory, and my client has a right to cross-examine the officer who prepared this report.

Prosecutor:

Your Honor, we wish to use the diagram on the lower third of the report as demonstrative evidence of the burglary scene and offer that portion of Exhibit N.

Judge:

The diagram part of State's Exhibit N is admitted as illustrative evidence. The verbal remarks and conclusions surrounding the diagram must be masked and not visible on the exhibit.

Prosecutor:

Your Honor, we have scanned the diagram into a computer which can be displayed on this monitor and shown.

Judge:

You may proceed.

---

5. *Objections to Computer Exhibits*

Objections regarding computer created or displayed exhibits may involve issues regarding authenticity and the original writing/best evidence rule (Fed.R.Evid. 1001–1106):

- Computer generated originals presented in a digitized alternative format (e.g. on a CD in a standard file format) are admissible if it can be shown that the conversion of the original was accurately reproduced from the first version.

- Scanned documents of computer documents and images are admissible if they can be authenticated and do not distort the original evidence.

- Charts summarizing data not itself introduced into evidence are admissible if the underlying voluminous data was made available to the opposing parties for review and a witness has laid the proper foundation.

- The rule of completeness for writings or recorded statements may require that the entire exhibit be introduced if the computer software only displays part of the relevant evidence in a document or recording.

- The rule of completeness may also apply to digital photographs which have been cropped or partially enlarged and require the contemporaneous introduction of other photos or parts.

CHAPTER 9
CROSS-EXAMINATION

REFLECTING ON ADVOCACY

Bromidic though it may sound, some questions don't have answers, which is a terribly difficult lesson to learn.

■Katharine Graham

A lie may live and even wiggle after it has been spiked, but not beyond the sundown.

—Heywood Campbell Broun

§ 9.1 INTRODUCTION

Cross-examination is the process of examining an opposing party or adverse witness. An effective cross-examination reveals information that supports the cross-examiner's case and that damages the opposing party's case. A primary purpose of cross-examination is to obtain information necessary to support statements made in summation.

There are two types of cross-examination:

- *Supportive cross.* Cross-examination develops evidence that supports the cross-examiner's case. Cross-examination questions can elicit favorable information not developed on direct examination and to repeat or bolster favorable evidence.

- *Discrediting cross.* Cross-examination also discredits the testifying witness or another witness. This may be accomplished in several ways, including attacking the credibility of the witness or testimony and reducing the evidentiary and persuasive value of the opposition's evidence.

A. *Supportive Cross–Examination*

Supportive cross-examination develops information helpful to the cross-examiner's case. Ask yourself these questions in formulating an effective cross:

- What statements to be made in summation rely upon the testimony of this witness? If a witness is the only source of helpful information, that evidence must be elicited during cross-examination. For example, if a witness is the only person who can identify a signature on a document, then that witness must be asked questions authenticating that document.

- What admissible evidence does the witness know? This information ought to be elicited through cross-examination. For example, if a witness has personal knowledge of the identity of individuals present during a conversation, the witness can be required to identify those individuals.

- What admissions has the witness made? If a witness has made written or oral statements, these admissions must be reviewed to determine which of them might be helpful to the cross-examiner's case. For example, in a breach of contract case, discovery may produce an admission that the opposing party failed to make an installment payment on time. One way to introduce this admission is to ask the opposing party about it on cross-examination.

● What information does the witness have to corroborate favorable evidence? An opposing witness may have information to support a favorable fact established by another witness. For example, an expert witness may support the methods used by an opposing expert who reached a contrary opinion.

● Can the witness bolster or rehabilitate the credibility of favorable witnesses? In addition to introducing proof of a fact through an adverse witness, testimony of that witness corroborating the testimony of a favorable witness may increase the credibility of the favorable witness. For example, if the testimony of a husband testifying in support of his wife can be corroborated by the opposing party, the credibility of the husband is enhanced.

● What portions of the direct examination were helpful? Helpful testimony from direct examination may be highlighted and expanded on cross-examination. For example, an eyewitness called by a plaintiff who observed a traffic accident which occurred during a rainstorm can be asked questions on cross-examination to establish poor visibility and slick roads.

B. *Discrediting Cross–Examination*

The purpose of discrediting cross-examination is to show that the testimony developed on direct examination and evidence introduced by the opposing party is inaccurate or incomplete, inconsistent, implausible, improbable, impossible, or unbelievable. Discrediting cross-examination undermines the other side's case and reduces the credibility of the other side's witnesses. It may be unlikely that the other side's case or the credibility of a witness will be totally discredited on cross-examination. More likely, bits and pieces of damaging information will be revealed that gradually erode the opponent's case. The basic goal of discrediting cross-examination is to discredit evidence or impeach a witness. See Section 9.4.

C. *Risks of Cross–Examination*

Cross-examination should be conducted with realistic expectations and with an assessment of the inherent risks. Cross-examination will not necessarily ''win'' a case or work miracles. Risky questions that have little hope of obtaining helpful information are often asked out of desperation because the cross-examination is not well conceived. Most of the risks involved in cross-examination arise because the witness is adverse, hostile or uncooperative. So, do not ask:

● Non-leading questions,

● Lengthy questions,

- Too many questions,

- Open ended questions that permit a witness to explain,

- Why or how or what happened next questions, and

- Questions that are asked out of curiosity with no expectation of what the answer will be.

D. Good Faith Basis

An advocate must have a good faith basis for cross-examination questions. An attorney cannot ask a question on cross-examination unless the attorney has proof of the underlying facts. The attorney must have a source of reliable information — a possible witness or document that supports the statement made on cross. For example, a cross-examiner cannot ask a witness, "You drank ten beers that evening, right?" unless the attorney has available evidence to prove that fact. The rationale for this requirement is to prevent the cross-examiner from suggesting false or fabricated facts through leading questions. While a cross-examiner cannot fabricate innuendos or inferences on cross-examination, and must have proof of the facts underlying the questions, the proof may not be or need not necessarily be actually admitted as evidence.

E. Myths About Cross–Examination

There are myths about cross-examination that arise from a misunderstanding of cross-examination strategies and tactics. The following explanations will clear up these misconceptions:

- *Myth: Only an experienced lawyer can be an effective cross-examiner.* Any advocate who thoroughly prepares and properly asks cross-examination questions can be effective. All advocates, regardless of experience, have the capability to conduct an effective cross-examination.

- *Myth: The cross-examiner need not be caring or sensitive.* Decision makers may identify with the witness. The witness may be perceived as a nice, decent person or may have a background similar to the background of the decision makers. They expect a witness to be treated courteously and respectfully, and not to be treated in an uncaring or insensitive manner.

- *Myth: Cross-examination should be conducted very aggressively.* An attorney who conducts an aggressive cross-examination may be perceived as manipulating the witness and the evidence. An attorney must be perceived as fair and should be politely insistent and assertive rather than overly aggressive. Not that many witnesses or situations require an overly aggressive approach.

- *Myth: The witness must be destroyed on cross-examination.* The purpose of cross-examination is not necessarily to make the witness look or feel bad, but to obtain information to win a case.

After a good cross-examination, a witness may leave the stand without feeling "destroyed."

- *Myth: The witness should always be shown to be a liar.* Attacking the credibility of witnesses by suggesting or inferring that they are lying is ill-advised unless there is direct evidence of their lie. Many witnesses make honest and good faith efforts to describe an event and will not look like or sound like they are making things up. However, it is not uncommon for witnesses who see or hear only a portion of an incident to add details they assume occurred. These witnesses may then blend their recollection of what actually occurred with the assumed details. This mistaken recollection and belief forms the basis for their testimony. The witness is mistaken, but not lying. A direct attack on the veracity of such a witness is inappropriate and ineffective.

- *Myth: The cross-examiner must know the answers to all the questions asked before asking them.* The reality is that often the lawyer will know the witness' prior statements and know what the witness will repeat at trial. But, just as often, there will be no complete, verbatim transcript or statement. The cross-examiner will still need to ask questions, and can effectively do so by accurately predicting what the witness will say.

- *Myth: Cross-examinations must produce dramatic results.* A cross-examination that does not leave the fact finder gasping, the witness crying, or the attorney exalting, does not indicate that the cross-examination has been ineffective. Some cases may involve such dramatic moments, but many do not.

- *Myth: Cross-examination is an opportunity to debate with the witness.* Argumentative questions are improper and likely to draw an objection. The cross-examiner wants to obtain "yes" or "no" responses from a witness and wants to avoid debating with the witness.

- *Myth: Cross-examination often escalates into a shouting match between the witness and the attorney.* There is no need for an attorney to ask questions in a loud or harsh manner, except in unusual circumstances. Few witnesses deserve or require this treatment.

- *Myth: Cross-examination should result in the witness "confessing."* Witnesses seldom "confess" their guilt or liability on the stand, certainly not with the frequency that Perry Mason achieved such results.

- *Myth: Cross-examinations that appear on television or in the movies are realistic and appropriate.* More often than not, cross-examination questions asked in a television program or motion picture are unrealistic and inappropriate. A witness does not deserve to be treated in the way commonly depicted in television and the movies.

- *Myth: Cross-examinations should always be short.* A cross-examination should be as long as necessary to obtain the required information from the witness. With some witnesses, cross-examination will be short, and with others, long. There is no set time limit for effective cross-examinations. The facts, witnesses, and circumstances determine the content and length.

- *Myth: Cross-examination should cover one point, and no more than a few points.* Some advocates suggest that cross-examination should only cover one or a few points. This is appropriate advice if that's all the information a cross-examiner needs to develop. Many cross-examinations require the development of more points. What one experienced advocate considers to be one point with six subpoints, another lawyer may consider to be seven points. Regardless of the semantics or the counting system used, a cross-examination should cover what is necessary.

- *Myth: Cross-examination is the most difficult advocacy skill.* Different advocates have different views about which part of the case is most difficult. A well-prepared cross-examination, seeking answers already known by the cross-examiner, need not be any more difficult than other parts of the case.

Cross-examination can become very difficult and very damaging if questions are phrased improperly, inappropriate areas are explored, or the attorney loses control over the witness. Proper planning, preparation, and an understanding of what works reduces these problems.

§ 9.2 PREPARATION

A. *Planning*

The preparation for a cross-examination begins during the preliminary stages of a case. Witnesses are interviewed, witnesses' statements are taken, and depositions are completed. The responses obtained from these discovery sources provide information useful for cross-examination. Before trial or hearing, the different areas of cross-examination are reconsidered and specific questions are planned. Preparation continues until the moment cross-examination begins. The cross-examiner listens carefully to the answers the witness gives on direct examination and adds, deletes or modifies questions to be asked during cross.

After the witness has testified on direct, the cross-examiner is usually able to ask a high percentage of the prepared questions. This occurs because the well-prepared cross-examiner already knows or can predict what the witness knows and does not know. Some modifications will be necessary.

Adjustments may also be necessary during the cross-examination itself. The witness may not respond as anticipated, or may give unresponsive or rambling answers. The attorney must listen carefully during the cross and flexibly adapt to the responses by asking follow-up questions that produce the desired responses. Form 9.1, which appears on the adjacent page, provides methods of planning a cross-examination. The remainder of this chapter explains the planning topics in detail.

B. Should There be a Cross–Examination?

The decision to cross-examine must be made during trial preparation and again during the trial or hearing. Whether cross-examination should be conducted as planned, or whether any cross-examination should be conducted at all, are questions that must be finally resolved after the witness has completed direct examination. The vast majority of witnesses merit some cross-examination. Consider the following factors in determining whether a witness should be cross-examined:

- Has the witness damaged the case? If the witness has not provided any evidence which damages the case, the cross-examination may not be necessary. A witness who did not appear credible, or whose story is not credible, or who has been contradicted by other evidence may not need to be cross-examined.

- Is the witness important to the other side? The more significant a witness is to the opposing side, the more likely it is that cross-examination will be necessary.

- Will the decision maker expect cross-examination? Witnesses who have provided damaging information or who are important to the other side need to be cross-examined to meet the expectations of the decision maker and to prevent opposing counsel from commenting on such failure during summation.

- Did the witness omit important adverse information on direct examination? Cross-examination regarding that information may be unwise. Occasionally, an opposing attorney may intentionally withhold evidence during the direct examination of a witness anticipating the evidence will be disclosed on cross-examination or redirect. If there is no cross-examination regarding this evidence, this information may never be disclosed. Some experienced lawyers set this trap for the inexperienced cross-examiner.

- Will cross-examination unavoidably bring out information that is harmful to the case? If cross-examination will yield more harmful than helpful information, it may be best not to cross-examine.

- Are questions being asked only for the sake of asking questions? If the cross-examination will serve no better purpose, then it ought not be conducted.

- Does this witness present any difficulties that may cause substantial problems? If a witness is very difficult to control or some other problem exists, the decision to cross-examine should be reconsidered.

FORM 9.1
CROSS-EXAMINATION WORKSHEET

Case _____ Witness _____ File_____

Supportive Cross-Examination Information:

Discrediting Cross-Examination:

    Implausible/Improbable/Impossible:

    Inconsistencies:

    Impeachment: Facts/Opinions/
                                        Modifiers/Synonyms

        Interest/Bias/Prejudice

        Competency Deficiencies

        Inadequate Observation/
          Lack of Perception

        Poor Recollection

        Inconsistent Conduct

        Criminal Record

        Specific Instances of Untruthfulness

        Prior Inconsistent Statements
          Written/Oral/Omissions

        Other Areas:

C. Full and Fair Opportunity to Cross–Examine

A party has a right fully and fairly to cross-examine a witness. Unusual situations may arise when a witness who has testified on direct examination cannot be cross-examined. These situations include: (1) the assertion of a privilege by the witness which properly permits the witness to refuse to answer questions, (2) a witness becoming ill or otherwise incapacitated before or during cross-examination, and (3) the refusal of a witness to answer a question which the judge or arbitrator orders the witness to answer. In these situations, the cross-examiner may request that the direct examination testimony of the witness relating to the cross-examination topics be stricken because no opportunity exists to cross-examine the witness regarding those matters.

D. Scope of Cross–Examination

The scope of cross-examination is usually limited to the following two areas: the subject matter of direct examination and matters affecting credibility issues. The law in most jurisdictions, including the federal system, limits cross to the scope of the direct and to matters that discredit the witness or the case. See Fed.R.Evid. 611. Judges and arbitrators, however, have broad discretion to permit inquiries into additional matters. Cross-examiners will typically have a lot of latitude to explore relevant areas which affect the case or the credibility of a witness.

While the rules of a given jurisdiction may appear to restrict the scope of cross-examination, practice often permits broader inquiries. Some judges and arbitrators strictly enforce the rules, however, and sustain an objection that the cross exceeds the scope of the direct. The cross-examiner should then advise the decision maker that the questions apply to a credibility issue which permit the examination to proceed.

If an area of inquiry on cross exceeds the scope of the direct examination and does not involve credibility issues, the cross-examiner has several options. First, the questions may be asked and the opponent may not object. Second, the question may be asked, the opponent may object, and the objection may be overruled, permitting the answer. Third, the cross-examiner can seek permission to allow a broader cross-examination. In this case, the attorney may advise the judge or arbitrator that the witness could be called back later to testify, and it would be more efficient if the examination was completed at one time. Fourth, if the questions are disallowed, the attorney can subsequently call the witness during the cross-examiner's next opportunity to introduce affirmative evidence.

E. Preparing Topics and Written Questions in Advance

Cross-examination is most effective when topics and questions are prepared in advance. Experienced lawyers may be able to effectively cross-examine by relying solely on a list of topics. Many lawyers, however, especially inexperienced advocates, need to write out questions to be most effective. The extent to which written questions should be prepared depends upon the nature of the question, significance of the topic, type of witness, and abilities of the attorney.

Effective cross-examination often demands that the attorney ask precise questions containing particular words. In these situations the attorney, particularly the novice cross-examiner, is well advised to write out the questions. Most prepared questions will not need to be altered significantly during the case, but an attorney must adapt the questions to changing circumstances. The attorney should avoid simply reading prepared questions and must pay attention to the witness' verbal and nonverbal responses in order to ask follow-up, clarifying or additional questions.

F. Structure

Cross-examination questions should be asked in an order that makes the cross-examination most effective, interesting, persuasive, and memorable. An effective way to organize cross-examination points is to:

- List all the points expected to be made.
- Divide the points into the two broad categories of cross-examination: supportive cross and discrediting cross.
- Within these categories, rank each point from most to least important.
- Of the more important points, decide which should begin or end the segment.
- Organize the other points in a sequence that works best.
- Select and structure any subtopics under the main points.
- Review all the listed points and determine whether the initial assessment of their rank, order, and sequence appears to be the most effective.

G. Order

If both supportive and discrediting questions are to be asked, the supportive cross-examination questions ought to be asked first for a number of reasons. These questions elicit helpful information and will be emphasized by being asked at the beginning of the cross-examination. These questions follow the pattern of questions asked on direct examination, which was just completed. The witness will be more likely to be more cooperative at the beginning of such a cross-examination. The credibility of the witness has not yet been attacked and the decision maker may perceive the witness to be more believable.

The order of the supportive cross-examination questions should follow a prepared structure, with important questions beginning and ending the line of questioning, and with the other points asked in the middle. The final point of supportive cross-examination should also serve as a transition into the discrediting category of cross-examination.

The shift from supportive to discrediting cross-examination may cause a problem. The cross-examiner wants the fact finder to believe the admissions elicited during the supportive cross-examination and to disbelieve the witness during discrediting cross-examination. With some witnesses, it might be advisable to omit or restrict the scope of the discrediting cross-examination to avoid the witness from being entirely discredited. The transition questions that begin the discrediting cross-examination should be selected to reduce this problem. With other witnesses, the discrediting cross-examination may render testimony so unbelievable that the fact finders will not believe the supportive cross-examination answers. In these situations, it may be better to avoid asking supportive cross-examination questions altogether, unless there is no other source for this information.

The order of the discrediting cross-examination questions should also follow a prepared structure. Important points should be made at the beginning and the end of this category of questions, with other points interspersed in the middle.

An alternative to a logical sequence of planned questions is to probe areas in a random fashion. This "jumping around" or "hop and skip" approach has the advantage of causing problems for witnesses who may be fabricating their responses. Such a witness, if asked questions in a logical or chronological order, may be able to maintain the fabrication, but if asked questions in a random order may be more likely to testify inconsistently. This approach has some disadvantages. The cross-examiner may have difficulty in remembering what has been asked, and the fact finder may find it difficult to follow an unstructured cross-examination. This approach requires a lot of practice or experience to be effective.

H. Concluding Questions

The concluding questions of a cross-examination should share the following characteristics: the questions should conclude the examination on a high note by making an effective point, should not be objectionable because sustained objections disrupt the conclusion, and should be of the type the witness will respond to favorably. If the cross-examiner has a doubt regarding whether the questions are effective, "safe" questions may be used for the conclusion, and risky questions asked earlier.

I. Recross Examination

The scope of recross examination is limited to the subject matter of the redirect examination. A primary purpose of conducting a recross is the same as conducting a cross-examination: Is there any information this witness has that is needed for summation? Recross examination questions usually refer to the previous redirect answers of the witness and compare these responses to contradictory evidence: "During the redirect examination by your attorney, you stated that . . . . ; however, it is true that . . . . " If no recross is necessary, the cross-examiner can say: "Your Honor, there is no reason for any further questions." There often is no need to conduct a recross, and a recross should not be conducted merely because redirect questions were asked. Recross questions should not be asked if the redirect was ineffective or if the examination of the witness has been overly lengthy, and the fact finder cannot absorb more information from this witness.

J. Location and Movement

The cross-examiner should be visible to the fact finder during the examination. The cross-examiner asks the questions containing the evidence the fact finders need to hear. Unlike direct examination, when the direct examiner may be inconspicuous, the cross-examiner should be conspicuous.

The cross-examiner may have the option to sit or stand. Many jurisdictions require the cross-examiner to stand behind a lectern and not move about the courtroom. Cross-examiners may approach the witness when showing the witness an exhibit or using a visual aid. Many jurisdictions require the attorney to remain seated behind counsel table, especially in administrative hearings and arbitrations. In some small hearing rooms, the cross-examiner may sit only a few feet away from the witness.

In jurisdictions where counsel has an option to stand and move around the courtroom or hearing room, the cross-examiner should determine what location is best. This will depend upon the nature of the questions asked and the demeanor and responses of the witnesses. If the cross-examiner wants the fact finder to observe the witness displaying guilt or uncertainty, the cross-examiner should stand in a location which requires the witness to look in the direction of the fact finder and which permits the fact finder easily to see both the witness and the attorney.

If the cross-examiner can move during cross-examination, movement should be purposeful. It may be effective to move closer to the witness during impeachment or when significant questions are asked to control the response of the witness. Further, the closer the cross-examiner is to the witness, the more likely the witness will become uncomfortable and appear anxious and not credible. The cross-examiner cannot stand too close or "crowd" a witness. Opposing counsel will probably object, and the judge or arbitrator will ask the cross-examiner to move away from the witness to a suitable distance.

K. Demeanor

Compassion and confidence are two important cross-examination traits. Many witnesses deserve to be treated compassionately because of the facts or merely because they are people. The decision maker may expect witnesses to be treated decently. If the witness perceives that the cross-examiner is confident, the witness is more likely to be agreeable and less evasive.

The most effective demeanor for a cross-examiner is to be firm, yet sensitive. This is especially true during the beginning of a cross-examination attempting to elicit supportive evidence. A "friendly" cross-examiner is more likely to elicit favorable information. Some witnesses deserve special treatment, including sympathetic witnesses such as young children, a victim of a crime, or a bereaved spouse.

Other situations may require more assertiveness on the part of the attorney, particularly during impeachment efforts or when controlling an evasive or rambling witness. The cross-examiner should avoid becoming combative with the witness and avoid displays of anger. Such conduct makes thinking difficult and will likely draw objections.

§ 9.3 TACTICS AND TECHNIQUES

Effective cross-examination requires the use of proper tactics and techniques. Many of these approaches are principles or "commandments" which should never be violated. All of these approaches are matters which need to be considered before and during the presentation of a cross. They include:

- Use proper question form,
- Select the right content,
- Seek agreement from the witness,
- Control the witness' responses,
- Emphasize helpful points,
- Utilize safe questions, and
- Specify questions for certain witnesses.

The tactics described in each category should be reviewed before every cross-examination to determine which should be employed. Not all of the techniques ought to be used in every cross, but many will be applicable. If a problem does occur during cross, it is usually because one of the tactics was not properly employed.

Cross-examination questions must be carefully crafted and precisely asked. The difference between an effective cross-examination question and an ineffective one is often very subtle. The use of one wrong word, the slight mistiming of a question, a momentary loss of control over a witness, all may cause problems that can lead to even more serious problems. A witness may properly refuse to answer a question, may rightfully claim a question is unclear, and may try to explain an answer, all because the cross-examiner failed to ask a precise question.

A. *Form of Question*

1. *Leading the Witness*

Only questions that suggest or contain the answer should be asked on cross. Questions that require a "yes," "no," or short, anticipated answers should be asked so the testimony develops as anticipated. The question "why" and questions which require explanations should almost always be avoided, because they call for open-ended answers that will reveal unnecessary information and the answers cannot be controlled.

Example:

Q: You are Chicago, correct?

A: Yes.

Q: You are hog butcher for the world?

A: Yes.

Q: Toolmaker, correct?

A: Yes.

Q: Stacker of wheat?

A: Yes.

Q: You are also a player with railroads and the nation's freight handler?

A: Yes.

Q: It is fair to say you are stormy?

A: Yes.

Q: Husky?

A: Yes.

Q: Brawling?

A: Yes.

Q: You are the city of the big shoulders?

A: Sure.

Q: And your poem was written by Carl Sandberg?

A: Of course.

A proper question requires the witness to respond "yes" or "no." An improper question permits the witness to describe, expand or explain the answer.

2. *Form of Leading Question*

Leading questions should be formulated to prompt responsive answers. An effectively phrased leading question requires the witness to agree with the question. There are a variety of ways leading questions can be asked. The more the question reasonably suggests the answer, the more effective it will be.

Example:

Ask: You saw Charlie Allnut on the African Queen?

Not: Did you see the defendant on the African Queen?

Phrases may be added to leading questions to obtain an answer. These prefaces or clauses may be useful in prompting a response. The repetitive use of these phrases ought to be avoided, however, because they may detract from the substance of the question. Examples of these phrases include:

Example:

You saw the defendant on the boat, isn't that true?

Or,

It is true that you saw the defendant on the boat?

Or,

Rosie Sayer, you saw the defendant on the boat, right?

Leading "questions" may also be asked in the form of statements which sound like questions because of the cross-examiner's voice inflection.

Example:

Q: You met Buddy Holly at the airport?

A: Yes.

Q: At about 11:00 p.m.?

A: Yes.

Q: That was the first time you met Mr. Holly?

A: Yes.

Q: And the last?

A: Yes.

The various forms of leading questions ought to be used during a cross-examination for variety and to prevent a cross from sounding monotonous.

3. *Simple, Short Questions*

Short, straightforward questions in simple, understandable language are most effective. Lengthy or rambling questions confuse everyone.

Example:

Ask:

Q: The fight began?

A: Yes.

Q: The referee stood in the middle of the ring?

A: Yes.

Q: Ali stood in one corner?

A: Yes.

Q: Frazier stood in the opposite corner?

A: Yes.

Q: Ali began to move toward the center of the ring?

A: Yes.

Q: Frazier also began to move towards the middle of the ring, right?

A: Yes.

Not:

Q: As the fight began both Ali and Frazier stood in their respective corners and then each of them began to move towards the center of the ring, isn't that what happened?

---

4.   *Avoid Multiple Negative Questions*

Questions that contain double or multiple negatives are misleading and should not be asked.

Example:

Do not ask:

Q: It is correct is it not, that you don't know who was on the Galactica?

Q: It is not true, is it, that you are not from Battle Star?

B.   *Content of Questions*

1.   *Fact Questions*

Questions which include the relevant facts prompt responsive answers. The factual words included in the cross-examination question must be provided and based on accurate information to force a witness to admit the accuracy of the question. Questions which seek a conclusion or employ words with multiple meanings permit the witness to be non-responsive or explain an answer.

Example:

Avoid asking:

Q: When you visited Michael Cory, you wanted to sell him as much insurance as you could?

A: He came to my office. I told him I could provide him with an insurance policy that met his needs.

Ask instead:

Q: You asked Mr. Cory to come to your office?

A: Yes.

Q: While he was in your office, he told you he needed insurance coverage?

A: Yes.

Q: You told him you could provide him with insurance?

A: Yes.

Q: You wanted to sell him insurance?

A: Yes.

Some words appear to be ''facts'' but are conclusory words. Each cross-examination question should be reviewed to determine whether the precise words used are facts or whether they include elements seeking a conclusion.

Avoid asking:

Q: Mr. Churchill read the lease agreement, correct?

A: He may have skimmed the lease.

Q: He understood the terms of the lease, didn't he?

A: I don't know.

Ask instead:

Q: You handed Mr. Churchill the lease agreement?

A: Yes.

Q: You saw him look at the lease agreement?

A: Yes.

Q: He sat there for some time looking at the lease?

A: Yes.

Q: The two of you discussed the lease for over an hour?

A: Yes.

Q: He asked you some questions about the lease?

A: Yes.

Q: You answered his questions?

A: Yes.

Q: You asked him if he had any other questions about the lease?

A: Yes.

Q: You asked him whether that lease met his country's needs?

A: Yes.

Q: And he said, "Yes it did"?

A: Correct.

Q: He signed that lease?

A: Yes.

---

2. *Properly Asking for Opinions*

An effective way to force a witness to provide an opinion is to first establish the factual basis for the opinion. For example, if you want eyewitnesses to admit they were tired at the time they made an identification, you first need to establish the factual basis for their being tired before you ask questions about their being tired.

Example:

Q: Mr. Chaplin, your wallet was stolen at approximately 8 p.m., correct?

A: Yes.

Q: You got up that morning about 6 a.m.?

A: Approximately 6 o'clock.

Q: You worked from 8 a.m. until 7 p.m.?

A: Yes.

Q: You worked hard during parts of the day?

A: Sure.

Q: Your normal work day is from 8 a.m. until 5 p.m., correct?

A: Yes.

Q: You worked later than usual that day, right?

A: Yes.

Q: Working 11 hours that day was a tiring experience?

A: Yes.

Q: You were naturally tired at the end of your work day?

A: Yes.

Q: You were going home and looking forward to resting?

A: Sure.

Q: Because you had a very tiring day at the office, right?

A: I was tired.

If the witness was asked the opinion question before the factual questions, the witness could have tried to bring up reasons for not being tired. Factual questions are needed to establish the conclusion that the witness was tired and to prevent the witness from explaining away an answer. Even if the witness refused to admit to being tired at the end of the day, the fact finder would believe the witness was tired and would not believe the witness' denial.

3. *Using Modifiers*

The use of adjectives and adverbs as modifiers may help in obtaining favorable responses from a witness. Different impressions may be created on cross-examination, if appropriate modifying words or phrases are used. For example, a witness may be willing to admit to different degrees of being tired depending on the sequence of questions asked and the modifying words used.

Example:

Q: You were somewhat tired after working a *full* day, correct?

A: Yes.

Q: Working *all* those hours made you feel *tired*?

A: Yes.

Q: Working those *additional* overtime hours made you *more* tired than usual?

A: Perhaps.

Q: The *hard* day you had made you feel *quite* tired at the end of the day?

A: Some, yes.

Q: Your work that *long, hard* day caused you stress?

A: Well, some.

Q: It's fair to say that you went through a *lot* of stress by the end of the day, correct?

A: At the end, sure.

Further questioning with some witnesses may have them agreeing to being "very tired" at the end of the day. Using various modifiers — a little, somewhat, quite, very — is an effective way to have the witness gradually agree to a position.

4. *Using Synonyms*

If a specific word is being sought on cross-examination, a synonym may be useful instead of trying to force the witness to admit to one specific word. A thesaurus provides alternative words that more effectively describe a situation. In the eyewitness example, having the witness agree to being "exhausted" at the end of the day rather than just being "tired" is more effective. Consider using synonyms which more accurately portray the event the jurors should perceive. In addition to the word "tired," other words such as exhausted, fatigued, worn out, weary, rundown, drained, listless, dull, or tuckered out could be used.

C. *Seek Agreement With the Witness*

1. *Being Compassionate*

Witnesses ordinarily deserve courteous treatment. Some witnesses may deserve righteous indignation, others may be verbally "attacked," but no one deserves to be questioned in an obnoxious manner. The cross-examiner can usually be much more effective by being politely assertive and persistent and by showing appropriate compassion rather than aggression.

Example:

Q: Ms. Lindberg, I understand this is a difficult time for you. We all know the kidnapping and death of your son was a terrible tragedy. You understand that I need to ask you some questions about the event so we can understand what happened?

---

2. *Flattering the Witness*

An effective way to obtain a responsive answer to a leading question is to ask a question that makes the witness look good. Witnesses are much more likely to agree with a position that serves their self-interest or flatters them in some way. For example, if the purpose is to get the witness to admit to being tired, then questions should be asked which show the witness had legitimate reasons to be tired.

Example:

Q: Tom Sawyer, you consider yourself a good worker?

A: Yeah.

Q: You work hard when your job requires it?

A: You bet.

Q: Sure. And your work is demanding?

A: I'll say.

Q: You want to succeed at your job, don't you?

A: I'd like to, yes.

Q: You try to do the best possible job you can?

A: I try.

These and additional questions lead to the inevitable conclusion that a hard working and dedicated employee who worked a full day would naturally be tired at the end of that day. Positive, supportive, and flattering questions usually result in an agreeable witness.

3. Establish Concepts

One of the purposes of cross-examination is to provide the fact finder with a different perspective and explanation of a situation. These perspectives and explanations can be established on cross-examination by asking questions that develop these "concepts." The cross-examiner wants the witness to show agreement with a "concept" by agreeing with the question. However, a witness may disagree with certain words used to establish the concept. The cross-examiner should then focus on establishing the concept and not necessarily force the witness to agree to specific terms. The technique of using synonyms described in section 9.3(B)(4) helps establish concepts.

Example:

Q: You were exhausted at the end of the game, Ms. Hopscotch?

A: No, I was not exhausted.

Q: You must have been tired?

A: Yes, a bit.

Q: All that hopping and bending did tire you out?

A: Yes.

Attempting to have the witness agree with a conclusory word before asking a sufficient number of appropriate fact questions is likely to backfire. It is much wiser to ask the predicate facts which establish the conclusion so the witness has to agree. The summation can then be used to explain that the ability of the eyewitness to make an identification was diminished.

4. Employ Indirection

Cross-examiners sometimes use indirection in asking questions. With indirect questions the witness does not perceive why a question is being asked or the purpose of a line of questioning until the point is made. During witness preparation, the direct examiner will advise the witness of the anticipated areas of cross-examination, and the witness may have some understanding of the purpose behind some questions. This advance information may not be sufficient to alert witnesses to all areas of cross-examination, and their nervousness and unfamiliarity with the legal process may reduce their ability to think clearly and anticipate questions, making indirection an effective tactic.

Example (Cross-examining the employee):

Presume the cross-examiner represents an employer who fired an employee who then sues the employer for breach of the employment contract. The employer in defense claims the employee was an "at will" employee and could be fired at any time without cause, and cross-examines the employee.

Q: You could quit your job at any time, Ms. Vanilla, is that correct?

A: Yes.

Q: The dwarfs could not force you to stay?

A: Not if I wanted to leave.

Q: Yes. If you no longer wanted to work there, you could leave?

A: That's true.

D. Control Responses and the Witness

1. Know the Answers

A cardinal rule of cross-examination is to ask only those questions to which the answer is already known by the cross-examiner. Many answers will be known because they appear in a witness statement, a deposition, a document, or are within the knowledge of another person. If the witness refuses to answer the question properly, the source of the information can be used to impeach the witness. Additionally, because the witness knows that a source of information exists, the witness will tend to answer the question to avoid impeachment. In this way, the witness' response can be controlled.

Example:

Q: You were driving your broomstick approximately 5 light-years an hour, isn't that correct Mr. Potter?

A: I'm not sure how fast I was going.

Q: You were going approximately 5 light-years an hour?

A: I don't know.

Q: You recall that you gave a written statement in this case to an investigator, correct?

A: Yes, I did.

Q: In that statement you said you were going approximately 5 light-years an hour?

A: Oh, that's right.

A corollary to this rule is that you may have to ask questions seeking answers you may not actually know. You may not have the complete statement of a witness; there probably were questions that were not asked during a deposition; you may be in an administrative hearing or arbitration without knowing the prior statements from the witness. These situations are common and frequent.

A successful cross-examination approach is to reasonably predict what the answers will be. You can prepare an effective cross based upon what the witness is likely, or very likely, to say. And this can be done with a fair amount of confidence.

Example:

Presume a witness views an accident while walking home on Valentine's Day. And presume the cross-examiner does not know the answers to the following questions but hopes to reduce the ability of the witness to observe and remember.

Q: The day of the accident was Valentine's Day?

A: Oh, yes.

Q: Did you have some plans that evening?

A: Well, yes, but not really much.

Q: While you were standing on the corner, were you thinking about your plans?

A: Yeah.

Q: And looking forward to the evening?

A: Yes. I was.

Q: And were those thoughts you were having, is it fair to say, enjoyable thoughts?

A: You could say that.

Q: While you were thinking about the plans and evening, the accident happened, correct, Ms. Cupid?

A: Well, yes.

---

2. *Avoid the Dangerous Unknown*

A cross-examiner might be tempted to ask important questions to which the answers are unknown and unpredictable. This temptation may arise because the cross-examiner has not properly prepared the case or because the attorney is playing a hunch or thinks any possible response can be handled. These temptations need to be avoided. If a witness on direct examination adds some new details which are unfamiliar to the cross-examiner, impeachment by omission may be available. See Section 9.4(E).

3. *Pursue the Anticipated*

Some cases do not involve extensive discovery and the advocate may not know a lot about what the witness will say on direct. Administrative hearings and arbitrations are examples of these situations. An effective cross-examination can still be conducted by predicting and preparing for the anticipated. In most cases, the advocate can predict what the witness will say and can prepare an effective cross-examination. A party or another witness can be an excellent source of information about what an adverse witness knows. Common sense and experience are other useful sources.

4. *Listen and Observe*

It is axiomatic that the cross-examiner should listen to the answers and observe how the witness responds. But there are many things going on during cross-examination to distract the cross-examiner. The cross-examiner must remember to concentrate on the task at hand, including listening to the exact answers and observing the subtleties and nuances of the responses. The attorney must remain alert in order to follow up on nonresponsive or ambiguous answers, to repeat or rephrase questions if a witness is perplexed, or to comment on the appearance and credibility of witnesses during summation.

Example:

Q: You were not at the studio, were you, Ms. Davis?

A: No.

[Does the answer "No" mean "No, I wasn't there," or "No, I was there"? The inflection the witness uses in responding may make the response clear. If not, the cross-examiner should follow up:]

Q: That means you were not there?

A: That's right.

Example:

Q: It is true that you don't remember what Mr. Hale said, right?

A: Yes.

[This question is awkwardly phrased because it contains the words "true," "right," and the negative: "don't." The attorney needs to clarify the response:]

Q: Your answer is that you don't remember?

A: Yes.

Example:

Q: Ms. Alice, you paid the restaurant bill?

A: I think so.

Q: Excuse me, your facial expression indicated that you may not have understood that question.

---

5. *Control the Witness*

The most effective way to control witnesses is to ask questions to which they must agree. Fact questions that are accurate will require the witness to agree. Questions that contain an answer that the witness has previously provided will also prompt the correct response. Examples in the previous sections which rephrased inappropriate questions illustrate this type of control. Lengthy or imprecise questions or questions that contain conclusions may give the witness reason to hesitate in responding.

Example:

Avoid asking:

Q: At the time the fight started you were standing behind the bar at the cash register giving change to a customer, isn't that correct, Mr. Gleason?

A: Not really. I was watching to see who started the fight, and I saw your client hit the plaintiff.

Rather ask:

Q: A fight broke out, didn't it Mr. Gleason?

A: Yes.

Q: You were behind the bar?

A: Yes.

Q: You were standing at the cash register?

A: Yes.

Q: You were giving change to a customer?

A: Yes.

Additional ways to maintain control include:

a. *Repeat the Question*

Example:

Q: You were standing behind the bar?

A: Well, yes, but I was looking up.

Q: You were standing behind the bar?

A: Yes.

b. Insist on an Answer

Example:

Q: You were giving change to a customer?

A: I heard this noise.

Q: My question was — you were giving change to a customer?

A: Yes.

c. Rephrase the Question

Example:

Q: You were giving change to a customer?

A: I heard this noise.

Q: Perhaps my question was not clear enough. Let me ask it again this way. When you heard a noise, you were handing change to a customer?

A: Yes.

d. Advise the Witness to Answer

Example:

Q: You closed the cash register drawer?

A: As I was looking over in the corner.

Q: You walked away from the cash register?

A: A customer called me over.

Q: Mr. Gleason, please limit your answer to the question I asked in order to help the jurors understand what happened?

A: All right.

Q: You did walk away from the cash register?

A: Yes I did.

Q: After you closed the drawer?

A: Yes.

---

e.   *Further Advise the Witness*

Example:

Q: The customer asked you for a drink?

A: She was thirsty.

Q: She asked you for a bottled beer?

A: We do not sell beer on tap.

Q: Mr. Gleason, in the interests of time, please answer the specific question asked. If you don't understand the question, tell me and I'll rephrase it so it is clear. If you cannot answer it yes or no, tell me and I will rephrase it.

---

f.   *Seek Cooperation From the Witness*

Example:

Q: Mr. Gleason, during your direct examination you answered the questions that your attorney asked you. You will be able to give me that same degree of cooperation you gave your attorney, won't you?

A: I'll try.

---

g.   *Request a Curative Instruction*

If a witness gives a nonresponsive answer, the judge can be asked to instruct the jury to disregard the answer that was not responsive to the question asked.

Example:

Q: You walked down to the far end of the bar?

A: But I'm sure your client started that fight.

Cross-Examiner:

Your Honor, we ask that you instruct the jury to disregard that last answer as being nonresponsive and improper.

---

h. Ask the Judge or Arbitrator for Further Assistance (if nothing else works)

Advocates can ask the judge or arbitrator to instruct the witness to answer the questions asked. Some judges and arbitrators may do this on their own to prevent a witness from being unresponsive. However, some may refuse to assist the attorney and tell the attorney to conduct the examination. It is ordinarily more effective to ask for assistance after a witness has failed or refused to directly answer a number of questions. Many judges and arbitrators expect an attorney to control the witness and to ask the judge for assistance only if those attempts fail. Others, however, will initially control a non-responsive witness.

Example:

Q: The bottled beer was in a refrigerator located below the bar, wasn't it?

A: I could clearly hear your client yelling.

Q: You bent down?

A: Just for a brief moment.

Q: You opened a refrigerator?

A: How else could I get the bottles out? It only makes sense. . . .

Cross-Examiner:

Your Honor, I object on the grounds of nonresponsiveness and ask that you instruct this witness to answer the specific question asked and not to ramble on.

---

6. Closing Loopholes

To increase the chances a witness will agree with a question, ask a witness a series of preliminary foundational questions to prompt responsive answers.

Example:

Q: You gave the police a description of the person you saw start the fight, correct?

A: Yes.

Q: The events were *fresh* in your memory?

A: Yes.

Q: The description you gave was *accurate*?

A: Yes.

Q: You wanted to *assist* the police in finding this person?

A: You bet.

Q: You did *not withhold* any information from the police about the description of this person?

A: I did not.

Q: You gave them the *best possible* description you could of that person?

A: Yes.

These preliminary questions lay a foundation requiring the witness to respond because no reasonable person would disagree with the resulting conclusion.

7. *Avoid Asking One Question Too Many*

Questions should be designed to produce necessary information. When that information is obtained, the attorney should stop asking questions. Asking too many questions may hurt the case because the witness is given another opportunity to explain an answer. Often, a point can be made in closing argument without having the witness answer a question regarding that point.

Example:

Q: After the fight, you gave a description of the person who started the fight to the police?

A: Yes, I did.

Q: You told the police that person was about 5′10″?

A: Yes.

Q: Had brown eyes?

A: Yes.

Q: Black hair?

A: Yes.

Q: Was of medium build?

A: Yes.

Q: Now that description fits many people who live in this community, doesn't it, Mr. Gleason?

A: I will never forget the face of your client who started that fight.

The last question is an example of one question too many. The attorney can make that point in closing argument without trying to get the witness to agree.

8. Avoid Explanations

Questions that permit a narrative response, or that ask "how" or "why," invite disaster in a cross-examination. A witness should not be given an opportunity to explain something that diminishes the point made on cross-examination. The opposing attorney may ask questions on redirect examination, but the cross-examiner should not ask questions that prompt explanatory responses.

Example:

Do not ask:

Q: So tell us *why* you say my client did it?

A: I've never seen anybody commit such a brutal act. I'll never forget that man as long as I live.

---

9. Anticipate the Unexpected

You may think witnesses will agree with your leading questions, but you need to be prepared in case they do not. If you have a prior statement they made, you can use that to refresh their recollection or impeach them. See Section 9.4. If you do not have anything to impeach them with, then you need to prepare for their lack of agreement with you.

There are some things you can do. First, prepare alternative questions, so you won't be stuck having to ask these questions spontaneously. If you expect a yes answer, presume they will say no and prepare questions to ask them if they disagree. If you expect a yes or no answer, presume they will say "I don't remember" and prepare questions for this possibility. This way, you have an effective cross-examination prepared for whatever they say. This can be a time consuming process, but it's easier if you are naturally paranoid. Second, focus on asking questions about concepts and not words. If they will not agree with your choice of words, change the words and get them to agree with your concept. See Section 9.3(C).

Whatever, you do, don't begin arguing with them or saying something like: "Do you expect us to believe. . . . " Those statement questions are argumentative and usually ineffective.

E. Emphasize Points

1. Expand a Point

It may be more effective in making a point during cross-examination to ask a few questions instead of just one question on a topic. You may want to do this with especially important facts. These additional questions may emphasize the point and may prevent the fact finder from missing a point because they missed the one question asked on that point.

Example:

Avoid asking:

Q: You had three drinks at the bar that evening?

Rather ask:

Q: You arrived at the bar at approximately 6 p.m.?

A: Yes.

Q: You ordered one martini?

A: Yes.

Q: And you drank that martini?

A: Yes.

Q: You ordered a second martini?

A: Yes.

Q: You drank the second martini?

A: Yes.

Q: Then you had a glass of wine?

A: Yes.

Q: You say you left the bar at approximately 7 p.m.?

A: Approximately.

Q: You had two martinis and one glass of wine during the one hour you were at the bar, Ms. Temperance?

A: Yes.

---

2.   *Save Point for Summation*

An effective cross-examination helps the fact finder remember and understand the point made during cross-examination. Therefore, questions should be designed so that at the end of a series of questions the fact finder understands the point being made. Sometimes, it is necessary or more effective to ask questions with points that may not be obvious or clear. The reasons for asking these questions can be fully explained in final argument.

Example:

Q: Officer Krupkie, you consider yourself a good police officer?

A: Yes.

Q: You take pride in your work?

A: Yes.

Q: You have been a police officer for ten years?

A: Yes.

Q: You graduated from the Police Academy?

A: Yes.

Q: You regularly attend police training programs?

A: Yes.

Q: You hope someday to become a captain?

A: That would be my hope.

Q: You were the detective in charge of the investigation in this case?

A: Yes.

Q: You spent many hours conducting that investigation?

A: Yes.

Q: You spent several weeks involved in that investigation?

A: Yes.

Q: You developed a profile of the person who you believe committed this crime?

A: Yes.

Q: It is fair to say that you had a feeling about the person who committed this crime?

A: That's just good police work.

Q: After further investigation, you selected two individuals who you thought may have committed this crime?

A: We initially narrowed our investigation to two.

Q: Yes. And you further investigated this first person on your list of suspects?

A: Yes.

Q: You later decided that this first person did not commit the crime?

A: That's right.

Q: You then investigated the second person on your list?

A: We decided to continue our investigation.

Q: And after still further investigation, you decided the second person could not have committed the crime?

A: Yes, that's correct.

Q: And then you began an investigation of Mr. Shrek, the defendant in this case?

A: Yes.

During summation defense counsel can argue how uncertain the police were regarding their suspicions about the defendant, how long it took to conduct their unsuccessful investigations, and how reluctant the police may have been to re-investigate the case if they had not arrested the defendant.

F. Ask Safe Questions

1. Repeat Supportive Direct Examination

The general rule is that direct examination testimony should not be repeated on discrediting cross-examination because the repetition of the direct will only emphasize the opponent's case. However, repetition of direct examination testimony will be effective if that part of the direct is supportive of the cross-examiner's case. Leading questions usually are the most effective way of presenting supportive evidence. Open ended questions may be effective only if the response is helpful, witness control is not a problem, and the answer will be short.

Example:

Q: Humpty Dumpty, you approached the wall on your own?

A: Yes.

Q: You then decided to sit on top of the wall?

A: Yes.

Q: You were able to climb the wall on your own?

A: Yes.

Q: You sat on the top of the wall, correct?

A: Yes.

Q: Then you fell off the wall?

A: Yes.

Q: There was no one around when you fell off the wall?

A: That's right.

Q: And that was a great fall?

A: Sure.

Q: Some people came immediately to help you?

A: Yes.

Q: All the King's men came?

A: There were a lot of them.

Q: And all their horses?

A: Apparently.

---

2. Ask "Neutral" Cross–Examination Questions

With some witnesses it is not necessary to cross-examine them after direct examination to obtain supportive information or to discredit them. Cross-examination, however, may be useful to spend some time with them so that the fact finder will not retain too favorable an impression of their testimony. With other witnesses problems may arise during cross-examination, possibly placing the cross-examiner in an awkward situation. The examiner may need some "safe" questions to get back on track. In these and other situations, the following cross-examination questions are appropriate and may fill the need for safe cross-examination inquiry.

Example *(Volunteer witness):*

Q: Ms. Wong, you were asked to be a witness in this case by the attorney for the plaintiff, correct?

A: Yes.

Q: You were not served with a subpoena ordering you to come to court to testify, were you?

A: No.

Q: You are voluntarily testifying for the plaintiff?

A: I suppose so.

Example *(Familiarity with evidence):*

Q: You have talked with the attorney for the plaintiff about this case, correct Mr. Olijuwon?

A: Yes.

Q: Have you discussed the testimony that you were going to give in this case?

A: Yes.

Q: You also previously talked to the plaintiff?

A: Yes.

Q: And you discussed with the plaintiff what happened in this incident?

A: Yes.

Q: And you talked with other witnesses in this case about this incident?

A: I may have.

Q: Before coming into court to testify today, you had some idea of what the plaintiff was going to say, didn't you?

A: Yes.

Q: And you also had some idea of what some of the other witnesses were going to say?

A: Yes.

Example *(Reviewed documents):*

Q: You were not present in court when the plaintiff testified, were you, Mr. Ahmed?

A: No.

Q: You had a chance to read the deposition of the plaintiff which was taken before this trial, didn't you?

A: I looked at it.

Q: And you had a chance to look at some written statements the attorney for the plaintiff showed you?

A: I did.

Q: And those statements contained the stories of some of the witnesses in this case?

A: I believe so.

Example *(Favorable testimony)*:

Q: You pretty much understood why the plaintiff had brought this lawsuit, Ms. Beyonce?

A: Yes.

Q: You knew that your testimony would help the plaintiff's case?

A: I suppose so.

Q: In fact, you understood that the plaintiff expected you to testify favorably?

A: Well, I assume that's why they asked me to come.

Q: And your testimony is helpful to the plaintiff?

A: I suppose so.

These questions and answers may not establish information useful for cross-examination purposes, compared to the other approaches and techniques explained in this chapter. However, they may be useful in situations where safe, neutral or indirect questions need to be asked. Arguments may be made, based on answers to the questions, that the witness appears biased, over-prepared by the other attorney, or has no real knowledge of the facts.

G. Design Questions for Specific Witnesses

1. Witnesses with Special Considerations

Certain witnesses require special consideration in both the formulation and delivery of questions. These witnesses include children, experienced witnesses, experts, and witnesses with communication problems. Special efforts should be made to employ tactics to deal effectively with problems these witnesses may create. Simple words, a softer or more assertive approach, technical mastery, a different location for questioning, are some tactics that may be useful.

2. Cross–Examining the Evasive Witness

Some witnesses may give evasive answers to cross-examination questions even though the questions are phrased as effectively as possible. They may display selective memory, forgetting information which hurts them and only remembering information which helps them. Rambling witnesses provide nonresponsive answers, defeating even the best efforts to control their responses. Occasionally, witnesses may take on an adversarial demeanor or hostile attitude, even though the cross-examiner is tactful and polite. Still other witnesses may repeatedly answer by saying "I am not sure," "I can't remember," "I don't recall," "Maybe," or "I don't know," even though the question is simple and direct. Efforts to control or to correct the behavior of these evasive witnesses may only result in more frustration.

These evasive witnesses, if allowed to continue, usually destroy their own credibility. Fact finders perceive these witnesses to be unreasonably evasive and disbelieve their story. One way to cross-examine them is to continue to ask them questions and permit them to continue to be evasive. The more a witness testifies in an unreasonable manner, the more likely it is that their testimony will be ignored.

The negative impact created by these evasive witnesses may extend beyond their story and adversely affect other parts of the opponent's case. Further, during summation, the cross-examiner can compare the selective memory of the witness during cross with the good memory on direct examination. However, if the cross-examiner needs specific answers, the questions can be narrowed in scope until the witness gives an answer. Then the cross-examiner can gradually increase the scope to continue to get responsive answers.

3. Cross–Examining Reputation Witnesses

Because the character of a party or witness is usually not an issue, few cases involve the examination of reputation witnesses. The credibility of each witness who testifies can be attacked by the testimony of another who states that the witness' reputation for telling the truth is poor. As a practical matter, this occurs infrequently because most people have decent reputations for telling the truth. Also, it is difficult to locate a person who can convincingly testify to a witness' propensity for being untruthful. Consequently, the opportunities to cross-examine reputation witnesses do not arise often.

When such opportunities arise, reputation witnesses can be cross-examined like any other witness. They may also be cross-examined as to specific instances of misconduct which contradict the character trait in issue. Cross-examination questions can establish bad acts, prior misconduct, convictions, and other instances of misconduct which contradict the reputation established on direct examination. Some cross-examination techniques are:

- If the reputation witness testifies that the witness has a good reputation in the community, the question, "Have you heard . . . " of specific instances of misconduct can be asked.

- If the reputation witness testifies that in the witness' opinion the reputation of the character trait is good, the question, "Do you know . . . " of specific instances of misconduct can be asked.

- Reputation witnesses can also be effectively cross-examined by questions which establish their lack of personal knowledge about the events of the lawsuit:

"You were not home when the beating occurred?"

"You did not see the defendant with Ms. Liwynske?"

Another line of questioning may establish the limited knowledge of the reputation witness and the narrow basis of the testimony:

"Thousands of people live in Hakuna Matata's community? You have only talked to a few of them about the defendant's reputation for truth?"

Or

"You only spend a limited amount of time with the defendant in politics? You are unaware of how the defendant treats his family at home?"

Some jurisdictions restrict the type of questions that may be asked on the cross-examination of a reputation witness. All jurisdictions require that the cross-examiner have a good faith basis and available proof to establish the prior misconduct.

§ 9.4 DISCREDITING CROSS–EXAMINATION

This section describes and provides examples of cross-examination techniques which discredit evidence and impeach witnesses. Section A explains how to attack a story that is implausible, improbable, or impossible. Section B describes how to establish inconsistencies between witnesses. Section C explains impeachment strategies. Section D describes common areas of impeachment. Some of these techniques overlap and may be combined when implemented.

A. *Implausibility, Improbability, Impossibility*

Cross-examination can establish that the story told by a witness ought not to be believed because it is implausible, improbable, or impossible.

1. *Implausible*

The story may be implausible because it does not make sense or reflect common life experiences. For example, a witness may testify that four years before the trial, while repairing floor tile in the hallway outside the office of the CEO of M & M Company, he recalled over-hearing the CEO say these exact words: "I just placed an order for 750 units at a price of $138,000, F.O.B. Los Angeles, and they agreed to send a letter of credit before sending the bill of lading and to pay for transit loss insurance." The cross-examination of that witness may include repeating the highlights of the direct examination testimony to demon-strate the implausible character of the story. The attorney may also argue in summation that the recollection of such detail is too implausible to be believed.

2. Improbable

A witness' version of a story, or part of a story, may be improbable. It may be unlikely the story could have occurred the way the witness describes. The more unlikely the story, the more easily a showing of improbability may be made. For example, a witness may testify that she was no more than 100 feet away from a building while peddling her bicycle at a speed of 15 miles per hour toward the building, when she saw the black smoke and heard the explosion. The cross-examination may consist of her repeating her direct examination testimony; and the attorney may place a mark on a diagram showing her position in the alley at the time of the explosion. During summation, the attorney can use a mathematical formula for the number of feet per second a bicycle travels at 15 miles per hour to show that either she was at least 300 feet away or that she was peddling over 30 miles per hour, which, while possible, is unlikely.

3. Impossible

Some witnesses may sincerely tell an impossible story. While they may honestly believe what they perceived and remember, they are still wrong. For example, a witness may testify that, while parked behind the crosswalk at the intersection of Oak and Elm, he saw the defendant's motorcycle traveling at a high rate of speed. The cross-examination may consist of the witness repeating the testimony. During the defendant's case, the cross-examiner may then call an investigator to introduce photographs taken through the car window from the spot where the witness said he was stopped showing a brick building blocking the witness' view.

B. Establishing Inconsistencies Between Witnesses

A witness' story may be inherently correct and complete, but may contradict the story told by another adverse witness. Cross-examination can establish these inconsistencies. For example, Police Officer Hernan-dez testifies that Sergeant Schultz was holding the shotgun in her right hand with the barrel pointed toward the ground. The defense cross-examiner may have Officer Hernandez repeat part of this testimony to highlight it for the fact finder. Officer Giribaldi subsequently testifies for the defense that Sergeant Schultz held the shotgun in both hands with the barrel pointed at the deceased. The defense can then argue these material inconsistencies during summation and point out why a particular witness (Officer Giribaldi) ought to be believed. It is usually ineffective, and often argumentative, for the cross-examiner to question Officer Hernandez directly as to why his testimony contradicts the testimony of Officer Giribaldi.

It is also improper to ask one witness to comment on the credibility of another witness or to ask whether a witness believes another. It is permissible to ask a witness if that witness agrees or disagrees with a story told by another witness. For example, asking: "Do you believe Officer Hernandez is telling the truth?" is improper. However, in most jurisdictions, one may properly ask: "Officer Hernandez testified that Sergeant Schultz held the shotgun in her right hand. Do you disagree with his statement?"

C. Impeachment Strategies

Impeachment is a tactic designed to reduce the credibility of the witness, the credibility of a story, or the credibility of another witness. Any witness may be impeached. Any declarant of a hearsay statement who does not appear as a witness may also be impeached. Federal Rule of Evidence 806 and similar state rules permit the impeachment of the credibility of a hearsay declarant to the same extent that a live witness can be impeached.

1. Using Material and Significant Issues to Impeach

Effective impeachment covers material and significant issues. If an issue is collateral — immaterial or insignificant — the impeachment is usually ineffective or disallowed. Whether impeachment evidence is collateral depends upon its impact on the issues in the case and on the credibility of the witness. Impeachment evidence ought to be introduced if the evidence relates to an issue, reduces the credibility of a witness or is otherwise important.

Impeachment is most effective when it relates to significant facts or opinions adversely affecting the credibility of the witness or story. A "reasonableness" test is the standard that ought to be used to determine the value of impeachment material. If it is reasonable that the testimony of a witness might be affected by a certain factor, or if the witness' testimony is unreasonable because the witness has testified differently on separate occasions, then the impeachment is reasonable and should be conducted.

The following examples illustrate the reasonableness factor:

- If a witness is a good friend of a party, it is reasonable that the witness may be biased in favor of that party. If a witness is merely an acquaintance of a party, that fact may not reasonably establish bias.

- In an attempt to establish bias on the part of the witness in favor of a party, a cross-examiner may succeed by showing that the witness is a current, satisfied employee of the party for whom the witness is testifying. On the other hand, it would be ineffective for the cross-examiner to attempt to establish bias if the witness had worked for the employer for one month ten years ago and had no contact with the employer since that time.

● Witnesses may be uncertain about an exact day of the week. For example, a witness may testify that the day of an event was a Tuesday when in fact it was a Wednesday. But, if a witness testifies at a deposition she was "pretty sure" it was the defendant who was driving the car, and then testifies at trial she "is certain" the defendant was driving a car, such a significant change in her opinion will make impeachment worthwhile.

● A witness to a crime may testify that she was standing at a "book rack" when she saw the defendant. Investigation reveals the rack she stood by was a magazine rack and not a book rack. An attempt to impeach the credibility of the witness by showing the rack was for magazines and not books may be so insignificant that it is worthless.

Impeachment efforts regarding marginal issues usually backfire because the fact finder may conclude that if the marginal issue is the best defense the cross-examiner has, the defense must be very weak. Cases involving highly significant impeachment material that destroys the credibility of a key witness usually will be settled. At the other extreme, many witnesses may have made prior statements that contain minor inaccuracies when compared with evidence. These inaccuracies may not be significant or worth the effort to impeach the witness.

2. Proving Impeachment Through Extrinsic Evidence

A witness may occasionally deny the impeaching evidence. For example, a witness may testify that she is not an employee of defendant corporation or a witness may deny having a felony criminal record. The cross-examiner is usually able to introduce extrinsic (meaning from a source other than the witness) evidence to establish the impeaching fact. For example, the cross-examiner may call the personnel director of defendant corporation to testify that the witness is an employee, or the cross-examiner may introduce a certified copy of the criminal conviction and ask the court to take judicial notice of that document.

Extrinsic evidence may not be admissible if the impeaching issue is collateral. An issue is collateral if there is no direct connection between the impeaching fact and the relevant issue in the case. For example, a witness may testify on direct examination that she saw a plate glass window crack as she was drinking her vanilla shake. The cross-examiner asks her whether, in fact, the shake was chocolate, not vanilla, and she denies that it was chocolate. The cross-examiner will not be able to call the fountain clerk to testify as to the flavor of the shake because the type of shake is only collateral and not related to any material issue.

However, if the same witness testifies on direct examination that she saw the plate glass window crack when she was sitting in a booth, the cross-examiner may ask her whether she was in fact sitting at the soda fountain. If the witness denies sitting at the soda fountain, the cross-examiner may call the fountain clerk as a witness to testify that the witness was sitting at the soda fountain with her back to the plate glass window, preventing her from seeing out. This issue is non-collateral because it directly relates to the ability of the witness to see and perceive.

3.   *Responding to Impeachment Evidence by the Direct Examiner*

The cross-examiner must consider the tactics available to the direct examiner who must deal with impeachment. The direct examiner has a number of options when facing impeachment evidence.

First, the direct examiner can object to the attempted impeachment. The area of impeachment may be immaterial or insignificant and an improper topic for impeachment. Second, the direct examiner may request the judge or arbitrator to allow related statements explaining the impeachment to be introduced immediately in an effort to reduce the impact of the impeachment. Jurisdictions commonly have a rule permitting the introduction of statements related to the area of impeachment contemporaneously with the introduction of the impeaching statement. See, e.g., Fed.R.Evid. 106. The rationale for this rule is to permit statements to be placed in proper and complete context.

For example, a witness may testify during a deposition: "The car was traveling around 30 miles per hour. But it may have been going slower." On direct examination, the witness testifies that the car was traveling "around 20 miles an hour." On cross-examination, the cross-examiner introduces the prior statement that the car was traveling "around 30 miles per hour" to impeach the witness. The direct examiner can ask that the prior statement — "But it may have been going slower" — be introduced at the same time during cross-examination to present the complete context of the statement. This request should be granted, and the statement can be read from the deposition transcript to the fact finder by the direct or cross-examiner.

Third, the direct examiner can explain the impeaching evidence during the direct examination. It is less harmful if the witness voluntarily explains a mistake or problem on direct examination. For example, it is a preferred practice for a witness who made a prior inconsistent statement to admit and explain the mistake during direct examination. Fourth, the direct examiner can have the witness explain the impeaching evidence during redirect examination. This may be necessary, even if the witness first explains it on direct examination, depending upon how damaging the information is and how it was elicited during cross-examination. For example, if a witness during direct examination testified there were three firefighters at the scene, and at cross-examination admits there were only two, a redirect examination question would be: "Why did you say there were only two firefighters at the scene during cross-examination?"

Fifth, the direct examiner may rehabilitate an impeached witness with a prior consistent statement, if it rebuts a charge of fabrication or improper motive or statement. See, e.g., Fed.R.Evid. 801(d)(1)(B). If there is a written prior consistent statement, the statement can be introduced as an exhibit. If the prior consistent statement was not written but made to another person, that individual may be called to testify to the prior consistent statement. Sixth, in a jury trial the direct examiner may request that the judge give the jury an instruction limiting the jury's consideration of the impeaching evidence to its effect on the credibility of the witness and not as substantive proof of the evidence. See Section 4.5(E).

D.   Common Areas of Impeachment

There are eight established areas of impeachment:

- Interest, Bias or Prejudice,
- Competency Deficiencies,
- Inadequate Observation/Lack of Perception,
- Poor Recollection (Lack of Memory),
- Inconsistent Conduct,
- Criminal Records,
- Specific Instances of Untruthfulness, and
- Prior Inconsistent Statements/Omissions.

1.   Interest, Bias or Prejudice Impeachment

Witnesses may have an interest in a case that motivates them to testify in a certain way. This interest might be financial gain if the case is resolved favorably, or an emotional reason, such as pride or revenge, that can be satisfied through successful litigation. Establishing these factors on cross-examination can demonstrate the underlying motivation behind a witness' testimony and may substantially reduce the credibility of that witness' testimony.

Bias and prejudice are factors which prevent a witness from being impartial. A witness may have a bias in favor of, or a prejudice against, a party or a case. Bias or prejudice can result from a variety of causes. The basis for the bias or prejudice is usually a relationship the witness has with a party or an interest the witness has in the case. The most common causes stem from family or personal relationships, employment situations, and life experiences. Establishing these factors during cross-examination reveals the underlying influences which make impartiality difficult or impossible for a witness.

If a witness denies the existence of an interest or a relationship, extrinsic evidence of the fact can be established. The cross-examiner can introduce such a fact through a witness or a document authenticated by a witness.

Example (*Prejudice*):

Q: Mr. Bluto, you do not consider Popeye a friend, do you?

A: He is not a friend.

Q: You have argued with him over the years?

A: Yes.

Q: You have had many fights with him?

A: Yes.

Q: Popeye has taken Olive Oyl, the woman you love, away from you?

A: He's trying.

Q: That makes you angry?

A: Yes.

Q: It is fair to say, Mr. Bluto, that you hate Popeye?

A: Without a doubt.

Example (*Bias and interest*):

In a personal injury case, the father of the plaintiff was a passenger in the car which the son was driving at the time of the accident. The father was not injured.

Q: You were the passenger in your son's car at the time of the accident. Correct Mr. McMurray?

A: Yes.

Q: Your son lived with you at that time?

A: Yes.

Q: And he lives with you today?

A: Yes.

Q: You have a close relationship with your son?

A: Yes.

Q: You talk to him about many things?

A: Yes.

Q: And you talked to him about this accident?

A: A few times.

Q: Your son has told you that he hopes to receive money in this case?

A: Yes.

Q: You and he were driving back to the university?

A: Yes.

Q: That is a private college?

A: Yes.

Q: Your son pays for part of his tuition at the college?

A: Yes.

Q: And you pay for the balance of the tuition?

A: Yes.

Q: And your son pays for all his expenses?

A: For most of them.

Q: The tuition and the expenses are quite high?

A: It is expensive.

---

2. Impeachment Based on Competency Deficiencies

Section 7.2(A) described the four competency requirements for a witness: oath, perception, recollection, and communication. Cross-examination may establish that a competent witness has deficiencies which render testimony of the witness less credible. The competency requirements of perception and recollection are two areas most frequently attacked on cross-examination.

The two other requirements of oath and communication are not usually areas for cross-examination inquiry. If a witness is unable or has difficulty taking an oath or affirmation, the opposing attorney will argue that the witness is incompetent. After the judge or arbitrator makes a determination that a witness has properly taken an oath or affirmation, that requirement will usually not be an effective area to be probed on cross-examination. Further, Federal Rule Evidence 610 explicitly prohibits evidence of a witness' beliefs or opinions on religion to be introduced for the purpose of reducing or enhancing the credibility of that witness.

Occasionally, a child witness or another witness who has difficulty discerning the truth may be asked cross-examination questions to establish an inadequate or inappropriate understanding of the oath or affirmation. Because of the delicate nature of the issue and the vulnerable status of the witness, cross-examination on the matter of oath or affirmation may cause the fact finder to empathize with the witness and to perceive the cross-examiner negatively. Effectively cross-examining a witness on the abstract notions of truth is difficult. Cross-examination can be effective when a record exists showing the witness has lied under oath or affirmation previously, or has told a story different from that told on direct examination. Section 9.4(D)(7) illustrates these cross-examination areas.

Communication problems that witnesses have will ordinarily not be effective areas for cross-examination. If a witness cannot communicate, an interpreter will be made available by the examining attorney or court to translate the testimony in an understandable fashion. See Section 3.6(D). If a witness has difficulty communicating because of a disability, cross-examination inquiries may make the fact finder more sympathetic toward this vulnerable witness rendering the cross-examination ineffective. If a witness has difficulty because of nervousness or some other reason, that factor may be self-evident and may not require any cross-examination questions.

3. *Inadequate Observation/Lack of Perception Impeachment*

To reduce their credibility, the ability of witnesses to observe an event or to perceive a situation may be challenged on cross-examination. Most witnesses do not observe or perceive everything, and the inadequacies of observations and the lack of perception may be established on cross-examination. Common causes for inadequate observation and lack of perception are:

- The witness was not expecting the event,
- The witness was distracted,
- The event happened quickly,
- The situation was unusual,
- The event scared the witness,
- The situation surprised the witness,
- The witness was doing something else during the event,
- The witness' perception based on sight, taste, hearing, smell, or touch was adversely influenced by other factors, and
- Details of the event or situation were not previously described by the witness.

If the witness denies the impeachment questions asked to establish a material fact, the cross-examiner can introduce extrinsic evidence of this fact through other evidence.

Example (*Car driver*):

Q: Professor Knapp, you were driving east on Summit?

A: Yes.

Q: You were on your way to school?

A: Yes.

Q: You approached the intersection of Summit and Victoria around noon?

A: Yes.

Q: Your class begins at noon?

A: Yes. When I get there.

Q: You were going to be late for that class?

A: Sadly, yes.

Q: You were anxious to get to school?

A: Yes.

Q: You were in a hurry?

A: A bit. But I wasn't speeding.

Q: You spend a fair amount of time thinking about your classes?

A: Yes.

Q: Sometimes you think about your classes when you're at home?

A: Yes.

Q: And sometimes when you are driving your car?

A: Yes. But I pay attention.

Q: Your class was on your mind as you drove east this day on Summit Street?

A: Yes, I suppose.

Q: As you approached the intersection of Summit and Victoria, the stop and go traffic light turned red?

A: Yes.

Q: You noticed there was a crossing guard standing on the sidewalk to your right?

A: Yes, she was on the southwest corner.

Q: While you were waiting at the intersection, you would from time to time glance up at the light to see if had changed?

A: Yes.

Q: And you looked around to see if there were any kids in the intersection crossing the street?

A: Yes.

Q: I believe you said on direct examination you saw two students to your right talking to the crossing guard?

A: Yes.

Q: Your radio was on in your car at this time?

A: I listen to public radio.

Q: It was noon time and the news was on the radio?

A: Yes.

Q: Cars were driving north and south through the intersection?

A: Yes, I saw some cars drive by and Dean Easley's limo.

Q: You were not expecting to see an accident at that time, were you?

A: No.

Q: That surprised you?

A: Yes.

Q: It is fair to say when you first heard the collision you naturally got a little frightened?

A: I was startled.

Q: You had a passenger in your car that day?

A: Yes.

Q: You were driving to school with another professor, Professor Juergens?

A: Yes.

Example *(Car passenger):*

Q: You were the passenger in the car with Professor Knapp, correct?

A: Yes.

Q: You both were on your way to school?

A: Yes.

Q: During the drive you talked with Professor Knapp?

A: Yes.

Q: He told you he was in a hurry because he was late for class?

A: He mentioned he was late.

Q: While the car was stopped at the intersection, Professor Knapp made some remark about the crossing guard?

A: Yes.

Q: He said he wished he were a crossing guard instead of a law professor?

A: Yes.

Q: And you said "There is not much difference"?

A: As a joke, obviously.

Q: After the accident, both of you drove one block to the school?

A: Yes.

Q: You don't recall Professor Knapp saying anything at all to you about the accident, do you?

A: No, I don't recall.

Q: You do recall that he said after the accident he was going to be late for class?

A: He said that, and he was sad.

4. Impeachment Based on Poor Recollection (Lack of Memory)

Most witnesses will not remember everything they observed or perceived. Some witnesses might not actually recall what they say they observed or perceived. Other witnesses may have had their recollection influenced by what they learned after an event. Cross-examination can reveal reasons why the witness' memory is lacking or unduly influenced. If the witness denies the underlying fact showing poor or absent memory, the cross-examiner can introduce a non-collateral fact through extrinsic evidence. Common factors that diminish the recollection of a witness include:

- The passage of time,
- The absence of any written record,
- Discussing the matter with others,
- Being involved in similar situations,
- Inability to distinguish this event from others, and
- Matters that adversely affect the memory of the witness.

Example (*Car driver*):

Q: After the accident, you immediately drove on to the law school?

A: Yes.

Q: You did not wait at the accident scene?

A: No.

Q: You did not give your name or address to anyone?

A: No.

Q: You did not tell anyone at that time what you saw?

A: No.

Q: Back at the law school, you discussed the accident with Professor Juergens, the passenger in your car?

A: Yes.

Q: You discussed what you saw?

A: We talked about it.

Q: You taught your two-hour class that day?

A: Yes.

Q: You stayed in your law school office and wrote some memos?

A: Yes.

Q: You bought some — I won't mention what — from eBay on the Internet.

A: For my collection.

Q: You did not talk about this accident with anyone else while you were at the law school?

A: No.

Q: After school, you went home for dinner?

A: Yes.

Q: You recall you told your wife, Ms. Jesson, and your children — Chris, Nathan, and John — that you saw an accident that day?

A: I mentioned it at dinner.

Q: You do not recall the details of what you told them, do you?

A: No.

Q: About a week later you talked to an investigator about this accident?

A: Yes.

Q: During that week after the accident you don't recall whether you talked to anyone else about the accident, do you?

A: No.

Q: Some time later you talked with an investigator, a Brad Cousins, and received an accident report form, didn't you?

A: Yes.

Q: That was a blank form with instructions to be completed?

A: I believe so.

Q: You never filled out that form, did you?

A: No.

Q: You never made any written notes about the accident, did you?

A: No, they're not a part of my memoirs.

Example (*Police officer*):

Q: Officer Marmaduke, you mentioned on direct that you thought the street lights at the intersection were not working at the time of the accident, correct?

A: Yes.

Q: This event took place approximately two years ago?

A: Yes.

Q: You arrived shortly after the victim had been injured?

A: Yes.

Q: You immediately began an investigation, correct?

A: Yes.

Q: As part of that investigation you talked with witnesses at the scene?

A: Yes.

Q: During an average week would you say you talked to over a hundred different people?

A: It is difficult to say, but that's possible.

Q: You may talk to more than a hundred different people during your week?

A: Some weeks more, some weeks less.

Q: When you conduct an investigation and talk with a witness you complete a report, correct?

A: Yes.

Q: You cannot possibly remember all the details these witnesses tell you?

A: That's true.

Q: You also have investigated many accidents over these past two years?

A: Yes that's true.

Q: It is impossible to remember all the details that you yourself see?

A: That's true.

Q: That's why you need reports?

A: Yes.

Q: These reports need to be accurate?

A: Yes.

Q: And complete?

A: Yes.

Q: The reports need detailed information?

A: Yes.

Q: If the reports don't have the details, an accident can be confused with another?

A: Yes, that can happen.

Q: You complete a report to make a record of the investigation?

A: Yes.

Q: That written report can help refresh your memory about the details of an investigation?

A: Yes.

Q: The investigation report you completed in this case included the important information the witnesses told you?

A: Yes.

Q: It also had all the important details that you saw?

A: Yes.

Q: There is no mention anywhere in your report that the streetlights were not working, correct?

A: There is no mention.

Example (*Salesperson*):

Plaintiff has sued defendant for breach of an express warranty made during a sale. The salesperson has testified under direct examination that he does not recall stating that the car had no major mechanical problems and denies that the plaintiff consumer asked whether the car had any major mechanical problems.

Q: You have been a salesperson with Courtesy Car Company for three years, Mr. Loman?

A: Yes.

Q: Would you say that you have sold three or four cars a week on the average over the three years?

A: That would be a fair average.

Q: You, of course, talked with each of these customers?

A: Of course.

Q: Some of these customers leave and come back to the car dealer a number of times before deciding to buy a car?

A: Yes.

Q: In addition to all these customers, you also talk with other potential customers who decide not to buy a car?

A: Yes.

Q: Would you say that you talk to another 20 or 30 potential customers during an average week?

A: That is more difficult to estimate. Some weeks more, some weeks fewer.

Q: With each one of these customers and potential customers you talk about the features of the cars they are interested in?

A: Yes.

Q: You talk about the exterior of cars?

A: Yes.

Q: You talk about the interior of cars?

A: Often.

Q: You talk about the engines?

A: Sure.

Q: You talk about gas mileage?

A: Frequently.

Q: You talk about many features of the various cars the customers look at?

A: Yes.

Q: The plaintiff, Betty Buckley, bought a used car from you two years ago?

A: Yes.

Q: When you first met her on the sales lot she was like any other customer to you, correct?

A: Yes.

Q: And when she returned to buy the car, she was also like any other customer?

A: Yes.

Q: Most customers ask you questions about the cars they are interested in?

A: Yes.

Q: And Ms. Buckley asked you some questions about the car she purchased?

A: I assume so.

Q: You cannot remember all the individual questions that all your individual customers ask you?

A: That's not possible.

Q: Customers often have questions based on what they want in a particular car?

A: Yes.

Q: You don't recall whether Ms. Buckley asked asked about a satellite radio that gets Broadway musicals, do you?

A: No, I don't.

Q: As a salesperson it's important for you to meet the needs of your customers?

A: Well, yes.

Q: You cannot anticipate all questions, can you?

A: No.

Q: But you try your best to satisfy your customers?

A: Yes.

5. *Inconsistent Conduct Impeachment*

Testimony of a witness may be discredited because the conduct of the witness may be inconsistent with the witness' direct examination. If the witness denies the inconsistent behavior, the cross-examiner can introduce extrinsic evidence of non-collateral conduct. Cross-examination can disclose that the actions of the witness contradict the testimony.

Example:

In a personal injury case, the plaintiff Joyce Simmons has testified regarding the extent of injuries to her lower back, including pain and suffering.

Q: Ms. Simmons, immediately after the accident you got out of your car?

A: Yes.

Q: You walked over to the defendant's car?

A: Yes.

Q: You then walked over to a gas station?

A: Yes.

Q: That was about a hundred yards from the accident scene?

A: I would guess so.

Q: You asked the gas station attendant to call the police?

A: Yes.

Q: You did not ask for an ambulance or for a doctor?

A: Not at that time.

Q: You then walked back to the accident scene?

A: Yes.

Q: You stood around and waited for the police?

A: Yes.

Q: The police arrived about fifteen minutes later?

A: Yes.

Q: You talked with the police?

A: Yes.

Q: You did not ask for an ambulance or a doctor at that time, did you?

A: No.

Q: A tow truck arrived?

A: Yes.

Q: You stood around and watched the tow truck tow your car away?

A: Yes.

Q: About an hour after the accident, the police drove you home?

A: Yes.

Q: You didn't ask to go to a hospital?

A: No.

Q: When you arrived home, you told your family about the accident?

A: Yes.

Q: You then ate dinner?

A: Yes.

Q: After dinner you and your husband went to a movie?

A: To relax.

Q: After the movie you went home and went to bed?

A: Yes.

Q: The next morning you got up?

A: Yes.

Q: You ate breakfast?

A: Yes.

Q: You went to work at the grocery store?

A: Yes.

Q: You did not go to see a doctor then?

A: No.

Q: You talked with some of your friends at work about the accident?

A: Yes.

Q: You worked a full day that day?

A: Yes.

Q: Later that day you decided to telephone your doctor?

A: Yes.

Q: You made an appointment to see your doctor three days later?

A: Yes.

6. Impeachment by Criminal Record

A witness may be impeached by introducing a prior criminal conviction of that witness. Federal Rule of Evidence 609 and similar state rules determine the type of criminal convictions that may be used to impeach and the discretion the judge or arbitrator has to deny the admission of such impeachment evidence. In general, convictions for a crime of fraud, dishonesty, false statements, or felony convictions (convictions of crime punishable by a term in excess of one year) may be used if the conviction or the release from confinement occurred within ten years from the date of the present trial. Convictions may be inadmissible if their unfairly prejudicial impact substantially outweighs their probative value. The fact a witness has been arrested or convicted of misdemeanors or juvenile offenses is usually inadmissible as a basis for impeachment.

Most jurisdictions allow all witnesses to be impeached through cross-examination questions revealing criminal convictions, but some jurisdictions permit only party witnesses to be impeached by prior convictions. Questions may be asked of the witness that reveal the crime involved, type of conviction, date and location of the conviction, and the sentence imposed. Some jurisdictions do not allow cross-examination of criminal defendants in regard to prior convictions and only permit impeachment to be proven by the introduction of a certified record of the criminal conviction.

Cross-examination questions cannot usually delve into the facts or details of the crime to avoid unfair prejudice. Ordinarily, direct or redirect examination questions may be asked of the witness to explain the circumstances of the conviction or crime to reduce the impact of the conviction and reduce the negative impact on the credibility of the witness. If the witness denies the conviction, the cross-examiner can introduce extrinsic evidence, commonly a certified copy of the judgment of conviction. Judges and arbitrators typically have reasonable discretion regarding the use of criminal records and information.

7. Impeachment by Specific Instances of Untruthfulness

Evidence relating to the untruthfulness of a witness may be introduced against that witness during the cross-examination of that witness. Federal Rule 608(B) and similar state rules provide a judge or arbitrator with discretion to permit a witness to be cross-examined regarding specific instances of misconduct that relate to the untruthfulness of the witness. The cross-examiner may ask leading questions which show the witness has committed acts establishing an untruthful character.

Example:

Q: Mr. Gandolf, you have lied in other situations in your life, haven't you?

A: I'm not sure what you mean.

Q: About three years ago, you applied for a job with Equilaw, correct?

A: Yes.

Q: You filled out an application form for a job with Equilaw?

A: Yes, I did.

Q: On that application form, you wrote that you had five years experience in human relations, right?

A: So.

Q: Well, you didn't have five years experience in human relations, did you?

A: Not necessarily in that type of job.

Q: What you wrote on the Equilaw application form was untrue?

A: I didn't have that experience.

Q: That statement was a lie, was it not?

A: It was incorrect.

Q: Two years ago you applied for a job with Mission Bay Enterprises, correct?

A: Yes.

Q: You interviewed with the personnel director at Mission Bay Enterprises, correct?

A: I believe so.

Q: You told that personnel director you had previously worked for Equilaw?

A: I may have said that.

Q: Equilaw never hired you?

A: I never worked there.

Q: That statement you made to the Mission Bay personnel director was untrue?

A: Yes.

Q: That statement was a lie?

A: Yes.

Evidence of the untruthful character of the witness may be introduced through opinion and reputation by witnesses called to testify on direct examination, as explained in sections 9.3(G)(3) and 7.10(D). These witnesses may be cross-examined like any other witness, and they may also be asked questions about specific acts of truthfulness by the witness who is being impeached. Further, to contradict the testimony of these impeaching witnesses, other witnesses may testify on direct examination to the reputation for truthfulness of the witness who is being impeached. These witnesses may also be cross-examined like any other witness, and may be asked questions regarding specific instances of untruthfulness by the witness.

These situations infrequently occur. The information needed to establish the untruthful character of a witness is seldom available. Even if the information is available, it may be inadmissible because it is unfairly prejudicial or collateral to the issues of the case. Further, the tactic may backfire, because the fact finder may perceive the attack to be unfair and unrelated to the issues they must decide.

Example:

A witness testifies on direct examination that a party has a reputation for truthfulness.

Q: Did you know the witness lied in the past to employers?

A: No, I didn't know that.

Q: Did you know he had lied to Equilaw when he falsely told them he had five years experience in human relations?

A: No.

Q: Did you know he lied to Mission Bay Enterprises when he told them he had worked for Equilaw?

A: No.

---

8. *Refreshing Recollection of an Adverse Witness*

The cross-examiner may want to establish a fact through an adverse witness by refreshing recollection. There are situations when the cross-examiner wants to prove a fact and will prefer to refresh the witness' recollection rather than impeach the witness. This may occur when the witness is not fabricating information but has made a mistake or cannot remember a portion of an event.

Refreshing recollection can be accomplished by showing the prior statement to the witness. If a witness on cross-examination forgets a fact the cross-examiner wants to establish affirmatively, it will be more effective for the cross-examiner to refresh the recollection of the witness through a prior written statement. The cross-examiner may use a leading question to introduce the answer, but displaying to the fact finder the source of the written prior statement may be more effective.

Example:

Q: On direct examination, you testified that the Forum arbitration clause was signed on November 17?

A: I believe so.

Q: Do you now recall that you signed the arbitration clause on October 17?

A: No, it was November.

Q: I show you the original of the National Arbitration Forum clause. Please look at the bottom of the page.

A: I see it.

Q: You did sign the arbitration agreement on October 17?

A: Apparently.

Q: October was the month you signed?

A: Yes.

E. Impeachment with Prior Inconsistent Statements

The credibility of a witness may be diminished on cross-examination by the use of prior inconsistent statements. To be used on cross-examination, prior statements must be inconsistent or contradictory. The obvious point to be made is that the witness provided testimony on a previous occasion that was different from the direct examination testimony. Effective cross-examination establishes and emphasizes the difference between a prior inconsistent statement and the testimony at the trial or hearing.

1. Impeachment Preparation

The cross-examiner has to be intimately familiar with the witness' prior statements so that prior inconsistent statements can be located easily in the case notebook during cross-examination. Proper indexing and thorough preparation assists in making prior statements available for impeachment.

2. Stages of Impeachment

The introduction of prior inconsistent statements usually includes four stages.

A. Reaffirm the Direct Examination Testimony

The cross-examiner commits the witness to the direct examination testimony by having the witness repeat the testimony to reaffirm the evidence. This ought to be done in a way that does not unnecessarily alert the witness to the cross-examiner's intentions. Direct examination testimony that differs from a prior inconsistent statement should be selected. Precise questions should be asked which restate as exactly as possible the direct examination testimony. The cross-examiner should avoid asking questions which paraphrase or improperly summarize the testimony to avoid disagreement from the witness. Repetition of the direct testimony will prevent the argument that there really was no inconsistency, will reduce the witness' ability to explain away some ambiguity in the direct examination testimony, and will highlight the contrasting answers.

B.   *Describe the Circumstances of the Prior Inconsistent Statement*

The cross-examiner can then lead the witness through a series of questions describing the circumstances and type of prior inconsistent statement. These questions establish the date, time, place, and circumstances of the previous statement. If the fact finders are to believe that the prior inconsistent statement is accurate, questions that establish the reliability of the prior statement ought to be asked.

Some prior inconsistent statements are admissible as substantive proof. Federal Rule of Evidence 801(d)(1)(A) provides that a prior inconsistent statement made under oath at a legal proceeding is not inadmissible hearsay, but is substantive evidence. Some states provide that other prior inconsistent statements may also be considered substantive evidence. If the cross-examiner does not want the fact finders to believe that either statement is true, then questions that establish the reliability of the prior statement need not be asked.

The Federal Rules of Evidence and similar state rules no longer require an attorney to call the witness' attention to the circumstances of the prior inconsistent statement. However, strategic considerations usually mandate such an explanation. These questions explain the circumstances of the prior statement, increasing the fact finders' understanding of what happened and the impact of the inconsistent statements. These background questions also reduce the witness' opportunity to explain away the prior statement, further increase the tension of the witness, and highlight the importance of the witness' mistake. There is no required number of questions that should be asked to establish the circumstances. The case, the witness, the prior inconsistent statement, and the theory of cross-examination determine how many and which questions will be asked.

C.   *Introduce the Prior Inconsistent Statement*

The cross-examiner then introduces the prior inconsistent statement. Usually, the most effective way is to read the inconsistent statement to the witness, while the witness reads silently along, and have the witness admit making it. Another way to introduce the statement is to have the witness read it aloud. The problem with having a witness read a prior statement is that the witness may not read it with the same degree of emphasis as the cross-examiner. Opposing counsel ought to be told of the source of the statement and either the page number or line number of the source. The prior inconsistent statement need not be marked (unless the judge or arbitrator insists), because it is not being offered as evidence. The reading of the prior written statement and the witness' affirmation of the answer is the evidence offered. See Fed. R.Evid. 615(a).

D. Obtain the Witness' Response to the Inconsistent Statement

Ordinarily a witness will admit to making the inconsistent statement. The direct examiner will most likely have instructed the witness to readily admit the statement. The direct examiner may even have covered it on direct examination, or plans to have the witness explain it away on redirect examination. Impeachment questions should not be asked on cross-examination which allow the witness an opportunity to explain away the inconsistency.

If the witness admits making the statement, the impeachment process is concluded. If the witness does not admit the prior inconsistent statement, the cross-examiner must prove that the statement was made. If the witness denies making the statement, or cannot recall making it, the cross-examiner will need to establish the witness made the statement. Usually, extrinsic evidence is introduced to prove the statement. The type of extrinsic evidence depends upon the type of statement made. The following sections describe the various types of prior inconsistent statements and the necessary extrinsic evidence.

It is highly unlikely that witnesses will deny they made a statement appearing in a transcript or that their signature does not appear on a written statement. A witness may attempt to be evasive and say the transcript may be inaccurate or the written statement is incomplete, but further questioning will usually be successful in having the witness admit the transcript or written statement is authentic.

Example:

Q: You have told us you saw both cars just before the crash?

A: Yes that's true.

Q: Are you sure you saw both cars before the crash?

A: Absolutely!

Q: Do you remember when Investigator Lestrade visited with you the day after the accident?

A: Yes.

Q: That was at your home, wasn't it?

A: Yes.

Q: He asked you some questions, didn't he?

A: Yes.

Q: And he wrote your responses down in a statement?

A: Yes.

Q: Investigator Lestrade gave you a chance to read that statement, didn't he?

A: Yes he did.

Q: And you did read it?

A: Yes.

Q: You signed that statement, didn't you?

A: Yes.

Q: You signed it because it was true and correct?

A: Yes.

Q: You wouldn't have signed it if it wasn't true and correct, would you?

A: No.

Q: Now, in about the middle of that statement you told Investigator Lestrade: "I only saw the Ford before the crash, and not the other car."?

A: If that is what it says.

This method of impeachment repeats the direct examination. An alternative method accomplishes the same thing but does not require that the direct examination be repeated. Repeating the direct examination may over emphasize that information. The following alternative technique avoids highlighting the direct examination.

Example:

Q: You only saw one car just before the accident, didn't you?

A: No.

Q: Are you sure you did not see just one car?

A: Yes I'm sure.

Q: Didn't you tell Investigator Lestrade you only saw one car?

A: I may have.

Q: Well, you do recall the day after the accident you told Investigator Lestrade you saw only one car?

A: I talked to an investigator after the accident.

Q: And you gave him a statement?

A: Yes.

Q: He wrote it down?

A: Yes.

Q: You read it?

A: Yes.

Q: It was true?

A: Yes.

Q: You signed it?

A: Yes.

Q: Because it was the truth?

A: Yes.

Q: I hand you a written statement and ask you to look at it. That is your signature on the statement, correct?

A: Yes.

Q: Read silently along with me. In that statement it is written: "I only saw the Ford before the crash, and not the other car."

A: Yes, I see that.

---

3. Significant Prior Inconsistent Statements

The nature of the impeaching material varies from significant to minor. Section 9.4(C) explained why impeachment efforts should be made only with significant, material evidence. If a witness testifies at a deposition that a car was a "light green" color and at the trial or hearing states the car was "green," it is ineffective to attempt to impeach the witness based on this minor discrepancy, unless the precise color of the car was significant. Minor inaccuracies will not adversely affect the credibility of the witness unless there is a pattern or a large number of them. Fact finders understand that witnesses do not have perfect recall.

4. Introducing Contemporaneous Prior Statements

The direct examiner can request that additional portions of the prior statement be introduced contemporaneously with the impeaching part of the statement to prevent a cross-examiner from introducing selective facts out of context. Federal Rule of Evidence 106 and similar state rules permit an opposing attorney to request that the judge or arbitrator require the reading of other relevant portions of the statement. See section 9.4(C).

5. Types of Prior Inconsistent Statements

There are five major types of prior inconsistent statements:

- Prior statements under oath,
- Discovery responses and verified pleadings,
- Written statements,
- Oral statements, and
- Omissions.

The following sections demonstrate examples of each of these types of prior inconsistent statements and the extrinsic evidence that is necessary to prove impeachment if the witness denies the prior statement.

A. *Prior Statements Under Oath*

Prior statements under oath include testimony provided at depositions, previous trials, motion hearings, preliminary hearings, grand jury hearings, inquests, and hearings before various boards.

Example:

Q: Ms. Westby, you testified on direct examination that you were traveling in your car at 25 miles per hour just before you entered the intersection?

A: Yes.

Q: You further testified that you knew the speed to be 25 miles per hour because you had just looked at your speedometer immediately before driving through the intersection?

A: Yes.

Q: That is your testimony under oath today before this jury?

A: Yes, that is what I said.

Q: Do you recall that you previously testified under oath regarding the facts of this case?

A: Yes, I remember.

Q: You remember we call that procedure a deposition?

A: Yes.

Q: There was a court reporter there taking down your statements just like there is a court reporter here today?

A: Yes.

Q: You took an oath and promised to give truthful answers?

A: Yes.

Q: You recall that your attorney was there with you?

A: Yes.

Q: And you recall that I was there?

A: Yes.

Q: Before that deposition, you had an opportunity to talk with your attorney about the deposition?

A: Yes.

Q: You had an opportunity to prepare for the deposition and think about what happened at the intersection?

A: Yes.

Q: That deposition occurred just a few months after the accident?

A: Yes.

Q: The events of the accident were still fresh in your mind at the time of your deposition?

A: Yes.

Q: During your deposition, questions were asked of you and answers were given by you just like today in court?

A: Yes.

Q: At the beginning of the deposition you were advised that if you did not understand a question to say so and it would be rephrased?

A: Yes.

Q: The questions and answers at the deposition related to what happened at the intersection of May Avenue and Ridge Boulevard?

A: Yes.

Q: You answered those questions at the deposition as best you could, correct?

A: Yes.

Q: You gave complete and honest answers?

A: I tried.

Q: You did not withhold any information, did you?

A: No.

Q: Ms. Westby, I'm handing you a document. Please look at it. Is this a transcript of your deposition?

A: It appears to be.

Q: Please turn to page 63 and look at line 10. You were asked this question then: "How fast were you driving when you first entered the intersection?" Do you see that?

A: Yes.

Q: And your answer to that question was: "About 25 miles an hour. I'm not real sure." Do you see that?

A: Yes.

Q: The next question you were asked was "Did you look at your speedometer any time before you entered the intersection?" And your answer was "I don't believe so." Do you also see that response?

A: Yes.

Q: Those were your answers a year ago, under oath?

A: That's what is written here.

Q: And those are your answers?

A: Yes.

Q: Do you recall several months after the deposition going to your attorney's office to read your deposition transcript?

A: Yes, I recall that.

Q: And you read over the answers that you gave?

A: Yes.

Q: And you understood at that time that you could make any changes if you had said anything incorrect or untrue?

A: I believe so.

Q: After reading your deposition you signed the deposition?

A: Yes.

Q: Your signature appears on the last page of that transcript, correct?

A: Yes, that's my signature.

Q: Thank you, Ms. Westby. That concludes my questioning.

The redirect examination can include the direct examiner's introduction of any segment of the deposition that helps bolster the accuracy of the direct examination testimony, reduces the impact of the prior statement, explains what the witness meant to say during the deposition, or shows that cross-examining counsel attempted to use a response out of context.

Example (Continued):

Judge:

Redirect, counsel?

Direct Examiner:

Q: Yes, your Honor. Ms. Westby, please turn to page 116 of that same deposition, and look at line 8. That question was asked of you later in the deposition and it reads "Do you have any other basis for determining how fast you were going just before you entered the intersection?" Do you recall that question being asked of you that day?

A: Yes.

Q: Would you please read from your deposition the answer that you gave that day?

A: I said, "My long years of driving experience. And it's possible, come to think of it, that I looked at my speedometer, which I often do."

Q: That was your testimony a year ago, under oath?

A: Yes.

Proof of Prior Testimony

If a witness denies giving a deposition answer, a statement appearing in a deposition may be proved by offering that portion of the original deposition transcript into evidence. In most jurisdictions, the original deposition is not part of the file or record. Usually, the attorney who took the deposition has possession of the original transcript. The certification page prepared by the reporter is attached to the original transcript certifying it to be the original.

There are three ways to place a deposition transcript into evidence.

1. The judge or arbitrator may take notice of the original transcript and receive it in evidence.

2. In other jurisdictions, the attorney must authenticate the document, overcome any hearsay problems, and establish the transcript as an original writing. The original transcript of the deposition, which contains an attestation by a notary public, is self-authenticating under the rules of evidence, and a copy is also self-authenticating. See Fed. R.Evid. 902(1) and 902(4). The transcript can be established to be an original writing or an admissible duplicate by the certification signed by the notary at the end of the transcript stating it is the original. See Fed. R.Evid. 1001(3) and 1001(4).

Hearsay problems may be overcome in one of two ways. If the deponent is an adverse party, the transcript can be offered as a party admission. See Fed.R.Evid. 801. If the deponent is a non-party, the transcript may be offered solely for the limited purpose of impeaching the witness (not for the truth of the matter asserted) rendering the transcript non-hearsay. See Fed. R.Evid. 801(c). If the witness is a non-party and the filed transcript is offered as substantive proof in addition to its impeachment value, the transcript can be offered in evidence as a public court record exception to the hearsay rule. See Fed. R.Evid. 803(8).

3. In a few jurisdictions, the reporter may have to be called as a witness to establish that the reporter is a qualified reporter, that the reporter was present at the proceeding and swore in the witness, and that the reporter prepared a verbatim record of all questions and answers.

Prior testimony that appears in a judicial or other proceeding may be proved by introducing a certified copy of the transcript of that portion of the proceeding containing the witness' testimony. The clerk of court or other administrator can provide a certified copy of the transcript prepared by the reporter. The judge or arbitrator may take notice of a certified transcript. In a few jurisdictions, the reporter who transcribed the testimony may need to be called as a witness and a foundation similar to that of a deposition reporter may have to be established.

The transcript should usually be marked as an exhibit and introduced in evidence. The portion of the transcript that contains the prior inconsistent statement ought to be read to the fact finder by the attorney.

B. *Discovery Responses and Verified Pleadings*

Prior inconsistent statements may appear in answers to interrogatories, responses to requests for admissions, a verified complaint, or other legal documents signed by the witness under oath.

Example:

On direct examination, a party testifies that he cannot remember whether he received a memorandum. An answer to an interrogatory states he did receive the memorandum.

Q: Mr. Kreskin, you testified on direct examination that you did not receive the Houdini memorandum, is that correct?

A: Yes.

Q: You do recall that as part of this lawsuit, you received some written questions from us?

A: I think so.

Q: Those questions are called interrogatories?

A: Yes, I remember them.

Q: You, with the assistance of your attorney, provided us written answers to those questions?

A: Yes.

Q: You swore under oath that the answers that you gave were true?

A: Yes.

Q: Do you recall question No. 5 which asked, "Identify all memoranda you received related to the Houdini file"?

A: That sounds familiar.

Q: Your sworn answer to that question in part was, "I recall receiving the Houdini memorandum."

A: If that is what it says.

Q: That is what you stated in writing under oath at that time?

A: Yes.

Q: You discussed your answers to those questions with your attorney?

A: Yes.

Q: You understood that you had to provide complete and accurate answers?

A: Yes.

Proof of Discovery Responses and Verified Pleadings

Discovery responses and verified pleadings that appear in the file can be proved by introducing those documents. Discovery responses that are not in the file may be proved by introducing the originals of those documents, which are usually in the possession of the attorney receiving the response. The opposing attorney will usually agree that the originals are accurate and authentic, and the court will receive them in evidence. The opposing attorney will usually also agree that the original is accurate and authentic and that stipulation will be sufficient for the court to receive the transcript into evidence.

C. Written Statements

Written statements include writings that have been signed, agreed to, or approved by a party. Writings include written statements given to a police officer or investigator, notes handwritten by the witness, typed statements that are signed by a witness, affidavits from judicial, administrative, or arbitration proceedings, memoranda prepared by the witness, letters, business records, and other documents.

Example:

The witness has testified that the defendant was not present at a meeting on December 1. In a memorandum the witness prepared and signed, the witness stated the defendant was present at the meeting.

Q: Mr. Marple, you have told us that the defendant, Ms. Krinkell, was not present during that December 1 meeting, correct?

A: That's right.

Q: You remember the other two people who were there but not the defendant?

A: She was not there.

Q: After that meeting on December 1, you prepared a memorandum?

A: I may have.

Q: It was your normal business practice to prepare a memorandum after a meeting that summarized the meeting?

A: Yes, it was.

Q: And after the December 1 meeting, you prepared such a memorandum?

A: I am not certain.

Q: I hand you what has been marked for identification as Defendant's Exhibit No. 6. Your initials appear on this memo?

A: Yes.

Q: It is dated December 1?

A: Yes.

Q: It summarizes a meeting that occurred at 3:00 p.m. that day?

A: It appears to.

Q: That is the memorandum you prepared after the December 1 meeting?

A: Yes.

Q: In the first paragraph of that memo, you identified the individuals who were present at the meeting?

A: Yes.

Q: You state in that memo: "Present were Sam Wilkins, Sam Shepard, and Dorothy Krinkell."

A: Yes.

Q: In that memo you identified Ms. Krinkell as being present at that meeting?

A: It appears so.

Proof of Written or Signed Statements

If a witness denies making a prior written statement, the prior statement can be proved by calling any witness who can identify the writing or the signature of the witness. The questions are the same as those needed to authenticate a document. See Section 8.6(B).

D. *Oral Statements*

Any oral statement a witness has made to anyone may be used as a source for impeachment. This includes oral statements made to investigators, police officers, business personnel during a meeting, friends at a social gathering, or to any person at any time at any place.

Example:

A witness to a robbery was interviewed by a police officer and told the officer that she did not see the person who robbed the bar. The prosecution called this witness and on direct examination she identified the defendant as the robber.

Q: On direct examination, you testified the defendant was the person in this saloon?

A: Yes.

Q: You identified the defendant as the person who robbed the saloon?

A: Yes.

Q: You believe it was the defendant who was in the saloon the day it was robbed?

A: Yes.

Q: Ms. Kitty, you do recall talking to Marshal Dillon shortly after the robbery?

A: Yes.

Q: Marshal Dillon asked you what you saw?

A: I think so.

Q: You wanted to help the Marshal find the robber?

A: Yes.

Q: You wanted to tell Marshal Dillon everything you knew?

A: Yes.

Q: Marshal Dillon was taking notes when he talked to you?

A: I'm not sure.

Q: Ms. Kitty, at that time you told Marshal Dillon that you did not see the person that robbed the saloon?

A: I don't recall saying that.

Q: Ms. Kitty, you told Marshal Dillon that you did not know who robbed the saloon?

A: I don't believe I said that.

Proof of Oral Statements

If the witness denies making the prior oral statement, the previous oral statement can be proved by calling any witness who can testify that the witness made the prior statement.

Example (Continued):

Q: Marshal Dillon, did you speak to Ms. Kitty shortly after the robbery?

A: Yes.

Q: Did she say anything about the robbery?

A: Yes.

Q: What did she say?

A: She said she did not see the person who robbed the saloon.

Q: Anything else?

A: She also said she did not know who the robber was.

E.   Omissions

A common method of impeachment involves the cross-examination of a witness regarding a matter testified to on direct examination that does not appear in a prior written statement. Witnesses frequently fail to include all important details in prior statements. The omission is significant because there is no record of this material statement in any report, statement or testimony. The absence of this important information can be revealed on cross-examination and be used to reduce the credibility of the witness.

The impeachment process by omission is similar to impeaching with a prior inconsistent statement except the omission does not appear in the prior statement. A witness who testifies to an important matter that does not appear in a prior written statement can be impeached by establishing the absence of this material matter from the previous statement. Common prior statements which may omit significant facts include reports by police officers, memoranda by investigators, deposition testimony, and testimony in other proceedings. The impeachment process can establish that the prior statement was made at a time when the events were fresher in the witness' mind and can suggest that the witness may be adding facts or making things up because the statements were not included in the prior statement. This process is a subtle form of impeachment because the cross-examiner is establishing the nonexistence of a fact or opinion.

Example:

In an automobile accident case, the plaintiff, Mr. Hardy, has testified on direct examination that the defendant said, "I am sorry. It was my fault." In his previous deposition the plaintiff never testified the defendant said those words.

Q: On direct examination, you stated the defendant, Mr. Laurel, said to you after the accident, "I am sorry. It was my fault."?

A: Yes, that's what he said.

Q: Your testimony is the defendant made that statement to you immediately after the accident?

A: Yes.

Q: Now, Mr. Hardy, you recall your deposition was taken in this case?

A: Yes.

Q: At that deposition you testified under oath just like you were testifying under oath today?

A: Yes.

Q: Your attorney was present at that deposition?

A: Yes.

Q: And I was there asking you questions about the accident?

A: Yes.

Q: You remember I told you if you did not understand a question I asked you should tell me and I would rephrase it so you understood it?

A: I believe so.

Q: That deposition was taken about three months after the accident?

A: Yes.

Q: And the accident happened over two years ago?

A: That's about right.

Q: Before that deposition you talked with your attorney about the accident?

A: Yes.

Q: And after that deposition you had an opportunity to read the transcript of what you said and make any changes on it?

A: Yes, I believe so.

Q: You recall that during the deposition I asked you this question — on page 35 line 16: "What did Mr. Laurel say to you immediately after the accident?"

A: I believe so.

Q: And you recall your answer: He said "I am sorry this all happened."

A: If that's what it says.

Q: I show you your deposition transcript and ask you to read the next question that was asked you on line 18.

A: "Did the defendant say anything else?"

Q: Please read line 19 with me as I read it out loud. It says "No, I don't believe so." Right?

A: Yes.

Q: Nowhere in these answers did you say the defendant said, "It's my fault."

A: That's correct.

Example:

On direct examination, a police officer testified he found a note in the defendant's pocket with the victim's name and phone number on it. That statement does not appear in his written report.

Q: Inspector Tragg, after you arrested the defendant, you searched his pockets?

A: Yes.

Q: On direct examination, you said you found a note in one of his pockets?

A: Yes.

Q: You also told us the victim's name and a phone number were on that note?

A: Yes.

Q: You are sure about that?

A: Yes.

Q: After you arrest someone you prepare a written report?

A: Yes.

Q: You have been trained on how to prepare such a report?

A: Yes.

Q: You were trained to include all important facts?

A: Yes.

Q: You were trained to prepare a complete and accurate report?

A: Yes.

Q: After you arrested the defendant, you prepared such a written report?

A: Yes.

Q: You wanted the report to include all important matters?

A: Yes.

Q: And you wanted that report to be complete and accurate?

A: Yes.

Q: Let me show you your report. This is your written report, correct?

A: Yes.

Q: After you completed the report, you read it over?

A: Yes.

Q: You made the corrections in your own handwriting on the report, right?

A: Yes.

Q: And after reading and correcting it, you signed it?

A: Yes.

Q: One of the purposes of this report is that the prosecutor relies on it to determine what happened, true?

A: Yes.

Q: Another purpose is to help you refresh your memory before testifying at trial?

A: Yes.

Q: You read this report before testifying here today?

A: I looked it over.

Q: You looked it over to help you remember what you did that evening?

A: In part, yes.

Q: Inspector Tragg, nowhere in this report did you state that you found a written note on the defendant?

A: That's not in the report.

Q: Nowhere in this report did you state that you found a note in the defendant's pocket?

A: That's not in there.

Q: Nowhere in the report did you state that you found a note with a name and phone number written on it?

A: That's not in the report either.

Proof of Omissions

Once the witness admits the information is missing, the impeachment is completed and the omission has been proved. If the witness denies the omission, the relevant portion of the transcript or the written statement must be introduced and shown to the fact finder to prove the absence of the significant fact or opinion. Omissions can be proved by introducing the prior written statement using the same methods to introduce deposition transcripts and documents described in the previous subsections.

CHAPTER 10
EXPERTS

REFLECTING ON ADVOCACY

Even when experts agree, they may well be mistaken.

—Bertrand Russell

Expert opinion . . . is only an ordinary guess in evening clothes.

—Hon. Curtis Bok in
Kerstetter v. Commonwealth

§ 10.1 INTRODUCTION

A. *Scope*

Expert witnesses are used when the scientific, technical, or other specialized knowledge of the expert will assist the fact finder in understanding the evidence or in determining a fact that is in issue. In both simple and complex cases, expert testimony may be needed in order for one or both parties to prove their case. For example, in personal injury actions, medical experts ordinarily testify. In criminal cases, scientific experts often testify on behalf of both the prosecution and defense.

In civil cases, parties know what the testifying experts will say. Discovery has produced written expert reports that likely resulted in the parties deposing all the experts. It is common in many cases for experts to appear through a DVD or video presentation, with the fact finders watching and listening to their testimony presented on monitors. This testimonial method assures that the fact finder will hear the expert testimony and avoid problems with scheduling experts for trial, and also reduces, to some extent, the overall costs of expert testimony at trial. Another aspect to this process is that a case may be more likely to settle after the parties evaluate the actual expert opinions.

Experts testifying in civil cases commonly have two deposition segments or two separate depositions. The first is discovery with an opposing party seeking information about the expert and the expert's opinions and bases of those opinions. The second is preserving trial testimony with the proffering party conducting direct examination followed by cross-examination conducted by the opposing party and concluding with redirect and recross. Objections are made on the record and the judge will later rule on the objections and the DVD disk or video tape will be edited to reflect the rulings. While this process takes time, it assures that the expert testimony will be available in a timely and efficient manner.

In criminal cases, both the prosecution and defense will exchange information about expert opinions and testimony as required by the applicable law. The timing often depends upon which side has the burden of proof on an issue. These experts testify in person in open court as required by due process and constitutional provisions.

B. *Expert Examinations*

Experts testify on direct and cross-examination. Many of the comments in the chapters on direct and cross-examination also apply to expert witnesses. This chapter explains additional and alternative tactics and techniques applicable to expert witnesses and has three parts:

Expert Witnesses

Direct Examination of Experts

Cross-Examination of Experts

EXPERT WITNESSES

§ 10.2 EXPERT WITNESSES

A. *Purposes of Expert Testimony*

Expert testimony serves several purposes in a trial, arbitration, and hearing. An expert may:

- Provide a fact finder with factual information. For example, a treating physician will testify to the injuries suffered by a civil plaintiff.

- Apply expert knowledge to the facts of a case and render an opinion. For example, a design engineer can explain information about product design and render an opinion regarding the defective design of a specific product.

- Explain scientific principles and theories. For example, in a homicide case, a forensic pathologist may explain the medical principles involved in determining the cause of death.

- Testify to test procedures and results. For example, a chemist can explain the testing procedures to identify cocaine and describe the test results which prove the substance to be cocaine.

- Explain real evidence introduced in the case. For example, a radiologist can explain an MRI to the jury.

- Interpret the facts and render an opinion regarding the likelihood of an event or occurrence. For example, an accident reconstruction expert may testify to the probability of causation in a civil case.

- Testify to the amount of recoverable damages in a civil case. For example, an economist can testify to the present value of projected lost earnings of an injured plaintiff.

- Render an opinion which contradicts the conclusions of an expert who testified for the opposing party. For example, a psychiatrist can testify that a defendant was not mentally ill at the time the crime was committed, which directly contradicts the expert opinion of a psychiatrist called by the defense.

B. Identity of Experts

A person who has specialized knowledge gained by education, training, experience, or skill may be qualified as an expert. Many professionals who have had extensive formal education and training may be readily qualified, such as doctors, engineers, and economists. Other individuals whose expertise has been derived primarily from experience or skill may also be readily qualified if they have the requisite experience and skill, such as mechanics and technicians. The specific laws of a jurisdiction determine who may or may not be an expert, as explained in Section 10.3.

C. Areas of Expertise

An area of knowledge that contains scientific, technical, or other specialized information may constitute an admissible area of expertise. A general test that most jurisdictions apply is: whether the area of expertise has gained general acceptance within the relevant scientific, technical, or other specialized expert community. A scientific theory which has gained general acceptance within the relevant scientific community or which has been verified by reliable experiments is ordinarily recognized as an admissible topic of expertise. These fields of expertise include medicine, engineering, economics, psychiatry, accounting, and law. Additional fields of generally recognized expertise include firearm analysis, ballistics, mechanical repairs, laboratory analysis, and property assessments.

An area of expertise will ordinarily be recognized by a decisionmaker if experts in the area and related areas recognize and accept the area as one reflecting specialized knowledge. Areas that are not traditionally considered areas of expertise or that are unusual may not be recognized by the decision maker as an area of expertise. For example, individuals proficient in operating lie detector machines are not usually considered experts because their opinions and lie detectors have not been recognized as accurate or reliable. Recently accepted areas of new expertise include expert testimony regarding child abuse syndrome and post traumatic stress syndrome.

Judges and arbitrators ordinarily recognize or take judicial or arbitral notice of the recognized area of expertise. Some fields of expertise are not widely accepted and many require proof of reliability. These fields include hypnosis and voice spectrograms. An expert may need to be asked questions to establish this reliability: "How well recognized is this area of expertise? Do experts like you recognize this area as reliable and accurate?" Again, the applicable law of a jurisdiction determines the scope of expertise, as further explained in the following section.

§ 10.3 THE LAW OF EXPERT TESTIMONY

Every jurisdiction has specific laws regarding the qualifications of experts and the recognized areas of expertise. The primary and common sources of this law for each jurisdiction are evidence rules and judicial decisions applying and interpreting the rules. In federal cases, Fed. R.Evid. 702 and related rules and federal case law regulate expert testimony, including controlling cases such as Daubert v. Merrell Dow Pharmaceuticals, 509 U.S. 579 (1993).

Two different approaches to admissible expert testimony are defined by the *Daubert* case and an earlier case, Frye v. United States, 293 F. 1010 (D.C.C.C. 1923). The *Daubert* case, presently used in federal court cases, has four primary factors to be reviewed by the trial judge in determining the admissibility of expert testimony to assist the trier of fact in understanding or determining a factual issue:

- Whether the theory has been subjected to peer review and publication,

- The potential rate of error of the theory in issue,

- Whether the underlying technique has been generally accepted as valid by the relevant expert community, and

- The potential rate of error of the technique.

Some state courts have adopted the *Daubert* approach. Others have modified it by adding more factors, such as: the extent to which the theory/technique relies on the subjective interpretation of the expert and the degree to which non-judicial uses have been made of the theory/technique.

Many other state courts continue to use the *Frye* test, also known as the "general acceptance test." These jurisdictions more broadly permit expert testimony if the opinion to be offered is based on a principle that has gained general acceptance in the particular field in issue; and these jurisdictions allow experts to testify whether such a principle has gained this general acceptance. Still other jurisdictions use a combination of approaches. Arbitrators and administrative law judges commonly follow the applicable evidence law to the case, ranging from *Daubert* to *Frye* to variations of these approaches.

DIRECT EXAMINATION OF EXPERT WITNESSES

§ 10.4 DIRECT EXAMINATION OF EXPERT WITNESSES

A. *Attorney Preparation*

The attorney should know the subject on which the expert will testify as well or better than the expert. Without this specialized information the attorney may miss critical information, present information that will subject the expert to devastating cross-examination, or will be unable to identify errors or discrepancies with the testimony of the opposition's experts. In addition to studying the area of expertise, the attorney must read other transcripts of expert examinations in the area to determine the areas of vulnerability that the particular type of testimony or the witness may have.

The attorney may hire consulting experts in the field to assist in this educational process. These experts need not be called to testify but only serve to educate the attorney and offer suggestions for the cross-examination of opposing experts. An expert may also act as both trial and consulting expert in appropriate situations to reduce costs.

Form 10.1 provides an example of a format to prepare for expert testimony.

FORM 10.1
EXPERT TESTIMONY PLANNING WORKSHEET

Case _____   File   _____

Name _____   Fees   _____

Qualifications   _____

Opinions   _____

Sources of Information   _____

Personal Knowledge   _____

Other Sources   _____

Bases of Opinions   _____

Exhibits   _____

Technical Terms to be Explained   _____

Treatises   _____

Probable Cross-examination Areas   _____

Redirect Examination   _____

B. Qualifying the Expert

The rules of evidence require that the expert must be qualified in the area about which the expert will testify. See Fed. R.Evid. 702. The decision maker rules on whether an individual is "competent" and qualified to be an expert witness. This means the decision maker determines that:

- The expert has the education, training or experience in a field that is beyond the general knowledge of the fact finder;

- The expert has sufficient information on which to testify in the particular case;

- The opinion is based on the education, training and experience of the expert as applied to the information and is not based on unfounded speculation or conjecture.

The foundation necessary to qualify an expert is relatively straightforward and generally not difficult to prove. Examples demonstrating the legal foundation for almost every area of expertise may be found in many articles and books on the subject of expert examinations. The following illustrates common areas of qualifications.

OUTLINE OF EXPERT TESTIMONY

Name

Title, degree

Personal Background

Address (work, home)

Family

Length of residence

Hobbies

Clubs

Social organizations

Charitable organizations

How, When Expert Becomes Involved

Treating physician

Consultant

Examination for trial (plaintiff or defense)

Neutral expert

Retained by plaintiff or defense

Fees

Occupation

Employer

Position/description/responsibilities—how long

Prior employers/positions/responsibilities

Education

Undergraduate degrees

Institution

Graduation date

Advanced degrees

Institution

Graduation date

Training

What

Where

When

By whom

Certificates/licenses

Professional Organizations

Name

Purpose

Length of membership

Authority in organization

Professional Achievements

Books

Articles

Teaching

Lectures

Consultations with other professionals

Awards/honors

Legal Experience

As Witness

Plaintiff or defense

Frequency of testifying

Consultant

Organization or parties

Frequency

Specialized Experience

Type of experience

Tests

Examinations

Study

Consulting with others

Personal interview

Number of tests

Results

Specific Examination or Tests Involved in Case

Why

When

Where

How

Reports

Date

Summary

Supplement

Exhibits

Exhibits already prepared

Exhibits to be prepared

Weaknesses

Weakness of profession

Weakness of expert

Weakness of opinion

Bias

Prejudice

Interest

Lack of information

Lack of testing

Opinions

Basis of Opinions

Sources of Opinion

Exhibits

After sufficient foundation has been laid to establish the qualifications of an expert, the attorney may continue with the questioning to elicit expert testimony. Some jurisdictions require that the examining attorney request the decision maker to accept the witness as an expert or "tender" the witness as an expert before continuing with the testimony: "Your Honor, we tender Dr. Watson as an expert forensic scientist." This motion should be made outside the hearing of the jury, in case the decision maker may decide the expert is not qualified, unless the attorney is certain the decision maker will accept the expert.

C. *Establishing Qualifications*

Qualifications may be presented in sequence at the beginning of the examination, or may be mixed throughout the examination and presented as they apply directly to a particular point. Whenever qualifications are established, an effort should be made to "humanize" the expert and show that the witness is also a good person as well as an expert. Some experts may appear arrogant when describing their background because in effect they are telling the fact finder how brilliant they are. The attorney should ask questions which personalize the expert, and the expert should answer in a modest, appropriate manner which establishes how much the witness knows but not how much smarter the witness is compared to the fact finder.

The following examples demonstrate two different ways of presenting an expert's qualifications.

1. *Qualifications at Beginning of Examination*

Example:

Q: The plaintiff calls Dr. Noah Carter.

Q: Dr. Carter, you are a medical doctor?

Q: Do you live in our city?

Q: How long have you lived in our city?

Q: Do you have family in the city?

Q: Where did you go to college?

Q: In what fields did you get your degree?

Q: Where did you go to medical school?

Q: When did you graduate from medical school?

Q: Did you continue your schooling after medical school? Where?

Q: Did you specialize?

Q: Explain what that means?

Q: Are you board certified?

Q: What does that mean?

Q: What experience do you have in your specialty?

Q: Have you done any lecturing or teaching in your specialty or related areas?

Q: Have you written any books or articles in the area or in related areas?

Q: Do you belong to any professional organizations?

Q: Have you ever testified in court before?

Q: How often?

Q: Have you testified for both the plaintiff and the defense?

It is more traditional, and usually easier, to present the qualification in sequence at the beginning of the examination. Many courts and arbitrators are familiar with an expert examination presented in this way and are comfortable with the sequence. This approach may not be the most persuasive way of presenting the expert. Long qualifications presented in the abstract may tend to bore the fact finder as they do not directly relate to the case.

2. *Qualifications During the Examination*

Example:

Q: Dr. Carter, you are a medical doctor?

Q: Where did you go to medical school?

Q: When did you graduate from medical school?

Q: Did you continue your schooling after medical school?

Q: Where?

Q: Did you specialize?

Q: Explain what that means.

Q: Now Doctor, at my request, did you examine the knee of Mr. Baryshnikov?

Q: When was that?

Q: Where did the examination take place?

Q: How long did the examination last?

Q: Did you have sufficient time for the examination?

Q: Tell us what you did to perform the examination.

Q: While you were at medical school, did you have training in conducting this kind of examination?

Q: Have you had any specific training or education in injuries of the type that Mr. Baryshnikov has?

Q: Was that training and experience helpful to you in diagnosing his injury?

Q: How?

Q: Have you ever lectured on the type of injury that Mr. Baryshnikov has suffered?

Q: Have you written any books or articles in regard to that type of injury?

Q: Does your lecturing and writing assist you in diagnosing and treating injuries of this nature? How?

---

3. *Early Introduction of Opinion and Qualifications*

With some opinions, it may preferable to introduce opinions very early during an expert's testimony, followed by a presentation of the specific qualifications for each opinion. Fed.R.Evid.705 permits an expert to give an opinion without first testifying to the underlying facts or data. The federal rules and similar state rules allow the early introduction of expert opinions. Advocates should do so when appropriate in a case.

Example:

Q: Dr. Harvey, what doctorate degree do you have?

Q: What, among other things, does this degree prepare you to do?

Q: Did you examine the KLT computer at issue in this case?

Q: Describe your examination.

Q: How long did your examination take?

Q: Do you have an opinion whether the 501 chip you examined in the computer violates the 5419 patent at issue here?

Q: What is that opinion?

Q: Where did you learn to analyze computer chips?

Q: At MIT, what courses did you take that helped you know how to analyze computer chips?

Q. What research did you conduct that assisted you in being able to analyze computer chips?

Q: What publications did you write explaining the computer chip analysis method you used in this case?

D. *Resumes and Stipulations*

Alternative ways to qualify an expert include submission of the expert's resume or stipulations to the qualifications of the expert by opposing counsel. Decision makers may allow the curriculum vitae of the expert to be introduced as an exhibit in addition to their oral testimony or in lieu of such testimony. If the case involves many experts, the attorneys may prefer, or the decision maker may require the attorneys, to submit complete or summary resumes of the experts instead of questioning the experts about their qualifications. This procedure saves time and allows the jurors to concentrate on the expert testimony.

An attorney may stipulate to the qualifications of an opponent's expert, making it unnecessary for that expert to be qualified. An attorney may tentatively decide a stipulation is preferable to having the fact finder hear the qualifications of the other side's expert. This will be particularly true if the opponent's expert has better qualifications than the attorney's expert. Some decision makers may urge the attorneys to stipulate to each other's experts in an effort to save time.

An advocate must consider whether the submission of resumes or an offer of stipulation is tactically wise. It may be more effective for the fact finder to hear the expert testify to qualifications. An attorney can refuse the offer of the opposing attorney to stipulate to qualifications and establish qualification through testimony. Discussions with the decision maker about the use of curriculum vitae and offers of stipulations should be conducted outside the hearing of the jury to avoid adversely influencing the jurors by comments made by the opposing attorney or rulings made by the decision maker.

E. Tendering the Expert

Some jurisdictions require a lawyer to formally "tender" the witness to the court as an expert before that expert may give an opinion. The judge then decides that the witness is not qualified or permits the witness to proceed to testify as an expert. An opposing lawyer could "pass" on the witness and not oppose the witness testifying as an expert.

Neither the federal rules nor most state rules require a proffering lawyer to make this formal request. It will need to be done in those state jurisdictions that follow this process.

§ 10.5 EXPERT OPINIONS

A. Opinions

After a decision maker is convinced that a witness is qualified to give an expert opinion, the direct examiner must convince the fact finder that the expert is worth believing. The establishment of this persuasive foundation requires the direct examiner to present the information in a way that is accurate, reliable, convincing, and authoritative. The examiner must establish that the opinion of the expert should be relied on by the fact finder and that the opinion of any expert called to testify for the opposition should not be believed.

An expert will usually testify to a number of opinions. A case may involve a major and several subordinate or minor opinions. Some decision makers may require the attorney to use specific traditional words (legal jargon) as a predicate to the introduction of an opinion.

Example:

Q: Do you have an opinion based upon a reasonable degree of medical (or psychiatric, accounting, or other) certainty?

A: Yes.

Q: What is that opinion?

Example:

Q: Doctor Grissom, based on your experience, training, and education in the area of fingerprint analysis and, in addition, based on your examination of the fingerprints that you found on the dashboard of the car and your comparison of those fingerprints with the known fingerprints of the defendant, do you have an opinion to a reasonable degree of certainty whether the fingerprints found on the dashboard of the car are the fingerprints of the defendant?

A: Yes, I do.

Q: What is the opinion?

A: The fingerprints that were found on the dashboard of the car identically match the defendant's left thumb and forefinger.

B. *Outline of Expert Opinion*

A summary outline of the direct examination of an expert ordinarily includes the following topics:

- The subject matter of the opinion,
- The theories or principles that support the area of expertise and opinion,
- The sources of information relied upon by the expert,
- Any standard tests or routine procedures used in the area,
- Specific tests or procedures used in a case,
- Other bases of the opinion of the expert,
- The opinion or conclusion, and
- An explanation of the opinion and conclusion.

Most direct examinations of an expert follow the sequence of this outline. Each direct examination should be reviewed to determine whether a different sequence would be more effective.

C. *Sources of Information*

An expert witness must explain the sources of information or facts which support the opinion of the expert. This information is critical to comply with the evidence rules and to convince the fact finder to accept and rely on the opinion. Federal Rule of Evidence 705 and similar state rules permit an expert to give an opinion without first having to provide the sources of the information or facts underlying the opinion. This rule permits some flexibility in the order of the expert testimony. The expert may explain the sources either before or after rendering the opinion, as previously explained in Section 10.4.(C)(3).

There are a variety of sources of information an expert may rely upon:

- Personal, firsthand information perceived prior to the trial or hearing.

- Information obtained from experts, documents, records, files, witnesses, and other sources, prior to or during the trial or hearing.

- Evidence including testimony heard by or told to the expert during the case.

- Hypothetical questions.

Whatever information the expert relies upon must be of a type "reasonably relied upon" by experts in the particular field in forming such an opinion. See Fed.R.Evid. 703. This broad standard permits an expert to testify to any source of information, whether it is admissible or inadmissible during the case, as long as experts in the area reasonably rely upon such information.

1. Personal, Firsthand Information

An expert may have personal firsthand knowledge of information learned or perceived prior to the hearing. The witness may testify to these sources after a proper foundation has been laid which includes the actual observations or perceptions made, when and where these observations occurred, how the expert made these observations and who was present, and a description of the observations.

Example:

Q: Fire Chief Gunble, were you at the scene of the fire?

A: Yes.

Q: When did you arrive at the scene?

A: We received the first alarm about ten minutes after the fire started, and I arrived at the casino about five minutes after we received the alarm.

Q: What did you see when you arrived at the casino building?

A: Flames were shooting out of all the windows on the west side of the building, and the walls on the east side had partially collapsed.

Q: What did you notice about the flames?

A: They were a very bright orange color and were spreading rapidly from north to south through the building.

Q: Who was at the scene of the fire when you arrived?

A: The owner of the casino, Ms. Burns.

Q: Did you talk with her?

A: Yes.

Q: What did she say?

A: She said, "It's all for the good. The World Poker Tour had cancelled." Then she tented her fingers and whispered "Excellent."

An expert who has firsthand knowledge about physical evidence may need to testify to establish the chain of custody of the exhibit. Section 8.4(C) describes establishing the chain of custody. For example, an expert who examined and tested strands of hair seized at the scene of a crime will testify to opening the sealed container containing the hair and resealing the container after the tests have been completed.

Experts who examine or tested an item of physical evidence may not be able to recall the specific exhibit. An expert who routinely handles and examines many physical objects may have no independent recollection of a specific exhibit. Notes made by the expert may be used to refresh a recollection of the expert. Questions may be asked which first establish the regular, standard or correct procedure always employed by the expert followed by questions which establish that those recognized procedures were followed with the specific exhibit.

2. Information Obtained From Other Sources Prior to the Trial or Hearing

An expert may rely upon information from other than personal observations and experiences, as long as the type of information is relied upon by other experts in the same area to reach conclusions. This type of information may include evidence that is inadmissible at trial. The most common form of inadmissible evidence will be hearsay. For example, in practice an expert may rely upon a multiple hearsay statement, which the rules of evidence would exclude as unreliable. If, however, experts ordinarily rely upon this source of information, this expert may rely upon this hearsay in forming an opinion.

An expert may explain to the fact finder these sources of information if they helped form the basis of an opinion even if they are not admissible. However, it is unclear to what extent an expert can explain the inadmissible sources of information. Federal Rule of Evidence 703 permits an expert to describe the source of the information and to testify that the information was relied upon as the basis of the opinion; however, judges and arbitrators disagree as to the admissibility of the actual information itself. Many decision makers permit the expert to testify that the expert relied upon information from another person, but do not permit the expert to testify to what that person said or wrote if it is inadmissible evidence.

Example:

Examining Lawyer:

Q: Doctor Dre, have you ever examined the plaintiff?

A: I did not.

Q: Have you done anything in regard to the plaintiff?

A: Yes, I have.

Q: What have you done?

A: I have read the entire medical record of the plaintiff. I have spoken with Dr. Hayson, and I have read her medical reports. In addition, I have read the accident reports prepared by the police department and I have read the statements given to the police by the two witnesses to the accident.

Q: Doctor, what did Dr. Hayson say in her reports?

Opposing Counsel:

Objection, your Honor, inadmissible hearsay.

Judge:

Sustained.

Q: Is this the type of information that experts in the field of orthopedic surgery, like you, normally rely on to reach a conclusion or to form an opinion about a person's injuries?

A: Yes, it certainly is.

Q: Based upon this information, and your experience, training, and education, do you have an opinion about the nature or type of injuries suffered by the plaintiff?

A: Yes, I do.

Q: What is that opinion?

A: I cannot find any evidence the plaintiff has suffered any injury whatsoever.

---

3. Information Perceived or Made Known During the Case

An expert may base an opinion upon evidence introduced during the trial or hearing. The expert may learn of this information by sitting through the case, or may be provided this information by the direct examiner. The substance of this information must also be the type of information that an expert in the same area relies upon to form an opinion.

Example:

Q: Dr. Jung, have you been here in court during the testimony of the defense psychiatrist, Dr. Freud?

A: Yes, the entire time.

Q: Have you been here during any other part of the trial?

A: No.

Q: Have you read any files or records concerning this trial?

A: Yes.

Q: What have you read?

A: I have read the court file of this case and the transcripts provided me by the court reporter at the end of each day of testimony.

Q: Is the type of information you received from listening to the defendant's psychiatrist and from reading the daily transcripts of the testimony of all the other witnesses, the kind of information a forensic psychiatrist generally uses to form an opinion as to whether the defendant knew what she was doing or whether she knew what she did was wrong at the time she shot the police officer?

A: Yes, it is.

Q: Based upon this information and your education, training, and experience, do you have an opinion whether the defendant knew what she was doing or if she knew it was wrong at the time she shot the victim.

A: Yes, I do.

Q: What is that opinion?

A: My opinion is that the defendant knew exactly what she was doing when she shot the police officer and she knew it was wrong when she did it.

D. Hypothetical Questions

An expert may base an opinion upon a hypothetical question. The direct examiner asks the witness the hypothetical question which contains facts that have been or will be introduced during the trial. The expert, not having personal knowledge of these facts and not having heard these facts during the trial, is asked to assume facts in forming an opinion. The Federal Rules of Evidence and similar state rules no longer require hypothetical questions to be used to introduce an opinion. They can be used, but are usually cumbersome and much less effective than relying on one of the previous sources of information experts can rely upon.

If used, hypothetical questions should be prepared in advance with the help of the expert. They should be written out in order to avoid mistakes and should be accurate, complete, and as short as possible. The attorney should practice reading the question so that the question can be presented in as interesting a way as possible. Long, complicated hypothetical questions usually serve little purpose as they become dull and very difficult to follow.

Example:

Q: Dr. Hubbard, I ask you for your opinion based on the following hypothetical facts: Assume that on April 3, 2004, a thirty-nine year old man was employed as a groundskeeper in the Ramsey school system. He was riding a lawnmower to care for the grounds at Quigley High School, which were hilly and wooded. This man was mowing at about a speed of two miles per hour. His hands were on the controls and he occasionally had to look back over his shoulder. The mower hit a stump that stuck out of the ground about eight inches high and twenty inches in diameter. The force of the impact knocked the man off the seat of the mower and he fell to the ground. He hit his head on the turf and became unconscious. A passerby saw the accident and came to his aid. When the man became conscious, after about five minutes, the passerby took him to Mounds Park Hospital where he was examined. The examination included an x-ray of his head. The x-ray revealed a fracture line on his skull which extends from the anterior side of the external auditory meatus through the middle of the right parietal bone about four inches. The man complains of severe headaches.

Dr. Williams, assuming all these facts, do you have an opinion based on a reasonable degree of medical certainty whether Mr. Simpson's injury to his head was caused by the fall from the mower.

A: Yes I do.

Q: And please tell us that opinion.

There is a tendency to oversell a case with a hypothetical question and ask the expert to give an opinion far beyond the expert's capability. The hypothetical question should not be used to argue the case. The more that is put in the question, the more there is a chance for exaggeration and error, and the more opportunities there are for the cross-examiner.

E. Questions Calling for Narrative Responses

The direct examination of an expert witness parallels many of the approaches and techniques applicable to a lay witness. There are, however, some differences in strategies. A direct examiner usually wants an expert to answer narrative questions with lengthy responses, and decision makers typically allow expert witnesses much leeway. Many experts testify as if they were a teacher explaining information to the fact finder.

Experts generally are permitted to testify with long narrative responses. This strategy does not mean the expert should be permitted to control the testimony. The attorney should retain control. The expert witness is not an expert in court procedure or tactics. Some experts with courtroom experience can provide useful suggestions regarding how their opinion ought to be introduced and what questions should be asked. A narrative answer should be monitored and interrupted if words or concepts need to be explained or if the expert is getting off the track or is boring.

F.　*Explaining Technical Terms*

The direct examiner must understand and know how to pronounce all of the expert's technical terms. The testimony of an expert may necessarily include the use of technical terms because they are required to lay a foundation for an opinion or because they buttress the credibility of the expert. The direct examiner must make certain that technical terms the expert mentions are explained in plain language that jurors understand. Either the expert should define these terms after using them, or the direct examiner should interrupt and ask the expert to explain the terms. It is critical to an understanding of the expert testimony that definitions of terms be fully explained to the decision maker.

Examples:

Q:　How does a stethoscope work?

Q:　What is a CAT scan?

Q:　You used the term "metacarpals." What are they?

Q:　Mr. Washington, how does a surveyor do a triangulation?

The terms and their correct spelling are also important for the record. The attorney should provide the reporter with a list of the terms the expert will use along with their definitions.

Demonstrative exhibits and visual aids may be effectively used to help experts explain information. Charts, diagrams, models, and videotapes may be prepared which illustrate what an expert describes. For example, a drawing of a gas chromatograph (a device which measures blood alcohol levels) helps the fact finder understand what an expert describes. A model of a human body allows a doctor to explain the relevant parts of a body. A videotape which shows a testing process makes clear what is very difficult to describe with oral testimony. An attorney may create a visual aid while the expert testifies by writing key words the witness uses on an easel pad or computer screen.

G.　*Treatises*

Treatises include books, periodicals, and pamphlets. A treatise may be used on direct or cross-examination. The authenticity of a treatise may be established by a reliable authority, through the admission of a witness, through another verifying expert or through judicial notice. A treatise may be introduced as evidence for any purpose. Treatises do not become exhibits, but the portions of a treatise offered in evidence are read into the record.

When a treatise is in general use and is relied on in a particular field, most experts will admit that it is an authority. An expert cannot prevent being cross-examined by a treatise by saying the particular treatise is not recognized as an authority. If one witness is able to testify that the treatise is authoritative, it may be used to cross-examine another expert, even though that expert refuses to recognize the authority of the treatise. The authoritative parts of the treatise may be read by the attorney or by the expert. It is the verbal testimony that is heard by the fact finder and may be admitted for any and all purposes. Whether used for impeachment purposes or as substantive proof of its contents, a treatise may substitute for a live expert and may corroborate another expert's opinion.

Example:

Examining Lawyer:

Q: Doctor, are you familiar with an article in the National Journal of Medical Research, entitled "The Diagnosis of Migraine Headaches Suffered by Law Students," by Dr. Langdell?

A: Yes, I am.

Q: Have you read that article?

A: Yes, I have.

Q: Have you used the information in that article in your work?

A: Yes, I have.

Q: Do you consider it authoritative?

A: It is a very reliable authority.

By the Attorney:

Your Honor, if I may, I would like to read to the jury one sentence on page 4 of that article entitled, "The Diagnosis of Migraine Headaches Suffered by Law Students."

Judge:

You may do so.

Examining Lawyer:

"The severity of a migraine headache of an average law student bears a direct relationship to the number of law school classes attended by the student."

CROSS-EXAMINATION OF EXPERT WITNESSES

§ 10.6   EXPERT CROSS-EXAMINATION

A.   *Preparing to Cross–Examine the Expert*

Thorough preparation for cross-examination of an expert begins during discovery and case preparation. Information must be obtained regarding the expert's identity, qualifications, opinions, basis for opinions, data and documents, supporting opinions, information relied on in forming opinions, publications, and fees. To effectively cross-examine an expert, the attorney must become knowledgeable about the area of expertise involved in the case. The attorney may acquire this knowledge and become an "expert" by studying the area, reading texts, and taking classes. The attorney's own expert in the case, colleagues, and other experts or attorneys can be useful sources of needed information. Additionally, the attorney can review treatises and articles in helping prepare for cross-examination.

B.   *Cross–Examination Areas*

The cross-examination approaches and techniques explained in Chapter 7 that apply to lay witnesses also apply to expert witnesses. Additionally, this section explains other tactics that can be used to cross-examine experts. These approaches include both supportive and discrediting cross-examination:

Supportive Cross–Examination

- Obtain concessions.
- Criticize the other side's positions.

Discrediting Cross–Examination.

- Disclose expert fees and financial interests.
- Establish bias or prejudice.
- Attack sources of information.
- Show unreliable or insufficient information.
- Dispute facts.
- Show lack of thoroughness.
- Show insufficient testing.
- Establish existence of other causes.
- Show inappropriate or insufficient expertise.
- Establish differences of opinions among experts.
- Establish subjective opinions.
- Introduce inconsistent prior statements.
- Discredit hypothetical questions.
- Expose other deficiencies.

- Expose unreliability of expertise.
- Use treatises.

The attorney must review these techniques and determine which of them are applicable. Experts do not often change their opinion or admit making a major mistake on cross-examination. Thus, attacking the opinion of an expert is difficult. However, an expert's opinion can be indirectly attacked by establishing a few significant deficiencies.

The attorney must also "control" the responses of the expert witness. Some experts have testified many times in court, and may know as much or more about a specific subject than the attorney. The attorney may therefore have difficulty controlling the responses from these experts if the attorney attempts to accomplish too much. The last part of this section presents questions that may be asked to reduce the risk of losing control of an expert while discrediting the testimony.

C. Developing a Plan

It is critical to develop a cross-examination plan and adapt it to the trial testimony. The following section explains a variety of approaches and techniques that form the basis of an effective plan. A successful plan may also incorporate possible, alternative lines of cross-examination depending on the expert's answer.

Cases commonly require an expert to conduct tests to ascertain and support their opinion. For example, an expert in a products liability case may be asked if she conducted a certain test. If she says "no," the cross can proceed to demonstrate what this test would have revealed. If she answers: "It wasn't necessary," the cross can continue to establish the choices and decisions she made and what information she did not obtain.

§ 10.7 SUPPORTIVE AND DISCREDITING CROSS-EXAMINA-TION

A. Supportive Cross–Examination

The cross-examiner ought to be able to identify some areas of agreement with the opposing expert. It is likely that the experts for both parties will agree on some matters, such as:

- Factual matters, such as some of the critical underlying facts.
- Sequence of events and the way things happened.
- Mixed fact and opinion positions that are consistent with the direct examination story.

The following examples illustrate supportive cross of an expert.

1. Obtaining Concessions

An opposing expert may be used to establish, agree with or corroborate positions and opinions propounded by supporting experts. Questions can be asked which obtain admissions regarding generally accepted theories, principles, and opinions among experts and which show that the opposing expert agrees with the cross-examiner's experts.

Example:

Q: Do you agree with Dr. Jekyll that schizophrenia can be effectively treated with certain drugs?

A: Yes.

Q: One of those drugs is Schizophryn?

A: Yes.

Q: Another one of those drugs is Psychophryn?

A: In many situations.

Q: You heard Dr. Jekyll state that the conduct of the defendant on the day of the crime was a classic reaction of a person with a schizophrenic personality.

A: Yes, I recall that statement.

Q: You do agree with that conclusion?

A: I do.

This concession can be effectively used during summation. "The prosecution's expert agreed with our expert. Mr. Hyde, who testified for the prosecution, testified in support of our position. He said...."

2. *Criticizing the Other Side's Position*

The opposing expert may be used to criticize a part of the opposing party's position, statements or conduct. Questions can be asked which establish that what the opposing party said or did was not appropriate or was otherwise deficient.

Example:

Q: After the butterfly valve failed to close completely, the defendant did not replace the valve, correct Mr. Papillion?

A: That is my understanding.

Q: Had the defendant replaced the butterfly valve at that time, this accident may not have happened?

A: That's true.

Q: After the accident, the butterfly valve marked as Exhibit No. 2 was left outside by the defendant?

A: Yes.

Q: And exposed to the sun and the wind and other elements of the weather?

A: Yes.

Q: Those elements affected the condition of the valve as it sat outside for approximately a month?

A: Yes.

Q: If the defendant had placed the butterfly valve in a safe protected environment, say inside a building, the condition of the valve would have been protected?

A: Yes.

Q: Did you conduct any tests on the butterfly valve?

A: Oh, yes.

Q: Why did you?

B. Discrediting Cross–Examination

The most effective way to reduce the impact that an opposing expert has in a case is by discrediting the expert testimony. There are a variety of sources within the testimony itself that can yield successful discrediting efforts, as explained with the following topics and examples.

1. Expert Fees and Financial Interests

An expert usually receives money for time spent in preparing for and testifying at the trial or hearing. The amount of money may be revealed on cross-examination, inferring that the testimony is influenced by the fee. Sometimes the fee is or appears to be excessive. Further, financial interests in a case can be exposed if the expert has testified in similar cases, or for the opposing attorney, or expects to testify in similar cases for the opposing attorney in the future. These fees and interests infer that the expert may be influenced to testify favorably in order to receive future income.

Example:

Q: Dr. Doyle, you received a fee from the plaintiff's attorney for the hours you spent in preparing for this case, correct?

A: Yes.

Q: And you received a fee for the hours you are spending in court during this case?

A: Yes.

Q: You will be sending your bill for these fees to the attorney for the plaintiff?

A: Yes.

Q: The amount of those fees that you receive will be more than $33,000?

A: Yes.

Q: You have been asked to testify in previous cases by the plaintiff's attorney, correct?

A: Yes.

Q: And you testified in several similar previous cases?

A: Yes.

Q: And you expect to testify again in the future?

A: I may.

The direct examiner will often bring out the existence of the fee, the amount of the fee, and involvement in previous cases during direct examination to reduce the impact of this area of cross-examination. In addition, the direct examiner may ask redirect questions allowing the expert to explain that the opinion has not been influenced by the fees or any financial interest. This may not be an effective area for cross-examination if the cross-examiner expects to call an expert to testify on direct examination and that expert has similar fees and financial interests.

The cross-examiner should avoid the question, "You are being paid for your testimony today, aren't you?" An experienced expert witness will reply that the payment is not for the testimony but is compensation for time, and that the charges are the same fee for time whether the expert is in the office or is testifying.

2. Bias or Prejudice

A professional expert witness who testifies frequently may have developed an apparent bias or prejudice because of involvements in previous cases. There are a number of experts who only testify for one side because of circumstances (e.g., treating physicians who testify for injured plaintiffs), and there are experts who testify because of choice (e.g., insurance defense experts). Other experts may not testify exclusively for one type of party, but still may testify more often for either plaintiffs or defendants or prosecutors or criminal defendants.

The extent of the bias or prejudice is influenced by whether the expert has somehow been involved with the facts before liability arose or whether the expert was hired as an advisor to plan or support the litigation, arbitration, or administrative law case. If an expert was a treating expert or was retained before the trial or hearing, the expert can be shown to have been a major participant in the case. If an expert was retained late in the case, the expert will have been influenced by the fact that the expert knew what opinion the attorney wanted the expert to form and assert.

Example:

Q: Doctor Mendoza, you have testified approximately 20 times in court before?

A: Yes.

Q: Of those 20 times, 18 have been on behalf of the defense?

A: I believe so.

Q: Approximately 90% of the times you have previously been in court have been in support of the defense?

A: Yes.

The direct examiner may anticipate this line of questioning and portray the expert as an independent professional and not as a hired gun. The direct examiner may also conduct redirect examination to disclose any favorable aspects of the expert's involvement with the other side of such cases.

3. *Inadequate Sources of Information*

Questions may reveal that an expert relied upon incomplete or inadequate sources of information in forming an opinion. The inference is that the expert did not have all the available information necessary to form a proper opinion, or did not know of a source of information essential to forming an objective opinion. The expert may have received the information primarily from the attorney who hired the expert; the expert may not have had information disclosed by other experts in the trial; or the expert may not have reviewed information essential to forming a proper opinion.

Example:

Q: Doctor Mcintyre, you based your opinion in this case on information that the plaintiff provided you, correct?

A: Yes.

Q: You were not present at the scene of the fire?

A: No.

Q: You never went to the scene of the fire, did you?

A: No.

Q: You never conducted your own investigation of the remains of the building?

A: I did not.

Q: You don't have any personal information about how the fire started?

A: No.

Q: You relied exclusively on the information the plaintiff who hired you provided you?

A: Yes.

Q: That information was contained in a written file?

A: Yes.

Q: You never talked to the owner of the building, who is the defendant in this case, did you?

A: No.

Q: You never talked to the fire marshal in this case?

A: No.

Q: You never talked to anyone except the plaintiff and members of the law firm representing the plaintiff, did you?

A: That's correct.

---

4. Unreliable or Insufficient Information

Some experts may base an opinion on subjective facts obtained from a party. This is particularly true of treating or examining physicians, psychiatrists, or psychologists who derive their information from a patient. The expert's reliance on this information suggests their opinion is unreliable because of the subjective, slanted nature of the information.

Example:

Q: Doctor, you examined Ms. Woo's lower back, correct?

A: Yes.

Q: She told you she had some pain in her lower back, correct?

A: Yes.

Q: She told you she thought the injury she suffered in the boat accident caused that pain?

A: Yes.

Q: You relied on her regarding her claim of lower back pain?

A: Yes.

Q: You looked at her lower back that day?

A: Yes.

Q: There was no bruising in the area of her lower back?

A: No.

Q: There was no apparent muscle spasm present, was there?

A: No.

Q: You took no x-ray of her back?

A: No.

5. Disputed Facts

During direct examination the expert reveals the facts that form the basis for the expert opinion. Some of these facts may be in dispute. On cross-examination the attorney can ask the expert if the opinion would change if the expert relied upon other facts. If the expert agrees with this conclusion, the attorney can argue in summation that the opposing expert agrees with this favorable conclusion. If the expert disagrees with the conclusion, the attorney can argue that the opinion of the expert is suspect because the expert stays with the same opinion regardless of differences in facts.

Example:

Q: Doctor Lavoisier, you based your opinion on the fact that the glucose content was five percent, correct?

A: Yes.

Q: If the glucose content were only four percent, would that fact affect your opinion?

A: It might.

Q: Would the fact that the glucose was less than three percent change your opinion?

A: Yes.

---

6. Lack of Thoroughness

Experts have limited amounts of time to spend in preparing and forming opinions. In many situations experts do not prepare all things carefully or thoughtfully. Questions can be asked which show how little an expert has done and how much more an expert could have done.

Example:

Q: Doctor Ramashad, you conducted a psychiatric examination of the defendant?

A: Yes.

Q: You met with the defendant for an hour and a half?

A: Yes, I interviewed her.

Q: The only time you spent with the defendant was those ninety minutes?

A: Yes.

Q: That is all the time you believed you needed to form an opinion?

A: It was a sufficient amount of time.

Q: If you had spent more time with the defendant you would have acquired more information?

A: Sure.

Q: That additional information may have affected the opinion that you formed about the defendant?

A: It's possible.

Q: You may have learned some things about the defendant you did not learn during your only interview with the defendant?

A: True.

Q: You could have given the defendant some tests?

A: There was no need to.

Q: You decided not to give any tests?

A: That's true.

Q: And those tests may also have given you more information about the defendant?

A: They may have.

Q: And, Doctor, you do not know what you may have learned, do you?

A: I don't know.

Q: And that additional information may well have changed your opinion today, correct?

---

7. *Insufficient Testing*

An expert may not have conducted sufficient tests or procedures to support an opinion. The cross-examiner's own expert can tell the examiner what tests an expert should have or could have conducted before being able to render an opinion. Questions on cross-examination can establish that the expert failed to conduct ordinarily necessary tests, did not obtain information that experts typically rely on before forming an opinion, and may not have obtained critical test results that would have changed the expert's opinion.

Example:

Q: Doctor McCoy, you removed the cast two weeks after the break?

A: Yes.

Q: At that time, you did not test to determine any loss of weakness in the muscle, did you?

A: Not at that time.

Q: You did not believe it necessary?

A: It wasn't.

Q: You choose not to conduct any test, correct?

A: That's right.

Q: You could have rather easily?

A: I suppose.

Q: And you did not conduct any test to determine any weakness with the nerve, did you?

A: No.

Q: You didn't think it was necessary?

A: No.

Q: And, again, you decided not to do any further tests?

A: That's correct.

Q: You placed a new cast on?

A: Yes.

Q: You removed this cast four weeks later?

A: Yes.

Q: Some fractures require much more time in a cast, don't they, Doctor?

A: Yes.

Q: Serious fractures?

A: Usually.

Q: When you removed this final cast, you did not perform an electromyography, did you?

A: No.

Q: Isn't it true an electromyography, if performed early enough, would make it possible to demonstrate a weakness in a muscle or nerve before a permanent loss of strength developed?

A: In some cases, yes.

---

8. *Existence of Other Causes*

Often there are alternative explanations for expert opinions. Cross-examination can reveal those alternatives by establishing other causes in addition to the cause the expert bases the opinion on. The cross-examiner's expert can provide other possible causes of an event.

Example:

Q: Doctor Zhivago, there can be other causes for back pain, can there not?

A: Yes.

Q: A degenerative condition can cause back pain?

A: Yes.

Q: Or stress?

A: Do you mean physical stress or mental stress?

Q: Physical stress.

A: Yes.

Q: And mental stress?

A: I suppose, yes.

Q: And infectious conditions?

A: Yes.

Q: Heredity?

A: Yes.

Q: Congenital conditions?

A: Yes.

Q: Even a preexisting injury?

A: Yes.

---

9. Inappropriate or Insufficient Expertise

The expertise of an expert may be in areas different from those directly involved in the case. An expert may have expertise in a very broad area, and the case may involve a very narrow area. Or an expert may have expertise in a very narrow area, and the case may involve a broader area of expertise. Some opposing experts may be vulnerable to these attacks based on the lack of education, training, experience, or skills in an area of expertise involved in the case.

The emphasis attached to this area of cross-examination depends upon how the opposing expert contrasts with the cross-examiner's own expert. If a broad area of expertise is applicable to the case, the cross-examiner should attempt to narrow the expertise of the opponent's expert. If a narrow area of expertise is appropriate to the case, the expert should attempt to broaden the expertise of the opponent's expert.

Example:

Q: Ms. Veranzano, your Master's degree is in structural engineering?

A: Yes.

Q: You did not major in electrical engineering, did you?

A: I did not major in it, but I had some courses in it.

Q: Your experience has primarily been in the field of structural engineering?

A: Primarily.

Q: More of your professional life has involved the area of structural engineering as contrasted with the area of electrical engineering?

A: Yes.

Q: You have published numerous professional articles?

A: Yes, many.

Q: You have written articles on structural engineering?

A: Yes.

Q: You have written articles on bridge construction?

A: Yes.

Q: And you have written articles that have appeared in structural engineering magazines?

A: Yes.

Q: None of those articles deal with the electrical engineering issues in this case, do they?

A: Not directly.

Q: You have not relied on any of those articles as a basis for your opinion in this case, have you?

A: I did not need to.

Q: Because those articles did not deal with the matters at issue in this case?

A: They did not.

---

10. Differences of Opinion Among Experts

Opinions in some areas of expertise are subject to significant and legitimate differences of opinion among qualified experts. This is especially true in fields of expertise involving subjective or interpretive fields, such as psychiatry or economics. Questions can be asked which establish different experts have legitimate differences of opinion and the testifying expert has been sometimes wrong and sometimes right in the past.

Example:

Q: Doctor Heller, it is difficult to predict with accuracy the rate of inflation for future years?

A: Yes.

Q: It is fair to say that prominent economists differ among themselves regarding the future rate of inflation?

A: Yes.

Q: This area of predicting the rate of inflation is subject to significant differences of opinion among experts?

A: Yes.

Q: You have been an expert economist for over twenty years?

A: Yes.

Q: During that span of time, you have had occasion to predict the rate of inflation?

A: Yes.

Q: Sometimes your predictions have been accurate?

A: Yes.

Q: And sometimes your predictions have been inaccurate?

A: Yes.

Q: You have disagreed with the predictions of experts whom you consider to be renowned in the field of economics?

A: Yes.

Q: And these experts who are authorities in their field and whom you recognize as authorities — have disagreed with your predictions regarding the rate of inflation in the past?

A: I suppose.

Q: And sometimes their predictions — and not yours—have been accurate?

A: Yes.

---

11. *Subjective Opinions*

An expert may admit that the opinion the expert reached is a matter of judgment and not based on some immutable principles. This technique is useful for areas of expertise that are more subjective in nature than scientific. For example, in areas of expertise that are based on interpretations, evaluations can effectively be attacked.

Example:

Q: The assessment of the value of real property is not a science, is it Ms. Monopoly?

A: No, it is not a science.

Q: There are many variables that affect the value of a piece of property, correct?

A: Yes.

Q: Some of these variables are based on subjective evaluations and not objective data?

A: That is true.

Q: Some of these factors require an appraiser individually to interpret property values, correct?

A: Yes.

---

12. Inconsistent Prior Statements

An expert witness can be cross-examined using any oral or written statement by that expert that contradicts or is inconsistent with a position taken on direct examination, as with a lay witness.

Example:

Q: Dr. Keynes, you testified on direct examination that the defendant properly used the FIFO method in this transaction because it is the "preferred method" employed by accountants, is that right?

A: Yes.

Q: Doctor, you prepared a written report summarizing your opinions of this case, didn't you?

A: Yes.

Q: The attorney for the plaintiff retained you and paid you for your time in preparing that report?

A: Yes.

Q: Before preparing the report you thoroughly reviewed all the facts, correct?

A: Yes.

Q: You consider yourself an expert with regard to accounting procedures, don't you?

A: Yes.

Q: The report that you prepared was accurate, wasn't it?

A: Yes.

Q: Doctor, I would like to show you your written report. You do recognize this report as the one you prepared, correct?

A: Yes.

Q: Your signature appears at the end of the report on page 5?

A: Yes.

Q: Please turn to page 3, second paragraph, 4th line.

A: Okay.

Q: You wrote what's contained on that line in that paragraph in that report, didn't you?

A: Yes.

Q: You wrote on line 4 that: "Neither the FIFO nor the LIFO method is preferred in a case such as this."

A: I see that.

---

13. Hypothetical Questions

If a hypothetical question is used on direct examination, an effective way to cross-examine the expert is to ask the expert concise hypothetical questions which contain facts different from the direct examination hypothetical. This approach is similar to the technique discussed in Section 10.5 and can be used with similar success. There are fewer opportunities to cross-examine the expert on the basis of the hypothetical facts because hypothetical questions are asked less often on direct examination.

14. Treatises

Treatises can be used during the cross-examination of an expert to impeach that expert as well as for other purposes. Federal Rule of Evidence 803(18) and similar state rules provide:

- Treatises may be used on cross-examination of an opposing expert, or on the direct examination of an expert.
- Treatises include treatises, periodicals, pamphlets, articles, and professional magazines.
- Treatises must be established as "reliable authority" by admission of a witness or by another expert or by notice.
- Treatises may be introduced as evidence for any purpose.
- Treatises are read into the record and do not become exhibits.

Some experts who have written extensively may have published a position contrary to their position taken at the trial or hearing. Other experts may be impeached by treatises another person authored. This impeachment process requires a thorough review of all the publications in the area and a detailed index of these publications for use during trial.

An expert on cross-examination need only admit that a treatise is a reliable authority generally recognized in an area. The expert does not have to have relied upon the treatise or professionally agree to its position. Leading questions which establish that the treatise has successive editions, is used extensively in professional schools, or appears in the offices of many experts, may establish this foundation.

If an expert on cross-examination denies the general reliability of the treatise, the treatise may still be used but will need to be established as authoritative by another expert, by notice, by the publisher of the book, or by a librarian. Some jurisdictions still require the witness on cross-examination concede that the treatise is authoritative and that the witness relies on it before it can be used for impeachment.

The attorney proffering the treatise may read it to the fact finder and it becomes part of the record. The treatise is admitted as evidence for all purposes: for impeachment, as substantive proof of its contents, to substitute for a live expert, or to corroborate another expert's opinion. The opinion of an author of a treatise or other learned publication can be introduced through the treatise even though the author does not testify. See Section 10.5(G).

Example:

Examining Attorney:

Q: Dean Dean, are you familiar with a text entitled, The Economics of Law Schools?

A: Yes.

Q: This text has been a reliable authority in the field of economics for many years, correct?

A: Yes.

Q: Do you consider this text to be authoritative?

A: It's one authority.

Q: Dean, do you agree with the following statement that appears on page 169: "The increase of law school tuition is in inverse proportion to the number of blue books graded by law school professors."?

A: In general, I agree.

To the Arbitrator:

I now would like to read a short paragraph from page 368 of the text.

Arbitrator:

You may do so.

Examining Attorney:

"A major factor which law school administrators use to determine a law professor's salary is based upon the formula equal to pi squared times the number of footnotes in the law review articles the professor has published during leap years." No further questions.

---

15. *Safely Exposing Deficiencies*

Additional areas that can be established on cross are topics that do not depend upon the facts and circumstances relating to the specific area of expertise. These areas include "safe" questions which can be asked if questions suggested in the previous subsections are not appropriate or are too risky.

- The late entry of the expert into the case. Perhaps the opposing attorney did not secure this expert until immediately before the trial or hearing.

- The very limited amount of time the expert spent reviewing the information and data.

- The fact the information the expert relied upon has been provided primarily by the party who retained the expert.

- The facts and information upon which the expert relied are not the facts upon which other testifying experts in the case relied.

16. *Lack of Reliability of the Field of Expertise*

This area may be available if the advocate does not present an expert in the field of expertise presented by the opposing party's expert. The attorney should then attempt to ask cross-examination questions establishing the unreliability of the field of expertise and the failure of experts in that area to accept and recognize the area as a reliable field of expertise. Topics that may be successfully covered using this approach include:

- Lack of education, experience, training, and the expert's skills;

- Differences between related areas of expertise that have been generally recognized and unrecognized;

- Unreliability of the procedures, tests, or opinions rendered; and

- The observation that the field of expertise is nothing more than the application of common sense that the fact finders may apply on their own.

CHAPTER 11
SUMMATION

K. Improperly
   Referring to
   Results in
   Similar Cases

L. Improper
   Comments

M. Improper In-
   terruptions

N. Admonishing
   Counsel

REFLECTING ON ADVOCACY

Facts, as such, never settle anything. They are working tools only. It is the implications that can be drawn from facts that count.

—Clarence Belden Randall

A good speech is a good thing, but the verdict is the thing.

—Daniel O'Connell

§ 11.1 INTRODUCTION

A. Scope

Summation is the final opportunity the advocate has to make an oral presentation to the fact finder. During summation, the advocate may explain the evidence, the law applicable to the evidence, and reasons why the jurors should render a verdict or why the judge or arbitrator should decide in favor of the advocate's client.

Summation usually occurs after the close of all the evidence. Summation is also known as closing argument or final argument, although the term "argument" may misstate the primary purpose of summation. It is not enough for the attorney to "argue" the rightness or wrongness of positions to the fact finder. The attorney must "advocate" and present a reasonable, persuasive explanation. Summation can never be a substitute for the facts and the law. Lawsuits are won by what happens during the entire case presentation.

B. Purposes

The purposes of summation are to:

- Summarize the factual theories of a case.
- Explain persuasively the significance of the evidence presented.
- Draw reasonable inferences, argue conclusions, comment on credibility, refer to common sense, and explain implications that the fact finder may not perceive.
- Explain the law, elements of the claims and defenses, and jury instructions in jury trials.
- Answer questions from a judge or arbitrator.
- Highlight the rational and emotional dimensions of the case.
- Integrate the theories, evidence, and law into a cohesive and comprehensive presentation.

C. The Summation Story

A case begins with the story told during opening statement and concludes with a story summarized during closing argument. The story of the case should be a story that moves the fact finders to want to render a favorable decision. An effective summation provides the decision makers with reasonable explanations, appropriately evokes the emotions of the events that occurred, and provides a motivation to return a favorable decision.

All cases involve reasons and emotions and have facts that support the telling of a compelling story. Criminal cases involve matters of freedom and liberty. Personal injury cases involve pain and suffering. Commercial litigation cases involve the economic livelihood of people. Antitrust cases involve public interest issues. The advocate must try to bring to life the emotions and feelings underlying the drama of those events.

D. The Human Dimensions

Decision makers base their conclusions not only on the logic and reasons supporting a position but also on the human dimensions of the case. An intellectual argument that reaches only the minds of the fact finder is usually not sufficient. The advocate must present an argument that involves the emotions of the decision makers as well as their intellects. Decision makers want to do what is right, and they also want to be fair. They want to do what is reasonable, and they also want to feel good about their decision.

The advocate must consider using these psychological and emotional influences. Every advocate has this ability. Every attorney, outside the courtroom and hearing room, has told a story to someone that touched the listener and produced appropriate feelings. This same ability will be needed during summation when the advocate must tell part of the story in a way that similarly influences the fact finders.

This goal of presenting a reasonable and emotional story is the art of presenting a compelling closing argument. An advocate has goals that are similar to the goals of speakers in other professions. Take a moment and think about effective speakers and consider their approaches. They not only presented information and advanced reasonable positions but also said something that appropriately tapped emotions that affected decisions.

An improper or inappropriate appeal to emotions must be avoided. Fact finders who hear an inappropriate appeal to emotions may conclude that the facts, the law, and reason do not support the attorney's position. The effects of a singular appeal to emotion are usually not long-lasting. Pure emotional appeals may be effective while in the courtroom or hearing room, but such appeals lose their impact after time passes.

E. Values and Viewpoints

Summation is no different than other aspects of trial advocacy. The focus must be on what is likely to most help the decision maker decide the case favorably. The values, norms, viewpoints, and life principles of each decision maker will have a profound influence on how the stories are heard and interpreted and what may be said in summation that successfully influences the final decision.

As a final decision is formed, it is unlikely that the judgment will be based on factors that contradict the core values and guiding viewpoints of the decision maker. And so a summation that includes reasons and explanations that reflect the beliefs and norms of the decision maker may be most influential.

§ 11.2 WHAT CAN BE PRESENTED

A. Facts and Opinions

All facts and opinions which are a part of the case, even those in dispute, may be described during summation. The attorney should discuss all important evidence and selectively discuss remaining evidence.

B. Inferences

Inferences are conclusions drawn from the evidence presented. Generally, the attorney may make and explain all reasonable inferences from the evidence so long as the inferences are related to the evidence presented.

C. The Story

The attorney should summarize the case story expressed in words and phrases used throughout the trial or hearing. The closing argument presents an opportunity for the attorney to connect the themes of the case with the evidence and applicable law.

D. The Law and the Legal Theories

During final argument, the attorney may explain how the law applies to the facts to support the decision sought and how the evidence supports the legal theories.

E. Theory of the Case

A focal point of closing argument is an explanation of the theory of the case. Opening was the first time the advocate expressed the theory of the case, summation is the last time the theory can be further explained. See Section 2.5.

F. Anecdotal References

The attorney has the opportunity during summation to present anecdotes, analogies, and metaphors involving common life experiences and to employ a variety of persuasive techniques, including the use of fictional stories, poems, and appropriate references from other works of literature and art.

G. *Underlying Values and Norms*

Explanations how a decision in favor of a client supports and is consistent with the values and norms of the decision maker will increase the chance of success. A decision based on contrary principles and beliefs will appear to be the wrong decision to that decision maker.

H. *New Explanations*

An important goal of summation is providing the decision maker with an explanation of the case that the decision maker has not thought of or considered. The advocate should strive to present new ideas, explanations, and interpretations of facts, law, and events. The art of advocacy is providing insights into a case which are not apparent from the facts and law.

I. *Urging a Result*

The closing argument is the last opportunity the attorney has to explain and ask for the specific result the client wants.

J. *No Requirement to Discuss Everything*

The attorney is not required to summarize or comment upon all the facts, opinions, inferences, and law involved in a case. A failure to comment on and refute a credible position or defense developed by opposing counsel, however, may be a mistake. A decision not to address an issue, an opponent's theory, or a particular fact should be based on an analysis of the importance of that subject and the ability of the attorney and the opponent to explain persuasively the position to the fact finder.

§ 11.3 PREPARATION

A. *Early and Continuing Preparation*

The planning of a case begins with the preparation of the closing argument. See Section 2.4. The final argument provides the focus for the entire case. Throughout the case, the attorney should be preparing the fact finder for what will be heard during the closing argument. A closing argument should reemphasize the theory of the case previously presented. The factual summary and legal theories of a case that were selected prior to the trial or hearing provide a framework of ideas for the closing argument. These concepts need to be refined and revised depending on how the evidence develops during the case.

1. *Jury Selection*

In a jury trial, the first opportunity to present a case to a jury is during jury selection. The attorney is prohibited from directly arguing the case in this initial stage of the trial, but may indirectly inform the potential jurors about the theories of the case. Through questions, the attorney prepares the jurors for what they will hear and see during the trial. References to jury selection responses may be made during summation. The attorney may attempt to persuade the jurors to find a favorable verdict by asking a question during jury selection and later, during closing argument, referring back to the answer, promise, or commitment the jurors gave. This technique creates a psychological inducement for the jurors to act consistently with their initial position.

For example, in a civil damage case, the plaintiff's attorney during jury selection ordinarily questions the jury members regarding their ability to return a verdict for a substantial amount of money if substantial damages are proven. The plaintiff's attorney during summation may refer to the juror's "agreement" or "promise" to award substantial damages based on the evidence presented.

2. Opening Statement

Opening statement provides an opportunity to lay a complete foundation for the closing argument. During an opening, the attorney, for the first time, explains the evidence that is subsequently discussed during closing argument. The explanation during opening must be consistent with the closing argument, otherwise the attorney will appear to have failed to prove the case.

3. Presenting the Evidence

Direct and cross-examination testimony develops the facts that were initially explained during the opening statement. The complete and credible presentation of evidence is the last step in preparing the fact finder for final argument.

B. Jury Trial Instructions

Prior to the closing argument in a jury trial, the judge informs the attorneys of the exact instructions of law to be provided to the jury. In most jurisdictions, the charge to the jury takes place after summation. In some jurisdictions, the judge charges the jury before summation. The attorney must review these final instructions and make certain the evidence explained in the final argument supports the law which will be explained by the judge. See Section 12.2.

All statements of law made by the attorney must be accurate. The judge will tell the jury that if the attorney has explained the law differently than the judge, the jury must ignore the attorney's statement. If the attorney misstates the law, the attorney loses credibility and diminishes the impact of summation. If the attorney states the law correctly, even using the same words as the judge, the result can raise the credibility of the attorney and positively reinforce the attorney's summation.

C. Identifying Central, Pivotal Issues

The advocate must simplify the issues for the decision makers. A review of the factual summaries and legal theories will determine which facts and what legal elements are undisputed and which important, controversial issues remain disputed. Evidence that has been stipulated, uncontradicted or unrebutted may resolve some issues.

The following checklist provides a framework to construct a closing argument based on the primary issues the fact finder must make in a case:

1. *Believable Story*

- Identify reasons why the story ought to be believed.

- Use analogies or common sense explanations to support the story.

- Rely on favorable legal principles.

2. *Credibility of a Witness*

- Summarize the testimony of the witness.

- Describe the favorable demeanor of the witness.

- Rely on exhibits introduced through the witness.

- Rely on corroborating testimony or exhibits.

- Use legal principles that support the credibility of the witness.

- Attack opposing witnesses with contradictory testimony.

- Describe the unfavorable demeanor of opposing witnesses.

3. *Reasonable Inferences*

- Summarize favorable testimony.

- Identify supportive physical and documentary evidence and lay and expert opinion testimony.

- Rely upon favorable law.

- Employ a supporting analogy or anecdote.

4. *Application of Law to Facts*

- Reasonably interpret the law.

- Specifically apply elements of the legal standards to the evidence.

D. Anticipating the Opponent's Position

The preparation of the case requires an attorney to anticipate the various theories and positions of the opposing case. The presentation of the case makes clear the exact positions taken by the opposing lawyer. By the close of the evidence, an attorney should know what the opposing attorney will argue in summation. The attorneys need to predict the most persuasive and compelling argument that opposing counsel could present and analyze how to counter this argument. The more accurate the prediction, the better the chances that a final argument can be constructed to rebut or reduce the impact of the opposing argument.

E. Selecting Exhibits and Visual Aids

The attorney must decide which exhibits and visual aids are to be used during summation. Consideration should be given to the impact the exhibits and visual aids may have on the decision maker, the importance of the exhibits in the case, and how effectively the visual aids can be employed. Real evidence, demonstrative evidence, deposition transcripts, witness statements, discovery responses, and any other exhibit that has been introduced during the case may be used during closing argument. Visual aids may also be created that highlight summation. These visual aids may include: a prepared chart; a summary of evidence or argument on a poster, a board, or monitor screen; handwritten notes by the attorney on a whiteboard or easel page; a power point presentation using a laptop; or an enlarged copy of the verdict form in a jury trial.

F. Length

Summation should be long enough to cover the essential arguments of the case, yet short enough to maintain the attention of the decision maker. The reasonable, optimum length for a closing argument varies depending upon the circumstances and complexity of the case and the speaking ability of the attorney. Many closing arguments last between twenty and forty minutes. Even in complex and lengthy cases, summations seldom take longer than a few hours. The longer a closing argument is, the more difficult it is to maintain the attention of the decision maker. In those jurisdictions that permit rebuttal, the attorney may need to reserve time for rebuttal by requesting permission from the judge or arbitrator.

Trial judges ordinarily ask the attorneys how long they anticipate the closing argument will take and usually allow lawyers a sufficient amount of time for summation. Trial judges have broad discretion in restricting the time available and will limit the time if the requested amount is unnecessarily long or out of proportion to the length of the trial or the issues to be resolved.

Some jurisdictions by statute or rules, and some judges by local practice, impose specific time limits on arguments. In these courts, the trial judge usually gives additional time if the attorney provides legitimate reasons for needing more time.

While administrative law judges and arbitrators may expect brief closing arguments, longer arguments, if effective, can be presented. Administrative cases and arbitrations may involve specific time deadlines, and summation needs to be completed during the available time.

G. Order and Sequence

The general rule is that the party who has the burden of proof closes last. Because the plaintiff/claimant/prosecutor has such a burden, they argue last. However, in a very few jurisdictions the order is different and the attorney must determine if the case is being tried in one of these locations.

In those jurisdictions which permit rebuttal argument, there are three summations: the first argument by the party with the burden, the opposing argument, and a rebuttal argument. In those jurisdictions that do not permit rebuttal, there are two summations: the defense argues first followed by the plaintiff/claimant/prosecutor. In civil cases, in which both parties carry the burden of proof, usually the plaintiff/claimant has the opportunity to have the final argument. If the burden of proof in a civil case rests with the defendant/respondent, the defense is permitted the last closing argument.

The attorney who argues last usually has an advantage because that attorney can rebut any argument the opposing lawyer makes. The lawyer who argues first and has no rebuttal has to anticipate what the opposing counsel will say in rebuttal and counter those points during summation. Counsel who has rebuttal can divide the argument and save some persuasive parts for rebuttal.

H. The "Opening" Summation

In jurisdictions that permit rebuttal, the advocate must decide what to include in the initial closing and what to save for rebuttal. Usually, the scope of rebuttal argument is limited to the points made during the opponent's argument that were not explained during the initial summation. Practically, however, the scope of rebuttal is very broad because the closing argument by the opposing lawyer generally covers all important issues in the case. A rebuttal lawyer may prefer to save some important points for rebuttal to reduce the chance opposing counsel may anticipate and counter them.

I. Rebuttal Summation

Rebuttal summation should emphasize the pivotal issues not covered during the initial closing and counter points made by the opponent. A rebuttal summation is more effective if begun by advancing positive reasons in support of a favorable decision, instead of beginning with defensive explanations. The points made by the opponent need to be countered during rebuttal, but rebuttal should primarily present an affirmative argument.

Rebuttal summation can be prepared in advance by predicting what the other attorney will argue. This advance preparation permits the integration of the counter arguments into a restatement of the case theory. Any appeal to emotion should also be prepared in advance to close summation with a dramatic conclusion appropriate for the case. The emotional appeal with the most potential impact may be best saved for the very end of the argument.

J. Written Outline and Detailed Script

The final argument outline that was prepared during case preparation may need to be revised. This final outline should include all parts of the closing argument to make certain that every matter that needs to be addressed has been included. Form 11.1 provides an outline of factors that can be included in summation.

Some lawyers prefer to write out or dictate a complete closing argument. This approach helps the attorney finalize the contents of the closing argument and helps determine whether some matter has been omitted. This script should not be used during the presentation of the closing argument. Reading a script of a closing argument bores the listeners and significantly diminishes the persuasive power of the attorney because the presentation appears dry and impersonal. The attorney should prepare a key word outline from the script. With practice and preparation, the outline should be all that is needed and used during final argument.

K. Rehearsal

The closing argument must be rehearsed. Oral practice permits the attorney to improve both the content and the style of delivery. The attorney may rehearse the closing argument before colleagues, in front of a mirror, or on videotape for review and critique. The attorney should practice until the summation can be presented in as persuasive a manner as possible. A thorough understanding of the argument comes through practice. When presenting the closing argument, the attorney should not necessarily attempt to recall the words used during the practice sessions, but express the ideas rehearsed in these sessions. A sincere, flowing, and persuasive argument can only be presented when the attorney is comfortable with the material and the delivery.

FORM 11.1
CLOSING ARGUMENT WORKSHEET

Case _____ File _____

Case Theories/Themes

Structure

Introduction

Argument

Inferences

Explanations

Evidence

Witnesses

Credibility of Witnesses

Circumstantial Evidence

Law/Jury Instructions

Special Interrogatories/Verdict Form

Analogies/Metaphors/Anecdotes

Exhibits/Visual Aids

Emotional Aspects

Case Weaknesses

Burden of Proof

Opposing Argument

Facts Not Proved/Promises Not Kept

Request for Order/Award/Decision/Verdict

Conclusion

Rebuttal

L. Specific Requirements

The attorney needs to determine before summation whether the judge or arbitrator has any special requirements or limitations or whether applicable rules regulate the final argument. Determining this avoids having the closing argument interrupted by objections from opposing counsel. Local practice and procedures, such as the prohibition of the use of some visual aids during closing argument or time restrictions, may limit what can be done during summation.

§ 11.4 ORGANIZATION

A. Structure

Closing arguments, like all other parts of the case, must be presented in a structured manner that most effectively achieves the purposes of the closing argument. Any number of structures may be used. The selection of a structure depends upon the theories, facts, law, circumstances, and strategies of the case. The following are some examples of different structures:

1. Chronology

The closing argument can follow the chronology of the story presented during the case.

2. Flashback

The closing argument can begin with the conclusion of the story, which the fact finder has already heard, and flashback to earlier events which explain and describe what happened.

3. Undisputed and Disputed Facts

The evidence can be explained first by describing the undisputed facts and then highlighting the disputed facts, with an explanation that the facts supporting the attorney's case are what actually happened.

4. Order of Key Witnesses

If key witnesses testified in a logical or reasonable order, summation can be structured based on their testimony.

5. Issues, Positions, Topics

Summation can be structured based on the order the issues, positions, or topics were presented in a case.

6. Claims or Defenses

The structure of a closing can be based on the claims or defenses asserted. For example, claimant's counsel in a breach of contract case can present an argument based on the factors that prove the existence of a breach of warranty. Defense counsel may organize a final argument based on the number of defenses supported by the evidence. For example, a criminal defense attorney can present a closing argument based on a number of reasonable doubts.

7. Liability and Damages

In civil cases, the closing argument could begin with an explanation of the liability issues followed by the damage issues, or vice versa.

8. The Law, Jury Instructions, Verdict Form

Summation can be based on the elements of the applicable law or order of the substantive jury instructions and verdict form. For example, in a criminal case, the prosecutor can structure a final argument by following the elements to be proved in a burglary case. In a breach of contract case, respondent's counsel can structure a final argument which rebuts the elements of contract law covering the creation of a contract, its breach, and damages. In a jury trial, a verdict form that contains special interrogatories provides an organized way of reviewing the evidence. The jurors will sequentially answer these questions as they appear in the form, and counsel can use the same format during closing argument.

9. Multiple Substructures

Many closing arguments employ a number of these alternative structures. For example, a closing argument may contain a description of undisputed facts, followed by a narrative chronology of the disputed facts, followed by an explanation of legal elements. Section 2.6 explained the various issues that can be decided in a case. Each of these issues may be described during summation by employing different structures.

B. Introduction of Summation

Summation should begin with an introduction that draws the attention and interest of the decision makers to the presentation of the argument. The attention level will usually be high at the beginning of summation as the case is drawing to a close. The introduction sets the tone for the final argument and should be designed to have a persuasive impact.

The proper tone of a case depends upon the facts and circumstances and the primary goal of the introductory statements. A common way to begin is a low-key approach, with passionate appeals reserved until later stages of the closing. Another approach is to establish an appropriate, dramatic tone at the beginning and periodically return to this theme during the closing.

The following examples demonstrate alternative introductory statements.

1. Case Theory

An effective way to begin the closing argument is to summarize in a few sentences the factual summaries and legal theories of the case. This approach reinforces what the decision maker has heard during the previous stages of the case.

Example (Civil Plaintiff):

This case is about a job that was arbitrarily taken from a hardworking woman. This case is about Libby Joyce and her right to be treated fairly and decently. This case is not about some abstract facts. What you heard from this witness stand and what you read from these documents really happened. It happened to this woman. It happened because of the poor judgment and mismanagement by this corporate employer. For the past two days you saw and heard this story unfold in this arbitration.

Example (Civil Plaintiff):

This lawsuit is about safety. Thomas Harvick had a right to the safe functioning of the products he bought from the defendant. He had a right to expect he would not be electrocuted by a defectively designed product — a tragedy that could have been prevented by inexpensive insulation. Insulation protects people against shock and could have — would have — prevented the unnecessary death of Tom Harvick. A small expense of $44.00 for a ceramic insulator on the chain of this window washer's harness — would have prevented the electrocution of Thomas Harvick. That is what this trial has been all about.

---

2. Dramatic Introduction

A dramatic introductory statement attempts to establish an atmosphere, set a tone, and grab the jury's attention. A dramatic statement that is appropriate to the case and presented in a sincere and natural manner can be effective.

Example (Civil Plaintiff):

What is more precious than the birth of a child? A child who is healthy and who has a full life to live. To love, to cry, to laugh, to fail, to succeed. What is more tragic than the birth of a child who is born without the ability to take care of herself, to ever tell her parents how much she loves them, to ever cry, to ever laugh, to ever fail or succeed at school or work?

Example (Criminal Prosecution):

Members of the Jury, that man (pointing to the defendant) on the morning of August 16 walked into his garage, opened up his toolbox, and pulled out a claw hammer. That man (looking at the defendant), grasping the claw hammer in his right hand, walked from his garage, through his kitchen, up the stairway, into the bedroom of his home, and deliberately stood over his wife, who was peacefully asleep. That man, the defendant Walter Simmons, intentionally raised that claw hammer in the air and with all his might smashed that claw hammer into the face of the woman who married him and lived with him until he ruthlessly killed her.

3. Outline of Argument

Summation may begin with an explanation of the outline of the presentation. The decision maker may find it easier to follow the argument if they know how it is organized and what structure the attorney will use.

Example (Plaintiff Contract):

This presentation consists of three parts — the same three parts I discussed during opening statement. First, I will show how the evidence establishes the existence of a valid and enforceable contract. Second, I will explain how the evidence clearly establishes how and why the respondent breached its contract with my client. Third, I will review with you all the damages my client has suffered which the defendant is obligated to pay.

4. Explanation of Summation for Jurors

In jury trials, final argument can begin with an explanation of the purpose of summation. The advantage of these preliminary remarks is that the jurors may better understand the reasons for closing argument. The disadvantage of these remarks is they may not be the most effective and persuasive way to begin summation.

Example (General):

We are now about to come to the end of this trial. Soon you will deliberate together and reach a verdict. This part of the trial — summation — provides me with an opportunity to speak to you for the last time. What I will say to you will be consistent with what I have said to you before and with what you have heard and seen during this trial.

Example (General):

Five days ago you knew nothing about this case. This week you have heard the testimony of several witnesses and have seen several documents. Five days ago I presented to you an opening statement — a story of what you would hear and see. Today I will summarize that evidence and explain to you how the facts and the law lead to the conclusion that my client is entitled to a verdict in this case.

These introductory remarks are sometimes used because attorneys need something easy to say to reduce their nervousness, or because they have heard another attorney make similar statements, or because they have not considered alternative introductory remarks. Many attorneys prefer not to begin summation with these explanatory remarks but may delay making such comments until after they explain their case theory or use an alternative attention-grabbing statement.

5. *Expressing Gratitude*

It is customary for some advocates during summation to thank the decision makers for their attention and time. A statement of appreciation should be sincere, brief and not patronizing. Whether the beginning of summation should include this statement or whether it should be mentioned later, if it all, depends on how the attorney wants to begin. Some lawyers believe there is no need to thank decision makers because they are doing their job or duty.

Example (General):

We have now come to the stage of the trial called closing argument. The witnesses have all testified. The documents have all been introduced. We, the attorneys, are almost done. You will shortly begin your deliberations to reach a just and fair verdict in this case. My client, Brenda Dunn, and I, and all of us involved in this trial, thank you for the time and attention you have devoted to this case.

6. *Defense Introductions*

Defense counsel can begin summation with any one of these suggested openings in jurisdictions where there is no rebuttal. In jurisdictions where there is rebuttal, defense follows the plaintiff/claimant/prosecutor. An alternative introductory statement may include an indirect or direct reference to a statement made by opposing counsel.

Example (Civil Defense):

You have just heard part of the story of what happened on August 1. You did not hear an explanation of the entire story. You will now, and when you do you will understand how the evidence supports the whole story told by the defendant Robert Kost and does not support the partial story told by the plaintiff Tom Kost.

Example (Defense Multiparty Case):

In some cases there are two sides to a story. In this case, there are three sides to the story. During the trial you heard and saw evidence introduced in bits and pieces supporting different versions of what happened three years ago during September. I will help you piece together the third story and show you how the bits of evidence lead you to the conclusion that it is the only accurate and reliable story of what happened.

Example (Criminal Defense):

The prosecutor used this chart to explain to you the legal elements of the crime the government had to prove beyond a reasonable doubt for you to conclude that my client is guilty of burglary. I will explain to you how the prosecutor failed to prove each of these elements, and then I will present to you six additional reasonable doubts why John Sapphire did not commit the crime that happened on June 15.

---

7. Rebuttal Introductions

The attorney who has a rebuttal argument can begin with a prepared introductory statement or can begin with remarks that contradict the opposing argument.

Example (Plaintiff):

Defense counsel wants you to think there are six reasons which show there is reasonable doubt in this case that her client did not steal over $50,000 worth of jewelry. There are no such six reasons. The evidence clearly establishes the guilt of John Sapphire. I told you during opening statement I would present evidence to you of the guilt of the defendant. I presented that evidence to you. I now want to clarify a few remarks counsel made during her closing argument and answer a few questions you may have in your mind about how John Sapphire committed the crime of burglary.

---

8. Alternative Introductions

The attorney should prepare introductory remarks that most effectively meet the primary goal the attorney wants to achieve during the beginning of the closing argument. The previous examples illustrate some possibilities. Other approaches should be considered. Attorneys may obtain ideas about other introductory statements from the world of art and literature, including plays, movies, books, or from arguments given by other attorneys.

An attorney may prepare a number of alternative introductory statements and, after selecting the most effective statement, modify the other statements and use them during some other stage of the closing argument. For example, an attorney may prefer to begin with an explanation of the case theory followed by an explanation of the purpose of closing argument. Or an attorney may prefer to begin with a dramatic statement followed by an explanation of the outline of the closing argument.

C. Body of Closing Argument

Section 11.5 provides numerous illustrations of the content of the main portion or body of summation. The topics to be covered during the summation need to be structured in an orderly, persuasive manner. An example of such a structure is:

- The introductory statement,
- Explanation of pivotal issues in the case,
- Summary of important facts, opinions, and inferences,
- Description of who, what, when, where, how, and why,
- Application of facts to support legal elements,
- Explanation of legal elements or key jury instructions and verdict form,
- Summary of strengths of the case,
- Explanation of weaknesses of opponent's case,
- Reference to burden of proof,
- Answer questions from judge or arbitrator,
- Explanation of reasons supporting favorable decision,
- Description of the remedy sought, and
- Conclusion.

D. Conclusion

Summation should conclude with a strong ending. The attorney should review the facts, the theories, and the law to create a conclusion that leaves the decision maker wanting to find in the favor of the client. The conclusion of the argument should be well thought out and should be designed to tie the argument together and be a clear and obvious ending. Even if there have been some problems in the argument and the attorney gets flustered or lost, a strong conclusion may help offset these problems.

Example (Criminal Defense):

Chuck's liberty and future are in your hands. We thank you for your time and the attention you have devoted to this case. Years from now when you look back at this trial, you must be able to conclude that your verdict was the right one, that it was fair and just. Years from now, the prosecutor may not remember this case, nor may the public. But the defendant cannot forget.

Chuck must live all his life with your decision, which can only be not guilty.

Soon you will go and deliberate. Let me tell you a story to help direct you. There was an old man and a young boy.

The old man was known to be very wise. The young boy was scheming of a way to prove that the old man was not wise about everything. And so the young boy trapped a little bird, and he took it in his hands and went up to the old man. He said, "Old man, old man, what do I have in my hands?" And the old man being wise, said, "You have a little bird." And the clever little boy said, "Tell me, old man, is the bird alive or dead?" And the young boy gleefully thought, "Now I have him. For you see, if the old man says it is alive, I will crush it and kill it and show him that it was dead. And if the old man says it is dead, I will open my hands and turn the little bird free, proving the old man is wrong." And the old man, being very wise, looked at the clever little boy straight in the eyes and said, "The answer is in your hands." And the liberty and future of Charles Bell Oaks is now in your hands.

Example (Criminal Prosecution):

Defense counsel has asked you to find his client not guilty and send him home to live his life. Defense counsel was here to speak on behalf of his client who sits here in the courtroom. But there is another person who is not here. Her life came to a brutal end by the hands of the man who now asks you for mercy, who now asks to go home. Where is the mercy he showed for Marni Winona? She will never go home. She will never see her six-year-old child, Olivia. Who will speak for her? Members of the Jury, you will speak for her when you return the only verdict supported by the facts and law in the case: a verdict of guilty of murder in the first degree.

Example (Civil Plaintiff):

I'm going to close now. Defense counsel for St. Paul Corporation told you a number of times that you were not to decide this case based on sympathy you might have in this case for Marci Mitchell. Indeed, the judge will instruct you that you are to base your decision upon the facts of this case and not upon passion or prejudice. It would be natural for you to have sympathetic feelings for Ms. Mitchell, who told you in this courtroom how she is struggling to maintain the operation of her neighborhood service station that she has worked hard to maintain for 10 years.

Members of the Jury, Marci Mitchell does not want your sympathy. Her family and friends can sympathize with her. You should not and need not decide this case based upon sympathy. Ms. Mitchell wants only what she is legally entitled to under the facts of this case. She has a right to her money from the defendant, the money that they owe her under the franchise agreement. Marci Mitchell deserves a verdict in the amount of $975,000, an amount supported not by sympathy, but by the facts, the law, and your wise judgment.

E. A Final Argument Critique

After constructing the closing argument, the attorney can review the following factors to determine if the argument is effective:

- Does the closing argument tell the decision maker why to find for the client?

- Does the closing argument make the decision maker want to find for the client?

- Does the closing argument tell the decision maker how to find for the client?

- Does the closing argument satisfy the common sense questions of the decision maker?

- Does the closing argument cover all factors the decision maker may consider during deliberations?

Advocates have difficulty constructing a closing argument that covers everything that needs to be said. Several barriers must be overcome to construct a comprehensive closing. First, the attorney who knows the case very well will have some difficulty in deciding what the decision maker, who does not know the case as well, needs to be told. Secondly, every case has some gaps, caused by missing evidence or natural omissions, which need to be covered during closing. If not, the fact finder will create their own conclusions and inferences, which may not support the decision requested by the attorney. Thirdly, the natural curiosity of the decision maker needs to be satisfied. Information that is not legally relevant to the case may need to be discussed to make a more complete story and to satisfy the fact finder's curiosity.

Conversations with decision makers after a decision (where permitted) sometimes reveal the decision makers deliberated over matters the attorney did not consider important or were not covered in detail during the case. These discussions provide an opportunity to learn from hindsight what should have been presented during the trial or hearing. The attorney should consider in advance what the decision maker may want to know, fill in these gaps, and answer potential questions during the closing argument.

One way of determining this information is to rehearse in front of colleagues or friends and ask them what is missing, what gaps exist, what prompts their curiosity, and what questions they have. The attorney can then present an argument that not only contains legally relevant evidence but provides the information that satisfies their curiosity. For example, the evidence in a theft case may include testimony by a victim that the defendant stole her purse as she walked home after work and that she called the police immediately after the theft when she arrived at her apartment. In order to add substance to an identification, the prosecutor should permit the witness to describe what she was thinking as she was walking before her purse was taken. The experienced prosecutor would also have the victim describe how she got in her apartment if her purse, which contained her keys, was stolen. This information prevents the decision makers from incorrectly filling in gaps and speculating about information that is legally irrelevant to the case.

§ 11.5   CONTENT

One of the primary goals of closing argument is for the advocate to provide reasons that support a favorable decision. The attorney has broad latitude in explaining these reasons which are based on the theories of the case, facts and opinions, inferences and conclusions, and the law applicable to the case.

A closing argument should involve the decision maker in the presentation. Summation is an opportunity for the decision maker to mentally participate in the case. An attorney should not approach summation thinking that the decision maker needs to be persuaded by all of the arguments. The decision maker may already have decided some factual and legal issues. An attorney needs to recognize this and employ techniques that take advantage of it. One technique is to suggest that some or much of what will be said during closing argument will only reaffirm what the decision maker is already thinking. Another technique is to acknowledge that the decision maker may have some unanswered questions and that the argument will attempt to summarize the evidence in a way that will resolve these concerns in the client's favor. In bench trials, administrative hearings, and arbitrations, the attorney may suggest the judge or arbitrator ask the questions that are unresolved.

This section lists many factors to consider when developing the final argument. The factors have been organized into seven categories for ease of analysis and application: argument, evidence, law, techniques, tactical considerations, criminal cases, and civil cases.

The advocate must consider which of these factors should be included and how they should be organized and presented in summation. Some of these factors — such as explaining the evidence and the law — will be included in all closings, while the inclusion of others will be discretionary.

A. *Argument*

1. *Types of Arguments*

The closing argument allows an attorney to say most anything that falls within the broad definition of argument. An attorney may:

a. *Draw Reasonable Inferences From Direct or Circumstantial Evidence*

Example (Civil Defense):

My client, Chris Commonwealth, received a hand-delivered letter at his home from the plaintiff at about 6 p.m. on July 20. The plaintiff claims Will threatened his life on that very day. I'm sure you will agree that someone supposedly in fear for his life is not going to hand-deliver a letter to his enemy's home after a supposed threat was made. What can we infer from these circumstances? The plaintiff's charge of assault is not supported by the facts.

b. *Suggest That Certain Evidence Implies a Reasonable Conclusion*

Example (Civil Plaintiff):

The fact that Summit State Bank hired five part-time file clerks, that the manager took Jeffrey Michael off his regular duties once the high school students were trained and put Jeffrey to work cleaning the office — a task degrading and not related to Jeffrey's job — and that Jeffrey was laid off during the same week two additional part-timers were hired all suggest one conclusion: Summit State Bank wanted to get rid of Jeffrey Michael.

c. *Present Conclusions Based Upon the Circumstances of the Case*

Example (Civil Defense):

Emma Elamein had drunk nearly a fifth of bourbon during the snowstorm. She had a cigarette in her mouth when she poured gasoline from a five gallon canister into the fuel tank of the Blizzard Snowblower. Emma Elamein failed to take adequate or reasonable steps for her own safety when she tragically and accidentally killed herself.

d. *Suggest the Decision Maker Apply Common Sense in Deciding a Case*

Example (Civil Defense):

You are to use your common sense when deciding this case. You are to rely upon your common sense in deciding how probable and how likely is our story. You are to use your common sense in concluding how unlikely and untrue their story is in this case. And when you do, you will reject the coincidences they want you to believe.

---

e. *Suggest That the Jurors Apply Life Experiences in Determining a Fact*

Example (Civil Plaintiff):

You know what it means in this society to be attractive. You know you cannot tell Rita Riley that her scars don't matter. Everything Rita confronts in life will remind her she is scarred — that she is not attractive. You know what value our society places on physical beauty. Rita will never meet another human being face-to-face without that other person's face reflecting the horror of her disfigurement.

---

2. *The Story*

The explanation of the facts may be told in a story form which includes descriptions of the scene, the characters, and the event. The goal of the attorney should be to summarize facts in a way that is reasonable and consistent with the recollection of the fact finder.

Example (Civil Plaintiff):

Elaine Pershowa began working part-time for Masssoit Bank when she was 55 years old in order to supplement her husband's income. Roger Pershowa's income was severely cut back because of his retirement due to a partial knee replacement. Elaine's work was praised; she received substantial raises each review period. But then Masssoit Bank was taken over by Summit State Bank. Suddenly Elaine was pressured into working nearly ten hours a day. Next she was given degrading tasks to do, such as cleaning the office, tasks having nothing to do with her skills as a filing clerk. Finally, Elaine was ordered to train in three young students, two of whom were still in college. After these three were trained, Elaine was laid off. Why? Because she is 63 years old. Summit State Bank has never recalled Elaine to work. Instead Summit State Bank has hired two more part-time high school students.

---

3. *Explaining Why Something Happened*

The evidence presented may tell the decision maker what happened and how something happened. The attorney may, during closing argument, need to explain why something happened.

Example (Civil Plaintiff):

You have heard the evidence in this case and you know what happened during the surgery and how Dr. Kildare conducted that surgery. You must decide why he performed the surgery the way he did. The evidence leads you to only one conclusion: Dr. Kildare was negligent. He made a mistake. Even though he is a doctor, he is still a human, and he made a serious mistake. He did not intend to hurt my client. He did not plan to make a mistake, but he did.

B. Evidence

1. Explanation of the Evidence

A substantial part of a closing argument consists of the attorney summarizing and explaining the evidence. This description should be consistent both with the facts described in the opening statement and with the evidence produced during the case. Some attorneys take closing argument to an extreme and try to argue that certain evidence has more value than a reasonable decision maker would ascribe to that evidence. This approach generally fails because it sounds unreasonable. The attorney should be careful not to exaggerate the nature of the evidence presented because decision makers easily recognize such overstatements and lose faith in the credibility of the attorney.

Example (Civil Defendant):

The judge and the lawyers refer to this part of the case as closing argument or summation. I do not intend to argue but rather explain the evidence to you. Time does not allow me to cover every bit of testimony, every piece of evidence, or every exhibit. I may not mention some things that you recall, but I am sure you will remember those matters and discuss them during your deliberation. Now I would like to summarize the evidence you have heard and seen.

2. Witnesses

The attorney may summarize the evidence by identifying the witnesses who testified to certain facts and opinions. Witnesses who were especially effective, persuasive, or credible should be referred to by name. If a trial involves a large number of witnesses who testify over a lengthy period of time, the decision maker may have some difficulty in remembering who testified about what. The attorney in such cases needs to not only identify the witness by name but also establish when they testified and the topics of their testimony.

Example (Civil Defendant):

We brought before you the testimony of the two people who talked to each other in the phone conversation on October 15. First, there was Louis Armstrong. Mr. Armstrong was the manager of the Cosmos Band. He took the stand and told you he had been managing the band for two years and during that October 15 telephone conversation he told Frank Hester the band was available to play on New Year's Eve. After he testified, Frank Hester testified. Mr. Hester was the manager of the Sylvan Lounge. Mr. Hester told you it was his job to contract with bands to play at the lounge. He also told you Louis Armstrong told him in that same telephone conversation on October 15 that the Cosmos Band was available to play on New Year's Eve.

3.　Credibility of Witnesses

An attorney may comment on the credibility of a witness, may demonstrate how an observation or statement is inaccurate, may attempt to show a witness is biased or prejudiced, or may comment on the witness' demeanor. Impeachment techniques may be used during the case to establish facts to reduce that witness' credibility. The attorney can restate the facts developed on cross-examination, which establishes why a witness should not be believed or that a witness' perceptions are improbable or implausible. In a jury trial, the attorney may also refer to the instruction on credibility that the judge will provide and explain to the jury how the facts in the trial match the factors of that instruction in reducing the credibility of a witness.

Example (Lie):

You heard the plaintiff's boss, Alberta Dowlin, testify that she fired the plaintiff because the plaintiff lied on his employment application. The plaintiff had lied on that application not once but on every page. Page one, the plaintiff was not honorably discharged from the Marines, he was never a Marine. Page two, the plaintiff was not laid off from the Forest Community College, he was fired for sexually harassing students. Page three, the plaintiff did not receive a PhD in linguistics from LaSalle University, the plaintiff's last degree was a B.A. in speech and communication from Hampton College. Plaintiff is not an honest or honorable person in his professional or personal life.

Example (Mistake):

The judge will tell you that you decide whether a witness is credible or not, whether a witness is to be believed or not. There are two key witnesses who testified for the plaintiff. Rosencrantz and Guildenstern both testified that they saw an accident. You have to determine whether they saw what they say they saw. The judge will give you an instruction regarding the credibility of witnesses which will help you in making your decision.

There are several factors which influence the ability of an eyewitness to see what actually happened. One factor is how close they were to the scene of the accident. Another factor is how clear a line of vision they had of the accident. Another is what they were doing immediately before the accident. Let's apply those three factors to the testimony of Rosencrantz and Guildenstern.

Example (Demeanor):

One of the factors you can consider in determining the credibility of the witness is the demeanor of the witness—the way they testify on direct and cross-examination. Do they appear to be telling the truth? Did they seem sure? Did they seem uncertain? Were they evasive? Did they hesitate? You will need to apply those standards to the testimony of Jessica Weston.

You will recall that she was the stockbroker who works for the defendant, and that she testified in this witness stand two days ago. During her direct examination, she appeared to be uncertain about the time of the day she met with the defendant in her office. Counsel for defendant had to suggest the answer to her. If she was uncertain about that key piece of evidence, perhaps she was uncertain about other matters. During her cross-examination, when I asked her questions, her attitude changed, and her memory became worse. She was not as cooperative in answering my questions and giving you information the way she was when she answered questions asked by opposing counsel. She remembered fewer details about conversations she had with her supervisor, the person for whom she is still working.

Example (Relationship):

We all heard the testimony of the defendant's wife. We all heard her testify in direct examination that her husband was with her the entire evening when the crime was committed. We all heard her testify in cross-examination that she loved her husband very much and continues to love him very much. There is nothing more beautiful than the bond that exists between a loving wife and husband. There is no doubt that Lorene Sentinel loved her husband, Gary, before the murder, and that she loves him after the murder. She loves him because he is her husband. She loves him even though he is a murderer. And she naturally wants to give him an alibi and tell you he was with her when he committed the murder. She would rather violate her oath to tell the truth than have you find him guilty.

4. *Circumstantial Evidence*

Evidence presented in the case consists of direct and circumstantial evidence. In a jury trial, the judge will give a jury instruction explaining circumstantial evidence to the jurors. The attorney may need to further explain circumstantial evidence.

Example (General):

Circumstantial evidence has the same value as direct evidence. An example of circumstantial evidence that demonstrates how accurate and compelling it is, is the story of Robinson Crusoe. You recall that Crusoe was on an island and he thought he was all alone. One morning he went down to the beach and he saw a footprint on the sand. Knowing that someone else was on the island, he became so overcome with emotion that he fainted. He didn't see anyone, but he knew because of the footprint there was someone else on the island. He woke to find Friday, the person who made the footprint, standing beside him, who was to be his friend on the island. The footprint — the marks on the sand made by a human foot — was circumstantial evidence. His seeing Friday was direct evidence. Both were true and compelling. Let's look at the facts of this case — the footprints that tell us what happened.

Example (Criminal Defense):

There is no direct evidence in this case which links my client to the crime. The prosecution has used circumstantial evidence in an effort to prove to you the guilt of my client, but that evidence proves nothing.

You know how weak, inaccurate, and misleading this type of evidence is. Some of you may recall the story from the Bible regarding Joseph and his brothers. Joseph was the favorite son of his father, Jacob. His brothers were very envious of him and they beat him and sold him into slavery. They wanted their father to believe that Joseph was dead, and so they took Joseph's coat and some goat's blood, and they smeared the goat's blood on the coat, and showed the coat to their father who concluded that Joseph had been killed by some evil beast. Of course, the truth was that Joseph was alive, but his father believed him to be dead. And so it is in this case. The truth is my client is innocent, but the prosecution attempts to convince you that he is guilty. You cannot rely on the weak circumstantial evidence in this case to find my client guilty. If you did, you would be making the same tragic mistake that Joseph's father did.

5. Detail and Corroboration

A detailed factual explanation has the advantage of refreshing the recollection of the decision maker and explaining the relationship between various types of evidence that may not have been obvious or made clear during the case. A detailed presentation has the disadvantage of increasing the risk that the decision maker's memory of the evidence differs from that of the attorney's explanation. A detailed description will be effective if the attorney accurately summarizes the details.

Summation provides an opportunity for the attorney to explain the primary source of the facts and to describe sources of circumstantial evidence and corroborating facts. This explanation will increase the persuasiveness of the evidence by explaining the connection between facts which the fact finder may have missed.

Example (Civil Defendant):

My client is not liable for the tragic death of Ms. Magdalen because the facts show Mr. Oxford was not using reasonable care for his own safety. You heard testimony from Mr. Hampshire, a friend of Mr. Oxford, that Mr. Oxford didn't know how to use the all-terrain vehicle, and that Mr. Oxford put the owner's manual — still in its unbroken plastic seal — on the shelf of the garage. Mr. Oxford's wife, Catherine, testified that Defense Exhibit No. 6, the owner's manual, taken from the Oxford's garage, remains unopened, just as Mr. Oxford had left it. You also heard Tom Cromwell, Mr. Oxford's neighbor, testify that after Mr. Oxford started the ATV, he said to Mr. Cromwell, "Well, here goes. I want to see how fast this thing can go."

---

6. Reference to Actual Evidence

The factual explanation may employ words used by the witnesses or words that appear in documents. The attorney should neither overstate nor understate the facts. Quoting the testimony of a witness and mixing that quote with a factual summary is often an effective approach. Reading testimony from a transcript of the case is permissible and may also be very persuasive. Reading from an exhibit or showing highlighted portions of the exhibit can be equally effective.

Example (Criminal Prosecution):

Yesterday you heard Mary Kay testify about meeting Curtis Brown after the Alinisi poetry reading. She testified that Curtis admitted his part in the crime. This transcript — which you heard yesterday — of what Curtis said proves what he did:

Q: When did you next see Curtis?

A: He picked me up right after my economics class, about 3:30.

Q: What did you do when you were driving?

A: I talked about my day. I mentioned that I was in Jordan Auditorium waiting for Alinisi to arrive for a poetry reading, when all of a sudden three police officers came in and told us to go down to the lobby.

Q: After you told him what happened, what was his reaction?

A: He laughed so hard he had to pull over to the side of the road. He said at 12:45, just before the 1:00 reading was scheduled, he called Max, the secretary and threatened that a bomb would go off in Jordan Auditorium if Alinisi went ahead with the reading.

Now, ladies and gentlemen, no reasonable person makes an admission like that unless he did what he admitted he did. Curtis wanted to impress Mary Kay. He wanted her to share in his secret.

C. *Summation to Jurors*

1. *Explanation of Law*

The judge will explain the law during final jury instructions. An attorney must summarize and explain pivotal instructions, and must accurately state the content of the instructions. The attorney can read from or quote the exact jury instructions. Many instructions will not adequately or clearly explain the law because the instructions contain abstract legal concepts. In these situations, the attorney may comment on the instructions and provide an expanded (and correct) description of the instruction and of its meaning in simple, easy-to-understand language.

An accurate explanation of jury instructions can be very persuasive. The final instructions come from the judge, whom the jurors usually respect and understand to be impartial and the source of the law. Jurors are likely to be persuaded by an explanation by a trial attorney that is supported by the instructions. A copy of the jury instructions is often given to the jurors for use during deliberations, and an argument based upon these instructions will more likely be remembered and discussed by the jurors.

Example (Civil Defendant):

The law provides you with legal guidelines and explanations to guide you and assist you in reaching a verdict. These explanations are called instructions on the law. The judge has explained some of them to you already. The judge will explain more of them to you after we have completed our summation. Now I would like to discuss with you how those instructions apply to this case.

This is an accident case. The judge will tell you about the law of negligence, and the judge will also tell you what it is not. I am quoting what the court will tell you:

"Negligence is lack of ordinary care. It is the failure to exercise that degree of care which a reasonably prudent or careful person would have exercised under the same circumstance." That is the standard. That is the law: A person must do what a reasonable person would do under the circumstances of the case. And that is what the defendant, Bonita Minnetonka, did in this case. She acted reasonably and prudently.

2. Special Interrogatories

A case may involve special interrogatories which require the jury to make specific findings of fact during deliberations. These interrogatories may accompany a general or special verdict. The attorney may read special interrogatories to the jury and urge the jurors to answer in a specific way. Rules and case law will determine whether an attorney can inform the jury that the answers to any one of the interrogatories may determine the outcome of the case. In most cases, the attorney can comment upon the effect of special interrogatories. In some cases an attorney may not be permitted to make such comments.

Example (Civil Defendant):

There are several things the plaintiff Morgan Bearpath has to prove to you before you can hold my client John St. Martin responsible for what happened in this case. To help you decide who is responsible for what happened, you will be given a list of questions you must answer in the jury room. The judge will give you those questions on a sheet of paper. I've had the piece of paper enlarged so that we can go through these questions together to discuss how these questions should be answered. Let me place this on the easel.

The first question is: "Did the plaintiff and the defendant enter into a contract on May 1? _____ Yes, _____ No." The judge will explain the elements that make up a contract. I've also had that explanation enlarged on this board. Let's apply the facts that all of us heard in this case to these elements to determine if a contract was entered into.

3. Explaining the Jury System

In jury trials, it is common for one or both attorneys to explain the purpose the jury serves in our system of justice and the importance of the jury's decision. These appeals, if done sincerely, can be effective.

Example (Power of the jury):

As jurors you are part of a tradition that is hundreds of years old. You are members of the community who come together and decide significant cases like this. Individually you are each a citizen. Collectively sitting here as jurors you are part of our system of justice. You hold in your hands the power to judge the difference between right and wrong. Today you will exercise that power to set right what has been done wrong.

Example (Conscience of the community):

Jurors, you are the conscience of the community. When you speak, the community speaks. You represent this community and its conscience and its attitudes. You shape and form the conscience of our community through your decision.

---

4. Request for Verdict

A closing argument must include an explanation of the specific verdict the attorney wants for the client. This explanation should be clear so the jurors understand what conclusion they must reach to find for a party. In most cases, the request will be a specific request for a verdict of guilty or not guilty or for a verdict for the plaintiff or defendant.

Example (General):

When you reach your verdict you must think it through and understand what it means. Verdict is a latin word meaning to speak the truth, so by your verdict you are going to speak the truth here today.

Once you write down your verdict, no one can change it. You can't be called back and told, "That's not right. You didn't do it right. Do it again." What you do here today is done forever.

It is also important that you reach your verdict for the right reason. Not only should the result be right — it is just as important that the reasons for it are right.

D. Techniques

1. Analogies, Metaphors, Anecdotes

The attorney may wish to refer to analogous situations, or use metaphors or tell an anecdotal story to make a point during summation. The images described by an attorney through an analogy, a metaphor, or anecdote may assist the decision maker in understanding the point of law or application of fact to law. An effective story will command the attention of the fact finders and will provide them with a comparison to determine the appropriateness of a point made during argument. An example of an anecdote to bolster circumstantial evidence is the story of Robinson Crusoe described in Section 11.5(B)(4).

Example (Civil Plaintiff):

They left a time bomb ticking at Dearborn Estates. It was just a matter of time before Jenkins would use his master key to get into Diane's apartment. It was just a matter of time before Jenkins would renew his acts of terror. That time struck on May 15 when Jenkins, hiding in Diane's kitchen, surprised her, held a knife to her throat and brutally assaulted her. Dearborn Estates lit that fuse and started that time bomb ticking when Dearborn negligently hired Jenkins on the basis of his letter with no references and no prior dates or places of employment. Even when the secretary of the Dearborn Board of Directors found Jenkins in a drunken and disorderly state and reported this to the Board, the Board did nothing. The Board could have defused the situation and spared Diane, but the Board did not make the one phone call to the police that would have stopped the disaster. One phone call would have informed Dearborn Estates that Jenkins was on parole for another assault. But the Board did not take the time to investigate and fire Jenkins, and that was all the time Jenkins needed. They are responsible for Jenkins exploding.

While a carefully drawn, common sense metaphor or analogy may assist the decision maker in understanding a concept, careful consideration should be given before one is used. If the analogy or metaphor is too simple or does not make sense, the point will not be made with persuasive impact. If there is an opportunity for the opponent to argue following the presentation of an analogy or metaphor, the opponent could make the use of these techniques appear simplistic or foolish.

Example:

Plaintiff's Attorney:

The agreement between Dolores Saki and Health Center, Incorporated was like a web. Doctor Saki, just finished with a residency, wanted to begin her pediatric practice. Health Center required her to sign an employment contract according to its terms: if she ever wanted to leave Health Center, she could not practice in a 100 mile radius of Santa Fe for two years. She knew she wanted to begin a practice in Santa Fe. What she didn't know was that Health Center, Incorporated was not the kind of practice she wanted.

After three months, Dee Saki resigned. She was caught in a web and she couldn't pull away. The more she struggled and tried to

reason with Health Center's administration, the more menac-
ingly loomed the spider.

When Dr. Saki ventured from Health Center, she started her
own office in Santa Fe. The spider let her build up a practice
and then flung out the web again. An injunction closed her
office and stopped her from earning a livelihood to support
herself and her six-year-old son in their modest home. She is
unable to practice; her medical school loans are in default; her
mortgage payments are overdue. Health Center, like a spider
that stores up victims for later consumption, wrapped Dee Saki
in its web as an example for the rest of its employees.

Defendant's Lawyer:

Members of the Jury, counsel has spent a lot of time talking
about voracious spiders and sinister webs. Let's consider the
reality. Doctor Dolores Saki is a competent, well-educated adult.
She knew what she was doing when she signed her employment
contract. She certainly could have sought advice from another
professional–a doctor friend or even a lawyer. She choose not to.
Society, and you, must hold her responsible for her obligations.
There is nothing menacing about Health Center. The Center
provides a vital service to the Santa Fe community.

---

2. Creativity

One of the primary tasks of the attorney in closing argument is to be
creative and innovative and explain the significance of inferences. While
the direct and circumstantial evidence may lead decision makers to clear
and obvious conclusions, the attorney's task is to explain the less obvious
conclusions. The advocate needs to highlight the subtle nuances of the
facts presented.

Example (Criminal Defendant):

*Presume that the defendant is accused of assaulting the victim in
an alley one block away from a bar where the defendant and
victim had a fight.*

My client, Gracie Allen, has been accused of hiding in an alley,
waiting for the victim to pass so that she could jump out and
attack the victim with a big stick because of something that
happened in the bar. My client did not hide in that alley, did not
jump out, did not attack the victim. It was somebody else.

You recall that the victim, Jack Benny, said that he had never
met my client before that night, did not know where my client
lived, and did not tell my client where he lived. And you recall
that Mr. Benny said he and my client never talked before or

after their argument in the bar, except to call each other names and yell at each other.

You also recall during my cross-examination of Mr. Benny, he told us that when he left the bar he could have left through the rear door on Mason Street, or he could have gone out through the front door and turned left and walked west toward Dixie Street, or could have gone through the front door and crossed the street toward Main Street. Instead, he testified that he went out through the front door and turned right toward Richmond Avenue.

You may have wondered why I asked those questions. His answers tell us that my client is innocent and did not assault him. My client, Ms. Allen, did not know where Mr. Benny lived. My client did not know which way Mr. Benny would leave when he left the bar that night. My client would not know to hide in a dark alley one block east on Richmond Avenue. There was no way my client would have known whether the victim would have left the bar through the front or the rear doors or which way the victim would have walked home — because my client did not know where the victim lived. Some stranger was waiting in that alley, ready to attack anyone who passed by. Mr. Benny was that unfortunate person who happened to pass by. Mr. Benny was tragically attacked by that stranger while my client was on her way home in a bus.

---

3. The Use of Exhibits

Section 11.3(E) described how to select visual aids and exhibits to be used in closing argument. The design, placement, and use in the argument can be as important as the visual aid or exhibit itself. The importance of the exhibit in the trial, the impact words and colors on the visual aids, the location in the room for clear viewing and easy access, the placement in the structure of the presentation, and the style of the lawyer in the use of and reference to the exhibit are important considerations in determining whether the exhibit will aid or interfere with the final argument presentation.

The use of exhibits and visual aids allows the attorney to approach a judge or arbitrator or walk over to the jury box and stand in front of the decision maker and point to, quote from, or use the exhibit there. This technique can enhance the summation impact of a point and add drama to the case.

Example (Defense Exhibit):

The most critical piece of evidence in this case did not come from the testimony of witnesses. The most critical piece of evidence is contained in Exhibit No. 1, this letter written by the defendant Ms. Roberto to plaintiff's employer. This letter was read to you during the trial, and each of you individually had an opportunity to read it yourself. We had this letter enlarged so that we can go over what the defendant wrote in that letter, and focus on the meaning of the words Ms. Roberto used.

Example (Defense Visual Aid):

Over the past two weeks of trial, you have heard from many witnesses and reviewed many documents. The judge will tell you that you must find my client not guilty if, based on all that evidence, you have a reasonable doubt that he committed a crime. The evidence in this case reveals there are at least eight reasonable doubts. We have prepared a chart which lists those eight reasonable doubts and the supporting evidence.

---

4. Personalizing Experiences

Decision makers will more likely accept an explanation of an event if something similar has happened to them. It can be helpful during summation to mention situations the decision makers might have experienced that resemble what happened in the case. For example, if the issue in a case is the eyewitness identification of the defendant, and the theory is that the witness misidentified the defendant, the attorney for the defendant can suggest this happens to people in other situations in life.

Example (General):

Have you ever been at a party and saw someone across the room and recognized them as a friend, only to approach that person and find out that it was not your friend, even though it looked like your friend from a distance?

Have you ever been at a restaurant and called for your waiter only to be embarrassed because the person you called was not your waiter, even though you had seen him and talked with him several times?

The witness here similarly picked out the wrong person. And that is perfectly understandable. The witness here was scared and frightened and did not expect to confront a stranger. At a party or at a restaurant that fear is not there. Reasonable people make many mistakes in identifying friends or people they meet. And the witness made the same mistake in this trial.

---

5. Reason and Emotion

Summation may include appeals both to reason and to emotion. An explanation of the facts and law can support a logical reason why a party is entitled to win. An appeal to emotion may create a motivating force to support a decision based on reason and logic. Appeals to emotion create an atmosphere in the room and feelings within the decision maker to render a favorable decision. Appeals to reason and logic provide a basis to return a decision. An approach that blends these two factors increases the chances of a victory.

An appeal primarily to logic and reason may diminish the human elements of the case. Appeals to compassion and empathy are as vital to an argument as appeals to reason and logic. Judges, arbitrators, and jurors do not leave their humanity at home but bring it with them to deliberations.

The extent to which an attorney relies upon both emotion and reason for an argument depends upon the circumstances of a case. With some cases it will be more effective for the attorney to emphasize a rational, logical explanation of the evidence and the law. In other cases, it will be more effective for the attorney to rely on the emotions and feelings created by the facts. An attorney must carefully balance the use of emotion in a case. An attorney may make the presentation of an argument more dramatic by relying upon its emotional aspects, but the attorney must also be cautious not to play to the passion and prejudice of the decision makers.

Example (Defense):

We all have feelings for what happened. Those feelings are natural and appropriate. You should use those feelings in your evaluation of the facts of this case. This is why you will never be replaced by a computer decision maker. Only a person can understand and appreciate the facts of this case. You are not a robot. And you are not required to act like a robot. You are to use your feelings just as you are to use your reasoning in deciding this case. That does not mean that you should decide this case on sympathy. Neither client is entitled to a decision based on sympathy. But, you may and you should have empathy for the parties in this case.

Two common basic emotions are like and dislike. Appeals to emotions during summation can be based on these two feelings. Generating a feeling of dislike or hate toward a party sufficient to support a decision against that party will be difficult, unless the facts justify such an attack. The positive emotion will be easier to establish on behalf of a client to persuade the decision maker that a party is entitled to win. The more effective argument is to show that a person is entitled to the benefit of a favorable decision, rather than trying to show that a person ought to be punished by losing a case.

Example (Civil Plaintiff):

Counsel for defendant has told you that there are some expenses Mr. and Mrs. O'Connor will not incur as a result of Danny's death, that there is some money they will not have to spend on their dead son. That is true. There are also some things they will never have to put up with because Danny is no longer with them. They will never have to sit in the heat of the sun on a hot, July afternoon, watching Danny play Little League baseball. They will never have to wait in long lines in some crowded toy store before the hectic days of Christmas buying Danny some toy that will break the day after Christmas. They will never have to lay awake at night, worrying about where their teenage son is and why he isn't home. They will not have to live through all that.

6. *Rhetorical Questions*

A rhetorical question can be an effective tool of persuasion because it directly involves the decision maker in the presentation. The essential aspect of a rhetorical question is that the answer should be obvious.

Example (Civil Plaintiff):

(*Counsel holding photograph.*) Mr. Franke is scarred. He is disfigured. His hands and arms will require grafting and plastic surgery. Can anyone look at this picture and fail to see years of anguish — emotional and physical — for Mr. Franke?

If the attorney believes the decision maker may not answer the rhetorical question the same way the attorney would, counsel should answer the rhetorical question.

Example (Civil Defendant):

Was Garfield House Apartments negligent in inspecting and maintaining the Ruud water heater? There is only one answer: No. Garfield House Apartments not only had a maintenance manager periodically check the system but also had a service contract to cover any repairs.

7. *Questions from Judges and Arbitrators*

A judge or arbitrator may ask questions during summation. This is usually helpful to the advocate because the questions reveal the issues the judge or arbitrator needs help in assessing. An advocate should answer these questions promptly and effectively, if possible. If a question is asked and the lawyer does not know or have an answer, the lawyer should directly say so and not try to avoid the problem or make a misstatement. The lawyer can move on to a related area and use the unanswered question as a transition to an effective part of the final argument. In general, advocates should welcome and encourage the judge or arbitrator to ask questions, however difficult they may be.

E. Tactical Considerations

1. Contradictions

It may well be obvious to the decision maker that a dispute exists between the parties. What will not always be obvious, however, is the specific factual contradictions in the case. Some cases do not involve apparent factual differences but involve subtle contrary inferences and conclusions. The attorney may need to highlight the inconsistencies between witnesses, to point out the contradictions in testimony, and to make certain the decision maker understands the factual disputes.

Example (Civil Defendant):

The issue in this case you must decide is whether a telephone conversation took place on May 2. The plaintiffs have raised another issue — a side issue which is not relevant to the merits of this case. That side issue might misdirect you from focusing on the real issue in this case. That misdirection is a magician's tool, a magic trick. And like a magic trick, that side issue is an illusion. It is not the real issue in this case.

---

2. Case Weaknesses

Every case will have some weak points which the attorney must address in closing argument. If an attorney can think of a reasonable interpretation that reduces the obvious weakness of a point, that explanation should be provided. If the attorney cannot think of any mitigating explanation, then the weakness can be conceded in a candid and forthright manner. This disclosure may enhance the credibility of the attorney and reduce the impact of the opposition's focus on such weakness.

Example (Civil Plaintiff):

It may not have been a good idea to let a six-year-old child ride a full-sized ten-speed bicycle. But Nicolas was ecstatic with his birthday present. Nothing could have kept that child from trying out that bike. His parents — preoccupied with the three-week-old baby and Nicolas' birthday guests — couldn't have known Nicolas was taking that bike onto the county road instead of the long farm driveway where he always rode his old bicycle.

---

3. Attacking Opposition's Positions

An effective technique may be to attack the logic and reasonableness of the opponent's contentions. An attorney may select one or more specific arguments of the opponent, demonstrate the weakness of the evidence or contentions, and explain how this information must be reconciled in favor of the attorney's client.

A significant portion of the closing argument should not be spent defensively responding to the opponent's issues, positions, and argument. The decision maker may perceive an attorney who does this as an advocate without any substantial positions. Arguments that attack the opponent's case must be balanced with arguments that support the attorney's case.

Example (Civil Defendant):

Counsel has tried to tell you how reasonable the substantial restrictions in Dr. Saki's contract with Health Center, Incorporated were. Let's review how unreasonable those restrictions really are. Two years of no practice within a 100 mile radius of Santa Fe means that Dr. Saki would have to terminate her credentials with United Hospital, would have to end the more than 500 doctor/patient relationships she has developed with people in this community who looked to her for aid and comfort, would lose the goodwill from her medical practice that she has developed over the past four years, and would leave this community short of a highly capable, very experienced general practitioner. Those restrictions are not reasonable.

---

4. Mentioning Negative Suggestions

The opposition's case may have some weaknesses that ought not to be used as a reason why the opponent should lose. These weaknesses may not be sufficiently relevant or material to be a significant point, or it may not be tactful to rely on a weakness because the decision maker may perceive the reliance to be a "cheap shot." For example, if an opponent in a contract case is a recovering alcoholic, it would be folly to use that former lifestyle as a reason why the opponent should lose. However, there are some weaknesses that can be briefly mentioned during summation that tactfully remind the fact finder of some problems.

Example (Civil Defendant):

You do not need to rely on other problems with the testimony of the plaintiff's major witness, Finley Bjorland to disbelieve his story. You need not consider the fact that he drove away immediately after the accident to get to the baseball game on time and did not stop to leave his name as a witness. You can disregard the fact he did not call the police until one week after the accident to tell what he says he saw. And you can ignore the fact he refused to talk to our investigator when she called and asked him some questions about the accident and that he willingly talked to counsel for the plaintiff. But, you can't ignore the fact that Finley Bjorland could not have seen what he said he saw.

This approach may work if the comments are presented in a way the fact finder does not view as unfair or sarcastic.

5. *Absent Evidence/Witnesses*

During closing argument an attorney may comment on facts which were described by opposing counsel during the opening statement, but that were not proven during the course of the trial. If the opposition has failed to offer evidence or introduce exhibits, an attorney may comment on the significance of that non-evidence. If a party could have called a witness, if that witness could have been subpoenaed, and if that witness was a material witness, an attorney may comment on the failure of the party to call such a witness. The failure of a party to call a witness may create an inference that the witness would have testified adversely to that party.

Some situations may prohibit comments about the lack of certain evidence. For example, it is unconstitutional for a prosecutor to comment on the criminal defendant's failure to testify. It may also be improper for a party to comment on the lack of certain evidence if that information is protected by a privilege.

Example (Civil Defendant):

Counsel for plaintiff told you they would prove to you the defendant committed discriminatory acts against the plaintiff. Counsel for plaintiff told you they would prove the defendant made racist statements. How did they try to prove that to you? Did they call one single witness to come to this courtroom and say they heard the defendant make racist statements? No. Did they bring before you one written piece of evidence containing any racist statement by the defendant directed to the plaintiff? No. It is not enough in our system of justice for somebody to claim something happened. It is not enough in our system for someone to say they will prove to you that something happened. Our system requires the facts be brought before you so you can determine what happened. Those facts were not brought before you, and the only reasonable conclusion you can reach is: what the plaintiffs say happened did not happen.

---

6. Lie vs. Mistake

Every trial involves contradictory evidence pitting the testimony of one witness against another. Some witnesses deserve to be called a liar. More often, a better tactic is to describe a witness as being mistaken about a fact. It may be sufficient to point out that everyone sees an event from different perspectives and that how the witness has perceived an event may be a mistaken observation based on an incorrect perspective.

When claiming that a witness has lied or is mistaken, an attorney should provide a reason to the jury why that person is lying or is mistaken. Merely asserting that a witness has made an intentional or negligent mistake is not enough. The facts established on the cross-examination of that witness must be summarized to demonstrate that witness' lack of credibility.

Example (General):

Michelle Turgenet told you under oath the salesperson said the warranty would cover all major mechanical problems with the car. You then heard from the salesperson, who denied making that statement to Ms. Turgenet. You have to decide whether that statement was made. Michele Turgenet remembers it was made because it was a very important factor in her decision to buy that car. Does the salesperson really remember what he said? You can easily conclude he is mistaken in what he remembers. He told you he has sold hundreds of cars and has talked to many hundreds of customers. He has no reason to remember what he told Ms. Turgenet when she asked him specific questions that were important to her about the warranty.

---

7. Jury Selection Commitment

In a jury trial, the attorney may refer to promises the jurors made during jury selection to remind the jurors of their commitments.

Example (General):

Several days ago during jury selection, we asked you some questions. And to some of those questions you answered "yes." You said you would decide this case based upon the testimony of the witnesses you heard from this witness stand. You said you would decide this case based upon the facts contained in documents that you have seen. All of us must rely on those promises that you have made, that you will not base your decision on other facts or other evidence or other things unrelated to this case.

---

8. Broken Promises

During opening statement in a jury trial, the opposing attorney may have made some promise to the jury which has not been met. An attorney during closing argument should review statements made during the opening and inform the jury the opposing counsel failed to do what was promised.

Example (Civil Defendant):

During this trial, counsel for Nicolas Burdock promised to prove the Whizzer bicycle was unreasonably dangerous. All counsel has shown you is that it was unreasonable for Nicolas' parents to let a child ride a full-sized ten-speed bicycle, unsupervised on a road where vehicles traveled at 55 miles an hour — and more — in both lanes. And that is part of the tragedy.

---

9. Anticipating Rebuttal Argument

In a jurisdiction where the party with the burden has an opportunity for rebuttal, opposing counsel may need to explain that there will be no opportunity to counter what the opposing party will say during the last closing argument.

Example (Civil Defendant):

Because the plaintiff has the burden of proof in this case, the plaintiff has the opportunity to again present an argument after I have finished. I anticipate plaintiff will question the ability of Abdul Maki to identify the truck involved in the accident. As you listen to Plaintiff's counsel you should ask yourself whether what the Plaintiff argues to you about the identification is supported by the evidence you heard in this case or whether it is clear Mr. Maki saw that truck. I will not have another opportunity to talk to you after plaintiff completes her closing argument, but I am confident you will believe Mr. Maki and not counsel's argument.

F. Criminal Cases

1. Burden of Proof

Both the prosecution and the defense may explain "beyond a reasonable doubt" burden of proof. Consideration should be given to a clear and simple explanation that will help the decision maker understand and properly apply the standard.

Example (Prosecution):

The term "beyond a reasonable doubt" does not mean proof beyond a shadow of a doubt or beyond all doubt. The prosecution need not remove all doubt in order to convict the defendant, for if that were the standard, convictions of criminals would be almost impossible.

The term "reasonable doubt" only applies to the elements of the crime that must be proved. If you have a doubt that is unreasonable, the defendant must be found guilty. If you have a doubt as to something that is not part of an element that needs to be proved, the defendant must also be found guilty. In this case, there is no reasonable doubt as to any of the elements of the crime of robbery.

Example (Defense):

The judge will tell you that a reasonable doubt is a doubt that would cause a person to pause in making an important decision or transaction in life. For example, an important decision is the purchase of a house. Imagine that the three witnesses for the prosecution are real estate agents selling a home and that the buyer of the home learns that one of the salespersons has never seen the home, another salesperson lied both to the police and under oath to a judge, and another salesperson is a convicted felon. A reasonable buyer would pause in entering into that transaction, reasonably doubt the accuracy of the statements made by those salespeople, and decide not to buy the house. Similarly, you should reasonably doubt and reject the testimony of the three witnesses for the prosecution and decide the defendant is not guilty.

2. Lesser Included Offenses

Lesser included offenses are difficult to explain without diminishing the strength of the argument in support of the most serious offense or of an acquittal on all charges. A prosecutor may have to decide how to deliver an argument seeking a premeditated murder conviction and, in the same argument, explain the elements of manslaughter. The defense must consider how to reduce the chances the decision maker will find a defendant guilty of premeditated murder and at the same time not concede a conviction based on manslaughter. These and other areas need to be carefully explained during summation.

Example (Prosecution):

We have proved the defendant committed the crime of murder in the first degree. He killed his business partner with premeditation and with intent. In this case, just like many others, there are other crimes involved. They are called lesser included offenses. When we proved murder in the first degree, we also proved these crimes.

G. Civil Cases

1. Burden of Proof

Counsel for both plaintiff and defendant must decide whether to discuss or describe the burden of proof. When making this decision the attorneys must consider the importance of the decision maker understanding and applying the correct standard of proof. Section 2.12 discussed whether the burden should be explained or relied on. In a jury trial, if an attorney decides the burden of proof should be explained during summation, consideration must be given to whether the judge's instructions defining the preponderance of evidence are clear and sufficient, whether they should be repeated, emphasized, and related to the facts, or whether an example and a more detailed definition should be given.

Many jurors may confuse the burden of proof in a civil case with the burden of proof in criminal cases and think that the phrase "beyond a reasonable doubt" (which they have heard countless times in movies, books, and television) should apply. The plaintiff's attorney should make certain the jury does not confuse the applicable burden of proof. In some civil cases, the burden of proof is the "clear and convincing" standard. See Section 2.12(C).

Example (Plaintiff):

In this case, we have the burden of proof — the burden of proving our case to you. The judge will tell you — and now I am quoting from what the court will read to you later in this case: "The party that has the burden of proof must persuade you by the evidence that the claim is more probably true than not true and that it outweighs the evidence opposed to it." Now that is the law.

As the plaintiff, our proof must outweigh the defendant's proof. The phrase, "preponderance of the evidence," means nothing more than the greater weight of the evidence, the greater likelihood of the truth. To prove our case all we have to do is to tip the scales in our favor. It may help you to visualize in your mind the scales of justice. One side of the scale holds the evidence of my injured client, Nicolas Burdock; the other scale holds the evidence of the defendant bicycle manufacturer, Whizzer. Little Nicolas Burdock doesn't have to topple the scales. He just has to tip them in his favor. All we have to do is tip those scales by the weight of the evidence, slightly in our favor, and we have carried our burden of proof.

The use of the "scales of justice" is usually effective because the description provides a visual explanation of an abstract concept and because the jurors have not previously heard this description. Another descriptive explanation can be equally effective. The attorney needs to determine what description, if any, of the burden of proof ought to be explained.

2. Liability and Damages

A plaintiff in a civil case may prefer to argue damages after explaining the basis for liability. This tactic may leave the decision maker at an emotional peak with a lasting impression of the damages the plaintiff has suffered.

A defense attorney may prefer to argue against damages initially in the closing argument and then argue the lack of liability on the part of the defense. This approach reduces the awkwardness of having to explain the possibility of damages after arguing the plaintiff has no right to recovery.

Example (Defendant):

Nicolas Burdock is a brain-damaged child who will need constant medical care and supervision. His condition is irreparable. This is a terrible tragedy. But Whizzer, the maker of the bicycle, isn't responsible. Nicolas was too small for the bike his grandparents bought him. His own parents never took the bike into a dealer to have the seat adjusted. Nicolas' bike did not malfunction. He was too small a child to control that bike. And his parents knew it.

---

3. Award of Damages

The plaintiff's attorney may need to explain why damages should be awarded to reimburse the plaintiff for the injuries suffered, income lost, or expenses incurred.

Example (Plaintiff):

A long time ago people were guided by the law of retribution in these matters. The law was to do to another what he did to you and your family. You may have heard it expressed as: "an eye for an eye, a tooth for a tooth, blow for blow." But with the development of our system of justice, we have become more civilized. We do not ask that the defendant be hurt.

All we ask is he fairly compensate the plaintiff for the wrong done with money damages. Why money damages? Because it is the only remedy the law provides. You have no other alternative than this under our system of justice.

4. Amount of Damages

The argument may contain a request for a specific amount of damages to be awarded with an explanation for the amount of money sought. Asking for a specified amount of damages is usually much more effective than leaving the assessment to the jurors. There are some cases where a request for a general amount of damages may be effective, but usually the better strategy is to request an amount of money or provide the decision maker with a range of adequate awards.

Example (Actual Damages):

And now, (pointing to monitor screen listing damages), here is a list of the damages Joyce Wharton has suffered. Your responsibility is to determine the amount of damages the defendant must rightfully pay to Ms. Wharton because she lost her leg. It is up to you to determine the amount of damages Ms. Wharton is rightfully entitled to as a result of the negligence of the defendant. The defendant's negligence prevents her from leading a full and complete life, and prevents her from continuing her lifelong dream of being a professional dancer. I will go through each of these types of damages and suggest a reasonable amount of money Ms. Wharton has a right to receive:

The nature and extent of the injury and physical disability	$350,000.
Loss of past earnings	$44,000.
Loss of future earnings	$700,000.
Past medical expenses	$95,000.
Future medical expenses	$55,000.
Disfigurement and inability to walk	$600,000.
Past pain and suffering	$200,000.
Future pain and suffering	$350,000.
TOTAL	$2,394,000.

This total of $2,394,000 is a substantial amount of money, but just think of the substantial pain endured by Ms. Wharton, the substantial loss of her professional career, and her substantial personal loss.

Example (Intangible Damages):

The tragedy in this case is that Timmy and Carol will never see their mom again. She died under the wheels of the defendant's truck. The further tragedy is that there is no way that Ms. Bachmeier can be brought back to life to live with her children. As I mentioned before, the only thing our society allows to compensate Timmy and Carol for the loss of their mother is money damages. In this jurisdiction, the judge will tell you

Timmy and Carol are entitled to receive an award of damages for the loss of the love and affection of their mother, for the loss of never being able to love, hug, be held by, laugh with, cry with, and just be with, their mother. You have to decide how much to award Timmy and Carol. How does one assess the loss of the love and affection of a mother? How does one put a dollar amount on such a terrible loss? Sometimes, stories about life help us determine the value of life. This story might help you determine the value of a lost mother.

This story requires us to go back in time, before this tragedy. Imagine that Timmy and Carol are on vacation with their mom along the ocean. Mom relaxes on the beach, and Timmy and Carol tell her they are going to go for a walk down the beach looking for shells. They walk about a block down the beach, and Carol stumbles over something in the sand. She looks down and sees something silver gleaming. Timmy says "What's that?" Carol says "Let's find out." And they begin to dig around this gleaming silver object. When they finish digging, Carol says "You know what this looks like? This looks like one of those magic genie lamps." And Timmy says "You mean one of those lamps you rub and a genie appears and grants your wishes?" And Carol says "I'm going to find out. I'm going to rub it." And so she rubs it, and magically a genie appears and says to them, "Today, Timmy and Carol, is your very lucky day. You have released me from the magic lamp and I am going to reward you by giving you two million dollars." You can imagine how excited Timmy and Carol are. They hug each other and Timmy says to Carol, "Mom will be so thrilled!" . . . . "Aaaahhh," the genie interrupts, "There is one condition. I will give you two million dollars, but you see your mother over there lying on the beach— you will never, ever see her again." Now, I ask you, members of the Jury, do you think Timmy and Carol would consider for one moment taking two million dollars, or any amount of money, and never see, hug, and love their mom ever again?

Example (Punitive Damages):

The judge is going to tell you that you may award punitive damages in this case if you find the conduct of the defendant wanton and willful and in gross disregard for the safety of others. The law allows you to award punitive damages in this case to punish the defendant. An award of punitive damages allows you to take away some money from the defendant to make the defendant and other future defendants realize this should not happen ever again. An award of punitive damages is not made to the plaintiff to give him something because he deserves it, but rather it is to act as a deterrence, that is, to send the message to the defendant and other future defendants not to do this in the future.

To send this message, the amount of punitive damages must be significant. The amount must be enough so the defendants feel they are punished. How do you set that amount of damages? It depends on the amount of actual damages, who the defendant is, how much of a profit it makes, and how much it is worth.

The defendant here is a corporation that is worth 60 million dollars and has average profits of 12 million dollars a year. Those are staggering amounts of money. But only a substantially large amount of punitive damages will affect the defendant and have an impact on its future conduct. If you took away from it 3 million dollars — which is 3 times actual damages and one quarter of one year's profit — the defendant would be properly punished under law. And when you consider how wanton, how willful, and how grossly indifferent it was to the safety of the plaintiff and others, you may conclude that even 3 million dollars is not enough money to fairly punish the defendant corporation.

---

5. Per Diem Argument

A plaintiff's attorney may use a "per diem" argument, which divides a period of time into small units and assesses a dollar value for each of these units. For example, if a party will suffer permanent injuries for the remaining thirty years of life, the plaintiff's attorney might argue the plaintiff is entitled to receive $100 a day for thirty years because of this continuing injury, for a total of $1,095,000.

Many jurisdictions prohibit per diem arguments. Some jurisdictions permit the argument when coupled with a mitigating jury instruction. Other jurisdictions permit the argument to be used by the plaintiff's attorney as an alternative way to determine certain damages. For example, the plaintiff's attorney could suggest that the decision maker may decide upon a value of $100 per day, or $200 a day, or more in determining recovery for pain and suffering. This attorney could not, however, in these jurisdictions suggest a total amount of damages based on a per diem formula.

Example (Plaintiff):

How do you arrive at dollar amounts for the intangible things — for pain and suffering? You have heard the testimony about the pain the plaintiff has suffered in this case. How do you determine how much to compensate the plaintiff for that pain? If a person goes to a dentist to have a cavity filled, the dentist might say, "I can drill your tooth without any novocaine or any painkiller, but for an additional $60 I can give you novocaine, and you will be free from pain for one hour." $60 for freedom from pain for 60 minutes. Who would refuse to pay $60 for freedom for one hour from such excruciating pain?

6. *Collateral Source Rule*

An injured party may have received partial recovery from sources other than a favorable verdict or judgment, including workers' compensation, health insurance, or government benefits. Many jurisdictions require the judge or arbitrator to subtract damages obtained from collateral sources from an award of damages. Other jurisdictions have statutes or rules which require the jurors to deduct collateral source payments from their verdict. The specific rules and practice of a jurisdiction determine whether and how collateral source payments affect what is said in closing arguments.

7. *Financial Status of Party*

The general rule is that the financial status of a party is irrelevant and cannot be referred to during summation, unless the financial status is an issue in a case. For example, if punitive damages are sought, the financial status of a defendant will be relevant because the assessment by the decision maker of punitive damages depends upon the financial status of the party.

8. *Impact of Tax Laws*

If the amount of the jury verdict is not taxable income, then the general rule is that tax law cannot be mentioned during summation nor considered by the decision maker. In some cases, the tax laws will have an effect upon the award or verdict. In these cases it might be appropriate for the decision maker to consider the impact of these tax laws, proper for a counsel to refer to the tax laws during summation, and proper, in a jury trial, for the judge to explain the tax laws during jury instructions.

9. *Existence of Insurance*

The general rule is that neither party may refer to the existence or non-existence of insurance during a case, and this rule includes summation. Insurance may only be mentioned if its existence is an issue in the case. The rules of evidence prohibit references to liability insurance. See Fed.R.Evid. 412.

§ 11.6   PRESENTATION AND DELIVERY

The more effective and persuasive an attorney is in presenting a closing argument, the greater the chance a favorable determination will be reached by the judge, arbitrator, or jury. If the evidence presented in a case is weak, the attorney will have little chance of convincing the decision maker in final argument to return a decision for the client. If the evidence presented during the case is strong, statements made by the attorney during summation will most likely match the conclusions the decision maker has already reached. If, however, the evidence presented by both sides is balanced, the closing argument becomes vitally important and may have a significant influence in the determination made by the decision maker.

Many of the factors that influence the presentation of an opening statement also affect summation. The following factors supplement factors of persuasive advocacy discussed in Sections 1.7 and 6.6, including confidence, sincerity, interest, honesty, dress, demeanor, voice, tone, use of simple language, and selection of impact words.

A. *Location of the Presentation*

The attorney needs to present the summation from a position that enhances its presentation. In general, the more effective location for an attorney is to stand or sit in front of the decision maker and avoid being hidden by a lectern or table. In administrative and arbitration forums, it may be common for the attorney to sit, but permission may be obtained to stand. In other tribunals, rules require the attorney to stand behind a lectern when presenting the closing argument. In these situations, the attorney can ask permission to stand away from the lectern in order to make a more effective presentation. If this request is denied, the attorney may use visual aids and exhibits which permit the attorney to stand away from the lectern and closer to the decision maker.

If a lectern must be used, it may be used as a tool, and all the effective communication techniques can be applied with the restrictions that a lectern places on such things as movement and gestures. A lectern may also provide a safe refuge for those attorneys who are uncomfortable with or have not had the time to practice speaking away from a table or lectern. It is too easy, however, to overuse notes while at a lectern or to use no gestures and remain frozen in one spot which may make both the attorney and argument appear boring.

B. *Movement*

Movement, if appropriate, can be effective during summation. The attorney may need to move to provide the decision maker with a different view, particularly if the summation is lengthy. Movement and stance must be orchestrated so as not to be distracting. Movement that appears random and purposeless should be avoided. An attorney should use movement as a transition or to make a point more emphatically.

C. *Appropriate Distance*

The attorney must maintain an appropriate distance from the decision maker. This distance should neither be so far away that personal contact is lost, nor so close that the decision maker feels uncomfortable. The appropriate distance will depend upon the size of the room, the location of everyone, and the circumstances of the case. During most of the closing argument, the attorney should maintain a personable distance of between five to ten feet, where possible.

In a jury trial, the attorney can move closer to the jurors and stand by the rail of the jury box. For example, it is possible to make part of the presentation right at the jury box. The attorney cannot remain too close for a long time and must use this closeness for emphasis. The attorney will need to speak quietly and must avoid making prolonged eye contact with any one juror, particularly those near the attorney. The attorney must avoid making a juror uncomfortable by being too close. One way to avoid this is to stand at the jury rail between two jurors and make eye contact with only the jurors in the back row, saving eye contact with the front row for the approach to and movement away from this brief, close presentation. The distance that an attorney maintains should be flexible and vary in different circumstances. An attorney should observe the jurors' reactions and move closer when appropriate and stand further away when necessary to avoid making jurors feel uncomfortable.

D. Gestures

An attorney needs to use appropriate gestures during summation to make the presentation more interesting. A lack of gestures or use of awkward hand movements or wild gesticulations needs to be avoided. Firm and purposeful gestures should be used, and those gestures should appear natural.

E. Eye Contact

One of the most effective ways to be persuasive and compelling is to look the decision makers directly in the eyes during summation. This also helps hold their attention and allows the attorney to observe their reactions. In jury trials, eye contact should be made with all jurors and not just a few selected jurors. Often an attorney can identify those jurors who appear to be dominant, one of whom is likely to be selected the foreperson. Eye contact should be directed towards these jurors when presenting important points during summation. Eye contact does not mean staring at or looking at jurors so intensely that they become uneasy.

F. Transitions

The closing argument is more effective if the attorney employs transitions during the presentation. Preparatory remarks, silence, a louder voice, a softer voice, visual aids, movement and gestures are all ways to make a transition.

G. Developing Own Style

An attorney must deliver the final argument in a style that reflects the attorney's abilities. An attorney should avoid copying and mimicking another lawyer's style but should be open to adapting and reworking what someone else has done if this style appears effective. Many parts of a closing argument may be taken from previous arguments or presentations made by other attorneys because of the similarity of the cases, the issues, or the quality of the ideas. This form of copying is not improper and can be most effective if the attorney appears to be presenting it in a spontaneous, fresh manner.

H. Observing the Decision Maker's Reaction

The attorney must observe the reactions of the decision maker during the closing argument and consider these reactions during the argument. An attorney who remains conscious of the observed reactions will more easily maintain interest and attention. The facial expressions, body language, and eye contact displayed by the decision maker communicate some information about attitude or position. These perceptions may not always be accurate and an attorney must be cautious when attempting to read the mind of the decision maker. Because it is difficult to determine accurately what someone is thinking, care must be taken not to overreact or completely change an approach because of a perceived reaction.

I. Notes and Outlines

It will be necessary in many cases for an attorney to rely upon notes or an outline during closing argument to ensure all important points have been covered. The longer the closing argument the more likely it is for an attorney to need to rely on notes. An attorney should never read a prepared closing argument or follow the notes so closely that eye contact is not established with the decision maker. Reading the argument will lead to a very boring and uninteresting presentation.

Occasional references to notes are appropriate as long as such references do not unreasonably interfere with or detract from the presentation. Often notes are only used as a crutch — which an attorney does not need. A persuasive, flowing argument usually is more effective, even if one or two points are omitted. Continuous use of notes to make sure that every detail is included often leads to a disjointed and ineffective presentation.

Prepared outlines can be effectively used in summation if combined with the use of visual aids. A prepared diagram, a whiteboard, easel paper, or a monitor screen may contain an outline of part or all of the closing which highlights important matters and assists the attorney in explaining the argument.

§ 11.7 OBJECTIONS

The lawyer is generally allowed wide latitude in discussing the evidence and presenting theories during summation. All the tools of oratory are at the lawyer's disposal, and tactics calculated to convince or persuade the decision maker may be used. Objections may be asserted during closing argument to prevent improper statements and conclusions.

If an attorney has an opportunity for a closing argument or rebuttal after the opposition, the attorney may prefer not to object but later comment on the inappropriate statement made by the opposing lawyer. If an attorney has no further summation, then an objection may be necessary to repair any damage and to preserve a matter for appeal. Many attorneys do not object during final argument unless the opponent is saying or doing something that is clearly improper and unfairly prejudicial to the case.

An objection to improper summation must be made in a timely fashion. Usually, the objection must be made immediately during or at the end of the summation. In a jury trial, the objecting attorney should also request a curative instruction. The trial judge may then attempt to reduce the prejudicial impact of the improper comments by instructing the jurors to disregard the comments. Some jurisdictions require the attorney to make the objection as well as request a curative instruction. The reason for the curative instruction is to provide an opportunity for the trial judge to rectify the error. The damage done by some improper comments may not be correctable by a curative instruction.

Appellate courts have reversed verdicts and granted new trials even where the trial judge gave curative instructions because the comments were so prejudicial as to deny the objecting party a fair trial. For example, comments made by an attorney regarding the existence of insurance in a civil case may be impossible to correct. Further, improper comments made in a case in which the issues are very close may be sufficient to support a motion for a mistrial. See Section 3.8(C)(9).

The facts and circumstances of each case determine whether the impropriety of the remarks is incurable. Appellate courts may reverse a verdict without objections being made to the closing argument where the substantial interests of justice require such a reversal. See Section 12.9. However, the trial attorney should not rely on such results because the granting of a new trial or an appellate court reversal for improper closing argument seldom occurs.

The following paragraphs describe objections that may be made to improper comments during summation to correct or reduce the impact of the errors.

A. *Arguing New Matters*

An attorney may not introduce or argue new matters during closing argument beyond the scope of admitted evidence. Section 11.2 described what can be presented in closing argument. References to facts or to the law which go beyond the evidence or legal issues are objectionable. References to evidence deemed inadmissible or to facts and opinions that were not introduced during the case are also improper.

Objection:

Counsel is improperly referring to matters not presented in this case.

Response to Objection:

- Explain the evidence or law that supports the comments made.
- Avoid referring to inadmissible or unproven evidence.

B. Misstating the Evidence

Misstating evidence is improper. An objection can be made if an attorney mischaracterizes the evidence.

In a jury trial, the judge may not recall the exact evidence or may permit the attorney broad latitude in characterizing the evidence because the judge has given or will give an instruction that what the attorneys say during summation is not evidence. The jurors will be instructed that they are to rely upon their own recollection of the evidence. In some cases, the judge may give a curative instruction during summation advising the jury to ignore an improper characterization made by the attorney.

Misstatements of evidence may also occur regarding evidence admitted for a limited purpose. The attorney, during argument, might use evidence admitted for one purpose to prove something else. An objection should be made to this improper characterization.

Objection:

Counsel misstated the evidence presented during the case.

Response to Objection:

- Explain the source of evidence supporting the comment.
- Explain the comment is a permissible inference that may be drawn from the facts presented.
- Argue the statement is a good faith belief by the attorney of what the evidence was.
- Remind the judge an instruction will be given to the jurors that what the lawyers say is not evidence.

C. Improper Legal Argument

The lawyer may not argue a personal interpretation of the law applicable to the case. It is proper for the attorney to correctly explain the applicable law and apply it to the facts. It is improper for the attorney to misstate or misinterpret the law or ask that the law be disregarded.

Objection:

Counsel is incorrectly stating the law.

Response to Objection:

- Refer to the legal elements or jury instruction counsel is explaining.

- Argue the explanation is a fair interpretation of the law as applied to the facts.

D. Improper Personal Argument

An attorney may not state a personal viewpoint or make personal remarks about the facts, credibility of witnesses, expert opinions, or other evidence. The decision maker is to decide the case upon the evidence and not upon the personal opinion of counsel. For example, the attorney may state: "There is no question in my mind that the plaintiff lied to you. I heard what you heard, and I saw what you saw. I am convinced the plaintiff lied." A prosecutor may not state: "I have prosecuted over 20 drug dealers over the years. I have never been as sure as I am in this case about the guilt of the defendant. I not only think he is guilty, but I firmly believe as an officer of the court that he is guilty as charged." While an inadvertent, occasional use of a statement prefaced by "I believe" may not call for an objection, any serious effort on the part of the attorney to influence the decision maker by a personal opinion should call for an objection.

Objection:

Counsel is stating improper personal opinions.

Response to Objection:

- Avoid making statements of personal opinion.

- Avoid using the word "I" in a statement referring to an opinion or conclusion.

- Preface such remarks with:

    "It is clear from the evidence...."

    "The only conclusion that can be reached is...."

E. Improper "Golden Rule" Argument

The "Golden Rule" argument is a statement by an attorney asking the decision maker to put themselves in the place of a party or witness. An example is "Put yourself in the place of the defendant in this case. How would you want yourself to be treated?" Decision makers are to decide the case based on the facts, not based upon how they personally want to be treated as a party or believed as a witness. For similar reasons, in a jury trial, an individual juror may not be singled out by name and addressed with a personal appeal.

Objection:

Counsel is improperly asking the decision makers to put themselves in the place of a party.

Response to Objection:

- Avoid making this statement.
- Do not use the word "you" (referring to the decision maker) during such a statement.
- Ask the decision makers to rely upon their common sense or how a reasonable person would respond and not how they personally would respond.

F. Appeals to Passion

Statements are improper if they serve only to inflame the passions of the decision maker. Attorneys may legitimately invoke emotions in a case, but may not rely on improper sympathy. The drama inherent in many cases will naturally result in appropriate emotional closing arguments. Empathy, sadness, and tears may naturally result from the atmosphere of the courtroom or hearing room. What is appropriate or inappropriate depends upon the case and the jurisdiction.

Objection:

Counsel is inflaming passion and prejudice.

Response to Objection:

- Explain that emotions are a natural part of the case.
- Present the argument in a less emotional manner.

G. Beyond the Proper Scope of Argument

Section 11.3(I) explained the scope of rebuttal may be limited in some jurisdictions. During rebuttal, the attorney may make statements that exceed the proper scope of the rebuttal.

Objection:

The argument by counsel exceeds the proper scope of the rebuttal argument.

Response to Objection:

- Explain that the topic raised by opposing counsel relates to the rebuttal argument.
- Include the arguments during the initial summation and do not save them for rebuttal.

- Ask the judge or arbitrator to exercise discretion and permit a broader rebuttal.

H. Improper References to the Invocation of a Privilege or the Failure to Introduce Unavailable Evidence

All jurisdictions recognize evidentiary privileges which prevent the introduction of relevant information. These jurisdictions differ regarding whether opposing counsel may suggest that the fact finders draw adverse inferences from the invocation of such a privilege. For example, in jurisdictions that recognize marital privileges and prevent spouses from testifying to confidential marital communications, opposing counsel usually may not refer to the excluded marital conversation and may not ask the decision maker to draw the inference that what was discussed must be harmful to the case.

In some cases, relevant evidence cannot be obtained by a party for legitimate reasons. The evidence may have been inadvertently lost by a third party. A key witness may not be able to be located after substantial efforts. Some evidence may be outside the subpoena power of the court, arbitrator, or agency. In many jurisdictions, it is improper for opposing counsel to ask that adverse inferences be drawn from the failure of the other attorney to introduce such evidence.

Objection:

Counsel is improperly asking that adverse inferences be drawn from the lawful invocation of a privilege.

Response to Objection:

- Check the laws of the jurisdiction to determine whether this is permissible before doing it. If it is, provide the judge or arbitrator with the citation to the permitting authority.

- Make a reference to the missing evidence without asking for any adverse inference.

I. Prosecutorial Misconduct

In criminal cases, the prosecutor must be careful not to overstep the bounds of fair argument. Prosecutors may be bound by a higher standard than defense counsel. Defense counsel may rely on the constitutional rights of the defendant which protect against an overzealous prosecutor. For example, it is a constitutional violation for a prosecutor to comment on the defendant's failure to testify. And it is improper for a prosecutor to say that, unless a conviction occurs, a lot of money will have been wasted in the case and that the defendant would not have been arrested if he was innocent.

Objection:

Prosecutor has made unfair prejudicial comments.

Response to Objection:

- Do not make such statements.
- Tone down the argument.

J. *Appeals to Prejudice*

It is a gross violation of the fundamental precepts of our system to appeal to the prejudices or biases of the decision maker regarding racial, sexist, economic, religious, political, or similar arguments. These comments are not only unconscionable but are also grounds for substantial ethical sanctions.

Example:

Plaintiff's Lawyer:

Whatever doubts you may have about the defendant's liability in this case can be resolved by considering the wealth of the defendant. This very rich and well-off defendant can clearly afford to pay the plaintiff a lot of money and should be made to do so, even if you aren't sure the defendant is negligent.

Defendant's Attorney:

Objection. Counsel is using gross prejudice to win the case.

Judge:

Sustained. And the jury is instructed to disregard those improper statements.

K. *Improperly Referring to Results in Similar Cases*

Attorneys may not cite or quote the results of similar cases when arguing to a decision maker. The case is to be decided based on the facts and law of the present case and not on what other decision makers have done in other cases, unless it is controlling precedent.

Example:

Plaintiff's Lawyer:

This is not the first case where the defendant's product injured someone. There have been other trials, where the defendant lost. You should do what those other jurors did.

Defendant's Attorney:

Objection. Counsel is making totally improper remarks about former verdicts.

Judge:

Sustained. And I am severely admonishing counsel for this malfeasance.

L. *Improper Comments*

The following statements represent examples of improper comments: mentioning insurance, referring to the financial status of a party unless punitive damages are in issue, implying that the jurors as taxpayers would ultimately be responsible for a damage award to a plaintiff who sued a governmental agency, telling the decision maker that the present case is not the first time litigants have asked for such damages, comments that denounce or degrade opposing counsel or the adverse party, a comparison between the resources of the opposing counsel's law firm and the lack of such resources of the other attorney's firm, and any other unprofessional statements.

M. *Improper Interruptions*

Objections may not be made merely to interrupt the attorney. If an attorney makes such harassing objections, opposing counsel should object to the objections.

N. *Admonishing Counsel*

If opposing counsel makes a number of improper comments or continues to make inappropriate comments after an objection has been sustained, objecting counsel should consider asking the judge or arbitrator to admonish counsel and instruct the attorney to stop such behavior. See Section 3.13(B).

CHAPTER 12

VERDICT AND APPEAL

REFLECTING ON ADVOCACY

Whereof you are a well deserving pillar, Proceed to judgment.

—Shakespeare
Merchant of Venice, Act IV,
Scene I

There are four sides to every answer: Right and wrong, yours and mine.

—Bo Hamilton

§ 12.1 INTRODUCTION

This chapter covers the procedures that occur after all evidence has been introduced and the parties rest. These procedures include final jury instructions, jury deliberations, the announcement of the verdict, post-trial motions, stays of proceedings, post-arbitration matters, post-administrative case proceedings and the appellate process.

§ 12.2 JURY INSTRUCTIONS AND THE VERDICT FORM

A. *Jury Instruction Conference*

After the attorneys have submitted their proposed instructions and verdict form to the judge, the judge decides what instructions are to be given and which verdict form is to be used. The instructions and verdict form the judge ultimately decides to use constitutes the "charge" to the jury.

The judge's decision is based on whether evidence has been introduced requiring or supporting a charge and what applicable law must be contained in the charge. The judge is also concerned that the charge is accurate, fair, and understandable. Section 2.7 explained the need for the attorneys to prepare proposed jury instructions early in the case and the procedures involved in submitting these instructions and verdict forms to the judge.

The judge must inform counsel before summation and before the charge to the jury what final instructions and verdict form will be given to the jury. Typically, the judge holds a jury instruction conference in chambers. During this conference, the judge advises counsel what revisions, additions, or deletions the judge made to the instructions proposed by counsel. Following this conference, the judge issues an order on the record specifying the instructions and verdict form the court plans to give to the jury. The order also notes the proposed instructions and verdict forms the court has refused to give. Frequently, when there are disagreements over instructions, the judge will work with the lawyers in an effort to reach a compromise or agreement.

Some judges provide each attorney with a copy of the final instructions and verdict form. Also, some judges note on the proposed instruction which points were granted, denied, modified, or granted or denied in part. The attorneys should know what exact charge will be given to determine what references or explanations they can make regarding the instructions and verdict form during summation. The proposed and the final jury instructions become part of the court file, in order to ensure their availability for possible appellate court review. In some jurisdictions proposed instructions do not automatically become part of the record, and attorneys should make certain that all instructions are made a part of the record.

During this jury instruction conference additional matters may be reviewed, including whether any anticipated problems may arise during closing argument, the time limits or restrictions regarding summation, the making or renewal of motions outside the hearing of the jury, which exhibits will be provided to the jurors during deliberations, and whether it's still not too late for settlement or mediation.

B. *The Judge's Charge*

The judge instructs the jury in open court before or after closing arguments. Most commonly, the judge instructs after summation. Many jurisdictions permit the judge to explain instructions before summation, particularly in cases involving factually or legally complex issues. An attorney may request that the judge instruct the jury periodically before trial, during trial, or both, as well as after summation if such instructions will help the jurors better understand the law. The trial judge has broad discretion in determining how and when to instruct the jury. See Section 2.9.

Most judges attempt to read the instructions and verdict form to the jury in such a way as to make the charge interesting and informative. Some judges explain the instructions to the jury by paraphrasing or summarizing the instructions. While this approach may make the explanation more understandable, it runs the risk an instruction will be misstated or an important word or phrase omitted.

In addition to instructing the jury regarding the law, federal judges and state court judges in some jurisdictions may comment on the evidence. These judges, instead of merely explaining the law, can refer to issues in the case and suggest interpretations of facts for the jury. In these jurisdictions, the jury still makes all factual determinations, not the judge. The scope of proper comments varies among judges and jurisdictions. Section 4.4(F) explained and provided examples of appropriate comments.

At the end of the charge, the judge may ask if the jurors understood the instructions and verdict form or if they have any questions. Some jurors may occasionally ask for a re-reading or an explanation, which the judge has discretion to do.

The written verdict form is given to the jury to take into the jury room to complete. Many jurisdictions require or permit judges to give the jurors a written copy of all of the instructions for the jurors to use during deliberations. This submission increases the chances the jurors will properly apply the law and reduces the chance the jury will need the judge to repeat certain instructions.

C. Objecting to Instructions and the Verdict Form

Errors made in jury instructions are a ground for the trial judge or appellate court to grant a new trial. The standard for a new trial and appellate reversal is whether an instruction was legally accurate and whether evidence supported the instruction. An attorney must make a timely and proper objection to preserve errors based on the jury instructions or verdict form. A party waives all errors unless the attorney objects and provides the court with an opportunity to correct the mistake.

Objections to instructions and the verdict form may be made at the time the judge informs the attorneys of the charge to be given, or, alternatively, objections may be made right after the jury has been charged, before they begin deliberations. In some jurisdictions, the objections must be made at both times. In most jurisdictions, objecting before the charge has been given is sufficient. If an error is first noted during the charge, the objection must be made after the instructions and before the jury retires to deliberate. This prevents an attorney from remaining silent and objecting later only if the verdict is not favorable. Whenever made, the objection must be made on the record and outside the hearing of the jury. Usually, this is done orally in the presence of the court reporter, either in chambers or in the courtroom.

The trial lawyer must specifically state the objectionable matter and the grounds for the objection. A general objection is usually insufficient. Examples of objections to proposed instructions include:

- No factual support in the record exists for the proposed instruction.

- The proposed instruction misstates the law.

- The proposed instruction fails to follow the pattern instruction approved in that jurisdiction.

- The proposed instruction is cumulative.

- The proposed instruction is argumentative.

- The proposed instruction will confuse the jurors.

The preferred practice is to identify the instruction that is faulty and provide controlling authority. The objection is made to allow the judge an opportunity to correct the mistake. For example, the written instructions given by the judge to the attorneys may be complete and proper, but during the final charge the judge may have misstated or omitted an instruction. The attorney must call the error to the court's attention to preserve a ground for a new trial or appeal. An exception to this rule may involve errors of fundamental law or mistakes that could not have been corrected by the judge.

After the attorneys have objected to the instructions given by the judge, the judge has an opportunity to modify or add to the instructions given. Explanations given by the judge that may have misled or confused the jury should be clarified.

D. Bench Trial

In a civil bench trial, the judge usually decides the case by making findings of fact and conclusions of law in writing or orally on the record. The drafting of proposed findings and conclusions by the attorneys parallels the considerations involved in drafting proposed jury instructions. Section 2.10 explained these considerations. The attorneys typically submit proposed findings of fact and conclusions of law which are consistent with the relief sought. See Fed.R.Civ.P. 52 and Section 3.11(E). To withstand a challenge at the trial or appellate court level, findings and conclusions should accurately reflect the supporting evidence and the law. They should also be clear and concise, balanced and not biased. A comprehensive draft of findings should follow the evidence introduced and assist in persuading the judge the facts have been proved. A comprehensive draft of conclusions of law similarly assists the judge in determining all the legal elements have been proved.

In a criminal bench trial, the judge will declare the defendant either guilty or not guilty. Defendants obviously much prefer the latter ruling. In some jurisdictions, the judge may have to prepare written findings. In some cases, the judge may explain the decision on the record or in writing, without making specific findings.

E. Administrative Decisions

An administrative law judge issues a decision, often called an order, with an accompanying explanation of supporting reasons or findings of fact and conclusions of law. The applicable statutes or rules determine the type of decision made and how detailed it is.

F. Arbitration Awards

An arbitrator issues an award after an arbitration hearing. The award describes the relief awarded to the prevailing party which typically is money damages and may be any form of relief, including injunctive relief. The arbitrator generally has the same power a judge has and can issue an award within the scope of the agreement, the rules, and the law. The award may be a short, summary statement or may include findings, conclusions, and explanations.

If the losing party fails to abide by the award, the prevailing party can seek to enforce the award in court. Arbitration awards can be confirmed into a judgment in any court with jurisdiction, including state or federal, by following the applicable statutory procedures. See Section 12.8(D).

G. *Jury Trial Stipulations*

Trial counsel may stipulate to certain procedures. Before the case is submitted to the jury, the judge may request, or the attorneys may suggest, the following stipulations be agreed upon:

- *The court, in the absence of counsel and the parties, may re-read and explain to the jury any instructions previously given or answer any relevant questions, if the jurors request such information while they are deliberating.* This stipulation speeds up jury deliberations and allows the judge to meet with the jury without requiring counsel to be present. It may be difficult or impossible for the attorneys to be located and advised of the jury request because of the attorneys' busy and conflicting schedules.

- *The parties waive the right to have the clerk or court reporter present when the jury returns a verdict.* The jury may deliberate outside of normal court hours when some court personnel are not present, and this stipulation allows such personnel to be absent. A judge must be present to accept a verdict from the jury. If the judge who presides at the trial is not available, a substitute judge must attend the return of the verdict by the jury.

- *A sealed verdict may be returned.* The judge who accepts the verdict may review it and place it in a sealed envelope. Some jurisdictions permit the parties to stipulate that a court employee (a clerk or bailiff) may accept and seal a verdict instead of the judge. The verdict will be opened in court later when the judge, attorneys, parties, and court personnel are available. This stipulation permits a jury to be discharged and the announcement of the verdict delayed until court is in session.

- *The parties waive their right to be present when the jury returns the verdict and allow the judge to announce the verdict in open court on the record.* If the parties or attorneys do not wish to be present or would have great difficulty in arranging their schedules to attend, they may consent to this procedure.

- *The parties waive their right to poll the jury.* This allows the judge to discharge the jury immediately after receiving the verdict from the jury.

- *A stay of entry of judgment for an agreed upon number of days shall be granted after a verdict.* This provision allows the losing party to serve post-trial motions without having to seek a stay of entry of judgment or a stay of execution on a judgment that has been entered. See Section 12.6(A).

While these stipulations are routine in some jurisdictions, they are uncommon or not even allowed in other jurisdictions. The parties in civil cases are usually free to waive any of their rights regarding the verdict return procedures. Defendants in criminal cases have the constitutional right to be present for all procedures and may or may not waive any of their rights depending upon the nature of the proceeding.

Ordinarily, nothing goes wrong with these procedures. If something unusual should happen, such an occurrence would rarely present grounds for a new trial. Because of this, many lawyers are willing to enter into these stipulations. Many other attorneys, however, reasonably believe that it is wise or necessary to be in court in case something does go wrong. Further, after all the excitement and emotion of a trial, the attorneys and parties may be eager to be present for the reading of the verdict.

§ 12.3 JURY DELIBERATION PROCEDURES

After the judge has instructed the jury, the jurors are sworn by the clerk to render a true verdict and are taken to the deliberation room by the bailiff. The jury room is typically adjacent to the courtroom. While deliberating, the jury is in the bailiff's custody.

A. *Deliberations*

Jurors typically deliberate during normal court hours on weekdays until they reach a verdict. If they deliberate more than one day, they usually go home and return for continued deliberations the following day. The judge instructs them not to discuss the case with anyone outside the courtroom, not to read any newspapers or articles about the trial, and not to watch television or listen to the radio, if the trial has engendered some publicity. Many juries deliberate during evening hours or over the weekend, especially if they are close to a verdict, or if there is some reason to accelerate the reaching of a verdict, for example, an upcoming holiday. Jurors are usually free to set their own pace and establish their own hours for deliberation, as long as the schedule is reasonable.

B. *Sequestering the Jury*

In major criminal cases and in well-publicized civil cases, the jury may be sequestered during deliberations and stay at a hotel or motel instead of going home to sleep. This does not happen often because of the expense involved and because most trials do not warrant such an additional safeguard. The bailiff, assisted by marshals or other court personnel, continues to be responsible for the jurors and arranges for transportation, lodging, food, edited reading materials, and edited television or video programs.

C. *Copy of Jury Instructions*

As explained previously, a judge may order, or an attorney may request, that a copy of the jury instructions be provided for use by the jurors during deliberations. Some portions of the original instructions, which are not needed by the jurors, may be removed, such as the number, caption, citations to authority, and other written comments.

D. Exhibits

The trial judge has discretion to decide which exhibits received into evidence will be allowed in the jury room during deliberations. In some jurisdictions, all exhibits are automatically provided to the jurors, unless the attorneys object and present a substantial reason for changing this practice. In other jurisdictions, only real evidence exhibits go to the jury. Demonstrative evidence such as diagrams that aid the jury in understanding certain testimony may or may not be allowed to go to the jury. Trial attorneys should review all exhibits to determine which, if any, should be provided to the jurors.

Favorable exhibits provide jurors with an available and visual statement as well as a reminder of the evidence and may have a useful impact on the jurors. Attorneys should request the court to have these exhibits provided to the jurors by arguing that the exhibits provide the jurors with an accurate and complete set of relevant facts which will expedite their deliberation process. On the other hand, if unfavorable exhibits will be provided to the jurors, trial counsel may argue against their submission by claiming that the jurors will give the exhibit undue weight and fail to consider oral testimony equally.

A judge may decide not to submit an exhibit to the jury because the jury might place undue emphasis on the exhibit, the exhibit may be dangerous, or because the exhibit would not help the jury to arrive at a verdict. The judge has broad discretion in making these decisions.

E. Jurors' Notes

The judge has broad discretion in deciding whether to allow jurors to take notes and whether the notes are allowed in the jury room. Many judges allow jurors to take notes during the trial and to use notes during deliberations. Some judges do not allow the jurors to bring these notes into the deliberation room. The exclusion of jurors' notes avoids the problems of notes being considered evidence and prevents note-taking jurors from exercising more power in deliberations than other jurors. Usually, jurors are instructed to rely on their own recollection of testimony, and if their notes are inconsistent with their recollection, to disregard their notes.

F. Questions by Jurors

A jury may have questions regarding the case or want to have some instructions re-read or explained by the judge. In these situations, the foreperson can write a note to the judge asking to meet with the judge or may reduce the questions to writing and submit them through the bailiff to the judge.

The judge has discretion to reinstruct, explain, re-read, provide additional instructions to the jury, or answer questions. The proper way for the judge to meet with the jury is in the courtroom and on the record. Usually, the judge telephones counsel or their offices, advises them of the jury's request, and asks whether they wish to attend. In civil cases, some judges may meet with the jurors without notice to the attorneys. In criminal cases, the defendant and the attorneys have a right to be present.

Many juries never have any questions for the judge. Some judges are reluctant to respond to jury requests because they do not want to interfere with the decision making of the jurors. Some judges, perceiving that a jury is having major disagreements, will attempt to assist the jurors in an effort to avoid a hung jury. See section 12.3(H).

The judge may not be able to resolve some problems the jurors may have. The jurors may want help on factual issues that are exclusively within their domain, or they may ask the judge to assist in the application of jury instructions to the facts, something only the jurors themselves may do. For example, if the jurors ask the judge to explain the meaning of a word or phrase in a jury instruction, the judge may do so. If the jurors ask the judge to decide a factual dispute, the judge must refuse this request. Resolving the facts of the case is the exclusive duty of the jury, and the judge may not infringe on that responsibility.

After the judge responds to the questions or problems, the jurors return to deliberate.

G. Unanimous Jury Verdict

In criminal cases, a jury verdict must be unanimous. In civil cases, verdicts are typically unanimous, but many jurisdictions allow non-unanimous verdicts in some situations. These jurisdictions, including federal courts, allow civil parties to stipulate to less than unanimous verdicts. Some jurisdictions, by statute or rule, allow a less than unanimous civil verdict to be returned after the jurors have deliberated for a certain period of time and have been unable to reach a unanimous verdict. For example, a jurisdiction may permit a civil verdict to be returned by five out of six jurors after the jurors have deliberated for a specified period of time.

H. Hung Jury

If the required minimum number of jurors cannot agree on a verdict after a significant amount of time, the jury is said to be "hung," and the judge may discharge them and declare a mistrial. What is a significant amount of time depends upon the facts and circumstances of each case. Usually, the judge will not declare the jury hung unless a lengthy period of time has passed and it has become clear that the jurors are unable to resolve their differences. The time period may be several days or several weeks depending upon the number and complexity of the issues, how far from agreement the jurors are, how the deliberations are proceeding, and how fruitless further deliberations are likely to be. In a simple case, a judge may declare a jury to be hung after several days of unsuccessful deliberations. In a complex case, several weeks of daily deliberations may pass before a judge will declare a jury hung.

Because the remedy for a trial resulting in a hung jury is a new trial with a new jury, courts are reluctant to declare a jury is hung. Judges will do what they can to explain jury instructions, answer appropriate questions from jurors, and encourage the jurors to reach a verdict to avoid having to go through another trial of the same case.

Many jurisdictions allow a judge to give the jurors a "dynamite" charge (also known as an *Allen* charge). This occurs when the judge brings the jurors in open court and firmly and assertively reminds them of their responsibilities and their need to reach a verdict in the case. Some jurisdictions prohibit this type of charge because of the undue pressure the judge may exert on the jurors' decision.

§ 12.4 RETURN OF THE VERDICT

The foreperson of the jury advises the bailiff when the jurors have reached a verdict. The bailiff advises the clerk or the judge a verdict has been reached, and they, in turn, contact trial counsel, who may want to attend. When the jury returns a verdict during regular court hours, the presiding trial judge or a substitute judge brings the jurors into the courtroom for the return of the verdict. If the jurors return a verdict outside of normal court hours, the bailiff will contact the judge who will then accept the verdict. Counsel may, however, stipulate neither they nor the judge need be present when the verdict is returned. In that case, the verdict is usually sealed and opened by the judge during working hours, with or without the lawyers being present, depending upon the stipulation.

When the jurors return to the courtroom, the foreperson typically hands the completed verdict form to the bailiff or clerk who in turn hands it to the judge who reviews it. If the verdict form is incomplete or inconsistent, the judge usually orders the jurors to return and properly complete the verdict form. If the verdict form is properly completed, the judge, or clerk, or foreperson reads the verdict in open court; and the judge or clerk may then ask the jurors if the verdict is true and accurate.

A. *Polling of the Jury*

After the verdict has been read, and before the jurors have been dismissed, the attorney who has lost may request that the jury be individually polled. The trial judge or clerk usually polls the jury by asking each individual juror whether the verdict is their true and correct verdict. If all the jurors agree, the judge dismisses them. If, and this rarely occurs, a juror dissents from the verdict, the judge usually orders the jurors to continue deliberations to reach a unanimous verdict. In civil cases where a less than unanimous verdict is permitted, only those jurors that supported the verdict need to affirm their position.

In some jurisdictions, polling the jurors is a routine procedure. In other jurisdictions polling is uncommon. Some lawyers do not do so unless they believe there were problems among the jurors during deliberations. There is no disadvantage for a losing trial attorney to ask the jurors be individually polled, except the pain of being repeatedly rejected by each juror in open court.

B. Discharging the Jury

After the verdict has been read and after polling, the judge discharges the jurors, thanking them for their participation, and advising them they may, but need not, speak to anyone about the case.

C. Contacting Jurors

A trial attorney may talk with the jurors after they have been discharged. The topics the attorney may discuss with the jurors vary among jurisdictions. Some jurisdictions prohibit the attorneys from talking with the jurors except to thank them for their time. It is common courtesy for the winning and losing attorneys to thank the jurors before they leave the courtroom. Other courts allow the attorneys to ask the jurors to comment on the evidence and trial strategies or to critique the trial skills of the attorney. Many jurors will be candid and the attorneys can learn much from these conversations. Some lawyers retain a professional to contact the jurors and ask them prepared questions seeking information on what went right with the trial presentation, or what went wrong.

Most jurisdictions prohibit attorneys from contacting jurors after they leave the courthouse if the purpose is to obtain information in support of a motion for a new trial. These jurisdictions typically enforce these restrictions by declaring these contacts by the attorneys improper and unethical and refusing to consider any evidence obtained in this manner.

Some jurisdictions are more liberal, and if the attorney suspects that an impropriety involving the jury has occurred, they permit attorneys to contact jurors after the trial and ask whether any prejudicial or extraneous matters affected the jury deliberations. Such information may be a ground for a new trial.

All jurisdictions prohibit attorneys and parties from pressuring or harassing the jurors and prohibit inquiries into the confidential jury deliberations.

D. Misconduct of the Jury

Misconduct occurs if the jurors allow their verdict to be influenced by factors other than the evidence admitted in the case or if the jurors fail to follow the law the judge gives them. If a nonjuror contacts a juror about the case before a verdict is reached, the juror must immediately inform the judge. If the contact prejudicially affects the juror's ability to be fair and impartial, the juror will be dismissed and replaced with an alternate. If there is no alternate juror and the trial is a civil case, the judge may declare a mistrial unless the parties agree to a verdict reached by fewer jurors.

Jurors may not decide the verdict on the basis of personal knowledge of the case. Any personal knowledge should be disclosed during jury selection, and the juror excused. Likewise, jurors may not base their decision on personal experiences as if those experiences were evidence to consider. For example, during deliberations in a product liability case, jurors may not rely on their personal use of the product to prove or disprove what actually happened in the case.

Jury misconduct is a ground for a motion for a new trial or a reason for appellate reversal of a verdict. The misconduct must be of such a nature that a party has been adversely and prejudicially affected. The mere occurrence of misconduct is usually not enough. The mistake must result in prejudicial error. See Section 12.9(D).

E. Impeaching a Verdict

The adversary system protects the sanctity of jury deliberations. Deliberations will not be interrupted, and a verdict will not be discarded, unless some extraneous prejudicial information or improper influence has affected the decision of the jurors. Examples of such improprieties include bribing the jurors or improper comments by a court official, such as the bailiff, telling the jurors how they should decide. Jury misconduct that occurs during deliberations is very difficult to discover.

Most jurisdictions follow the federal rule which prohibits a juror from testifying to any statement made during the course of jury deliberations, or to the effect of anything that may have influenced the juror's minds or emotions, or to any matter concerning the juror's mental processes. See Fed.R.Evid. 606(b). The federal rule and similar state rules permit jurors to testify only in unusual situations where some extraneous prejudicial information was improperly brought to the jury's attention or where some outside influence was improperly brought to bear upon any juror. These restrictions severely limit the ability to impeach a jury verdict and insure that verdicts will be final and stable. These limitations also reduce the chances that jurors, after a trial, will change their minds about their verdict because of pressures placed on them by a party, attorney, or third person.

F. Motion to Question the Jurors

A trial attorney who learns that prejudicial matter may have adversely affected jury deliberations may move the court for a hearing regarding such matter. The moving attorney must first establish that such information is reliable. Many jurisdictions accept hearsay information as sufficiently reliable if the information shows the existence of improper and extraneous information which may have prejudiced the verdict. If a judge agrees a hearing is warranted, the judge usually calls the jurors back to be questioned individually about the extraneous, prejudicial matter. The judge usually conducts the questioning, with the attorneys submitting proposed questions to be asked by the judge. The attorneys may also be able to ask some questions of the jurors after the judge has completed questioning. These hearings are infrequently granted because of the difficulty in learning about extraneous matter and showing that it probably had a prejudicial effect on the verdict.

§ 12.5   POST–TRIAL AND POST–HEARING MOTIONS

After a final order, award, or verdict, one or all parties may submit post-trial or post-hearing motions requesting the court to review the decision. These motions are usually required to preserve the right to appeal based on trial or hearing errors.

A.   *Motion to Dismiss*

A defending party may bring a motion to dismiss during a trial or hearing to seek the dismissal of a bench trial, administrative hearing, or arbitration. Section 3.8(C)(7) explained motions to dismiss. It would be unusual and usually unnecessary to bring a motion to dismiss after a trial or hearing before a judge or after an arbitration because there is no advantage in so doing. All the parties have already completed presenting their evidence, and they prefer a final decision be made by the judge or arbitrator, not a ruling on a motion.

B.   *Motion for Judgment as a Matter of Law (JAML)*

A party may bring a motion for a judgment during a jury trial at the close of the opponent's evidence, at the close of all the evidence, or on both occasions. Or a party may bring a motion after the jury has returned a verdict. These motions request the judge to review the evidence in a light most favorable to the nonmoving party and rule that the evidence is insufficient to sustain a verdict for the opponent.

In federal courts and in state courts that adopted recent federal rule changes, these motions are known as motions for judgment as a matter of law (JAML), whenever they are brought. In most state courts, a motion brought during the trial or at the end of all evidence is known as a motion for a directed verdict; and a motion brought after the jury has returned a verdict is known as a motion for judgment notwithstanding the verdict (judgment n.o.v. or j.n.o.v. from the Latin "non obstante verdicto"). In all courts, the grounds for these motions, however named or whenever brought, are the same.

C.   *Motion During Trial*

The basis for determining whether a judgment as a matter of law or directed verdict motion should be granted is whether any reasonable person could find on behalf of the respective party. There is no reason for the jury to decide a case if no reasonable juror could find for a party. That party should lose, and the judge can and should make that decision.

If a motion brought by the defendant after the plaintiff has rested is granted, the defendant need not introduce any evidence and judgment is granted for the defendant. If the motion brought by either party after both sides have rested is granted, there is no need for closing argument or jury deliberations, and a judgment is entered for the prevailing party.

Judges are not inclined to grant verdict-motions but prefer to allow cases to go to the jury and then grant post-trial motions to remedy any problem. Judges will grant a motion in part and dismiss some claims in a multiple count lawsuit if the evidence supports some but not all the causes of actions.

D. Motion After the Jury Verdict

The same reasonable person standard for determining whether to grant or deny a JAML or j.n.o.v. motion is identical to the standard explained in the previous Section (12.5. C). The judge must find that, as a matter of law, the only reasonable conclusion that could be reached from the evidence is the moving party is entitled to judgment and the jury's determination of the evidence was unreasonable.

There usually is some reasonable evidence to support the verdict and judges cannot merely substitute their judgment for that of the jury, and so these motions are seldom granted. If the JAML or j.n.o.v. is overturned on appeal, the jury's verdict is reinstated and becomes the final verdict in the case.

In many jurisdictions a motion for a verdict before the jury deliberates must be made before a judge will consider a verdict motion after the jury has returned. In other jurisdictions, either or both motions can be made.

E. Motions in Bench and Criminal Trials

In civil bench trials, a motion to amend findings, conclusions, and the order is brought, not a verdict motion, because there is no verdict. In criminal cases, the defense brings a motion for judgment of acquittal to challenge the verdict. A prosecutor cannot bring such a motion because the government cannot challenge the insufficiency of the evidence, and a judge cannot reverse a verdict rendered in favor of the defendant.

F. Motion for New Trial

A party may seek a second trial if some error or misconduct regarding the law, facts, rules, or procedure occurred during the first trial. Ordinarily a losing party brings a new trial motion, but a prevailing party might also seek a new trial on all or some of the issues if the verdict did not provide the winning party with complete or sufficient relief. A new trial motion may raise questions of law and fact. See Fed.R.Civ.P. 59 and Fed.R.Crim.P. 33. The exact grounds vary from jurisdiction to jurisdiction, but generally, a new trial may be granted if:

- A party was deprived of a fair trial because of irregularities in the proceedings caused by the judge, referee, jury, or prevailing party.

- The jury, judge, or prevailing party committed misconduct.

- The trial was prejudiced by a surprise situation that could not have been anticipated or prevented by using ordinary care.

- Material evidence has been newly discovered which, with reasonable diligence, could not have been found and produced at the trial.

- Excessive or insufficient damages were awarded by the jury based on passion or prejudice.

- Errors of law occurred at the trial, including wrong evidentiary rulings and incorrect jury instructions.

- The verdict is not justified by the evidence, or is contrary to the law.

- A verdict is otherwise fatally defective.

Commonly, a motion for a new trial is brought at the same time as a motion for j.n.o.v. or a motion to amend. In some jurisdictions, when a motion for a new trial is not made to the trial court, the appellate court will only review the case to determine if the evidence and law support the verdict. Other issues, including errors of law and fact, may not be reviewed unless the attorney has made a motion for a new trial. A party may also bring a new trial motion before a judge in a bench trial based upon some of the above applicable grounds.

G. *Rulings on Post–Trial Motions*

A losing party may bring a motion for a judgment as a matter of law and a motion for a new trial. In ruling on these motions, the trial court has four options:

- The court may grant the JAML and also the new trial,

- The court may grant the JAML and deny the new trial,

- The court may deny the JAML and grant the new trial, or

- The court may deny both motions.

The alternative motions present separate and distinct questions to the trial court as described in the preceding sections. The most common ruling is the last and fourth option listed; the others are not often granted.

H. *Motions to Reduce or Increase the Jury Award in Civil Cases*

In some civil cases, the losing party or unhappy prevailing party may not want a new trial on the merits but may want a different dollar award. A losing party may seek a reduction in the award by bringing a motion for a new trial requesting a remittitur. This motion requests that the court determine the verdict amount is unreasonable or is based on errors and that the court conditionally grant a new trial, unless the opposing party accepts a reduced judgment.

For example, if a jury returns a $1,000,000 verdict in favor of the plaintiff, defense counsel may request the court to order a remittitur to $400,000 or grant a new trial. Faced with this remittitur, the plaintiff must either accept the reduced $400,000 judgment or proceed with a new trial.

Some jurisdictions, but not federal courts, permit a post-trial motion to increase the dollar award of a jury verdict for an unhappy prevailing party. This procedure, known as additur, is similar to a remittitur but has the opposite effect. The verdict winner requests that the court order an additur or grant a new trial.

For example, a plaintiff who received a verdict of $250,000 may request an additur of $50,000. Faced with this additur, defense counsel must either accept the increased judgment of $300,000 or proceed with a new trial.

I. Motion to Amend Court Findings and Conclusions

In a bench trial and in some administrative hearings, a party may move to amend the findings of fact, the conclusions of law, or an order a judge has entered. The motion must explain which findings are not supported by the evidence, which conclusions are not supported by the law, and why the order is improper. The motion should also suggest revised findings and conclusions. Some jurisdictions require this motion be made to preserve issues for appeal. Section 3.11(E) explained the procedure for submitting proposed findings, conclusions, and orders to the judge. Motions to amend ask for a change of mind and heart, an unlikely event. A judge is not likely to do so unless the advocate accurately shows the record does not support a factual finding or the law is clearly contrary to the conclusion the judge reached.

J. Motion to Modify an Arbitration Award

In arbitration, a party may bring a motion to reopen an award under very limited circumstances. These alternative situations include:

● The award is not final.

● The award is ambiguous or contains evident material mistakes.

● A party was not served with the claim documents.

● The arbitrator did not decide a submitted issue.

● All the parties agree to reopen the award.

K. Timing

When a post-trial motion must be made depends upon rules of the court or administrative agency which vary from jurisdiction to jurisdiction. The time available to submit post-trial and post-hearing motions is ordinarily limited to no more than 10 or 15 days after a verdict or after a party has been notified of the filing of the decision. See, e.g., Fed. R.Civ.P. 59; Fed.R.Crim.P. 29, 33, 34, & 45. These time limits are usually strictly enforced. If an untimely motion is made, the motion will not be considered. The reason for such short, strict time limits is that these motions must be brought and considered by the judge while the events are still fresh in the judge's mind and because there is an administrative need to close cases and not let them drag on.

L. *Supportive Memorandum*

The submission of a supportive memorandum explaining the factual and legal grounds for the motion may be required and will increase the chances of obtaining a favorable ruling from the judge. In some cases, supportive affidavits will be necessary to establish the grounds for a motion. See Section 3.8(A)(2).

§ 12.6 ENFORCEMENT OF JUDGMENT

A. *Stay of Entry of Judgment*

A losing party ordinarily needs to obtain an order from the judge staying entry of the order or judgment or the enforcement of a judgment or administrative decision until the post-trial or post-hearing motions have been decided and an appeal taken. Judges commonly grant stays to preserve the status quo until they rule on the post-trial or post-hearing motions or an appeal is taken. See Fed.R.Civ.P. 62 and Fed.R.Crim.P. 34. After a verdict has been reached by the jury or a decision made by the judge, the losing party should bring a motion to stay entry of the judgment or decision based on the verdict or order. A stay will prevent the winning party from obtaining and enforcing a judgment. If the judge denies a motion for stay of entry of judgment or judgment has already been entered, the losing party should bring a motion to stay enforcement of the judgment. If that motion fails, the losing party may be able to bring these motions before an appellate court.

B. *Enforcing Civil Judicial Decisions*

The winning party will seek voluntary compliance with the judgment by the losing party after it has been entered and the appeal time has expired or the judgment has been upheld on appeal. Or, the winning party may enforce the judgment. See Section 12.8(A).

C. *Enforcing Administrative Decisions*

The nature of the administrative decision and the applicable statute determines how it is to be enforced. Some administrative decisions are self-enforcing, others may be enforced by the administrative agency, and others may be enforced by a court in the same way a judicial order is enforced.

D. *Enforcing Arbitration Awards*

An arbitration award may be enforced by having it confirmed into a judgment. If the losing party refuses to abide by the award, the prevailing party can easily bring a motion or petition in court to confirm the award into a civil judgment and enforce the judgment. See Section 12.8(D).

§ 12.7 COSTS, INTEREST, AND ATTORNEY'S FEES

A. *Costs and Expenses*

A prevailing party in a civil case or arbitration is entitled to receive reimbursement for the costs incurred during the case unless the court orders otherwise. See, e.g., Fed.R.Civ.P. 54; National Arbitration Forum Code of Procedure Rule 37. Recoverable expenses typically include witness fees, reasonable expert witness fees, service fees, filing fees, deposition expenses, the cost of transcripts used during the case, and related expenses. An arbitrator can include costs in an award. Administrative judges may be able to assess costs depending upon the applicable law.

Courts commonly have forms available from the clerk or administrator which the prevailing attorney may complete to obtain reimbursement for costs. The clerk will automatically add (tax) these costs to the judgment unless the losing party, within a limited period of time, challenges the costs, or the clerk believes the costs are not recoverable. A party may request a hearing before the trial judge to determine whether the expenses are recoverable.

B. *Interest*

A victorious party is usually able to recover interest in a case. There are two major forms of interest: prejudgment or prehearing interest and post-judgment or post-hearing interest.

Prejudgment/prehearing interest usually covers the period of time between the date the cause of action arises and the entry of order, award, or judgment. This period of time covers the trial or hearing procedures and may cover several years.

Some jurisdictions, as a part of prejudgment/prehearing interest, have a separate statute authorizing post-verdict or post-order interest, which covers the period of time between the rendering of a verdict by a jury or the decision made by a judge and the date judgment is entered. This period of time usually covers the post-trial motion proceedings and may cover a few weeks or a few months.

Post-judgment/post-hearing interest covers a period of time from the date of entry of judgment, order, or award until it is paid. This time period covers the appellate process and may cover a year or more in duration.

Prejudgment/prehearing interest is recoverable if a contract between the parties provides for interest or if the law allows such interest. The general rule in most jurisdictions is that prejudgment/prehearing interest is recoverable for liquidated damages (i.e., contract cases) and not available for unliquidated damages (i.e., tort cases). Many jurisdictions have enacted statutes which modify this general rule and permit interest to be recovered in many different types of cases. Some statutes establish the amount of the interest by setting a fixed percentage of six percent, eight percent, or more. Other statutes, which are more common, call for courts to adopt a floating method of calculating interest, based upon treasury bills or some other financial instrument. Attorneys may contact an administrator or clerk to determine the applicable rate of interest.

Post-judgment/post hearing interest is available for all federal court money judgments and is usually also available for state court judgments, arbitration awards, and some administrative monetary orders. The amount of the interest is usually set by statute or rule similar to the way the percentage is set in prejudgment/prehearing situations.

C. *Attorney's Fees*

The prevailing party is usually not entitled to recover attorney's fees. This rule, known as the American rule, prevents the winning party from recovering attorney's fees unless a statute, contractual agreement, or judicially created exception permits the recovery of attorney's fees.

There are many situations when attorney's fees are recoverable. Cases involving consumer law issues, securities law matters, antitrust problems, and civil rights violations may permit the recovery of attorney's fees based upon specific federal and state statutes. Civil cases involving contractual agreements may include contract terms that permit the prevailing party to collect attorney's fees from the losing party. Judicially created doctrines that permit the recovery of attorney's fees are few and limited. A prevailing party may be able to recover attorney's fees in cases brought or defended in bad faith by the opposing party.

When available, the prevailing party may ask to recover attorney fees from a judge or arbitrator, who have the power to determine the reasonable amount recoverable and to add that amount to the judgment or award. The party seeking attorney's fees usually must bring a motion requesting an award of the fees. In determining the proper recoverable fee, judges and arbitrators may use a formula which multiplies the number of reasonable, compensable hours worked by the normal hourly billing rate of the attorney or a reasonable attorney (called the "lodestar" formula), or a combination of these methods. This formula may be adjusted upward or downward depending upon several factors including: the complexity of the case, the quality of legal services rendered, the issues litigated, the likelihood of success, the opportunities foregone by counsel, and related factors. Judges and arbitrators have reasonable discretion in establishing the amount of attorney's fee awards.

§ 12.8   CIVIL AND CRIMINAL JUDGMENTS

A. *Entry of Civil Judgment*

A judgment is not effective or enforceable until entered by the clerk or administrator. See, e.g., Fed.R.Civ.P. 58. In a jury trial, if a general verdict form is used, the clerk automatically enters the judgment unless the court orders otherwise. If a special verdict form or general verdict form with interrogatories is used, the judge must issue an order entering judgment. In a bench trial, the judge must direct that judgment be entered based upon the order of judgment decided by the court.

Entry of judgment is critical in order to permit the filing of a notice of appeal or to permit a party to execute on the judgment. In many jurisdictions, unless judgment is entered, no appeal may be taken from that judgment. In all jurisdictions, a prevailing party cannot execute on a judgment until the judgment is entered. As previously explained, a losing party who plans to appeal or prevent the opposing party from executing on a judgment pending appeal must obtain a stay which stops enforcement of the judgment. This stay may be obtained from the trial judge. In some jurisdictions, after an appeal has been filed, this stay must be obtained from the appellate court because the trial judge no longer has jurisdiction over the case.

B. Entry of Administrative Decision

An administrative decision becomes final when it is issued by the administrative law judge or when it is filed or entered with an administrative agency. The applicable statute determines how it becomes final and how it is enforceable as a judgment.

C. Entry of Arbitration Award

An arbitration award becomes final when it is issued by the arbitrator or when it is entered by the administrative organization. An arbitration award can readily be converted into a civil judgment by a court with jurisdiction through a confirmation proceeding.

D. Confirmation of Arbitration Award

The prevailing party may bring a motion or petition to confirm the arbitration award in a jurisdiction where the losing party resides, does business, or has property. Federal and state arbitration acts govern the procedures. Federal Arbitration Act, 9 U.S.C. Section 15. The confirmation process is a simple process with the court reviewing the written documents and entering judgment on the award, and ordinarily does not require a hearing. After the award is confirmed by the court, the award becomes a judgment and can be enforced like any civil judgment.

E. Satisfaction of Civil Judgment

A judgment is satisfied when it is paid by the losing party. A judgment may be satisfied upon partial payment. A winning party may accept partial payment on a judgment to avoid an appeal or to obtain immediate recovery on a judgment that may not be collectible in the future.

F. Execution of Civil Judgment

If the losing party fails or refuses to voluntarily pay a money judgment, the winning party may need to enforce the judgment to collect the amount of the award. A variety of remedies and methods to enforce a judgment exist in every jurisdiction by statute and rule. Common remedies include execution, garnishment, attachment, replevin, and other forms of statutory or judicially enforced collection. If a trial results in an injunctive decree, the remedy for failure to abide by the decree is for the defendant to be held in contempt of court.

G. Entry of Criminal Judgment

A verdict of not guilty will be entered as a final judgment. A verdict of guilty does not necessarily mean a judgment of guilty will be entered and reflected on a defendant's record. The method of entry of judgment depends upon local law and practice.

A judge may:

● Stay entry of judgment until the completion of the defendant's appeal,

● Enter judgment and stay sentencing until the end of the defense appeal,

● Stay entry of a judgment and continue a matter for later dismissal if the defendant complies with probation terms,

● Enter judgment of guilty and stay imposition of a sentence, and place the defendant on probation,

● Enter judgment, impose a sentence, and stay execution of sentence with probation, or

● Enter judgment, impose and execute a sentence.

Sentencing options available to a judge are based on statutory sentencing limitations, administrative or legislative guidelines, and constitutional provisions.

§ 12.9 APPEALS

A. Judicial Appeals

Advocates are involved directly or indirectly in appellate practice. All trial advocates must make certain that a record of appealable issues has been properly preserved. See Section 3.12(A). Many trial lawyers write the appellate brief and argue the appeal. Other trial lawyers have another member of their firm who specializes in appellate practice participate in the appeal. Still other trial lawyers refer the appeal to another law firm. It is the client, of course, who decides which attorney will handle the appeal. The winning party will usually stay with the winning attorney. The losing party, however, may decide that a change in talent and expertise may be what is needed to improve the chances of succeeding on appeal.

Clients also decide, in consultation with their attorneys, whether an appeal should be taken or whether a cross-appeal should be filed if the opposing party appeals. An explanation of the appellate process and the decision of whether to appeal extends beyond the scope of this book. There are several appellate considerations that a lawyer must understand, however, and the remainder of this chapter briefly explains these matters.

B. Administrative Appeals

Administrative decisions are usually appealable. Some administrative decisions are appealable to another level of the administrative agency and will be reviewed by another administrator or administrative law judge. Many administrative decisions will eventually be appealable to a judicial judge.

C. Arbitration Appeals: Modifying or Vacating an Award

Arbitration awards are final and binding and usually not appealable. Arbitration awards may be reviewed by a court in limited circumstances. A party may seek to modify or vacate an arbitration award on limited grounds. The Federal Arbitration Act and state arbitration acts specify the reasons supporting a motion to modify or vacate. The reasons are usually narrow in scope and include:

- The award was procured or obtained by corruption or fraud.
- The arbitrator exceeded the power provided by the agreement, the rules, and the law.
- The arbitrator did not follow the applicable substantive law.
- Manifest injustice under the law has occurred.

These limited grounds protect a party from being denied a fair arbitration proceeding. The judge who considers a motion to vacate or modify is limited to these grounds and cannot second guess the arbitrator or change the award because the judge disagrees with the arbitrator. Nor may a court typically review and reverse or alter the factual determinations of the arbitrator.

There is no direct appeal of an arbitration award to a judicial appellate panel. A losing motion to modify or vacate an award can be appealed to an appellate court. Alternatively, the parties may agree in an arbitration agreement to appeal an award to a panel of three arbitrators. A party cannot collaterally attack an arbitration award by bringing a judicial action against the adverse party, the arbitrator, or the arbitration organization.

D. Whether to Appeal

The major factors that influence the decision whether a verdict or order ought to be appealed include the following:

- Type and degree of the error,
- The economic resources of the client, and
- The chances of success on appeal.

1. Type and Degree of Error

A party is not entitled to a perfect trial but is entitled to a fair trial. Mistakes and errors occur in every trial. Minor or inconsequential mistakes do not support the granting of a motion for a new trial or a reversal on appeal. The errors must be serious and substantial to obtain a new trial and to win on appeal. There are three types of errors most jurisdictions recognize:

a. Prejudicial Error

Prejudicial error occurs when the substantial rights of a party have been adversely affected. Any error short of depriving a party of substantial justice is not prejudicial error and is insufficient to overturn the verdict or judgment. An example of prejudicial error is the failure of the trial judge to allow a key witness to testify who has highly relevant and credible testimony. Another example is the refusal of the judge to give a jury instruction, requested by a party, which correctly explains the law on a pivotal issue in the case.

b. Harmless Error

An error that the appellate court does not deem to be prejudicial error is known as harmless error. This type of error is a mistake that occurred at the trial level but which did not deprive a party of a substantial right. This type of error is not sufficiently harmful to warrant a new trial. Incorrect rulings by the trial judge regarding the use of leading questions on direct examination would be an example of harmless error. Another example is the erroneous refusal by the judge to allow certain exhibits to be provided the jury during jury deliberations.

c. Plain Error

The "plain error" doctrine allows an appellate court to review an error even though the error was not properly preserved on the record. This type of error must severely prejudice a fundamental right of a party that ought to be protected, even though it was not properly made a part of the trial record. An example of plain error is when a prosecutor comments in closing arguments on the failure of the defendant to testify, and the error is not objected to by defense counsel or corrected by the judge.

2. Economic Resources

A client who has expended substantial resources for the trial may decide it is not economically worthwhile to take an appeal. A losing party may be able to negotiate the payment of an amount less than the judgment by agreeing not to take an appeal. The winning party may accept less than the judgment to avoid the risks of an appeal.

3. Chances of Success

The chances of success depend upon the nature of the issues to be appealed and the prior decisions of the appellate court. The issues may be of such a nature that little precedent exists to support reversal. Statistics from each appellate court reveal that certain types of appeals have a greater chance of being successful. For example, in some jurisdictions issues of law may be reversed on the average of twenty to thirty percent of the time by a court of appeals. Trial lawyers need to consider specific precedents in the appellate jurisdiction and the prior decisions of the appellate judges.

E. Finality of Judgment and Order

The general rule is that a case is not appealable until a final judgment has been entered. This requirement prevents piecemeal appeals from rulings the trial judge makes as the litigation and trial progress. Exceptions authorizing intermediate appeals are explained in the following subsection.

The entry of a final judgment permits an appeal to be taken from the judgment and from any order entered by the judge during the trial prior to the entry of judgment. The final judgment incorporates all previous orders, rendering all pretrial and trial rulings by the judge appealable. Rulings on post-trial motions may precede or follow the entry of final judgment, depending upon whether the judge delays entering judgment until after ruling on the post-trial motions. The normal appeal procedure is to appeal from the entry of final judgment and the orders denying the post-trial motions. The appeal from the judgment makes appealable all pretrial and trial rulings. The appeal from the post-trial order preserves all errors raised in the post-trial motions.

F. Intermediate Appeals

Pretrial and trial orders entered by a judge are generally not appealable during the trial. They are appealable as of right after a final judgment has been entered. Some pretrial and a rare trial order may be appealable prior to the final judgment if one of the exceptions permitting an intermediate appeal is met. These exceptions are:

1. An Order Which Determines Some of the Claims

An appeal may be taken from a judgment entered in a multiple party or multiple claim lawsuit if the judge declares there is no reason to delay entry of judgment on fewer than all of the parties or claims and enters a judgment. Federal Rule of Civil Procedure 54(b) and similar state rules codify this procedure. This rule recognizes that a judge may make a final decision in a complex case that ought to be appealed prior to completion of the entire case.

2. Immediate Appeal Designated by Federal or State Statute

Other orders immediately appealable vary among jurisdictions but generally include interlocutory orders involving injunctive relief and other equitable remedies. These statutes recognize that in order for the status quo to be preserved, an order may need to be immediately appealable.

3. The Collateral Order Doctrine

Many jurisdictions permit a small number of collateral orders to be appealable. These collateral orders are final determinations of claims collateral to and severable from the main claims in the lawsuit, but which are too important to be denied review and too independent of the case to require that appellate review be deferred until the entire case is adjudicated. The scope of these appealable orders varies significantly among jurisdictions. In federal courts, appealable interlocutory orders include rulings granting or denying motions in limine and orders denying joinder of claims for parties. In state courts, appealable orders may include discovery orders and procedural orders affecting substantive matters.

4. Writs of Mandamus or Prohibition

All jurisdictions permit a losing party to request the appellate court to order a trial judge to do something (mandamus) or to restrain a judge from doing something (prohibition). These writs are available in extraordinary situations where substantial rights of the parties are being adversely affected, or substantial injustice occurs, or if the judge makes a bizarre ruling. For example, these writs may be available to review a motion granting or denying a change of venue or pretrial rulings excluding or denying evidence or establishing trial procedures.

5. Petitions for Discretionary Review

Some jurisdictions, by court rule, permit a party to bring a petition for discretionary review requesting the appellate court immediately to review an order of the trial judge. The rules in each of these jurisdictions describe the scope of appealable orders, which typically include orders appealable under the collateral order doctrine.

6. Intermediate Appeals in Criminal Cases

A defendant's constitutional right to a speedy trial and the procedural rules of a jurisdiction determine whether an intermediate appeal is available. The government and the defendant may appeal adverse pretrial rulings if the rulings have a substantial and prejudicial effect on the appellant's case.

G. Standard of Review

The standard of review is the standard employed by the appellate court in determining whether to affirm or reverse the decision of the trial court. The party losing on an issue carries the burden of establishing that the applicable standard, justifying a reversal, has been met. Most jurisdictions apply three standards of review depending upon the type of error the judge is claimed to have made.

1. If the issue is a legal issue and involves an error of law, the appellate court will review the conclusion of the trial judge "de novo." Under the de novo standard, the appellate court substitutes

its judgment for the trial judge and determines the proper applicable law.

2. If the issue is a factual issue and involves a factual error, the appellate court will review the finding of the trial judge to determine if the factual finding is "clearly erroneous," that is, if it is against the manifest weight of the evidence.

3. If the issue is a mixed question of law and fact, and involves a discretionary decision, the appellate court will reverse the decision of the trial judge only if the trial court "abused its discretion," that is, if there was no reasonable basis to support the judge's decision.

§ 12.10 APPEAL PROCEDURES

A. *Initiating the Appeal*

An appeal is usually initiated by filing a "notice of appeal" in the trial court and with the appellate court within a prescribed period of time, for example, thirty days in a civil appeal and ten days in a criminal appeal. Many appellate courts also require the submission of a statement of the appeal or a docketing statement or the completion of an information form. These documents provide the appellate court with information about the judgment and orders appealed from, the issues, the nature of the case, and other data.

B. *Appeal Bonds*

In civil appeals, the appellant may need to post a cost bond or a supersedeas bond, or both, with the notice of appeal. A cost bond ensures payment to the appellee if the appellee prevails on appeal and ordinarily covers the costs of printing and submitting the briefs. An appellant typically has to file a cost bond, or provide other security, to ensure payment of these costs incurred by the appellee on appeal. The specific amount of this cost bond is established by statute or rule or by motion brought by the prevailing party before the trial judge.

An appellant may also have to file a supersedeas bond, or provide other security, to ensure that the judgment, enforcement of which is suspended during appeal, will be paid or enforced if the appellant loses the appeal. A supersedeas bond makes whole the prevailing party if the appeal is unsuccessful. See Fed.R.Civ.P. 62; Fed.R.App.P. 7 & 8. The amount of the bond is often equal to the amount of the money judgment (which may be substantial) and is fixed by the trial court in determining the risk to the prevailing party during the appeal process. The supersedeas bond is usually secured by one or more sureties which submit to the jurisdiction of the court and are available to pay the amount of the judgment if the appellant loses.

Some jurisdictions do not require cost or supersedeas bonds unless the prevailing party brings a motion for such bonds. The parties to the appeal may stipulate to alternative methods of security instead of the posting of a bond. An appellee may not be concerned with either bond if the appellant has substantial financial assets or will remain solvent during the pendency of the appeal.

C. Stays

The filing of a notice of appeal does not ordinarily stay the enforcement of a judgment or order. If the appellant has not obtained a stay of execution on the judgment from the trial court, the appellant will need to obtain a stay from the appellate court during the pendency of the appeal. See Section 12.6(A).

D. Record

The appellant usually must order the record from the court reporter for the appeal. The record typically consists of the pleadings, the written rulings and orders appealed from, the relevant portions of the trial transcript, and trial exhibits. The appellee may also designate other parts of the record to be included in the record for appeal. The mechanics of gathering and transmitting the record to the appellate court varies among jurisdictions, and usually requires a cooperative effort among the appealing parties, the trial court clerk, and the appellate court clerk.

The appellant also must make arrangements with the trial court reporter to transcribe those portions of the trial record needed for appellate review. Not all of the trial transcripts need be included in the appellate record. Only those portions of the transcript that contain the issues raised on appeal are included in the appellate record. The appellant ordinarily provides a list of the designated portions of the record that need to be transcribed, and the appellee may designate other portions of the transcript that need to be transcribed. Since the court reporter is paid for transcribing the record, the appellant must also make satisfactory financial arrangements with the reporter.

E. Briefing and Argument Schedule

After or during the completion of these procedural steps, the appellate court provides the attorneys with a briefing schedule indicating the deadlines for submission of the briefs and oral argument.

*

Index

References are to Sections